W9-BBB-721

Frederick Barbarossa

BY THE SAME AUTHOR

The Place of Hooker in the History of Thought
Relationship and Solitude
Problems of Religious Knowledge
The Origin of the Carolingian Empire
Life in the Age of Charlemagne

Frontispiece A contemporary likeness of Frederick I, Barbarossa. Copper bust from the Klosterkirche, Cappenberg. (Courtesy of Erich Müller, Kassel.)

Frederick Barbarossa

A Study in Medieval Politics

Peter Munz

CORNELL UNIVERSITY PRESS
ITHACA AND LONDON

First published 1969

Library of Congress Catalog Card Number: 69-20392

Printed in Great Britain

To my nieces and nephew
Alice, Bridget and Timothy

Contents

Illustrations

Plates

Maps

Preface

Owing to the paucity of the sources, it is difficult to write a real biography of Frederick I, surnamed Barbarossa. The present book is therefore more a study of the politics of his reign which lasted from 1152 to 1190.

Frederick was a contemporary of Henry II of England and in many ways one could fruitfully compare these two men. Both spent much energy in extending the scope of their power – Henry II across the Channel to his possessions in France; and Frederick I, across the Alps to northern Italy. Moreover, the second half of the twelfth century provided both opportunity and incentive for transforming the ancient institution of kingship into an administrative system, which might eventually create the conditions necessary for improving the subjects' standard of living and quality of life. As a result of their attempts at state building Henry and Frederick both became involved in a lengthy struggle with the church. Each came to the throne after long years of civil war in England and Germany and both were men of unusual physical and mental strength and resourcefulness. Soon after their deaths it turned out, however, that the Channel as well as the Alps proved geographical barriers too formidable for the kind of kingdom they had envisaged – a fact which was dramatically underlined by the accident that both Henry and Frederick were succeeded by sons who wanted to continue the policies of their fathers without possessing either their intelligence or their adroitness.

There is, however, little point in a systematic pursuit of such comparisons. For Henry II succeeded to a kingdom which, though in a state of disarray by the middle of the century, was a kingdom based upon the Norman Conquest. Given this initial foundation, the history of law and government in England has been continuous from Henry's reign to the present day. Frederick I, by contrast, became king of Germany in 1152 and was crowned emperor by Pope Hadrian IV in 1155 – but, because of the absence of systematic feudalism his kingdom and empire were at that time titles and dignities rather than established institutions. Unlike Henry therefore, Frederick had to face tasks which were very largely undefined and which made great demands upon his inventiveness and enterprise. Although he acquitted himself of these tasks with intelligence and determination, the results of his labours did not long survive him.

In writing this book I have endeavoured to render as many Latin and German expressions in English as possible. I hope thus to have gained in intelligibility whatever may have been lost in technical precision. Only a few words, such as *Vogtei*, *Landgraf* and *ministerialis*, have been used in their German and Latin form because I have not been able to find sufficiently unambiguous English equivalents. The names of ecclesiastical princes appear in an English form, e.g. Bishop Otto of Freising; but the names of lay princes appear in their German form, e.g. Otto von Wittelsbach.

I wish to apologize for citing some sources according to different editions. The book was written on several continents and I had to avail myself of the editions I could find wherever I happened to be. As the editions are always clearly mentioned, no inconvenience should result.

First I wish to thank my publishers, Eyre & Spottiswoode, who suggested that I write this book and took the most painstaking care in helping me to revise it. I also wish to thank my colleague Professor Keith Sinclair for making many useful comments on an early draft; the staff of the Niedersächsische Staats – und Universitätsbibliothek in Göttingen; and Professor H. Fichtenau for allowing me to work in the Institut für Österreichische Geschichtsforschung in Vienna.

I also owe a very special debt to the Research Fund of the Victoria University of Wellington for providing the means of obtaining the necessary books and microfilms for my work; and to the Deutsche Akademische Austauschdienst of the German Federal Republic for a generous grant towards a sojourn in Germany. Last, but not least, I must thank Professor F. L. W. Wood, the Head of the Department of History in the University of Wellington, for the moral support and practical encouragement without which I could not have written this book while engaged in teaching duties.

Wellington,
New Zealand,
January 1969

P.M.

List of Abbreviations

ADB	*Allgemeine deutsche Biographie*
AdM	*Annales du Midi*
ADR	*Archivio della Regia deputazione Romana*
Ae	*Aevum*
AfD	*Archiv für Diplomatik Schriftgeschichte, Siegel-und Wappenkunde*
AFD	*Archiv für Diplomatik*
AGDG	*Archiv der Gesellschaft für ältere deutsche Geschichtskunde*
AGGW	*Abhandlungen der göttinger Gesellschaft der Wissenschaften*
AH	*Agricultural History*
AHDL	*Archive d'histoire doctrinale et littéraire du moyen âge*
AHES	*Annales d'histoire économique et sociale*
AHP	*Archivium Historiae Pontificiae*
AHR	*American Historical Review*
AIS	J. F. Boehmer, *Acta Imperii Selecta*, Innsbruck, 1870
AKG	*Archiv für Kulturgeschichte*
ANHVN	*Annalen des historischen Vereins für den Niederrhein*
AOG	*Archiv für Oesterreichische Geschichte*
AP	*Analecta Praemonstratensa*
APA	*Abhandlungen der preussischen Akademie der Wissenschaften*
ASI	*Archivio storico Italiano*
ASL	*Archivio storico Lombardo*
ASPN	*Archivio storico per le provincie Napoletane*
AU	*Archiv für Urkundenforschung*
AZ	*Archivalische Zeitschrift*
BDL	*Blätter für deutsche Landesgeschichte*
BEFAR	*Bibliothèque des écoles françaises d'Athènes et de Rome*
BHF	*Bonner historische Forschungen*
BISI	*Bulletino dell' istituto storico Italiano per il medio evo*
Boso	Boso, *Liber Pontificalis*, Duchesne ed., Paris, 1955
Bouquet	M. Bouquet and others, *Recueil des historiens des Gaules et de la France*, Paris, 1738–1904
BRG	Ph. Jaffé, *Bibliotheca Rerum Germanicarum*, Berlin, 1864–
BZ	*Byzantinische Zeitschrift*
CCh	*Cisterzienserchronik*
CHJ	*Cambridge Historical Journal*

Chronicle	Otto of Freising, *Chronica sive de Duabus Civitatibus*
CMH	*Cambridge Medieval History*
CSSH	*Comparative Studies in Society and History*
DA	*Deutsches Archiv für Erforschung des Mittelalters; vols. I–VII* as *Deutsches Archiv für Geschichte des Mittelalters*
DALV	*Deutsches Archiv für Landes- und Volksforschung*
Döberl	M. Döberl, *Monumenta Germaniae Selecta*, IV, München, 1890
Dölger	F. Dölger, *Corpus der griechischen Urkunden des Mittelalters und der neueren Zeit*. A. Reihe, *Regesten der Kaiserurkunden des oströmischen Reiches von 565–1453*, II, 1925
DZG	*Deutsche Zeitschrift für Geschichtswissenschaft*
EHR	*English Historical Review*
EHS	*Eberings historische Studien*, Berlin
ELJ	*Elsass-Lothringisches Jahrbuch*
Eu	*Euphorion*
FbpG	*Forschungen zur brandenburgischen und preussischen Geschichte*
FDG	*Forschungen zur deutschen Geschichte*
FRRGI	J. Ficker, *Forschungen zur Reichs- und Rechtsgeschichte Italiens*, 1868–74, Neudruck, 1961
FS	*Franziskanische Studien*
GA	*Geistige Arbeit*
GDV	*Geschichtsschreiber der deutschen Vorzeit*, ed. G. H. Pertz and others, Leipzig
Gesta	Otto of Freising, *Gesta Friderici I Imperatoris*
GGA	*Göttinger gelehrte Anzeigen*
Giesebrecht	W. v. Giesebrecht, *Geschichte der deutschen Kaiserzeit*, 2nd edition, Braunschweig, 1877–
Gretser	J. Gretser, *Opera Omnia*, VI, *Defensio Romanorum Pontificum*, Regensburg, 1735
GRM	*Germanisch-Romanische Monatsschrift*
GSLM	*Geschichtsblätter für Stadt und Land Magdeburg*
GV	*Vergangenheit und Gegenwart*
HB	K. Hampe, *Deutsche Kaisergeschichte in der Zeit der Salier und Staufer*, 10th edition, ed. F. Baethgen, Heidelberg, 1949
Haller	J. Haller, *Das Papsttum*, III, Stuttgart, 1952
Hauck	A. Hauck, *Kirchengeschichte Deutschlands*, IV, 8th edition, Berlin, 1954
Helmold	Helmold, *Chronica Slavorum*

HG	*Hansische Geschichtsblätter*
HJ	*Historisches Jahrbuch der Görresgesellschaft*
HS	*Historical Studies, Australia and New Zealand*
HT	*History Today*
HV	*Historische Vierteljahrsschrift*
HZ	*Historische Zeitschrift*
JDR	H. Simonsfeld, *Jahrbücher des deutschen Reiches unter Friedrich I*, I, 1908
JGMOD	*Jahrbuch für die Geschichte Mittel- und Ostdeutschlands*
JKGV	*Jahrbuch des kölner Geschichtsvereins*
JL	Jaffé-Löwenfeld, *Regesta Pontificum Romanorum*, II, Leipzig, 1885–8
JRH	*Journal of Religious History*
MA	*Le Moyen Age*
MAe	*Medium Aevum*
Mansi	J. D. Mansi, *Sacrorum Conciliorum Collectio*, Venice, 1776
MF	C. V. Kraus, ed., *Des Minnesangs Frühling*, Leipzig, 1954
MGH, Const.	*Monumenta Germaniae Historica, Constitutiones*
MGH, LdL	*Monumenta Germaniae Historica, Libelli de Lite*
MGH, SS	*Monumenta Germaniae Historica, Scriptores*
MGS	M. Doeberl, *Monumenta Germaniae Selecta*, IV, München, I, 1890
MGSL	*Mitteilungen der Gesellschaft für salzburger Landeskunde*
MIOG	*Mitteilungen des Instituts für oesterreichische Geschichtsforschung*
MJbK	*Münchner Jahrbuch der bildenden Kunst*
NA	*Neues Archiv der Gesellschaft für ältere deutsche Geschichtskunde*
NAV	*Nuovo archivio Veneto*
NAWG	*Nachrichten der Akademie der Wissenschaften in Göttingen*, phil-hist. Klasse.
NDB	*Neue deutsche Biographie*, Berlin, 1960
NHJ	*Neue heidelberger Jahrbücher*
Nitzsch	K. W. Nitzsch, *Geschichte des deutschen Volkes*, 2nd ed., II, Leipzig, 1892
NJDW	*Neue Jahrbücher für deutsche Wissenschaft*
NJL	*Niedersächsisches Jahrbuch für Landesgeschichte*
NRHD	*Nouvelle revue historique de droit français et étranger*
Pez	B. Pez, *Thesaurus Anecdotorum Novissimus*, II and III, 1721; IV, 1729, Augsburg und Graz

Pflugk-Harttung	J. V. Pflugk-Harttung, *Acta Pontificum Romanorum Inedita*, II, Abt. I, Stuttgart, 1884
PhJ	*Philosophisches Jahrbuch*
PJ	*Preussische Jahrbücher*
PL	Migne, *Patrologia Latina*
QuF	*Quellen und Forschungen aus italienischen Archiven und Bibliotheken*
RB	*Revue Bénédictine*
RAC	*Rivista di archeologia cristiana*
RHDFE	*Revue historique de droit français et étranger*
RHE	*Revue d'histoire ecclésiastique*
RHEF	*Revue d'histoire de l'église de France*
RHM	*Römische historische Mitteilungen*
RIFD	*Rivista Internazionale di filosofia del diritto*
RIS	L. A. Muratori, *Rerum Italicarum Scriptores*
RSI	*Rivista storica Italiana*
Robertson	J. C. Robertson, *Materials for the History of Thomas Becket, Archbishop of Canterbury*, London, 1875–85
RF	*Romanische Forschungen*
SA	*Stader Archiv*
Sae	*Saeculum*
SBaG	*Schweizerische Beiträge zur allgemeinen Geschichte*
SBA	*Sitzungsberichte der bayrischen Akademie der Wissenschaften*, phil.-hist., Klasse
SHA	*Sitzungsberichte der heidelberger Akademie*
SHDB	*Mémoires de la société pour l'histoire du droit et des institutions des anciens pays bourgouignons, comtois et romands*
Simonsfeld	H. Simonsfeld, *Jahrbücher des deutschen Reiches unter Friedrich I*, I, 1908
Sp	*Speculum*
SPA	*Sitzungsberichte der preussischen Akademie der Wissenschaften*, phil.-hist., Klasse
SPAA	*Spicilegium Pontificii Athenaei Antoniani*
SRG	*Scriptores Rerum Germanicarum in Usum Scholarum ex Monumentis Germaniae Historicis separatim Editi*
SSV	*Studi Storici Veronesi*
Stumpf	K. F. Stumpf-Brentano, *Die Reichskanzler, vornehmlich des X., XI. und XII. Jahrhunderts*, Innsbruck, 1865–83
Sudendorf	H. Sudendorf, *Registrum oder merkwürdige Urkunden für die deutsche Geschichte*, I, Jena, 1849; II, Berlin, 1851

SWA	*Sitzungsberichte der wiener Akademie der Wissenschaften*
SZG	*Schweizerische Zeitschrift für Geschichte*
SSWG	*Schriften der strassburger wissenschaftlichen Gesellschaft in Heidelberg*
Tengnagel	S. Tengnagel, *Vetera Monumenta contra Schismaticos*, Ingolstadt, 1612
TAPhS	*Transactions of the American Philosophical Society*
Tr	*Traditio*
UJ	*Ungarische Jahrbücher*
VAHVN	*Vaterländisches Archiv des historischen Vereins für Niedersachsen*
VSW	*Vierteljahrschrift für Sozial- und Wirtschaftsgeschichte*
VuG	*Vergangenheit und Gegenwart*
Watterich	J. M. Watterich, *Vitae Pontificum*, Leipzig, 1862 II
WDGB	*Würzburger Diözesan-Geschichtsblätter*
WVH	*Würtembergische Vierteljahrshefte*
Z	*Zeitwende*
ZAGV	*Zeitschrift des aachner geschichtlichen Vereins*
ZDA	*Zeitschrift für deutsches Altertum*
ZFSL	*Zeitschrift für französische Sprache und Literatur*
ZGNKG	*Zeitschrift der Gesellschaft für niederrheinische Kirchengeschichte*
ZGO	*Zeitschrift für Geschichte des Oberrheins*
ZGS	*Zeitschrift für die gesamte Staatswissenschaft*
ZHVN	*Zeitschrift des historischen Vereins für Niedersachsen*
ZKG	*Zeitschrift für Kirchengeschichte*
ZSG	*Zeitschrift für schweizerische Geschichte*
ZSKG	*Zeitschrift für schweizer Kirchengeschichte*
ZSSRGger	*Zeitschrift der Savigny Stiftung für Rechtsgeschichte,* germanistische Abteilung
ZSSRGkan	*Zeitschrift der Savigny Stiftung für Rechtsgeschichte,* kanonistische Abteilung
ZThGA	*Zeitschrift für thüringische Geschichte und Altertumskunde*
ZVLGA	*Zeitschrift des Vereins für lübeckische Geschichte und Altertumskunde*
ZWLG	*Zeitschrift für würtembergische Landesgeschichte*

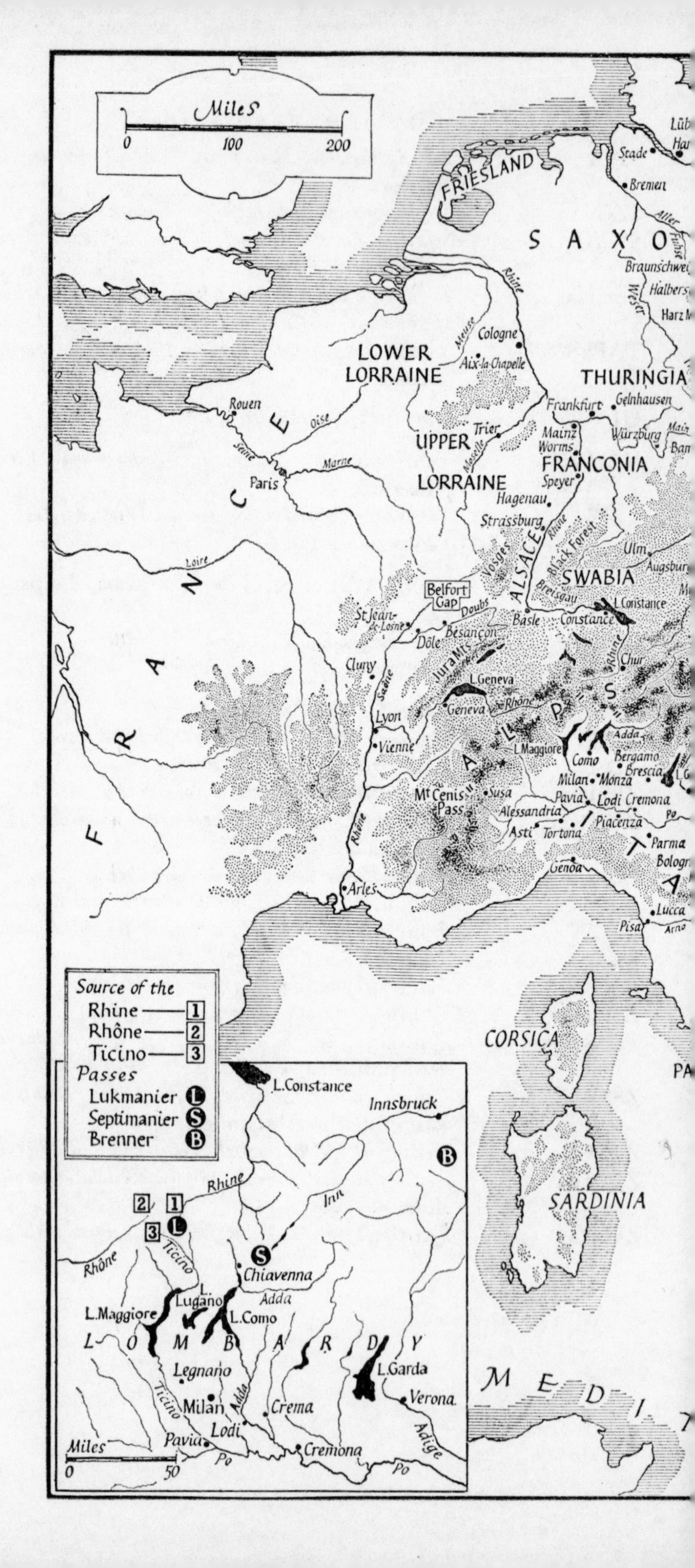
Miles
0
100
200
FRIESLAND
SAXO
LOWER LORRAINE
UPPER LORRAINE
THURINGIA
FRANCONIA
SWABIA
ALSACE
FRANCE
ALPS
ITALY
CORSICA
SARDINIA
MEDIT
Stade
Bremen
Braunschweig
Halbers
Cologne
Aix-la-Chapelle
Frankfurt
Gelnhausen
Mainz
Worms
Würzburg
Speyer
Trier
Rouen
Paris
Hagenau
Strassburg
Vosges
Black Forest
Breisgau
Ulm
Augsburg
Belfort Gap
St Jean-de-Losne
Dôle
Besançon
Doubs
Basle
Constance
L.Constance
Jura Mts
Chur
Cluny
L.Geneva
Geneva
Lyon
Vienne
Arles
Mt Cenis Pass
Susa
L.Maggiore
Como
Bergamo
Brescia
Milan
Monza
Pavia
Lodi
Cremona
Alessandria
Asti
Tortona
Piacenza
Parma
Genoa
Lucca
Pisa
Arno
Po
Adda
Rhine
Rhône
Meuse
Moselle
Seine
Oise
Marne
Loire
Saône
Aller
Weser
Source of the
Rhine 1
Rhône 2
Ticino 3
Passes
Lukmanier L
Septimanier S
Brenner B
L.Constance
Innsbruck
Rhine
Inn
Rhône
Ticino
Chiavenna
Adda
L. Lugano
L.Maggiore
L.Como
LOMBARDY
Legnano
L.Garda
Milan
Crema
Verona
Adige
Pavia
Lodi
Cremona
Po
Miles
0
50

EUROPE
during the reign of
FREDERICK
BARBAROSSA
FB
POMERANIA
POLAND
Oder
SILESIA
Pleissenland
Chemnitz
Erzgebirge
Prague
BOHEMIA
MORAVIA
Danube
AUSTRIA
Vienna
Salzburg
HUNGARY
Drava
Sava
Spalato
Ancona
Tivoli
Anagni
Benevento
APULIA
ADRIATIC SEA
SERBIA
BYZANTINE EMPIRE
Danube
KINGDOM OF SICILY
Palermo
SICILY
RANEAN
SERBS
BULGARS
Danube
BLACK SEA
Constantinople
Bosporus
BYZANTINE EMPIRE
ARMENIA
Rhodes
Crete
Cyprus
COUNTY of TRIPOLI
Jerusalem
SALADIN
W.Bromage

FREDERICK BARBAROSSA

A Study in Medieval Politics

CHAPTER I

The Kyffhäuser Legend

In Thuringia, to the north of the river Unstrut, stands the imposing Kyffhäuser mountain. Its northern slopes rise steeply from the plains, and its heights command a view of the whole land. According to a legend the Emperor Frederick Barbarossa never really died but is asleep inside that mountain. Over the centuries his red beard has grown through the table at which he is sitting, and outside the ravens circle the peak. One day, so the prophecy goes, the ravens will stop flying; and then the emperor will awake, emerge from the mountain and restore the glory of the German empire.

During the nineteenth century this Kyffhäuser legend cast a tremendous spell both on the German public in general and on the minds of historians. Societies were formed to propagate the legend. The Kyffhäuser was called 'that most German of all German mountains';[1] and when Germany was finally united and the empire re-established, an enormous monument was erected on the peak. It shows the new Emperor William I on horseback, with the front hooves almost leaping out over the plains. The historian Dahn[2] nicknamed him *Barbablanca* to underline the parallel with *Barbarossa*; and under William's pedestal, in a sort of cavern, there is an over life-size figure of the sleeping Frederick Barbarossa carved into the face of the cliff. The new emperor of 1871 is obviously the old emperor *redivivus* and the gigantic monument was to prove that the old prophecy had at last been fulfilled.

The less said about this aberration of nineteenth century patriotism the better. Even so aggressive and militant a nation-

[1] Quoted by A. Timm, 'Der Kyffhäuser im deutschen Geschichtsbild', *Historisch-politische Hefte der Ranke Gesellschaft*, Göttingen, 5, p. 24.
[2] Quoted by A. Timm, *op. cit.*, p. 22.

alist as Treitschke[1] publicly dissociated himself from the Kyffhäuser cult in its vulgar form. But the spell cast by this legend on the minds of historians is less understandable and more deserving of attention, for from the middle of the nineteenth century almost down to the present day, the picture of the Emperor Frederick Barbarossa as drawn by the majority of historians has been coloured and contaminated by it. It is the picture of a patriarchal ruler, benign as well as stern.

The first major biography of Frederick was written in the eighteenth century by Bünau.[2] It is a sober and, by the standards of the time, impeccable work of scholarship. It tells the story of Frederick's reign, but the emperor does not emerge from it as an especially heroic or politically beneficial figure. Almost a hundred years later Raumer[3] devoted a large part of his work on the Age of the Staufen to Frederick. There again nothing very spectacular is attributed to Frederick, and his reign does not appear to have been particularly golden. But after Raumer, Frederick's image became completely transformed. In 1871 Prutz produced his major work and stated boldly in his preface that his conception of the emperor was greatly indebted to the Kyffhäuser legend, for unless Frederick had been a heroic figure and his reign a golden age, that legend would never have formed itself in the mind of his people.[4] And in 1880 when the final volume of Giesebrecht's *Geschichte der deutschen Kaiserzeit* appeared its editor and redactor (for Giesebrecht did not live to conclude it), although he admitted he had doubts as to the genuineness of the legend, said that the existence of the legend proved that to the German people the Emperor Frederick was the most brilliant of all the emperors and that no other emperor had lived or died so whole-heartedly for the splendour and dignity of the imperial ideal. By this imperceptible transition, popular belief became the judgement of the modern historian; and the picture which emerged from Prutz and Giesebrecht has never really been abandoned.[5]

[1] *Briefe*, Leipzig, 1913, Vol. II, p. 369.
[2] Leipzig, 1722.
[3] *Geschichte der Hohenstaufen*, 1823.
[4] *Friedrich I*, 1870.
[5] One cannot help suspecting that even so critical a historian as P. Rassow must have been under the spell of the legend. What else would have prompted his *Honor Imperii*, 1940, in which he argues in favour of Barbarossa's splendid new conception

At first sight there seems nothing wrong in considering legends as part of the historian's material. Legends and folk tales must have some origin, and provided one can be satisfied that they do indeed reflect contemporary popular beliefs and impressions, their value as a source of information is great. But it so happens that in this case the legend originated a good hundred years after Frederick Barbarossa's death.

Frederick's death in 1190 did not make a deep impression. He had gone on a crusade, did not return and was succeeded by his son Henry VI. He had left affairs in Germany and Italy fairly settled and as a result people did not really take much notice of his disappearance. There was no cataclysm, no terror occasioned by his death. There was no more than the ordinary expression of sadness and if the author of the Annals of Reinhardsbrunn wrote that there were various and conflicting and confused opinions abroad about the actual manner of his death[1] he only stated a sad truth to which modern historians also have to subscribe. Frederick had been dragged dead from the river Saleph in Asia Minor. But there was no telling whether he had fallen in, whether the sudden immersion in the water had caused him to have a heart attack, or whether he had been overcome by the current and drowned. There are several accounts, but they are a little vague and they are not consistent with each other. But there is no evidence for the belief that the strange manner of his death gave rise in Germany to weird stories that he might still be alive.[2] For, so the history of mythology teaches, people imagine a resurrection or a return after death only of men who died terribly and whose disappearance is associated with sudden terror and apocalyptic fears; such men were tragic heroes and were, when alive, the very opposite of successful. The end of Frederick Barbarossa's reign was peaceful and uneventful, and he appeared to have been a successful ruler.

---

of empire in 1152, and caused him to overlook the decisive refutation of his argument contained in the fact that Otto of Freising, writing in the late 50s, makes no mention of the treaty of Constance in 1153, which according to Rassow, constitutes the evidence for the new conception, see p. 136 below.

[1] *Cp.* G. Voigt, *Die deutsche Kaisersage*, HZ, 25, 1871, p. 135.

[2] S. Riezler, *Der Kreuzzug Kaiser Friedrichs I*, FDG, 10, 1870, pp. 132 ff is wrong on this point.

The beginnings of the legend about the emperor in the Kyffhäuser are to be sought in a number of prophecies which were circulated immediately after the death of the grandson of Frederick Barbarossa,[1] the Emperor Frederick II. Frederick II died suddenly in Italy in 1250, sixty years after his grandfather, at the height of a titanic struggle between empire and papacy for the control of Italy. His supporters responded immediately by producing a Sibylline prophecy in which Frederick II was described as the emperor of the last age in history in whose reign the golden age[2] had all but dawned: the soil had been fertile, the starving had been fed and all nations had been subjected to Christianity. People were therefore invited to rally to his successor Conrad IV. Frederick's death had been a disaster, but, like the sun itself, Frederick had left a new sun which was about to rise: *sol invictus*. Hence, despite the change of person, the reign of the sun was to continue.[3]

There is no explicit mention of immortality or of Frederick's return in this prophecy. But the ingredients of the story that his death had not *really* occurred are all present. Moreover, Frederick II had neither produced abundance and peace nor subjected the world to Christianity. The whole prophecy was conceived in strenuous opposition to the facts. It originated among the citizens of Tivoli who were still holding out against Rome and who were then hoping that Frederick's successor Conrad would protect them. Given this political situation, the impulse for the prophecy is intelligible.

What is much less intelligible, at first sight, is that his opponents also indulged in prophecies about Frederick's return from death, or, rather, tried to persuade people that Frederick was not *really* dead. There were many circles among the Friars Minor in the thirteenth century who, as the true followers of St Francis' ideal of total poverty, had fallen foul of the established Church. In

[1] There is no need to search anywhere else, because there is no doubt now that before the sixteenth century nobody believed the emperor of the legend to be anybody but Frederick II.

[2] Virgil, *Ecl.*, IV, 39; Ovid, *Metam.*, I, 109.

[3] For all this *see* K. Hampe, *Eine frühe Verknüpfung der Weissagung vom Endkaiser mit Friedrich II und Konrad IV*, SHA, 1917.

these circles the prophecies of Joachim of Flora that the end of all history and the reign of the Church was about to take place had found fertile ground. According to the Joachimite prediction, the end of this reign would be preceded by the coming of the Antichrist. It so happened that the end had been predicted for the year 1260; and Frederick, for obvious reasons, was cast in the role of the Antichrist. His death in 1250 was therefore considered premature. And lest the Joachimite calculations be confounded, Joachimite and Friar Minor circles were anxious to believe that Frederick was not dead. Immediately after his death, the saying *vivit, non vivit* began to circulate in Italy[1] and people began to believe that Frederick was not dead but had merely been magically removed. Later the story arose that he was actually roaming the country in disguise; and within a decade or so of his death the story emerged that he had been seen entering Mount Etna in Sicily to the accompaniment of the weirdest natural phenomena.[2]

In Germany, Frederick II had neither been popular nor greatly important and his sudden death did not create much of an impression – and there is no very obvious reason why such a legend should have arisen. Nevertheless two special reasons emerge. The first is provided by the existence of Waldensian and other dualistic sectarians who all believed that the world of matter and flesh was totally evil, and that Christians ought to live in complete poverty and renounce the world.[3] Their teachings belonged to the mainstream of twelfth and thirteenth century heresy and had been for almost a century the object of active ecclesiastical persecution. It appears that Friars Minor carried the story about Frederick's return from the dead, or from the mountain, to Germany, and that the image of Frederick was transformed from that of an Antichrist into that of a protector of the

[1] *See* O. Holder-Egger, *Italienische Prophetien des 13. Jahrhunderts*, NA, 15, 1890; E. Kantorowicz, *Zu den Rechtsgrundlagen der Kaisersage*, DA, 13, 1957. *Cp.* also the earlier argument by M. Brosch, *Die Friedrichsage der Italiener*, HZ, 35, 1876, p. 21, who expresses some justified doubts as to how popular and how widespread the beliefs reported by Salimbene were in thirteenth-century Italy.

[2] *Cp. Gervasii Tilberiensis Otia Imperialia*, Leibniz ed., SS rerum Brunsvicarum, I, p. 921; *Ex Thomae de Eccleston Libro de Adventu Fratrum Minorum in Angliam*, MGH, SS, XXVIII, p. 568.

[3] *Cp.* A. A. Hauck, IV, p. 409.

persecuted heretics.[1] If Frederick as Antichrist was the enemy of the church, he was likely to be welcomed by other enemies of the church as a Messiah. The story was thus adapted to suit both the heretics and the partisans of the Staufen. Frederick II was prophesied to return as a reformer of the church, and, by implication, as the harbinger of the golden age; he had also been well known as an enemy of the papacy and there was therefore enough historical plausibility in the belief that on his resurrection he would lead the cause of the persecuted heretics to victory. The Staufen party did not exactly share in these heretical hopes; but necessity makes the strangest bedfellows and after the collapse of all Staufen ambitions in 1268, they were prepared to believe in the legend.

What is really striking is the list of things Frederick II was expected to do on his return. He would persecute the clergy and reform the corrupt church; he would equalize incomes by forcing the rich to marry the poor and would protect orphans and widows. He would find husbands for nuns and Beguines and force monks to hide their tonsure with cow-dung. He would banish monks and after a restoration of his empire he would travel to the Mount of Olives and lay down his imperial insignia in front of a barren and dried-up tree and thus cause it to sprout again.[2]

In this programme the mingling of religious and economic ideals is apparent, and is combined with a longing for religious purity as well as for social justice. Frederick II appears not as the Antichrist but as the good emperor who immediately precedes the

[1] For the connection of the legend with the heretics of Schwäbisch Hall in the thirteenth century see D. Völter, *Die Sekte von Schwäbisch-Hall und der Ursprung der deutschen Kaisersage*, ZKG, IV, 1880; and M. W. Bloomfield and M. E. Reeves, *The Penetration of Joachism into Northern Europe*, Sp, 29, 1954, p. 791. For the connection with the flagellants of 1340, *see* P. Hosp, *Ketzertum und deutsche Kaisersage beim Minoriten Johann von Winterthur*, FS, 3, 1915. For the connection with the heretics in the early fifteenth century and the testimony of Rothe, see H. Eberhardt, *Die Kyffhäuserburgen in Geschichte und Sage*, BDL, 96, 1960, p. 93.

[2] This list of objectives is taken from John Winterthur, F. Baethgen ed., MGH, SRG Berlin, 1955, p. 280. Apart from minor variations it is fairly identical with the objectives reported in other accounts, e.g. Ottmar's rhymed chronicle in Pez, *Script. Rerum Austriac.*, III, p. 290; and Jordanus of Osnabrück, *De Prerogativa Romani Imperii*, AGGW, pp. 79 ff. For the latter *cp.* also E. Dümmler, HZ, 29, 1873, pp. 491–2. John of Winterthur was an educated man and expressed great indignation at the superstition upon which the legend was based.

Antichrist. Prophecies about the coming reign of a 'good emperor' had been current in Germany for centuries, mostly in the form given to them by Abbot Adso,[1] that the last emperor would reign happily, and finally depart for Jerusalem and deposit his crown and sceptre on the Mount of Olives. In the late thirteenth century therefore the prophecies concerning Frederick II and the more ancient prophecies concerning the final emperor appear to have coalesced. The older prophecy encouraged people in the belief that there was truth in the new version; and the new version reinforced the belief in the old.

In view of the ultimate transformation of the whole legend, there is another feature which is of particular interest. It was said that after the completion of the social and economic reforms the emperor would journey to the Holy Land and there divest himself of his imperial dignity and make a voluntary surrender of his power to God.[2] With this part of the legend, we can see that the programme was assuming an archetypal shape: in the end, universal love will reign and there will be no need for empires.

There was no question here of a restoration of empire; or, if

[1] Abbot Adso of Montier-en-Der, if he was the author of the work *De Vita Antichristi*, wrote in 948. Sackur, *Sibyllinische Texte und Forchungen*, Halle, 1898, p. 164, believes that these prophecies first originated in the age of Constantine. For their content and vogue *cp.* J. Adamek, *Vom römischen Endreich der mittelalterlichen Bibelerklärung*, Würzburg, 1938, pp. 64–5. S. Riezler, *Zur deutschen Kaisersage*, HZ, 32, 1874, pp. 67 ff., was the first to point out the influence of these prophecies on the formation of the legend.

[2] The intrusion of the image of the barren tree into the legend deserves special mention. In Adso's original version, the emperor would travel to Golgotha or the Mount of Olives and deposit crown and sceptre. But in the thirteenth and fourteenth-century versions, the emperor was to travel to the Holy Land and hang up his shield on the barren tree which would then bloom. If an emperor divested himself of the crown, he gave up his power. (*Cp.* F. Kampers, *Vom Werdegang der abendländischen Kaisermystik*, 1924, p. 122, for the many possible variations on the theme that a ruler must lay down his insignia in the navel of the world.) This was an ancient and well-known symbolism. But if an emperor hung up his shield on a tree, he prepared to sit in judgement. (*Cp.* F. Kampers, *Kaiserprophetien und Kaisersagen im Mittelalter*, München, 1895, p. 137, note 1.) The substitution of the one image for the other may or may not be significant. But the really striking innovation is the introduction of the image of the barren tree. One can explain it only by assuming that in the popular imagination the memory of the story of the tree Ygdrasil and its connection with the twilight of the gods was more lively than the Mount of Olives. The prophecies of Adso were propagated in more or less learned circles. But our present legend was very much a matter for the popular imagination and the lower classes. Hence the re-emergence of ancient Germanic and pagan folk-lore. *Cp.* also F. Kampers, *ibid.*, pp. 137–138.

there was, the restoration was to be purely temporary. For the rest, the programme was not visionary but sociologically fairly precise and concrete.

It is no wonder that before long the story about Frederick's eventual return was to be treasured not only among the sectarians but also among the lower classes in general. This was particularly notable at the time of the Peasants' War in the early sixteenth century. The so-called *Volksbuch* of the Emperor Frederick, published first in 1519, tells, for instance, that when the emperor laid siege to Jerusalem, the city was taken after a ten days' assault through the efforts of the son of a Bavarian miller who was carrying the flag of the *Bundschuh*. And during the revolt of 1525, the peasants of central Germany congregated at the foot of the Kyffhäuser mountain which by that time was well established as the place in which the emperor was asleep. This peasants' army was destroyed in the battle of Frankenhausen; but even after the battle it was believed in that region that on Good Friday an assembly of peasants would take place on the Kyffhäuser, and that the Emperor Frederick would be resurrected, and would avenge the innocent blood which had been spilt at Frankenhausen.[1] It is impossible to tell whether the peasants congregated spontaneously at the Kyffhäuser because of the legend, or whether Thomas Müntzer, their leader, knowing the legend's power, chose the Kyffhäuser. Whatever the answer, there can be no doubt of the legend's powerful role in the Peasants' War.[2]

The second explanation for the formation in Germany of the legend is based on much more concrete political circumstances. There lived in Thuringia from 1269 to 1324 a grandson of Frederick II, Friedrich der Freidige, who, after Conradin's death in 1268, was considered the natural heir of the Staufen cause. At the end of the *Interregnum* there were people who even considered the possibility of electing him emperor. Nothing came of such plans. But already during his lifetime there were stories abroad in Italy and in Thuringia that this Friedrich would be the third Frederick and that under him the Staufen empire would be

[1] Quoted by H. Eberhardt, *op. cit.*, p. 97.
[2] *Ibid.*, p. 97, and A. Timm, *op. cit.*, pp. 12–13.

restored.[1] After his death the legend that sooner or later a Frederick would return and inaugurate the golden age, gained ground. Such stories were circulated until the middle of the sixteenth century.[2] It was said that the right Frederick would have a golden cross marked on his back[3] and all manner of prophecies were put forward relating first to Friedrich der Freidige[4] and eventually to Fredericks in general. As a result there was a succession of pretenders who claimed to be the subjects of these prophecies,[5] and there is no doubt that within a hundred years of the death of Friedrich der Freidige people were confused as to whether they expected the new Frederick to be a descendant of Frederick II or whether they expected him to be Frederick II resurrected.[6] But whatever was believed, it is clear it was not Frederick Barbarossa who was expected to return.

Nevertheless four problems remain. First, how and why did the legend come to be attached to the Kyffhäuser mountain? Second, why and when was Frederick Barbarossa substituted for Frederick II? Third, when and why was the content of the prophecy connected with the resurrection changed from the punishment of the clergy to the restoration of imperial power? And fourth, when and why did historians begin to consider the legend a source of historical knowledge?

As far as the first problem is concerned, any answer must take

[1] Grauert, *Zur deutschen Kaisersage*, HJ, 13, and F. Kampers, *Kaiserprophetien und Kaisersagen im Mittelalter*, pp. 127 ff.

[2] *ibid.*, p. 129. [3] *Loc. cit.*

[4] Grauert, *op. cit.*, passim.

[5] For these false Fredericks who came forward because there was a legend see e.g. Michelsen, *Die Kiffhäuser Kaisersage*, ZThGA, I, 1854, pp. 147 ff. At the time of the Emperor Sigismund, one rumour had it that the pope would not anoint him because he was not called Frederick (*ibid.*, p. 145). The most pathetic case of a false Frederick is the one of the tailor from Langensalza who was lunatic. He appears to have been found on the Kyffhäuser and the villagers insisted that he was the Emperor Frederick come back. The authorities investigated and found that he was a harmless lunatic on whom people were trying to foist the identity of the emperor. *See* H. Eberhardt, *op. cit.*, pp. 98–9.

[6] Grauert, *op. cit.*, p. 140 ff, and F. Kampers, *Die deutsche Kaiseridee in Prophetie und Sage*, München, 1896, p. 107, believe that at first the man in the mountain was believed to have been Friedrich der Freidige. But there is no written evidence for this. It is more probable that people expected a Frederick and when Friedrich der Freidige turned out not to be the emperor, they concluded that the Frederick they were expecting was Frederick II and took him to be asleep in the mountain.

into account not only the physical topography of the Kyffhäuser but also its history. The Kyffhäuser is a numinous mountain, and it is not surprising that the excavations conducted on the mountain before the second world war have brought to light prehistoric settlements which go back to pre-Germanic times. When the Teutonic Swabians first vanquished the local Celts, they established cults on similar mountains to celebrate the victory of their gods over those of the Celts,[1] and it is probable that such a cult developed also on the Kyffhäuser.[2] Eventually the mountain came to be associated with Wotan[3]; and when the Germans were Christianized, the story went that Wotan had taken refuge in the mountain and was biding his time there to reappear and vanquish the priests – an ominous background for the later imperial legend![4] The ravens which were later said to be flying around the mountain while Barbarossa was asleep are clearly Wotan's birds. It is impossible to say how early people saw the ravens, but to people living in the plains, the clouds which at certain times accumulate around the peak were an indication that Wotan was alive controlling the weather for good or for ill.[5]

But it was not only the Wotan legend that made the mountain notorious. A large number of legends of the region elaborate on the theme of a mysterious man who went in search of metal or treasure – the two are always associated – and, falling to his death in a cave or crevice, was devoured by the mountain. The occasional disappearance of such mysterious prospectors often gave

[1] A. Götze, *Führer auf die Steinsburg bei Römhild*, 3rd ed., Hildburghausen, 1934.

[2] G. Neumann, *Kyffhäuser Studien*, ZThGA, 42, 1940, p. 371. See also the same author's 'Die Kelten in Thüringen', *Der Thüringer Erzieher*, 3, 1935, pp. 9 ff. *Cp.* also B. K. Meyer, *Die ehemalige Reichsburg Kyffhäusen*, Rossla, 1868, pp. 31 ff., and E. Rodhe, *Psyche*, London, 1925, p. 93.

[3] A. Fulda, *Die Kyffhäusersage*, 1889, believed to have discovered documentary proof that the Kyffhäuser used to be sacred to Wotan.

[4] *Cp.* W. Erben, *Untersperg – Studien. Ein Beitrag zur Geschichte der deutschen Kaisersage*, MGSL, 54, 1914, p. 16.

[5] J. Praetorius, *Alectryomantia*, p. 70, records an old local saying: 'Hoho! the emperor Frederick is brewing; the weather is going to be heavy!' The peasants of the surrounding plains are even today thinking of Wotan when they look at the weather:

Steht der Wode ohne Hut,'
Bleibt das Wetter schön und gut;
Ist er mit dem Hut zu sehn,
Wird das Wetter nicht bestehn.

rise to terrible rumours. The metal or treasure itself is ambivalent. People wanted to bring it to light; but the physical dangers surrounding the digging gave rise to the belief that there was a magic spell which prevented it from being found. And at times the metal was 'heard' and interpreted as an army of iron-clad warriors living in the mountain. If gold diggers and necromancers had inhabited the mountain, Christians felt its attraction for religious purposes. It developed into a place of pilgrimage and was used as such until the time of the Reformation.[1]

The Kyffhäuser mountain was also important strategically because of its commanding view over the plains. According to an old legend, the castle on its peak was first built by Julius Caesar.[2] This cannot be true; but the story proves that, as long as anybody could remember, the mountain was associated with military power. The castle, the ruins of which are still visible, was probably built in the late eleventh century and occupied by imperial *ministeriales*. As such it remained until the middle of the fourteenth century as an outpost of imperial power in a region which was increasingly becoming divided among the various territorial princes who were developing their independence at the expense of the empire.[3] When the empire lost its last vestiges of power in Thuringia during the late fourteenth century, the castle seems to have been abandoned. By the fifteenth century, like so many other Thuringian castles, it was used as a quarry for stones; and even then the chronicler John Rothe, who died in 1434, called it a 'deserted and ruined castle'.[4]

So first of all, the castle was associated with imperial power. Second, by the time the legend was beginning to take shape the castle was beginning to be neglected and was falling into ruins, which made it easy for people to imagine that the old emperor might be asleep in the mountain. The castle had been his. Also, the ancient association with Wotan must have encouraged the

[1] L. Bechstein, *Mythe, Sage, Märe und Fabel*, III, p. 186; Rothe, *Düringische Chronik*, R. v. Liliencron ed., Jena, 1859, p. 679, reports that after Easter 1433 the church organized pilgrimages in order to exorcise the imperial ghost. For the chapel *see* H. Eberhardt, *op. cit.*, p. 89.

[2] G. H. Behrens, *Hercynia Curiosa*, 1st ed., 1703.

[3] H. Eberhardt, *op. cit.*, p. 79 ff.

[4] *Düringische Chronik*, R. v. Liliencron ed., p. 426.

belief that someone lay asleep there. And as progressive Christianization tended to weaken the belief that that person was Wotan, the idea that it was the emperor was taken up with all the greater enthusiasm. There can be no certainty about the exact date of the localization of the legend on the Kyffhäuser. But we know that it was well established there by 1434.[1]

When and why people began to think that the man asleep in the mountain was Frederick Barbarossa and not Frederick II is a more complicated problem. The date can be settled fairly easily. The first time Frederick Barbarossa is mentioned as the subject of the legend in a written document was in 1519, when the so-called *Volksbuch* was published. It had a very wide circulation in the sixteenth century and went through many editions – but we can also be fairly certain that it drew on an oral tradition and probably, therefore, even before 1519 some people thought that the man in the mountain was Barbarossa.[2] Even so, the truth took a long time to die. A Broadsheet of the year 1537 mentioned that the man in the mountain was Frederick II and the publicist Fischart (d. 1590) knew that the legend concerned him.[3] Similarly, in a collection of anecdotes published by Drautius in 1642, the man is said to be Frederick II. But other antiquarians were less sure. In 1600 Johann Wolf wrote that the Frederick in the mountain was the elector Frederick the Wise of Saxony.[4] Johannes Praetorius, writing in the second half of the seventeenth century, was in two minds. In one of his earlier works in 1666, he believed the Frederick in the mountain to be Frederick II[5] but in his *Alectryomantia* he spoke of him as Frederick I.[6] Tentzel, in 1689, admitted there was no telling which of the two Fredericks was believed to be in the mountain[7] and Behrens, at the beginning of the following century, reported that opinion was divided.[8] The same

[1] Leibniz ed., *Scriptores rerum Brunsvicarum*, II, p. 1115.

[2] The *Volksbuch*, Pfeiffer ed., ZDA, V, went through many editions in the sixteenth century. It was used in 1531 by Sebastian Frank and in 1572 by Caspar Hedio.

[3] *Gargantua.*

[4] *Lectionum Memorat. Tomus II*, Laningal, 1600, p. 114.

[5] *Neue Weltbeschreibung*, etc., Magdeburg, 1666, pp. 353–4.

[6] Frankfurt and Leipzig, 1681, pp. 67 ff.

[7] *Monatliche Unterredungen*, Leipzig, 1689, p. 719.

[8] *Hercynia Curiosa*, Nordhausen, 1712, p. 151.

division of opinion was mentioned by the so-called Melissantes who added that, for all he cared, it was probably the devil himself who was in the mountain.[1] Eventually, the philosopher and historian Leibniz was alone in his certainty that the legend concerned Frederick II.[2]

During the eighteenth century the confusion appears to have increased. Behrens and Praetorious had both expressed their doubts, but their books were widely used by less discerning readers, and so the story that it was the Emperor Frederick Barbarossa who was in the mountain was disseminated. Finally it was made famous throughout Germany by Rückert's poem published in 1817[3] and given the seal of scholarly approval by the publication of J. Grimm's *Deutsche Mythologie.*[4] Soon after Grimm it gained further currency through the collection of Thuringian legends by Ludwig Bechstein,[5] and it must have been at that time, fortified by the opinions of such authorities on myth and legend as Grimm and Bechstein, that historians began to wonder what information such a popular legend might yield about Frederick Barbarossa.

It is remarkable that it did not occur to Grimm, who knew so much about mythology and the patterns on which myths were constructed, that the identification of the emperor in the mountain as Frederick Barbarossa must be of recent origin. For to anybody acquainted with mythological patterns, it should have been clear that this particular type of legend was not likely to have formed

[1] *Das erneuerte Alterthum,* Frankfurt and Leipzig, 1713, p. 550.

[2] See his note to Engelhusius, *Scriptores rerum Brunsvicarum,* II, 1710, p. 1115.

[3] 'Der alte Barbarossa, der Kaiser Friedrich. . . .' Novalis, writing *circa* 1800, knew that the legend concerned Frederick II. See *Schriften,* Samuel ed., Stuttgart, 1960, I, pp. 337, 340–8. But Görres, writing in 1907, did not hesitate to identify the emperor in the mountain as Frederick Barbarossa. He had found the legend in Otmar's *Volcks-Sagen,* Bremen, 1800, where the emperor is simply called Frederick and said to have a red beard. Görres, no doubt, jumped to his conclusion because of the red beard. *Cp.* E. Koch, *Die Sage von Kaiser Friedrich im Kiffhäuser,* Grimma, 1880, p. 19.

[4] J. Grimm, *Deutsche Sagen,* 1st ed., 1816, Grimm drew his material mainly from Praetorius. But where Praetorius had been doubtful about the identity of the emperor, Grimm had no hesitation in lending his scholarly authority to the identification of the emperor as Frederick Barbarossa. In his later *Deutsche Mythologie* he was aware of the mythological echoes of the story about the removal of heroes to mountains, etc.; but he did not betray the slightest doubt in regard to the mythopoeic fallacy of identifying the emperor as Barbarossa.

[5] *Die Sagen des Kyffhäusers,* 1st ed., 1835.

itself around the figure of a *successful* emperor. Grimm did state that in some versions of the legend it was said that the emperor who would return was Frederick II, and he thought that people had probably mixed the two up.[1] But he did not conclude anything more from this observation.

The first to notice the substitution and its comparatively recent origin was the antiquarian Michelson.[2] And in 1871 the historian G. Voigt published an article in the *Historische Zeitschrift* which proved the substitution beyond doubt.[3] But many nineteenth century historians were naïve rationalists and had little or no knowledge of the logic of mythopoeic thinking. One example of this is a tortuous explanation put forward by Bernheim in 1895. Bernheim admitted that the legend originally had concerned Frederick II but went on to say that the substitution was fully justified for he believed that the legend implied that the emperor in the mountain *must have been* a successful emperor. And since Frederick Barbarossa had been a successful emperor, the substitution was actually an improvement on the original version![4] Bernheim must have imagined that if the returning emperor was to be a messiah, he must have been a great and triumphant emperor before his death – how else could anyone believe him to achieve triumphs in the future? Bernheim was unaware of the basic mythological principle that a Resurrection must be preceded by a Fall.

Bernheim's reasoning, however, is only a special instance of the kind of rationalization which was responsible for the initial substitution of Frederick Barbarossa for Frederick II, first evident in the *Volksbuch* of 1519. Voigt provided a curious and purely cir-

[1] *Deutsche Mythologie*, 2nd ed., II, p. 910.

[2] *Die Kiffhäuser Kaisersage*, ZThGA, I, 1854.

[3] Vol. 26, 1871.

[4] *Die Herrscher der deutschen Kaiserzeit in den ursprünglichen Volksüberlieferungen*, PJ, 1895, 81, p. 357. L. Bechstein believed that the confusion arose because both men died in foreign lands and were equally qualified for the role of hero. See his *Mythe, Sage, Märe und Fabel*, III, p. 183. S. O. Riezler, *Der Kreuzzug Kaiser Friedrich I*, FDG, X, 1870, p. 126 ff., was not aware of the substitution and therefore went with a fine tooth-comb through all the accounts of Frederick's death in Asia Minor in order to discover what features in these accounts could have given rise to the legend. At least Riezler was more perceptive than Bernheim, for it did occur to him that if the legend had originally attached itself to Frederick Barbarossa, it must have had something to do with the peculiarly tragic manner of his death rather than with the fact that he was a greatly successful ruler.

cumstantial explanation.[1] He noted that in post-medieval times the legend stressed more and more that on account of the length of time the emperor had been waiting in the mountain his beard had grown to an enormous length. Voigt concluded that people got confused by the beard: they knew that Frederick Barbarossa had a beard and therefore jumped to the conclusion that if a beard is mentioned, the beard must belong to Frederick Barbarossa. Kampers, another historian, was more vague. In early times emperors were not clearly numbered and there are a number of occasions in the late thirteenth and fourteenth centuries when chroniclers and historians simply confused the two Fredericks. Kampers concluded that the substitution owed its origin to a similar carelessness.[2] In contrast to these views, a close examination of the *Volksbuch* of 1519 provides a more cogent and particular reason for the substitution. For the author of the *Volksbuch* relates that Frederick Barbarossa was a truly famous ruler and the greatest since Charlemagne. He did not die but merely disappeared and is said to be in the mountain. One day he will return and punish the clergy and hang his shield on the barren tree in the Holy Land. For this reason the sultans are keeping that tree under constant watch.

The author reasons that if the emperor is to return and triumph, he must have been a triumphant emperor in his lifetime. But since he knew that Frederick II was *not* triumphant and that Frederick Barbarossa *was* triumphant, he concluded that the legend cannot refer to Frederick II. Ironically, none of the stories he relates redound much to the credit of Frederick Barbarossa or encourage the belief that he was a successful emperor. But once the author had attached the legend to Frederick Barbarossa, he had to conclude, *in defiance of his own evidence*, that Frederick Barbarossa was indeed a great emperor.[3]

[1] Voigt, *op. cit.*, p. 185.

[2] For example see *ibid.* pp. 189–90. Even Bartolo of Sassoferrato confused the two Fredericks.

[3] Both Sebastian Brant (1458–1521) of Strassburg and the physician Adelphus writing in the early sixteenth century believed that Frederick Barbarossa was, after Charlemagne, the greatest of all emperors because of his crusade. Adelphus was the author of a history of Frederick Barbarossa which was very largely based upon the thirteenth-century chronicle by Burchard of Ursberg.

The hope held out by the legend also changed its content. We have seen that originally people had hoped that the emperor would return and punish the clergy and inaugurate the end of history by causing the barren tree to blossom; and the author of the *Volksbuch* says quite clearly that on his return Frederick Barbarossa would do precisely these things. There is no indication in the *Volksbuch*, however, that, on his return, the emperor would carry out a work of practical political reconstruction. Those hopes came only much later. One can indeed surmise that the rationalized myth began to lose its popular appeal in the seventeenth and eighteenth centuries and that when it came to be resurrected in the nineteenth century, it was resurrected for political purposes and given a new content. When precisely this happened is impossible to say. According to Behrens, writing in the beginning of the eighteenth century, the current story was that the emperor in the mountain is only half asleep and will wake well before the Final Day of Judgement and will return to rule his empire.[1] How he will rule was not mentioned. But he will re-assume the empire, and there is no reference to the punishment of the clergy or the barren tree. We have a recorded instance of the year 1810 when, on the occasion of a musical festival in Frankenhausen at the foot of the Kyffhäuser, the singer Methfessel and some of his friends climbed the mountain and invited the Emperor Frederick Barbarossa to awake soon and liberate Germany from the Napoleonic yoke.[2] Methfessel knew nothing about the punishment of the clergy and the barren tree in the Holy Land. He took it for granted that if Frederick Barbarossa were to come back, he would come back to defeat Napoleon. When giving expression to this hope, Methfessel completed the process of de-mythologization which had been begun by the *Volksbuch*. And from here it was a small step, after the fall of Napoleon, to the belief that the return of Frederick Barbarossa would signify the restoration of the empire or the unification of Germany. When the de-mythologization was thus complete, the nineteenth century version bore very little resemblance to the original: Frederick Barbarossa had been substituted

[1] *Cp.* Voigt, *op. cit.*, p. 183, n. 2.

[2] Louis Spohr, *Selbstbiographie*, Kassel und Leipzig, 1860, I, pp. 159 f.

for Frederick II; and the desire for social justice and the eschatological expectations had been replaced by a very practical political programme. It was in this vulgarized shape that the legend began to influence the judgement of historians in the nineteenth century.

The earliest historian of Frederick Barbarossa who conceivably could have heard of the substitution of Barbarossa for Frederick II, was the physician Adelphus,[1] writing in the early sixteenth century. But at that time the hope connected with the return of the emperor was still so clearly eschatological that Adelphus, who was exclusively concerned with the then fashionable humanistic nationalism, took no notice of the legend at all. The next major work on Frederick Barbarossa appeared in the early eighteenth century and was written by Heinrich von Bünau.[2] Bünau was a real eighteenth century rationalist. He firmly believed in enlightenment and he too was proof against the legend, most probably because of its eschatological significance. Raumer's volume on Frederick Barbarossa appeared first in 1823 and, chronologically, one might expect him to have been the first victim of the new vogue. But Raumer,[3] although he was in touch with Tieck and other romantics, appears to have taken no notice of the legend. As a result his portrait of Frederick Barbarossa was considered weak and colourless.[4] But by the middle of the nineteenth century the combined efforts of Rückert, Grimm and Bechstein had changed the climate of opinion. When Prutz produced his major biography he said in his preface that he had allowed himself to be influenced by the Kyffhäuser legend because such a legend would not have arisen if there had not been a germ of truth in it.[5] And when, soon after, B. v. Simson completed Giesebrecht's volumes on Frederick Barbarossa, he too felt obliged to pay oblique tribute to the power of the legend.

One can see from this that historians did not begin to take notice when Barbarossa was substituted for Frederick II – for the

[1] His *Barbarossa* appeared first in 1520.

[2] *Probe einer genauen und umständlichen Kayser – und Reichshistorie oder Leben und Tathen Friedrichs I, römischen Kaysers*, Leipzig, 1722.

[3] *Geschichte der Hohenstaufen*, 1st ed., 1823.

[4] F. X. Wegele, *Geschichte der deutschen Historiographie*, p. 1028.

[5] *Friedrich I*, 1870, Preface.

substitution of one emperor for another in a weird medieval legend was of no interest to the critical minds of historians. They began to take notice when the eschatological content of the legend was being replaced by a practical political programme – be it the expulsion of Napoleon or the unification of Germany. But by that time there really was nothing left of the original legend, except perhaps the story that the emperor was asleep in the Kyffhäuser. And that localization of the legend on the Kyffhäuser, as we have seen, is by no means the oldest part. Thus the legend which Prutz believed to yield some information about Frederick Barbarossa stands revealed as a modern concoction. The fact that the original does not concern Frederick Barbarossa is significant enough. But in its modern form, looking forward to the restoration of the empire, it could not even have been used as an indication of the feelings people had about Frederick II. For Frederick II was supposed to come back not to restore the empire but to punish the clergy, to equalize incomes and then to hang up his shield on the barren tree and bring all history to a final conclusion.

It is, of course, difficult to say in precisely what ways the legend has cast its spell over the picture of Frederick Barbarossa which has come to be accepted. The documentary evidence about his reign, as is to be expected in medieval history, shows enormous and tantalizing gaps. Historians intent upon an overall picture of his reign have therefore always had to resort to a great deal of interpretation, to fill those gaps and to arrive at a coherent picture. In this respect the legend in its modern form has proved a baneful influence. For it says that Frederick Barbarossa will return and restore the empire *because* in his own time he was so successful in building up the empire. When historians approach the source material for the reign of Frederick Barbarossa with the idea that people in the late twelfth century used to believe that he had built up a huge and powerful empire and that he had been a greatly triumphant ruler, their interpretation of the material will naturally be influenced. The picture of Frederick which has thus emerged suggests the more or less tacit use of the modern legend in several ways.[1]

[1] K. Hampe in his standard text, *Deutsche Kaisergeschichte*, 11th ed., revised by F. Baethgen, Heidelberg, 1963, p. 220, admits that although the Kyffhäuser legend

One can pin-point this influence in three general features. There is, first, the widespread belief that Frederick's accession marked the beginning of a new epoch – if he was so triumphant as emperor, his power and vigour must have been felt right from the start. Historians are therefore apt to apply the words of Frederick Barbarossa's twelfth-century biographer, Otto of Freising, to the effect that a new age was beginning, to the *whole* of his reign. Secondly, historians have tended to see the political manœuvre which led in 1180 to the fall of Henry the Lion as a final measure taken by Frederick to chastise an over-mighty subject – a measure which they suppose prepared and completed the final triumph of the powerful emperor.[1] Thirdly, the legend has predisposed historians to see the crusade as issuing from the fullness of Frederick's power, a sign of final triumph from which he unfortunately did not return. But it seems more likely that his decision to undertake the crusade at the age of 65 is proof of the ultimately transcendental direction of his political aims. Viewed from that angle, his death and his failure to return appear almost like poetic justice – at any rate as something that might have been expected; as something that set a transcendental seal on his political efforts. Far from going on a crusade because he was the great and successful emperor – as the modern legend has it – he went because he had allowed feudalism to grow and flourish so that he would be freed from attending to his daily tasks as a ruler and administrator. Without the modern legend, the crusade on which he died appears not as the crowning glory to a successful political career, but as the antithesis to a political career.

In this book therefore an attempt will be made to present a

---

does not go back to Barbarossa in such matters 'fantasy must overrule reason'. He repeated this thought on p. 103 of his *Herrschergestalten Deutschen Mittelalters*, 6th revised edition, Heidelberg, 1955: 'The picture of his (Frederick's) personality has pressed itself deeply into German and, substituted by legend for the person of his grandson as the emperor waiting in the mountain for the day of his return, was able to inspire . . . as late as the nineteenth century the movement for unification.'

[1] In truth, if one looks at what little evidence there is about the reasons for the fall of Henry the Lion, it seems that Frederick proceeded to destroy Henry because Henry was an obstacle to the growing feudalization of Germany – a feudalization which Frederick wanted to develop so that he could be free to go on a crusade.

picture of Frederick Barbarossa's[1] political efforts freed from the spell of the Kyffhäuser legend. But in order to be able to sift and interpret the scanty source material, one is compelled to make an assessment of the general nature of the sociological developments that took place in the twelfth century. The historian must form an impression of the atmosphere and the environment in which Frederick Barbarossa worked and moved. If he wants to reconstruct the course of Frederick's political activities, he must seek to connect the isolated pieces of evidence with one another and gauge their meaning. The meaning they have is the meaning they had in Frederick's mind. Therefore one has to begin by trying to understand Frederick's mind and asking what his plans were; and since plans are usually formulated in response to problems, one must begin by asking what were the problems which confronted Frederick.

At this point it is equally necessary to make clear some of the problems which historians have when dealing with this period. The documentary evidence is sparse, and therefore to get a full comprehensible picture of Frederick, the historian must make certain assumptions about the character of the period and the man.

I have refused to take my cue from the Kyffhäuser legend and merely investigate the nature of the empire over which he was supposed to have presided so gloriously. I have instead taken my cue from the observation that he thought and planned and that these thoughts and plans provide the connecting links between his political actions. The actions which are not thus connected, such as his abortive campaigns in Poland, are treated as incidents without special significance. Most of his plans could not be realized. This does not prove that he had none; but that other people, too, had plans which crossed his.

[1] Frederick was the grandson of Frederick von Büren who was made duke of Swabia in 1079 by Emperor Henry IV. The Büren family henceforth called themselves the Staufen after the rock near Göppingen in Swabia on which they erected their family castle. Frederick was surnamed Barbarossa by the Italians because of his red beard.

CHAPTER II

To Begin at the Beginning . . .

The central feature of Germany in the twelfth century is the enormous social transformation that was taking place. Its most likely and most direct cause was probably the enormous and spectacular increase in population.[1] But whatever its precise cause, the outcome is clear – at least in outline. Society was proliferating in all directions. Class distinctions were being multiplied and a large number of new classes emerged where before there had probably been no more than half a dozen. A limited number of large families or clans whose personal association had provided the skeleton of political organization[2] split up into so many groups and subgroups that a purely personal association as a basis for political organization was no longer possible. The increase in quantity was also to cause a change in quality.[3]

[1] The population of Germany is estimated to have risen from four million in 1100 to seven million in 1200. J. C. Russel, *Late Ancient and Medieval Population*, TAPhS, 1958, NS, 48, Pt. 3, pp. 111–12. See also p. 99. The population increase was not confined to Germany. M. K. Bennett, *The World's Food*, 1954, p. 9, Table I, considers that between 1100 and 1200 the population of Europe rose from forty-eight million to sixty-one million. According to B. H. Slicher van Bath, *The Agrarian History of Western Europe*, London, 1963, p. 79, the five decades from 1150 to 1200 (i.e. the exact period of Frederick's reign) are one of the three periods of the steepest increase in population in European history. The other periods are the fifteenth century and the eighteenth, nineteenth and twentieth centuries. The highest index of population increase ever is for the period 1850–1900, i.e. 150·8 per cent. The index for 1150–1200 was 122 per cent and was surpassed before the nineteenth century only once, in 1400–50, when it reached 133·3 per cent. G. Duby, *Economie rurale et la vie des campagnes*, Paris, 1962, I, p. 214, cites an example from Lombardy which shows that in 1181 as much as 12 per cent of the agricultural labourers were not residing in the village of their ancestors. This suggests a very high rate of mobility in the rural population.

[2] 'The numerous dispensations that were required for such marriages show that by 1100 all the royal houses and the more powerful princely houses were related by blood. They formed one great family.' Otto Forst de Battaglia, *The European Nobility*, CSSH, V, 1962–3, p. 64.

[3] As against the older views of Inama-Sternegg and Lamprecht that there also took place a revolution in agrarian economy, both A. Dopsch, *Herrschaft und Bauer in der*

As far as politics and government were concerned, these social changes required a completely new form of organization. In the Germany of the twelfth century, therefore, any energetic ruler was faced with the task of having to devise a new scheme of government and of political organization. In front of him there was a vacuum which had to be filled. But with society proliferating and with the old methods of cementing the bonds of association becoming rapidly ineffectual, the task of reorganization and of finding new political forms had to be completed rapidly. Alternately, if the new task could not be completed, society would generate spontaneously its own bonds of association designed to produce some kind of effective security and protection for its individual members. And when indeed no new overall scheme of government was devised, the development of feudal bonds progressed more and more rapidly and more and more universally. Feudalism was people's spontaneous reaction to the governmental gap. The historian looking backward can, therefore, safely approach the history of the second part of the twelfth century with the idea that he is looking for efforts to form new ways of government either by devising a new scheme of government or by actively promoting the growth of feudal bonds.

The improvisation of new forms of government in competition with the rapidly evolving feudalization of society could, however, be no simple and straightforward task. There were also new social and ideological forces struggling against one another. Any improvisation of a new scheme of government would have to be successful in adjusting those forces with one another. In order to understand the vigour and the incompatibility of these forces, we have to examine their origins some two and a half centuries before.

---

deutschen Kaiserzeit, Jena, 1939, p. 135, and Ch.-E. Perrin, *La société rurale allemande du Xe au XIIIe siècle*, RHDFE, 4th ser., XXII, 1944, p. 101, insist that no economic revolution of any kind took place and that Germany remained economically backward. It is very important to bear this in mind, for it was the population explosion which created many of Frederick's problems. Moreover, the lack of an accompanying economic revolution prevented any far-reaching adjustments and ultimately allowed no more than the evolution of a feudal monarchy, so that one cannot but return to M. Bloch's description of the German monarchy as 'archaic'. See his *Feudal Society*, London, 1961, p. 426. Frederick's efforts were necessitated by the population explosion but many of them were wasted because of economic stagnation in Germany.

From the beginning of the tenth to the end of the eleventh century, the kings and emperors of the Saxon and Salian dynasties had laboured to erect their power in the lands between the Rhine and the Elbe. Their efforts were not based upon conquest and could not appeal to any kind of national consciousness or solidarity. Their only assets were the odd memories and traditions of Carolingian kingship and the fear of the Hungarian invaders, both of which, from the middle of the tenth century onward, had been transformed into an aggressive missionary zeal to convert the Slav heathen who lived beyond the Elbe. On this basis the grandiose scheme of a theocratic kingship had been built. The kings and emperors did not call themselves the equals of the Apostles, as the rulers of Byzantium had been wont to do; and the expression 'sacred empire' did not become customary until after the second half of the twelfth century. But in substance and conception, the rule of the Saxon and Salian kings was built upon a static religious order. God, the Supreme Judge, had charged the king with the rule of Christendom. To discharge this function, the king was anointed and crowned the supreme lord over clergy and laity. This was a massive and sacred order, something like a material realization of the city of God, with the Christians inside and the heathen outside – a fortress, very much a religious fortress, symbolized by the romanesque cathedral, with the towers like a bastion at the west end, and the altar at the east end; the faithful, led by their emperor, inside; and the demons of Satan, battling against the ramparts, outside. The structure was Byzantine, unitary, solid and hierarchical – if one may compare the land-locked regions that stretch between the Rhine and the Elbe, to the flourishing empire centred upon Constantinople, the most fabulous city of the Christian east. Given the wide social and economic differences between the eastern and the western empire, any comparison between the two must be confined to the theory which was shared by both: the supreme ruler was anointed to be more than a secular magistrate. He was the representative of God on earth and to him both clergy and laity owed obedience. There was nothing specifically spiritual or morally Christian in this theory; and the order to which it gave rise was Christian only because the God by Whom it was alleged to have been ordained was thought of as a Christian God. But in the western empire, this theocratic conception was given concrete substance by the way in which royal and imperial power operated through the princely bishops. It was to those bishops that the rulers had delegated a large number of their powers which otherwise would have been usurped by dukes and counts. In material expression of their supreme, divinely sanctioned overlordship, the kings invested the bishops not only with secular powers and treated them like feudal vassals, but also with the ring which signified their spiritual office. And whatever one might think of the importance of the theocratic theory on which this empire was built, one can have no doubts as to the theocratic practice by which it lived.

Ironically enough, it was in the shadow of this theocratic empire that the papacy had begun to espouse the cause of a spiritual reform, the avowed purpose of which was to free the bishops from the meshes of the feudal system, to make the church independent of the empire and to allow it to be guided by standards and considerations other than the glorification of this religious imperialism. In the course of this campaign, the reformed papacy finally insisted – or was obliged to insist by the stubborn imperial refusal to relinquish its hold over the bishops – that a king and an emperor is no more than a secular ruler, and a satanic one at that, unless he has obtained the blessing of the pope. By this standpoint, the papacy abandoned all ideas of substituting itself for the emperor as the head of the theocratic order and set itself instead on a course which before long tore the whole order, both in theory and practice, completely asunder. As a result, by the end of the eleventh century, people were beginning to learn to distinguish the sacred from the profane, the papacy from the empire, the supernatural from the natural, religion from politics. Instead of seeing the world as hierarchically ordered, with the emperor – under God – at the apex, people were beginning to discern the presence of at least three quite independent forces: spiritualism, naturalism and sacerdotalism.

There was, first, *spiritualism*. This was the conviction that a religious and God-fearing life had to be a life in poverty and humility;

and that such a life was incompatible with the pomp and wealth of feudalism, be it that of the princely bishops and popes or be it that of the king and emperor, anointed and ecclesiastically consecrated. Under this heading there began in the twelfth century a large number of developments ranging from the heretical sects that flourished in northern Italy and southern France to the eventually more orthodox preaching of St Francis of Assisi.

Secondly, we find the development of what we might call *naturalism.* Under this heading we should place the growth of a number of political institutions which were, instead of being guided by their memberships of the Holy Order, beginning to be propelled by purely rational considerations of secular utility. The manifestations of naturalism range from the forceful growth of the various Norman states in Britain, Normandy and Sicily to the minor territorial ambitions displayed in Germany, for example, by the princes of the house of Zähringen; and in Italy by the growing communes. In every one of these political organizations we find that the over-riding consideration is secular advantage. Instead of being content with forming a more or less spurious membership of the Holy Order, kings and dukes and citizens were bent upon evolving a machinery which would ensure the suppression of violence, the elimination of feuds, speedy justice, easy collection of taxes and, last but not least, a territorial compactness of their powers. For only with such territorial compactness could the political monarchy function efficiently. As far as the emperor was concerned, he agreed eventually that no matter how anointed he was, and how sacramental a ritual the coronation was, he was not competent to invest bishops with the ring of their office. In other words, he was obliged to concede that he was no longer quite the apex of the Holy Order; or at any rate, that as far as the priesthood was concerned, they had a warrant independent of him. And such an admission implied, or seemed to imply, that even an emperor was only a secular magistrate and that he existed for a rational mundane purpose rather than for a religious one.

The third force was *sacerdotalism.* Under its heading come not only the bishops' growing independence from the power of the kings and emperors, but especially the pope's growing overlordship of the clergy. Independent and free, the clergy tended to appear more as the intermediaries between God and man than as the clerical members of the Holy Order, subject to the anointed of God, the new David, the emperor. This development crystallized the purely sacerdotal and mediating functions of the church and tended to remove the clergy from the orbit of the old hierarchical order. It tended to establish and confirm the church not only as an indepedent institution but also as a rather superior institution which was to give soul to the body and guard the spirit from the flesh.[1]

It would, however, be a gross oversimplification to think that these three forces were always mutually hostile and opposed to each other. The Holy Order was breaking up; but this did not necessarily mean that the new forces were all incompatible with one another. On the contrary, the thirteenth century was to show very clearly that each derived some strength from the fact that each of the other two supported it in at least one respect. Thus spiritualism, though opposed to sacerdotalism in its insistence on ecclesiastical poverty, countenanced the power and influence of priests in their spiritual capacity and helped to free them from the trammels of both feudalism and the Holy Order. For the spiritual teachers objected only to the priesthood discharging secular and political functions, and their influence proved a vigorous support for the spiritual claims of priests. In the eleventh century, therefore, Gregory VII had welcomed the spiritual teachers in Milan as allies; and 150 years later, Innocent III was to try his best to make the Franciscan Friars available for preaching and missionary work, even though he thus offended the dignity of bishops and of the secular clergy.

[1] On the purely practical level, *sacerdotalism* was the strong tendency in the twelfth century for canon law to invade the spheres of public and private law. The conception of God's truce came to be applied to politics; the peace granted to the clergy came to be extended to peasants and merchants and the theft of ecclesiastical property came to be regarded as sacrilegious as if it were theft of an object of religious cult. All this amounted to an enormous extension of sacerdotal power and jurisdiction. The crusades, too, advanced sacerdotalism, for a layman who took the Cross became 'clericalized' and could benefit from certain provisions of the canon which ordinarily applied only to people in holy orders or to monks.

Similarly, spiritualism, at times, though believing that the Christian life was incompatible with the pursuit of temporal power and wealth, countenanced the growth of naturalism. For when it insisted that the clergy should cease to busy themselves with politics, it favoured by implication the complete control of politics by the secular authorities. Thus Arnold of Brescia, a radical preacher and advocate of the need for the complete poverty of the clergy, who had become the ideological leader of the Romans' rebellion against the pope, invited Conrad III to Rome and suggested that he deprive the pope of all territorial power and assume it in the pope's stead.

Sacerdotalism was however opposed to naturalism; for it claimed that the priesthood alone could provide the ultimate justification of all political power. But since it argued against the theocratic conception of imperial and royal power, it ended up by freeing kings, emperors and princes from all but utilitarian and naturalistic considerations and thus encouraged such triumphs of naturalistic reasoning as were to be found in the early fourteenth century in the *Defensor Pacis* of Marsilius of Padua, or in the aggressive anti-papal policies of Philip the Fair of France.

These three forces were jostling each other, competing with each other and struggling against each other, each deriving a certain measure of support from one against the other. But the fact that there were three rather than just two complicated any issue that was to arise and made the task of filling the vacuum a very complicated one which required a great deal of tact and ingenuity as well as a great deal of good luck.

Frederick's reign almost exactly spans the period between the second and the third crusades. The second crusade had ended in failure and disaster in 1148 – four years before his election to the throne. And the third crusade was first undertaken by Frederick himself in 1189, at the very end of his reign.

In spite of the initial universal enthusiasm, the second crusade had proved a complete failure from the military point of view. The crusaders had not been able to re-conquer Edessa and both Conrad III and Louis VII of France had been forced to return to Europe in early 1149 without restoring this much needed eastern bastion to the Christian knights. When the second crusade proved such a failure, there was an almost universal outcry of sorrow and indignation throughout Christendom.[1] There was a general feeling of depression and pessimism, and everybody realized that sooner or later a new crusade would have to be undertaken. Frederick became king and emperor in the wake of this despair and as emperor he knew that it was his duty eventually to go on a new crusade. He knew therefore from the beginning of his reign what the outcome ought to be. And this knowledge of the future enabled him to survey the present and understand that he would have to undertake the function of government in such a way that he would be able to depart for a new crusade. Somehow or other he would have to make ends meet – and if one plan proved unsuccessful he would have to try another. We can see therefore that his knowledge of the probable future made him approach the immediate governmental task in hand with a feeling of experimentation – there was a gap which ought to be filled.

But there was more to it than that. He not only kept the ultimate aim of his reign firmly in mind and approached all government problems as so many makeshifts to fulfil this ultimate aim. He also knew enough about the functions of an emperor to understand this ultimate end as more than a political expedient to assist the kingdom of Jerusalem or what was left of it.

Ever since the late tenth century, the prophecy that the reign of the Antichrist would be preceded by the reign of a final emperor had been current. The final emperor, a king of the Franks, would govern the Roman empire. He would be a great king and the last of all kings. After a happy reign he would travel to Jerusalem and deposit his sceptre and crown on the Mount of Olives. The act of voluntary surrender of the supreme power would immediately precede the coming of the Antichrist – and the coming

[1] 'The most convincing evidence of the disillusionment and discouragement which followed the failure of the Second Crusade is found not in the literary sources but in the poor response which greeted the efforts of Bernard and Suger to organize a new expedition for the relief of the Holy Land in 1150 and in the reduced number of new Cistercian monasteries established after 1147.' G. Constable, *The Second Crusade as seen by Contemporaries*, Tr., IX, 1953, pp. 275–6. But Constable's survey of the literary sources is equally convincing.

of the Antichrist would be the beginning of the last and final stage of all history. There is ample evidence that in the middle of the twelfth century this and similar prophecies were widely current. A popular play about the Antichrist introduced this theme in a very dramatic fashion, and all serious historical thought was preoccupied with the attempt to calculate exactly how and when the Antichrist and the final emperor would appear. The major and most influential work of universal history, the *Chronicle* of Bishop Otto of Freising was deeply concerned with this issue and we know that in a great crisis in his life Frederick asked the author, his uncle, to let him have a copy.

According to Otto's conception, the age of the *civitas permixta*, in which the good and the bad had managed to exist side by side, had come to an end with the pontificate of Gregory VII and the Investiture controversy. Otto was clearly aware that it had dissolved one stage of history. Ever since then the outcome of the second crusade and the persistent threat of civil war in Germany had proved that the forces of evil were becoming more dominant. But the traces of the *civitas dei*, of goodness, were all the more discernible now that they were so clearly separated from the *civitas diaboli*: the growth of the contemplative religious orders, especially the Cistercians, and the development of the crusading ideal were proof that goodness was trying to disentangle itself more and more from the rest of the world. For Otto did not simply console himself with contemplating the end, but traced the history of the forces which were bringing about that end. Eventually the crusading ideal and the contemplative ideal would prevail and the final day of judgement would arrive, heralded by the reign of the final emperor who would be succeeded by the Antichrist. After this, the post-historical age of eternity would commence. Otto of Freising was therefore convinced that his own age was almost the last age of history, and we cannot avoid the conclusion that Frederick, well acquainted with the ancient prophecy, was confirmed in his belief that he was to be the last emperor. This conviction nourished his determination to go on a new crusade, and the necessity of going on a new crusade in turn nourished the conviction; hence the pragmatic attitude he adopted to the schemes of government which he had to devise. None of them he considered as an ultimate end; and every time a scheme proved too difficult, he was able to give it up and devise a new one without suffering a personal failure. He was personally committed only to the ultimate end; but never to the scheme of government he had to devise in order to fill the political vacuum. Therefore he emerged from every crisis and every failure unscathed.

Neither Frederick nor any of his advisers knew enough sociology to analyse the vacuum of the second half of the twelfth century in precisely the terms in which we have analysed it above. They knew only that the old system of government was no longer functioning and that there was a vacuum. They were therefore satisfied with a knowledge of its particular manifestation and with the general explanation that the age of the *civitas permixta* had come to an end. But what is essential for the present argument is that they too had their foreknowledge of the future and were able to see the years of Frederick's reign stretching in front of them as a gap to be filled. The only difference between them and the modern historian is that the latter sees the end of the age of *civitas permixta* in sociological rather than in moral terms. But there is complete agreement that there was a gap to be filled.

In Frederick's and his contemporaries' view, the gap had been created by the disastrous end of the civil war caused by Pope Gregory VII's opposition to the Emperor Henry IV. The papacy had not emerged much more triumphant than the empire. But by providing leadership for a new spiritual tenor among the clergy and by encouraging princely rebellion against the king in Germany, it had managed to undermine the theocratic basis of the old order in which the king was the representative of God on earth and during the civil war a number of powerful dynastic families had arisen to compete for the great prize, the royal and imperial crown.

It had fallen first to one family and then to another – but the prize had, for the most part, not proved worth having. The reign of Conrad III (1137–1152), Frederick's immediate predecessor, had been a lamentable failure. He had tried valiantly to appease the families who were in opposition to him and to quell their feuds.

He had tried to oblige the papacy and had finally gone on a crusade from which he returned defeated and reduced in prestige, only to have to continue his vain struggles at home. His failure, however, had not necessarily been his fault. His own reign had started under the most inauspicious circumstances possible.

His predecessor Lothair had not been able to resolve the party strife that had torn Germany apart. He had hoped to keep control and to pass it on to his successor by advancing the fortunes of the Welf family to whom he was closely related. But instead of leading to pacification, such attempts had merely bred further opposition. On his death in 1137, the princes and bishops had been most reluctant to recognize his heir as king because such recognition would have deprived them of their right of free choice. Thus the archbishop of Trier summoned an assembly at Coblenz, at which Lothair's rival was chosen – without the support of a very considerable section of princes and bishops whose goodwill was vital for a king; and picked for no better reason than that he had been Lothair's rival. Dependent on the bishops to whom he owed his crown and unable to enlist a large body of voluntary support, Conrad struggled for fifteen years, trying to discharge his duty. There was nothing much wrong with his character or personality. He was said to have shrewd judgement, great sincerity and candour; piety, clemency, moderation, generosity, intellectual ability, even a sense of humour; and finally, courage and tireless energy. This was the whole gamut of qualities considered essential for a good ruler. But under the circumstances it was not enough.

For the Welf opposition had taken Conrad's election badly. Henry the Proud, duke of Bavaria, a Welf, was married to the daughter of the old Emperor Lothair and through her he had become duke of Saxony as well. When Conrad was elected, Henry the Proud happened to have the royal insignia in his keeping. He surrendered them but refused to pay homage to Conrad since Conrad demanded that he gave up at least one of his two duchies. Conrad in a weak position, tried a radical solution: he deprived Henry the Proud of both Saxony and Bavaria. Thereupon Welf VI, Henry the Proud's brother, made an alliance with

King Roger of Sicily against Conrad and started a rebellion in Swabia. Unable to overcome the formidable Welf faction in battle, Conrad at this late hour thought of a compromise. When Henry the Proud died, Conrad arranged for his widow Gertrude to marry his, Conrad's, half-brother, Henry von Babenberg (surnamed Jasomirgott) who had become duke of Bavaria in Henry the Proud's stead. And Henry the Lion, son of Henry the Proud, was invested with the duchy of Saxony, of which his father had been deprived. But Henry the Lion could still not reconcile himself to having been prevented from succeeding to the duchy of Bavaria as well, and the compromise therefore did not work. As a result there was more or less open civil war before, during and after Conrad's absence on the second crusade. In 1151 Conrad tried once more to weaken Henry the Lion's position in Saxony – but to no avail. It was this constantly explosive situation which prevented Conrad from going to Italy to be crowned emperor, and when he died in February 1152 he had still not become an emperor. With all his good qualities, he had been ineffectual. To reconcile the factions he would have had to be considerably stronger in resources. And to provide a new plan for a constitutional order, he would have to have had more imagination. As it was he battled along until he was prevailed upon to join the second crusade. This expedition summed up the failure of his whole reign. His army was destroyed in Asia Minor before it even reached its objective; and Conrad made his way back to Germany, a complete failure. He lived on for another three years; but when he died in 1152 there was nobody to regret him: under him, a chronicler reported laconically, 'the country began to be ruined by misfortune'.[1] One may well debate whether the misfortunes actually began under him. But that they continued and that he did nothing to stop them has ever since been the unanimous opinion of historians.[2]

It was at this point that the princes and bishops of Germany got together and elected Frederick, the nephew of Conrad, to succeed

[1] *Chron. Reg. Col.*, GDV, 69, p. 60. '*Huius regis tempora admodum tristia fuerunt*', *loc. cit.*

[2] For a criticism of the customary poor estimate of Conrad *see* F. Geldner, *Monumentum Bambergense*, Festgabe für B. Kraft, 1955, pp. 395–412.

as king. The almost unanimous choice was determined by personal considerations. Frederick was a powerful young man who well might be able to ride the storm and eventually calm it. But, what is more, he was related to both the Welf and Staufen families. On his mother's side he was the cousin of Henry the Lion; and on his father's side he belonged to the Staufen family. In view of the fact that under the primitive political conditions prevailing in the twelfth century virtually all political matters boiled down to family affairs, it was more than reasonable to hope that this double connection would enable Frederick to succeed where Conrad had failed. He was thus elected with wide support, in the hope that he would once more provide peace and stability. There is no indication that at that time either he or any of his electors had a plan for the reform of the constitution.

This is precisely the point at which the interest of the historian begins to be aroused. For Frederick reigned for thirty-eight years – a long time even by modern standards. It seems that he was not only physically indefatigable; he also had a mind which was elastic to an unusual degree. He was neither a bully nor a fanatic; and he was certainly not dogmatic. He was an extreme pragmatic empiricist in politics, but an empiricist of the finest kind: whenever he found that a policy he was trying could not work or that the cost began to be too high, he scrapped it. And such scrapping was invariably followed by the invention of a new policy. His ability to invent and improvise was indeed remarkable. During the thirty-eight years of his reign, he tried three completely different approaches to the problems of politics and power.

The first plan was conservative and traditional. Most of its features were inherited from his predecessors; it was only that he brought a stronger will to its pursuit, and that the constellation in 1152 was luckier than it had been before. Even so, the plan could not and did not work. Thereupon, in the summer of 1156, he made a swift and radical decision. He invented a new plan which I shall call the Great Design. He embarked on its realization with vigour and ruthlessness – until he found that it provoked more opposition than he could cope with. At this point, by now well middle-aged, he seems to have worried and hesitated. He could not throw the Great Design overboard and could not think of a new plan quickly enough. This hesitation led him close to disaster. But he rallied in time and once again, within one single month in 1175, he dropped the policies he had tried to pursue for the preceding twenty years. And from then onwards, more slowly this time but with remarkable sureness, he evolved a new plan, the third.

What strikes one in this pattern, first of all, is the remarkable physical achievement. Frederick, like most early medieval rulers, had to rule from horseback. There was no bureaucracy and no capital from which to administer; no forum or palace in which to conduct diplomacy.[1] Given the primitive technology of the period, the poor horses and the bad roads and the very imperfect conditions for resting on the way, Frederick performed during these thirty-eight years a tremendous physical feat. To be a ruler was not only a matter of wisdom and diplomacy but, in a quite literal sense, a matter of stamina.

The second quality that strikes one is his adaptability, his phoenix-like power to rise from the ashes; not to admit defeat, but to interpret a defeat merely as a falsification of a hypothesis. Every time he changed his mind, he abandoned a hypothesis that had proved false. And with untiring ingenuity, he put forward a new one and pursued it with the same vigour. He might of course be thought an opportunist. But this is unwarranted – because he went to enormous physical trouble and expense in order to test each hypothesis, whereas a real opportunist would have changed horses every time the going was tough. Again, he might simply be considered a power-mad politician, who had no principle other than the desire to stay in power. But once more this conclusion would be a mistake. Frederick tried one idea after another, and no single idea ever worked out. But this does not prove that he was power drunk. It merely means that other people had different

[1] The imperial chancellery, such as it was, kept no register before the reign of Henry VII in the early fourteenth century, H. Bresslau, *Handbuch der Urkundenlehre*, 2nd ed., i, p. 130, and even archives were unknown before the reign of Henry VI at the end of the twelfth century, *ibid.*, p. 166. Legal proceedings at the imperial court were always improvised and purely oral. *Cp.* H. Appelt, *Kaiserurkunden und Fürstensentenz unter Friedrich Barbarossa*, MIOG, LXXI, 1963, p. 35.

ideas which deflected Frederick's ideas from their purpose. But Frederick was ruthless in their pursuit and always ready to formulate new ones until, in the end, one of them seemed to 'work' – or, at any rate, work long enough for Frederick to gain the required respite to go on a crusade. By that time he was in his late sixties and he died, it seems, as the result of an accident in Asia Minor. This death put a stop to his endeavours – and we may therefore conveniently suspend an inquiry as to whether his last solution proved more durable than the others.

At the beginning of Frederick's reign it was questionable whether a German emperor could safely venture to Italy to aid a pope. By the end, Italy had been drawn into the orbit of the empire and Milan had become one of the great imperial strongholds. In Germany, at the beginning of the period, feudalism had been developed only on a private scale, and the monarchy itself was not a feudal institution in any sense of the term. By the end, feudalism had become the law of the land and the basis of the German monarchical constitution. Towards the end of the century, there had also emerged in Germany more precise territorial boundaries than there had ever been before and the territories were parcelled out in a way which nobody had anticipated in 1152. Moreover, an entirely new class of princes had emerged, socially and constitutionally distinct from the old German dynasts and the nobility, the so-called estate of imperial princes.

If these changes are impressive enough, one will be even more struck by the transformation of the mind. When Frederick grew up, he cannot have been treated to more inspiring a literary production than the *Kaiserchronik*, a lengthy and tedious list of imperial lives. It bears witness to crude social customs, to violent and uncontrolled displays of emotion. By the time he departed for his crusade, there had begun to develop in Germany a courtly epic, with all its conventional refinements and the overriding idea that love is not only the most powerful and irresistible of all passions, but at once the most destructive and the most beautiful one. As far as Frederick himself was concerned, one ought not to attribute too much importance to the emergence of courtly romance. Not even

Frederick's mind and heart could have been totally elastic. When he was young he had listened, we presume, to the older kind of recital. When he attended the celebrations in Mainz in 1184, where courtly poetry was first produced publicly in Germany, he must have reacted to this new kind of literature perhaps with bemused tolerance but with complete incomprehension.

But it was not only in society, politics and literature that the change was so marked. The spiritual life inside the empire also was undergoing enormous changes. At the beginning of his reign, Frederick had set upon Arnold of Brescia as a crazy preacher who advocated subversion in the church. During the half century of Frederick's reign, spiritualism had spread. The church had begun to oppose it by administrative measures, the problems of 'heresy' had been faced at the Lateran Council of 1179; the first inquisitions had been started and, last but not least, the seminal career of St Francis of Assisi was just about to begin.

Despite these changes, it would not be correct to attribute them to his planning. Nothing was further from Frederick's mind. He improvised his political plans in order to make ends meet, in order to keep his head above water. However, it would be equally wrong to argue that these changes came about in spite of him. For this could suggest that he was on the whole a staunch conservative who opposed change. The truth of the matter seems to be this. Changes were taking place – but the very dissolution of old ties and the growth of new ones created a state of flux and uncertainty. And it was in the midst of this state of uncertainty and flux that Frederick operated; and it was this state which provided the opportunity for his political virtuosity. Had there been less flux, his inventiveness would never have been called into play, and his experimentation would never have reached its farthest extension. We may therefore conclude that the far-reaching changes that took place during his long life provided the opportunity for his political talents; and that, in turn, the very flexibility of those talents eased, in the long run, the changes that were taking place.

The Kyffhäuser legend has tended to prevent historians from seeing Frederick operating in this context and displaying his political dexterity and inventiveness to the full. They have often seen him rather as a man presiding over and serving an established institution with determination and faithful perseverance. One need only compare the two pictorial images of Frederick – the contemporary bust where he is aloof and smiling, lean and erect, ironically detached, and the nineteenth century paintings in which he was invariably depicted as a benign old man, *pater patriae*, a patriarchal ruler whose stern and wrathful eye was forever watching lest someone disturb the peace or infringe his imperial rights and dignity. As a result, those historians have been guilty of what one might describe as a historical *synecdoche*: instead of seeing him over a period of thirty-eight years, they see him static, standing from the beginning to the end for a single set of ideas.[1] And thus the real Frederick, the political inventor and the man who was always resilient after every set-back, has remained hidden. The real clue to his mind is not that he had either no all-embracing idea at all or that he had only a single one; but that he fashioned all-embracing ideas and changed them when they proved unsuitable. Giesebrecht, Prutz and Hampe have all seen him as the single-minded servant of the established empire. E. Otto, in his biography of Frederick, has allowed for one change in thirty-eight years, when Frederick gave up the pursuit of good old law for the pursuit of purely dynastic interests. Friedrich Heer breaks off his account at the point where the bloodthirsty German tyrant, which he took Frederick to be, would presumably have changed his tune, and R. Folz admits that Frederick, Janus-like, faced both forwards and backwards in history and that some of his policies were conservative and others progressive. But not a single historian has seen him as a dexterous and ever-changing politician. They have all seen him as the servant of an institution, the laws and legitimate claims of which were all more or less fixed. Tacitly

[1] My objection to historical *synecdoches* is of some methodological importance. Throughout I have used Frederick's theoretical pronouncements as clues to the particular political situation which caused him to make them, rather than as considered statements of his permanent philosophy of life or politics, to be analysed for their abstract meaning or to be treated as contributions to a body of political thought. Taking each formulation as a momentary pronouncement relevant to a particular situation, I have, for example, guarded against viewing his actions in the autumn of 1158 in the light of his theories propounded to the Roman senators in the summer of 1155.

they have all assumed that, as the legend says, if Frederick is expected to rise from the dead or awake from his sleep in order to restore the empire, he must have presided over an imperial institution in his own lifetime.

When Frederick was elected in 1152, he was not quite thirty years of age,[1] and thus it must be presumed that he was born in the mid-twenties of the twelfth century. We have a bust of him, the so-called Cappenberg bust, a very fine specimen of twelfth-century art. It is highly stylized in the romanesque manner – but there is every reason to believe that in spite of its highly formalized quality it portrays Frederick's real likeness, or at least some very essential parts of it. It is well known that modern painters like Picasso or Modigliani are able, in spite of their completely unnaturalistic and formal technique, to catch the most characteristic features of a face and there is no reason for concluding from the extreme formalism of the bust that it cannot represent a genuine likeness. Moreover, Frederick's contemporaries were unanimous in describing him as a man with a smiling countenance; or as one who looked as if he was about to smile. And it is this quality which is portrayed most strikingly in the bust.[2] The smile is almost ironical and conveys an impression of great detachment.

[1] This was the opinion of Wibald, BRG, I, No. 505. A. Hofmeister, *Puer, Iuvenis, Senex,* Kehr Festschrift, *Papsttum und Kaisertum,* München, 1926, works out that Frederick was only twenty-two in 1152. But H. Grundmann, *Der Cappenberger Barbarossakopf,* Köln, 1959, p. 29, thinks that Wibald's estimate must have been correct.

[2] H. Grundmann, *op. cit.*, shows that the bust corresponds in almost every detail to Rahewin's description. Rahewin, *Gesta,* IV, lxxxiv: '*totaque facies*| *laeta et hilaris*'. Einhard, c. 22, says exactly the same of Charlemagne. But there is no reason why it should not have been true of both emperors. They were both men who found it easy to make friends and who had outward-going and genial personalities, not mistrustful or suspicious and not dominated by hatreds and resentments. Morena agrees: MGH, F. Güterbock ed., 1930, p. 167. Most valuable is the opinion of Richard of London who knew Frederick towards the end of his (Frederick's) life. His face expressed '*constantia animi, semper idem et immobilis permanens, nec dolore obscurior, nec ira contractus, nec dissolutus leticia*'. MGH, SS, XXVII, p. 204, 34. H. Naumann, *Versuch über welfische und staufische Dichtung,* ELJ, 8, 1929, p. 82, interprets Rahewin's and Morena's description of Frederick's smile as the *hohe Mut* of later courtly literature and attempts to see Frederick as an example of courtly culture. But, first, the translation is wrong. Secondly, the phrase in Rahewin comes from Einhard, c. 22, and Einhard cannot possibly have thought of courtly literature. Thirdly, it is certain that neither Rahewin nor Morena was acquainted with courtly literature. H. Fillitz, 'Der Cappenberger Barbarossakopf', *Münchner Jahrbuch f. bildende Kunst,* 3. Folge, 14, 1963, seeks to prove that the bust is

His contemporaries were also unanimous in their praise of his intellectual qualities. John of Salisbury wrote that before the schism Frederick had no equals in excellence.[1] Arnulf of Lisieux said that he was more active and cleverer than any other ruler.[2] Boso, an inveterate enemy, admitted that he was clever, astute and worldly wise.[3] Morena, a strong supporter, wrote that there had not been an emperor like him for a long time.[4] Wibald, his trusted adviser during his early years and a thoughtful man in every respect, described him as '*affabilis et liberalis et splendide disertus iuxta gentile idioma linguae suae*'.[5] His eloquence was universally praised[6] – and this is all the more noteworthy as he seems to have been fairly ignorant of Latin.[7]

Of his character we know very little. By the somewhat intemperate standards of his age he seems to have had a great deal of self-control. At times he could affect indignation in order to frighten an ambassador[8] and at other times he could show the utmost restraint in face of provocation.[9] There are also frequent reports of how his steadfastness and imperturbability saved the situation.[10] On other occasions, he allowed anger to force him into

---

a conscious attempt to imitate emperors' busts from late antiquity. He believes that Frederick had this bust made in order to counter papal theocratic pretensions and to propagate that he was one of the ancient emperors.

[1] Ep. 185, I, 321.

[2] Sermon to Council of Tours, Hefele-Leclercq, V, p. 970.

[3] Boso, p. 405.

[4] MGH, SS, XVIII, p. 640.

[5] BRG, I, p. 505. Niketas Choniates' description (Bekker ed., *Bonner Corpus*, pp. 84 ff.) must be dismissed as prejudiced. Whatever truth there was in the report that Frederick was boastful and arrogant was based on the reputation which Frederick had acquired during his brief sojourn in Constantinople when he had accompanied Conrad III on the second crusade. Frederick was very young then and may not have shown himself under these strange circumstances to his best advantage.

[6] Wibald, Ep. 375, MGH, Const. I, No. 138; Acerbus Morena, F. Güterbock ed., 1930, p. 167. Rahewin, *Gesta*, IV, lxxxvi; Richard of London, MGH, SS, XXVII, p. 204. Burchard of Ursberg was to describe him later on the basis of authentic information, as '*ingenio subtilis*': MGH, SS, XXIII, p. 345, 10.

[7] Rahewin says he understood it better than he was able to speak it, *Gesta*, V, lxxxvi. Richard of London, MGH, SS, XXVII, p. 204, says he had to have an interpreter. Saxo Grammaticus, MGH, SS, XXIX, p. 113, agrees. *Cp.* Giesebrecht, V, p. 839.

[8] *Gesta*, II, x.

[9] *Cp.* e.g. Morena, MGH, SS, XVIII, p. 609, lines 3 and 4.

[10] At Besançon, 1157, Roland was saved by Frederick's coolness. In April 1162, Frederick remained outwardly friendly to Eberhard of Salzburg, in spite of the latter's

a more extreme course than he had contemplated, or even into acts of real cruelty. As far as cruelty is concerned, one has to resign oneself to the fact that the twelfth century was still a very barbarous age and that people frequently shed blood, mutilated prisoners and sought brutal revenge even for minor insults.

The most complete contemporary description we have of Frederick is to be found at the end of the book begun by his uncle Otto of Freising and completed after Otto's death by Rahewin:[1]

> Now divine, august Frederick is (as a certain writer says of Theodoric) in character and appearance such a man that he deserves to be studied even by those not in close touch with him. The Lord God and the plan of nature have joined to bestow lavishly upon him the gift of perfect happiness. His character is such that not even those envious of his powers can belittle its praise. His person is well proportioned. He is shorter than very tall men, but taller and more noble than men of medium height. His hair is golden, curling a little above his forehead. His ears are scarcely covered by the hair above them, as the barber (out of respect for the empire) keeps the hair on his head and cheeks short by constantly cutting it. His eyes are sharp and piercing, his nose well formed, his beard reddish, his lips delicate and not distended by too long a mouth. His whole face is bright and cheerful. His teeth are even and snow white in colour. The skin of his throat and neck (which is rather plump but not fat) is milk white and often suffused with the ruddy glow of youth; modesty rather than anger causes him to blush frequently. His shoulders are rather broad, and he is strongly built. His thighs supported by stout calves are proper and sturdy.
>
> His gait is firm and steady, his voice clear, and his entire bearing manly. Because of his figure, he has an air of dignity and authority, standing or sitting. His health is very good, ex-

refusal to support Frederick's pope. In 1164 in Pavia, Gerhoh of Reichersberg attacked Frederick's pope. Several bystanders threatened to lynch him. But Frederick remained calm and listened to both sides. (*See* MGH, LdL, III, 408).

[1] *Gesta*, IV, lxxxvi. Many of Rahewin's phrases are borrowed literally from other writers such as Einhard, Sidonius Apollinaris and Jordanes. But Rahewin used these phrases only when they applied to Frederick, and H. Grundmann, *op. cit.*, shows that his portrait of Frederick is carefully assembled, like a mosaic, from these phrases.

cept that sometimes he is subject to a day's fever. He is a lover of warfare, but only that peace may be secured thereby. He is quick of hand, very wise in counsel, merciful to supplicants, kind to those taken under his protection.

If you ask about his daily routine when abroad, he attends matins at church and the services of his priests, either alone or with a very small following, and worships so earnestly that he has set a pattern and an example to all the Italians of the honour and reverence that are to be paid to bishops and to the clergy. He shows so great respect to divine services that he honours with becoming silence every hour in which psalms are sung to God, nor does anything venture meanwhile to trouble him about any business matter. His devotions ended and, after celebration of the Mass, having been blessed by the holy relics, he dedicates the rest of the morning to the task of governing his empire. If he engages in the chase, he is second to none in training, judging, and making use of horses, dogs and falcons and other such birds. In hunting he himself strings the bow, takes the arrows, sets and shoots them. You choose what he is to hit, he hits what you have chosen.

At meals there is both restraint and royal abundance; moderate rather than excessive drinking prevails, but the hungry cannot complain of frugality. When it is time for play, he lays aside for a little while his royal dignity, and is in such a humour that his condescension is not open to criticism, his severity is not bloodthirsty. Towards the members of his household he is not threatening in his manner of address, or contemptuous towards profferred counsel, or vindictive in spying out a fault. He earnestly searches the Scriptures and the exploits of ancient kings. He generally distributes with his own hand alms to the poor and scrupulously divides a tenth of his income among churches and monasteries. He is very eloquent in his mother tongue, but can understand Latin more readily than he can speak it. He wears his native costume and is neither extravagant nor frivolous in dress – yet is not meanly clad. It pleases him to have his camp display the panoply of Mars rather than of Venus.'

CHAPTER III

In the Footsteps of Conrad III

On 4 March 1152, the Tuesday after *oculi mei semper*,[1] the princes elected Frederick king. The election was almost unanimous and had been well prepared. It was indeed something in the nature of a family compact. Frederick was neither in the direct line of descent nor the most powerful of the princes, but his mother had been a Welf and his father a Staufen; and since the ancient Teutons were in the habit of tracing their descent bilaterally,[2] Frederick was really a member of both families. Ever since his accession in 1135 Conrad III had plotted and manœuvred to deprive the Welfen of as much of their power as he could. But to no avail. And during the last years of his reign, and certainly as he lay dying in Bamberg, it must have become clear to him that the only way of composing the feud was by making a family compact and that his nephew Frederick was the one person whose accession was acceptable to both families.

Frederick himself had prepared for such an eventuality. Although he counted and called himself a Staufen, he had quite openly favoured the other side of his family and thus proved to them that he recognized his ties with the Welfen too.[3] When Conrad lay dying, Frederick, in association with Conrad's closest advisers, Abbot Wibald and Bishop Eberhard of Bamberg, had entered into negotiations with the Welfen and produced a number of concrete proposals to prove that he was well inclined towards them. Henry the Lion, son and heir of Henry the Proud, was promised both duchies, Saxony and Bavaria. Count Welf VI was

[1] There is some doubt as to the actual date of the election. *Cp.* R. Holtzmann, *Die Wahl Friedrichs I zum deutschen König*, HV, 1898.

[2] *Cp.* P. Munz, *Medieval History in Australasia*, HS, XI, 1963, p. 8.

[3] For examples *see* J. Jastrow, *Welfenprozesse und erste Jahre Friedrich Barbarossas*, DZG, 10, 1893, especially p. 311.

promised a free hand as margrave of Tuscany and duke of Spoleto; and Henry the Lion's father-in-law, Berthold von Zähringen, was similarly encouraged to regard Burgundy as his sphere of influence.[1]

As against this powerful party, the opposition was weak. It was led by Henry, the archbishop of Mainz, whose see was traditionally opposed to the Salian and Staufen families and who resented the growing influence of Eberhard of Bamberg whom he suspected of trying to gain independence from his metropolitan authority.[2] He was supported in his opposition by the Babenberg faction and by their followers in Bavaria, because Henry von Babenberg, surnamed Jasomirgott, suspected rightly that the election of Frederick would mean the installation of Henry the Lion in Bavaria.[3]

According to a later story, Conrad was supposed to have designated Frederick on his death-bed as his heir.[4] If the story

[1] J. Jastrow, *op. cit.*, p. 312.

[2] The real reasons for Henry's opposition are not known and there has, therefore, been a great deal of speculation. Giesebrecht, V, 313, believed that there was tension between Eugene III and Henry, and that Henry opposed the election of a king who might be acceptable to Eugene. P. Rassow, *Honor Imperii*, 2nd ed., München, 1961, p. 10, believes that Henry tried a legalistic ruse and pretended to guard the interests of Conrad's son who was a minor. It is not clear why Rassow, uncritically, accepts this version, based entirely on later, mainly Welf sources. J. Haller, *Papsttum*, Stuttgart, 1952, p. 138, stresses the rivalry between the see of Mainz and Bishop Hillin of Trier, a close friend of Frederick's. It is also true that Henry was on very good terms, perhaps too good terms, with Henry the Lion. R. Holtzmann, *Die Wahl Friedrichs I zum deutschen König*, p. 197, believes that Henry opposed Frederick because he hated both Wibald and Bishop Arnold of Cologne, friends of the pope and of Frederick.

[3] The heads of the Babenberg faction kept away from Frederick's court after the election. Giesebrecht, V, 9.

[4] For the origin of the story *see* J. Jastrow, *op. cit.* It seems to have been circulated after 1180, at a time when Frederick had quarrelled with Henry the Lion. As against this, after 1180 there arose also a Welf version according to which Frederick had gained the crown through fraud. A still later version, end of thirteenth century, *Chronicon Fratris Balduini*, in Hugo, *Sacrae antiqu. Mon.*, II, p. 171, reports that Frederick had declared arrogantly that he would resort to violence if not elected. The story in Gislebert, *Chronicon Hanoniense*, MGH, SS, XXI, p. 516. is obviously due to a confusion of the 1152 election with the election of Lothair III. My own account follows Otto of Freising, *Gesta*, II, ii, together with the amendments of Jastrow, *op. cit.* The latter shows quite clearly that Frederick had played a much more active role than Otto of Freising admits. But Jastrow sees in Frederick's election a mere victory of the Welf faction. He is not sufficiently sensitive to the importance of the fact that the Teutons traced their descent bilaterally and that according to their reckoning Frederick literally belonged to both kins.

was invented to prove that Frederick succeeded by inheritance, there was no foundation for it. But if the story means merely to convey the impression that the transition from Conrad to Frederick was smooth and prearranged, we can accept it.[1] For Frederick's path was smoothed by Conrad's adviser Wibald[2] and by Eberhard of Bamberg[3] whom he met at Conrad's death-bed.[4] Nor must one overlook the important role played by Wibald's friend Arnold, the archbishop of Cologne.[5] As a result, there was no problem about the handing over of the insignia; and after Conrad's death, Frederick agreed that Conrad should be buried in Bamberg – a great triumph for the prestige of Bishop Eberhard – and not in Lorsch where Conrad had wanted to be buried among the members of his family. Both Wibald and Eberhard continued as close counsellors of Frederick and thus the continuity of the two reigns was firmly established.

Wibald had been an indefatigable counsellor and servant of Conrad's. He was abbot of two large and important monasteries, Stablo and Corvey. He seems to have known everybody and spent most of his time travelling and negotiating. A firm supporter of the papacy, he had always promoted close relations between king and pope.[6] But there is no doubt that both Conrad and Frederick held him in the greatest esteem. Arnold von Wied had been chancellor until 1151 when he had become archbishop of Cologne. He, too, was strongly pro-papal and one of the main supporters of Frederick's early policy to follow in the footsteps of Conrad. He accompanied Frederick on his first expedition to Italy and, in

[1] See Frederick's letter to the Emperor Manuel, BRG, I, No. 410, '*Sanctissimus . . . imperator Conradus, moriens, cum nos declarasset imperii sui successores. . .*'.

[2] On his coronation day Frederick rewarded Wibald with a generous privilege for his abbey of Stablo: Giesebrecht, VI, p. 325. See especially Wibald's own letters, BRG, I, Nos 364–6.

[3] H. Fichtenau, *Bamberg, Würzburg und die Stauferkanzlei*, MIOG, 53, 1939, p. 245, for the close relations between Eberhard and Frederick.

[4] W. Föhl, *Bischof Eberhard II von Bamberg*, MIOG, 50, 1936, p. 91.

[5] See especially BRG, I, No. 381. For this friendship *see* F. Hausmann, *Reichskanzlei und Hofkapelle*, 1956, p. 121–2.

[6] There is indeed no evidence for H. Zatschek's judgement that Wibald was a vain and unscrupulous go-getter who pushed himself forward and influenced politics without ever occupying a responsible post (*Wibald von Stablo*, etc., MIOG, Suppl. Vol. X, 1928, p. 471. *Cp.* also H. Gleber, *Papst Eugen III*, Jena, 1936). For a positive evaluation of Wibald *see* F. Hausmann, *Reichskanzlei und Hofkapelle*, p. 256.

1155, was one of the few people who strongly pleaded for a continuation of the old policy and a war against Sicily.[1] Bishop Eberhard of Bamberg was a gentle but firm man, reputed to be completely honest and pious, perhaps a little more of a theologian than most bishops of the twelfth century and there is probably truth in the statement that politics did not really satisfy him. He was not only an astute politician but also a shrewd administrator of his see. Pope Eugene probably would have liked to have drawn him completely into the papal circle – but without ever becoming antagonistic to any pope, Eberhard remained a close and personal supporter of Frederick.[2] He was prominent in the diplomacy of Frederick's first period when Frederick followed in the footsteps of Conrad[3] and was on every occasion remarkable for his wise and conciliatory approach. Even later, when Frederick had been obliged to turn against the papacy, Eberhard continued to hope for reconciliation.[4] Eventually, during the period in which Frederick developed aggressive and uncompromising policies, he withdrew from Frederick's councils, to re-emerge in the late 1160s to help Frederick reach a compromise with Pope Alexander III.

The character of these close advisers throws a telling light on the temper of Frederick's first plan. All his advisers were judicious, gentle and conciliatory, largely men of the church who still belonged to the era of St Bernard and of Pope Eugene[5] and on the whole much more attractive than, and very different from, the more secular minded princes of the church who emerged prominent in Frederick's councils after the complete failure of the first plan. Looking back one can easily see many reasons why a policy based upon the advice of such men was not likely to be very

[1] R. Knipping, *Die Regeste der Erzbischöfe von Köln im Mittelalter*, II, 1901, No. 598.

[2] *Cp.* A. Hauck, *Kirchengeschichte Deutschlands*, 8th ed., 1954, IV, p. 207.

[3] K. W. Nitzsch, *Geschichte des deutschen Volkes*, Leipzig, 1892, II, pp. 246 and 270; Fichtenau, *op. cit.*, and especially Helmold, I, 80 and *Gesta*, IV, 29. *See* also P. Wagner, *Eberhard II, Bischof von Bamberg*; Halle, 1870, pp. 66–7.

[4] J. M. Watterich, *Vitae Pontificorum Romanorum*, Leipzig, 1862, II, p. 454, and M. Maccarone, *Papato e Impero*, Rome, 1959, p. 340.

[5] It is very misleading to represent Eugene III, as Gleber, *op. cit.*, has done, as a pope who laid the foundations for the later victory of the papacy over the empire. P. Rassow, reviewing this book, HZ, 159, 1939, p. 181, pointed out that Eugene belonged to the movement which opposed Abelard and Gilbert de la Porrée; and that the later Pope Alexander belonged to those very forces which Eugene had opposed.

successful in filling the gap. But it is a great tribute to Frederick's statesmanship that his first thought should have been to work through the help and advice of such men and that he resorted to more ruthless plans only after the gentler methods had failed.

None of the advisers with whom Frederick surrounded himself were, however, simply yes-men. Frederick not only tolerated but even encouraged a certain amount of divergence of opinion and valued the fact that Eberhard of Bamberg and Wibald represented different aspects of the policy he had chosen to pursue. Eberhard was pro-papal in the sense that he wanted to bridge any possible difference of opinion between king and pope. Wibald was pro-papal in a much more positive sense, so much so that at the *curia* he was considered a reliable spokesman of papal interests.[1] Wibald himself was well aware that Eberhard's line was closer to Frederick and that his and Arnold von Wied's influence was perhaps not quite so strong as it had been under Conrad.[2] But Frederick was anxious to retain both men. Wibald was generally considered to be extremely influential with Frederick[3] and if Frederick felt that Eberhard's opinion was personally preferable, he also valued Wibald's. Wibald was indeed a very diplomatic and adroit politician. Under Conrad he had been hostile to the Welfen and had considered them disturbers of the peace.[4] After the family compact which he had done so much to bring about, he knew how to change his mind. In 1153 he played a major role in the conclusion of the Treaty of Constance between Frederick and Pope Eugene and was responsible for making several alterations in Frederick's favour in the text of the treaty.[5] This shows not only that he was no blind slave to papal policies but also that he must have done it in such a way as not to offend the *curia* in the least; for he remained on excellent terms with the papal legates at Constance and managed to persuade them to order the bishop of Halberstadt to excommunicate two enemies of Corvey.[6]

[1] JL, 9606 and 9696. F. Hausmann, *op. cit.*, pp. 237–8.
[2] BRG, I, No. 377.
[3] F. Hausmann, *op. cit.*, p. 244.
[4] E. Rehfeldt, *Die politische Stellung Wibalds von Stablo und Korvei*, Greifswald, 1913, pp. 44–5.
[5] W. Ohnsorge, *Zu den aussenpolitischen Anfängen Friedrich Barbarossas*, QuF, 32, 1942, pp. 16 ff.
[6] F. Hausmann, *op. cit.*, p. 239.

The new reign had begun as a family compact and it was hoped that this ancient and tried method of establishing order would again achieve the desired results. Neither Frederick nor anybody else at that time could possibly have understood that the major families had split into too many sub-groups and that the population had grown to such an extent that a simple agreement among the heads of the several branches of the leading families would not suffice. As it was, the clergy had been drawn in to support Frederick's election and this meant papal support and a good beginning for the new reign.

Indeed, quite apart from all considerations of public utility and politics, there was great rejoicing that there was a king who owed his kingship to unanimity and universal support. It is customary in Rome to shout in rejoicing, when a new pope has been elected, *habemus papam*, for what really matters is that there should be a pope, a ruler. Equally, the people might have shouted in March 1152 *habemus regem*; for what mattered first and above all was that there should be, physically, a king. His existence provided the visible embodiment of the divine power that sustained the universe. His presence guaranteed fertility, prosperity and justice – not in the rational sense that he would provide the political, judicial and military services that made prosperity and justice possible; but in the irrational and mystical sense that he embodied the vivifying power from which all these things were derived. 'In the king's righteousness,' Alcuin had written to King Aethelred in 793, 'is the common weal, victory in war, mildness of the seasons, abundance of the crops, freedom from pestilence.'[1] It is true that this had been said three hundred years before Frederick. There

[1] Jolliffe, *Constitutional History*, N.Y., 1947, p. 43. When Waldemar I of Denmark travelled through Germany in 1164 on his way to the Synod of Dôle, mothers carried their babies to him and peasants their wheat, because his touch would make them grow. (Saxo Grammaticus, Holder-Egger ed., 1886, p. 537). *Cp.* also M. Bloch, *Les rois thaumaturges*, p. 58. The *Kaiserchronik* holds up the *rex iustus et pacificus* as the highest ideal, the guarantor of internal and external peace. This is precisely what Frederick was, for Fridericus = peace:

> Ortu teutonicus romanus rex Fridericus
> Augusti nomen pacis possedit et omen,

quoted by F. Heer, *Die Tragödie des heiligen Reiches*, Zürich, 1952, p. 203. Frederick was very conscious of his role as guarantor of peace: 'Divina clementia ex pacis abundantia feliciter regnandi felicia nobis concessit tempora'. *Cp.* Giesebrecht, V, p. 99.

had been clear undertones of pagan corn-king conceptions in Alcuin's letter. But the notion that the king embodied the power that sustained the universe had not died. It had accommodated itself with Christianity. The unction provided the divine charisma for a king – he was God's vicar on earth[1] and as long as there *was* a king, this divine power was available for the society over which he presided. Whether his crown was the symbol of the sun or whether it represented Christ did not matter – for there was no clear logic in the concept either way. The king was the image of God – and as late as 1198 Walter von der Vogelweide wrote some celebrated lines about the fact that King Philip was a walking image of the Trinity:

Da gienc eins kaisers bruoder und eins kaisers kind
In eine wat, swie doch die namen drige sint.[2]

One may well look on such lines as a literary conceit; but if the memory of such thoughts had not still been alive, the conceit would have failed in its literary intention.

And thus what mattered first and foremost in March 1152 was Frederick's slow progress through his new kingdom, the way he showed himself to the crowds and his coronation in Aix-la-Chapelle. In Frankfurt after he had taken oaths of loyalty from all the princes present, he dismissed most of them. On the 6th he left Frankfurt by ship. He sailed down the Main and then the Rhine and disembarked at Sinzig. From there he proceeded on horseback to Aix-la-Chapelle where a huge crowd had gathered. People had come not only from many parts of Germany – that was natural enough. They had also come from western Gaul – people who owed no allegiance to Frederick either in a feudal or a political sense. They had come to see the coronation of a king – a religious ceremony and a visible proof that God's power was available to men.

The coronation was performed in the cathedral by Arnold, the

[1] *Rex imago Dei* and *rex assimilandus est Deo* were frequent formulas. *Cp.* W. Berges, *Die Fürstenspiegel des hohen und späten Mittelalters*, Stuttgart, 1938, pp. 31–4.

[2] 'There walked an emperor's brother and an emperor's son. As *one* appearing, though the persons are three.' H. Böhm ed., *Die Gedichte Walthers von der Vogelweide*, Berlin, 1955, p. 25.

archbishop of Cologne and Frederick was 'seated on the throne of the realm of the Franks that was placed in the same church by Charles the Great'.[1] A diadem was placed on his head and he was sacramentally anointed. 'But this too, should not be veiled in silence, that on the same day and in the same church the bishop-elect of Münster (also named Frederick) was consecrated by those same bishops who consecrated the king. So it was believed that the highest king and priest were actually participating in the present rejoicing; and this was a sign, that in one church one day beheld the anointing of the two persons who alone are sacramentally anointed, according to the ordinance of the New and of the Old Testament, and are rightly called the anointed of Christ the Lord.'[2]

But it would be quite wrong to believe that Frederick and his closest advisers did not also have some more utilitarian and concretely practical purposes in mind. If Frederick had been ambitious and had wanted the crown, he had been no foolish adventurer, full of vainglory and arrogance. If he was willing to present himself to the assembled crowds as the embodiment of the divine power which assured their prosperity and peace he was also and perhaps primarily and basically a shrewd politician, determined to discharge the practical and utilitarian functions of kingship.

One should perhaps not try to distinguish too clearly between the mystical and the utilitarian purpose of kingship in the middle ages – for the mystical function could not well be performed by a king who was weak and politically unsuccessful. Only if the king himself prospered and was strong could he feed the faith that he represented something of the divine power that sustained the universe. Hence the successful discharge of his political duty was intimately bound up with the fulfilment of his mystical purpose.

What then were Frederick's political intentions? Generally speaking, he saw himself as the chief arbiter of conflicting interests; as the king whose power and glory would force all contestants to seek his justice. He would pacify, by arbitration if possible and by stern military repression if necessary. In this general conception,

[1] *Gesta*, II, iii. [2] *ibid.*

Frederick started his reign in a completely traditional spirit. He had no plans or designs beyond the fulfilment of the customary functions of a king – to maintain law and promote peace. He hoped to achieve success in this policy by gaining the imperial crown in Italy which Conrad had always wanted. Pope Eugene III had been willing enough to receive him; and so were the citizens of Rome with whom Eugene lived in almost permanent conflict. But Conrad's position in Germany had been so precarious that he simply had been compelled to postpone the journey time after time.

Frederick, in conformity with his intention to pursue the aims of his predecessor, proposed, on the day following his coronation, an Italian expedition. His clerical supporters were keen; but the lay princes objected. Not in principle; but they dreaded the burdens and strain which such an expedition would impose on them and they felt that he first ought to attend to the various quarrels and conflicts in Germany. And so it was decided that in the meantime Frederick should send an embassy to Rome to announce to Eugene that he had been elected king. Both Lothair III and his immediate predecessor Conrad III had done more than that. They had begged the pope to confirm their election. But both of them had been elected in the teeth of a strong princely opposition and explicit papal approval had been invaluable to them. Frederick, whose choice had been practically unanimous, was in a much stronger position and it was therefore decided not to ask the pope for confirmation but merely to inform him of the election. Bishop Hillin of Trier, Bishop Eberhard of Bamberg, and a Cistercian abbot were chosen to carry the message to Rome.[1] The first draft of the message was prepared by Wibald and contained a request for confirmation. Wibald was very much of a traditionalist and was convinced that some kind of papal approval was necessary. Eberhard of Bamberg, less ecclesiastically minded than Wibald, redrafted the message and omitted the request for confirmation as well as a promise of a campaign to help the pope in Rome if the pope promised to crown Frederick emperor.[2] One can see how

[1] K. W. Nitzsch, *op. cit.*, p. 236.

[2] W. Föhl, *Bischof Eberhard II von Bamberg*, MIOG, 50, 1936, pp. 109, 112. Föhl's

the more secular minded Eberhard of Bamberg was advancing in the counsels of Frederick. His attitude represented a subtle nuance in tone as against Conrad's and Wibald's subservience to the pope. But Wibald was an astute diplomat. Being older than the others, he thought himself wiser. He felt that if not the letter, then at least the spirit of the custom ought to be obeyed. He recognized the subtle shift of tone implied by the fact that Eberhard was allowed to make the final draft; but then he wrote to the pope a private letter to conciliate him and suggested that he express his consent in spite of the fact that the customary form had not been observed.[1]

The choice of Eberhard as head of the mission is significant. He was a strong upholder of a close co-operation between king and pope and an old enemy of Archbishop Henry of Mainz, the chief opponent of Frederick's election. Wibald's orientation was more clerical than Eberhard's. But he too was retained as a counsellor.

---

attempt to isolate the sentences due to Eberhard is ingenious, but is not conclusive. We know from Wibald's letter to Ebehard that the latter was concerned with a change in the original wording, BRG, I, No. 374. The letter which it is alleged was eventually sent is in MGH, Const., I, No. 137 and contains also a promise made by Frederick to 'honour and love' the church of Rome and to look after widows and orphans. Pope Eugene III, in his reply (MGH, Const., I, No. 139) does not refer to this promise. Hence the suspicion that the letter which was actually sent to the pope differed from Wibald's original draft and also from the draft printed in MGH, Const., I, No. 137, in that the promise to honour and love the church of Rome and to look after widows was omitted. Jaffé, BRG, I, p. 499, note 1, as well as Giesebrecht, VI, p. 326, and Weiland, MGH, Const., I, p. 191, all believe that the letter was sent as printed. Simonsfeld, p. 43, note 103 and p. 54, note 56, however, doubted whether the promises made by Frederick contained anything about the church of Rome. E. Eichmann, *Die 'formula professionis' Friedrichs I*, HJ, 52, 1932, has examined the question and comes to the following conclusion. None of the known formulas used in twelfth century coronations contains anything direct about widows and orphans and nothing whatever about a promise to honour and love the Roman church, *op. cit.*, pp. 139–40. Hence one sees that Wibald must have concocted his version, printed in MGH, Const., I, No. 137, according to his own lights, since Eichmann sees no reason for believing that Frederick's formula should have differed in any way from the formulas used on other occasions. Eberhard, therefore, had to alter Wibald's draft in order to bring it into line with the truth. Eberhard omitted the promises in order to make sure that the letter to the pope would be factually correct. Hence Eugene's failure to acknowledge these promises. Eichmann's reasoning, though based on much learning, is not at all cogent. The election and coronation of Frederick were surrounded by so many circumstances different from those which had surrounded the coronations of Lothair and Conrad that it is by no means unreasonable to presume that he might have thought it wise to use a different *formula professionis*.

[1] BRG, I, No. 375, p. 505: 'Et sit vobiscum magni consilii angelus, declaretis eum in regem ac defensorem Romane aecclesiae.' In the same letter Wibald painted, for the pope's benefit, a most flattering picture of the new king.

Eberhard's style of writing was the official expression of policy: Frederick was prepared to assume all the responsibilities of protection towards the pope and his church and honour all of Conrad's promises.[1] In his private letter Wibald suggested to Eugene that he invite Frederick to undertake the expedition to Rome at the earliest opportunity.[2] There was obviously neither tension nor contradiction between the policies expressed by Wibald and Eberhard. There was merely a slight difference of emphasis. Eugene was well disposed towards Eberhard's mission and if he had any doubts as to Frederick's intentions, they were completely allayed by Wibald's letter. Eugene's relations with the citizens of Rome were far too precarious for him to stand upon ceremonies.

In the meantime Frederick applied himself vigorously to the talks in hand, that is to the settling of all the disputes outstanding from Conrad's reign. He scored a number of very notable successes in regard to the succession to the Danish throne and to the affairs in Lorraine. His agreement with Berthold von Zähringen about Burgundy is particularly instructive. With the help of Wibald[3] Frederick concluded a treaty with Berthold von Zähringen by which Berthold was entrusted with the overlordship of Burgundy down to the mediterranean coast. He was to consider himself the lieutenant of the king and was to have *dominatio*, *potestas*, *ordinatio*.[4] Frederick even promised aid for an attempt to win back certain parts of Burgundy, i.e. Provence, and a campaign was planned for that purpose in the summer of 1153. Certain archbishoprics and bishoprics were mentioned as exempt from Berthold's power[5] but the remainder were to be dependent on Berthold. It was indeed stated explicitly that if any of the Burgundian nobles claimed the right to invest bishops, Berthold was to take the power to himself. The spirit of this agreement is entirely in accordance with Frederick's willingness to make wide

[1] The *Vogtei* over the Roman church was the specific difference between *imperium* and *regnum*. *See* G. Tellenbach, *Römischer und Christliche Reichsgedanke in der Liturgie des frühen Mittelalters*, SHA, 1934–5. [2] BRG, I, No. 375.

[3] H. Büttner *Staufer und Zähringer im politischen Kräftespiel zwischen Bodensee und Genfersee während des 12. Jahrhunderts*, Zürich, 1961, pp. 34–5.

[4] MGH, Const. I, p. 199, No. 141. This document is known only through Wibald's draft in BRG, I, p. 514.

[5] H. Hirsch, *Urkundenfälschungen aus dem Regnum Arelatense*, Wien, 1937, p. 130.

concessions to Henry the Lion in the north and in Bavaria. Frederick was not anxious to secure more direct power for himself. He was prepared to tie the German magnates to himself by making wide concessions to them – a very similar charter concerning the bishoprics and churches east of the Elbe was issued to Henry the Lion in 1154.[1] Like Henry the Lion, Berthold was to be allowed an enormous expansion of power and in two charters he was even referred to as duke of Burgundy.[2] Frederick wanted, at this stage, above all, help for the projected expedition to Italy and in the pact with Berthold the nature of this help was minutely specified. The pact was negotiated by Wibald; and, since Wibald was one of the keenest promoters of the Italian expedition in aid of the pope, he took particular care to state the exact contributions which Berthold was to make to the expedition. For the rest, Frederick wanted to reserve for himself the role of arbitrator – so much so that when in February 1153 two of Berthold's greatest enemies appeared before Frederick, he treated them with friendship and forbearance at the risk of deeply annoying Berthold.[3] But Frederick was an astute diplomat and when he finally prepared for the Italian expedition, Berthold had become completely reconciled to him.[4]

Frederick also tried to compose the quarrel between the count of Flanders and the bishop of Cambray – but owing to clerical pressure seems to have been less than just to the count. His most notable success, however, was scored in regard to the old feud between Margrave Albrecht the Bear of Brandenburg and Henry the Lion. These two princes had been fighting over the inheritance of two families who had died out. Eventually Frederick persuaded the one to be content with one inheritance and the other with the other. It seemed a reasonable compromise and one wonders why it had taken the strong arbitration of Frederick to achieve it. But in those centuries men often fought and feuded for the sake of fighting and feuding – it was one of the great and very few pastimes then available.

[1] MGH, Const. I, No. 147, p. 206.

[2] Ulm, 1152. H. Büttner, *op. cit.*, p. 35, note 1.

[3] H. Büttner, *op. cit.*, pp. 36–7.

[4] E. Heyck, *Geschichte der Herzoge von Zähringen*, Freiburg, 1891, p. 343.

Frederick, however, did not quite trust the agreement. When, in 1152, the archbishopric of Magdeburg fell vacant he decided to put it into the hands of Bishop Wichmann of Naumburg-Zeitz, because Wichmann was related to all the major families in eastern Saxony and would therefore be likely to exercise enormous influence and power in that region. Since the archdiocese of Magdeburg was situated between the spheres of action of Margrave Albrecht the Bear and Henry the Lion and, whatever the future might hold, Frederick thought it best for the balance of power in northern Germany if these two princes were separated by a third, a princely bishop, devoted to the king.

Wichmann was descended from the house of Seeburg.[1] His father's great-grandfather Burchard had had a sister who was the ancestor of the Supplinburg family and a descendant of that same Burchard had been archbishop of Magdeburg until 1142.[2] To a modern reader these connections may appear somewhat remote; but in an ancient Teutonic society in which descent was traced bilaterally, they were real enough. Apart from these family connections, Wichmann was also a suitable man in every other respect. He had great military talent and was to prove himself an adroit diplomat: whenever possible he preferred negotiation to violence.[3] He was a good ecclesiastical administrator and both the church and city of Magdeburg were to have good reason for being grateful to him.[4] He also loved worldly splendour[5] and good living

[1] J. Hartung, *Die Territorialpolitik der Magdeburger Erzbischöfe Wichmann, Ludolf und Albrecht, 1152–1232*, GSLM, 21, 1886, p. 10. Also O. V. Heinemann, *Albrecht der Bär*, Darmstadt, 1864, p. 193.

[2] K. Uhlirz, *Wichmann*, ADB, 42, p. 781. For Wichmann's relations with the Billung family see Giesebrecht, V, 12, and H. Fechner, *Wichmann*, FDG, 5, 1865, p. 425. Wichmann had also owed his first 'election' to the see of Naumburg to family connections. He had not even been a member of the Naumburg chapter. He had, however, had relatives in the chapter and his uncle, Margrave Conrad, had various connections with the see of Naumburg. *Cp.* F. Winter, *Erzbischof Wichmann von Magdeburg*, FDG, 13, 1873, p. 119.

[3] Godfrey of Viterbo, *Gesta Friderici*, MGH, SS, XXII, p. 333, V, 1207. There is a 'portrait' of Wichmann on his tomb in Magdeburg cathedral.

[4] W. Hoppe, *Erzbischof Wichmann von Magdeburg*, GSLM, 43–4, 1908–9, pp. 261 ff. Wichmann had greater success in the territorial growth of Magdeburg than any of his predecessors. He not only promoted both commerce and colonization east of the Elbe but also acquired Jüterbog after 1157, the abbey of Nienburg in 1166 and the allodial property of the Sommerschenburg family in 1179. *Cp.* A. Brackmann, *Magdeburg als Hauptstadt des deutschen Ostens im frühen Mittelalter*, Leipzig, 1937, pp. 63–6.

[5] *Chron. Mon. Ser.*, MGH, SS, XXIII, p. 163. In the *Relatio de Pace Veneta*, MGH, SS,

and it seems that under his administration clerical celibacy was not too strictly enforced in Magdeburg.[1] But this was nothing very unusual in the twelfth century and the fact that Magdeburg was known for its secular liveliness rather than for strict piety merely served to increase the reputation of its archbishop.

Wichmann was a tough, determined and ambitious man. He had entered the chapter of Halberstadt probably in 1140. In 1145, or 1146, Wigand, a member of the chapter, was killed by the men of Martin, the chapter's provost, because there had been a dispute between chapter and provost over the extent of the latter's fief. Although Martin himself was absent at the time of the murder, he was identified with the murder, and the chapter, led by Wichmann, agitated for his removal and eventually Wichmann was appointed to his office. Martin's guilt was never proved – but Wichmann was not a man to allow such an opportunity to pass.[2]

The next step was his election to the see of Naumburg through family influence – for Wichmann was at that time not even a member of the Naumburg chapter.[3] The see of Magdeburg fell vacant in January 1152 through the death of the archbishop. Owing to a clash of principles a double election had resulted. On one side there was provost Gerhard, who stood for the ideals of ecclesiastical reform inaugurated in Magdeburg by Archbishop Norbert. On the other side there was Hazeko, the leader of the worldly party and a man who had in the past made many difficulties for Norbert.[4] These two men who claimed to have been elected to the see were both old and neither of them inspired Frederick with much confidence. For Frederick knew that the precarious agreement between Henry the Lion and Albrecht the Bear was not likely to last. Count Sommerschenburg whose lands were situated in that region was likely to die in the foreseeable

XIX, p. 462, he is described as a mild, good and modest man. For his worldly bearing see Hoppe, *op. cit.*, p. 220. His glory was sung in the *Carmina Burana*, A. Brackmann, *Magdeburg als Hauptstadt des deutschen Ostens im frühen Mittelalter*, Leipzig, 1937, p. 63. *Cp. Annales Marbacenses* ad 1183.

[1] *Chron. Mon. Ser.*, MGH, SS, XXIII, p. 163.

[2] F. Winter, *op. cit.*, pp. 118–19.

[3] *Cp.* p. 56, note 2.

[4] F. Winter, *Die Zisterzienser des nordöstlichen Deutschlands*, pp. 45 ff., 354.

future without heirs and there was bound to be a contest over his lands.[1] He decided therefore to invoke what he maintained to be his right under the Concordat of Worms,[2] i.e. to adjudicate in cases of disputed elections. He set both candidates aside and nominated Wichmann. Gerhard thereupon appealed to the pope who was happy to support such an ardent advocate of ecclesiastical reform. But the supporters of the ageing Hazeko were easily won over to Wichmann's cause.[3] There was enough inflammable material to make a first major quarrel between king and pope. But since neither side felt quarrelsome, it needed only the diplomatic tact of Wichmann to settle the matter to everybody's satisfaction. Wichmann himself wanted to take up the archbishopric but not without papal consent. In the end he travelled to Rome where the pope put the *pallium* on the altar and stated he would not object if Wichmann took it, as long as his papal face was saved by not actually having to hand it to Wichmann. And thus the matter was solved. Wichmann became the legal archbishop of Magdeburg and administered his see for many decades and rendered invaluable services as a diplomat and adviser to Frederick – always proving his skill as a negotiator and arguing for careful methods and sensible settlements.

The one great question, indeed the greatest of all questions, however, Frederick failed to settle. He had had high hopes for succeeding in pacifying the Welf opposition by surrendering to them, in addition to their tenure of Saxony and Tuscany (the so-called Matildan lands were in the possession of Welf VI) the duchy of Bavaria. The latter duchy had been held by the Babenberg family ever since Conrad had managed to deprive the Welf family of it. The present duke, Henry Jasomirgott – thus surnamed by virtue of his favourite form of swearing – was Frederick's uncle. It appears very probable that this surrender had been promised by Frederick

[1] F. Winter, *Erzbischof Wichmann von Magdeburg*, FDG, 13, 1873, p. 117.

[2] The exact provisions of the Concordat of Worms of 1122 were sufficiently in doubt to allow all sides a certain freedom of interpretation. *Cp.* the remarks of P. Rassow, *Honor Imperii*, new edition, München, 1961, p. 22, especially note 21.

[3] F. Winter, *op. cit.*, p. 116. It seems that Eugene III did not mind the royal investiture (BRG, No. 401), but he considered Wichmann's translation from Naumburg to Magdeburg uncanonical. Eugene appealed to Gregorian sentiments when he objected to Frederick's policy; see BRG, I, No. 403, p. 538.

already before his election and that Henry the Lion had counted on it. But Frederick had been a bit too rash, and obviously did not have the support of the other side of his clan. For it is very noticeable that from the first, Duke Henry Jasomirgott began to absent himself from Frederick's courts; and when finally called upon to appear and invited to surrender his duchy, he refused. He was summoned time and again; and time and again he disobeyed. Finally the duchy was given to Henry the Lion by some sort of formal judgement. But there the matter rested, for Henry Jasomirgott would not surrender it nor depart from his castles in Bavaria. Short of force, nothing could dispossess him. But force was just the very thing which Frederick wanted to avoid. He had hoped to act as arbiter and peace-maker, and seems to have been somewhat astonished to find that, in this particular instance at any rate, mere arbitration and peaceful persuasion were not enough.

In the meantime, Frederick's fame as an arbiter had spread. Already at a court in Ulm, towards the end of July 1152, several plaintiffs from Lombardy had appeared to seek justice. And in Würzburg, in mid-October, an even greater number had gathered. They urged him to come to Lombardy to compose the endless quarrels between the various cities and to confirm certain bishops and counts in their fiefs. There were also refugees from Apulia, deprived of their lands by the intransigent policies of King Roger of Sicily. And finally there was a letter from a certain Wezel, a disciple of Arnold of Brescia, in which Frederick was blamed for having failed to seek the confirmation of his election from the citizens of Rome. The letter was clearly an invitation for Frederick to come to Rome and support the cause of the citizens and of Arnold of Brescia against the pope. Wezel indeed argued that in Rome not even the market vendors and fishwives believed in the Donation of Constantine according to which the pope claimed the lordship of the city.[1]

The pope himself was becoming more and more anxious that Frederick should come to Italy and Rome and restore order in the city. The immediate occasion for the Romans' rebellion against Pope Eugene had been the latter's refusal to raze the city of Tivoli

[1] BRG, I, pp. 539–43, No. 404.

to the ground after he had conquered it to please the Romans. But there were deeper reasons for this rebellion which was to last, off and on, for so many decades.

Until the middle of the eleventh century, every pope had been firmly connected with one or the other of the great Roman families who had always considered the papacy to be the greatest prize of their incessant feuds. But with the triumph of the reform party in Rome during the second half of the eleventh century,[1] the papacy had come more and more often into the hands of men who were not Romans and who could not count on any of the Roman factions for support. Instead, they had to base their power upon the support and obedience of the universal church and thus they lost their close connections with the inhabitants of the city they wanted to rule. As a result of the reform movement, the papacy in Rome had become a foreign institution. At the same time, the Roman noble families themselves had exhausted their resources during their long struggles with one another and thus, by the early twelfth century, had lost their dominant position in the city. Hence the growing importance of the 'middle classes'. Though in this respect the city of Rome did not differ fundamentally from other north Italian cities of the twelfth century, this development was strongly aided and reinforced by ancient memories of republican traditions and thus, in 1143, when the people of Rome were irate at the pope's refusal to consent to the destruction of Tivoli, they stormed the Capitol and re-established the senate. Ironically, they misunderstood the ancient significance of the senate. They ignored the fact that the senate had been the noble section of the city. They simply seized upon the expression *senatus populusque romanus* and concluded that any popular movement must aim at its restoration.[2] Pope Innocent II objected to the senate, but to no avail. Later, in 1144 Lucius II tried to secure the support of King Roger of Sicily when his relations with the senate were precarious. Eventually the senate demanded the exercise of sovereignty. They proposed that the pope, like any other bishop, was to content himself with the Tenth and with voluntary gifts. They elected a

[1] I follow mainly J. Haller, *Das Papsttum*, Stuttgart, 1952, III, pp. 62 ff.

[2] J. Haller, *op. cit.*, III, p. 66.

patricius to be governor of Rome and declared the city an 'imperial republic'.

This was too much for Lucius II. He appealed to Conrad III but before Conrad was able to reply, Lucius had died, victim of an outbreak of public violence on 15 February 1145. A successor was elected in secrecy and haste and the new pope, Eugene III, was only able to take possession of the Lateran. But a consecration in St Peter's was impossible, for the populace would only allow him to enter if he recognized the proposed constitution of the imperial republic. Eugene, therefore, departed from Rome with the cardinals and was consecrated elsewhere. As a result, the fury of the populace knew no bounds: in the ensuing riots there was general looting of papal property and many churches were destroyed.

In December 1145 Eugene finally reached an agreement with the Romans at Sutri, to the effect that he would recognize the senate but that the senate was to pay homage to him. This arrangement lasted for just over one year. In March 1147, Eugene had to emigrate again. And when he tried to return in the autumn of the following year, he found that the rebellion had spread further through the preaching of Arnold of Brescia. Arnold had been well known because of his advocacy of clerical reform, insisting that the clergy ought to live in complete poverty. Wherever he had preached, he had attacked the clergy's wealth. Now he had been attracted to the centre of the church and in Rome his campaign was directed not only against the wealth of the clergy but also against the temporal power of the popes. No wonder that he had become a rallying point for the rebellion.[1]

[1] St Bernard and Gerhoh of Reichersberg had often attacked the church's wealth. But Arnold's connection with the Roman rebellion against the pope's temporal power lent a specially sharp edge to his radical insistence on complete poverty. Arnold, however, was not the author of the rebellion as Otto of Freising, *Gesta*, I, xxviii, maintains. (In *Gesta*, II, xxviii, Otto corrects himself and says that Arnold arrived after the first outbreak and merely added fuel to the flame). When Otto wrote the *Gesta*, Arnold had been executed by Frederick, and Otto was therefore anxious to attribute as much blame as possible to Arnold for the rebellion. In the 40s, when writing the *Chronicle*, he had not even mentioned Arnold in connection with the rebellion: VII, xxxi and xxxiv. G. W. Greenway, *Arnold of Brescia*, Cambridge 1931, p. 106, noted the contradiction without, however, being able to explain it by the fact that the *Gesta* were written after Arnold's execution at the request of the pope. For that matter, Arnold's relations with the senate were far from peaceful. In September 1152, Eugene III reported to Wibald that Arnold had tried to instigate a rebellion of the common folk against the

Once the rebellion had gained an ideological focus, Eugene realized that he would have to seek military aid. He had the choice between King Roger of Sicily who, in return, asked for nothing less than to be invested with the kingdom of Sicily and for complete power over the churches and bishoprics of southern Italy and Sicily; and King Conrad of Germany who would have asked for nothing more than the imperial crown. Roger's help would have been effective, but he was expensive. Conrad's was not likely to be as useful, but he was cheap. And therefore, in 1149, Eugene had approached Conrad. Conrad made it clear that he would support the pope against the Romans,[1] but unfortunately he was fully occupied in Germany and the proposed expedition could not be undertaken. Luckily, Eugene had enough money in hand to negotiate an agreement with the Romans without Conrad's aid. He agreed to recognize the senate, who in return for a payment of five hundred pounds would pay homage to him and recognize his sovereignty in the city. And thus by Christmas 1149, Eugene had been able to return to Rome.

All the same, the peace was unstable. In July 1150 Eugene once more had to leave Rome and once more took up negotiations with both Roger and Conrad. In 1151, Wibald on behalf of Conrad had made a firm treaty with Eugene, promising help in return for the imperial coronation. Moreover, at a court in Würzburg in September 1151, Conrad had made a public announcement that he intended to go to Italy within a year with the ultimate aim of a campaign against the Norman kings of Sicily. In this way, Conrad wanted to free the pope from all his difficulties, Roman rebels as well as Norman kings, and had intended to fulfil the terms of

---

senate. (BRG, No. 403, p. 538). The senate, it seems, might have accommodated themselves to imperial rule in Rome, provided it recognized the senate. But Arnold was more left-wing and preferred a real commune.

[1] Arnold of Brescia, about that same time, had also written to Conrad and invited him to come to Rome and put himself at the head of the senate and the popular movement. The letter is in BRG, I, No. 216. It is the only piece of writing by Arnold which we have. K. Hampe, *Zur Geschichte Arnolds von Brescia*, HZ, 1924, 130, pp. 58–9, accepts it as genuine and gives good reasons why at this stage Arnold should describe himself as a 'senator' to Conrad. Conrad's reply is also in BRG, I, No. 345, and exactly foreshadows Frederick's reply to a similar letter by one of Arnold's friends written in 1152 (see p. 59, note 1 above). Being firmly committed to the pope, neither Conrad nor Frederick could entertain these tempting invitations.

the treaty of Thessalonica which he had concluded with the Greek emperor on his return from the crusade.[1] Eugene, on his part, had exhorted the princes of Germany to support their king in these plans. But Conrad had died before they matured.

Frederick was confronted by all these problems at the court he held in Würzburg in October 1152. Whereas he kept a fairly open mind as to the quarrels in Lombardy he was quite clear what he ought to do in regard to the refugees of Apulia and the pope. He considered himself bound by the agreements made between Conrad and the Byzantine emperor to wage war on the kingdom of Sicily; and he took it as a matter of course that he had to restore papal power in Rome, because it was the pope and the pope alone who could lawfully crown him emperor.

As to the agreements between Conrad and Byzantium, it is not easy to see them in a clear light. According to most German sources, the Byzantine emperor had taken advantage of Conrad when the latter was passing through Byzantium on his way home from the unfortunate second crusade. Sick and beaten, Conrad had been cornered and forced to sign a treaty in which he promised to help the Byzantine emperor to destroy the power of the Norman kings of Sicily.[2]

If one consults Byzantine sources, one gets a very different picture. There it is stated that the crude Teutonic barbarian, on his way home from the Holy Land, had inveigled the Byzantines into a treaty against the king of Sicily, because Conrad wanted support for his forthcoming Italian campaign. And in order to add insult to injury, the Byzantine emperor had to seal the agreement by allowing the marriage of the cultivated and beautiful Byzantine Princess Theodora to Conrad's unkempt half-brother, Henry Jasomirgott.[3]

However this may be, Frederick considered himself bound. And

[1] *See* Kinnamos, II, 19. There is some doubt as to where the treaty was concluded and, therefore, as to its name. *Cp.* P. Rassow, *Honor Imperii,* new ed., München, 1961, p. 97, note 35. *Cp.* p. 64, note 2 below.

[2] *Cp.* S. Runciman, *History of the Crusades,* Cambridge, 1952, II, p. 285. *Cp.* the opinion of Gerhoh of Reichersberg, quoted by P. Classen, *Gerhoch von Reichersberg,* Wiesbaden, 1960, p. 157.

[3] Chalandon, *Les Comnène,* II, i, pp. 326–7. The bride's mother received messages of condolence. Henry Jasomirgott's first wife Gertrude had died in 1143.

there is no doubt that the campaign against the king of Sicily was, apart from the coronation in Rome, the avowed objective of his first Italian expedition. So much so, that it was expressly mentioned in the treaty which he made with the pope at Constance in 1153.

Following negotiations which had been carried on in the second half of 1152, early in 1153 papal legates had met Frederick in Constance where the treaty was formally sworn to and signed on 23 March.[1] It was a perfect agreement of concord between king and pope. The king promised not to make peace with either the citizens of Rome or with the king of Sicily without papal approval. He also promised to restore papal power in Rome and do everything to advance the *honour* of the pope. The Greeks were not to be given any territorial concessions in Italy. On the other hand, the pope promised to advance the *honour* of the empire and to crown the king in Rome; to excommunicate all those who defied the king; and equally not to concede any territories to the Greeks in Italy. All this was to be observed by both parties without feud or bad faith, unless changed by free and mutual consent.[2]

[1] For the date *cp.* H. Zatschek, *Beiträge zur Geschichte des Konstanzer Vertrags*, Wien, 210, 3, 1930, p. 7.

[2] Wibald's draft is in BRG, I, No. 407. For the edited, full text *see* P. Rassow, *op. cit.*, pp. 115 ff. There is nothing fundamentally new in the Treaty of Constance and I think Rassow's interpretation of the term *honor imperii* (*op. cit.*, pp. 60 ff) as having a geographical meaning, untenable. I think that Grundmann's criticism of Rassow is justified: HZ, 164 pp. 580–1. *Cp.* also the sound views of M. Maccarone, *op. cit.*, p. 73. But even if Rassow's interpretation were correct, there is nothing really new in the treaty. Frederick merely agreed to follow Conrad's policy to destroy the Norman kingdom in Sicily. The only new feature is that Frederick promised – in contradiction to the Treaty of Thessalonica – not to make territorial concessions to the Greeks. But that was a minor point (*cp.* p. 65, note 1 below), for the Treaty of Constance *did* reiterate the major purpose of the Treaty of Thessalonica, i.e. to make war on the king of Sicily. By the Treaty of Constance, Frederick may have altered the letter of the Treaty of Thessalonica, but not the spirit. It was possible for him to do this, because in 1153 he was in a stronger position than Conrad had been in 1147, and he therefore felt that he might be able to fulfil the objects of the Treaty of Thessalonica without making territorial concessions to the Greeks in Italy. In the final redaction of the Treaty of Constance, Frederick had Wibald's description of him as *rex* replaced by the expression *imperator Romanorum*. W. Ohnsorge, '*Kaiser' Konrad III*, MIOG, 46, 1932, p. 358, has a very learned reason to justify the use of *imperator* before the coronation: he says that since 1139 it had been customary to use a secularized *imperator* (equals *rex*) concept in correspondence with Constantinople. But it is doubtful whether Frederick was as learned as Ohnsorge and more likely that he simply felt that Wibald was too cautious. Hence the alteration. And in any case, the Treaty of Constance was not a letter addressed

The agreement was clearly one of mutual assistance between pope and king. However, as far as the Greeks were concerned, the mutual promise not to make them any territorial concessions in Italy must have presented a problem. For if they were to take part as allies in the expedition against the Norman king, it might prove difficult not to make territorial concessions to them on the peninsula. But one can only suppose that both Frederick and Eugene at that juncture decided to cross bridges when they came to them.[1]

---

to Constantinople, and Frederick was not consistent: he referred to himself as *dominus rex* in the actual text of the treaty. The Greek emperor was also called simply *rex*, whereas Frederick and Wibald in addressing him directly used all the most formal imperial titles: BRG, I, p. 550. It must also count as criticism of Rassow's view (that the concept *honor imperii* marked a new departure in imperial policy and that the Treaty of Constance therefore proves that Frederick did not intend to follow in the footsteps of Conrad) that the expression *honor imperii* is perfectly balanced by the expression *honor papatus*. For that matter, the whole treaty is a genuine bilateral agreement between two parties. *See* H. Mitteis, *Politische Verträge des Mittelalters*, ZSSRGger, 67, 1950, pp. 92–3.

[1] It is quite clear that in the Treaty of Thessalonica Conrad had made some kind of territorial promise to the Greeks in Italy. *Cp.* W. Ohnsorge, *Zu den aussenpolitischen Anfängen Friedrich Barbarossas*, QuF, 32, 1942, p. 21, and the literature cited in note 1. Immediately afterwards Wibald used all his diplomatic skill to persuade the pope that he had nothing to fear from that treaty. Conrad had merely wanted to tie the Greeks firmly to himself and make sure that the pope would not have to expect unpleasant surprises from the Greeks in Italy. During the last two years of Conrad's reign, Wibald planned to cement an alliance with the pope as well as with the Greeks. *Cp.* Ohnsorge, *op. cit.*, p. 27. Wibald wanted Conrad's son Henry to marry a Greek princess; and after Henry's death he thought that Conrad himself might marry a Greek princess. The persistence of his efforts shows that there was something equivocal in the Treaty of Thessalonica, which he wanted to straighten out. This is also proved by the conflicting reports of the reasons for the conclusion of the treaty (*cp.* p. 63, notes 2 and 3 above). But there is no doubt about Wibald's efforts to mollify both pope and Greeks about these equivocations. And when the Treaty of Constance was concluded, these efforts were continued. Frederick was most anxious that the Greeks should not be antagonized by the new treaty with the pope, and therefore caused Wibald to write a conciliatory letter in which he declared his readiness to consolidate his friendship with the Greeks and his hostility to the Normans of Sicily, by wanting to marry a Greek princess, i.e. by wanting to follow in the footsteps of Conrad. (*See* M. Doeberl, *Monumenta Germaniae Selecta*, München, 1890, p. 81, No. 28, and BRG, I, No. 410). Wibald wrote a personal letter to Constantinople to assure the Greek emperor of the friendship between the two empires and of his own efforts in that direction, especially on behalf of the marriage plans. (BRG, I, No. 411) We must therefore conclude that as far as the thorny question of any eventual territorial concessions to the Greeks in Italy was concerned, it was not directly mentioned, and Frederick must have hoped that time would bring some kind of solution. The Treaty of Constance can, therefore, in no way be regarded as inconsistent with Frederick's Byzantine policy. Nor did the Greeks consider it to be, for the ambassadors who were to discuss the marriage plan left Constantinople in the middle of 1153, that is, well after the conclusion of the Treaty of Constance. *Cp*, W. Ohnsorge, *Zu den aussenpolitischen Aufängen Friedrich Barbarossas*, QuF, 32, 1942, pp. 15–16.

At that time, the concord between pope and king was such that the papal legates readily concurred in two other matters which were much in Frederick's mind. They pronounced his marriage to his wife null and void and agreed to hold a court in Worms in June in order to deprive a number of bishops of their sees.

Some time after June 1149, Frederick had been maried to Adela von Vohburg, the daughter of Margrave Dietpold II von Vohburg. This marriage had been intended as an act of reconciliation. The margrave died in April 1146 and had left two sons who were minors. The Vohburg family, in spite of earlier changes, had been steady supporters of the Staufen and the Babenberg families, and at that time the duke of Bavaria, a Babenberg, was fighting the bishop of Ratisbon. Because the Welfen and their followers were in full opposition and the Staufen needed all the able-bodied supporters they could muster, Conrad had granted the margravate to his own brother-in-law, Gebhard von Sulzbach, since the Vohburg heirs were still minors. Some time after June 1146 Berthold von Vohburg came of age and Gebhard handed the margravate back to him. In order to confirm the Vohburgs in their adherence to the Staufen cause, Berthold's sister Adela was married soon after to Frederick and it was agreed that the imperial fief of the Egerland should be her dowry.[1]

When Frederick came to power largely as the candidate of the Welf faction, he considered the Vohburg alliance of minor significance. Indeed, he almost immediately granted the dowry to his cousin Frederick IV, duke of Swabia[2] and as mere margraves the Vohburg family had become expendable. Frederick's personal relations with Adela had never been close. It seems that she was older than Frederick and since she was never mentioned in any charter[3] and was never crowned, one must conclude that Frederick had had very little to do with her.[4] When it became known to him

[1] A. Mardus, *Die Eheschliessungen in den deutschen Königsfamilien von Lothar III bis Friedrich II*, Greifswald, 1909, p. 27; H. Simonsfeld, p. 156, notes 18 and 19.

[2] H. Heuermann, *Die Hausmachtpolitik der Staufen von Herzog Friedrich I bis König Konrad III*, Berlin, Diss., 1939, p. 94. As a result, the Vohburg family never became *Reichsfürsten*, for without the Egerland, the Nordgau did not amount to much.

[3] With one exception, Stumpf, 3684; H. Simonsfeld, *op. cit.*, I, p. 217, note 22.

[4] W. Kowalski, *Die deutschen Königinnen und Kaiserinnen*, Weimar, 1913, p. 9.

that she was committing adultery, he decided to have the marriage dissolved, even though at that time he had no clear idea whom he wanted to marry.[1] It is impossible to prove beyond doubt from the statements in contemporary chronicles that Adela was guilty of adultery. But the fact that the marriage had been childless and that Adela married immediately after her divorce a man who was beneath her station and little more than a household retainer and that she bore him many children[2] seems to make the adultery fairly certain.

Although Germanic custom would have allowed Frederick to kill or repudiate his wife for committing adultery, Gratian had said quite expressly that adultery was no ground for divorce in canon law.[3] So there remained only the possibility of having the marriage annulled on the ground of consanguinity. Frederick was in fact related to Adela in the sixth degree[4] and according to the canonical custom of the twelfth century – a custom which the church did not manage to uphold in the long run – even the seventh was still a prohibited degree. If the upper classes of medieval Europe had observed this canonical rule punctiliously they would have been hard put to find what they would have considered a suitable marriage partner, for real exogamy was unknown and, if practised, would have dissolved the bonds of society too quickly. There is therefore no reason why Frederick should suddenly have had scruples about prohibited degrees. For that matter, when Frederick did re-marry, his new wife was also related to him in the sixth degree.

Eugene was not keen on dissolving marriages on such grounds[5]

[1] Adela's adultery is mentioned in *Chron. Mon. Ser.*, MGH, SS, XVI, p. 149. E. Rundnagel, *Die Ehescheidung Friedrich Barbarossas*, in Festschrift f. R. Holtzmann, 1933, has shown that the *Chronicon Montis Sereni* is based, for the years 1151–1181, on the *Ilsenburger Annalen*. Hence the notice that adultery had taken place goes back to a fairly contemporary source which, moreover, was pro-Staufen and had therefore no reason to invite bad rumours.

[2] She married Dietho von Ravensburg, a *ministerialis*. Giesebrecht, V, 27. According to Burchard of Ursberg, *Chronicon*, SRG, p. 26, Adela's new husband was a Staufen *ministerialis*. But according to Simonsfeld, p. 169, n. 68, he was a Welf *ministerialis*.

[3] C. 32, Qu. 7, c. 1.

[4] For Adela's pedigree see BRG, I, No. 408.

[5] According to Gratian even the seventh degree was prohibited. But Gratian was not binding and it is certain that the sixth degree was in the twelfth century a debatable matter. The annulment was therefore not mandatory.

and it seems that Frederick could have followed the example of the French king whose marriage was dissolved in 1152 without papal authority. But at that time, Frederick was sincerely anxious to accommodate himself with the pope; and the pope, though he need not have complied, was equally anxious to please Frederick, and thus the papal legates were empowered to annul Frederick's marriage to Adela.

Pope Eugene also willingly obliged Frederick in another matter. Frederick was determined to strengthen his position in Germany by relying on as many bishops as he could. And therefore he wanted to take the opportunity, early in his reign, of removing a number of bishops in order to appoint nominees of his own. The matter must have been discussed in Rome at the time when the preliminaries of the Treaty of Constance had been discussed[1] and the depositions were carried out immediately after the conclusion of that treaty by the papal legates. The archbishop of Mainz was the first victim. It was not possible to advance any reason or to prove that he had been a bad archbishop. St Bernard, in one of the last letters he ever wrote, testified in his favour[2] and the action of the legates was criticized by many people who seem to have understood that Henry was dispossessed because he had led the opposition to Frederick's election. And in June 1153 Frederick nominated – there was hardly the appearance of an election[3] – his chancellor Arnold von Seelenhofen to the see of Mainz.

The other deprivations had better reasons: Bishop Henry of Minden was accused of a crime;[4] Bishop Burckard of Eichstätt seems to have been senile; and Bishop Bernhard of Hildesheim, blind. But even in these cases there is no doubt that Frederick used their failings in order to create vacancies to which he could promote the election of, or appoint, his own men.

Frederick's predecessor, Conrad, had been very much dependent on his bishops. But, owing to the strength of the princely opposition, he had been compelled to rely on their voluntary support – which fact had always given the bishops a decisive and

[1] P. Rassow, *op. cit.*, p. 18.
[2] For St Bernard's letter see Giesebrecht, V, 28.
[3] P. Rassow, *op. cit.*, p. 18.
[4] K. Löffler ed., *Mindener Geschichtsquellen*, 1917, Vol. I, p. 156, note 1.

independent voice in politics, so much so that Conrad had become known as a *Pfaffenkönig*, the priests' king. Frederick, by contrast, was able to create a solid episcopal phalanx which he could trust and whose support was not to remain conditional. Frederick kept a very close watch on episcopal elections[1] which, in many cases, were almost nominal. Indeed, it was taken for granted that Frederick simply appointed bishops,[2] and as a result, throughout his reign the German episcopate's support was assured. The episcopate was tied to his person even though they took little notice of the various anti-popes whom Frederick was to be compelled to sponsor for a long period.[3]

The episcopate's firm personal support helped Frederick to weather the ecclesiastical storm of the sixties and made the final compromise with the papacy possible. Frederick not only relied on his bishops for general political support – but also drew heavily upon their personal and military services. In fact, it turned out (and Frederick was probably able to foresee this quite early in his reign) that the bishops were to be the chief suppliers of soldiers and knights and the very backbone of his military machine. If the arrangements made at the very beginning of his reign with the German princes were to last and if Frederick was to be no more than a general supervisor and arbiter, he would at least have to be able to count on firm military support from his bishops. This policy was not exactly in keeping with the Gregorian reform programme for the church, but there was no opposition to it. And, what is more, while many people were to object to many things Frederick was to do, nobody ever challenged his ecclesiastical arrangement.

All things considered, Frederick could claim, by the end of 1153, after one and a half years of power, a fair amount of success in his policy of peace-making and arbitration. Thus he was determined to follow it up by the long intended expedition to Italy to gain the

[1] *Cp. Chron. reg. Col.* for 1173.

[2] Almost all of Frederick's chancellors were 'elected' to bishoprics and the following bishops were relatives of Frederick: Dietrich IV of Metz, Hermann II of Bamberg (cousin), Otto of Brixen, later of Bamberg (House of Andechs), Henry of Passau (House of Berg), Diepold of Passau (House of Berg), Otto II of Freising.

[3] *Cp.* R. Jordan, *Die Stellung des deutschen Episkopats im Kampf um die Universalmacht unter Friedrich I*, Würzburg, 1939.

imperial crown, to restore papal power in Rome and to fight the king of Sicily. It was only natural that on his way through Lombardy he should intend to continue his peace-making and his arbitration. The earlier complaints from Lombardy had multiplied before the king and the papal legates at Constance;[1] and Frederick must have intended to sit in judgement and to settle feuds in Lombardy on his way to Rome.

The lawlessness prevailing in northern Italy was well known[2] and at Constance a deputation from the city of Lodi had appeared to beg Frederick to restore peace and justice in Lombardy.[3] There were no conflicts of principle between Frederick and the north Italian cities. It all turned on whether they would accept him in his role of peace-maker or not. The Veronese, for instance, sent profuse apologies for any misdemeanour they might have been guilty of[4] but the Milanese did not. And it was this failure to accept him in the role which he wanted to play which predisposed him at that time against Milan. But Frederick's intentions were completely peaceful[5] and the Italians themselves encouraged him to think that they expected him to arbitrate. When Frederick eventually put Milan to the ban of the empire he took from it all the rights it had exercised so far, such as coining, levying customs and all secular jurisdiction. With the exception of the right of coinage, which he gave to Cremona, he decided to retain all these rights for his own purposes. But[6] this decision was based upon the judgement of his *curia* and there was no suggestion that Milan had not exercised those rights legally. They were now taken away not because their use had been illegal but because Milan had been disloyal in refusing to accept Frederick's arbitrations and had to be punished.[7]

[1] Morena, *De Rebus Laudensibus*, MGH, SS, XVIII, p. 588.

[2] *Cp.* e.g. Peter the Venerable, in a letter quoted by W. Lenel, *Der Konstanzer Friede von 1183*, HZ, 128, 1923, p. 220.

[3] Morena, *op. cit.*, pp. 588–9.

[4] *Gesta*, II, xlv.

[5] *Gesta*, II, xi; especially last sentences.

[6] MGH, Const. I, pp. 216–17.

[7] H. Koeppler, *Frederick Barbarossa and the Law Schools of Bologna*, EHR, 54, 1939, p. 582. In view of later events and of the reasons for which Frederick was to put Milan to the ban of the empire again in 1158, it is important to emphasize that in 1155, Frederick did *not* deny that Milan was legally entitled to the possession of the *regalia*.

If his role in Lombardy could not be fulfilled, this was due to the fact that the social conditions in which his arbitration could work had to be feudal or quasi-feudal. But in northern Italy at that time conditions had changed and urban culture had sufficiently progressed for the simple concept of royal arbitration to be no longer applicable. On his first expedition to Italy, Frederick had a poor understanding of these new conditions. He did not know that the economic development had drawn the landed nobility into the cities. He believed that the nobles would have preferred to defend themselves against urban encroachments but had unfortunately failed to escape from the authority of the cities.[1] There could have been no greater misconception of north Italian conditions; but his policies were based upon this misconception and therefore his arbitrations were not widely welcomed.

At the same time, one cannot but wonder whether it had not already occurred to him that his policy of arbitration would not prove wholly successful in the long run. For as far as military expeditions were concerned, the German princes had at first been reluctant to go to Rome with him after his election, though by the end of 1153 they had consented, because the imperial crown was at stake and it was in their own interest to encourage Frederick to acquire such an accretion of prestige. But on two other occasions, where the purpose of the intended military expedition had been purely utilitarian, they had refused their support altogether: Frederick had had to call off the campaign against the king of Hungary[2] as well as the campaign against the duke of Barcelona.[3] In this respect there had been an open check to Frederick's plans and he may well have reckoned with the possibility of similar refusals once the immediate objective of the Italian expedition, the imperial coronation in Rome, was achieved. However, for the time being, if he had such doubts he did not give way to them. Neither the death of Pope Eugene in July 1153 nor the death of

---

In 1155 he did *not* consider this possession a usurpation. In 1158 he was to claim that it was. See H. Appelt, *Friedrich Barbarossa und die italienischen Kommunen*, MIOG, LXXII, 1964, p. 317.

[1] *Gesta*, II, xvi.

[2] Giesebrecht, V, p. 14. See *Gesta*, II, vi and BRG, I, No. 391.

[3] Giesebrecht, V, pp. 13–16.

King Roger of Sicily in February 1154 altered anything in the situation. Frederick was determined to proceed to Italy. In October 1154 he collected his army on the Lechfeld near Augsburg and took the road across the Brenner pass to Italy.

The tasks which confronted Frederick upon his arrival in northern Italy towards the end of 1154 were fraught with considerable difficulties. As he came not just as an arbiter and protector but also with well defined objectives, he had brought a largish army with him. This tended to encourage suspicions of any further, perhaps purely incidental, aims he might have.

Moreover, the restoration of papal power committed him against the citizens of Rome; and the projected war against Sicily forced him to seek the goodwill of Pisa and Genoa and Venice, the only cities which had the seapower so essential for a successful attack upon the Norman kingdom.[1] Even in his role as an objective arbiter, Frederick had already entertained, before his departure from Germany, so many complaints against the city of Milan's high-handed aggression against its smaller neighbours, that he was practically committed to a hostile attitude from the start. In addition, the army itself was a problem, for it required to be fed. His soldiers had already foraged on their way down the southern slopes of the Alps. Frederick had ordered full restitution to be made to people who had suffered much damage, but when he took survey of the situation at the first halt on Lake Garda, he decided that in future systematic provision for the feeding of the army would have to be made. Thus he decided to insist on the customary *fodrum*, a contribution for the upkeep of imperial armies on their way to Rome. The messengers who were sent to collect the *fodrum* were not well received. In some places they met with a bland refusal, and in others were given less than the full amount demanded. As a result the army seems to have been short of food, and there was an increasing incidence of disorderly looting on the part of individual soldiers. Although eventually Frederick issued very severe orders to restore discipline in the army,[2] he

[1] Frederick treated Venice, Genoa and Pisa almost as equals. Pisa was promised far-reaching territorial concessions in southern Italy. (H. Meyer, *Die Militärpolitik Friedrich Barbarossas*, EHS, 200, Berlin, 1930, Ch. 5 and p. 102) In December 1154,

could not solve the problem merely by threats; and there is no doubt that in more than one instance Frederick gave way to the army's clamour for loot by laying siege to a castle or destroying a city to satisfy their demands.

Frederick collected his army and held court on the plains of Roncaglia. There were some belated reinforcements from Germany – but Frederick noticed that more than one of his princes had failed to appear. More important, however, was the fact that a large number of embassies arrived with complaints about local quarrels and feuds. Especially important were the accusations made by the citizens of Como, Lodi and Pavia against Milan. Frederick tried to persuade the Milanese to accord a fairer treatment to the victims, but in vain. And so he was finally forced to put Milan to the ban of the empire.

So extreme a measure does not seem originally to have been intended by Frederick. He had come to Italy to be crowned in Rome and to make war on the king of Sicily. The passage through Lombardy was necessary but he was unlikely to have planned to become involved in lengthy conflicts there. As it was, the actual collision with Milan was almost incidental. Like other cities, the Milanese had sent an embassy to Frederick when he was holding his court near Roncaglia. When he decided to break camp, he requested two Milanese consuls to act as guides to the army. The path led through a region which had been devastated by the warfare between Milan and Pavia and the army suffered from lack of supplies. Frederick's soldiers, irritated by hardship, began to suspect that the consuls had led the army into these regions on purpose and their ill-humour and hunger led to violence. Firstly, Frederick refused to free the Milanese prisoners which the citizens of Pavia had surrendered to him as arbiter. Then the Milanese pedlars and bakers who had followed the army were molested, and finally, when the army reached the vicinity of Rosate, a Milanese castle, he demanded that the castle be vacated by its inhabitants.

---

when Frederick was besieging Galliate he concluded a treaty with Venice, making the largest possible concessions without asking for much in return. (A. Baer, *Die Beziehungen Venedigs zum Kaiserreich in der staufischen Zeit*, Innsbruck, 1888, pp. 5–12.)

[2] Giesebrecht V, p. 46.

In pouring rain, men, women and children departed and the following morning Frederick's soldiers entered the place, looted it completely and then burnt it down.

The citizens of Milan themselves were startled by the violent turn of events. When the two consuls who were alleged to have caused this incident returned to Milan they were almost lynched and an embassy was immediately despatched to Frederick to pay him a sum of money and restore peace. But Frederick was angered by now and demanded that Milan allow full freedom to Lodi and Como. This the Milanese could not concede without abdicating their whole position in Lombardy and so there occurred a complete breach between Frederick and Milan, with Milan being put to the ban of the empire.

From then on, Frederick had to proceed carefully: he had to maintain friendly relations with the sea-power cities, Genoa, Pisa and Venice. But he was also prudent enough to avoid a physical showdown with Milan. Therefore he carefully by-passed the city and turned westwards to take revenge on their lands and to allow his army some looting. He assailed first Galliate, then Trecate and finally Torre di Momo, all of which had been fortified by the Milanese. Then keeping westwards to avoid Milan as far as possible, he crossed the Po near Turin, and turned back, south-eastwards. At the news of his approach the citizens of both Chieri and Asti simply vacated their towns, even though they were well fortified. Frederick and his army took possession of both towns, looted them completely and then destroyed them. Then retracing his steps further eastwards on the other side of the Po, he finally came to Tortona.

The city and fortress of Tortona is situated on the northern slopes of the Appenines and dominates the road which leads from Genoa to Milan. In that region of Lombardy, the Pavians held sway; but Tortona had stood out against them, a faithful ally of Milan. When Frederick was approaching with his army, aiming to reach Pavia before finally turning south to cross the Appenines, the citizens of Pavia approached him with complaints about Tortona. In passing, Frederick therefore decided to humiliate Tortona, thereby inflicting another blow on a Milanese outpost.

1 (*a*) Frederick I. Relief in the Porta Romana. (Museo d'Arte Antica, Milan.)

1 (*b*) Frederick I. Relief in the cloisters of the Convent of St Zeno. (Mansell Collection.)

2 Rainald von Dassel, bishop of Cologne and Frederick's Chancellor, bust from Cologne Cathedral. (Courtesy of Rheinisches Bildarchiv.)

Tortona, however, was heavily fortified. On one side it was well protected by nature. The castle itself was situated on high cliffs, and these natural defences had been augmented by a series of strong towers, the most outstanding of which was known, since it was made of red bricks, as the red tower. Tradition alleged that it had originally been built by the Roman king Tarquin. To the south, on the lower slopes, there was the city itself, protected by both walls and towers. Confident of Milanese support and relying upon their fine fortifications, the citizens of Tortona refused to attend Frederick's camp when summoned. Frederick put the city to the ban of the empire and when the citizens continued in their defiance, Frederick laid siege to Tortona. Once more, it would seem, he was about to get involved in a diversion.

The lower city was easily stormed and taken. The inhabitants retreated to the castle on the cliffs and the siege began. Milan had sent a small detachment, consisting of 100 knights and 200 bowmen and with the help of these, the Tortonans made daily excursions and attacks upon the besieging army in order to fetch water from an outside well. Determined to put a stop to the resistance of the city, Frederick soon resorted to brutality: he had several prisoners of war hanged publicly and finally had corpses and pitch-torches thrown into the well to render the water undrinkable. The castle itself could not be assailed. Frederick tried an ingenious scheme to have tunnels dug under the towers in order to undermine the foundations and make them crumble. But the besieged dug tunnels of their own to meet those of the assailants and thus caused them to cave in. In this way the siege dragged on. It had begun on 13 February and over a month later, at Easter, Frederick was no further forward.

During the four days' Easter truce, a delegation of priests and monks came from the city to negotiate. Frederick would not receive them in person, but deputed several of his bishops to talk to them. They described the hardships they were suffering in the besieged city and begged the king to be merciful. But Frederick would make no concessions and thus the fighting resumed. It was not until three weeks after Easter that the citizens were finally impelled by hunger and disease to make an offer of surrender.

Frederick agreed to allow the inhabitants to leave the city, taking with them as much as they could carry. The city itself and the rest of their property was to be left to Frederick's army. Abbot Bruno of Chiaravalle, who had acted as a mediator, seems to have been promised that the castle itself was not to be destroyed. But the promise was not kept, for the citizens of Pavia had paid Frederick a handsome sum in return for an undertaking that the castle would be razed to the ground. One cannot gain a clearer insight into the petty and sordid circumstances which Frederick had helped to create. Short of money and supplies for his army, he was forced to hire it out, so to speak, to some of the Lombard cities in order to perform repressive actions against their enemies which they did not have the military resources to undertake themselves. In 1154 and 1155 Frederick himself seems to have had no personal plans in Lombardy and it is conceivable that he might have helped Milan to establish her rule in Lombardy once and for all. As it was, he acted for the enemies of Milan.

The physical dismantling of the castle took some time, and it was not until 20 April that Frederick could actually proceed on his way towards Pavia. Even so it took the Pavian soldiers who had joined him another week to complete the levelling of the site. The complete destruction of a city or castle was an arduous task in the days when there were neither bulldozers nor explosives. Even so, no permanent change in the power constellation could take place. Milan, as cautious as Frederick himself, had wanted to avoid a direct military clash and therefore had not rendered any great help to Tortona. A Milanese army had been despatched, but had not proceeded as far as Tortona itself. It arrived only after Frederick's departure, and no sooner had the Pavians completed their labours of destruction than the Tortonans and the Milanese army re-occupied the site and began to rebuild both castle and city on 1 May.

From Tortona, Frederick moved to Pavia whose citizens gave him a tremendous welcome and on Sunday, 24 April, he held a crown-wearing festival there in the church of St Michael. After three days of celebrations he continued on his journey – now a little more anxious to avoid further conflicts. The citizens of Pavia seem to have wanted him to attack their enemy, Piacenza, but Frederick refused and merely devastated the country around Piacenza. For that matter, with the example of Tortona fresh in mind, many other cities sent him embassies with rich presents. The one notable exception was Genoa, whose consuls insisted that they would not give Frederick a single penny. Far from being angered, Frederick spent some time in consultation with a Genoese consul, giving him assurances of his goodwill as long as Genoa was prepared to support the campaign against the kingdom of Sicily.

In mid-May, Frederick celebrated Pentecost near Bologna. The citizens seem to have received Frederick and his army in a friendly way, bringing both presents and supplies. The brief sojourn at this encampment is noteworthy, for at that time Frederick established his first contact with the law school of Bologna. The doctors, together with their pupils, came out in a long procession to pay their respects. Frederick received them graciously and showed great interest in their activities. During the ensuing discussions it might well have dawned on him that there were as yet undreamed of possibilities in the revived study of Roman law. Teachers and pupils, when they noticed Frederick's obvious interest in their pursuits, begged him to use his authority to protect them in one particular matter against the citizens of Bologna who otherwise treated them well. Apparently, the citizens had used the fact that so many students from other cities were within their walls to collect outstanding debts incurred in their home cities. The students felt, not unnaturally, that this practice was unfair and the teachers feared that its continuation might well keep future students away. Frederick considered their request just, and asked the citizens of Bologna to refrain from the practice and to honour the students as their guests. There is no doubt that he was extremely interested in the law school and did his best to assure its vigorous development.

After his brief sojourn in Bologna, Frederick was determined not to delay any longer. He now had a sufficient assurance of supplies for his armies and seems to have been confident of reaching Rome without the necessity of further entanglements. Pope

Anastasius who had succeeded Eugene III in 1153 had died in the meantime and Hadrian IV had succeeded him. Hadrian had the unusual distinction of being the only Englishman ever to have been a pope; but he was a distinguished man also in other, more important respects. He had worked his way up from very lowly origins in England and had left his home country for lack of patronage. His obvious gifts had succeeded in securing preferment for him on the continent and eventually in Rome, and as he had just accomplished an important diplomatic mission in Sweden he seemed a suitable candidate for the papal throne. Hadrian was a mild and gentle man, though determined and strong in his decisions. Continuity of administration and policy in the *curia* had been assured for some time by the presence of Cardinal Roland, the papal chancellor. Roland had already been prominent in the counsels of Eugene, had served Anastasius and continued in office under Hadrian. It is tempting to think of him as the real power behind the throne – for Hadrian was not given to great displays of vigour. Hadrian wrote to John of Salisbury to complain of the burdens and hardships of his high office.[1] Historians have always been prone to interpret this letter in a political sense, imagining that Hadrian was referring to the difficulties of the papacy, caught between Romans and Sicilians and exposed to the questionable protection of Frederick. It seems more likely that Hadrian meant the complaint in a personal sense: elected pope, he had to follow the firm line laid down by Roland,[2] with little opportunity for a quiet life. He wished, he wrote, that he had never left England or that he had remained in the Abbey of St Rufus near Valence where he had first found refuge. It is not easy to form a very clear picture of Hadrian. If in his communication to John of Salisbury we find him soft and sensitive, aware of sorrow and pain, we have also evidence that he could be tenacious and stubborn in politics. Perhaps the two traits go together; he might have overcompensated in politics for his softness in private life.

[1] *Polycraticus*, VIII, 24. Boso says that Hadrian was affable, mild, patient, slow to yield to anger, quick to forgive.

[2] Nevertheless it is clear from all the evidence that Roland and Hadrian co-operated without discord. According to Mathew Paris, MGH, SS, XXVIII, p. 437, they were very cordial friends.

It is certain that in late 1154 – he had only just been elected – he continued papal policy and put all his trust in Frederick. He immediately urged Frederick not to waste time in Lombardy but to hurry to Rome[1] and in early 1155 he rejected all offers for a peaceful settlement made by King William of Sicily and even refused to recognize William as king.[2] He was indeed anxious to have a formal renewal of the Treaty of Constance because he wanted the concord between pope and emperor to be as explicit as possible.[3] Putting his full trust in Frederick's approach he decided to confront the unruly citizens of Rome with the full vigour of his wrath, thus publicly proclaiming that he relied entirely on Frederick. If through his attitude to the Romans and to the king of Sicily, he committed himself entirely to Frederick, he had nevertheless his personal and private reservations: he seems to have disliked Frederick as a man for his self-assurance[4] and also had a certain distrust of some of Frederick's ecclesiastically minded advisers.[5] This does not prove that he was two-faced but shows merely that he was an intelligent man who could distinguish his personal feelings from the demands of prudence and politics.

Immediately prior to Frederick's approach to Rome, the situation in the city had become extremely dangerous for Hadrian. Arnold of Brescia was then at the height of his influence over the citizens. Hadrian had demanded that he be banished, but in vain. But when a follower of Arnold of Brescia physically assaulted a cardinal during Easter, 1155, Hadrian dropped all prudence and lashed out: Rome was placed under an interdict. Only then were the citizens prepared to treat with the pope. They offered to expel Arnold unless he made his submission to the pope. Arnold refused.

[1] Godfrey of Viterbo, *Gesta Friderici*, MGH, SS, XXII, p. 310, v. 133. BRG I, No. 439.

[2] Romuald of Salerno, MGH, SS, XIX, pp. 427–8.

[3] For the renewal of the Treaty of Constance see P. Rassow, *op. cit.*, pp. 66–8. The text is in H. Zatschek, *Beiträge zur Geschichte des Konstanzer Vertrags, 1155*, SAW, 1930. Rassow's comments, *op. cit.*, pp. 70–1, are implausible. Hadrian may have been nervous, at Frederick's approach, but Frederick was anxious to allay the pope's fear. For Wibald's active part in the renewal *see* Hausmann, *op. cit.*, p, 243.

[4] Boso, p. 325.

[5] A. Hauck, *op. cit.*, IV, p. 214, note 2: Hadrian did not trust Wibald.

He was expelled and the interdict was revoked. Thus it became possible for Hadrian to leave the Leonine City and celebrate Easter in the Lateran.

On the news of the approach of the army, Hadrian decided to go to meet Frederick. But he seems to have been a bit wary and wanted to avoid a meeting until such time as Frederick had given proof that he would punctiliously observe the Treaty of Constance. So he demanded first that Frederick capture and hand over Arnold of Brescia, who had left the city but had found refuge in the neighbouring countryside. Frederick immediately obliged. Hadrian however was still not assured. He had already gone to Viterbo to meet Frederick when he heard of a royal embassy to him. Therefore he withdrew to Civita Castellana where the embassy followed him. He had sent an embassy of his own to Frederick and was not willing to give Frederick's embassy any assurances until he had heard of the results of his own embassy. Eventually the two embassies met and decided to interview Frederick who had by now reached Viterbo. The interview produced all possible assurances for Hadrian. Even though we know of these assurances only from a source very hostile to Frederick, there is no reason to doubt his sincerity. What is much more surprising is the over-cautiousness of Hadrian. But even that is explicable. As pope he had only one great bargaining point against a powerful king, the imperial coronation. Once the coronation was duly performed, all the trump cards were with the emperor. A pope could issue a sentence of deposition and excommunication, but given the religious character of a coronation ritual, such a sentence might be no more effective than the de-frocking of an ordained priest. In the popular eye, at least, the coronation bestowed powers and qualities which could never be quite annulled.

Hadrian, in the end, seems to have felt reassured. On 8 June Frederick and Hadrian finally met face to face near Sutri. Upon meeting Frederick did not hold the pope's stirrup and lead his horse as was customary; but once Hadrian had dismounted and was seated on a throne, Frederick prostrated himself before him and kissed his feet. He expected that Hadrian would then raise him and offer him the kiss of peace and was very much taken aback when Hadrian refused.

It was a very old custom which went back at least to the days of King Pipin, that a king should act as *strator* to the pope's horse and lead it as far as one could throw a stone. The performance of such a service was a mark of respect for the head of the church;[1] but at the same time also a mark of the greatest distinction for the person honoured to be chosen to perform it. Thus it had been practised on a great many occasions. But during the half century preceding the meeting at Sutri, two new elements had arisen which had altered the simple situation. First, stirrups had been introduced and to hold a stirrup for a man mounting or dismounting from a horse was a marshall's office, and rather different from merely leading the horse. Secondly, with the growth of feudal custom, people had begun to associate the holding of the stirrup with a feudal service and had in fact come to consider it not as a simple mark of respect but as a specific act of service rendered by a vassal to his lord. When Lothair III had met Pope Innocent II in Liège in 1133, he had acted both as *strator* and as a marshall. Given the peculiar relations between Lothair and Innocent at that time, there is no doubt that Lothair had been willing to allow everybody to think that he considered himself the pope's vassal.[2] But in 1155, though Frederick was prepared to observe the Treaty of Constance and was prepared to prostrate himself before Hadrian, he did not wish to convey the impression that he considered himself Hadrian's vassal. For that reason, and that reason alone, he refused the service in question.[3]

[1] M. Maccarone, *op. cit.*, p. 119 especially note 37. When Frederick was sure there was no feudal interpretation, he never minded the service. He rendered it to Victor IV in Pavia and to Alexander III in Venice. (Boso, p. 440 and Romuald of Salerno, MGH, SS, XIX, p. 453, lines 15–17).

[2] I follow R. Holtzmann, 'Der Kaiser als Marschall des Papstes', *Schriften der Strassburger wissenschaftlichen Gesellschaft in Heidelberg*, D.F., 8. Heft, 1928, and the same author's *Zum Strator- und Marschalldienst*, HZ, 145, 1932. Holtzmann was criticized by E. Eichmann, *Officium Stratoris et Strepae*, HZ, 142, 1930. Eichmann's approach to the problem is legalistic. He does not distinguish the political circumstances of the meeting of 1155 from those of the meeting between Frederick and Victor IV in 1160. Similarly he misses the significance of the political changes which, although Frederick had refused an oath to the Romans in 1155, made him very willing to take one in 1167.

[3] Frederick was by no means alone in believing that if he rendered the service people might interpret it as an admission of feudal dependence. Gerhoh of Reichersberg,

There was no incipient conflict in Sutri at this time. Frederick, unlike Lothair, had not owed his election to the influence of the clergy. He saw no reason for wishing to give nourishment to what he considered false ideas and therefore refused to perform an act which might be, in fact was very likely to be, interpreted as a feudal service. However, Hadrian was adamant and in retaliation, refused the kiss. He refused the kiss not because he wanted Frederick to proclaim himself his vassal; but because he realized that Frederick's refusal might be interpreted as proof of a lack of respect for the pope. What with the various embassies which had preceded the meeting, one might have thought that suitable protocol would have been arranged.[1] But the matter had to be straightened out. Once the error had been committed, Hadrian became very suspicious and wanted to make sure that it was no *more* than this.

Frederick consulted with his princes. Most of them, especially those who were old enough to remember the days of Lothair, con-

---

MGH, LdL, III, 393, 35, would have agreed with him and therefore held that the service ought not to be rendered. Gerhoh, however, was less interested in the consequences the service might have for the emperor's reputation than in the light its exaction might throw on the pope. Gerhoh thought that no pope should demand it, for such a demand is proof of worldly pride, *ibid.*, 393, 13. A pope, to him, was a spiritual lord and as such could not be a feudal lord.

[1] Helmold, I, 80, makes Frederick say: 'Tell him [the pope] that it was a defect not of devotion but of knowledge'. Helmold's whole account of the *strator* incident is very condensed and even confused in details, but in substance likely to be true. Helmold's account is based upon the report of eye witnesses and breathes the authentic air of a misunderstanding which both parties regretted. Helmold's report of Eberhard of Bamberg's speech is also noteworthy for its sensible attitude, and one has every reason for believing it to be authentic. Many historians have doubted its authenticity, e.g. H. Reuter, *Geschichte Alexanders III*, 1860–4, new ed., Vol. I, p. 9, and H. Prutz, *Friedrich I*, 1870, Vol. I, p. 70. But Hirsekorn, *Die Slavenchronik des Presbyters Helmold*, Halle, 1874, and P. Wagner, *Eberhard II, Bischof von Bamberg*, Halle, 1876, Excurs I, accept it as authentic. It certainly fits in well with everything we know of Eberhard. Otto of Freising does not mention the incident at all and merely reports that Frederick and Hadrian met near Viterbo, *Gesta*, II, xxviii. Frederick's autobiographical letter to Otto mentions that the meeting took place in Sutri but states that the pope met Frederick 'joyfully'. The only sources for the incident other than Helmold are Boso, p. 391 and Albinus-Cencius, *Liber Censuum*, Watterich, II, 342. Giesebrecht, VI, 341, thinks that Boso copied from Albinus-Cencius' official report; Duchesnes, *Liber Pontificalis*, II, 391, note 1, thinks that Albinus-Cencius copied from Boso. In another place, Duchesne, BEFAR, 2ème série, VI, p. 414, note 1, thinks that Boso might have been the author of both versions. However, this may be, Boso and Helmold are consistent with one another. Given the fact that Frederick eventually gave in to Hadrian, it is not difficult to see why after 1156 (see Chapter IV, below) both he and Otto preferred to suppress all knowledge of the incident.

sidered that Hadrian's request was reasonable and that he should not be accorded less honour than Innocent II had received. Thus Frederick was persuaded to give in: but in order to avoid the impression that anything remotely denoting a feudal dependence was intended, he insisted that the service be said to be performed by him not for Hadrian in person, but to the glory of the Apostles Peter and Paul.[1] And so camp was broken; Frederick departed and pitched his tents in the vicinity. The next day Hadrian followed him, to be met once more. This time Frederick led Hadrian's horse a short distance and then helped him to dismount by holding the stirrup.

This whole embarrassing incident has been accorded far too much importance. In view of later developments, historians have seen here the first clash between empire and papacy. But nothing could be further from the truth. Frederick and Hadrian were substantially one and in complete agreement – otherwise there would have been no such easy settlement of the dispute. The real importance of the incident lies merely in the fact that it throws some light on the clumsiness of twelfth-century diplomacy. The two embassies which had been exchanged had overlooked the question of protocol – which after all was very important. Protocol nowadays (when most people get their ideas of the importance of powers and institutions from textbooks and newspapers), often appears ridiculous and superfluous. But in the twelfth century, the punctilious observance of protocol was the only known way in which authorities could make public what they thought of each other.

What was much more important in the long run was the fact that Frederick failed to reach a similar understanding with the citizens of Rome. In order to have the interdict removed, they had broken with Arnold of Brescia. But this did not mean that they had reached an agreement with Hadrian. And it appears that they now tried to make a direct approach to Frederick.[2] They

[1] Gerhoh wrote that many people took the *strator* service to be a sign of the king's or emperor's feudal dependence on the pope. (MGH, LdL, III, 393, 35). Hence he objected to it.

[2] Helmold, I, 80; Otto of Freising, *Gesta*, II, xxix.

sent an embassy to him and declared that they would be happy to welcome him in the city and elect him emperor provided he conducted himself as an emperor. They said that a prince who comes to Rome to be crowned ought to come in a fitting way, that is in a golden chariot, clad in purple, leading with him the tyrants he had conquered and bearing with him the riches of their people. He also ought to honour the city which is, after all, the capital of the world and give the senate the sum of fifteen thousand pounds of silver.[1] Frederick replied, smilingly, that the promise was flattering, but the price too high. 'You men of Rome,' he said, 'make large demands upon our emptied treasury.'[2] He obviously saw the irony of the situation and realized that the Romans had a point in suggesting to him that if he wanted to be emperor, he ought to be richer and more triumphant in war than he actually was. But then he added in a sterner tone: 'You will act more advisedly if, by giving up these demands, you try our friendship rather than our arms.'[3] But the Romans would not unbend and informed him openly that if he did not comply the gates of the city would remain shut to him.

There was something to be said for the attitude of the Romans. They, like everybody else, had heard that Frederick had come to

[1] Otto of Freising, *Gesta*, II, xxix, reports that the Romans asked Frederick to take three oaths and admits that the oaths were required by the 'Old Order'. But the Old Order required one oath to be sworn three times; not three different oaths. There seems no doubt that the Romans asked for money, and such a demand was not part of the *Ordo Cencius II* – if that was the 'Old Order' referred to. But it had become customary for the Romans to demand a sum of money from the popes (J. Haller, *Das Papsttum*, Stuttgart, 1952, III, p. 124), and they may have simply felt that if Hadrian had not been able to pay, Frederick ought to; and Otto of Freising lumped this demand for money together with the customary oath. Gerhoh of Reichersberg was aware that the custom of money being paid by the popes to the Romans dated back to the pontificate of Gregory VII, i.e. had something to do with the triumph of the reform party over local factions. He wrote that Gregory VII had given money to the Romans in order to enlist their support against Henry IV. Gregory VII had thus countenanced the triumph of avarice in Rome and had helped to unleash Satan. MGH, LdL, III, pp. 389, line 2, 390, line 37, 509, line 31. From then onwards, popes had been obliged to buy the fealty and obedience of the Romans. Hence papal greed for money. Gerhoh held that it would have been better for the popes to give up the city and deplored the fact that popes and cardinals had always felt that they had to preserve their rule over the city at any price. MGH, LdL, III, pp. 388 ff., 391. There is a very wide disagreement as to the origin of the *Ordo Cencius II*. Eichmann, *op. cit.*, dates it 962; R. Holtzmann, *op. cit.*, HZ, 145, 1932, believes that it originated as late as 1192.

[2] Helmold, I, 80. [3] *loc. cit.*

arbitrate and establish peace. It was reasonable for them to hope that he would listen to their complaints about the pope. If he could not redress their grievances he might at least pay them the sum of money which it was customary for a pope to pay them on his accession and which Hadrian had not been able to pay. They reasoned that if he expected them to live in peace with Hadrian he ought to pay the money on Hadrian's behalf and thus restore order and amiability to Rome in the least violent manner possible. As it was, they had miscalculated in thinking that Frederick had the necessary financial means. He had come empty handed. He made no bones about this[1] and had no choice. As it turned out, the Romans' approach was not at all unrealistic, for they did control the city and in view of the difficulties Frederick was to have in gaining entry and the impossibility of staying there, one cannot help thinking that the Romans were arguing, after all, from a position of strength.

What happened had all the makings of a wild west shooting match. Frederick and Hadrian and the army encamped, as was customary, on the Monte Mario. The Leonine City seems to have been controlled by Hadrian; but the rest of Rome was in hostile hands. And therefore Frederick and Hadrian had to hatch a plot in order to perform the coronation at the traditional place in St Peter's. They agreed to perform the ceremony, not as the Romans expected and as was customary, the following Sunday, but on the Saturday instead. In order to be sure that the Leonine City would remain peaceful, Cardinal Octavian, a distant kinsman of Frederick's,[2] secretly led a small troop of soldiers into the city through a small gate and occupied the cathedral and its environs. The next morning Hadrian and the cardinals followed into the city in order to be ready to receive Frederick. Frederick himself followed at eight o'clock in the morning on horseback and

[1] Unlike the straightforward Helmold, Otto of Freising sought to disguise Frederick's poverty and instead made him deliver a high-sounding speech to the effect that he was like Charlemagne and has come as a conqueror and that he will not buy the crown like a pedlar. In view of Helmold's sober statements, one cannot take Otto's account as correct. It must be considered part of the propaganda campaign which Otto undertook on behalf of Frederick after the change of policy in 1156. *Cp.* Ch. IV, below.

[2] Octavian, the later Pope Victor IV, was already then considered by everybody a reliable partisan of Frederick; *Gesta*, II, xxxi.

was received by Hadrian at the steps of St Peter's. In the church of St Mary in Turri Frederick took the oath that he would be a faithful protector of the Roman Church and then everybody moved back to St Peter's where he was anointed and, at mass, given sword, sceptre and crown by the pope.[1] The warriors present shouted their applause – according to one witness it sounded like a roll of thunder; but in view of the fact that it is reliably reported that the citizens of Rome remained completely unaware of what was going on in the Leonine City, it is more probable that the soldiers had been instructed to hush their voices and refrain from any loud expression of their joy. By midday all was over: the emperor returned to his encampment outside the gate and began to celebrate the occasion with a banquet.

During the afternoon the news of the coronation spread, and the people of Rome congregated on the bridge of St Peter and poured into the Leonine City, wreaking their first vengeance upon two imperial soldiers they came across, assaulting several cardinals and then beginning to loot. When Frederick heard of the rising he interrupted his meal and called his men to arms in order to assist Pope Hadrian. He tried to prevent further people coming

[1] This is Boso's account, p. 392. The account in *Gesta*, II, xxxii, is less detailed and probably inaccurate in stating that the coronation took place after the mass. According to the Old Order both unction and coronation were performed during the mass. In 1155 the unction was performed before the mass. It is not known when this devaluation of the unction was first begun. E. Eichmann, *Die rechtliche und kirchenpolitische Bedeutung der Kaisersalbung im Mittelalter*, in: *Festschrift f. Hertling*, München, 1913, p. 270, says that during the twelfth century the unction tended to lose its importance and the imposition of the crown by the pope became the central part of the ceremony. The papalization of the imperial *Laudes* was a long drawn out process and 'the abrogation of the priestly essence resident in the emperor's office presents itself as a long process at the end of which we find the name of Innocent III'. (E. H. Kantorowicz, *Laudes Regiae*, Berkeley and Los Angeles, 1958, p. 143.) The ultimate papal aim was to establish that the unction, consecration and coronation of an emperor was *not* a sacrament. W. Ullmann, *The Pontificate of Adrian IV*, CHJ, XI, 1953, pp. 240–1, attributes the introduction of most of these changes to Hadrian. But whatever changes Hadrian made, if he did make any, were in line with the general tendency, were continued and emphasized after him, and were expected by Frederick. For there is no indication that Frederick was surprised or angered by the fact that he was anointed before mass; that the unction took place before a side altar; that he had his shoulders and arms anointed, instead of his head; and that the oil used was not chrism but only unconsecrated catechumen oil. If Hadrian's changes were as dramatic and unsuspected as Ullmann suggests, Frederick would have surely remarked on it. The fact that he did not could almost be taken as proof that the desacramentalization of the whole ceremony was already well established by 1155.

across St Peter's bridge; but the Leonine City was soon full of Romans, who were now also streaming in from the Trastevere side. A terrible massacre ensued and only when night fell did Frederick remain in command of the Leonine City. But even this small victory was of no use to him. Shortage of food and a complete failure to gain entrance into Rome proper obliged him to depart, together with Hadrian, the next day. In order to have the coronation performed Frederick literally had hacked his way into the Leonine City; and in the end, had to hack his way out again.

Frederick and Hadrian marched around the countryside describing a wide circle around Rome, and subjecting the smaller cities. On the feast of the Apostles, 29 June, they proclaimed to the world their complete accord and Hadrian said mass and absolved all those who had been guilty of killing Romans. Whoever kills in defence of the empire is not a murderer, he said, but merely a just avenger. During the time of this tour, Hadrian handed Arnold of Brescia to the prefect of Rome who had him executed. At that time Frederick did not yet have any doubts as to the continuation of his plans and policies, otherwise he might have wondered whether it would not be politic to keep Arnold alive, albeit under arrest. For in any change of plan, the great popular figure of Rome might prove useful. It was indeed alleged later that Frederick regretted the execution[1] – and since it is not likely that this regret should have been occasioned by any humanitarian feeling, it can only mean that he realized later that circumstances had changed and that Arnold would have been a useful ally against the pope. For the time being, however, both emperor and pope were bent upon the war against Sicily, which, after the coronation, was the final object of the whole Italian expedition.[2]

The opportunity seemed propitious, for a Sicilian army had

[1] This regret is mentioned in the so-called Bergamo Epic, first published under the title *Gesta di Federico I in Italia*, E. Monaci, ed., Rome, 1887, p. 34.

[2] P. Rassow, *op. cit.*, pp. 72 ff., committed by his own theory that Frederick's 'new' policy began in 1152, is compelled to seek tortuous arguments to prove that at that time the question of the lordship over Farfa and Tivoli caused serious friction between Hadrian and Frederick. But in both cases amicable agreement was reached. For Farfa, Hadrian seems to have given in. *Cp.* P. Kehr, *Urkunden zur Geschichte von Farfa im XII. Jahrhundert*, QuF, 9, 1906, p. 181. In Tivoli, Frederick gave in: MGH, Const. I, p. 215.

begun to withdraw as Frederick was approaching Rome and an uprising against King William had been organized under no less a person than his own nephew, Robert of Bassavilla. But at this point Frederick was brought face to face with the political realities of Germany. The German princes declared roundly that they had had enough and insisted on an immediate return to Germany. Frederick was appalled. He pleaded, he argued – but he had to give in. His whole power in Germany depended on the goodwill of the princes and on their goodwill alone. If they abandoned him, he had neither army nor resources to do anything, least of all to undertake the campaign against the king of Sicily. Hadrian also was disappointed, but he was equally powerless. He decided instead for the time being to make the best of a bad bargain and to appear grateful for what little the Germans had done for him. He showed himself generous to many German bishops – above all to Hillin of Trier whom he appointed permanent apostolic legate in Germany. At Tivoli Frederick and Hadrian bade each other farewell – the one to turn northwards, 'not without bitterness of heart'[1] as his biographer says; and the other to remain near Rome, wondering what to do next about his unruly Roman subjects who would not let him come back into the city.

Frederick's army, which had been suffering severely from the summer's heat, literally disintegrated. The princes were granted leave to go home and the whole army dispersed: some took ship across the Adriatic, others moved towards western Lombardy and others again made for the Great St Bernard – obviously everyone was anxious to take the shortest route to his home. Frederick himself moved slowly with the small contingent that was left. Again he was short of food and demanded the *fodrum* from the city of Spoleto. The citizens of Spoleto appear to have had an understanding with the king of Sicily, for they refused to surrender a friend of Frederick whom they had captured on his return from a mission to Apulia. And when they finally produced the *fodrum*, Frederick found that the demanded sum had not been paid in full and that what had been paid consisted partly of counterfeit coins.

[1] *Gesta*, II, xxxvii; Boso, p. 393, says that Frederick abandoned the campaign against Sicily because the princes demanded it.

Frederick thereupon decided to punish Spoleto and laid siege to the city. The inhabitants were too sure of themselves, or at any rate, they thought they could easily deal with the remnants of Frederick's army: they met him in open battle. Frederick attacked and soon the Spoletans began to retreat – not fast enough though, for as they regained the gates, Frederick and his followers were upon them and entered the city with them. Spoleto was looted and burnt down – and the citizens fled in panic to a neighbouring hill.

From Spoleto he made his way northwards along the Adriatic coast. On his way through Lombardy he issued a number of generous privileges to the cities that had been faithful to him: above all, he forbade the Milanese to coin money and granted that right to their old opponent, the city of Cremona. It is important to note, in view of the jealousy with which Frederick was later to guard his *regalia*, that at that time he showed no great intention to keep them in his own hands.

When he approached Verona, he found that the citizens had built a bridge across the Adige to tempt him to cross the river without entering the city. Frederick accepted the offer of the use of the bridge – only to find that it had been meant as a trap. The Veronese had released a large number of logs up-river and hoped that these logs would reach the bridge at the moment when Frederick and his soldiers were right on it.[1] It seemed a hazardous undertaking, not likely to succeed, as it depended on such precise timing. As it was, Frederick reached the other bank safely and the bridge gave way only after some Veronese soldiers had also crossed and attacked Frederick's rear. The whole thing was a completely amateurish plot. The soldiers were captured and immediately executed.

As Frederick approached the narrow gorge where the Adige had cut its way deeply into the rocks and where even today both railway and road have to pass through a tunnel, he met with a further obstacle. There was a castle on top of the rock and from that castle the passage through the gorge could be controlled. Alberic, a

[1] *Gesta*, II, xxxix, gives the impression that this bridge was near Verona. But it seems that the bridge was further up, near the famous gully in which Frederick was to be ambushed. *See* L. Simeoni, *Veronesi mutilati durante la prima discesa del Barbarossa*, SSV, II, 1950.

Veronese, was in command of the castle and he decided to demand a ransom from Frederick. It is improbable that he had any designs on Frederick's life; he merely did not want to miss a good opportunity for extracting a ransom. Frederick however decided upon a ruse suggested to him by a couple of friendly Veronese knights: there was a rock high above the castle and some of his men volunteered to scale it. Once on top, they displayed the imperial banner and at that sign, the soldiers below stormed the castle, which now came under attack from above and below. Thereupon Alberic and his men lost courage and abandoned the castle. Most of them fell off the steep face of the rock. The remainder were captured and executed.

With this inconsequential event the Italian expedition came to an end. Frederick regained the other side of the Alps without further incident and by the end of September 1155 he was back in Augsburg. It had taken him a year to become emperor – but in all other respects one can hardly say that the campaign had been a great success. He had made many enemies in Italy; he had found that his efforts at arbitration and peace-making had met with no greater success than his attempts in Germany to end the quarrel between Henry the Lion and Henry Jasomirgott. He had also failed in the second important objective of the journey, the war against Sicily. He had not been of much use to the pope, who was still at odds with the Romans and in conflict with the king of Sicily. And finally, the weakness of his whole position had been demonstrated when the German princes had forced him to break off the campaign. Obviously, his power in Germany itself did not have solid foundations.[1] If Frederick had been a lesser man, he would simply have continued to muddle through, hoping that sooner or later a lucky accident would enable him to be more successful. If he had been unreasonably stubborn, he would have persisted with his anti-Sicilian and pro-papal policy and hoped for an opportunity to prepare a second expedition. But Frederick was neither lacking in determination nor unreasonably stubborn.

[1] Otto of Freising, *Gesta*, II, xliii, reports that during Frederick's absence in Italy there had taken place all kinds of feuds, arsons and other disturbances. Frederick himself complained about these things, Stumpf, 3728.

Having recognized the complete bankruptcy of his first simple plan to follow in the footsteps of Conrad, he now decided to abandon it and think of something new. Undaunted by failure, he set out to fashion a new scheme.

CHAPTER IV

The Change of Plan

It is not easy to determine exactly when Frederick decided upon his change of plan; nor is it possible to say to what extent he was influenced by other counsel, or whether he took the decision on his own. The change of plan and the formulation of what I will call the Great Design occurred during the course of the year 1156. By the middle of that year he had given up all thought of continuing the Greek alliance, and that in itself is an indication of the new course. In June of the same year, Pope Hadrian, cutting his losses as far as Frederick was concerned, made a treaty with the Normans of Sicily.[1] This may have precipitated Frederick's own decision to embark upon a new policy. But it is unlikely that this event by itself caused Frederick's change of plan – for there were weighty reasons for a change other than the behaviour of Hadrian. Again, in May 1156, Frederick chose a new chancellor and appointed Rainald von Dassel – the man who was to remain supreme in his counsels for the next eleven years and whose name is insolubly linked with the Great Design and with the policies which Frederick pursued to realize it. It is more than likely that the Great Design owed something to Rainald; and it is certain that Frederick appointed him at the very moment when he was thinking of changing his policy. All evidence points to the conclusion that the change was beginning about May 1156 when Rainald first became chancellor and was complete by July, when the Greek connections were finally severed.

[1] Helmold, I, 81, makes Hadrian demand the Sicilian expedition before the coronation; but the princes refused and therefore Hadrian had to crown Frederick first. This version may be wrong. But the two salient features stand out correctly: the Sicilian campaign was part of the bargain; and Frederick was very much at the mercy of the princes who did not like the Sicilian plan.

Rainald von Dassel[1] came from a family which did not belong to the great princely families of Germany. He was born about 1118–1120[2] – which would make him just over thirty-five in 1156 and five or six years older than Frederick. Nothing much is known of his early career. It seems that he studied in Paris sometime between 1140 and 1146,[3] and that by 1147 he was provost of the cathedral chapter in Hildesheim.[4] Rainald must have been ambitious and determined to rise socially and politically – and since he was not high born, he sought preferment through personal contacts. He was present at a royal court in Würzburg in 1149 and it seems that he met the future King Frederick there.[5] At that time the see of Cologne was vacant, and there was some doubt as to who the next archbishop of Cologne would be. Rainald seems to have had some information on the subject, which he thought might be useful to Wibald,[6] and we may presume that his connection with Wibald dates from that time. Together with Wibald he also got to know Arnold von Wied, who in fact became the archbishop of Cologne. He kept in touch with these important statesmen – at first for purely personal reasons. There is a remnant of a correspondence between Wibald and Rainald from 1150 – a correspondence mainly about ancient literature. It seems unlikely that Rainald was genuinely interested in such matters, but he did have access to some books which Wibald wanted and Rainald wished to make himself agreeable. Wibald's interest was genuine, for he could not have had any reason for wanting to cultivate Rainald. And, moreover, pious cleric that he was, he always felt he ought to justify his mundane interests in pagan authors. At one stage Rainald asked for a loan of the *Attic Nights*. Wibald wrote back to say that he could not find the book and sent a military manual instead.[7] One wonders whether the gentle abbot was

[1] Various forms of the name have been used: Reinaldus, Reinnaldus, Reginold, Regenold, etc. *Cp.* R. Herkenrath, *Reinald von Dassel*, Diss. (typed), Graz, 1962, p. 416 ff. – There is a sculpture of Rainald in Cologne Cathedral, but the nose has been flattened and its appearance is thus somewhat distorted even if we assume that it is a genuine likeness.

[2] W. Föhl, *Studien zu Rainald von Dassel*, JKGV, 17, 1935, p. 235. [3] *ibid.*, p. 241.

[4] *ibid.*, p. 245. C. Schambach, *Forschungen zu Rainald von Dassel*, ZHVN, 1913, p. 353, doubts this. [5] W. Föhl, *op. cit.*, pp. 248–9. [6] *ibid.*, pp. 250–1.

[7] *ibid.*, p. 253, *Cp.* BRG, I, Nos. 207, 208, 212, 213.

being ironical and thought that military matters were more to Rainald's taste.

At the end of 1152, just after Frederick had become king, Rainald was sent to Rome by his bishop on diocesan business. It is more than probable that he was in unofficial touch with the royal embassy which was then in Rome to prepare the Treaty of Constance. It has even been surmised that Rainald was entrusted with negotiating those parts of the agreement between king and pope which could not well be mentioned in writing, i.e. the divorce and the deposition of the bishops. If so, Rainald's diplomatic talent was tested, and the results prove that he must have given a good account of himself.[1] In this way, Rainald had become well known to the politicians and statesmen around Frederick. And when Frederick in early 1156 looked around for someone to promote the change of plan, both Wibald and Arnold von Wied must have recommended Rainald. It is doubtful whether they were clearly aware of the views of Rainald and of the impetuous temper with which he was to put them forward. If they had known him well, they might have hesitated to recommend him. But Rainald had probably been astute enough not to reveal himself fully to these men and to dissimulate especially his views on ecclesiastical affairs. At the same time, Wibald knew that Rainald was politically uncommitted to the old course, and that Frederick wanted to change it. He himself was obviously not going to play a leading part in the new era; and, for that matter, he was getting old.

Frederick's choice of Rainald is in every way remarkable. Rainald was not a career diplomat and had never been a member of the royal chapel. Thus he was chosen not because he was the next in line of seniority or because he had impressed the king with his ability. He was an outsider and must have been brought in for purely political reasons. Rainald had trodden carefully; he had made friends with the right people but had always taken care not to be identified with their views and policies. And when Frederick needed a new man, his old advisers recommended Rainald. We do not know when exactly he became chancellor; but he appears for the first time in his new capacity in a charter of 10 May 1156.[2]

[1] W. Föhl, *op. cit.*, pp. 255–6.

[2] Stumpf, No. 3740.

Rainald had extraordinary talents. He was inventive, lively and incessantly active,[1] a good speaker and an astute negotiator.[2] His friends even described him as generous, serene and sincere.[3] But perhaps Acerbus Morena was nearer the mark when he wrote that Rainald's chief characteristic was his avid desire to serve the emperor.[4] To this one ought to add the qualification that he was to prove himself more than a mere servant and sought often to give imperial policies a sharp anti-papal twist. He himself had no great taste for the clerical life[5] and treated his vocation in a fashion which was cynical even by the standards of the twelfth century.[6] Whatever clerical interests he had, they were focused upon ecclesiastical pomp and the magic of relics rather than on pastoral care. The pomp and the magic fascinated him, and it was one of the great moments in his life when he carried the relics of the three Wise Men from Milan to Cologne where they are still installed in the cathedral.[7] His real passion, however, seems to have been for the military life and he acquired a great reputation as an intrepid and fiery soldier, which he himself did his best to broadcast.[8] In fact, he appears to have been obsessed by his own military prowess and wanted it to be looked upon as a direct sign of the divinely ordained invincibility of his cause.[9] No wonder that Frederick seized the chance of obtaining the services of such a man. For Rainald, this was the opportunity he had waited for; and for the next ten years, the two men became inseparable.

The outcome of the Italian expedition alone had provided weighty grounds for a complete revision of policy. For when Frederick had

[1] *Annales Egmundani*, MGH, SS, XVI, p. 464.

[2] Archipoeta; H. Watenphul and H. Krefeld ed., *Die Gedichte des Archipoeta*, Heidelberg, 1958, pp. 66–7.

[3] *Annales Egmundani, loc. cit.*

[4] SRG, F. Güterbock ed., Berlin, 1930, p. 168.

[5] He could have become bishop of Hildesheim in 1153, but preferred to wait for a better chance. *Cp.* W. Föhl, *op. cit.*, p. 258.

[6] For his pluralism *see* C. Schambach, *Das Verhältnis Rainald von Dassels zum Empfang der höchsten Weihen*, ZHVN, 80, 1915.

[7] P. Munz, *Frederick Barbarossa and the Holy Empire*, JHR, 3, 1964, p. 31. Rainald was also mindful of his debt to Hildesheim and in 1164, munificently, he let them have three fingers of the Three Wise Men. *Cp.* J. Ficker, *Rainald von Dassel*, Köln, 1850, p. 9.

[8] For Rainald's prowess in Ravenna in 1158 *see Chron. Col.*, GDV, 69, p. 68. For his feats in Tusculum in 1167, *see* Morena, MGH, SS, XVIII, p. 609 and *ibid.*, for his bravery during the Milanese rebellion.

[9] *Cp.* P. Munz, *op. cit.*, p. 35, note 40.

been compelled by the princes to abandon the projected campaign against Sicily and had to leave Hadrian helpless *vis à vis* both Rome and the king of Sicily, Hadrian had been compelled to revise *his* ideas and to agree to a complete diplomatic revolution.

In order to understand the far-reaching effects of this revolution, it is necessary to go back a few years in the relations between the papacy and Sicily. In 1149 Eugene III and King Roger had agreed to a four years' truce and in 1150, at a meeting in Ceprano, King Roger had conceded to Eugene the right to decide disputed episcopal elections in his kingdom. But even then Eugene had still refused to recognise Roger as king and to invest him with his kingdom. Thus matters had stood at the beginning of Hadrian's pontificate. The new pope was no more friendly to Roger's successor, William, than Eugene had been. Early in his pontificate, Hadrian called Roger *dominus Siciliae.*[1] He would not address him as king and as a result of this attitude open war broke out between the papacy and the kingdom of Sicily. Hadrian allied himself with those south Italian barons who were hostile to the king. And when the Greek emperor threatened Apulia, and Frederick attempted to carry out the Treaty of Constance, the position looked really desperate for the king of Sicily. By June 1155, even though it seemed clear that Frederick could not pursue the Sicilian plan, Hadrian received the homage of the ex-prince of Capua and of other south Italian barons who were rebels against King William, and at this point William was prepared to make peace. Hadrian and Cardinal Roland, his chief adviser, were diplomatic enough to know that the moment was opportune and that they ought not to tempt fate, for William at this time offered good terms. He was prepared to render homage to the pope and pay him enough money to accommodate himself with the Romans. Further, he offered to cede three castles in order to strengthen Hadrian's hold on Benevento and to restore the liberty of all churches in his kingdom.[2] But in spite of Hadrian's and Roland's sagacity, there were considerable difficulties in the way of an agreement. To begin

[1] *Cp.* M. Maccarone, *Papato e Impero,* Rome, 1959, p. 141.

[2] P. Kehr, *Die Belehnung der süditalienischen Normannenfürsten durch die Päpste, 1059–1192,* APA, Berlin, 1934, p. 46.

with, Hadrian was also in touch with William's enemies, the Greeks and the Apulian rebels.[1] He was keeping all doors open. For it was no easy matter to reverse the whole system of alliances. William's predecessor, King Roger, in the eyes of all thoughtful men, had been a tyrant,[2] and there was considerable objection among the cardinals to any proposal of peace with the successor of such a man.[3] There may also have been other reasons for their opposition to Hadrian and Roland: some were genuinely frightened of making any concessions lest William ended up by demanding too much,[4] and others probably hesitated because they realized that William was in a weak position in October 1155 and hoped that before long they might extort even better terms from him.[5] However this may be, the opposition was not only strong, but consisted of the majority of the cardinals and thus carried the day.[6] Cardinal Roland alone stood out, even then, as the upholder of a Sicilian alliance. For he had sized up Frederick's impotence correctly and realized that only a complete diplomatic revolution would provide the papacy with an effective protector.[7]

At this stage Roland advocated a policy the pursuit of which was to provide its own justification. For although Frederick's first attempt to fulfil the Treaty of Constance was a failure, there was no certain proof that a second attempt might not be more successful. But if the papacy now changed sides and concluded an alliance with Sicily, such a policy would demonstrate to Frederick beyond the shadow of doubt the foolishness of continuing in the footsteps of Conrad. And once Frederick decided not to follow in those footsteps, Roland's diplomatic revolution would be fully vindicated.

During the spring of 1156, however, the situation in southern Italy changed. William had been sick during the winter. But in

[1] M. Maccarone, *op. cit.*, pp. 144–5.

[2] *Cp.* H. Wieruszowski, *Roger II of Sicily, Rex-Tyrannus, in 12th Century Political Thought*, Sp, 1963, xxxviii, p. 38.

[3] Fliche et Martin, ed. *Histoire de l'église*, Paris, 1946, IX, p. 23.

[4] O. Vehse, *Benevent als Territorium des Kirchenstaates*, QuF, 22, 1930–1, p. 156.

[5] P. Kehr, *op. cit.*, p. 46.

[6] Boso, p. 394.

[7] M. Pacaut, *Alexandre III*, Paris, 1956, p. 90.

the spring he had recovered and resumed his campaigns. He defeated a Greek army and by the end of May 1156, Hadrian was besieged in Benevento. Frederick was on the other side of the Alps. Hadrian and Roland, enclosed in Benevento, realized that now they had no choice[1] and were therefore more than ever forced to come to terms with William. In order to gain a free hand for the negotiations, they persuaded most of the cardinals to leave Benevento by pretending to be concerned for their safety.[2] And so, with only three cardinals in attendance on Hadrian (Roland, Hubald, the later Lucius III, and Julius), the final peace negotiations were begun.

The Treaty of Benevento between William and Hadrian was concluded in June 1156. It settled all territorial disputes and established the territorial unity of the Norman kingdom. A team of shrewd diplomats also settled the ecclesiastical disputes to more or less mutual satisfaction. The various parts of the Norman kingdom were listed, and it was stated that the pope invested William and his heirs with them. In return, William undertook to pay homage to the pope and to pay a large yearly tribute. Strictly, in feudal law, there ought to have been a provision for a new formal

[1] Boso and Romuald of Salerno say that William 'venit' to Benevento. William of Tyre says that William 'obsedit' Benevento. O. Vehse, *op. cit.*, p. 156, follows William of Tyre and believes that Hadrian was forced into the treaty. It is more probable that William acted with a great deal of restraint and showed much deference to Hadrian whom he knew to be willing to come to terms. There was no need to force him. *Cp.* V. Epifanio, *Sul preteso assedio di Benenvento e sul concordato tra la chiesa e lo stato normanno del 1156*, ASPN, n.s. XXVIII, 1945, pp. 49–74. Boso's account of William's first approaches to Hadrian is completely partisan in favour of William. He insists on William's humility and goodwill. Such partisanship might invalidate his historical testimony. But it shows that there was quite clearly a pro-Sicilian party – that Boso was a member, and that we are right in inferring that his friends (e.g. Roland, etc.) must also have belonged to it. Boso says that William beat the Greeks and the Apulian barons, and that his victory was God's reward, as it were, for his humility towards the pope. See Duchesne, II, 394; Lamma, *Comneni e Staufer*, Roma, 1955, I, 185. – The same note of William's humility was struck again after the signature of the Treaty of Benevento, when William had been victorious. Both he and the Sicilian party wanted to give a nice moral cloak to the diplomatic revolution. See MGH, Const. I, 588. – Boso writes as if all the cardinals had agreed to the treaty. So does Gerhoh, MGH, LdL, III, p. 405. It is not likely that this is true. If it were true, Hadrian would have kept more than three cardinals with him in the besieged Benevento. Some of Victor's cardinals wrote a letter to explain their position and put it quite explicitly that the division among the cardinals had had its origin in the debate about the Treaty of Benevento, *See Gesta*, IV, lxii.

[2] H. Simonsfeld, JDR, p. 453; J. Haller, *Papsttum*, III, p. 127.

investiture upon Hadrian's death. But nothing was said about this. All that was considered necessary was that the heirs of William should pay homage to the pope.[1]

If Hadrian and Roland had had their way in late 1155, they could have obtained better terms.[2] But despite the terms, there is no doubt that the Treaty of Benevento represented the fruition of Hadrian's and Roland's intentions. The rest of the world was less pleased. Thomas à Becket called the treaty a 'tyrannous usurpation'.[3] The Apulian exiles were bitterly disappointed.[4] They were furious with Hadrian and declared that they had been betrayed by him and, according to Romuald of Salerno, Frederick '*molestissime tulit*'[5] the news of the treaty. He certainly considered that the pope had been the first to break the Treaty of Constance.[6] Frederick's anger and consternation – although it is technically true that Hadrian had been the one to take the initiative in the reversal of alliances – was hardly justified. For it had been his own failure the year before which had forced Hadrian into the position in which he had to conclude the treaty, and ultimately, if the turn of events in Italy was distressing, Frederick was intelligent enough to realize that it was intimately connected with his own lack of power and with his own failure to carry on in the footsteps of Conrad. And if one considers that the appointment of Rainald to the chancellorship dated from May 1156 (i.e. preceded the conclusion of the Treaty of Benevento by one month) one cannot but conclude that Frederick, like Hadrian, was prepared to face the consequences of the failure of his first plan regardless of Hadrian's policy. The Treaty of Benevento now simply reinforced his determination to change his plan of government – for his services as protector of the church of Rome were no longer required and in any future design upon the kingdom of Sicily he would have to reckon with papal opposition. Yet it was the precariousness of his

[1] P. Kehr, *op. cit.*, pp. 47–8.

[2] According to E. Caspar, *Die Legatengewalt der normannisch-sicilischen Herrscher*, QuF, 7, 1904, p. 206, the treaty was a triumph for the Normans.

[3] Bouquet, XVI, p. 300.

[4] William of Tyre, PL, 201, c. 717.

[5] MGH, SS, XIX, p. 429.

[6] P. Rassow, *Honor Imperii*, new ed., München, 1961, p. 81.

command over the German princes which was the ultimate cause of the unsatisfactory conclusion of the Italian expedition, and which eventually led to Hadrian's defection.

Frederick was therefore obliged not only to revise his policies in Italy; but also to examine very carefully his position in Germany. His kingship in Germany was indeed based upon the simplest and most traditional formula possible. He wanted to be a strict and impartial dispenser of justice – no more and no less. And chroniclers and historians have usually seen in his refusal to be merciful rather than just, on the day of his coronation, an act typical of his unbending and straightforward attitude. All this was an application of an ancient Germanic conception. Peace and law meant that old customs were being kept. The king's duty was merely to protect all the subjective rights everybody had. It was not his business to issue laws of his own and to supplement the subjective rights by objective duties. He was supposed to play a purely passive role as law protector; and was not expected to make new laws or initiate administrative changes. The German nobility was opposed to the idea of a written law, and in the education of their sons they preferred to rely upon emphasizing the personal and moral virtues which would keep society together.[1]

Well over one hundred years before Frederick's reign, Wipo, writing for the benefit of Henry III, had advised the kings to pay more attention to Roman law and explore the possibilities for a more active conception of rulership. It is hard to say how necessary this advice had been during the first half of the eleventh century. But there is no doubt that by the middle of the twelfth century such advice had become absolutely imperative.

The traditional conception of passive kingship could only prove effective in a limited social world. As long as the king was the head of a more or less corporate body of a limited number of noble families who between them owned and controlled all the cultivated land, the royal function could indeed be performed in a purely passive way by the protection of subjective rights. Until the end of the eleventh century the class of dynastic proprietors had been comparatively small. It is estimated to have contained no more

[1] K. W. Nitzsch, *Geschichte des deutschen Volkes*, Leipzig, 1892, Vol. 2, p. 37.

than a few hundred families.[1] These dynasts were welded together by ties of blood and marriage into something like a closed corporation and thus the German monarchy had been an essentially personal institution – a personal association of a comparatively small number of specific men. This small body of men sustained the monarchy, and the king in turn only had to deal with this group, who in turn dealt with their dependants. But these dependants had originally not counted as far as the monarchy was concerned. Before the twelfth century these dynasts were an 'absolute aristocracy of property, of personal freedom of movement, of political influence', a closed caste,[2] completely separated from the rest of the population.[3]

By 1150 these social conditions had begun to change. A large number of these dependants had come to assume an independent life, and *ministeriales* had, for instance, begun to be considered capable of holding office.[4] Hence the old distinction between free and unfree had begun to break down, for, when unfree people were capable of holding office, it was rendered meaningless. Eventually this emancipation of the *ministeriales* led to complete personal independence: they became capable of making contracts and of entering into feudal relations with the older dynasts. Thus they swelled the ranks and numbers of the old ruling families and made the continuation of the old order impossible.[5] As a result, during the twelfth century, the old closed corporation of dynasts or princes was breaking up. Families disintegrated and split up and thus the number of families proliferated. By 1180 the family names of the German dynasts ran into thousands. And as a result of the unevenness of the economic resources of the multiplying branches of the original families, there occurred an ever increasing social differentiation: some sank and others rose in the social scale. Countships and dukedoms had been the exclusive preserve of the old families. They had been a nobility of birth and their prerogatives had been their birthright. Given the fact that their privileges were

[1] O. v. Dungern, *Constitutional Reform and Reorganization under the Hohenstaufen*, p. 208, in G. Barraclough, ed., *Medieval Germany*, Oxford, 1938, Vol. II.

[2] O. v. Dungern, *Der Herrenstand im Mittelalter*, 1908, p. 383.

[3] *ibid.*, p. 401. [4] *ibid.*, p. 337. [5] *ibid.*, p. 257.

theirs in their own right, there had not been much else to do for the king but to respect and protect them. But with the multiplication of the families and with the increasing social differentiation between them, there must have been also an ever increasing number of families who could not claim any privileges as their birthright. They must have been either content not to have any; or hoped to gain some from the king.[1]

It is impossible to form any precise view of this situation. But the little we know seems to indicate that it was highly unlikely that the old simple and passive conception of royal obligation could have remained effective. The king could no longer just ride around and protect the peace, for the community was no longer supported so strongly by purely internal ties. To keep it together, more than simple overlordship was required, for social conflicts and mobility were bound to increase once there were so many different families and so many more variations in their affluence and economic resources.

It is very unlikely that Frederick should have known all this. But in some vague way he must have sensed that the traditional conception of a king's function was fast becoming outmoded and not likely to prove effective as the twelfth century progressed. Medieval people were not given to social analysis or even to much factual observation. And when they tried quantitative estimates they usually miscalculated. But this does not mean that Frederick and his advisers were completely ignorant. At any rate, Frederick's failure to command sufficient support for his policies during the first years of his reign brought him face to face with the problem and compelled him to revise the traditional conception of kingship. Whether he was aware or not of the social revolution in Germany – for this was what it amounted to – his political failure had made it imperative by the end of 1155 to fashion a more enterprising and more positive conception of his royal duties. In response to this challenge he conceived what I am calling the Great Design.

The Great Design was based on a bold and ingenious geograph-

[1] O. v. Dungern, *Constitutional Reorganization and Reform under the Hohenstaufen*, p. 223, in G. Barraclough ed., *Medieval Germany*, Oxford, 1938, Vol. II.

ical vision. On a range of mountains in southern Switzerland, there are in close proximity the sources of three large rivers. The Rhine flows northwards, through the lake of Constance towards Cologne and the North Sea. The Rhone flows westwards at first, through the Lake of Geneva; and then turns south, past Arles, and reaches the Mediterranean. And the Ticino flows due south, passes through Lombardy not far from Milan and eventually joins the Po. Frederick decided to establish his imperial administration in the basins formed by these three rivers. Swabia, Burgundy and Lombardy, as these regions were known then, were to form something like a *terra imperii*. He intended to weld these lands together as best he could and have their churches and monasteries, their manors and estates and their cities administered and ruled by his personal servants and officials. It is difficult for us today to contemplate the feasibility of such a design, for Lombardy is part of Italy, Burgundy is in France, the Rhineland in Germany and the southern portions of old Swabia are now in Switzerland. These modern, post-medieval distinctions have so much come to be taken for granted that Frederick's plan seems to us more like that of a visionary than that of a political realist. For that matter, it was bold even in the days of Frederick. But it was not fantastic; for the physical contiguity of the lands of the three rivers gave it a clear geographical basis.[1] If it had materialized, there would have

[1] The one great physical obstacle, formidable even at the present time, was the Alps which separated Lombardy from Swabia, Alsace and Burgundy. Frederick was aware of the obstacle and took pains in order to cope with it. Wherever he could, he tried to make the fortresses commanding the mountain passes into imperial fortresses (*reichsunmittelbar*). His constant preoccupation with the passes during the period during which he pursued the Great Design is collateral evidence that the Great Design had a territorial and geographical foundation. Until 1155, Frederick clearly preferred the passes which led into the Adige valley because they were not so high. But as experience had taught (see p. 89, above) the Adige valley was completely controlled by Verona and when it became increasingly difficult to tie Verona to imperial politics, Frederick, after 1157, relied more and more on the more western passes leading to the Lake of Como. But even in the east, he sought to counteract the power of Verona over the Adige valley by relying on the support of the bishops of Trento and Brixen who controlled the actual passes and by furthering the small communes of Sirmione and Brenzone on Lake Garda and by founding the county of Rivoli. Further to the west, on Mont Cenis, Frederick depended very much on the loyalty of the Marquis of Montferrat and of Count Biandrate, *see* H. Büttner, *Die Alpenpasspolitik Friedrich Barbarossas bis zum Jahre 1164–5*, in Th. Mayer, ed., *Grundfragen der alemannischen Geschichte*, Konstanz, 1955, pp. 243–76. The shortest route from Swabia to Lombardy

emerged, in the very heart of Europe, a fairly centralized state which would have been, at least by the standards of the twelfth century, bureaucratically administered. And there is no doubt that if Frederick's plan had been successful the political history of Europe would have been appreciably different. As it stood, it was one of the most constructive and imaginative political plans ever mooted in Europe.[1]

---

was from the Lake of Constance over the Septimer Pass to Maloia or, alternatively, over Chur and the Splügen Pass. On both routes, Chiavenna was vital. As long as Frederick merely followed in the footsteps of Conrad, he was fairly unconcerned about Chiavenna. In 1152 the question about the county of Chiavenna was brought before him and Frederick decided that the consuls of the city were entitled to the county. He thus rejected the claim of the bishop of Como. (Simonsfeld, p. 118–19.) The following year, the question came up again and this time Frederick decided in favour of the bishop. The consuls of Chiavenna sought to support their claim by arguing that the county belonged to the duchy of Swabia and ought therefore not be entrusted to the bishop of Como. But Frederick would not consider this argument and rejected it by explaining that neither the city nor the consuls had ever received a charter of investment for the county from any duke of Swabia. (Simonsfeld, p. 175.) In 1158, that is after the inception of the Great Design, the question came up again. And this time Frederick was fully alive to its implications. Several Swabian counts and barons now urged Frederick to restore the county to Swabia and in 1158 Frederick needed little persuasion to do so. The bishop of Como lost the county and the consuls of Chiavenna were formally invested with it as a Swabian fief. Simonsfeld, pp. 509–10 and P. Scheffer-Boichorst, *Zur Geschichte des 12. und 13. Jahrhunderts*, Berlin, 1897, pp. 120 ff. Frederick's willingness to revise his earlier policy is instructive. It must have been of great help to Frederick that his friend Rudolf von Pfullendorf managed in 1166 to acquire the *Vogtei* of St Gall. Incidentally, he was also the *Vogt* of Chur. For the importance of Count Rudolf's power in helping to secure these roads *see* A. Schulte, *Geschichte der mittelalterlichen Handels-und Verkehrsstrassen zwischen Deutschland und Italien*, Vol. I, 1900. p. 86. – Later, at the height of the schism, when he was hard pressed, he took pains not to alienate Bishop Egino of Chur, even though the latter refused to commit himself openly in favour of Frederick. But Frederick was aware of the strategical importance of Chur for the Alpine passes and would not exercise pressure on him. *Cp.* H. Büttner, *Churrätien im 12. Jahrhundert*, SZG, 13, 1963, pp. 19–20. Similarly, Frederick showed complete tolerance to Archbishop Peter of Tarentaise, who sided openly with Alexander. Frederick was too conscious of the importance of the Alpine passes which lay in Peter's diocese, *ibid.*, p. 20. Not the least of the reasons why it was a great blow to Frederick that Como in 1168 was forced to join the Lombard League was the fact that it could control the access to Italy *via* the Septimer Pass.

[1] Unfortunately K. Bosl, who in his *Die Reichsministerialität der Salier und Staufer*, Stuttgart, 1950, has done so much for the investigation of Frederick's state-building programme has remained too absorbed in a purely national preconception and in his conclusions he does less than justice to his own findings. On p. 617 Bosl maintains that the Staufen aimed at turning the whole of Germany into a territorial state, bureaucratically administered by their servants. If one follows Bosl, one gains a clear appreciation of Frederick's intention to create the foundations of a 'modern' state. But one also comes away with the idea that the region in which Frederick sought to implement these intentions corresponded more or less to Germany. In fact, Bosl's own maps as well as his own summary tell us quite clearly that Frederick's efforts were confined to the

The first step towards the implementation of this Great Design was, however, a decisive move to settle the old German problem of the Bavarian duchy. As we have seen, no attempt to persuade Henry Jasomirgott to surrender the duchy to Henry the Lion had been successful. When summoned to appear before the emperor, Henry Jasomirgott had either refused to attend or claimed that the summons was legally faulty. He had proved tough and resilient, and had evaded all possibilities of a confrontation. Frederick himself must have realized that he could not expect the forty-six-year-old Henry Jasomirgott to content himself with the mere margravate of the East Mark of Bavaria in virtue of which he would have owed homage to the much younger Henry the Lion. Henry Jasomirgott, husband of a Byzantine princess and uncle of the Emperor Frederick, would have to be established in a position in which he remained at least the equal of Henry the Lion. And as long as these two men were at odds, the old family rivalry could not be considered solved. And as long as both of these men were not contented, Frederick could not proceed towards the measures required by the Great Design in Burgundy and Lombardy.

On his return from Italy he had at first continued his old efforts to persuade Henry Jasomirgott to surrender Bavaria, but in vain. Once his plan was conceived, however, a final settlement between Henry the Lion and Henry Jasomirgott was urgent and imperative. Frederick, therefore, produced a completely revolutionary proposal which was at once adopted and which proved successful for many years to come. In June 1156 – at the very time when Hadrian was preparing for the Treaty of Benevento with King William – Frederick met Henry Jasomirgott at Ratisbon and submitted the following proposal to his uncle: Henry Jasomirgott was to surrender Bavaria to Henry the Lion; but the eastern parts of

---

upper Rhineland and to Alsace, with a few tentative efforts in the direction of the Danube basin and towards Chemnitz. Hence, from Bosl's own evidence it is quite clear that Frederick was not thinking in terms of the whole of Germany when he was thinking of his new 'state', but only in terms of a new region. If one bears this in mind and then abandons national viewpoints altogether, one can link his plans for the upper Rhineland and Alsace to his plans for Lombardy and arrive at an understanding of his geographical vision.

the duchy were to be established as a separate duchy for Henry Jasomirgott. By this plan, the latter received much more than mere compensation. For the new duchy was to be created by an imperial charter.[1] Henry Jasomirgott's ducal dignity in Austria was not to be based upon odd remnants of tribal feeling or on an ill-defined conglomeration of rights and immunities such as other dukes had managed to collect in their hands over the centuries. The new ducal authority was to be clearly defined in terms of a well marked-out territory.[2] Inside that territory Henry Jasomirgott and his heirs were to become almost 'sovereign' rulers. All this was to be issued by Frederick in the form of a charter – a special privilege which would set the new duchy apart from all other previous duchies. With this plan Henry Jasomirgott was well content.

It would be quite wrong to think that the issue of the *privilegium minus* – as the charter came to be known – was the last stage in Frederick's desperate efforts to reach an agreement between Henry the Lion and Henry Jasomirgott. It was the very reverse – no less than the beginning of a new development, for it was markedly different from previous unsuccessful proposals, and was based upon a wholly new conception of dukedom.

In terms of constitutional history, the issue of the *privilegium minus*[3] was a revolutionary step of the most far-reaching significance. In Germany there had been known, before 1156, only the most rudimentary form of territorial 'states'. Under Lothair III, there had indeed appeared many *Landgrafschaften* in which the *Landgraf* was a little bit like a duke governing a certain circum-

[1] There is now no doubt that the *privilegium minus* is genuine. *See* K. J. Heilig, *Ostrom und das deutsche Reich um die Mitte des 12. Jahrhunderts*, in Th. Mayer ed., *Kaisertum und Herzogsgewalt im Zeitalter Friedrichs I*, Leipzig, 1944, passim and especially p. 172.

[2] The *privilegium minus* grant of all justice in Austria was directed against the other Austrian dynasts (H. Mitteis, *Der Staat des hohen Mittelalters*, 3rd ed., Weimar, 1948, p. 298), and the expression *ducatus Austrie* referred to a territory, not a function. (Th. Mayer, *Fürsten und Staat*, Weimar, 1950, p. 284) The change of meaning of *ducatus* had taken place. Thus the Babenbergs achieved by royal grant in 1156 what Henry the Lion struggled all his life to achieve in Saxony.

[3] The whole charter was the result of tough bargaining and laborious negotiations; *cp.* Th. Mayer, *Mittelalterliche Studien*, Lindau und Konstanz, 1959, p. 225. There is a great legal and verbal similarity between the *privilegium minus* and the Würzburg ducal diploma of 1168, for the Hochstift Würzburg had a great influence on the chancellery of Frederick; *cp.* H. Hirsch, *Kaiserurkunde und Kaisergeschichte*, MIOG, 35, 1914.

3 The Empress Beatrix, Frederick's second wife.
(From a coin now in the Staatliche Museum, Berlin.)

4 Frederick with his two sons, Henry VI (right) and Frederick, duke of Swabia (left). (Hessische Landesbibliothek Fulda.)

scribed territory. He was supposed to exercise the rights the king claimed to be his. But the *Landgraf* was not a prince; and, significantly, we find him establishing himself only in those regions in which there was a preponderance of free men and free peasants. This was clearly an early instance of the conception of territorial power – as against power based upon an accumulation, in one hand, of a number of rights. When Frederick looked around for a solution to the conflict between Henry the Lion and Henry Jasomirgott, he decided to avail himself of this concept and to elaborate it.[1]

For there was a difference. Henry Jasomirgott became, with the issue of the *privilegium minus*, the prototype of a completely new type of imperial prince,[2] and thus the *privilegium minus* became the *magna carta* of the German territorial state.[3] The new conception gained ground very rapidly. The Zähringen family availed themselves of the idea[4] and in 1168 a similar document was issued for the bishop of Würzburg, transforming his bishopric into something like a territorial state.[5] In this way a wholly new era in the constitutional development of Germany was inaugurated. But there is no reason for believing that this new development which eventually was to become virtually universal by the issue of the Gelnhausen Charter in 1180, was at this stage planned by Frederick. In 1156 Frederick issued the *privilegium minus* because it seemed the only expedient way of composing the strife between the Welf and Babenberg families, and because he *had* to compose it if he wanted to embark upon the realization of his Great Design. He did not issue the charter because he wanted the territorial conception of the state to gain ground; but this

[1] *See* Th. Mayer, *Die Ausbildung der Grundlagen des modernen deutschen Staates*, HZ, 159, 1939, p. 476 and the same author in *Kaisertum und Herzogsgewalt*, Leipzig, 1944, p. 417.

[2] Heilig, *op. cit.*, p. 172.

[3] Th. Mayer, *Friedrich I und Heinrich der Löwe*, in Th. Mayer ed., *Kaisertum und Herzogsgewalt*, Leipzig, 1944, p. 440 and the same author's *Die Ausbildung* etc., HZ, 159, 1939, p. 481 and 487.

[4] Th. Mayer, *The State of the Dukes of Zähringen*, in G. Barraclough ed., *Medieval Germany*. Oxford, 1938, II, p. 199.

[5] *Cp.* Th. Mayer, *Friedrich I und Heinrich der Löwe*, in *Kaisertum und Herzogsgewalt*, Leipzig, 1944, p. 417. How exactly new the powers granted to Würzburg in 1168 were, is still controversial; *cp.* E. Schrader, *Vom Werden und Wesen des würzburgischen Herzogtums Franken*, ZSSRGger, 80, 1963.

conception gained ground because he issued the charter.[1] In a less explicit manner, Frederick used the same expedient in order to reconcile Duke Berthold von Zähringen to his policy. Under the first plan, Berthold had been allowed to roam widely over the whole of Burgundy.[2] But now that Frederick was planning to incorporate most of Burgundy in the Great Design, he had to find ways and means of accommodating Berthold, and he did it by persuading him to confine himself to a much smaller region and to exercise in that smaller region a much more real and defined authority which explicitly excluded all royal rights.[3] Unfortunately, the text of that agreement has not been preserved.[4] Berthold was easily reconciled[5] to this arrangement which established him as something like a territorial prince in the region comprising the bishoprics of Lausanne, Geneva and Sitten, and immediately set to work and increased his efforts to strengthen his position in this smaller region in accordance with the new conception of the territorial state – speaking of his rights as *per totam terram et dominium meum.*[6] The original ducal title of the Zähringen family[7] had been said to have been an 'empty' title[8] but this new arrangement gave it some substance, albeit in a smaller and more circumscribed region.

When we finally turn to Saxony and Henry the Lion, we find that for all practical purposes he, too, was beginning to consider himself as a territorial duke in Saxony[9] and to lay there the

[1] Th. Mayer, to whom one owes so much for the elucidation of this aspect of twelfth century politics, is so obsessed with the notion that the territorial state is better than any other form of political organization, that he always puts the cart before the horse and writes as if Frederick and his fellow princes took these measures *in order* to promote the territorial state. However, they took these measures because they were politically expedient and the territorial state resulted from them.

[2] See above, Ch. III.

[3] M. Chapuis, *Recherches sur les institutions politiques du pays de Vaud du XIme au XIIIme siècle*, Lausanne, 1940, pp. 101–2. *See* also H. Büttner, *Waadtland und Reich im Hochmittelalter*, DA, 7, 1944, pp. 79–132, especially pp. 111 ff.

[4] It is, however, described in *Gesta*, II, xxix.

[5] E. Heyck, *Geschichte der Herzoge von Zähringen*, Freiburg, 1891, pp. 384 ff.

[6] H. Büttner, *Staufer und Zähringer im politischen Kräftespiel zwischen Bodensee und Genfersee*, Zürich, 1961, p. 43. [7] *Cp.* p. 55.

[8] *Cp.* Th. Mayer, *The State of the Dukes of Zähringen*, p. 181, in G. Barraclough ed., *Medieval Germany*, Oxford, 1938, Vol. II.

[9] Helmold, I, 73, wrote in connection with an incident in the early 50s: 'In haec enim terra sola ducis auctoritas attenditur.'

foundations of a territorial state.[1] Henry, however, was a very practical man and as far as his Bavarian duchy was concerned, he did not really pursue similar designs. The possibility was certainly there. For the *privilegium minus* had brought about the separation of the East Mark from Bavaria and had thus dissolved the old and traditional unity of the Bavarian tribe, and it seems clear that Frederick would not have minded the full establishment of Henry's territorial power in Bavaria.[2] But in Bavaria Henry had few personal possessions[3] and he realized that the pursuit of any new territorial design would have been too much of an uphill fight.

Frederick had drawn the inspiration for such a revolutionary step from two sources. There was first the immediate urgency for reaching a settlement, for without a settlement the Great Design could not be initiated. And secondly there was the clear realization that by embarking on the Great Design, Frederick would be able to wash his hands of Germany as such. The early attempts to allow Henry the Lion the possession of two duchies as against Frederick's kingship had involved a very precarious balance of power. Under the old, first plan, according to which the king was to be a mere arbiter and overlord, this might well have made little difference. But now with Henry the Lion firmly entrenched in both Bavaria and Saxony, and with the emergence to the east of yet another duchy in which Frederick had literally abdicated most powers as arbiter and overlord, Frederick was prepared to remain little more than a nominal king in Germany proper. His new aim was to establish himself as a powerful ruler in the lands of the three rivers instead. In the light of the Great Design his conception of his duty towards Germany as a whole had changed. And it was this altered conception which made it possible for him to put forward the revolutionary issue of the *privilegium minus* plan for Henry Jasomirgott. As we shall see, he was going to find it very difficult

[1] For details see p. 262 below,

[2] Having granted Henry Jasomirgott the *privilegium minus*, Frederick felt that he ought to allow similar privileges to Henry in Bavaria. Thus, in 1158, he issued a diploma in which he recognized Henry's brutal suppression of Föhring.

[3] For Henry's few possessions in Bavaria *see* C. W. Böttiger, *Heinrich der Löwe*, Hannover, 1819, Exkurs II, and Heigel and Riezler *Das Herzogtum Bayern zur Zeit Heinrichs des Löwen und Ottos I von Wittelsbach*, Munich, 1867, p. 248.

to abide by this altered conception; for the implementation of the Great Design was to involve him in a conflict with the papacy which sent its ripples not only through Italy but also through France and Germany. And in the end it turned out that the Great Design could not be enforced without gross interference in Germany proper. But in 1156 this could clearly not have been anticipated either by Frederick or by anyone else.

The main principle of the Great Design was that Frederick should build up his own state – thus following more or less clearly the line of development which had been mapped out for the Babenberg dukes in Austria, for Henry the Lion in Saxony,[1] for Berthold von Zähringen in the region of the Jura mountains and, a little later, for the bishop of Würzburg. The only difference was that the geographical sweep of Frederick's Design was very much more ambitious; and, if successful, would have made him the most powerful ruler in Christendom.

It is important to survey Frederick's concept region by region. The two northern regions, Swabia and Alsace, were divided by the Black Forest mountains and by the river Rhine,[2] and in each Frederick was firmly established because of his family possessions. He therefore started with a double advantage because crown property and family property had all been indistinguishably united in the hands of the Staufen and were administered together.[3] The central part of these regions was described by Otto of Freising as *vis maxima regni*, and modern research has confirmed the soundness of his view.

Frederick's plan and efforts to build up these regions into a

[1] W. Schlesinger, *Mitteldeutsche Beiträge zur deutschen Verfassungsgeschichte*, Göttingen, 1961, p. 234. Frederick's aims in Swabia were not very different from those of Henry the Lion as described by R. Hildebrand, *Der sächsische 'Staat' Heinrichs des Löwen*, EHS, 302, Berlin, 1937, passim. For Frederick *see* e.g. K. Weller, *Reichsstrassen des Mittelalters*, WVH, N.F., 33, 1927 and M. Ernst, *Miszellen zur Geschichte Ulms*, ZWLG, 1941, pp. 433 ff.

[2] As an additional obstacle, Lothair III had also planted the Zähringer between Swabia and Alsace. *Cp.* Th. Mayer, *Die historisch-politischen Kräfte im Oberrheingebiet im Mittelalter*, ZGO, N.F., L. II, 1938 pp. 15–16.

[3] For Swabia *see* K. Weller, *Die staufischen Städtegründungen in Schwaben*, WVH, N.F., 36, 1930, p. 151; for Alsace *see* H. W. Klewitz, *Geschichte der Ministerialität im Elsass bis zum Ende des Interregnums*, Frankfurt, 1929, p. 53. *Cp.* also H. Niese, *Die Verwaltung des Reichsguts im 13. Jahrhundert*, 1905, pp. 22 ff.

compact territory is all the more remarkable when one recalls how comparatively unsuccessful his Staufen ancestors had been in their efforts. When Frederick's ancestor, Frederick von Büren, was first established as duke of Swabia, he had received an immediate blow to any territorial ambitions when both Zürich and the upper Rhine bank were taken away from his duchy and given to the Zähringen family as an independent sphere of influence. Similarly, other dynasties like the Welf and the Pfullendorf families became independent of the duchy – thus the power of the Staufen dukes extended over little more than their unsubstantial possessions in northern Swabia and Franconia.[1] As a result, Welfen, Zähringer and Staufer had fought for predominance in Swabia, and during the reign of Lothair, who was consistently partisan to the Welf and Zähringen families, whatever progress the Staufen had made under the Salian kings was rendered null and void. Nor had Conrad III succeeded in eliminating the Welf influence in Swabia. In short, during the seventy-three years between the nomination of Frederick von Büren as duke and the accession of Frederick as king, the Staufen had not succeeded in establishing themselves territorially in Swabia in any real sense.[2]

Frederick pursued a hundred and one different methods in order to enlarge his holdings and in order to connect scattered ones. He took fiefs from the church, at first in the name of other members of his family, and eventually in his own name.[3] His

[1] Th. Mayer, *Die historisch-politischen Kräfte im Oberrheingebiet im Mittelalter*, ZGO. N.F., L II, 1938, p. 14.

[2] *Cp.* H. Heuermann, *Die Hausmachtpolitik der Staufer von Herzog Friedrich I bis König Konrad III.* Diss., Berlin, 1939. K. Bosl, *Reichsministerialität der Salier und Staufer*, Stuttgart, 1950, p. 624, says the contrary, but inexplicably, quotes Heuermann in support. For the very limited power of the Staufen in Swabia before Frederick *see* also Th. Mayer, *Friedrich I und Heinrich der Löwe*, p. 407, in Th. Mayer ed., *Kaisertum und Herzogsgewalt*, Leipzig, 1944.

[3] For church fiefs *see* K. Weller, *Die staufischen Städtegründungen in Schwaben*, WVH, N.F., 36, 1930, p. 155. For the *vogtlose* Cistercian and Praemonstratensian houses Frederick assumed a *defensio specialis*: thus they became dependent on him. *See* K. Bosl, *op. cit.*, p. 155 and H. Hirsch, *Klosterimmunität seit dem Investiturstreit*, Weimar, 1913, p. 114. For the way in which Frederick exercised *Vogtei* over certain monasteries because he held the neighbouring castles of Rothenburg and Staufen, see Stumpf, Nos. 4132 and 4323. – Since nobody could be invested with a fief by an inferior, a king could not directly hold a fief from an abbot or bishop. But this was changed under Frederick who held directly from ecclesiastical institutions. *See* A. Boos, *Die Kirchenlehen der staufischen Kaiser*, München, 1886, p. 43, and H. Fein, *Die staufischen Städtegründungen*

efforts to create territorial connections between separate holdings in general followed the major routes of communication.[1] He often tried to gain a foothold inside a bishopric by granting special privileges to *ministeriales* who held fiefs from the bishop. In this way he made the *ministeriales* of the bishops of Worms, Speyer and Würzburg more dependent on himself.[2] He was also an indefatigable castle-builder. These castles were administered by his own *ministeriales*, and from their strategic positions he extended his influence and power over the surrounding regions.[3] Frederick also helped to promote the fortunes of *ministeriales* in every direction.[4] They, in turn, helped with the building of roads[5] to connect newly-founded cities and other holdings. They helped to clear land and to settle free peasants there whose 'freedom' was not derived from ancient rights but was the privilege of the new colonist. At times Frederick negotiated an exchange of estates in order to produce greater compactness. In 1158 he exchanged Badenweiler manor in the Breisgau for his possessions around Goslar[6] with Henry the Lion. Badenweiler was situated among Zähringen lands and had come to Henry as part of the dowry of his wife Clementia von Zähringen. It was useless to Henry; but invaluable to Frederick because it helped to build a bridge between Swabia and Alsace. Frederick, in general, gradually formed a wholly new conception of territorial government.[7] It was no longer enough to accumulate more and more holdings and lordships, he had also to evolve a

im Elsass, 1939, p. 81. For the vast extent of the church fiefs from Chur, Constance, Bâle, Strassburg, Speier, Würzburg, Bamberg, Ratisbon, Fulda, Ellwangen, held by the Staufen, *see* J. Ficker, *Heerschild*, pp. 39 ff.

[1] For detailed examples *see* K. Bosl, *op. cit.*, p. 153 and H. Dannenbauer, *Das Verzeichnis der Tafelgüter des römischen Königs*, ZWLG, 12, 1953, pp. 1 ff.

[2] K. Bosl, *Würzburg als Reichsbistum*, p. 175, in *Aus Verfassungs- und Landesgeschichte*, Th. Mayer Festschrift, Lindau, Konstanz, 1954.

[3] K. W. Nitzsch, *Geschichte des deutschen Volkes*, Vol. II, Leipzig, 1892, p. 280; K. Weller, *op. cit.*, p. 158; L. Bruhns, *Hohenstaufenschlösser*, 1937, *passim.*

[4] *Cp.* K. Bosl, *Die Reichsministerialität der Salier und Staufer*, Stuttgart, 1950, *passim.*

[5] By this exchange agreement, Henry obtained the castles of Herzberg, Pöhlde and Scharzfels with everything that belonged to them. Stumpf, 3792. *Cp.* K. Weller, *op. cit.*, p. 153 and K. Jordan, *Goslar und das Reich im 12. Jahrhundert*, NJL, 35, 1963, p. 71.

[6] K. Weller, *Reichsstrassen des Mittelalters*, WVH, N.F., 33, 1927 and M. Ernst, *Miszellen zur Geschichte Ulms*, ZWLG, 1941, p. 433 ff.

[7] K. Bader, *Der deutsche Südwesten in seiner territorialstaatlichen Entwicklung*, 1950, p. 31. It is remarkable that already in the thirteenth century the chronicler Otto of St Blaise commented on this aspect of Frederick's policy: SRG, pp. 30–1.

new conception of administration extending over a compactly organized territory in which the authority and influence of all other lordships was eliminated.[1] By using these methods, Frederick aimed at building up a state which was to stretch on a broad front from the upper Rhine over the northern parts of south Germany, to end in a wedge in the south-east with some weaker connections stretching northwards, down the Rhine.[2] Last but not least, Frederick became an active and indefatigable founder of cities in Swabia and other regions of his territory.[3]

Towards the north-east of the Danube lie the Pleissenland and the Erzgebirge. Previous to Frederick, Lothair III and Conrad III had shown an interest in these as yet scarcely settled regions and had thought of turning them into a royal domain.[4] It seems that in 1158 – very shortly after the initiation of the Great Design – Frederick began to take the plan for building up an imperial domain in the Pleissenland very seriously. In the following years the speed of colonization and of peasant settlement was increased rapidly, especially in the region of the Erzgebirge. In these lands Frederick took pains to guard his forest rights. Eventually he even deprived the margrave of Meissen of upper Lusatia and of the *Vogtei* of Chemnitz and invested a family of imperial *ministeriales* with their administration. Other *ministeriales* were charged with the supervision of the new peasant settlements.[5] In the twelfth century the country around Chemnitz was a royal forest which was being cleared by *ministeriales*. As such it was directly administered by the king and no dynast had been able to establish himself there.[6] It appears that the foundation of the city of Chemnitz took place about 1165 in order to encourage the settlement of merchants at a time when the peasant settlements in the Erzgebirge were still in their infancy. Frederick wanted to encourage trade and sought to promote the commercial development of the

[1] K. Bosl, *op. cit.*, pp. 20–1.

[2] *ibid.*, p. 632. An examination of Frederick's itineraries shows that his main concern in Germany was: Ratisbon – Nuremberg – Würzburg – Frankfurt. *See* Th. Mayer, *Das deutsche Königtum und sein Wirkungsbereich*, pp. 57–8, in *Das Reich und Europa*, Leipzig, 1941.

[3] K. Weller, *Die staufischen Städtegründungen*, WVH, N.F., 36, 1930, *passim*.

[4] W. Schlesinger, *Die Anfänge der Stadt Chemnitz*, 1952, pp. 210–11.

[5] *ibid.*, p. 203–4.

[6] *ibid.*, pp. 52 ff.

region under his patronage and protection.[1] He acted with the same intentions that Henry the Lion showed in the north when he encouraged the foundation of Lübeck.

In central Swabia Frederick's territorial policy was based upon a peaceful and friendly understanding with the families of Pfullendorf, Lenzburg and Andechs and many others. His relations with all these men, especially with Count Rudolf von Pfullendorf, were cordial and personal. He could always rely on Count Rudolf's services and support, and when it became apparent that he would die without heirs, Count Rudolf left his possessions to Frederick.[2] Other peaceful opportunities for acquisition of more property in Swabia occurred when many members of the nobility died in the disastrous epidemic in Rome in 1167. These friendly relations contrasted very markedly with the open hostility with which so many Saxon nobles met Henry the Lion's similar efforts.

In Alsace, Frederick pursued an identical policy. His ancestor, Duke Frederick II, had laid there the foundations of Staufen influence and during the twelfth century Alsace had become in a real sense a Staufen province. The Staufen had married into the Egisheim family and had founded many monasteries. They had taken possession of the Odilienberg and its monasteries, and from there they had extended their possessions to Rosheim. Another complex of Staufen lands was in the Gregorienthal in upper Alsace which reached into the plains, to Münster, Türkheim and Colmar. They also owned lands as imperial fiefs which they had obtained through their support of the Salian kings when Duke Frederick II had defended Henry V in 1115.[3] Their power was

[1] W. Schlesinger, *Die Anfänge der Stadt Chemnitz*, 1952 p. 172. On p. 187 Schlesinger points out that Chemnitz's foundation was very different from that of Lübeck, for in Chemnitz there was no *Unternehmerkonsistorium*. The phrase is Rörig's, who stressed that Lübeck did not owe its existence to the initiative of Henry the Lion: *Heinrich der Löwe und die Gründung Lübecks*, DA, I, 1937. R. Hildebrand, *Der sächsische 'Staat' Heinrichs des Löwen*, EHS, 302, Berlin, 1937, takes the opposite view. The whole controversy is really only a matter of emphasis. Both Frederick and Henry promoted actively the foundation of these cities. But they could not have done so if in some capacity or other there had not also been a merchants' association. *Cp.* H. Beumann, *Neuere Forschungen über Heinrich den Löwen*, HJ, 59, 1939. However, Lübeck was more fortunate in its geographical position than Chemnitz.

[2] K. Schmid, *Graf Rudolf von Pfullendorf und Kaiser Friedrich I*, Freiburg, i. Br., 1954.

[3] A. Meister, *Die Hohenstaufen im Elsass*, 1890.

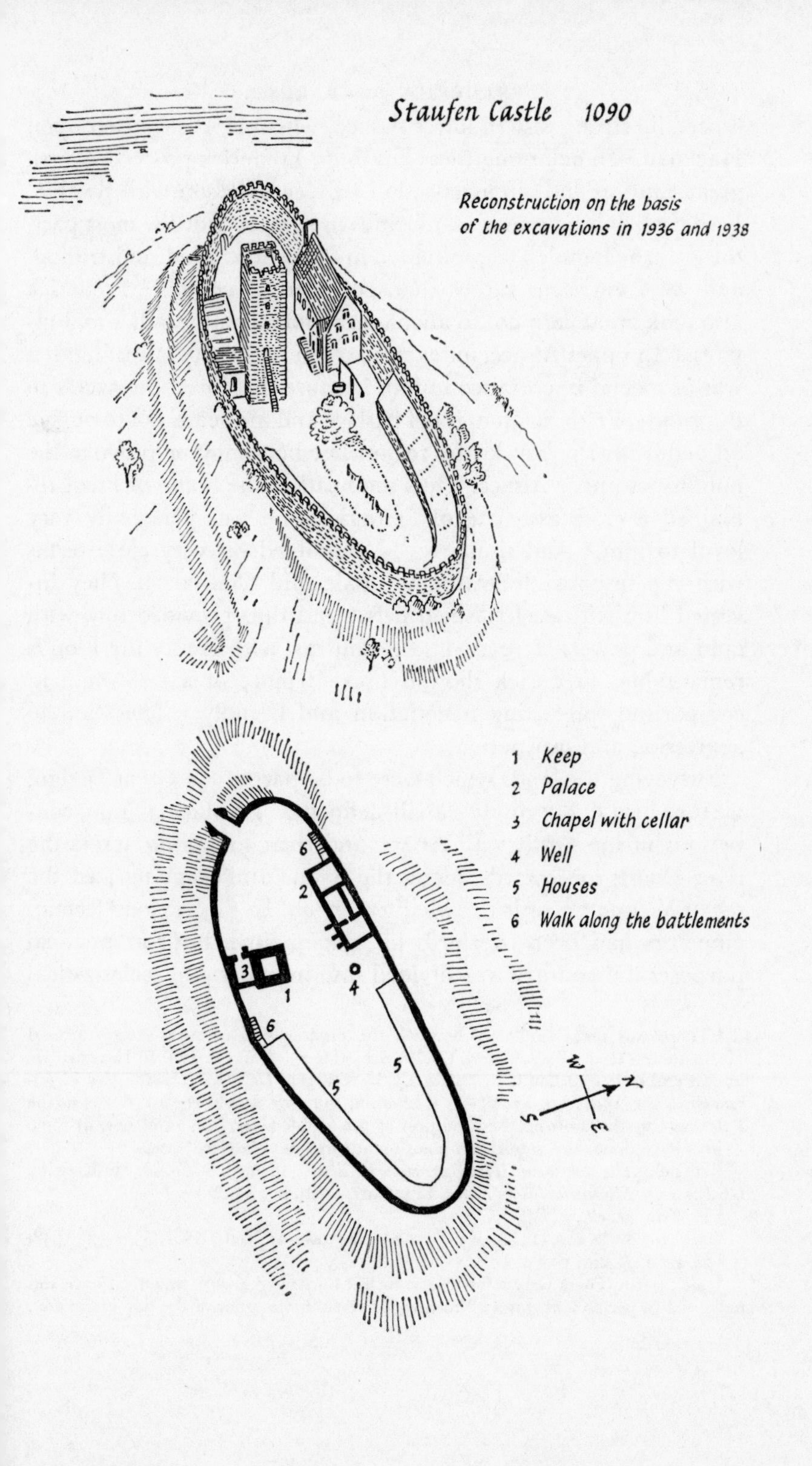
Staufen Castle 1090
Reconstruction on the basis
of the excavations in 1936 and 1938
1 Keep
2 Palace
3 Chapel with cellar
4 Well
5 Houses
6 Walk along the battlements
1
2
3
4
5
5
6
6
N
S
E
W

especially strong also in lower Alsace, where it was centred upon Hagenau.[1] In enlarging these holdings, Frederick proceeded with great caution and circumspection.[2] By comparison with Swabia, Frederick did not found many cities in Alsace.[3] For the most part, the cities he founded were situated in the centres of administration, and were garrisons rather than commercial centres.[4] Frederick also took great care not to alienate the important families and interests. In upper Alsace, for example, where the city of Mülhausen was of special importance to him because it secured the access to Burgundy, Frederick remained passive and took care not to pursue an acquisitive policy in the region lest he annoy or provoke the nobility of upper Alsace. Thus the head of the house of Pfirst remained a close associate of Frederick and was personally very loyal to him.[5] And similarly, he remained on very close terms with the bishops of Strasbourg, Bâle and Constance. They invested him with ecclesiastical fiefs,[6] and thus provided him with land and power. Here again, the contrast with Henry the Lion is remarkable. Frederick showed himself more of a statesman in comparison, preferring negotiation and friendly cooperation to aggression and usurpation.

Surveying the lands which were to be part of the Great Design, we turn next to Burgundy – an ill-defined geographical region, contiguous in the north with Alsace and then stretching across the river Doubs southwards, along the Saône and reaching past the see of Vienne towards the Mediterranean. In this region German emperors had been overlords for a long time, but for practical purposes the country was divided into innumerable ecclesiastical

[1] There was great similarity between the organization of royal estates around Hagenau and in the Pleissenland. *Cp.* W. Schlesinger, *op. cit.*, p. 129. In Hagenau we have a real code of urban law of 1164. *Cp.* F. Keutgen, *Urkunden zur städtischen Verfassungsgeschichte*, 1901, pp. 154 ff. – It is essential that one should regard Trifels in the Palatinate as the most northern outpost of the Staufen 'territory' and not, as some writers have done, as a southward pointing advance into 'foreign' lands.

[2] H. Fein, *Die staufischen Städtegründungen im Elsass*, 1939, p. 8. *Cp.* H. W. Klewitz, *Geschichte der Ministerialität im Elsass*, Frankfurt, 1929, pp. 53 ff.

[3] H. Fein, *op. cit.*, p. 64.

[4] *ibid.*, p. 68, *Cp.* also H. Thieme, *Staufische Stadtrechte im Elsass*, ZSSRG ger. 58, 1938.

[5] H. Fein, *op. cit.*, p. 55.

[6] *ibid.*, p. 81. There were a few frictions. But they were always smoothed over and never led to permanent states of hostility as became the order of the day in Saxony.

and lay lordships. Under Lothair the Zähringen family had gained much influence; and during the first years of his reign Frederick had confirmed this arrangement with Berthold IV.[1] But in 1156, in order to inaugurate the Great Design, Frederick's attitude to Burgundy changed completely. The initial treaty with Berthold IV was abrogated and replaced by a different agreement, directing Berthold's attention to a much smaller and more compact region.[2] Frederick himself thereupon decided to marry Beatrix, the daughter of Count Rainald. Count Rainald's heirs had always contested the promotion of the Zähringen family in Burgundy. With this new arrangement Frederick not only sought to put an end to the old feuds but clearly intended to place himself in a position where he would be able to assume personal government in Burgundy. For with his marriage to Beatrix, he could not only claim the traditional suzerain rights pertaining to the empire, but could also rule more directly as Beatrix's husband. Beatrix, as the heiress of Count Rainald, did indeed possess a very widely scattered series of rights and lordships in that region.

The marriage was proposed and celebrated, in some haste, in Würzburg in the June of 1156. Beatrix was extremely attractive[3] – but she was really too young to marry; and, indeed, her first child was not born until 1164.[4] The marriage seems to have been a happy one and Beatrix, unlike most other queens of Germany, spent most of her life travelling around with him. And when politics or sickness forced her to stay behind somewhere, she always rejoined Frederick at the first opportunity.[5] But at that time,

[1] See above, Ch. III.

[2] See p. 108 above. *Cp.* H. Hirsch, *Urkundenfälschung aus dem Regnum Arelatense*, Wien, 1937, p. 134 and especially p. 145.

[3] *Sigberti Continuatio*, MGH, SS, p. 407. *Cp.* F. Keszycka, *Kaiserin Beatrix*, Freiburg i.Ü., p. 25. In *Sigberti Continuatio*, MGH, SS, 6, p. 407, it is stated that Frederick married 'virginem elegantem'.

[4] According to J. Y. Mariotte, *Le comté de bourgogne sous les Hohenstaufen*, Paris, 1963, p. 69, note 52, Beatrix was then between twelve and sixteen years of age. But A. Hofmeister, *Puer, Juvenis, Senex*, in: Kehr Festschrift, *Papsttum und Kaisertum*, München, 1926, p. 312, believes her to have been only ten years old. In view of the fact that her first child was born only in 1164, Hofmeister's calculation is more likely to be correct than Marriotte's.

[5] W. Kowalski, *Die deutschen Königinnen und Kaiserinnen*, Weimar, 1913, pp. 104, 123. Beatrix's devotion to Frederick made her personally share Frederick's misfortunes. Her sorrows, which must have been considerable after the Roman disaster in the sum-

there can be no doubt that the marriage was entered into for purely political reasons: it was mutually advantageous to both partners. It enabled Beatrix to vindicate her claims in Burgundy more successfully; and it provided Frederick with the opportunity of making Burgundy part of the Great Design.[1]

The establishment of Frederick's lordship in Burgundy, however, was not a simple affair. Frederick had practically no personal possessions; and those of his wife were not sufficient for him to simply follow those policies which were being employed in Swabia and Alsace. With some members of the Burgundian nobility, for instance the house of Mâcon, Frederick's relations were friendly because they were closely related to Beatrix.[2] But there is no one single formula to cover his methods, except that he mainly sought to advance the fortunes of monasteries and bishoprics at the expense of the lay nobility. By generous grants and by issuing exemptions from lay control as well as from papal control,[3] he promoted the independence of the Burgundian church *vis-à-vis* local authorities and, in turn, their dependence on the empire. In this way the power of the lay nobility was curbed, and the great sees were treated as if they were part of the imperial church.[4] According to the evidence of Rahewin, by 1157 Frederick had established his authority in Burgundy as far south as Arles. As a result, in a country where previously there had been disorder and anarchy because of too great a love of liberty, there was now peace and submission to the empire. The archbishops of Vienne and Lyons and the bishops of Valence and Avignon had appeared

---

mer of 1167 and again after the battle of Legnano in 1176 when Frederick went missing for several days, evoked the sympathy of the poet Gautier d'Arras:

> Dont est bien drois que de doel fonde
> Par la millor de tout le monde.
> *Ille et Galeron*, V, 130 f.

[1] Otto of Freising relates the marriage and the settlement with Henry Jasomirgott in one breath: *Gesta*, II, xlvii–xlviii.

[2] H. Hirsch, *op. cit.*, p. 134.

[3] *ibid.*, p. 125. Hirsch tried to prove that a great many of the relevant charters were forged in an effort to ante-date Frederick's policy and make it appear more traditional than it was. But Hirsch's arguments do not appear to be sound. *Cp.* V. Brumm, *Zur Frage der Echtheit der ersten Stauferdiplome für südburgundische Empfänger*, MIOG, 57, 1949.

[4] H. Hirsch, *op. cit.*, p. 139.

at the court in Besançon and paid homage to Frederick.[1] Such homage was indeed customary in Germany; but in Italy it was widely opposed, and in Burgundy it had never been taken for granted.[2]

At the beginning of the Great Design at least there was no real opposition to these policies in Burgundy. At the court of Besançon in 1157 both the church and the lay nobility showed themselves reconciled to their fate and firm in their support of Frederick and Beatrix.[3]

As regards Lombardy, we are fortunate in having a full list of Frederick's intentions in the form of the famous decrees officially promulgated at Roncaglia in November 1158. Although it is probable that these decrees were more or less improvised, they were sweeping in scope and encompassed a new conception of government. It is conceivable that such decrees had first occurred or been suggested to Frederick when he had met the lawyers of the Bologna schools on his way to Rome in 1155. But at that time any ideas he might have had could only have been academic, for as long as he was pursuing his first plan, he could have had no intention of reducing Lombardy to complete and direct subjection.

For this is exactly what the theory of the Roncaglia decrees amounted to, even though their practical application, as we shall see, was intentionally capable of a great many interpretations to suit political circumstances. By these decrees Frederick proclaimed that he would resume all *regalia*, that is all the powers ever exercised by his predecessors in virtue of their conquest of Lombardy. He claimed the entire power of *bannus*, that is the full

[1] *Gesta*, III, xii. [2] V. Brumm, *op. cit.*, pp. 333–4.

[3] Girard de Vienne, count of Mâcon and Heracle de Montboissier, archbishop of Lyon, the two most powerful lords of Burgundy rushed to Besançon in the autumn of 1157 in order to commit themselves to Frederick. They hoped to use his support to subdue several minor lords east of the Saône to their jurisdiction. *Cp.* G. Duby, *La société aux XIe and XIIe siècles dans la région Mâconnaise*, Paris, 1953, p. 536. In 1157 Frederick created titles and offices to give substance to the idea of a royal court in Burgundy. *Cp.* R. Folz, *L'empereur Frederic Ier et le royaume de Bourgogne*, SHDB, 18, 1956, pp. 120 ff. Folz, *op. cit.*, p. 119, takes pains to point out that there was a considerable difference between Frederick's treatment of Burgundy proper and his treatment of Provence. Only the former, we may presume, for geographical reasons, was to become encompassed by the Great Design and somehow assimilated to Alsace. Provence was too far to the south and Frederick showed only a formal interest in it.

exercise of jurisdiction over all matters affecting property, life and liberty. Next, he insisted that he had the sole right to appoint dukes, margraves and counts, as well as the judges and consuls of the cities. Thirdly, he claimed all the minor *bannus* such as the authority to erect mills and ovens; the control over weights and measures, the rights to dispose of the forests; authority over markets, highways, navigable rivers together with all the revenues from ports and tolls, full power over all commerce and the sole right of coinage. Finally, he claimed all contributions for warfare incurred by the empire – soldiers, taxes, wagons, ships, horses, and so forth. He also requisitioned all imperial property for his direct disposal, the royal houses in the various cities, the palaces, domains and lands as well as direct authority over the settlers on royal property. The list was exhaustive. If enforced, these decrees would have made Frederick, at least in Lombardy, the most autocratic head of any state in twelfth-century Europe and, what is more, not just of any state, but of one of the wealthiest. With his authority thus secure in Lombardy he could easily have afforded to allow the Welf and the Babenberg and the Zähringen families the full ownership of their duchies, no matter how large. He would always have been able to raise armies for any purposes he might have had in mind and would have been completely independent of any need for support from the princes of Germany.

There was something paradoxical in the proclamation of the Roncaglia decrees, for they were promulgated with the full semblance of being good traditional law. Frederick had gone to a considerable amount of trouble to provide all the legal precedents necessary; and if one examines the decrees clause by clause, from a purely legal point of view, they contained nothing which Frederick did not claim as his titular right by virtue of being king of Lombardy and Roman emperor. But it is doubtful that Frederick could have been as naïve as countless modern historians who have asserted that he came to Lombardy in 1158 demanding no more than his legal rights, a simple-minded ruler taking his stand on traditional law. Frederick was fully aware of the fact that there had been economic and social changes in northern Italy between 1050 and 1150. Whether he understood the precise historical causes and whether he appreciated the extent to which this revolution had been countenanced by the growth of the heretical sects who, under Gregory VII, had found papal support against imperial overlordship, is another matter. But in his biography of Frederick, Otto of Freising showed himself fairly well informed about conditions in Lombardy. He provided quite a shrewd account of the unusual social and political developments which had taken place, and it would be unreasonable to assume that Frederick was more ignorant than Otto of Freising. It is much more probable that he was determined to subjugate Lombardy and that he knew that a struggle lay ahead. But in order to start with as much advantage as possible, he thought to provide himself with all the appearances of legality he could find. By digging far enough into the past, he could find quite genuine precedents for his claims.

This then, was the outline of the Great Design – a bold plan of constructive statesmanship. It was a forward looking plan in every respect: Frederick wanted to create a tightly organized state in a geographically defined region. In some parts, as in Swabia, he based himself mainly on traditional practices. In Burgundy he used political measures to advance the fortunes of those bishops and nobles most likely to pay homage to him and support him. In Lombardy, finally, he resurrected ancient laws which were valid but which he knew to be outmoded. If he had succeeded in this Great Design, there would have been nothing in medieval Europe to compare with it either in territorial compactness or in the closeness and directness of sovereign powers.

Frederick's aims ran parallel to those of the Zähringen dukes, to the aims allowed to Henry Jasomirgott in Austria and to the aims pursued by Henry the Lion in Saxony. The desire to found such centrally administered states was, of course, part of the political atmosphere of the second half of the twelfth century and in this respect the Great Design must be seen as the product of the political and administrative revolution which was initiated first by the Norman kings in England and promoted, to a slightly lesser extent, by the Capetian kings in France.[1] In order to understand

[1] A. Brackmann, *Die Ursachen der geistigen und politischen Wandlung Europas im 11. und*

correctly the scope of this revolution in the empire, however, one must keep in mind that Frederick intended to follow the lines of this revolution not in Germany as a whole, and much less in the empire as a whole. To do so would, given the poor means of twelfth century communication and the vast extent of these lands, have been completely impracticable. By the Great Design in the land of the three rivers, Frederick intended nothing less than to put himself at the head of a new state. And as far as Lombardy was concerned, he meant to do this not by creating new institutions or laws or by building new castles, but simply by declaring himself the source and authority of existing ones. He intended to pursue the Great Design in a limited geographical region, and he encouraged other princes to follow the lead of this revolution in their own, similarly compact territories. If this is granted, one is forced to the conclusion that, as far as the Great Design is concerned, Frederick can hardly be considered a German ruler; for the application of this revolution was, as far as he was concerned, intended for regions mostly outside Germany.

Frederick knew that the success of his aims would depend to a very large degree on the personnel he could find for their implementation. And it is in this respect that Frederick's position was, from the very outset, weak; so weak, indeed, that in retrospect one can understand how little chance of real success he had. The kings of England and France, even in the second half of the twelfth century, were able to employ trained bureaucrats. They employed bureaucrats and professional administrators who brought not only their professional expertise to bear on the task but were also socially pre-conditioned to complete loyalty to their royal employers. But owing to the social and cultural backwardness of Germany, Frederick was not able to find such a class of men. He had no trained lawyers and administrators to call upon. He had to rely entirely upon a class of unfree servants, described generally as *ministeriales*. These men owed their advancement entirely to him and thus initially formed a reliable instrument of direct rule and

---

12. Jahrhundert, HZ, 149, 1936, and *Die Wandlung der Staatsanschauungen im Zeitalter Kaiser Friedrichs I*, HZ, 145, 1932, has stressed the importance of the Norman example for Frederick.

administration. But even so, they were socially something like country squires. If Frederick advanced their fortunes and promoted them in the social ladder, such promotion was bound to turn them into a lesser aristocracy.[1] Eventually they were accommodated in the feudal hierarchy. But at no stage did they become a professional bureaucracy. Moreover, and this is equally important, these men had no educational qualifications for the tasks assigned to them. They could administer castles and supervise peasants. They could govern an Italian city and run a manor.[2] But they had no legal training and their whole cultural outlook remained bucolic and rural.[3] In the end, as the example of one of the most enterprising and ruthless servants of the crown in Alsace was to show, they became a threat to royal authority[4] and

[1] O. v. Dungern, *Constitutional Reorganisation and Reform under the Hohenstaufen*, p. 223, in G. Barraclough ed., *Medieval Germany*, Oxford, 1938.

[2] K. Bosl, *Reichministerialität der Salier und Staufer*, Stuttgart, 1950, pp. 617–18, 625–8.

[3] H. Heimpel, *Kaiser Friedrich Barbarossa und die Wende der staufischen Zeit*, Strassburg, 1942, noted that the Staufen empire did not have the organs of government and the personnel necessary for following the Norman example. Kienast, reviewing Heimpel in HZ, 167, 1943, p. 405, contradicts and quotes such odd instances of royal officials as some *baillis* known to have existed in 1184, a *iudex terrae* in the Pleissenland in 1172, a *procurator* in Swabia in 1173, etc. But one swallow does not make a summer and Kienast puts too sanguine an interpretation upon the evidence collected by Bosl, *op. cit.* G. Kirchner, *Staatsplanung und Reichsministerialität*, *DA*, 10, 1954, p. 468, points out that though Bosl may be right in stressing the importance of the colonizing efforts of Staufen *ministeriales* in Egerland and the Pleissenland and Vogtland, it does not necessarily follow that these efforts resulted in a material increase of power for Frederick. For these *ministeriales*, most probably, soon became fairly independent landowners in practice, if not in theory. For Frederick had no central office from which to control them and in which to check their accounts. Hence any comparison with the French *baillis* is misplaced. Even Bosl admits that Frederick's efforts at state-building cannot compare with similar developments in France and England at that time: *Das Hochmittelalter in der deutschen und europäischen Geschichte*, HZ, 194, 1962, p. 545. *Cp.* the remarks by H. Appelt, *Friedrich Barbarossa und das römische Recht*, RMH, V, 1961–2, p. 32.

[4] The example of Wölflin von Hagenau, a generation after Frederick, shows the *ministeriales* as enterprising and rather unscrupulous men. Wölflin was in fact described as *prefectus Alsatiae* (*Richeri Gesta Senoniensis Ecclesiae*, MGH, SS, XXV, p. 302; *Cp.* Niese, *Die Verwaltung des Reichsguts*, 1905, p. 273). He looked well after his and his master's interests. He came from very lowly origins and owed his career, which led him to influential positions in the royal court, to his intelligence and vigour. He administered the royal estates in and around Hagenau and eventually was put in charge of all imperial estates in Alsace. He founded cities and castles, attracted new citizens to existing cities, built walls around villages and turned them into cities. He began as *sculteltus* of Hagenau and ended as a *procurator* or *prefectus* of Alsace who drew cases to his court and, at times, forwarded them to the royal court. In the end, he was imprisoned by the

when they were used to serve in foreign lands, they tended to lose their bearings, frequently behaving in such a scandalous and brutal manner that they helped to brand Frederick's rule as oppressive, unjust and extortionate.[1]

In the *terra imperii*, Frederick aimed to be the supreme sovereign and thus to exclude all rights, powers and authorities exercised by any dynast in his own right. He wanted to be a real territorial lord and not merely a landowner or liege-lord. In order to achieve this he used *ministeriales*, who took a servants' oath instead of a vassals' oath.[2] Their services made it possible to dispense with granting rights of holding courts, *Vogteien* and rights of manning castles to members of the indigenous nobility. As a result, this method of creating a royal administrative service was most successful in newly-cleared lands on which peasants were settling but on which the older aristocratic families had not yet established themselves.[3] But the very success of this experiment in the Erzgebirge region, for instance, should have been proof that similar methods would not be equally successful in lands where there were dynasts, and least of all in lands where there were cities which had been accustomed to self-government and where *ministeriales* would have to be imported from abroad. The success of the employment of *ministeriales* in other regions depended on their being not a class of minor rural gentlemen but professional and educated administrators. But this is precisely what they were not. For education was almost impossible to obtain in Germany at that time. It is true some people journeyed to the schools in Paris and Chartres, but this was exceptional and was a privilege reserved to the very few.[4] The *ministeriales* were and remained rough men who had neither opportunity nor inclination to acquire an educa-

---

emperor because he extorted money. For his career, see K. Bosl, *Reichsministerialität der Salier und Staufer*, Stuttgart, 1950, pp. 194–7. If these men behaved like this at home, it is no surprise that they should have been even more unscrupulous when in charge of foreign lands.

[1] See p. 275, below.

[2] K. Bosl, *op. cit.*, p. 621.

[3] Kirchner, *op. cit.*, p. 470, doubts even this.

[4] Bishop Otto of Freising was well known to be a product of French education and he may not have been altogether exceptional. But he himself is evidence that modern education was very imperfectly assimilated.

tion. And as a result there could be nothing in Frederick's 'state' remotely similar to the English Exchequer or to the *baillis* and *sénéchaux* employed by Philip Augustus in France.

It is difficult to assess to what extent Frederick was personally responsible for the Great Design.[1] There was a definite change of personnel among his advisers, and it was no accident that Rainald von Dassel became Frederick's chancellor a month before the Treaty of Benevento. It is tempting therefore to see in him the main inspiration of the Great Design. He was certainly to become its most indefatigable and radical propounder and strategist. But if one examines his career from the day of his appointment to his death in Rome in 1167, it is evident that Rainald was always in the forefront whenever the pursuit of the Great Design implied attacks on the papacy. And one wonders, therefore, whether Rainald, for all his statesmanship, was not obsessed by his hostility to the papacy. Together with his hatred of popes, he showed a pompously reiterated belief in the empire as a sacred institution[2] and an unrealistic desire both to display the mystical and theological foundations of royal power[3] and to emphasize that the empire was superior to the papacy.[4]

It is true that Frederick relied more and more heavily on him.[5]

[1] Rainald had no direct influence on the text of the *privilegium minus*. It was written by the old chancellery before Rainald took full charge. W. Erben, *Das Privilegium Friedrichs I für das Herzogtum Österreich*, 1902. The one direct evidence we have is due to the Archipoeta, a fine poet, but a professional flatterer employed by Rainald. It must be discounted: 'Through the light of his [Rainald's] brilliance, the Emperor's mind was lit up.' Manitius ed., Munich, 1929, p. 54, v. 44 and p. 28, v. 2.

[2] For Rainald's responsibility for the magic pomp of the canonization of Charlemagne in 1165, when all pragmatic policies had failed, see p. 242 below.

[3] E. Otto, *Friedrich Barbarossa in seinen Briefen*, DA, 1942, has tried to isolate Frederick's personal and sober contribution to some of his letters. The rest, presumably by Rainald, consists of high-sounding, empty phrases about the splendour and sublimeness of imperial power.

[4] Rainald was outspoken about what he thought an emperor could do to a pope: 'In tali statu Deus vos in praesenti constituit, quod, si vultis, et Roman destruere et de papa et cardinalibus omnem vestram voluntatem habere', MGS, IV, p. 123.

[5] Acerbus Morena, MGH, SS, XVIII, p. 640, called Rainald 'ad sublimandum imperatoris honorem cupidissimus'. Perhaps the expression 'sublimandum' hits the nail on the head. Frederick might have preferred someone who was more concerned with practical politics. But Frederick made no bones about this reliance on Rainald, *cp.* Stumpf, 4018) and held him up as an example. (Stumpf, 4072) He always treasured Rainald's services and after his death wrote a sort of public testimonial for him: Stumpf, 4089. – For other men's judgement that Rainald was the chief adviser of

But, though this cannot be proved, Rainald appears to have remained an instrument rather than the inspirer of the Great Design. True, he was not always easily controlled, for he forced Frederick's hand on more than one occasion and by always following the most extreme course possible, made the pursuit of the Great Design increasingly precarious. It is plausible that Frederick, realizing that the implementation of the Great Design would cause a complete breach between emperor and pope, used Rainald because of his antagonism. But Rainald's fanaticism ultimately forced a course of action which was orientated much more to the humiliation of the papacy than towards the realization of the Great Design. And yet it would be quite wrong to see Frederick as forced against his will by Rainald towards the humiliation of the papacy (as represented by Hadrian and by Alexander III, his successor). In the heat of battle Frederick became angered. And when this happened he was always prone to act in a way that was not necessarily either prudent or conducive towards the realization of the original plan. It was on such occasions, as the destruction of Milan in 1162, and the court of Würzburg in 1165 which inaugurated the era of ecclesiastical persecution in Germany, that Rainald's counsels prevailed.

The relationship between Frederick and Rainald is, therefore, an essential part of the total situation. Rainald was employed initially as a tool. But a tool has a force of its own; and the tactics necessary for the realization of ultimate objectives also tend to acquire a momentum of their own. As it happened, by the time Frederick and Rainald had got themselves involved in a military and political situation that was fast eluding their control, Rainald suddenly died. Frederick was therefore left free to reconsider the whole plan. Whether he would have been able to do so with Rainald alive is impossible to say. Given his outbursts of anger, one is inclined to think that Frederick was more emotional than the contemporary sources about him liked to admit, and that

Frederick, *see* F. Güterbock, *Le lettere del notaio Bucardo*, BISI, 61, 1949, p. 63; *Chron. reg. Col.* ad 1167; *Cat. Archiepisc. Colon.*, I, MGH, SS, XXIV, p. 343; Otto Morena, p. 168. Not the least important service which Rainald always rendered Frederick was that he kept providing soldiers for Italy. *Cp.* W. Martens, *Rainald von Dassel*, ADB, 27, pp. 730–1.

therefore, while Rainald was alive, he might well not have been able to extricate himself from the desperate situation he had got into by the middle of 1167. And while he was no superman who could have calmly brushed aside Rainald's influence, he was certainly determined enough to start a complete re-examination once Rainald was gone. We need not criticize him for failing to stand aloof from Rainald's hopeless, but inevitable, confusion of ends and means. It is much more remarkable and worthy of respect that, once Rainald was dead, Frederick succeeded in cutting his losses for a second time in his life and start afresh.

With the ascendancy of Rainald, there went the gradual withdrawal of both Wibald and Eberhard of Bamberg from Frederick's councils. Although these two men had not always seen eye to eye with one another, they had both, each in their own way, been responsible for the policy of the Treaty of Constance. The failure of Frederick's first plan and the conception of the Great Design was a new departure and so, without palace revolution or a dramatic dismissal, both men moved into the background. Wibald, in pursuit of his old policy, had gone on a mission to Greece in August 1155. When he left, the change of plan had not yet been mooted. But on his return in the middle of 1156, it was complete. We know little of his business in Constantinople. But he did bring back a Greek embassy to discuss marriage plans. By that time, however, everything had changed and Frederick would not even receive the Greeks who had come with Wibald. They had to be left behind in Salzburg. Wibald himself joined Frederick in Würzburg in June, only to find Frederick preparing for his wedding with Beatrix. Finally in July, and probably to please his old friend Wibald, Frederick consented to receive the Greeks in Nuremberg. By that time, of course, the whole object of the embassy had disappeared. Wibald knew this; but as he was not a man given to sudden and radical measures, he hoped at least for a continuation of a friendly understanding with the Greeks. And, on the face of it, there was nothing absurd in this hope. For the Greeks were the enemies of the Normans in Sicily; and the Normans in Sicily had just allied themselves with the pope who was now no longer on friendly terms with Frederick. As it was, Wibald's hopes were to be dashed, for in the spring of 1158 the Greek emperor and the king of Sicily concluded an alliance.[1]

When Wibald saw how unlikely it was that his policies would prevail, he retired from court circles of his own accord. The withdrawal was very gradual and took a long time to become known. For as late as January 1157 Pope Hadrian wrote to Wibald to ask him to use his influence to heal the conflict between pope and emperor.[2] In March that year, Frederick himself wrote to Wibald to assure him that he still valued his advice highly and apologized for not having summoned him for a long time. He said that he had been mindful of Wibald's age and had not wanted to tire him out. He then told him that the expedition to Apulia in pursuit of the obligations to the Greeks had been cancelled, and that henceforth all efforts were to be directed against Milan.[3] The letter was polite and friendly – but at the same time a very clear indication of the change of plan and personnel. In August Frederick wrote again. And this letter is proof of Frederick's caution designed to antagonize as few people as possible. He assured Wibald that, as far as the Greeks were concerned, he would not do anything rash without first consulting Wibald.[4] But by then Wibald knew full well that the time for a Greek alliance had definitely passed.

Eberhard of Bamberg's withdrawal was even more gradual and more voluntary. He was still employed in the difficult negotiations with Hadrian, which followed the first clash after the reversal of alliances. For as long as the breach between emperor and pope was not final, a man like Eberhard was more useful in finding a formula for compromise than anyone else. But as time went by and as the new policies were defined more and more clearly, Eberhard seems to have become increasingly unwilling. And eventually he complained in a letter to his friend Eberhard, the archbishop of Salzburg, that he felt he could not adjust himself to

[1] F. Hausmann, *Reichskanzlei und Hofkapelle*, Schriften der MGH, 14, 1956, p. 250.
[2] JL, 10246.
[3] BRG, I, No. 456. H. Zatschek's opinion, *Wibald von Stablo*, MIOG, Suppl. Vol. X, 1928, pp. 429, 471, that Frederick's letter was ironical, is without foundation.
[4] BRG, I, No. 465.

the new world.[1] He was not to re-emerge until after the death of Rainald.

In September 1156, when the conception of the Great Design had been completed and the first steps towards its implementation had been taken, Frederick met his uncle, Bishop Otto of Freising, in Ratisbon. Otto of Freising was one of the most learned men in Germany at that time and had written a monumental chronicle of world history entitled *The Two Cities*. When Frederick contemplated how fundamentally new the character of his plan was, he became interested in history, studying how the new plan would compare with previous policies and how its value might be assessed historically. Most probably as he was embarking on a new policy, he felt the need to learn his job by seeing how others had tackled problems before him. He therefore asked Otto for a copy of his chronicle, and Otto promised to have one made for him and send it as soon as it was ready. But Frederick at that time, stimulated by his own historical studies, also felt the need for a propaganda tract to inaugurate the Great Design and to justify its conception. Moreover, he was painfully aware of the revolutionary character of the Great Design – negatively, in its abandonment of the papal alliance which had been based upon the Treaty of Constance, and, positively, in the administrative plans for the lands of the three rivers.

Frederick was, by instinct, a good statesman. We have seen that he took great care never to antagonize people needlessly and that he always preferred smooth negotiation to brutal measures. He realized that it would help the execution of the Great Design enormously if he could persuade people to accept it as a peaceful evolution of older policies. He therefore felt that it would not be desirable for the radical change of plan to become public knowledge. Anyway, in an age in which politicians and statesmen were not judged by their reasonableness, but by the mystical power they represented, Frederick knew that it would damage his prestige, perhaps irreparably, if it became known that he was in fact an innovating statesman. If the whole truth ever became

[1] The letter is in *Gesta,* IV, xxxiv.

known, people would think of him, at best, as an opportunist; and, at worst, as a pusillanimous and vacillating ruler. Neither reputation, if spread, would make the execution of the Great Design any easier.

For these reasons Frederick and Rainald decided to seek ways and means of disguising the true nature of the contemplated changes and of presenting a picture of the early years of the reign, which was to be nothing less than a subtle falsification of the truth. Frederick's attempt to follow in the footsteps of Conrad III was to be played down as much as possible. The emergence of the Great Design was to be, more or less vaguely, antedated to 1152 so as to appear to have started, if its outlines emerged explicitly at all, at the beginning of the new reign. In this way people would become more readily reconciled to it, and Frederick would appear much more of a conservative than he actually was. At least he would appear conservative in his own intentions and his policies would be looked upon as forming a consistent pattern from the day of his election onward. Frederick and Rainald thought that the man most likely to help them in this propaganda campaign was Otto of Freising. Otto was therefore approached and asked whether he would consider writing a history of Frederick's reign. Otto was not young at that time, and there was no reasonable hope of his ever living to complete a full life of Frederick.[1] If Frederick and Rainald had intended anything larger than a tract to persuade people of the essential continuity of imperial policies, they would not have approached Otto.

Otto of Freising must have been, at first, extremely embarrassed by such a proposal. It was a great honour. But as it happened, Otto's views of history were anything but sanguine, and the conclusions he had reached at the end of his *Chronicle* were so pessimistic that they could not possibly be used as a starting point for propagating the Great Design. It was not only that Otto's assess-

[1] The work was originally conceived in four books. Otto did not live to complete all four. But his secretary Rahewin did and worked to Otto's original plan. For when he came to the successful conclusion of the synod of Pavia, he suddenly broke the narrative off and writes 'But as we do not propose to have the books of this work exceed the number of the evangels . . .' (IV, lxxxv). He then winds up with a description of Frederick's character. Rahewin's way of keeping to the original scheme is literarily clumsy. But it is obvious that he followed a preconceived plan.

ment of Conrad's reign had been extremely poor. Such an assessment might indeed form the starting point for justifying Frederick's change of plan either for 1152 or for 1156 – in fact, a poor assessment of Conrad's reign would only serve to make people realize how imperative a complete change was. But the assessment of Conrad's reign was only one small element in the general argument of the *Chronicle*: the whole *Chronicle* was written in order to show that the end of all history was approaching and the reign of the Antichrist imminent. On such a premise it was, indeed, difficult to convince anyone that there could now arise an emperor with a Great Design to inaugurate a period of material and administrative progress. Like St Bernard of Clairvaux, like Gerhoh of Reichersberg and Hugh of St Victor, Otto of Freising believed that he was living near the end of time. All these men had bemoaned the spread of heresy, the schism in the earlier part of the twelfth century, the failure of the second crusade and the vanity of all wordly pleasures, and had agreed *taedet vivere*. Otto had argued in his *Chronicle* that the conflict between empire and church had been resolved in the long period from the reign of Constantine to the reign of Henry III; but that the great conflict between Pope Gregory VII and Henry IV, the so called Investiture Controversy, had broken up this unity and that ever since the world was in its death throes and the power of evil increasing. 'But we, set down as it were at the end of time . . .' he had written in the prologue to his *Chronicle*.

Basically, and this is of fundamental importance, Otto was a Cistercian monk whose main end was a life of contemplation which was designed to extricate the individual from the mutability and hence the misery of earthly existence.[1] His acquaintance with contemporary philosophy in France enabled him to interpret the monastic ideal in terms of the concepts of mutability and stability.[2] Having described the whole of history as teaching that

[1] Otto of Freising had entered the Cistercian Order on his way back from France. He was travelling with fifteen companions, and they stopped to spend the night at the monastery of Morimund, and here they all joined the Cistercian Order. J. Spoerl's (*Grundformen hochmittelalterlicher Geschichtsanschauung*, München, 1935, p. 38) opinion that Otto's entry into the Cistercian Order has no significance can only be described as perverse.

[2] *Chronicle*, Prol. I: 'For it is the part of a wise man not to be whirled about after

things are in constant change, he considered the forces of goodness to be present in the newly emerging Cistercian and Praemonstratensian orders. For these orders made it possible for individuals to withdraw from mutability and enter upon a life of stability. Hence the progress of these orders in the twelfth century was to Otto a sign of hope – but not of hope for history and human society, but of hope that society and history would now soon come to an end. As more and more men were becoming members of these orders, he reasoned, the citizens of the city of the devil would decrease in numbers until it would eventually become extinct.[1] He considered that the antidote to history, society and change consisted in the asceticism and self-denial of monasticism.[2] Hence the *Chronicle* abounds with invitations to the monastic life.[3] The monk is a full citizen of the city of God, and through his flight from the *mutabilitas* of the life of sin into the city of God he partakes of *requies*. And *requies* is identified with virtue.[4] Otto believed that the present age of history in the twelfth century was the seventh age in which the mixing of good and evil men in the *civitas permixta* had come to an end. Monks and crusaders were extricating themselves from the city of the devil. They were indeed preparing for the last decisive battle, and hence the appearance of the Antichrist who would emerge as the ruler of the city of the devil was imminent.

With these views, one can imagine how Otto must have been concerned by Frederick's requests. For if his historical analysis in the *Chronicle* was correct, there was very little ground for believing that the Great Design would be successful. Indeed, very little ground for wanting it to be successful. Its success would be, at best, only temporary; but while it lasted, it would merely delay the

---

the manner of a revolving wheel, but through the stability of his powers to be firmly fashioned as a thing foursquare. Accordingly, since things are changeable and can never be at rest, what man in his right mind will deny that the wise man ought, as I have said, to depart from them to that city which stays at rest and abides in eternity?' Ch.Ch. Mierow tr., New York, 1928, p. 93.

[1] There was a New Order of Knighthood from 1100: *Chronicle*, VII, 7; VII, 9. Evil, the temporal order, mutability, will all come to an end: *Chronicle*, Prol. II *Cp.* also Prol. V.

[2] *Chronicle*, A. Hofmeister ed., II, p. 34, p. 108. *Cp.* also IV, 4, p. 190; II, 23, p. 98; VII, 35, p. 373; VIII, 26, p. 433.

[3] *Chronicle*, pp. 6, 9, 98, 119, 129, 190, 223, 226 ff., 242, 260 f., 271, 278, 320.

[4] *Chronicle*, VI, 36, p. 306. Also VII, 35, p. 373.

final struggle and the advent of the Antichrist. And, at any rate, with such views, Otto was not really in a frame of mind suitable for propagating the new spirit of government and for writing a book in which the Great Design was to be given a positive evaluation.

Otto, however, appears to have been deeply impressed by the new plans and by the vigour and imagination with which Frederick and Rainald went to work on them. So much so that he seems to have been won over completely. And during the winter of 1156–7 he went through something which one can only describe as an intellectual, if not spiritual, revolution.[1] This change of mind is all the more remarkable as by that time Otto was a mature man approaching the age of fifty, and moreover a man who thought that he had already completed what he must have considered his *magnum opus*. But the air of activity and hopefulness

[1] Otto of Freising has been variously interpreted by historians, all intent upon explaining the ultimate consistency of his thought. Needless to say, these attempts have often led to strange views. J. Spörl, *op. cit.*, sees Otto as the upholder of the metaphysics of the Staufen Empire, lay and absolute. J. Schmidlin, *Die Philosophie Ottos von Freising*, PhJ, 18, 1905, sees him as an exponent of papal theocracy. At a pinch even the *Gesta* fit into this interpretation, because Otto was always very reluctant in his support of anti-papal measures. P. Brezzi, *Ottone di Frisinga*, BISI, 54, 1939, maintains that Otto's central aim was to realize on earth a city of God in which there would be scope for both sacerdotal and civil authority. E. Bernheim, *Der Character Ottos von Freising und seiner Werke*, MIOG, VI, 1885, sees him as a man of compromise. Otto took up Augustinian philosophy of history, and in his hands it became a compromise between hieratic and laical attitudes. But it was only his monkishness which made him give way to hieratic ideals. His readiness to compromise enabled him to produce two such different works as the *Chronicle* and the *Gesta*. J. Hashagen, *Ottos von Freising als Geschichtsphilosoph und Kirchenpolitiker*, Leipzig, 1900, says that Otto changed his conception of the city of God from a mystical one to a historical one. Hence the difference between the *Chronicle* and the *Gesta*. E. Otto, *Otto von Freising und Friedrich Barbarossa*, HV, 31, 1937, thinks that Otto's views are Augustinian and that he saw the emperor as supreme in secular matters and the church as a state. He proceeded in the same spirit to the *Gesta*. J. Koch, *Die Grundlagen der Geschichtsphilosophie Ottos von Freising*, in W. Lammers ed., *Geschichtsdenken und Geschichtsbild im Mittelalter*, Darmstadt, 1961, interpreted the philosophy of history of the *Chronicle* in terms of the philosophical realism of the school of Chartres reported in the *Gesta*. He thus manages to provide the appearance of consistency by overlooking the fact that Otto purposely omitted the account of the school of Chartres from the *Chronicle* – although he had first-hand acquaintance of it; and considered it important to mention it only in the *Gesta*. – The historians' apparent determination to ignore Otto's biography, to by-pass the evidence of his early conversion to the Cistercian Order and to overlook the profound impression acquaintance with the Great Design must have made on him, is dismaying. In contrast, the interpretation of the *Chronicle* by H. M. Klinkenberg, *Der Sinn der Chronik Ottos von Freising*, in G. Kallen Festschrift, *Aus Mittelalter und Neuzeit*. Bonn, 1957, is both subtle and profound.

had been so infectious, and Rainald's and Frederick's enthusiasm so powerful, that it had been communicated in a very vital way to Otto. When he returned home, he probably set to work immediately. First, he caused a copy of the *Chronicle* to be written and introduced a number of important changes into it.[1] The copy he eventually sent to Frederick is therefore nothing less than a revised edition; or, at least, as revised as was possible in a short time and compatible with the general framework of the book. For he could not contemplate, at that stage, re-writing the whole work. But he was able to add to it some information about his new intellectual discoveries. In order to soften the general impact of the impression that the heralds of the new age were the contemplative monastic orders, with their insistence on withdrawal from the world, Otto added information about the importance of Aristotle's logic.[2] He wanted to show that the new orders were not the only thing that had happened in the early twelfth century, and that there were also developments of a more mundane and secular nature which might herald a purely utilitarian renewal of history. He also wrote a new prologue in which he stated that previously he had written 'in bitterness of spirit'. He now added: 'I shall not be slow to prosecute this joyous task [of writing a history of the reign of Frederick] with joyful mind.' A more complete change of view can hardly be imagined.

His next task was to write the history of Frederick's reign. It had been agreed that Frederick was to supply Otto with a rough sketch of the outlines of events. Otto received this outline early in 1157, and we are fortunate to have it preserved.[3] It is a plain

[1] A. D. v. d. Brincken, *Studien zur lateinischen Weltchronik bis in das Zeitalter Ottos von Freising*, Düsseldorf, 1957, p. 223 and 225. Unfortunately the revised version is the only copy which has come down to us. *Cp.* also Ch. Ch. Mierow, *The Two Cities*, New York, 1928, pp. 18–19. R. Wilman, AGDG, X, 143, points out that none of the changes made in the revised copy were important. Bernheim, *op. cit.*, p. 24 f., agrees with him. But it depends on what one is looking for. See next note.

[2] A. Hofmeister, *Studien über Otto von Freising*, NA, 37, 1911, p. 677, points out that these passages, II, 8 and V, 1, were added in the 50s by Otto himself. Hofmeister speculated that they were added because Otto knew that they would interest Rainald. It seems more probable that Otto added them for his own satisfaction. With the new developments afoot, news of philosophical innovations was worth reporting.

[3] Printed in Ch.Ch. Mierow ed., *The Deeds of Frederick Barbarossa*, New York, 1953, pp. 17–20.

recital of the facts which Frederick wanted to have incorporated in the new book. There is no mention of ideas or of any mystique of rulership. Its sentences are lapidary and unadorned. And the most noteworthy feature is that the Treaty of Constance is not mentioned. It is unsubtle in tone and concerned entirely with Frederick's honour and pride and with power politics. This is indeed a true product of Frederick's own mind. When Frederick wrote to Otto to thank him for sending a copy of the *Chronicle*, he commented on the prowess and bravery of the emperors it described. But there was not a single word about the general concept of history which had been so dear to Otto.[1]

It seems, however, that Rainald took a more sophisticated interest in the plan to write a history of Frederick's reign as part of a propaganda campaign. And it is probable that he himself supplied Otto with a fuller outline.[2] This outline became the source for a great many other historical productions of the period, and it is a great pity that, unlike Frederick's autobiographical sketch, it has been lost.[3] It must have been fuller than Frederick's sketch,

[1] E. Otto, *op. cit.*, p. 52.

[2] It seems clear that Otto was not supplied with source material. For Book I, i.e. for the years before Frederick's reign, he used nine pieces he himself had collected for his *Chronicle*; but for Book II, for Frederick's reign, he only had two pieces. These, moreover, were not specially collected but were documents which had come to him in the course of events: one, a circular letter to all German bishops, and the other, a letter addressed to him personally. See next note.

[3] R. Holtzmann, *Das Carmen de Federico I Imperatore aus Bergamo und die Anfänge einer staufischen Hofhistoriographie*, NA, 44, 1922, argues very convincingly that Rainald produced a rough sketch of the history of Frederick's early reign, and that John of Cremona's *Chronicle* (now lost), the source on which the Ligurinus was based, the *Carmen* and the *Gesta* were all dependent on Rainald's sketch. It is certainly remarkable that there is such an abundance of historical works for the early period, and that they all follow identical lines. After that there is a real dearth of narrative histories. If one examines all subsequent historiography from the thirteenth to the twentieth centuries, this fault has never been remedied. Burchard of Ursberg, for example, has a real history of Frederick down to 1162. After that he proceeds in mere annalistic form. And it seems that the fate of the modern *Jahrbücher* also depends on this circumstance: Simonsfeld in 1908 produced a first, most elaborate volume for the early period. But nobody has felt equal to the task of continuing the work. W. C. Davis, reviewing Simonsfeld's first volume in EHR, XXIV, 1909, complained then that if the work was to be continued with the same detailed elaboration, it would take 50 years for the next volume to appear. More than 50 years have elapsed and there is still no second volume. The explanation is probably not in Simonsfeld's exaggerated elaboration which nobody wants to rival, but in the fact that for the period after about 1162 there is no adequate source material, for there was no Rainald, and, after the revolution in 1156, no further incentive for providing it. R. Holtzmann was criticized in details by E. Ottmar, *Das*

and must have contained a general recital of facts and also a general hint as to the purpose of the planned book. The Treaty of Constance was unlikely to have been mentioned.[1] The idea was to give the impression that there had never been a real concord between emperor and pope, that the quarrel was endemic in the whole situation and that the real beginning of the new policy was to be found in 1152, at the very accession of Frederick.[2] In this way, the story that there had been no revolution in 1156 was propagated. There is clear evidence of Rainald's influence here. For it was Rainald who wanted to give the Great Design a specifically anti-papal twist. And when one looks at Otto's finished product, one sees indeed that the conflict with the papacy is the underlying theme of the whole book. It begins with the omission of the Treaty of Constance and ends (the final books were completed after Otto's death by his secretary Rahewin) with the triumph of Frederick's anti-pope Victor IV at the synod of Pavia. Moreover, Otto was quite explicit in stating that Rainald had had much to do with the whole plan of writing the book: the revised version of the *Chronicle* contains a special dedication to Rainald, in which Otto acknowledges his debt to Rainald's inspiration.

And so Otto set to work. 'I consider those', he wrote in the prologue, 'who write at this time as in a certain manner blessed, because after the turbulence of the past, there has dawned the unheard calm of peace.' Such was his estimate of the new prospects and the new situation brought about in 1156 by the inception of the Great Design. The result was a book which breathes an almost renaissance-like determination to set the world in order

---

Carmen de Frederico I Imperatore aus Bergamo und seine Beziehungen zu Otto – Rahewins Gesta Friderici, Gunthers Ligurinus und Burchard von Ursbergs Chronik, NA, 46; but Holtzmann's general theory must be accepted.

[1] As a result the Treaty of Constance did not find its way into history until the first attempt at a critical history of Frederick was made by H. v. Bünau in 1722.

[2] P. Rassow, *Honor Imperii*, new ed., München, 1961, fell victim to the myth propogated by Otto of Freising. Rassow is convinced that the revolution took place in 1152 on Frederick's accession. As there is no real evidence for it in the early years of Frederick's reign, Rassow was compelled to resort to unlikely interpretations of the term *honor* in the Treaty of Constance. It is remarkable that Rassow did not even mention the fact that Otto omitted the Treaty of Constance.

and to bring about an era of perfection, happiness, prosperity and peace,[1] and which was as far removed as possible from the eschatological pessimism of the earlier *Chronicle*. Otto provided the ideological background himself. In order to create a positive image of Frederick, he represented him as a *rex iustus*, as a man intent upon the maintenance of traditional law, and thus distracted the readers' attention as much as was possible from the *raison d'état* and the calculating statesmanship of the Great Design.[2] But most important of all, Otto was true to his word: he did not mention the Treaty of Constance and thus lent his pen to a gross deception in the interests of the Great Design. Frederick, throughout, is represented as a traditionalist and a conservative. And there is no clear trace of the diplomatic revolution.

Or almost no trace. Otto was an honest man. And no matter how convinced he was of the value of Frederick's and Rainald's plans, he was also a good historian, and on two occasions he almost let the cat out of the bag. When he had to relate the change of alliances and Frederick's growing coolness towards the Greeks, he first produced the official version.[3] But a little later he added, presumably from his own knowledge, the real reason, i.e., that Frederick had married Beatrix[4] and reported that there had been a change of plan. And similarly, there is a passage in the second book in which Otto almost undoes the good work done by his omission of the Treaty of Constance. He states openly that in 1156 an entirely new plan was conceived.[5]

[1] For the humanists' great interest in the *Gesta* see F. J. Schmale, *Die Gesta Friderici I Imperatoris Ottos von Freising und Rahewin*, DA, 19, 1963, p. 211.

[2] As a result of Otto's and other chroniclers' efforts to represent Frederick in an archaic rather than 'modern' light, there is a corresponding poverty of source material about Frederick's down-to-earth statesmanship. *Cp.* A. Brackmann, *Die Wandlung der Staatsanschauungen im Zeitalter Friedrichs I, Gesammelte Aufsätze*, 1941, pp. 347–50.

[3] II, xlix: the official version was that in 1155 the Greeks had falsely declared, with the help of 'surreptitiously secured letters' that Frederick had granted the Greek emperor certain regions along the Italian sea coast. Not even Otto suggests that the letters had been forged. They were probably genuine enough and Frederick now merely used their undiplomatic use by the Greeks as an excuse for breaking off relations.

[4] *Gesta*, II, xlviii.

[5] II, liii. In the following, last chapter of Book II, Otto wrote: 'When the emperor met his uncle on the field where the latter was encamped under tents nearly two German miles from the town, with all the great and important men present, the plan which had for so long been kept secret was announced.' The plan was the issue of the *privilegium minus* and, we must presume, the whole of the new policies. In Chapter xlix

But these minor lapses into truthfulness apart, Otto completed – or rather began – his work in great style. He prefaced his account of Frederick's reign by a long book on the preceding years. And there he wrote, in complete contrast to the version he had given of these same decades in the *Chronicle*, that Conrad's reign had been a real success.[1] This was not necessarily a complete falsification: Otto simply had changed his mind. He now saw Conrad's reign as a preparation for Frederick's and wanted to produce as much evidence as possible for continuity. Secondly, he took the opportunity for introducing a glowing account of the emergence of the Staufen family in history as if it were a ray of light in the realm of darkness prevailing at the beginning of the twelfth century.[2] In the *Chronicle* there had been no corresponding account. Thirdly, and this is most important, he gave great prominence to the reports about the teaching of Peter Abelard and Gilbert of Poitiers. One might at first be surprised that he should think it necessary to introduce such thorny philosophical problems into a history of the reign of Frederick. But Otto was determined to show that the reign was connected with the emergence in the twelfth century of a new spirit in general, and that it had something to do with what later historians were to call the Renaissance of the twelfth century. We have a new departure in thought as well as in government, he seems to be saying.[3] Fourthly, again in marked contrast with his views in the *Chronicle*, he tries to justify the second crusade. True, he wrote, it did not have the desired effects. But it must all the

---

Otto wrote in similar vein: upon learning that William had beaten the Greeks (and made an alliance with the pope), Frederick 'changed his plan and directed his wrath against the people of Milan, to quell their arrogance'. Otto could not have been more explicit in stating the truth about the revolution at the end of Book II had he been writing in a completely disinterested spirit. He speaks of the new policies as a new plan in two places. – *See* also *Gesta*, II, xlix and I.

[1] *Gesta*, I, lxx. [2] *Gesta*, I, viii.

[3] Rahewin, completing the *Gesta*, reports that on his death-bed Otto asked for the passages in Book I about Abelard and Gilbert of Poitiers to be altered. He regretted having written as he did because he might thus have given offence to the church: IV, xiv. We do not know whether what we are reading now in Book I is Rahewin's redaction in accordance with Otto's wish or not. But the fact that Otto, when dying, had regrets about these chapters proves that Otto knew that what he had originally written there was written in the 'new spirit' of dialectical philosophy. And this is clear proof that he considered those philosophical developments somehow connected with the new plan, for the sake of which he was writing the whole work.

same have been good for a great many souls.[1] This was a back-handed compliment, but he felt that he owed that much to the memory of Conrad and to his revised estimate of Conrad's reign.

The *Gesta Friderici Imperatoris* is not only one of the finest biographies of the middle ages, but also our chief source of information for the early years of Frederick's reign. In a few places, however, it must be treated with caution. First of all there is the omission of the Treaty of Constance and the resulting bias it gives to the first phase of the reign. Then, the Treaty of Benevento is also omitted. Since it was the immediate occasion for the conception of the Great Design, Otto thought it wiser not to mention it, lest the reader might wonder whether this change of papal policy had not produced a response in imperial policy. And then there are several incidents which Otto decided to magnify enormously in order to provide an opportunity for setting out Rainald's ideology of the grandeur of the empire, his belief that the emperor is superior to the pope and his conviction that all his policies were consistently informed by his high-minded conception of law and the imperial dignity.[2] In one place, also, Otto saw fit to charge Arnold of Brescia (wrongly) with the authorship of the Roman revolution in order to justify Frederick's harsh treatment of Arnold.[3] He also completely revised his opinions of the Wittelsbach family. Otto von Wittelsbach was a close associate of Rainald and became a loyal servant of Frederick. In the *Chronicle*, Otto of Freising had vented his hatred on the whole family.[4] There is none of this in the *Gesta*.

These things apart, Otto's *Gesta* not only served its immediate

[1] *Gesta*, I, lxv. This is in marked contrast to his lamentations about the second crusade in the *Chronicle*.

[2] I am thinking especially of the way in which Otto let himself go on the Wichmann affair and on Frederick's quarrel with the Roman senate in 1155.

[3] It seems that Otto knew the real truth about Arnold's connections with the Roman rebellion. He accused him of the authorship of this rebellion in *Gesta*, I, xxviii. And in *Gesta*, II, xxviii, he says that Arnold 'as he found it [Rome] aroused to rebellion against its pope, he incited it all the more to revolt'. But in the *Chronicle*, VII, 31 and 34, he described the outbreak of the rebellion without reference to Arnold and obviously did not consider him responsible for it.

[4] *Gesta*, VI, xx. It is true, however, that Otto von Wittelsbach appears as the faithful servant of Frederick and friend of Rahewin first in Book III, written, most probably, by Rahewin.

purpose of promoting the Great Design, but is of great value in its own right. Without it, the history of Frederick could never be written. Because inadvertently – in fact in flagrant opposition to the intention for which it was composed – it provides incontrovertible proof of the change of plan in 1156 and of the inception of the Great Design. For its omission of the Treaty of Constance brands it as a tract for the times, written and conceived in a partisan spirit in the years 1156 and 1157, when it was vital to Frederick and Rainald to parade in front of the world as if the Treaty of Constance had never been signed and as if no change of plan was being contemplated. Without Otto's *Gesta* we would perhaps never really have understood the magnitude of the intended revolution. For without the *Gesta* we would never have known exactly *how* important it was, at this stage, to falsify history. For that matter, the story of the life of Otto of Freising, which we have been able to plot, shows the far-reaching and revolutionary nature of the change of plan in 1156–1157. For there is no other explanation of the fact that an ageing Cistercian bishop should suddenly revise his whole conception of history and substitute an outward going hope for a world-denying withdrawal. Such a substitution is psychologically almost implausible, for it is usually young men who are optimistic; and ageing men who are pessimistic. If it were not for Frederick's and Rainald's infectious enthusiasm, Otto of Freising's intellectual development would be psychologically completely inexplicable.

In the meantime, the first effect of the change of plan and the reversal of alliances was a clash with Pope Hadrian. This clash was very largely brought about by Pope Hadrian and his chancellor Roland, for reasons which were entirely connected with the internal policies of the *curia*. There had been a very serious conflict in the cardinals' college over the Treaty of Benevento and the Sicilian alliance. It had only been with great difficulty that Hadrian and Roland had been able to have their way and conclude the alliance, for there were many cardinals who were bitterly opposed to it. And it was for this reason that Roland and Hadrian decided upon a political manœuvre which would teach them a practical lesson and prove to them how dangerous the emperor was to papal aspirations and, by implication, how justified and necessary the Sicilian alliance was.[1]

When Hadrian, just prior to his election to the papal see, had been in Sweden, he had made friends with Eskil, the archbishop of Lund. When the latter heard of Hadrian's election, he decided to make the long journey to Rome to pay his respects. Returning from Rome in 1156, on his way home through Germany, he was set upon by robbers who not only deprived him of his property but also held him in captivity and demanded a ransom. It seems a curious coincidence that robbers, acting in their own interest, should at that very moment have provided an occasion for a conflict – for although Eskil's journey to Rome had been undertaken without ulterior motive, it so happened that Frederick saw in Eskil an enemy. For Eskil had been responsible for the withdrawal of the northern churches from the primacy of the see of Hamburg. This withdrawal, it was held, had diminished the authority of the empire, since the see of Hamburg was clearly an imperial see. As a result, Frederick did not rush to Eskil's rescue[2] and Eskil himself was not anxious for the ransom to be paid, whether because he liked to see himself as a martyr, or because he did not mind being the occasion for the planned conflict between Hadrian and Frederick. For Hadrian immediately took up his cause and

[1] I follow M. Pacaut, *Alexandre III*, Paris, 1956, pp. 92–3. Pacaut's version is particularly plausible when one follows it up by reading what Rahewin says in *Gesta*, III, xvi. On his return Roland reported the Besançon incident in Rome and the clergy there were very divided among themselves, for there was a party who favoured the emperor and a party who upheld the wishes of their pontiff. Several years later a pro-imperial writer stated that the journey to Besançon had been engineered by Roland. *Cp. De Schismate*, etc. in Sudendorf, No. XXII, pp. 62 ff. W. Ribbeck, *Der Traktat über die Papstwahl des Jahres 1159*, FDG, 25, 1185, considers it to have been written by a supporter of Victor IV in 1161–2.

[2] There is considerable disagreement as to whether Frederick had a hand in the capture of Eskil or not. Alexander III was to insist that Frederick had engineered the whole incident: J. M. Watterich, *Vitae Pontificum Romanorum*, Leipzig, 1862, II, p. 491. A. Hauck, IV, 223, n. 5, thinks this to have been a libel. But what really matters is not who caused the incident, but how it was exploited. K. Schambach, *Friedrich Rotbart und Eskil von Lund*. HV, 13, 1910, says that Frederick hated Eskil because Eskil was hostile to King Sven of Denmark, a vassal of Frederick. H. Simonsfeld, *Friedrich Rotbart und Eskil von Lund*, HV, 15, 1912, believes that Frederick hated Eskil because Eskil had opposed the aspirations of the archbishop of Bremen in Sweden. Simonsfeld, pp. 497 ff, thinks that Frederick was innocent of Eskil's capture, but admits that Frederick refused to help Eskil. Hadrian's own statement is, diplomatically, ambiguous about the degree of Frederick's guilt in this affair.

interpreted the whole incident as a calculated attack upon papal prestige. Letters were exchanged and when no conclusion was reached Hadrian sent two special legates to Besançon where, in September 1157, Frederick was holding a great court.

Hadrian obviously attached the greatest importance to these negotiations, for one of the legates he sent was no less a person than Cardinal Roland, the man who had always been his closest counsellor. Frederick officially received the legates in the presence of a large assembly of princes, and at that assembly the legates read a letter which Hadrian had sent through them. In this letter Hadrian complained about the treatment of Eskil and reminded Frederick that such treatment was an insult to the papacy, all the harder to forgive in view of the fact that he, the pope, had given him the imperial crown and the full power of empire, and that, if it had been possible, he would have given him even greater *beneficia*.

It is more than likely that Hadrian and Roland knew that the word *beneficia* had a double meaning and hoped that in Besançon Frederick and his associates would take offence. They knew from their experience in Sutri over the *strator* incident that Frederick was particularly sensitive to the suggestion that the emperor was a papal vassal and that the empire was a papal benefice. On an earlier occasion, Frederick had also begged the pope to have the paintings in the Lateran, on which the Emperor Lothair was represented as a papal vassal, removed.[1] It was therefore very

[1] These notorious paintings have not survived but are mentioned as a bone of contention between Frederick and Hadrian in *Gesta,* III, xi. Rahewin there says expressly that people were led to accept the literal meaning of *beneficia* in Besançon because they remembered those paintings. In 1155, in Rome, Frederick had taken exception to these paintings and Hadrian had promised to have them removed. The paintings present Lothair III and the pope. In the first Lothair comes to the City, in the second the emperor 'homo fit papae' (as the inscription ran), and in the third he is crowned. There is some doubt as to the precise scene represented in the middle one. P. Schramm, *Die deutschen Kaiser und Könige in Bildern ihrer Zeit,* Leipzig, 1928, p. 219, believed it to be a coronation scene rather than a feudal act of homage. In this interpretation he followed the description of Lothair's coronation in the *Chron. reg. Col.* But, first, this explanation does not do justice to the inscription for the middle part. And a drawing of the three pictures by Panvinio of the sixteenth century shows quite clearly that the author of the *Chron. reg. Col.* could not have seen the paintings and believed that the second and third were one single picture. G. Ladner, *I mosaici e gli affreschi ecclesiastici-politici nell'antico palazzo lateranense* RAC, II, 1935, says that the middle painting does not show the imposition of the crown but an act of *commendatio.* This is in keeping with the inscription and such an act was performed by Frederick in 1155 as well as by

probable that now, too, Frederick would not resist the opportunity of protesting. If he did protest, Roland and Hadrian could then turn to the other cardinals who were opposed to the Sicilian alliance and point out that the emperor was indeed unreliable and even hostile to the pope. And even if the worst came to the worst, Roland and Hadrian could always claim that the narrow, feudal meaning of *beneficia* had not been intended and that the whole incident was based upon a misunderstanding.

As it happened, Rainald and his friend Otto von Wittelsbach completely fell into the trap.[1] Roland immediately sensed his advantage. And instead of apologizing at once by pointing at the double meaning of the word, he continued to provoke Rainald by adding that, after all, the emperor *had* received his crown from the

---

Lothair. But in that case, M. Maccarone, *op. cit.*, p. 135, points out, the emperor would be shown on his knees (cp. Boso's description, p. 392), whereas in the Panvinio sketch of the painting he is standing. E. Eichmann, *Die römishen Eide der deutschen Könige*, ZSSRGkan, VI, 1916, p. 191, believes that the painting showed an act of *commendatio*; but not for the coronation, but for the investiture with the Matildan lands. Rainald and Frederick knew this, but objected to the paintings because they disliked the close association between a feudal investiture, albeit for the Matildan lands, and the coronation. M. Maccarone, *op. cit.*, p. 135–6, makes this last view even more plausible by pointing out that in Panvinio's sketch the middle painting shows actually an investiture *per anulum*, as is indeed recorded to have taken place when Lothair received the Matildan lands (MGH, Const. I, p. 169). P. Classen, reviewing Maccarone, HZ, 195, 1962, p. 380, says that if this were true, we would see the ring clearly. Because, he adds, it is not compatible with the principles of medieval iconography that the most important feature of the ceremony depicted is not shown. Classen must have overlooked the fact that we know these paintings only through Panvinio's sketches and that Panvinio was not a medieval iconographer but a sixteenth century draughtsman who was less interested in symbolism than in the artistic composition of the work. Hence there is no reason why he should not have omitted the ring. At any rate, the emperor's outstretched finger is clearly visible and that makes Maccarone's view completely plausible, for it is compatible with Panvinio's drawing, with the text of the description of the way in which Lothair was invested with the Matildan lands, and with the inscription. F. Kempf, *Kononistik und kuriale Politik im 12. Jahrhundert*, APH, I, 1963, p. 24, n. 20, prefers Ladner's theory to that of Maccarone. But whatever the precise meaning of the paintings, Frederick had reason enough to object because of the inscription 'homo fit papae', even if it did refer to the investiture of Lothair with the Matildan lands.

[1] M. Maccarone, *Papato e Impero*, Rome, 1959, p. 208 ff., believes that Rahewin's account of the Besançon incident was inspired by Rainald. But P. Classen, reviewing Maccarone, HZ, 195, 1962, p. 381, points out that this is very unlikely. Rahewin, at that time, was living in Freising and all his personal connections were with Otto's successor, Bishop Albert, with Eberhard of Salzburg and Eberhard of Bamberg, that is, all men who were less than friendly with Rainald and did not favour his policies. It is more likely that the *Chron. reg. Col.* account of the incident was inspired by Rainald.

pope, thus suggesting the narrowest possible papalist interpretation of the coronation. At this, there was an immediate tumult. Otto von Wittelsbach is said to have drawn his sword against the cardinals, and it was only due to Frederick's personal interference that bloodshed was avoided. As the news of the insult got around, there was even popular clamour against the cardinals. It was only with some difficulty that they regained their lodgings safely.

The legates were ordered to return straight to Rome, partly to prevent their making contacts in Germany, and partly to assure their personal safety, for Rainald and Otto von Wittelsbach had seen to it that the antagonism against them had become very noticeable.

The following day a manifesto was publicly issued, in which Frederick attacked the pope for his violation of the peace and asserted that he was emperor by the election of the princes and the grace of God,[1] and that anyone who suggested that the emperor

[1] The manifesto is in *Gesta*, II, xi and also in MGH, Const, I, No. 165. *See* K. Hampe, *Deutsche Kaisergeschichte*, Baethgen ed., Heidelberg, 1963, p. 161, and R. Jordan, *Die Stellung des deutschen Espiskopats im Kampf um die Universalmacht unter Friederich I*, Würzburg, 1939, p. 40, believe it was written by Rainald. R. M. Herkenrath, *Rainald von Dassel als Verfasser und Schreiber von Kaiserurkunden*, MIOG, LXXII, 1964, p. 56, is more cautious and says that Rainald had a hand in its composition. N. Höing, *Die 'Trierer Stilübungen'*, AfD, II, 1956, p. 125 f. believes that it was written by Eberhard of Bamberg. Höing admits that this does not necessarily mean that Rainald did not assist. Indeed, Eberhard did not draw away from the inner circle for another year or so. – It is noteworthy that this manifesto is the first occasion on which it was stated clearly that the emperor owed his power to the election of the princes. *Cp.* H. Bloch, *Die staufischen Kaiserwahlen*, Leipzig, 1911, pp. 11 and 19. – Since Gregory VII, it was taken that *ecclesia sacerdotium* was superior to *regnum*. The Besançon quarrel was concerned with this. Hadrian sided with Gregory VII, and Frederick opposed Gregory's view. For Frederick, *regnum* was independent of *sacerdotium*. This is the core of the manifesto. – F. Heer, *Aufgang Europas*, Wien-Zürich, 1949, pp. 605–6, argues that the dispute shows that it was due to a genuine misunderstanding caused by the changing meaning of words. Rainald, he says, was all caught in the old, feudal meaning of *beneficium* and with his traditional style of thinking could not understand that Roland used the word in its new sense, in which it meant a 'favour'. Heer believes that the dispute was due to the clash of the old world of thought with the new world of thought. – Whatever Hadrian and Roland meant by the word *beneficium*, it is noteworthy that Honorius Augustodunensis, for instance, had interpreted the Donation of Constantine to mean precisely that after Constantine had divested himself of the empire, it had been given back to him by the pope. Here then, as also in St Bernard and John of Salisburg, we find something like a feudal interpretation of the coronation. And Carlyle, *A History of Medieval Political Thought*, London, 1922, Vol. IV, pp. 334–6, notes that these thoughts are in harmony with Rainald's interpretation of Hadrian's letter. *Cp.* G. Laehr, *Die konstantinische Schenkung in der abendländischen Literatur*, EHS, 166, 1926, p. 59. Reading the *Chronicle*, IV, iii, one cannot help feeling that Otto of Freising had his doubts as to

was the feudal vassal of the pope offended against the doctrine of God as proclaimed by St Peter. For the time being, nothing further was done. Hadrian wrote to the German bishops to defend himself, and eventually he tried to withdraw by insisting that he had meant the word *beneficium* in the general and vague sense, in which it meant a 'favour'. Letters went to and fro, and the breach did not become final. Hadrian appears to have been concerned to avoid a complete rupture, as was Frederick also. Hadrian formulated various demands to Frederick; Frederick rejected them, but was obviously willing to negotiate. And there the matter stood by the middle of the following year when Frederick decided to set out for the campaign to Lombardy, to proclaim the Great Design publicly and use force in the event that some cities would not accept it.

---

the validity and genuineness of the Donation of Constantine. *Cp.* H. V. Voltelini, SWA, Vol, No. 4, p. 31, and ZSSRger, 50, 1930, p. 440. Frederick may well have shared these doubts. By the time of the Besançon incident he was certainly acquainted with the *Chronicle*.

CHAPTER V

The Great Design

In Swabia and Alsace there was no need for special measures and policies to pursue and implement the Great Design. Even if the ultimate aim was new and revolutionary, there was nothing very startling in the methods required to realize that aim. Frederick persistently and steadily continued to collect more and more lordships, to extend the range of existing ones, to collect church fiefs and to found cities in order to develop his holdings into one single compact territory.

In Burgundy the court held at Besançon in 1157 proved a milestone. Combining his imperial rights with the more material lordships enjoyed by him through his marriage to Beatrix, Frederick managed to rally the ecclesiastical lords of Burgundy and a great many of the lay nobles. The nature of his rule in Burgundy was less concrete than his rule in Alsace and Swabia. But, for the time being, it sufficed to have it recognized and to receive the homage of the Burgundian clergy and nobility.

There remained Lombardy, the centre piece of the new state, a land rich in cities and teeming with a population who had money, with people who were to be persuaded to pay real taxes to the emperor. But for that very reason Frederick was aware that the inhabitants of Lombardy were likely to put up a stiff resistance to the Great Design. They did not mind recognizing Frederick as the general overlord of Lombardy and paying homage to him in some vague manner. But Frederick knew that the more concrete implications of the Great Design might not be generally popular in Lombardy, and he was therefore prepared to meet the challenge, if necessary, with military force. It is improbable that he knew in early 1158, when he assembled his army at Pentecost, near Augsburg, for the expedition to Italy, how stiff that resistance would be.

For it is unlikely that Frederick or any of his advisers was able to form an accurate assessment of the social and economic development which had taken place in Lombardy during the preceding century.

The social and economic transformation of Lombardy had indeed been rapid and profound. Old Roman cities had begun to revive, and dozens of smaller, village-like settlements had expanded and developed into towns. By the middle of the twelfth century, the whole of Lombardy was covered with these cities, the largest of which was Milan – but even Milan was, by modern standards, a smallish town. The others were even smaller – but each was surrounded by walls; and some of them were quite impregnable fortresses. This growth seems to have been caused, first, during the preceding century by a steep population increase[1] which, in turn, had made a more intensive cultivation of the soil necessary; secondly, towards the beginning of the twelfth century, by a very marked increase in commercial activity resulting from the crusades and the opening up of the Mediterranean. The ports had been the first to benefit; but as goods were seeking their way inland, other cities had developed in the wake of Venice, Genoa and Pisa.

We are unfortunately ignorant of the precise cause of this economic development and of the rise of towns in northern Italy. Cipolla believes that the ultimate origin of this movement was something like a change of heart – an almost mysterious combination of optimism, confidence and concord.[2] Schumpeter might have described this period as one of 'the creative reactions of history'. But such notions do not really explain, they only draw attention to the tremendous psychological vigour which must have been operative during those early centuries – a factor which the historian cannot afford to overlook. Doren reminds us of a number of concrete factors. First, the remnants of ancient cities were

[1] It is estimated that during the twelfth century the population of many Italian cities increased from 5,000 to 30,000. *Cp.* G. Luzzato, *An Economic History of Italy*, London, 1961, p. 80. *Cp.* also P. J. Jones, *La storia agraria italiana nel medio evo*, RSI, LXXVI, 1964, p. 290. The population increase reached its peak between 1150 and 1250. *Cp.* J. C. Russell, *Late Ancient and Medieval Population*, TAPhS, N. S., Vol. 48, Pt. 3, p. 109.

[2] C. M. Cipolla, ed., *Storia economica italiana*, Torino, 1959. Introd. p. 9.

available.[1] Secondly, Italy had easy access to the Mediterranean orient, and during the century which preceded the first crusade, the Saracens were being cleared from the Mediterranean, especially from Corsica, Sardinia and Sicily. This fact by itself was no doubt a strong impetus to commercial revival.[2] Thirdly, feudalism had never gained a complete hold in northern Italy and therefore tended to disappear more rapidly. Hence there was no very strong resistance to urban communalism.[3] And last, but not least, there had taken place in the eleventh century the spread of popular heretical movements. Pope Gregory VII, for political reasons, had supported these popular movements and his support had appealed to the working classes and seems to have mobilized them for commercial enterprise.[4] It is possible that the original impulse to economic growth had come from an agrarian crisis and an agrarian revolution which had made both manpower and capital available. An increase in intensive and extensive agricultural cultivation might have made it possible for urban populations to be fed; and the rural population's increased wealth had provided a market for the products of the cities.[5]

Whatever the exact causes, the urban development of Lombardy in the twelfth century had a number of very distinctive and remarkable features. During the eleventh century there had been vast conflicts of classes. But by the early twelfth century the class struggle disappeared almost completely. The town acted like a magnet to all classes of people.[6] The landed aristocracy lived in the city, and the merchants of the city owned land. Hence the two classes did not draw apart because there was a community of interests.[7]

[1] A. Doren, *Italienische Wirtschaftsgeschichte*, Jena, 1934, I, p. 164.

[2] *ibid.*, p. 147. [3] *ibid.*, p. 164. [4] *ibid.*, p. 151.

[5] *Cp.* the stimulating papers by D. Herlihy, *The History of the Rural Seigneury in Italy, 751–1200*, AH, 33, 1959; *The Agrarian Revolution in Southern France and Italy, 801–1150*, Sp, XXXIII, 1958; and the remarks by P. C. Jones, *La storia agraria italiana nel medio evo*, ASI, LXXVI, pp. 300 f., 333, on the close interdependence between rural and urban growth in eleventh and twelfth century Italy.

[6] W. Goetz, *Die Entstehung der italienischen Kommunen*, SBA, 1944, 1, pp. 96–7.

[7] The lower nobility drifted towards the cities not only because there was wealth to be made there, but also because the lower nobility's estates tended to lose their labourers to the city. *Cp.* W. Goetz, *op. cit.*, p. 97; H. Pirenne, *Les villes et les institutions urbaines*, Bruxelles–Paris, 1939, pp. 393 ff. *See* also M. Weber, *Die Stadt*, pp. 649 ff., and E. Ennen, *Frühgeschichte der europäischen Stadt*, Bonn. 1953, pp. 251 ff., pp. 261, 266; R. Lopez, *Aux origines du capitalisme Génois*, AHES, 9, 1937, p. 448; M. Merores, *Der*

This community of interests[1] between all classes had very important political and social results. There was, first and foremost, a great deal of social mobility. It was comparatively easy for people to rise in the social ladder. Moreover, this social fusion found an important and direct expression in the military situation. The estate of warriors or knights, originally a class of feudal and landed people, joined harmoniously with the merchants, and this made for good armies.[2] This common military service, in turn, increased the tendency towards social mobility and helped to stop the erection of rigid class barriers.[3] It is equally remarkable that during the twelfth century the petit-bourgeois artisans disappeared as a class from active politics – to re-emerge again at the very end of the century.[4] The reason for the disappearance of these men as a class with separate interests is that they did not *have* separate interests. In that age of rapid economic expansion, they too were easily drawn into the growing community. Hence the internal life of the cities was comparatively peaceful and harmonious. This social mobility and harmony of interests led to a peaceful expansion of each town until the point was reached when this expansion came into geographical conflict with the areas in which other towns were expanding equally peacefully. There was a double movement around each city, in the twelfth century. On the one hand the commune invaded the *contado* in order to protect its interests and extend its authority beyond the walls and suburbs of the town. On the other hand, there was a massive migration from the *contado* to the town.[5]

Indeed, this harmony of interests and this social mobility had important political repercussions. Before the age of the Investiture Contest the Lombard bishops had, theoretically at

---

venezianische Adel, VSW, 19, 1926, p. 231; C. W. Prévité-Orton, CMH, V, 1926, pp. 235 ff.

[1] G. Luzzato, *op. cit.*, p. 67: 'Despite the evident part played by merchants (in the rise of the commune) there is clearly nothing in these events to indicate the triumph of business over landed interests. It would be truer to speak of merchants buying their way into the middle class of land-owners with the proceeds of trade.'

[2] H. Delbrück, *Geschichte der Kriegskunst*, Berlin, 1923, Pt. III, p. 348.

[3] E. Ennen, *op. cit.*, p. 262. *Cp.* W. Goetz, *op. cit.*, pp. 83, 91, 92, 94, 97, 101 for examples of social mobility.

[4] A. Doren, *op. cit.*, I, pp. 250–1.

[5] G. Luzzato, *op. cit.*, pp. 78–80.

least, exercised the rights and functions of counts. But with the emergence of the communes, the inhabitants of the towns had eventually wrested the right to elect their own town magistrates from the bishops, and thus a complete system of self-government had emerged. In the eleventh century there had been bitter strife and frequent warfare over the emergence of such independence. But in the twelfth century, the evolution of self-government was proceeding smoothly. In practically all cities the detachment of the citizens from their lords took place without a struggle. In Genoa and many other cities, the archbishop, far from opposing the free election of town officials, joined the commune.[1] It seems that this peaceful evolution of self-government had something to do with the comparative primitiveness of the economic life of the towns. Before the thirteenth century it was indeed very exceptional for the economic life of any one town to support a single class of merchants, let alone of artisans, powerful enough and numerous enough to take the lead in any political conflict and seize hold of urban government.[2] Hence urban government consisted of a fusion of all classes. In Milan, for instance, the consuls were composed in 1135 in the following way: there were seven consuls belonging to the *capitanei*, the large landowners, seven consuls belonging to the lesser nobility, and seven consuls belonging to the class of ordinary citizens.[3] High and low, consuls and bishops, merchants and nobles were all acting together.[4]

It is interesting to examine the extent to which Frederick and his advisers were acquainted with the peculiarity of these conditions in the twelfth century. Frederick certainly knew of the enor-

[1] W. Goetz, *op. cit.*, p. 101. 'The Investiture struggle in Italy had destroyed the power of the bishops. In order to secure the fealty of their vassals, the bishops had been forced to surrender the property of their churches to them. The episcopal positions in the cities were further undermined by the schisms: the decision whether a bishop was to be papal or imperial was left in the hands of the wealthy families, for the bishops for the most part had become dependent on them. Thus the cities were the real beneficiaries of the Investiture contest . . . Thus the bishops were no longer able to support an imperial policy . . . Only in places where the odd bishop had managed to retain the *regalia* in his own hands, was it possible for the old close relation between bishop and emperor to persist'; I. Ott, *Der Regalienbegriff im 12. Jahrhundert*, ZSSRGkan, 35, 1948, p. 273.

[2] G. Luzzato, *op. cit.*, p. 68.

[3] E. Ennen, *op. cit.*, p. 276.

[4] W. Goetz, *op. cit.*, p. 83. *Cp.* also pp. 120–1.

mous social mobility in these Lombard cities.[1] But he was not able to understand the implication of this mobility. If there is mobility and no social strife worth mentioning, it follows that the nobility for the most part had joined or were joining the citizens peacefully. But Frederick was not aware of this. Accustomed as he was to the rural conditions of Germany, he believed that the nobility had been forced into the cities against their will and were being subjected to the commune by force.[2] His ignorance of this implication also made him blind to the fact that in none of these cities was there a party permanently opposed in principle to a ruling party. As a result, he did not know that he could not count on the firm support in any city of any one group or class. Any city, if sufficiently provoked, was therefore likely to present a common front to the emperor. This situation, of course, was very different from the conditions which were to prevail in the following century. During the thirteenth century, class struggle was once more to become the order of the day in each city. And it was therefore possible for a genuine party-system to emerge. Then, too, every city came to be split into an imperial (Ghibelline) and a papal (Guelf) party, and Frederick's grandson, Frederick II, was therefore able to count everywhere on a certain amount of support. But during the age of Frederick I the emperor's only chance was to rely on the incessant inter-urban rivalries, on the hatred of one city for another. But these inter-urban rivalries, unlike the later urban class struggles, were fortuitous and unstable. They depended entirely on the aggressive policies of one town against another town and could therefore, when political prudence commanded it, be easily composed. Although such rivalries could be bitter they lacked any element of permanence and did not provide a stable ground on which Frederick might have been able to build up a solid party in support of his policies and of the Great Design.

Frederick also knew that the self-government of the towns was of comparatively recent origin.[3] He concluded that there might still

[1] *Gesta*, II, xiii. [2] *loc. cit.*

[3] *ibid.*, II, xv. E. Ennen, *op. cit.*, p. 275, gives the following dates for the origin of consuls: Lucca, 1091; Pisa, 1081; Milan, 1094; Asti, 1095; Genoa, 1099; Arezzo, 1098; Pavia, 1105; Bergamo, after 1122; Bologna, 1123; Siena, 1125; Brescia, 1127; Modena, from 1135–6; Verona, 1135–6; Florence, 1138.

be time to check this development. But he was ignorant of the economic and social conditions which had caused this political development and attributed it instead to mere wilfulness and to arbitrary disobedience.[1] In this attribution he was wrong. He also ignored the strong emotional undercurrent of this development. Ever since the days of the Investiture contest, when the Emperor Henry IV had counteracted popular movements in the cities by supporting the local bishops and archbishops against the heretics, and when Pope Gregory had supported the heretical movements because he disapproved of the emperor-sponsored, simoniacal bishops, the people in the towns had identified the authority of the emperor with the heresy of simony, and had considered their own resistance to the empire as a form of religious rectitude. The ecclesiastical reform movement of the preceding century had indeed made a strong appeal to all citizens who wanted to gain independence from episcopal government, and thus the political revolution and the ecclesiastical reform movement had joined forces.[2] In the twelfth century, the bishops had been drawn into the city government and the old conflict between citizens and bishops had been peacefully composed.[3] But the emotional undertone had remained, and any emperor who attacked the right to self-government had to reckon with the possibility of being identified by the citizens as a heretic supporting and advocating simony. And during the struggle against Frederick's attempt to impose the Great Design in Lombardy, this undertone came to be expressed in a general formula: the emperor was regarded as a heretic, and all heretics were Arians. The citizens of Milan, fighting for their independence, chose as their symbol their saintly Archbishop Ambrose who had chased the Arians from the city. When the walls of Milan were finally rebuilt in the early 70s, a relief depicting this event was displayed on them.[4] Frederick was

[1] *Gesta*, II, xv. [2] W. Goetz, *op. cit.*, p. 48. [3] *ibid.*, pp. 83–4.

[4] These sculptures are now in the *Museo Civico* of Milan. For the connection between ecclesiastical reform and the movement for civic liberty, *see* C. Violante, *La pataria milanese e la riforma ecclesiastica*, Rome, 1955. To the Lombard cities, the emperor appeared ever since the second half of the eleventh century as (a) the head of an oppressive feudal hierarchy, (b) the chief exponent of the sin of simony, (c) the oppressor of civic liberties. *Cp.* L. Chiapelli, *La formazione storica del commune cittadino it Italia*, ASI, 1930, 14, p. 54. By the middle of the twelfth century the feudal hierarchy had ceased

not aware of these associations and was therefore not able to gauge the strength of the purely emotional and religious resistance to his plans. He saw that resistance as a form of disobedience to a lawful ruler.

Frederick had had first hand experience of a more or less popular commune when he had met the citizens of Rome in 1155 before his coronation.[1] But he had obviously not learnt the lesson. Moreover, his general assessment of the situation in Lombardy was partially wrong. He believed that ancient law, under which the people of Lombardy had been governed by their bishops exercising the power of counts bestowed on them by the emperor, had simply been discarded and that no new law had emerged to take its place.[2] Although this idea was partially correct, for the rivalries between the cities were indeed fierce, and no ordered system of government and no system of adjudicating between these rivalries existed, inside each city there *was* a new law. And Frederick was quite wrong in thinking that the state of lawlessness was universal.

There was one other aspect in the situation which was to prove troublesome to Frederick. The wealth of these cities, such as it was, was mostly based on trade and agriculture. There was very little manufacture. Each town extended, so to speak, beyond the city walls, and the so-called *contado* spread around it with a radius of approximately ten to fifteen miles. The owners of the land had gone to live in the towns; but had by no means relinquished agricultural activities or discontinued their control of them. This meant that a very large number of city families owned and derived their income from owned manors and farms outside the city. This unusual feature of Lombard city life aided the undoing of Frederick. For it meant that his policy of destroying towns when they proved too defiant was ultimately completely unsuccessful. True, when a city was razed to the ground there was much lamentation; but the citizens simply dispersed in the countryside and probably found shelter in the farms and manors. When

to be oppressive and the bishops had ceased to be simoniacal and had instead been drawn into the movement for city self-government. But the old associations continued to exercise their spell and in the 60s, Alexander III made the most of them.

[1] *See* Ch. III, p. 84 above. [2] *Gesta*, II, xiii.

Frederick's army departed, they came out again and started to rebuild. And since the buildings in the city were for the most part fairly primitive ones, the rebuilding was neither too onerous nor too laborious. In this way, any direct retaliation against a city proved rather fruitless. Frederick, of course, was not a simpleton. At times he pursued a scorched earth policy. But he could never scorch the earth for more than a season at a time and he realized that such primitive measures could not intimidate the people permanently.

The cities had evolved a form of complete self-government. They controlled their own affairs and administration of justice and elected their own officials. They enjoyed the revenue from their own markets and tolls, and tried to increase it by encroaching upon those of their neighbours. In this way some of them had built up little empires, the most formidable of which was that of Milan. The Milanese had subjected the city of Lodi, and continuously threatened Cremona by supporting Crema, situated opposite Cremona. Brescia was pro-Milanese and therefore her neighbour Bergamo, was anti-Milanese. Both Pavia and Piacenza were anti-Milanese. But there was nothing permanent in this pattern, even though it was based roughly on geographical logic.

There was nothing in the Great Design that was incompatible with the existence of these cities as such. It is a mistake to think that Frederick was opposed to urban development on principle, or that, as a rustic squire from the Teutonic forests, he failed to appreciate the importance of city life. He was on the contrary most appreciative of the fact that with cities and trade a ruler might collect taxes in cash; and that cash might increase a ruler's freedom of movement. An imperial administration entirely dependent upon the collection of supplies in the form of feudal dues in kind was not nearly as elastic as one which could command revenue in money. It was not the intention of the Great Design to stop city development or even impede it. The Great Design was merely intended to assure that the cities should recognize Frederick as their real lord and allow him to be the primary beneficiary of their wealth. It was directed against the independence of the cities and at their self-government. Lombardy was included in the Great Design not just because it was geographically convenient to do so; but mainly because it happened to be economically advanced and progressive. In Lombardy cash was available and a ruler might therefore be able to collect large sums of money in the form of taxes and contributions. All the other lands over which Frederick ruled in one capacity or another were still deeply embedded in a purely natural economy. But a reassertion of imperial rights in Lombardy would yield enormous financial benefits.[1]

In spite of the imperfect knowledge[2] at Frederick's disposal when he ventured into Lombardy in 1158, the venture was not entirely foolhardy. It was based on the belief that the people of Lombardy were themselves suffering from the complete absence of an overlord and that the internecine warfare and the incessant rivalries between the towns were depriving their inhabitants of the finest fruits of the economic growth which was taking place. Frederick knew that in almost every Lombard town there were men who knew there had been an enormous increase in agricultural production and that all that was now needed for a 'take-off' was a centralized and efficient government[3] which would provide enough internal peace for people to go about their business and enrich themselves. These people looked towards Frederick and hoped he would provide this political framework.[4] The

[1] For the enormous financial benefits which Frederick expected to derive from Lombardy, *see* A. Dopsch's review of G. v. Below, *Die italienische Kaiserpolitik* in ZGS, 85, 1928, p. 596; R. Scholz, *Beiträge zur Geschichte der Hoheitsrechte der deutschen Könige zur Zeit der ersten Staufer*, Leipzig, 1896, p. 120; K. Lamprecht, *Deutsche Geschichte*, 3, p. 136. G. Deibel has provided a systematic survey of the sums involved: *Die italienischen Einkünfte Friedrichs I*, NHJ, 1932, and *Die finanzielle Bedeutung Reichsitaliens für die staufischen Herrscher des 12. Jahrhunderts*, ZSSRGger, LIV, 1944.

[2] It is worth noting that Otto of Freising inserted his information about conditions in Lombardy before his account of the first expedition of 1155. This was wise in view of his determination to give the impression that there was no change of plan in 1156. But since the 1155 expedition was directed to Rome and against Sicily, this information is really out of place in Book II.

[3] *Cp.* W. W. Rostow, *The Stages of Economic Growth*, Cambridge, 1962, p. 30: '. . . the central government has essential, major technical tasks to perform in the period of preconditions . . . the government must be capable of organizing the nation so that unified commercial markets develop; it must create and maintain a tax and fiscal system which diverts resources into modern uses, if necessary at the expense of the old rent-collectors . . .'

[4] It seems that Frederick first became acquainted with some representatives of this

two Morenas, father and son, have left an enduring monument to the opinions of these people and their support of Frederick in the shape of a history of his campaigns in Lombardy.

Otto and Acerbo Morena were citizens of Lodi. They represent a realistic and tough-minded and businesslike body of opinion in Lombardy, which did not consider that there was an essential conflict between Frederick's plan for Lombardy and the prosperity of the Lombard towns. They hoped that Frederick's rule would restore enough freedom to the smaller towns of Lombardy to enable them to live in peace with their oppressive neighbours, and that peace would be beneficial to all. The history they wrote is therefore openly partisan for Frederick. But there is one important feature in it which has to be stressed. Eventually the conflict with Lombardy precipitated a bitter conflict between Frederick and the papacy, which resulted in a schism. Hence Frederick's attention came to be diverted from the Lombard issue to the pursuit of the pope whom he considered to be responsible for the schism. Rainald urged this diversion and became the foremost exponent of the anti-papal policy of the early 60s. But in the history of the Morenas, the conflict with the papacy and the schism are treated as a side issue. The Morenas certainly considered the conflict and the schism as a diversion and probably deplored it. At any rate, they refused to take sides, even though they were so deeply committed to the cause of Frederick. They referred to both Victor IV

'party' at his court in Constance in early 1153. Two ambassadors from Lodi happened to be in Germany at that time and attended the court almost by accident. Encouraged by what they saw, they begged Frederick to help Lodi against Milan. Frederick listened sympathetically and promised help. On their return to Lodi, they met with a poor reception because everybody in Lodi was afraid of provoking Milan. And at that time Lodi had little ground for believing that Frederick would send more than promises to Lodi and threats to Milan. Such, at least, is the account given by Otto Morena at the beginning of his book about Frederick, MGH, SS, XVIII, pp. 587 ff. Simonsfeld, p. 173, points out that this version shows that the two ambassadors had acted on their own initiative and had not had an official commission from Lodi to approach Frederick. We may go further and conclude that the steps taken by these two ambassadors is proof that there was a 'party' in Lombardy who were persuaded that what Lombardy needed was an imperial authority to establish peace and justice. It would not go too far to see in this party the early forerunners of Dante's political thought. A century and a half later, Dante himself warned Florence that if they continued in their defiance of Henry VII they would rightly suffer the same fate as Milan had suffered in 1162. *Cp. Le Opere di Dante*, Florence, 1921, VI, 5, 20.

and Alexander III as popes.[1] One must therefore conclude that the history of the Morenas represents the Great Design in its initial, practical shape. Whereas the *Gesta* of Otto of Freising, inspired by the basically anti-papal preoccupations of Rainald, have for their main theme the conflict with the papacy, the history of the Morenas has for its main theme the establishment of a just and peaceful administration in Lombardy.

They begin their narrative with the court held in Constance in 1153, at which ambassadors from Lodi had appeared before Frederick in order to implore him to establish justice in Lombardy. They do not mention the Treaty of Constance which was concluded at that time – for they were willing to play along with Rainald's propaganda campaign and disguise the magnitude of the revolution of 1156. And they depict Frederick's campaign of 1155, as well as his campaign of 1158, as undertaken in direct response to the complaints made before him at his court in Constance in 1153. This historical deception apart, the existence of this history is proof that there was a group of men in Lombardy who welcomed Frederick's intentions and who hoped that he would promote, not hinder, further economic growth.

Encouraged by the knowledge of such support in Lombardy, Frederick prepared his campaign and the implementation of the Great Design very carefully. First of all he tried to make sure of a certain measure of support from the German princes. But, unfortunately, a campaign to Lombardy to implement the Great Design was not the same as a campaign to Rome undertaken for the sake of an imperial coronation. Hence he worded his invitation to the princes very cautiously: he wrote to them to inform them that there had been a change of plan, and that he would relieve them of their earlier oaths of undertaking a campaign against Sicily so that they could be prepared for other tasks of the empire. 'However, be assured that we shall compel neither you nor any of your princes to cross the Appenine-range.'[2] The last sentence is significant. For Frederick was fully aware of the fact that the princes

[1] F. Güterbock, *Das Geschichtswerk des Otto Morena*, Berlin, 1930, p. xix, explains this as 'historical objectivity'. I prefer to see it as proof that the Morenas considered the schism an unfortunate side issue.

[2] *Gesta*, II, 1.

were rather reluctant and he considered, on the whole, that their full support was not vital. He was hoping for some initial support in Lombardy, but was planning that before long he need not ask any German prince for further assistance.

It was just as well that Frederick was aware of their reluctance. For from the moment at which the war against Milan was proclaimed, the princes either excused themselves altogether or explained that they could not be of much help. Arnold von Seelenhofen, the archbishop of Mainz, for instance, found it very difficult to raise enough money and men, and in seeking support from his city he alienated the citizens of Mainz. The new king of Bohemia, when he announced in Prague that he had promised Frederick military support, found that his vassals threatened his advisers' lives. Only when King Wladislaw announced that he would not compel anyone to join him, did he find volunteers. On the Lechfeld itself, where the army was supposed to assemble, Frederick had to accept further excuses. Otto of Freising pleaded illness – and this was a genuine excuse. Hartwig, archbishop of Bremen, remained absent and Henry the Lion was given permission to join the imperial forces at a later date. Several other Saxon ecclesiastical princes were, like Hartwig, allowed to stay at home. Archbishop Eberhard of Salzburg appeared to be sick. Welf agreed to join later. As to Wichmann, the archbishop of Magdeburg there is no clear record as to whether he followed Frederick or not.

Frederick's next preparatory step was to make it clear to Lombardy that he was coming in order to protect the weaker cities against their oppressors and in order to establish a just overlordship. In order to accomplish this, he sent, at the beginning of 1158, Rainald von Dassel and Otto von Wittelsbach to Italy as ambassadors.[1] Without an armed force, they were to visit the friends and supporters of Frederick, take oaths of loyalty and stiffen the resistance of various cities to Milan. They met with a favourable reception in Verona, which was still intimidated after the failure of their attempts against Frederick in 1155. In Ravenna they were

[1] The report of the ambassadors is contained in *Gesta*, III, xix. A different version was found in two sixteenth-century MSS. This was published in Sudendorf, II, pp. 131 ff., and Simonsfeld, p. 718, believes that it was the original report issued by Rainald.

received warmly by the archbishop, though at that very time the *podestà* was away, treating with the Greeks in Ancona. On their return from Ravenna, Rainald and Otto had run into the returning *podestà* and, though they had been practically without an armed escort, had managed to capture him. Eventually they had forced him to take the oath and had thought this was quite a success, as they believed that no citizen of Ravenna had taken an oath to an emperor since the days of Otto the Great. They wrote triumphantly to Frederick that things were going well for his cause. But a more important success of the ambassadors was the conclusion of a treaty with Piacenza, the old antagonist of Milan. By this treaty, Piacenza first promised to furnish soldiers to Frederick for a siege of Milan. Secondly, she agreed to break all her agreements with Milan by 15 June, so that after that date only those Milanese who had commercial business in the territory of Piacenza would be tolerated there. As soon as Frederick himself would appear in Italy, Piacenza undertook to declare open war against Milan and seize both Milanese property and Milanese citizens in Piacenza. The latter were to be surrendered to Frederick, and the former to be retained by Piacenza. As long as Frederick remained in Italy, Piacenza was not to conclude a separate peace with Milan; but if Frederick had not arrived by 1 August the whole treaty was to be null and void.

All this was very clever diplomacy. For, in return for the imperial sanction of a war against Milan, Piacenza was to supply Frederick with a small army. And to compensate for the expense, Piacenza was to be allowed to retain Milanese property when seized; and in the meantime Piacenza was also to make a cash payment to the emperor: 600 marks of silver to Frederick on his arrival; and 60 marks to his officials within fourteen days of the agreement. Piacenza must obviously have been very anxious to fight Milan under imperial sanction. Her only insurance was that neither cash nor men were due if the emperor did not appear.

Not only did Frederick's ambassadors score successes in Italy before his arrival. The army itself which Frederick led across the Alps was of a considerable size. In fact, it was large enough to be divided and take several different routes to Lombardy. Frederick took the route across the Brenner. The lords from Lorraine took that through the Great St Bernard; those from Austria and Carinthia proceeded through Friuli. This seems to indicate that the assembly on the Lechfeld had been one of leaders only; and that the military contingents they provided had waited in their home lands, to be led to Italy by the geographically most convenient route.

When the various contingents began to assemble in the vicinity of Lake Garda, Frederick directed his activities against Brescia, a close ally of Milan. Its territory was devastated; the citizens of the neighbouring Bergamo, an enemy of both Brescia and Milan, were invited to join in the plunder, and eventually the citizens of Brescia promised to swear fealty to the emperor and furnished sixty hostages, a sum of money and some soldiers to assist in the campaign against Milan. Frederick then gave Milan a last opportunity to make a voluntary submission but to no avail. Milan sent an embassy to him. But the ambassadors failed to give satisfactory assurances that Milan would cease the oppression of other cities and were not able to buy Frederick's goodwill. With the approval of the German princes as well as of the representatives of several anti-Milanese cities, Frederick put Milan to the ban of the empire.

The stage set, a major attack upon the city was prepared. The Adda crossing proved hazardous but was eventually completed. Next, the castle of Trezzo was taken, and on 31 July Frederick and his army were encamped on the Lambro, very close to the place where the city of Lodi had stood before it had been destroyed by Milan. Two days later, the former citizens of Lodi staged a ceremonial procession. They appeared, accompanied by numerous clergy, in large masses, each carrying a cross as a sign of the misery in which they were now living. They begged Frederick to take revenge against Milan, the author of their misfortunes; and asked for permission to reconstruct their city. Needless to say, Frederick was more than willing to grant both requests. He asked them on which place they wanted to rebuild Lodi, and the citizens indicated a hill near the Adda, somewhat east of the old Lodi. The hill, protected both from the river and the swamps, seemed suitable enough. On the following day, at an appropriate ceremony on that hill, Frederick granted the land in question as a fief to the consuls of Lodi. A heavy downpour was interpreted as a divine blessing of the proceedings and Frederick in person then planned the size of the city and the construction of walls and moats. Work was begun at once, and for a little while Frederick supervised it with the greatest of interest. There can be no doubt that he was planning to build himself a veritable fortified capital in new Lodi and use it as a residence in Lombardy as well as a centre of operations.

When Frederick had crossed the Adda, the Milanese began to take fright. They destroyed the bridges over the Ticino and prepared their city for a siege. But they wanted to make one last attempt to gain the imperial favour and sent yet another embassy to the imperial camp. When the ambassadors offered terms, the German princes were on the whole inclined to accept them. They wanted an early conclusion of the campaign and saw no advantage in extreme policies. But the archbishop of Ravenna counselled caution and insisted that Milan was not to be trusted and ought to be destroyed as she had destroyed other cities. And thus both Frederick and the princes refused to negotiate. Frederick threw down the gauntlet and the princes, though still reluctant, gave in. The very next morning, 5 August, a small detachment of soldiers reached the walls of Milan. And as the citizens remained quiet, they reconnoitred and chose sites for the camp. Eventually they returned to join the main army, but in retreating some strayed from the other soldiers. At this moment the Milanese, who had been watching closely from the walls, broke out and slaughtered them. Thus the battle began.

The next day the combined army moved towards Milan and began to surround the city.[1] The Milanese made no move, only kept the gates firmly shut. In the evening there was a surprise attack. The main body of the army had encamped itself near the monastery of San Dionisio, between the Porta Orientale and the Porta Nuova. It was at this place that the attack took place.

[1] At the siege of Milan, 1158, there was present a small contingent of Romans under the prefect Pietro. (Vincent of Prague, *Annals*, MGH, SS, XVII, p. 673, 41–4.) This might have been agreed upon when a Roman embassy had met Rainald in May 1158 in Ravenna. It was proof of Frederick's new policy towards Rome.

Fighting was heavy, and only when darkness descended did the Milanese try to regain their city. The attack, however, had been unable to prevent the almost complete encirclment of the city. Only in the north and the west were the approaches still open.

As the siege proceeded, there were many picturesque incidents. Opposite the Porta Romana there still stood an ancient Roman triumphal arch. The Milanese had turned it into a fortress and about forty soldiers had been installed on it. Frederick's men managed to gain entrance into the three passages and proceeded to demolish the columns with hammers and axes. When the columns began to give way, the soldiers on top offered to surrender. Thereupon the arch was occupied by imperial soldiers who erected a catapult on it from which they slung heavy stones into the city. The Milanese then built a catapult of their own with which they managed to demolish the catapult on the arch, and eventually forced the abandonment of the whole installation.

In the meantime, Frederick caused a complete devastation of the countryside, and the Pavian and Cremonese contingents which had joined his army distinguished themselves by the fury with which they unleashed themselves against all Milanese property. The ferocity of their destruction was nothing new. They merely employed the methods which the Milanese on earlier occasions had used against them. By the middle of August the situation had become desperate. Hunger was in sight for the Milanese and disease and despair caused them to give in. But in the imperial camp, too, there was considerable suffering. The summer heat had become unbrearable. Here, too, was disease and the stench of corpses made the situation quite intolerable.

The archbishop of Ravenna, instigator of the uncompromising attack on Milan, suddenly died on 12 August. The voices of the German princes who wanted to return home were heard once more. And thus peace negotiations were begun. It was probably no accident that Bishop Eberhard of Bamberg was among the imperial negotiators. But even Rainald von Dassel and Otto von Wittelsbach favoured peace. None of them saw any point in a complete destruction of the city. Indeed, if one considers the brevity of the siege and the discomfort experienced by both sides and recalls how many years it was to take Frederick to conquer the city when general war had finally broken out, one must conclude that the peace negotiations at this stage were in the nature of a compromise rather than a victory for Frederick.[1] All appearances indicate that those men who favoured a general agreement with Frederick in terms of the Great Design, because it would afford Lombardy a period of peace and order in which to develop economically, came now forward in Milan.

On 7 September the agreement was ready: Milan was to pay a fine and to surrender hostages and allow Como and Lodi to be rebuilt. All citizens between the ages of 14 and 70 were to take an oath of loyalty to Frederick and all *regalia* such as the right to mint coins, dues from markets and tolls and all fines were to be surrendered to the emperor. And last but not least, though the present consuls were to remain in office for the remainder of their term, the new consuls, due to be elected on 9 February of the following year, were to seek confirmation from Frederick.[2] In short, Milan, by this treaty, gave the lead to Lombardy for a peaceful accommodation to Frederick's wishes. But it did more than that. The treaty was intended to preserve for Milan, under Frederick's aegis, the leading position in Lombardy. Thus, the substance of self-government was preserved and the imperial overlordship recognized. By this compromise Frederick turned Milan from the chief enemy into the chief ally.

The day after the conclusion of the treaty, peace was celebrated

[1] *Cp.* Cusani, *Storia di Milano*, 1861, p. 128. The treaty contained an attempt at an enumeration of the *regalia* which Milan was to surrender (MGH, Const. I, p. 243, c. 9), but a complete enumeration was abandoned in favour of a vague formula. *Cp.* H. Appelt, *Friedrich Barbarossa und das römische Recht*, RHM, 5, 1961–2, p. 21. H. Koeppler, *Frederick Barbarossa and the Schools of Bologna*, EHR, 54, p. 586, very plausibly suggests that it was this experience which prompted Frederick's decision to charge some lawyers at the forthcoming court of Roncaglia with the task of providing a complete and systematic list. If this is so, the decrees of Roncaglia are an even greater improvisation than has been supposed.

[2] The following elaborate provisions for the future prove that the September agreement was intended to be permanent. The present consuls were to remain in office until 1 February of the following year. But in future, the new consuls, though elected by the people of Milan, had to be confirmed in office by the emperor. If the emperor was in Lombardy, half of the elected consuls each year were to appear before him in person to be confirmed. If he was abroad, two consuls were to make the journey and take an oath of loyalty on behalf of their colleagues. MGH, Const. I, p. 242, c. 6.

in a festive manner. The archbishop of Milan received Frederick's kiss of peace and was allowed to sit down with the other assembled archbishops. This act was meant to proclaim the political eminence of the archbishop and to restore to him the exceptional position which he had had of old as the representative of imperial power – whereas by contrast the consuls were merely tolerated. The latter were made to approach barefoot, their swords hanging round their necks. Frederick took their swords, gave each a kiss of peace and absolved the city formally from the imperial ban. After this the archbishop celebrated mass in a huge tent. The celebrations were ended by a crown-wearing festival at Monza, in which both Frederick and the king of Bohemia, the only other anointed ruler present, appeared. Frederick wore a crown and the king of Bohemia a precious diadem. A crown-wearing festival was a very special occasion on which the king presented himself as the living embodiment of divine power. It is significant that Frederick decided to hold such a festival after his agreement with Milan and before the formal promulgation of the 'new' law at his court near Roncaglia. At the time of this festival, Frederick was at the height of his success with the Great Design.[1]

Thus Milan became an imperial city; and though Frederick himself did not enter the city, the imperial banner was flown from the steeples of the cathedral. With this general celebration the important first step for the implementation of the Great Design had been taken successfully. All that remained to be done now

[1] Crown wearing festivals were very special occasions. During the preceding 250 years we know of only 38 such festivals, mostly held at Christmas, Easter and Pentecost. But some were held on the occasions of a victory, a meeting with a pope or a consecration of a cathedral. Frederick held such festivals more often than his predecessors. *Cp.* H. W. Klewitz, *Die Festkrönungen*, ZSSRGkan, 28, 1939. In 1158, Frederick issued a *privilegium* for Monza along the lines of similar charters for royal *palatii* in Hagenau and Aix-la-Chapelle. He would have liked it to have become the crown wearing festival centre of his empire in Italy. *See* H. C. Peyer, *Friedrich Barbarossa, Monza und Aachen*, DA, 8, 1950–1. Folz, *La chancellerie de Frédéric Ier et la canonisation de Charlemagne*, MA, 1964, p. 27, points out that the Aix-la-Chapelle diploma of 1165 was similar to that for Monza, Vienne and Arles. One should note that Monza, Vienne and Arles were in the land of the three rivers. Hence Frederick's desire for 'capital' cities. But Aix-la-Chapelle was outside; and it is significant that the Aix-la-Chapelle diploma was issued in January 1166, when Frederick's policies were being completely deranged by the schism. He found it opportune then to bestow honours and privileges on a city which really lay outside the Great Design. *Cp.* Ch. VI, p. 243 below.

was a cautious political manœuvre to persuade the other cities to follow the example of Milan.

Not unnaturally, Frederick consulted his newly won friends. And they, mindful of the extraordinary position they had now acquired in the Great Design, advised him to single out those men who were faithful to him in every city and to nominate them consuls.[1] In other words, they advised Frederick to rely on those elements in each city who were favourably impressed by the Great Design and to make sure that in future they would hold power. Incidentally, the advice also implied that the position of the other cities would in future be rather less independent than the position of Milan, for the Milanese under the treaty of peace were to elect their own consuls and merely seek confirmation afterwards. There was nothing particularly Machiavellian in this Milanese advice. As the first to rally to Frederick, they naturally expected a somewhat privileged position. And for the rest, they assumed that Frederick's and their plans would be promoted reasonably and effectively if Frederick chose the consuls himself from among those citizens who were faithful to him and who favoured the Great Design.

With this triumph fresh in mind, Frederick proceeded to hold a formal court. On 11 November he arrived in the territory of Piacenza and encamped on the fields of Roncaglia.[2] After some initial deliberations with a large number of bishops who had appeared as the formal bearers of political authority in Lombardy, the court was officially opened. An interpreter translated the words of the emperor to the effect that it was Frederick's intention to make law prevail and not to tolerate ever again the usurpation of imperial rights by single cities or to allow the disturbance of the peace such as had until quite recently been customary. The assembled men were asked to co-operate in finding all the old laws, some of which had actually fallen into oblivion.

[1] Vincent of Prague. MGH, SS, XVII, p. 675. I follow A. Erler, *Die ronkalischen Gesetze des Jahres 1158*, ZSSRGger, 61, 1941, p. 140, in believing that Vincent's report refers to negotiations which took place before the court of Roncaglia.

[2] F. Güterbock, *Die Lage der ronkalischen Ebene*, QuF, 9, 1906, believes that in the twelfth century imperial assemblies were held in the Roncaglia which is east of Piacenza and not in the Roncaglia which is up-stream of Piacenza.

All this sounded good enough. The words were received with applause, and the archbishop of Milan replied that Italy was lucky to have such a ruler and that it was quite true that in ancient Roman law all authority belonged to the emperor, and so forth.

On the following day, the emperor first of all began to act in his judicial role. Countless people appeared before him, carrying a cross in order to indicate that they were the victims of injustice; and Frederick is alleged to have made the ironical comment that he was surprised to see Italy, the land of lawyers, so full of law breakers. But after the labours of jurisdiction – a surprising number of which, by the way, amounted to declarations in favour of the imperial power – Frederick proceeded to the real purpose of his court. The doctors of the Bologna law school had been summoned; and Frederick demanded from them a full declaration of all the ancient laws of Lombardy. They hesitated at first and stated that they could not give a list without full deliberations with the judges from all the cities. Frederick therefore caused two judges to be selected from each city. This commission retired to a nearby place in order to find the traditional law. It was a law-finding, not a law-making commission. For Frederick had decided, for political reasons, to make the Great Design appear as a mere resumption of the law which had prevailed in Lombardy before the towns had wrested self-government from their bishops.

The decrees which were eventually promulgated at Roncaglia as a result of the work of this commission fall into two major parts. There was first of all an enumeration of all the royal rights – *regalia* – which were to be conceded to Frederick. They comprised rents from certain estates which had originally belonged to free Lombards;[1] tolls to be levied on public roads and navigable rivers as well as in ports, wharves and markets; the right to coin money, the right to levy fines and the ownership of estates without lords. Further, the right to confiscate the property of criminals and the property of persons who had contracted forbidden marriages. The emperor was also allowed to demand horses, ships

[1] For the meaning of *arimanniae*, i.e. rents from these estates, *cp*. Th. Mayer, *Die Ausbildung der Grundlagen des modernen deutschen Staates*, HZ, 159, 1939, p. 471. *Arimanniae* were contributions due from a certain type of free men known in Germany as *Arimannen*.

and wagons as well as extraordinary subventions for purposes of war. He was declared the sole owner of silver mines and salt mines and of all the fisheries, and the half owner of any treasure which happened to be found on royal or ecclesiastical soil, and the sole owner of any treasure which was discovered as the result of a search. With this wide definition of royal rights, Frederick was out to ensure for himself a very large share of the financial revenue of Lombardy.[1]

The second part of the Roncaglia decrees concerned the nomination and confirmation of the public magistrates in the cities. It consisted of a so-called *lex omnis* which stated that all judges and magistrates must hold their power and authority from the prince. They could not exercise jurisdiction without imperial consent. But the formulation was fairly vague. A magistrate or judge could be deemed to have imperial consent when he was appointed to his office by the emperor; and he could also be deemed to have imperial consent when he was appointed or elected by someone else or had inherited his office, provided the emperor had invested him with his judicial and official functions. This latter method of regarding an official as possessing imperial authority for his office was specifically Germanic and was quite unknown to Roman law.[2]

These decrees were promulgated in a form strongly reminiscent of Roman law. Their wide definition of *regalia*, as well as the theory that all authority must proceed from the prince, owed undoubtedly something to Roman law conceptions.[3] But their

[1] Technically, the concept of *regalia* had originated in the disputes between the spiritual and temporal powers about the foundations of the empire in the eleventh century. In Germany the *regalia* were those rights which the bishops exercised because they had been invested with them by the king. Frederick extended this concept of *regalia* in Burgundy to include all the rights a ruler may claim in general. In Italy it received yet a different meaning. The concept was reformulated to mean single, imperial rights which used to be exercised by emperors but which had fallen into disuse during the century preceding the reign of Frederick. The rights thus enumerated as *regalia* were mainly rights that could be used for financial yields, and their financial use was the main consideration. *Cp.* I. Ott, *Der Regalienbegriff im 12. Jahrhundert*, ZSSRGkan, 35, 1948. The newness of the doctrine of *regalia* in Italy is further evidence for the improvised character of Frederick's policy.

[2] 'The separate *Bannleihe* is intelligible only in terms of Germanic law.' H. Appelt, *op. cit.*, p. 29.

[3] This was stressed and, unfortunately, overstressed by P. Arras, *Die ronkalischen Beschlüsse*, Leipzig, 1862, p. 30, and by Savigny, *Geschichte des römischen Rechts im Mittelalter*, IV, pp. 174 ff. P. Koschaker, *Europa und das römische Recht*, 3rd ed., München

outward appearance should not blind one to their actual content. To begin with, they were promulgated as a result of a law-finding commission.[1] Hence they were promulgated not as innovations but as ancient custom. And many of these ancient customs were of Frankish or Lombard origin[2] and had never been part of Roman law. Next, one must recall the political situation just prior to the court of Roncaglia. Frederick had made it quite clear in his arrangement with the Milanese that he was perfectly willing to allow them the continuation of their self-government, provided it was *theoretically* agreed that such self-government did not depend on a usurpation by the commune of rights which had

---

1958, p. 73, says that in the *constitutio de regalibus* a derivation of *regalia* from Roman law was 'attempted', because if the *regalia* could be made to appear to be based on Roman law, they might become part of a unified theory of government. It is worth recalling that the story which the Roman law jurist Martinus, alleged to have been a pupil of Irnerius, told Frederick, was added to the Morena Chronicle only in 1220 or 1221. *See* F. Güterbock, *Zur Edition des Geschichtswerks Otto Morenas und seiner Fortsetzer*, NA, 48, 1930, p. 146. Martinus was said to have told Frederick that according to Roman law, the emperor is the unconditional master of the world.

[1] The commission consisted of four eminent Bologna professors and of two judges from each of fourteen towns. This commission was bound by oath – not unlike an English inquest of sworn recognition. It drew up a list of *regalia*. The information was considered authentic because it was local, and sworn to by oath. This shows clearly that the Roncaglia decrees were not simply an arbitrary enactment of Roman law, but were based upon a medieval law-finding procedure. The Roman lawyers merely lent their techniques. *See* H. Koeppler, *op. cit.*, pp. 586–7. *Cp.* also H. Appelt, *Friedrich Barbarossa und das römische Recht*, RHM, 5, 1961–2, p. 23. Frederick simply used what happened to be available in Bologna for his own purposes. His plan was not inspired by Roman law nor did the revival of Roman law in the school of Bologna owe anything to Frederick. *See* W. Goetz, *Italien im Mittelalter*, 1942, II, p. 122. For practical purposes both Frederick and the communes got on very well without Roman law. As late as the second half of the following century a judge like Albertus Gandinus who wrote glosses on Roman law made no use, in his capacity of judge, of the *Corpus Iuris*. W. Goetz, *Das Wiederaufleben des römischen Rechtes im 12. Jahrhundert*, AKG, X, 1912, p. 35. Whatever use Frederick made of Roman law was child's play in comparison with the influence of Roman law on ecclesiastical government during the second half of the twelfth century. For the real heir to the Roman empire was the pope and under Alexander III the whole idea of papal government was based on the idea of re-establishing in the church the centralized government of the empire. *Cp.* G. Le Bras, *Le droit romain au service de la domination pontificale*, 1949, p. 392. Alexander was to develop a truly 'imperial' legislative activity. During his pontificate, 1159–1181, he issued 470 decretals. – W. Holtzmann *Über eine Ausgabe der päpstlichen Dekretalen des 12. Jahrhunderts*, NAWG, 1945, p. 34, counts as many as 713. By comparison, there are only nine pieces of papal legislation for the period 1143–1159 and 215 for the period 1181–1198. Innocent III finally stepped it up to 596. *See* M. Pacaut, *Alexandre III*, Paris, 1956, p. 260.

[2] H. Appelt, *op. cit.*, p. 30, points to the specifically Italian components of the decrees. On p. 25, Appelt speaks of a 'mixture of laws'.

originally belonged to the bishop as the representative of imperial authority in Lombardy. Provided that the derivation of all rights and powers from the imperial power was recognised, Frederick had been willing to accept the *status quo*. We ought to interpret the intention of the Roncaglia decrees in this sense. According to these decrees it would be perfectly possible for a magistrate who was elected by the citizens of a commune, to obtain from the emperor the authority to exercise his functions. And thus we see that whatever Roman law element there was in the theory of the decrees, in practice they were based upon an old Germanic principle which allowed anybody to exercise royal rights even though he was not a royal appointee, provided these rights appeared formally to have been granted to him.[1] If the Roncaglia decrees appeared in theory as an enormous accession of power to Frederick, they enabled him in practice to recognize all autogenous, judicial and political authority as he saw fit. We must therefore not exaggerate their importance, and we need not be surprised to find that on the whole they met with general approval in Lombardy. For the decrees by themselves, it was widely recognized, left almost everything open. If Frederick wished, there need be no fundamental change in the political and judicial set-up in the Lombard cities at all. The decrees were on purpose vague as to whether officials and magistrates were to be appointed by the emperor or elected freely and merely confirmed in their office by the emperor. Equally vague was the provision about the kind of assent the cities were to give to these officials. It might mean no more than the old Germanic practice that the people were to acclaim and thus confirm the appointment of a magistrate, or it might mean that they were to be allowed to elect him in the first place.[2] Above all, the decrees were not promulgated in writing. The imperial chancellery did not even keep a rough copy of the text. For future reference people had to rely on memory and on what notes were made at the time.[3]

[1] P. W. Finsterwalder, *Die Gesetze von Ronkalia*, ZSSRGger, 51, 1931, pp. 44–5.

[2] *loc. cit.*

[3] These notes are all we have. They are printed in MGH, Const. I, No. 174. For the casualness of the promulgation and for the lack of a properly executed charter see H. Appelt, *op. cit.*, pp. 22, 25.

All in all, the Roncaglia decrees appear as nothing more than a public declaration of Frederick's determination to establish himself as the real government in Lombardy.[1] The court was held in order to establish the general and theoretical principles of the Great Design and in order to communicate them to a vast number of people from all over Lombardy. But there was nothing more either to the court or to the decrees. For the rest, everything depended on political decisions, that is on the interpretation and execution of these decrees and upon the measures which Frederick would decide to take in order to apply the decrees. Their terms were such that the widest possible choice was open to him.

Eventually the original plan to interpret them in the sense of the agreement with Milan of September 1158 completely miscarried. And by the time Frederick's policy had led to the complete destruction of Milan in 1162, these decrees were generally taken in Lombardy to have been a tyrannous attempt to abrogate in practice every vestige of self-government and to restore the social and political conditions of the early part of the preceding century. It was then, but only then, that these decrees acquired their sinister reputation and that resistance to them became the rallying-point for the fight against Frederick's Great Design.

The period between the agreement with Milan in early September and the conclusion of the court near Roncaglia was the high water mark of the Great Design in Lombardy.[2] But Frederick made his first serious political mistakes during the months immediately following the conclusion of the court. For instead of doing everything possible to make the Lombard cities realize that he did not want to interfere materially with present conditions, Frederick soon found himself in a position in which he appeared as the protagonist of the narrowest and most tyrannical interpretation of the Roncaglia decrees. As far as the financial benefits,

[1] A. Erler, *op. cit.*, p. 141, says that the decrees were intentionally vague and unclear. G. Blondel, *Les droits régaliens et la constitution de Roncaglia*, Mélanges Paul Fabre, Paris, 1902, p. 225, called them a 'bastard work', and Visconti, *Storia di Milano*, Milan, 1937, p. 183, describes them as 'theoretical assertions'.

[2] This is quite clear from the *Gesta*. Otto of Freising had ended the second book with the announcement of the change of plan; and Rahewin, who had taken over the completion of the work, ended the third book with the crown wearing festival at Monza, just prior to the court of Roncaglia.

which he undoubtedly meant to acquire, were concerned, the cities would probably have had no objection. As it was, the constant inter-urban warfare must have cost them a great deal of money, and many cities had frequently paid the emperor vast sums in order to carry out a punitive expedition against a neighbouring rival. For that matter, there even seems to have been an understanding that Frederick would confirm any elected consul in office on the payment of a sum of money,[1] and in September 1158 the consuls seem to have been prepared to pay to Frederick a sum of money if he did not insist on their appearing before him barefoot.[2] These constant financial contributions appear to have been looked upon as so many expenses for the maintenance of peace, and were considered, in the long run, a sound investment. It is therefore improbable that the financial implications of the Roncaglia decrees by themselves should have caused resistance.

The real opposition to Frederick's Great Design was prompted by political considerations. When it became known how Frederick went about obtaining the submission of elected magistrates and forcing appointed ones upon various cities, there developed a general feeling of disquiet. For Frederick was making a grave mistake. He was aware, as he must have been, that there was a certain body of opinion in favour of the Great Design. But he failed, immediately after Roncaglia, to base his policies upon the sole support of this body of opinion. He refused to treat all cities alike and continued to favour those cities who had been enemies of Milan and therefore friendly towards the emperor. Such a policy of discrimination was justified before the agreement with Milan. But after early September 1158 it had lost its *raison d'être*. Frederick's failure to alter his tactics deprived him of the immediate benefits he could have reaped after Roncaglia.

After Roncaglia he began his efforts to follow up the decrees by dispatching a commission to visit the various cities. He ordered the commission to see to it that in each city the elected consuls were to be replaced by two *podestà*. They were to consent to the election of the *podestà* from among the local citizens. In Cremona

[1] A. Erler, *op. cit.*, p. 141, note 46.
[2] Giesebrecht, V, p. 168. Genoa paid a large sum, *ibid.*, pp. 184–5.

and Pavia, the commission met with no resistance. In Piacenza there were murmurs – not so much on account of the *podestà* as on account of a further order to have the moats filled in and to have all towers above a certain height destroyed. This latter provision was quite reasonable from Frederick's point of view – for if the laws of Roncaglia were to be observed, there would be no further need for these elaborate defence measures to which the Lombard cities had grown accustomed. However, even Frederick must have realized that such demands were extreme; and for that reason they were perhaps in the first instance confined to those cities which had in the past sided too openly with Milan. This policy of special consideration for the enemies of Milan was to arouse active opposition. For when the order for the razing of the fortifications was proclaimed in Crema, there was a disturbance. The city of Crema was situated directly opposite Cremona. The latter city had been a staunch supporter of Frederick because Crema was an ally of Milan. The rivalry between the two cities had been intense, and, with Milanese support, Crema had been turned into a specially-built fortress. After Roncaglia, Cremona thought the opportunity had come for a final elimination of her rival. The citizens of Cremona offered Frederick the very considerable sum of 15,000 marks in silver if he would order the destruction of Crema's fortifications. The request fell on sympathetic ears – for it corresponded to Frederick's policy. Even so, however, it is possible that he would not have proceeded against Crema at this juncture without the bribe. But 15,000 marks in silver was a large sum, and Frederick found it impossible to resist the temptation. It was a fatal mistake, for it strengthened the hand of the party in Milan which was opposed to the new policy and weakened the influence of the consuls who had, in September 1158, come to terms with Frederick.

This threat to Crema precipitated resistance not only in the city itself but also in Milan. No sooner had the Milanese heard of the order than their own resistance to Frederick's policies began to gather strength.[1] When the commissioners arrived in the new

[1] *Annales Mediolanenses*, MGH, SS, XVIII, p. 366: 'Quo audito Mediolanenses plurimum sunt turbati et mesti.'

city of Lodi, they found the citizens busy building and willing enough to abide by Frederick's proposed magistrates. But the commissioners were told that rumours of opposition from Milan had reached Lodi. They therefore directed their steps to Milan.

Rainald von Dassel and Otto von Wittelsbach, as the heads of the commission, summoned the consuls and told them that in future Milan was to be governed by appointed *podestà*. The commissioners were anxious to have this established before the election of the new consuls, which was scheduled for 1 February. In substance, this demand did not amount to much, for even under the September agreement of the preceding year, which had allowed the free election of consuls, these consuls had been supposed to take an oath of loyalty to the emperor.[1] The commissioners' demand amounted to little more than a shift in emphasis. But owing to the recent events, the consuls asked for time to deliberate. Eventually they returned and declared that the city was not willing to accept the appointed *podestà* and would insist on free elections. But they were willing to have the consuls thus elected take an oath of loyalty to Frederick. Again, there was no disagreement in substance in these counter-proposals, only a different emphasis. The commissioners were almost ready to agree to this counter-proposal. They said that the emperor would allow Milan to elect their magistrates, provided the Milanese would agree to these elected magistrates being invested with their authority by the emperor. In other words, Frederick would not mind who would be chosen, provided he was recognized as the source of the authority to be exercised by the chosen magistrates.[2]

[1] MGH, Const. I, p. 242, c. 6.

[2] See Giesebrecht, V, p. 187, for the reconstruction of these events. Vincent of Prague is the main source because he himself was in Milan with Rainald and the other commissioners. *Cp.* Giesebrecht, VI, p. 373, for critical comments on the sources. But whatever the precise sequence of events, and whoever the commissioners accompanying Rainald and Otto von Wittelsbach were, it is instructive to compare the standpoints of the main accounts. To Rahewin, *Gesta,* IV, xxiii, the most important factor in the commotion was that 'these disturbances come not from the nobility, but from the people'. In other words, the influence of the people makes for unreliability. He does not say explicitly what the bone of contention was, except that the commissioners had been ordered to install the *podestà* and consuls. 'Install,' of course, may mean 'choose' or 'confirm'. Vincent of Prague, GDV, 67, p. 53, is equally ambiguous: after reporting the consuls' first remonstrance, he makes the commissioners say that all this is much ado about nothing because the Milanese can choose freely and call their officials

When the consuls communicated these proposals to a large popular assembly in the cathedral, there arose a tumult which degenerated into a riot.[1] There were shouts of 'fora! fora! mora! mora!' – which meant: 'let us have the commissioners, they must be killed!' The crowd then moved to the municipal palace in which the commissioners were residing. The commissioners and, presumably, the consuls' officers in the palace, barricaded doors and windows. But the crowd seemed in a violent mood. The consuls attempted to quell the riot, but in vain. Then they tried to assure the commissioners that they themselves had no hand in this outbreak of violence and offered a sum of money as a fine for the insult. Eventually it became possible to remove the commissioners safely from the palace to their lodgings. And from there, under cover of night, they fled from Milan in disguise. Only Rainald, who as usual was intrepid, stayed for another day in his lodgings near the church of St Ambrose. There he was visited by several Milanese knights who assured him that eventually the city would be certain to accept the imperial policy. Then he too departed.

anything they like (i.e. *podestà* or consuls), provided the choice took place under the guidance of the commissioners. Again, he does not think it worth mentioning whether 'guidance' means merely supervision or 'by command'. Otto Morena is equally vague. He writes, MGH, SS, XVIII, p. 609, that the commissioners had come to Milan in order to 'create' from among the citizens, the *podestà*. Hence the riot. As against these accounts, the *Chron. reg. Col.*, GDV, 69, p. 73, does not mention the *podestà* and their method of selection at all. It reports that the riot occurred because the Milanese refused to pay the tribute which had been imposed on them at their defeat. This chronicle is close to Rainald and we may conclude that Rainald wanted to present Milan in as bad a light as possible, and did not consider that the dispute about how the consuls were to be appointed was sufficiently clearly a bone of contention to be elaborated upon. Finally, the *Annales Mediolanenses*, MGH, SS, XVIII, p. 367, say that the commissioners had come to persuade Milan in quite general terms to accept *potestatem Theotonicam*. They do not even mention the problem of the election or the appointment of officials. Taking all these accounts together, we find that Vincent of Prague, Rahewin and Morena are completely vague about the officials' method of appointment; and that the two chronicles written by adherents of the two opposing parties respectively, are actually silent about the problem of the method of appointment. We are thus forced to conclude that this problem was not considered important and that the riot broke out because of a growing general resistance to imperial policies in general. – Last, not least, one must bear in mind that the Roncaglia decrees had not been written down (*Cp.* p. 169, note 3) and that not only their original formulation in this respect had been ambiguous, but also that there was no text to which anybody could have referred.

[1] According to the *Annales Mediolanenses*, MGH, SS, XVIII, p. 367, the following men were the authors of the insurrection: Martinonus Malaopera, Azo Bultrafus, Castellus de Ermenulfis.

There can be little doubt as to what had happened. As a result of the proceedings against Crema, the opposition party in Milan had gained the upper hand. They had vainly opposed the consuls' policy in September of the preceding year and their opportunity had come when public opinion had become sufficiently inflamed by the news from Crema. They staged a riot, and as a result the consuls' more prudent and more cautious policy was discarded. The consuls tried to temporize and assured Rainald of their loyalty and other members of their party visited Rainald in order to tell him that with a bit of patience everything would be well. But Rainald was no fool. He gauged the nature of the outbreak correctly and came to the conclusion that a change of leadership in Milan was imminent.

When the commissioners reported back to Frederick, he was intensely perturbed. This was indeed the second occasion on which his commissioners had met with violence. Just before the riots in Milan, other commissioners had been assaulted in Crema. When Frederick heard of this incident, he had kept calm.[1] When he was told of the Milan riots he again kept quiet.[2] He ordered an inquiry into the events in Milan, and in the middle of February a Milanese embassy appeared before him in Marengo.[3] He reminded them that Milan had, after all, agreed to the Roncaglia decrees and that the Milanese themselves had offered Frederick the

[1] Morena, MGH, SS, XVIII, pp. 608–9.

[2] *loc. cit.* Morena's account of Frederick's prudence at this moment is in complete contrast with the version reported in the *Chron. reg. Col.*, a source close to Rainald. According to this version, GDV, 69, p. 73, Frederick flew into a rage and immediately decided to make war on Milan. In fact, this decision was taken only after considerable thought had been given to the matter. It is revealing that a source close to Rainald wants to give the impression that this far-reaching decision was taken in a rage and on the spur of the moment.

[3] Vincent of Prague, GDV, 67, p. 54. Vincent says that at the inquiry the Milanese expressed their regrets for the incident. Against this, Rahewin, *Gesta*, IV, xxvii, says that their representatives were men of 'much eloquence but little wisdom' and then reports their seemingly impertinent reply to Frederick. According to his report, the decision to make war had already been taken before Marengo, and at Marengo, Milan was to be given one last chance which they failed to take. In Vincent's account, at Marengo, Milan obviously was represented by the old party who wanted to work with Frederick. But in Rahewin's account, Milan was represented by the new men who refused to work with Frederick and who had come to power through the riots of January. Whichever version is correct, it is clear that Frederick, in spite of Rainald's fury and indignation, did not take the decision to make war on Milan lightly.

advice to appoint magistrates from those people who were faithful to him. The ambassadors replied that it was true that they had taken an oath but that they had never promised to observe that oath.[1] The meaning of this reply is not immediately obvious – for it seems improbable that the ambassadors should have answered Frederick in a cynically impertinent way with a mere statement that an oath was not necessarily an oath. What the ambassadors must have meant was that it was true that Milan had taken an oath, but that in view of the ambiguity of the Roncaglia decrees there was no telling what the oath exactly implied and what they were thus bound to observe.[2] In other words, they told Frederick now – and one must presume that these ambassadors had been sent by the party who were now in control of Milan – that they wanted the Roncaglia decrees interpreted in the sense most favourable to them rather than in the sense most favourable to Frederick.

If Frederick had allowed prudence to reign, he would have continued negotiations on this basis. But he was angered by the affront to his imperial authority and in his anger was open to Rainald's pressure. For Rainald had been mortally offended by the riots and, in spite of the personal courage he had shown in Milan, he had probably received quite a shock when the mob had demanded his death.[3] As a result, prudence was not allowed to prevail and Frederick decided there and then to make an example of Milan.

Frederick made a rapid tour of Lombardy in order to inspect cities and make preparations for a renewal of the war. He visited Lodi and prevailed upon Cremona, Novara and Pavia to assist Lodi in the building of their fortifications. Then he appeared in Piacenza – to intimidate the citizens, some of whom had robbed the imperial messengers who had been carrying a large sum of money paid by Genoa to Frederick. When he was celebrating Easter (12 April) in Modena, while he was watching a tournament, news arrived that Milan had laid siege to the fortress of

[1] *Gesta*, IV, xxvii. [2] A. Erler, *op. cit.*, p. 141.

[3] The *Annales Mediolanenses*, MGH, SS, XVIII, p. 367, attribute Rainald's violent hatred of Milan to these incidents.

Trezzo.[1] This was the straw that broke the camel's back. The games were interrupted and Frederick at once repaired to his army near Bologna. There, surrounded by the judges of the city and the professors of the law school, Milan was formally condemned. The city was put to the ban of the empire because it had committed high treason, had been guilty of rebellion and had defied the law. The property of Milan was to be looted and its citizens sold into slavery. Next, Frederick hastened to the relief of Trezzo. While passing through Lodi he learnt that the fortress had been captured, its German occupants taken prisoner and its Italian inmates massacred. Therefore he returned to the main army and led it at once into the territory of Milan. His army was not large enough to commence a regular siege; and Frederick had to be content with the devastation of the fields. But Milan was making ready: Crema, Brescia and Piacenza had resumed their old alliance with Milan and the war was in full swing. The Milanese attacked Lodi; Brescia invaded Cremona; and Frederick spent forty days scorching the area around Milan. Far from intimidating Lombardy, the harsh sentence against Milan had merely stiffened the determination of Milan and caused her old allies to rally. When the whole situation was thus once more in the balance, several attempts were made on Frederick's life. The would-be assassins were believed to have been sent by Milan; but no evidence has ever come to light to confirm this suspicion. Especially the second attempt was wholly mysterious, and since repeated torture of the perpetrator proved fruitless, some historians have been inclined to connect the attempt with the activities of the Lebanese assassins who might have decided to eliminate Frederick on account of some oriental intrigues in connection with the crusades.

Frederick seems to have realized that he needed to plan his strategy in a more decisive way and therefore decided to give way to the repeated requests by Cremona for the destruction of Crema. Crema had defied Frederick's orders for the destruction of its fortifications. Its citizens trusted the strong natural protections afforded by the river in the east, the swampy regions, and the help

[1] Vincent of Prague, GDV, 67, p. 55.

of Milan. In June, Frederick formally put Crema to the ban of the empire and charged the Cremonese with its execution. Thus the siege of Crema was begun. By September Frederick had joined the Cremonese with a largish army, reinforced by new contingents which had arrived from Germany.

The siege took a long time. Crema did not finally surrender until the end of January 1160. As time went by, Frederick got more and more agitated and eventually the siege was pursued with the most barbarous acts of cruelty on both sides. Frederick had prisoners either hanged or hacked to pieces. The besieged, in retaliation, killed their prisoners on the walls in full sight of their friends. At one stage, in order to protect one of his war-machines, Frederick had several Cremese prisoners suspended on ropes from its rafters, and at night these unfortunate people were lit up with candles. Frederick thus hoped to discourage the Cremese from hurling weapons and torches at the machine. To no avail. The people thus suspended were killed by their own kinsmen from the city. The ferocity displayed on both sides was the result of Crema's bitter resistance and of Frederick's recognition of his own impotence. The resistance was all the more bitter because Crema had been put to the ban of the empire and the punishment thus threatened went far beyond a mere application of the Roncaglia decrees. The methods employed during the long siege suggest that Frederick was already beginning to lose his equanimity and the steady determination with which he was planning to pursue the Great Design. Instead he allowed himself to be provoked and angered, and gradually assumed the shape of an avenger and tyrant rather than of a cool and level-headed statesman. The knowledge of the deterioration of his relations with Pope Hadrian during the second half of 1159, of Hadrian's death in November of that year and of the double election in Rome contributed to his growing fury.

The siege of Crema is also remarkable for the technical expertise displayed on both sides. According to one source, the besiegers constructed a rolling tower of considerable height and tried to move it towards the walls. The besieged countered the threat by building a movable bridge on their walls, with the help of which they hoped to capture the approaching tower. Frederick also had a special protective roof built, and under its cover the moats of Crema were filled. Eventually the besieged managed to set the roof on fire and also tried to undermine it by digging a tunnel towards it from inside the city walls. This latter move proved double edged, for Frederick's men nearly gained entry into the city through that tunnel. One day Frederick succeeded in having a breach made into the walls by a ramming block; but the Cremese were quick to erect an earthen wall behind the hole and thus frustrated the attack.

By the end of the following January hunger and disease proved to Crema the hopelessness of her position. The Cremese offered to surrender and were allowed to keep as much property as they could carry out of the city on their backs. Then the work of demolition was begun. The citizens of Cremona and Lodi who had participated in the siege joined in with alacrity and the Cremonese were alleged to have destroyed the churches as well as the other buildings. Frederick himself broadcast that a similar fate would befall all his opponents and stressed that the citizens of Crema had saved literally nothing but their bare lives.

If it had been difficult to reduce Crema,[1] Milan proved an even tougher military problem. Frederick resumed the campaign against Milanese territory almost at once, in the spring of 1160. But no decision could be reached. The city itself could not be properly besieged because Frederick's army was not large enough to surround it. He did obtain, from time to time, reinforcements from Germany; but never in sufficient numbers to clinch the matter. As it was, he had to confine himself to devastations of the countryside. These devastations, however, also deprived his own army of the necessary food. In this way, the campaign was continued throughout the summer and autumn of 1160. During the winter it came to a stop, and it was resumed in the spring of 1161.[2]

[1] Frederick's army found the siege of Crema so exhausting that no further immediate operation was possible. H. Delbrück, *Geschichte der Kriegskunst*, Berlin, 1923, Pt. III, p. 351.

[2] Frederick's army was too small to start a regular siege. Hence Frederick's tactics to intimidate Milan by cutting off the supply of food, *ibid.*, p. 355. In the twelfth century it was very common not to lay a strict siege to a city but to make a loose encirclement. A series of improvised castles was built in a wide circle around the city in

By the middle of 1161, when there was still no end in sight, several German princes, bitterly opposed to Rainald's determination to pursue the siege to its conclusion, attempted to begin negotiations with Milan. In August[1] Frederick's brother Conrad and Conrad's brother-in-law, Louis, the *Landgraf* of Thuringia, had promised a safe conduct to the consuls of Milan to enable them to start negotiations. But on their way, in the vicinity of the monastery of Bagnolo, the consuls were set upon by Rainald's men. The German princes who had promised the safe conduct were so irate at this high-handed interference with their plans that they swore to kill Rainald.[2] When the matter came before Frederick, Rainald tried to excuse himself by protesting that he had had no knowledge of the safe conduct. This was most probably untrue[3] but Frederick accepted the excuse and managed to compose this quarrel between his closest advisers. But the mere fact that it should have taken place shows that there was a group of men in opposition to Rainald's policies. For Conrad's and the *Landgraf*'s opposition was not confined to Rainald's intransigent policy against Milan. The year before, these two men had promoted the election of Christian von Buch to the see of Mainz, and Frederick, mindful of the fact that they were in opposition to Rainald, had refused in 1161 to confirm this election. Frederick at this stage was very deeply committed to Rainald and would not tolerate Rainald's opponents gaining influence.[4] Two years later, these same princes began military operations against the archdiocese of Cologne. Rainald was then still in Italy. He

---

order to cut off the food supply. In this way one could avoid pitched battles and save men, *ibid.*, p. 341.

[1] I accept Giesebrecht's date: VI, p. 404.

[2] Morena, MGH, SS, XVIII, p. 637.

[3] J. Ficker, *Rainald von Dassel*, Köln, 1850, p. 40.

[4] C. Varrentrapp, *Erzbischof Christian I von Mainz*, 1867. Scheffer-Boichorst, *Gesammelte Schriften*, II, p. 275, points out that Christian's election was rejected by Frederick in June 1161, whereas Conrad and Rainald became enemies only in August 1161. While it is true that Frederick had also other reasons for objecting at that time to Christian (*Cp.* p. 267 below) who later became one of his most faithful followers, Scheffer-Boichorst's objection to Varrentrapp is not really justified. It is very likely that Conrad disliked Rainald's policies well before August 1161 and that the August incident was a result, not the cause, of this dislike.

instructed his men in Cologne to resist strongly, and Conrad's and the *Landgraf*'s attempts came to nothing.[1]

The attempts at negotiation having failed, the siege was continued throughout the year 1161. Very gradually Frederick succeeded in gaining the upper hand. But even so it was not before the beginning of 1162 that the situation of Milan had become sufficiently desperate to make surrender imperative. The citizens were then indeed at the end of their tether and had begun to fear the worst when Frederick allowed six Milanese prisoners to return home: five of them had been blinded, the sixth had been deprived of his nose but allowed to keep his eyes in order to lead the other five home. Their treatment was to be a warning.

Under these conditions negotiations were begun in February 1162. At first the Milanese offered to accept all the conditions imposed by Frederick in pursuance of the Roncaglia decrees and to agree to the appointment of a *podestà*, Lombard or German, as the emperor might choose. The walls and towers and moats were to be razed and rebuilt only with the emperor's express permission. Milan was even prepared to reduce the size of its population by emigration. The only thing they wanted to salvage was the city itself, their property and the lordship over the surrounding countryside.

Frederick was sympathetic to this offer and submitted it to his advisers. They, on the whole, were inclined to accept it. Only Rainald protested and demanded an unconditional surrender.[2] Eventually prudent counsel prevailed against Rainald and everything was prepared for a treaty. Unfortunately at this point the consuls who had been conducting the negotiations lost control of events in Milan. The surrender negotiations had been too protracted, and by the time they were beginning to yield fruit, despair and disorder had gained the upper hand. The disorder issued into

[1] A. Busson, *Conrad von Staufen, Pfalzgraf bei Rhein*, AHVN, 1868, p. 14.

[2] Frederick wanted a conditional surrender and a negotiated peace. See Giesebrecht, VI, p. 407. The *Chron. reg. Col.*, GDV, 69, pp. 84–5, a source close to Rainald, seeks to disguise Rainald's standpoint as one of great prudence: Rainald argued that if Frederick wanted to save Milan he could easily do so after an unconditional surrender. What he failed to see at this stage – or did he see it? – was that once there was an unconditional surrender, Frederick would be open to the irresistible demand by Milan's old enemies to destroy Milan.

an insurrection and the consuls barely managed to escape alive. As a result of the riots it became clear that the political situation in Milan was so unstable that no treaty was worth making. It looked as if Rainald's protest against a negotiated surrender had been justified,[1] whereas in reality it was probably that protest which had caused the lengthy debates in Frederick's camp, which, in turn, had been responsible for the riots. And so it was that Rainald's opposition brought about its own justification.[2]

Under the circumstances, Milan had no choice but to surrender unconditionally. On 1 March the consuls appeared before Frederick in Lodi, carrying their naked swords round their necks. They threw themselves at his feet and admitted that they had committed high treason. They promised an unconditional surrender of the city, the citizens and all their property, and swore to obey every imperial command. On the following Sunday, they returned together with 300 knights who threw themselves at Frederick's feet and begged him to show mercy to their unhappy city. They surrendered their flags, and Frederick retained many of them as hostages.

Finally, on 6 March, about one thousand soldiers appeared on foot before Frederick and brought with them their *caroccio*, a heavily built, somewhat clumsy wagon, large enough to enable soldiers to use it as a shelter in times of battle. In the middle of it there was a huge mast topped by a cross and carrying a flag with a picture of St Ambrose. For the last time two trumpeters on the *caroccio* sounded their trumpets – the customary sign for the promulgation of civic ordinances – and then handed over their trumpets. Eventually the mast was lowered, and Frederick in person removed the flag. Thereupon all the Milanese fell on their knees and raised their crosses and begged for mercy. They were joined by Count Guido of Biandrate, a close friend of Frederick's. The emperor himself made no response; but Rainald reiterated that the surrender was unconditional and insisted that everyone took the

[1] The *Chron. reg. Col.*, *loc. cit.*, does indeed not mention the riots in Milan but simply says that the Milanese themselves accepted unconditional surrender in order to avoid further delay.

[2] The account in the *Chron. reg. Col.*, GDV, 69, pp. 84–5, makes it quite clear that the delay was due to Rainald's arguments.

oath of complete obedience which the consuls had taken earlier. They were told to come back the following day, and in departing they threw their crosses in the direction of the place where the empress was living, hoping thus to enlist her sympathy.

On the following day they were told that Frederick planned to be merciful. According to law, he said, they all had deserved death. But he would grant them their lives and absolve them from the ban. The present consuls and their immediate predecessors were to remain in captivity, together with a large number of notables. The knights were to furnish hostages, and the walls and moats were to be destroyed sufficiently to allow an easy entry to his army into the city. Thus the Milanese were dismissed and a commission consisting of six Germans and six Lombards was sent into the city to administer the oath to all citizens above the age of twelve.

On 13 March, Frederick left Lodi and held an assembly at Pavia. Here he met a large number of delegates from the towns which had been staunchly loyal and they, it is alleged, old and bitter enemies of Milan that they were, persuaded him to have Milan destroyed. Frederick gave in: on 19 March he issued an order that all inhabitants were to leave the city, and on the following day the work of demolition was begun. The various enemies of Milan were each assigned a special quarter for destruction, and their zeal was so great that the heavy labour of demolition was carried out in record time. Even churches were razed, and Frederick had to interfere in person in order to assure the safety of several holy relics. The most valuable ones, the bones of the Three Wise Men, were given to Rainald who later carried them in triumph to his archiepiscopal see of Cologne.

Frederick celebrated Palm Sunday on the ruins of Milan. But for the Easter celebrations he returned to Pavia, where he held court in great splendour. A great many bishops and archbishops were present, and even Eberhard of Salzburg had obeyed Frederick's orders to attend. He had brought with him Gerhoh of Reichersberg, a scholar and a controversialist of great renown, and Bishop Hartman of Brixen, a man whose spiritual advice Frederick had sought on earlier occasions. A similar array of lay princes was present, and at the festive procession Frederick wore the crown which he had vowed three years ago he would not wear until Milan had fallen. Pavia was full of joy and jubilation, the whole of Lombardy was at his feet, and Easter was celebrated in full triumph. Frederick promised to inaugurate a golden age of peace, and there are several charters which were dated such and such a day 'after the destruction of Milan'.

However, one ought not to be misled by appearances. Frederick, it is clear, had not intended the total destruction of the city. In his first negotiations with the consuls in February 1162 there had been a chance of negotiated surrender, even though the terms would have been harsh. The unfortunate and inopportune riot in Milan, however, revealed how precarious the consuls' authority had become. Frederick wavered; and as he was wavering, Rainald had seized his chance to encourage a more brutal course. Frederick then insisted on unconditional surrender, for he realized that no confidence could be placed in the consuls and their ability to abide by any terms to which they might agree. Even then, no complete destruction was intended. After all, the complete destruction of Milan would make the decrees of Roncaglia lose their relevance.

It was then, and only then, that the weakness of Frederick's position stood revealed. When he met the delegates of the other Lombard cities in Pavia, he found himself confronted by their irresistible demand for the total destruction of Milan. Irresistible, for Frederick's army was not sufficient to keep the whole of Lombardy in subjection; and unless he wanted to risk the emergence of ill-feeling and possible resentment against the Roncaglia decrees in those towns which had accepted them, he had to give in and allow them to vent their hatred on the city which had tyrannized them for decades. If the surrender had not been unconditional Frederick could easily have resisted the demand for total destruction without fear of offending the old enemies of Milan. He could then simply have sheltered behind the terms of the surrender. But now there were no terms: a refusal to allow the destruction of the city would look like a gratuitous insult to Milan's enemies. Once Frederick had followed Rainald's advice to insist on unconditional surrender, he could think of no good argument to protect Milan from the hatred of her old enemies.

Frederick, at that time, was probably not aware that he had put himself in a position in which the enforcement of the Roncaglia decrees had ceased to be the guiding principle of his policy. With the destruction of Milan, he had clearly gone beyond the objectives of Roncaglia and had started on a path which was to lead in a completely different direction.

But the physical destruction of Milan was not all. As he stood in triumph in Pavia, the victorious and invincible emperor, he suddenly must have remembered the pope. Hadrian had died towards the end of 1159. Owing to the growing turmoil in Lombardy at that time, a double election had taken place in Rome,[1] and although Frederick had tried his best to solve the dispute, he had not succeeded. By the time of his triumph over Milan, there were two popes in existence, competing with each other for the obedience of Christendom. The schism had begun. In his attempt to set his house in order in Lombardy, Frederick had managed to set it on fire.

[1] See p. 211 below.

CHAPTER VI

In Pursuit of Alexander III

In order to understand fully the extent to which Frederick had jeopardized the Great Design when he stood upon the ruins of Milan at Easter 1162, it is necessary to go back to the time immediately following the court held at Besançon in 1157. Cardinal Roland had staged the *beneficium* incident in order to prove to those of his fellow cardinals who opposed his Sicilian policy that Frederick was a really dangerous man. The incident had been a total success from Roland's point of view, for Rainald and Otto von Wittelsbach had more than obliged him. Otto had even threatened Roland and his companion with the sword. But it seems that the real purpose of Roland and his companion had been to proceed from Besançon to Germany and carry out a visitation of the German church. In his anger, Frederick even accused the two cardinals of planning to denude the altars of the churches of the Teutonic realm, to carry off the vessels of the House of God and strip the crosses of their coverings.[1] It is certain that the cardinals carried a number of letters to the bishops of Germany.[2] It seems that they had never thought that the incident

[1] *Gesta*, III, xi.

[2] The expression used in *Gesta*, II, xi, is *paria litterarum*. Mierow's translation, *The Deeds of Frederick Barbarossa*, New York, 1953, p. 185, prejudges the issue; for there has been a great deal of speculation about what the expression precisely means. Simonsfeld, p. 574, believes that the legates were carrying a large number of identical letters to be distributed in Germany, in order to mobilize opposition to Frederick on account of the Eskil affair – i.e. he takes it that the letters were proof of a systematic propaganda campaign against Frederick. K. Zeumer, *Par Litterarum*, NA, 35, 1909, suggests that the expression means 'a lot of written things'. See also N. Hilling, *Paria litterarum*, H. Finke Festgabe, Münster, 1925. Schrörs, *Untersuchungen zu dem Streit Kaiser Friedrichs I mit dem Papst Hadrian IV*, 1157–58, Bonn, Universitätsprogramm, 1915, believes that the pieces all dealt with the same subject. He argues very convincingly that Roland and the other legates meant to proceed to Germany in order to inspect the German bishops and to vindicate in Germany the authority of the pope. With this intention they did no more than continue the policy of Eugene III who had frequently interfered with ecclesiastical administration in Germany and who had often collected money

would work so well and arouse so much anger as to make their journey to Germany impossible. Their luggage was searched and the following day they were ordered to return to Rome. The visitation of the German church, whatever its ultimate purpose, could not take place.

It was very much part of Rainald's policy to prevent such a visitation and to reassure the bishops of Germany that they would not be subject to any close papal scrutiny. Hadrian in all innocence had imagined that the old policies of Pope Eugene III could be continued and that the papal supervision of the German church, which had been customary under Conrad III, would remain in order. He probably remembered the role played by papal legates at the court held in Constance in early 1153,[1] at the beginning of Frederick's reign, and took it for granted that these arrangements would also be observed in the future. But 1157 was not 1153; and by the time of the court in Besançon, the Great Design had been conceived. It is probably a measure of Hadrian's ignorance of the Great Design that he naïvely presumed that the old policies would prevail, no matter how great the diplomatic revolution caused by the Treaty of Benevento in 1156 had been. But if Hadrian was naïve in this regard, it had become a matter of urgent importance to Frederick and Rainald to assure the bishops of Germany that henceforth they would not be subject to papal supervision. Just as Frederick was to rely on their military support and political loyalty,[2] so they were to rely in future on his protection against papal control and papal demands for money. Whatever had been Frederick's need of episcopal support under the first plan (1152–1156) there was, after the inception of the Great Design, an urgent necessity for close co-operation between emperor and German bishops. For under the Great Design the German magnates were allowed a very free hand in their territories. They were likely to become more and more independent and, possibly, withdrawn

---

from the German bishops. HB, p. 160, note 1, and P. Rassow, *Honor Imperii*, new ed., München, 1961, p. 78, support this view. Frederick had never protested against this policy, but in Besançon he and Rainald made it clear that it could not continue.

[1] See above, p. 68.

[2] *Cp.* Nitzsch, p. 281 and R. Jordan, *Die Stellung des deutschen Episkopats im Kampf um die Universalmacht unter Friedrich I*, Würzburg, 1938, *passim.*

from imperial policies. All the more need, therefore, for securing at least the firm support of the bishops.

It is not possible to form a precise estimate of the extent to which Frederick and Rainald, at that stage, were determined to secure the independence of the German bishops from the papacy. But it is worth examining in this respect a series of curious documents which have come down to us. The first of these is a letter purported to have been written by Frederick to the archbishop of Trier. The letter declared that in future Trier was to be the head see of the German church and that all papal control in Germany was to come to an end. The second document purports to be a letter from the archbishop of Trier to the pope, notifying him of the emperor's intention. The third document is supposed to be the pope's reply – a reply in which all papal claims are so exaggerated as to provoke immediate antagonism to them. The whole empire of the Germans, it was stated, had been created by the popes for the express and sole purpose of being at the beck and call of the papacy. And if the emperor did not take heed, the pope might re-transfer the empire to the Greeks, especially since the emperor had been powerless to destroy the Norman kingdom in southern Italy and Sicily.

For a variety of reasons it is certain that these letters were not from the people by whom they were purported to have been written;[1] but they do throw a light on the situation. They may

[1] A. Werminghoff, *Nationalkirchliche Bestrebungen im deutschen Mittelalter*, Stuttgart, 1910, believed these letters to be genuine documents showing Frederick's intention, after Besançon, to establish, if necessary, a national church. HB, p. 158, note 3, points out that Frederick never had such thoughts and that the letters in question were no more than stylistic exercises, at best an indication of a trend in public opinion. Haller, p. 138, takes them more seriously. He believes they were written by a Trier 'journalist' who wanted to make the most of the Besançon incident in order to inflame public opinion in favour of the ambitions of Hillin, the archbishop of Trier. W. Ullmann, *The Pontificate of Hadrian IV*, CHJ, p. 241, speaks of the 'fabrication' of this correspondence in the months following Besançon and says that it is not difficult to prove that Rainald stood behind these letters. But he gives no proof. N. Höing, *Die 'Trierer Stilübungen'*, AfD, I, 1955 and II, 1956, agrees with Hampe that these letters originated as stylistic exercises but argues that they did not originate in Trier. He attributes them to the circle of the Bamberg chancellery school, and is inclined to connect them with the imperial chancellery and to regard them as propaganda instruments. The same author argues in *Der angebliche Briefwechsel Papst Hadrians IV und Kaiser Friedrichs I*, AfD. 3, 1957, that these letters were composed by no less a person than Eberhard, the bishop of Bamberg. They were, however, not be to be used as propaganda instruments. Eber-

have been inspired by Rainald in order to make public the threat of a complete severance of the German church from Rome; they may have been written by one of Rainald's critics, in order to reveal the ultimately dangerous end of Rainald's policies. Whatever the explanation, the existence of the letters proves the existence of the idea that papal power over the German bishops should be curtailed. The intentions expressed in these letters lack the legal precision of the English *Constitutions of Clarendon* (1164) but they do show that in Germany as well as in England the possibility of pruning papal authority was being contemplated.

When Roland and his companion were forced to return to Rome Hadrian must have been very embarrassed. Roland's manœuvre in Besançon had really been so successful that the real purpose of the journey had been placed in jeopardy. For Frederick had made it quite clear that he would not allow these two cardinals into Germany.[1] On their return to Rome, the party favourable to Frederick, far from being convinced that Frederick was indeed as

hard, on the contrary, wrote them in order to show up, in their complete absurdity, the ultimate ends of Rainald's Besançon policy. He wrote them to ridicule Rainald. W. Goez, *Translatio Imperii*, Tübingen, 1958, pp. 148–51, suggests that these letters were written by a young man as stylistic exercises for his training in the chancellery. But he assigns them to the early 60s rather than to the aftermath of Besançon because one of them was obviously penned in answer to a threat made by Alexander III that he might transfer the empire to the Greeks if Frederick did not behave himself. R. Folz, *La chancellerie de Frederic Ier et la canonisation de Charlemagne*, MA, LXX, 1964, p. 22, argues convincingly that the style of these letters is very different from that of Eberhard of Bamberg. Folz prefers to think of these letters as having originated in the school for chancellery notaries of Würzburg. – My own preference is obviously for Höing's theory, because if Eberhard of Bamberg wrote them in order to warn, by a *reductio ad absurdum*, of the ultimate consequences of Rainald's policy, this is consistent with the general view I have taken of Eberhard's political role. But there is a great strength in Folz's doubts. However, both he (pp. 24–5) and Goez make too much of the threat, in the letter purporting to have been written by Hadrian, to transfer the empire to the Greeks. The same letter, in its insistence on the notion of *translatio* by the papacy, is also very anti-Sicilian; and as such not likely to represent an authentic papal view of the early 60s. All in all, one must not overlook the possibility, suggested by Haller, *loc. cit.*, that the way in which the first letter obviously favours Trier at the expense of the senior see of Mainz, leads one to think that these letters may have to do more with the ancient rivalry between Mainz and Trier than with the question of empire and papacy. One could, however, argue against Haller that in the late 50s and early 60s Frederick was forced to brush aside any claims Mainz may have had to the primacy in Germany because of the murder of Arnold von Seelenhofen, the archbishop of Mainz and the generally unstable situation in Mainz as a result of this murder.

[1] *Gesta*, III, xi.

dangerous to the papacy as Roland had argued ever since the treaty with Sicily, blamed 'the thoughtlessness or inexperience of those who had been sent'[1] and urged Hadrian to make a more conciliatory move. Hadrian, therefore, despatched a letter to the bishops of Germany in order to defend himself and to explain that the emperor's anger at Besançon was unjustified. He did not at this stage actually apologize for the Besançon interpretation of the word *beneficium*, but criticized Frederick for issuing an edict 'that no one from your realm should approach the apostolic see'.[2] Hadrian then appealed to the German bishops to prevail upon the emperor to return to the 'right way' and to force Rainald and Otto von Wittelsbach to apologize.

Upon receipt of this letter, the German bishops took counsel. They expressed great dismay at the quarrel which had arisen between emperor and pope, but stated clearly that with all respect to Hadrian they were gravely perturbed by the ambiguity of the expression *beneficium*, which had been used in Besançon. Then they consulted Frederick who, with the help of Rainald, let them have a reply which the bishops communicated to the pope. In this reply Frederick stated that there were good and sacred laws which set certain limits to the church. The emperor owed his crown to the free election by lay and ecclesiastical princes, and if one must think of the empire as a *beneficium*, it is a *beneficium* given by God and by no other person. The road to Rome would not be closed; but all abuses 'by which all the churches of our realm have been burdened and weakened, will be resisted'. The doctrine that the imperial crown was a feudal tenure of the papacy was rejected categorically, and the pope was blamed for having come to an agreement with Sicily. For the rest, the bishops added a request to the pope to be more conciliatory in his next letter.[3]

[1] *Gesta,* III, xvi. [2] *Gesta,* III, xvi.

[3] *Gesta,* III, xvii. The letter is from June 1158 and was put together by Eberhard of Bamberg. *Cp.* W. Föhl, *Bishop Eberhard von Bamberg,* MIOG, 50, 1936. E. Otto, *Friedrich Barbarossa in seinen Briefen,* DA, 1942, seeks to disentangle Frederick's own words from those contributed by Rainald. While one cannot accept his conclusions with complete certainty, they are nevertheless very plausible. Otto suggests that the middle portion in which the bishops report to the pope what the emperor said, was composed by Rainald on the basis of a personal statement by Frederick. Rainald has a lengthy introduction about how the realm ought to be governed, a piece about the relations between

With this letter the quarrel, which was supposed to be a quarrel as to whether the German bishops and the papacy could communicate freely with each other, became enlarged into a major dispute over matters of principle. Rainald could not resist this opportunity, nor the temptation of attacking the pope's fundamental position by stating that the church had, in the first place, been exalted by the power of the empire, and that it was therefore wrong for the church now to destroy the empire. Rainald was thus making the most of what, according to Roland, was to have been a passing incident.

When Hadrian realized what was happening, he decided to withdraw. There was no point in continuing a quarrel over matters of such weighty political and ecclesiastical principle, especially as in Rome the pressure of the anti-Sicilian party was considerable. This party could now prove to Hadrian that, if the policies of Roland were persisted in, there was a real danger of a permanent breach with Frederick, a breach which would serve no purpose at all. Hadrian therefore decided to send another mission to Frederick, and this time chose Cardinal Henry and Cardinal Hyacinth, 'men of prudence in secular matters and much better qualified for dealing with affairs of state than those previously sent'.[1] These two cardinals did in fact belong to the pro-imperial party, and with their despatch it was hoped in Rome that the whole matter could be settled amicably.

---

church and empire, and a harangue about the Lateran paintings. Frederick's own contribution was much more sober. He wanted to stick to the actual bone of contention: abuses in the German church, freedom of access to Rome, the Treaty of Benevento – all matters mentioned by the bishops on their own account in this letter. Frederick was practical and matter of fact. Rainald was given to high-flown theory and willing quarrel over matters of principle rather than over concrete and real details. One can fill in this picture of Rainald from other pieces of evidence. (1) His behaviour at the Council of Rheims (J. Spörl, *Rainald von Dassel auf dem Konzil von Reims*, HJ, 60, 1940) about clerical dress. (2) His transfer to Cologne of the Milan relics, see below, p. 239. (3) His employment of the Archipoeta in order to have the extravagant praises of Frederick's pretensions to universal power sung. *Cp.* P. Munz, *Frederick Barbarossa and the 'Holy Empire'*, JHR, III, 1964, p. 31. (4) His role in the canonization of Charlemagne, below, p. 242. (5) His exploitation of the battle of Tusculum in order to build up his military charisma, below, p. 250. All these incidents could add up to a character sketch of Rainald and show him to have been temperamentally quite out of tune with the sober Frederick.

[1] *Gesta*, III, xviii.

However, Rainald and Otto von Wittelsbach, who by that time had been in Italy preparing for Frederick's arrival in the autumn of 1158,[1] tried their best to prevent a reconciliation. In fact as soon as Rainald had tested opinion in northern Italy and scored his first successes at Ancona and Ravenna, he wrote to Frederick to warn him of the conciliatory intentions of Henry and Hyacinth. He advised Frederick not to make hasty concessions to these cardinals, for the whole of Italy would soon be at his feet. Moreover, he had good reason to believe that the imperial party among the cardinals would soon win over the citizens of Rome, and he was indeed expecting daily an embassy from the Roman senate. If an agreement with the citizens of Rome could be made, Hadrian would really be threatened and Frederick could dictate terms to him.[2] Rainald knew, however, that the German bishops were in favour of a peaceful settlement with the papacy and he suspected, rightly, that the two cardinals would find a favourable reception in Germany. He himself was in Italy while in Germany Frederick's chief advisers were now Eberhard, bishop of Bamberg, and Otto, bishop of Freising – both men of peace and friends of the papacy. He therefore thought that it might be wiser not to take any chances. The two cardinals directed their steps respectfully to where he was residing in Modena and 'made a show of humility'.[3] He dismissed them non-committally. But as soon as they were on their journey northwards, he spread the rumour that these cardinals were enemies of the empire and that anybody who might waylay them and hold them for ransom might thus not only fill their pockets but also perform a task that would please the emperor. He had calculated well. When the two cardinals were travelling through the Tyrol, they were seized by brigands, robbed and kept in chains: it required some very high-powered intervention for them to be freed.

It is difficult to condemn Rainald at this stage. He was anxious to prevent a reconciliation because he hated the papacy, and he did his best to exaggerate the quarrel over the visitation of the German church for he knew that in the long run it was easier to make political capital out of a conflict over matters of principle

[1] See above, p. 158. [2] Döberl, p. 116. [3] *Gesta*, III, xxi.

than from a purely practical problem. But at the same time Rainald was most probably mindful of a purely pragmatic problem. He knew that the public proclamation of the Great Design was imminent. He also realized that after such a proclamation the chances of a peaceful understanding with the papacy would be negligible and therefore calculated that a sudden reconciliation with the pope would be a mere waste of time. Hence his determination to prevent it.

At Augsburg where Frederick received the two cardinals after their hazardous journey, Frederick's advisers were less politic. The two cardinals produced a letter from Hadrian, which was given to Otto of Freising to read and interpret. Otto was a man who could be relied upon for rendering it in a spirit favourable to Hadrian. Not that any favourable interpretation was necessary. For Hadrian was by now persuaded that nothing was to be gained by continuing the quarrel.

The letter contained indeed no less than a full apology. Hadrian took pains to explain etymologically that the feudal sense of *beneficium* had not been intended, and that he had wanted to convey no more than the notion that with the coronation he had done 'a good deed'.[1]

Frederick was 'mollified'.[2] He gave the cardinals the kiss of peace and many gifts and sent them back to Hadrian with an assurance of friendship. He added, however, that there were certain purely practical disputes which ought to be settled, and the cardinals promised to have them considered. Thus the quarrel over political theory was settled and there was every hope for a peaceful understanding on the purely practical question as to the relationship between the papacy and the German churches. Rainald's attempt to elevate the quarrel to a theoretical level in order to gain the greatest possible propagandistic advantages for Frederick from Roland's manœuvre in Besançon had failed. It is well to bear this in mind. For the new rupture between empire and papacy, which was to come in the following year, had nothing to do with matters of theory.

The problem thus settled, Frederick proceeded to Lombardy to

[1] *Gesta*, III, xxiii. [2] *Gesta*, III, xxiv.

lay siege to Milan and conclude the mutually satisfactory agreement with Milan of 7 September 1158. It so happened that during the siege of Milan in August that year the bishop of Ravenna, Anselm of Havelberg, died. Anselm had been promoted to the see of Ravenna with the agreement of Hadrian in 1155. He was a great supporter of Frederick, and during the early part of 1158 Rainald and Otto von Wittelsbach had used Anselm's position in Ravenna in order to establish that city's adherence to the Great Design in face of a certain amount of popular opposition.[1] Rainald's comparative success is a measure of the importance of the city to Frederick. When Anselm died during the siege of Milan, Frederick almost at once sought to have another faithful friend elevated to the see. He chose Guido, the son of Count Guido of Biandrate, one of his closest friends and followers. Cardinal Hyacinth, still fresh from his successful mission to Augsburg and anxious to continue the newly established concord between emperor and pope, went to Ravenna in person in order to persuade the electors to agree to Frederick's wishes, and thus lent the cloak of papal authority to Frederick's canonically not wholly legitimate interference with a free election.[2] But Hyacinth was acting in good faith. The agreement between Hadrian and Frederick was established.

Hadrian, however, was of a different opinion. Since the agreement reached at Augsburg, Milan had been subdued and Frederick had established himself firmly in Lombardy. It had become clear to Hadrian that a new policy was being inaugurated in Italy. He understood, therefore, that Frederick's determination to have Guido installed as archbishop of Ravenna was part of it and decided to object to the latter's election. As yet, he was somewhat hesitant in his opposition, and when he wrote to Frederick to tell him, he was careful to explain that he had nothing against young Guido and that he was sure that Frederick himself would prefer an even more honourable career for Guido, perhaps one which would bring him into closer relation with the pope.[3] Here was

[1] P. Lamma, *Comneni e Staufer*, Rome, 1955, Vol. I, pp. 298–300.
[2] M. Maccarone, *Papato e Impero*, Roma, 1959, p. 279.
[3] *Gesta*, IV, xx.

papal opposition to imperial policy – but couched in cautious terms and in agreeable language. It did not concern matters of principle. Indeed, everybody was clearly aware that it merely concerned Frederick's new policy in Italy – for Rahewin (who was continuing Otto of Freising's *Gesta*) reports this incident after stating that Hadrian's opposition to Frederick was being caused by the fact that 'the *regalia* had been sent to the emperor by the bishops and abbots and the cities and the notables'.[1] In other words, Hadrian's new attack upon Frederick was a direct response to Frederick's territorial policy in northern Italy.

Hence a new stage in the deterioration of relations between Frederick and Hadrian began. The next occasion for a dispute arose over the matter of imperial suzerainty in Lombardy. There had been an old feud over the possession of some castles in the Val Camonica between Bergamo and Brescia, which had been settled to the detriment of Bergamo in March 1156, and both parties had then agreed that the matter should not be referred to the emperor. Some time during the spring or summer of 1158 this agreement had been sanctioned by papal legates.[2] But after the inauguration of the Great Design, Frederick could not let the matter rest there, because it would have implied at least a tacit recognition of the suzerain authority of the pope. And thus, towards the end of 1158, he encouraged Bergamo to reopen the matter and bring it to his court, only in order to pronounce a new judgement in favour of Bergamo. Hadrian, naturally, was angered because this constituted not only an affront to his legates' competence, but also a clear attempt to exclude papal jurisdiction from Lombardy. He wrote to Frederick and had the letter delivered by an ordinary messenger, in disregard of diplomatic convention. He knew that this would provoke Frederick. But by this time Hadrian was beyond caring. For, although it is not known with certainty when this incident took place, it must have occurred either immediately before or immediately after Roncaglia – that is, at a time when the nature of the Great Design was no longer hidden from Hadrian. It was clear by now that Frederick meant to include at least Lombardy in his territorial kingdom and that that intention was a

[1] *Gesta*, IV, xviii. [2] Giesebrecht, V, p. 218, and VI, p. 382.

direct challenge to the territorial ambitions of Hadrian. And thus, at this stage, the conflict between empire and papacy was reopened on a completely different plane.

Hadrian, like so many other rulers during the second half of the twelfth century, had formed intensive and concrete territorial plans. And as the territorial implications of imperial policy became known, no further demonstration of the fact that the empire was a threat to the papacy was necessary. From this moment onwards, that is immediately after Roncaglia, the imperial party's influence in Rome was declining. The wisdom of the Sicilian alliance and of Roland's policies was fully vindicated by the promulgation of the Roncaglia decrees.

Boso, the papal biographer, made a special point of emphasizing the success and the importance of papal territorial acquisitions under Eugene III and Hadrian IV.[1] Under Hadrian there was no doubt of the systematic nature of these acquisitions and of the extension of papal authority. Concrete claims were put forward to a territory which included the Matildan Lands in Tuscany, the area from Acquapendente southwards to Rome, the duchy of Spoleto, Ferrara, Sardinia and Corsica. There is proof that these claims were well thought out, for territories to which Hadrian could never hope to vindicate his rights were excluded: there was no mention of Ancona and Ravenna.[2]

Hadrian had not exactly been the innovator of a territorial policy. Papal territorial supremacy in Sabinia, for instance, had been secured by the middle of the twelfth century. The popes had acquired castles where they had wanted to secure the roads.[3] But the vigour of the methods employed in the pontificate of Hadrian to secure these ends was something altogether new. There was an increase in purchases of land and of castles for military and strategic purposes and increasing foundations of new urban communities, in order to counterbalance the influence of the local

[1] For Eugene, *see* Boso, p. 381; for Hadrian, *ibid.*, p. 396; for Alexander, *ibid.*, p. 422 f.

[2] For these geographical limits see the letter by Eberhard of Bamberg, *Gesta*, IV, xxxiii. *Cp.* D. Waley, *The Papal State in the 13th Century*, London, 1961, p. 5.

[3] O. Vehse, *Die päpstliche Herrschaft in der Sabina bis zur Mitte des 12. Jahrhunderts*, QuF, xxi, 1929–30, p. 171.

barons.[1] Hadrian certainly enlarged the number of firmly held territories around Rome[2] and in 1156 he acquired places both in Tuscany and Campania.[3] In some places the newly acquired territories were administered by a chatelain who was directly responsible to the pope. His appointment was designed to eliminate baronial and other local influences and he could be removed by the pope at will.[4] On two occasions, Hadrian employed cardinals as *rectores* in Campania[5] and here we have an exact equivalent to Frederick's employment of a *iudex terrae* in the Pleissenland.[6] Most remarkable is Hadrian's policy in regard to the towns. Tivoli swore an oath of fealty to the pope, and so did Orvieto.[7] Lauri, a new community in Sabinia, owed military service and counsel. It had to receive papal *nuntii*, pay six pounds a year and *fodrum* when levied and the pope reserved to himself cases of murder and adultery which were to be heard by his representatives twice a year. There is no mention of a *rector*, and we may presume therefore that the town was administered directly by the pope.[8] Another example is Montasola. In a letter by Hadrian of May 1157, the city is described as a *civitas*, and must have achieved some form of corporate existence as a commune under papal lordship. Pope Nicholas II had reserved to himself the whole administration of justice; but Hadrian was anxious to retain only jurisdiction over cases of murder and adultery, which were to be heard twice a year, as in Lauri, by his ambassadors. He regarded the whole community liable to a yearly money payment, and considered himself entitled to *fodrum*, the shelter of papal officials and to various other services. There were, moreover, no communal rectors and Montasola too was directly governed by the pope.[9] By comparison with King Roger of Sicily, with Frederick or with Henry the Lion or even with Henry Jasomirgott in Austria, Hadrian's policy was not spectacular. Montasola was no Milan and no Lübeck. But nevertheless, no matter how small, the

[1] D. Waley, *op. cit.*, p. 12.
[2] *Liber Censuum*, Fabre-Duchesne ed., I, pp. 385 ff.
[3] O. Vehse, *op. cit.*, pp. 168–9.
[4] *ibid.*, p. 169.
[5] P. Kehr, *Italia Pontifica*, II, p. 171; *cp.* also *Liber Censuum*, *ed. cit.*, I, pp. 587–8.
[6] See above, p. 113.
[7] P. Kehr, *op. cit.*, II, p. 80.
[8] D. Waley, *op. cit.*, p. 13.
[9] O. Vehse, *op. cit.*, p. 171.

additions which Hadrian made to papal territory were tenable and their effectiveness is illustrated by the account of his biographer. At one time Hadrian went to the southern borders of his 'state' to receive the homage of his Norman vassals, accompanied by a splendid 'army of counts and other nobles from Rome, Campania and other neighbouring parts'.[1]

Given these facts, it did not take much acumen for contemporary observers to understand that after the proclamation of the Great Design at Roncaglia there was very little chance for a peaceful understanding between empire and papacy. Bishop Eberhard of Bamberg, though a supporter of Frederick, grew more and more unhappy about the turn events were taking. He disapproved of the anti-papal implications of the Great Design, though he recognized in his heart of hearts that they were inevitable. 'We greatly fear', he wrote, 'that he (Frederick) has changed'[2] and admitted that he was being displaced in Frederick's councils by 'men who are ignorant of things divine'.[3]

On the other side, his opposite number, Cardinal Henry, replied in a similar vein. He bemoaned the Roncaglia decrees: 'The records of another time are consulted, the imperial titles are read perhaps in the form which suited that age and the goodness as well as the simplicity of those times. . . . But now all things are changed.'[4] Eberhard of Bamberg even wrote to Hadrian directly and referred to the common danger which threatened the peaceful understanding between emperor and pope. Although he must have known that there was now no chance of the peace continuing, he implored the pope to write again to Frederick 'kindly and gently . . . and with paternal affection . . . for he is ready to show you all reverence'.[5] But Eberhard knew then that he was working for a lost cause, and not long after he wrote to his friend Eberhard, the archbishop of Salzburg, that his labours had all been in vain and that his soul was now weary of life.[6] By the time Rainald was trying to install imperial commissioners in Milan,[7] it had become clear that the men of peace, Eberhard of Bamberg on Frederick's

[1] Boso, pp. 393–4. [2] *Gesta*, IV, xxii. [3] *loc. cit.*
[4] *loc. cit.* [5] *loc. cit.* [6] *Gesta*, IV, xxxiii.
[7] See above, p. 174.

side, and Cardinals Henry and Hyacinth on Hadrian's side, were playing a losing game; and that in future policies would be fashioned by Rainald and Roland: 'perilous times seem to be coming', wrote Eberhard of Bamberg, quoting John, XXI, 18. But how perilous neither he nor anybody could foresee. For the worst that anybody expected was a clear rupture of relations between Hadrian and Frederick.

This rupture was finally brought about by Hadrian. Towards the end of May he sent a new embassy to Frederick, led by Cardinal Octavian, the leader of the imperial party among the cardinals, the purpose of which was to make demands so intransigent that he must have known them to be completely unacceptable. This new approach served no other purpose than to bring about a final rupture of relations. Hadrian now not only defined the territory which he claimed for complete papal overlordship in Italy, but also insisted that Frederick should never communicate again with the citizens of Rome without papal consent, never collect *fodrum* in papal territory, that the bishops of Italy render Frederick only an oath of fealty and never render him homage, and that imperial commissioners were never to be received in their palaces.

Frederick was somewhat taken aback by the intransigence of these demands. It is difficult to say whether he was really unaware of papal territorial aspirations in Italy and therefore hoped that it would be possible to reach a compromise, or whether he suggested a compromise arbitration merely in order to place himself in as innocent a light as possible. Whatever the answer, the rupture was now imminent. The papal envoys explained that they were not empowered to entertain a compromise – although Octavian was the head of the imperial party, the Sicilian party was now in complete ascendancy in Rome, and Octavian had been told firmly not to allow himself to be beaten down. Frederick, in turn, charged Hadrian with all the old misdemeanours, such as entertaining appeals to Rome and allowing his envoys to travel freely through imperial lands and living off 'imperial' churches. In fact, the dispute showed itself more and more clearly to concern the notion of territoriality. Frederick maintained that papal envoys were to confine themselves to papal lands, but had no business to visit and no right to live off bishops whose property lay in imperial lands.[1] It was being made quite clear that if there was something new in this dispute, it was this new conception of exclusive territoriality. In order to make political capital, Frederick also charged the pope with having broken the Treaty of Constance.[2] If Hadrian demanded a renewal of the treaty, this was sheer hypocrisy, for it was Hadrian who, by making peace with Sicily, had been the first to break the treaty. Frederick was on good ground here: by omitting to mention the military situation which, in 1155, had obliged Hadrian to come to terms with King William,[3] he could indeed claim that theoretically Hadrian had been the first to break the Treaty of Constance. But all in all, Frederick reiterated that now the pope was making 'new and unheard of demands'.[4] And in this he was correct. For the demands amounted to a rejection of Frederick's conception of territorial exclusiveness in northern Italy and as such they had never figured in the older dispute between pope and emperor. They were in fact made in order to bring about a final rupture.

Both sides had prepared carefully for this final rupture. When Milan had decided to resist the Great Design, and when control had passed from the consuls who were anxious to co-operate with Frederick to the revolutionary party, Hadrian had entered almost at once into negotiations with the citizens of Milan. Already in June 1158, before Frederick's arrival in Italy, Hadrian had sent two cardinals to Milan, most probably in order to encourage their determination to resist.[5] At that time, when the men willing to co-operate with Frederick were still in power, such papal encouragement had proved ineffectual. But these overtures were renewed early in 1159, and this time Milan was ready to make an alliance with Hadrian. Hadrian, through the good offices of King William

[1] *Gesta*, IV, xxxv.

[2] Rahewin, *Gesta*, IV, xxxvi, refers to it as *concordia*. This is the only oblique reference in the *Gesta* to the Treaty of Constance of 1153. That it occurs at all must no doubt be explained by the fact that Book IV was written by Rahewin who, on this issue (*cp.* p. 137 above) had not fully understood Otto of Freising's original intention.

[3] See above, p. 98. [4] *Gesta*, IV, xxxvi.

[5] G. Dunken, *Die politische Wirksamkeit der päpstlichen Legaten in der Zeit des Kampfes zwischen Kaisertum und Papsttum in Oberitalien unter Friedrich I*, EHS, 209, Berlin, 1931, pp. 35–8.

of Sicily, was now able to offer money to Milan, and during the first half of 1159 a real 'conspiracy' was concluded between Hadrian, King William and Milan.[1] And when, during the summer of 1159, it became clear that Hadrian's health was failing, the conspiracy was extended to include an agreement that in the event of his death the Sicilian party among the cardinals were to see that a successor was elected who could be relied on to continue the alliance.[2] Indeed, this conspiracy was an important factor in hardening Milan's determination to risk a confrontation with Frederick, and they could not reasonably be expected to risk this

[1] There can be no doubt that this conspiracy was made. In July 1158, two cardinals had been sent to Milan. We do not know the purpose of their mission, but it appears to have something to do with stirring up opposition to Frederick. *Cp.* Dunken, *op. cit.*, pp. 35–8. A few months later, Hadrian and King William of Sicily together encouraged the Milanese with money to rebel against Frederick. And during the first half of 1159, a real 'conspiracy' was agreed upon. The participants were 'most of the cardinals', William of Sicily, 'and nearly all the cities of Italy with many barons and other magnates'. (Burchard of Ursberg, SRG, Hannover and Leipzig, 1916, p. 40. He says that he obtained this information from a Cremona chronicle which has since been lost.) We know further that there was a *societas Lombardorum,* for Frederick wrote about it to bishop Albert of Freising in a letter of August 1159. *See* Dunken, *op. cit.*, pp. 44–7, and Ribbeck, *Friedrich I und die römische Kurie in den Jahren 1157–1159*, Leipzig, 1881, pp. 64–65. Gerhoh of Reichersberg testified that money had passed hands and that Hadrian had promised to excommunicate Frederick. *Cp.* P. Brezzi, *Lo scisma inter regnum et sacerdotium al tempo di Federico Barbarossa*, ADR, 63, 1940, p. 36. There is also the explicit statement in the *Annales Mediolanenses*, MGH, SS, XVIII, p. 368, that such an agreement was made at the time of the siege of Crema. – Money, of course, was always a touchy point. The sympathizers of Frederick suspected money everywhere. Hadrian and William, they maintained, had given money to Milan to make her rebel. Someone gave money to Hadrian, to make him excommunicate Frederick. They continuously suspected both the Greeks and the Kings of Sicily to be offering money to Frederick's enemies. This was a field in which Frederick never could compete, because he had none. Hence his and his friends' incessant indignation at this financially supported diplomacy.

[2] The agreement to elect only a man who would continue Hadrian's policy is the second part of the conspiracy. There is no direct evidence for it. Giesebrecht's argument, V, p. 228, that there cannot have been such an agreement because it was uncanonical, seems somewhat naïve. I entirely agree with Ribbeck, *op. cit.*, that the sources in which this second conspiracy is mentioned add up to a very convincing picture. His arguments are perhaps a bit careless, e.g. when he takes the opinions of Roland's enemies, expressed at the council of Pavia, that there was such a conspiracy, as complete proof. Gerhoh of Reichersberg was certain that there had been a *double* conspiracy, i.e. one between William, Hadrian and Milan (see note 1, above), and another, to elect only a suitable man to the papal see. *Cp.* MGH, LdL, III, p. 361. But quite apart from the general plausibility of the sources, there remains the fact that without this second conspiratorial agreement to limit the election to a pope of the right party, the whole first conspiracy with Milan and the Lombards would have made no sense. And of the first conspiracy, there is no doubt. Given that Hadrian was dying at the time of the first conspiracy, what else can one expect but such a second conspiracy?

unless they had good assurance that Hadrian would be succeeded by a pope who would be equally sympathetic to their cause.[1] Any agreement as to who was to be elected as successor of Hadrian was uncanonical; but at that time the political situation made such an agreement imperative.

This conspiracy not only amounted to a total victory of the Sicilian party at the *curia*, but was also an explicit attempt to perpetuate that victory after Hadrian's death. In order to execute it, it was necessary to seek an excuse for the removal of Cardinal Octavian, the head of the opposition, from the papal court.[2] For this reason, Octavian was entrusted with the last mission to Frederick. This mission, with its intransigent demands, must have been very distasteful to him. But he went willingly, because he hoped to be able to conduct the negotiations with Frederick in a way which might leave a door open for a compromise.[3] He probably knew that if he had remained with Hadrian he would still not have been able to prevent the conspiracy. As it was, he was not able to leave a door open either; but at least Frederick remained sincerely cognizant of Octavian's and his family's devotion to the imperial cause, and this last fatal mission which Octavian undertook on Hadrian's business did not cloud the close and cordial understanding between him and the emperor. On the contrary, Frederick immediately decided not only to show his gratitude to Octavian, but also to show it in a way which would demonstrate that he intended to cut right across Hadrian's territorial policy. A month after the unsuccessful mission he issued a generous grant to two of Octavian's kinsmen and thus installed them in a place which threatened one of Hadrian's major roads from Umbria to Rome.[4]

[1] I repeat that I consider the reasonableness of such an assurance as part of the 'evidence' that there was a 'conspiracy' to that effect.

[2] It was during Octavian's absence that the *curia* moved from Rome to Anagni where the conspiracies took place. *Cp.* W. Holtzmann, *Quellen und Forschungen zur Geschichte Friedrich Barbarossas*, NA, 48, 1930, p. 395, note 3.

[3] Lamma, *op. cit.*, II, p. 43 comments rightly on the strange fact that Hadrian should have entrusted the mission with the last, intransigent demands, after Roncaglia, to Octavian. But there is a very obvious explanation: the Anagni conspiracies could be made successfully only in Octavian's absence.

[4] In May 1159, just after Octavian's mission, Frederick issued a charter to Octavian's brothers, giving them the city and country of Terni together with all *regalia* as an

Given the location and the timing of this grant, it seems likely that Octavian had suggested it to Frederick himself in order to avenge his removal from the *curia* and the insult which this particular mission must have been to so imperial-minded a man as Octavian. It would seem that at least on this point Octavian managed to double-cross Hadrian and Roland.

If Hadrian forged an alliance with Milan, Frederick, at the same time, proceeded to forge a corresponding alliance with the citizens of Rome against their so-called lord, the pope. Such an approach required, of course, a complete change of policy in

---

imperial fief. The most recent edition of the charter is in E. Rossi-Passavanti, *Interamna dei Naarti, Storia di Terni dalle origini al medio evo*, Rome-Orvieto, 1933, II, pp. 99 f. Rossi-Passavanti considered the charter a forgery; but K. Zeillinger, *Zwei Diplome Barbarossas für seine römischen Parteigänger*, DA, 20, 1964, pp. 575 ff., gives very convincing reasons for its genuineness. The charter clearly mentions the borders of the grant, and it appears that the country in question dominated the major roads from Umbria to Rome. The charter also elevated the Monticelli family to princely rank. *See* also M. Maccarone, *op. cit.*, pp. 308–9. By this charter, Frederick and Octavian crossed Hadrian's territorial plans and disposed of lands and rights which the popes had considered part of the *Patrimonium Petri*. In Octavian's mission, Hadrian had expressly demanded recognition of papal sovereignty in that area (*See* F. X. Seppelt, *Geschichte der Päpste*, 1956, III, p. 235), for Terni was part of the Matildan lands. There can be no doubt that Octavian chose this particular place as a demonstration against Hadrian. – Long after the beginning of the schism, on 1 April 1160, Alexander III wrote to Arnulf of Lisieux that Frederick had planned to make Octavian pope already during Hadrian's lifetime. The letter is in JL, 10627. There is no other evidence for such a plan except Alexander's testimony which dates from a time when Alexander had every reason to discredit both Frederick and Victor. But it is true that when Frederick issued the above charter to Octavian's brothers, he also issued a charter to the canons of St Peter (*See* K. Zeillinger, *op. cit.*, pp. 570–1) who subsequently became ardent supporters of Octavian and were physically responsible for his election. It appears, therefore, that Octavian made good use of his mission to Frederick. He was not interested in his official business; but managed to double-cross Hadrian. – Even after Octavian's death, the Monticelli did not give up the struggle. They were present in 1167 when Frederick conquered Rome and Octavian's brother witnessed Frederick's charter for Rainald after the battle of Tusculum (Stumpf, Reg. 4086). After the Peace of Venice in 1177, the Monticelli continued their opposition to Alexander. The lords of Monte Albano and of Palombara belonged to their clan, and when Calixtus III could no longer stay in Viterbo, he was sheltered in the castle of John of Monte Albano, near Monticelio. Christian of Mainz had to lay siege to the castle. When Calixtus surrendered in August 1178, the count of Palombara elevated Landus of Serre, under the name of Innocent III, as the fourth anti-pope. Thereupon Alexander bought both the castle of Palombara and the new anti-pope for a large sum from the lord of the castle and had poor Landus incarcerated. This aftermath shows very pointedly to what extent the existence of anti-popes was determined by the resistance of the nobility to the growing territorial sovereignty of the pope.

regard to the citizens and the senate of Rome. In 1155 Frederick, rather imprudently, had made short shrift of their demands[1] and had shown himself anything but sympathetic to their aspirations for self-government. Now, in 1159, this policy was to be reversed. It is impossible to say who took the initiative; but it was clear that with the impending rupture of relations between pope and emperor, an alliance between Frederick and the Romans was a reasonable step. The Romans may have taken their cue from Frederick's complaint, made in late 1158, in justification of the new policy, that the pope had come to terms with the Romans as well as with the king of Sicily.[2] For if such an agreement had been a stumbling block to an understanding between Frederick and Hadrian, the rupture between them opened the road to an agreement between Frederick and the Romans whose alliance with Hadrian had been extremely precarious and only temporary. And thus, when Octavian was presenting to Frederick Hadrian's final demands, there was present also an embassy from the citizens of Rome who lost no time in expressing their amazement and indignation.[3]

Frederick shrewdly decided to use the presence of the Roman envoys to bring pressure upon Hadrian. He received them well and sent them home.[4] And then, turning to Octavian, he said that he would send an embassy to Rome to negotiate peace with Hadrian; but that if Hadrian did not wish peace, he would empower this same embassy to negotiate with the citizens and the senate instead.[5] Thus encouraged, the senate of Rome sent another mission to Frederick at the time when the siege of Crema was already underway.[6] This time Frederick not only received them graciously but gave them presents and entertained them for several

[1] *See* above, p. 84.

[2] Frederick resented Hadrian not only for the Treaty of Benevento, but also for his having come to terms with the citizens of Rome and for having implicated them in his agreement with William of Sicily. There is a clear reference to this in a letter reproduced in *Gesta*, III, xvii. But neither Rahewin, who wrote that part of the *Gesta*, nor MGH, Const. I, No. 167 have the correct text. Simonsfeld, p. 617, p. 58, amended the text correctly to read: 'de concordia Romanorum et Wilhelmi Siculi' and rejected the suggestion that Rahewin's *Ro* refers to Roger of Sicily. Maccarone, *op. cit.*, p. 241, note 86, has some doubts whether *Ro* really stands for *Romanorum*. P. Classen, reviewing Maccarone, HZ, 195, 1962, p. 382, produces additional evidence to dispel all doubts.

[3] *Gesta*, IV, xxxvi. [4] *Gesta*, IV, xxxiv. [5] *ibid.* [6] *See* above, p. 161.

days. And on their departure he sent Otto von Wittelsbach with them to Rome and ordered him to deal with the senate and arrange with them for the admission of an imperial prefect to Rome. Otto was well received in Rome by both people and senate.[1] He even got in touch with the pope. But very soon after Otto's arrival in Rome, on 1 September 1159 Hadrian breathed his last in Anagni, where he had moved a few months earlier because Frederick's encouragement of the senate had made his sojourn in Rome very difficult.

Even if Hadrian had not died at this particular moment, it is doubtful that the choice of Otto von Wittelsbach who had been one of the chief perpetrators of the Besançon incident, was likely to have furthered peaceful negotiations. Now, once Hadrian was dead, and a successor had to be chosen, there can be no doubt that a man like Otto would use all his resources in Rome to secure the election of a man antagonistic to Hadrian's and Roland's policy. Otto was most probably not aware of the so-called conspiracy. But even if he had been, this would have been only all the more reason for attempting to frustrate its execution.

When Frederick chose Otto as his representative in Rome, he could not have known that Hadrian would die and that Otto might thus be called upon to use his discretion in a situation the delicacy of which far surpassed his political acumen. Otto was a straightforward country squire; a bit of a roughneck; a man more given to action than to thought and reflection. If Frederick had intended extreme measures in Rome, he could not have chosen a better man. But the situation which developed upon Hadrian's death called for subtle manœuvres, not for brutal action.

There is no record of Otto's activities in Rome during that crucial month. But his presence alone must have been an encouragement to the imperial-minded cardinals and the senate and to all other opponents of Hadrian and Roland. Given Otto's character, it is unlikely that he kept quietly in the background. What exactly he did and how exactly he interfered with the regularity of the

[1] *Gesta*, IV, xlix–1. At this point Frederick may have had the regrets about Arnold of Brescia's execution, reported in the Bergamo Epic, *Gesta di Federico I in Italia*, E. Monaci ed., Rome, 1887, p. 34.

election of the new pope we shall never know. But there can be little doubt that he decided quickly and thoughtlessly that he would serve his master best by seeing to it that Cardinal Octavian should be the next pope.[1]

If Otto had been able to bring about Octavian's election in an unequivocal and more or less orderly way, this would obviously have suited Frederick best and would have been very much in his interest. But in view of the fact that there had been a conspiracy and that Roland and his party were determined to abide by its terms, the election of Octavian could not be considered a foregone conclusion. And given Roland's stubbornness and determination, it might have been safer, from Frederick's point of view, to allow Roland to be elected in an orderly manner and then try to come to terms with him over the territorial dispute – for as the earlier negotiations had shown there was no other more fundamental dispute. But Otto could only see matters in terms of black and white. To him, Octavian was white and Roland black. It probably – and this must be said in his defence – escaped his understanding that if Octavian were elected, Roland, bound by the conspiracy, would seek his own ways and means to oppose Octavian and cause a schism in the church. The possibility of a schism was again beyond him; and so were the likely consequences of a schism for the emperor. It need not even be assumed that Otto wanted to have Octavian elected. Octavian was anything but a puppet of Otto. Otto was merely determined to prevent the election of Roland and thus frustrate, unwittingly, the conspiracy made at Anagni. But to prevent the election of Roland was to give a free hand to Octavian, whose standing in Rome was such that any hesitation or dissent among the electors would almost certainly result in an attempt to elevate him.[2]

Octavian, indeed, was no ordinary cardinal. He belonged to the noble Roman family of the Monticelli[3] who were a related line of

[1] W. Holtzmann, *Quellen und Forschungen zur Geschichte Friedrich Barbarossas*, NA, 48, 1930, p. 397.

[2] Hauck, 1954 ed., IV, p. 245, suggests very plausibly that Frederick's agents were merely trying to prevent the election of Roland. K. Hampe, HZ, 106, p. 359, thinks they had positively wanted to have Octavian elected.

[3] P. Kehr, *Zur Geschichte Victors IV*, NA, 46, 1926, pp. 58–9.

the Tusculum counts, that is of the house of Maroza and Alberic.[1] From approximately 950 to approximately 1050, this family had treated the papacy as if it was their personal property. The popes who had ruled under the aegis of this family had all been simonists and anathema to the movement for reform – in fact it would not be an exaggeration to say that the growth of the reform movement and its capture of the papacy, ever since the days of Nicholas II and Leo IX in the middle of the eleventh century, was a direct reaction against the pernicious predominance of that family.

The Monticelli family seat was a castle on a high rock from which they had tried to extend their power over the region and into the city of Rome. From the beginning of the eleventh century there is evidence of their attempts to do so by worming their way simoniacally into monasteries and bishoprics and the college of cardinals, and by supporting several anti-Gregorian pretenders to the papacy. In short, the Monticelli and the counts of Tusculum were the feudal nobility from whose clutches the Gregorian reform party had been striving to free both papacy and church.

But this was by no means the whole of Octavian's background. He was also related to the greatest families in Bavaria, Provence and Champagne.[2] He was related to Richilde, the widow of Alfonso VII of Castile and the wife of Count Raimund. Richilde was the daughter of Agnes of Austria, sister of Henry Jasomirgott. She was the grand-daughter of the daughter of the Emperor Henry IV and hence a niece of Conrad III and a cousin of Frederick.[3] Moreover, through Adela of Blois, whom Louis VII of France married in 1161, Octavian came to be related to both the kings of France and England.[4] Similarly, Octavian was related to Henry of Troyes, who was to make himself the protagonist of his cause in France,[5] and to Guido of Crema who as Paschal III was supposed to succeed him as pope in 1164.[6]

[1] *See* P. Munz, *The Coronation of Otto the Great*, HT, XII, 1962, P. Kehr thinks that the Monticelli were a collateral of the Tusculan counts, *op. cit.*, pp. 80–3. J. Haller, *Papsttum*, III, p. 504, doubts this.

[2] Kehr, *op. cit.*, pp. 53–83.

[3] Victor referred to Richilde as *consanguinea*, Kehr, *op. cit.*, pp. 84–5.

[4] John of Salisbury, *Hist. Pont.*, MGH, SS, XX, p. 531.

[5] Hugh of Vézelay, MGH, SS, 26, p. 147.

[6] John of Salisbury, *loc. cit.*

Given these connections, it is not difficult to see that Octavian should have had special sympathies with German imperial circles. He had always represented imperial interests in the cardinals' college. In 1155 it had been Octavian who had led the knights who conquered the Leonine City to make the coronation of Frederick possible,[1] and at that time Hadrian had commended Octavian to Frederick as a man 'most faithful to you'.[2] A few years later, when Rainald and Otto von Wittelsbach were preparing Italy for the Great Design, a nephew of Octavian had been a member of the embassy from Rome which had approached the imperial commissioners.[3] Otto von Wittelsbach was thus personally acquainted with Octavian's Roman circle and it is not surprising that Octavian was widely known as a special friend of the Germans.[4]

Octavian's family connections and his general place in the social and political alignments of his age are clear enough. It is much more difficult, however, to form an impression of his character and personality. If one takes an overall view and sees him as a member of the European aristocracy, one might readily agree with the judgement of Bishop Arnulf of Lisieux, who considered him a mere tool of the feudal aristocracy's attempts to regain control of the church and undo the Gregorian reform movement.[5] By the time Frederick had firmly committed himself to the support of Octavian as pope, this was probably the only light in which one could see the situation: Roland as Alexander III on one side, the supporter of the Gregorian reform movement and the protagonist of the freedom of the church; and Octavian, as Victor IV, on the other side, the servant of the European lay aristocracy, bent upon allowing the church to be used for worldly ends. But there were people who thought well of him personally. William of Tyre, for instance, reports that Octavian had been one of the very few cardinals who had not been corrupted by the Knights Hospitalers when an embassy from Jerusalem had complained about these knights in

[1] *See* above, p. 85. [2] *Gesta,* II, xxxi.

[3] Döberl, p. 116.

[4] 'Specialis amator Theutonicorum'; *Gesta Alberonis Treviren. Auctore Balderico,* ad 1147, MGH, SS, 8, p. 255.

[5] *Arnulfi Lexoviensis Episcopi Epistolae,* ed., J. A. Giles, p. 116.

1156.[1] Gerhoh of Reichersberg thought well of him;[2] among the citizens of Rome he seems to have been well liked,[3] and Abbot Adam of Ebrach, at a time when Octavian was not yet a controversial figure, had written that if Octavian had a fault it was that he was too zealous.[4] As against such favourable opinions, there is a host of adverse judgements. John of Salisbury, a dedicated supporter of Alexander III, painted a very dark picture of Octavian and was specially negative about Octavian's legatine activities in Germany in the early 1150s.[5] But we know that just in regard to this legatine mission in Germany, Gerhoh was prepared to defend Octavian.[6] If anything, Octavian had been too strict an upholder of ecclesiastical discipline, as Abbot Adam of Ebrach, at least, had thought. During the months preceding the papal election of 1159, Octavian's relations with the imperial party were obviously close, and, like Hadrian and Roland, he had accepted money from his supporters.[7] But money was necessary to pursue Roman politics, and it does not necessarily follow that a man who accepts financial support is personally corrupt.

As soon as Hadrian's death became known in Rome, the remainder of the cardinals, including Octavian and several senators, rushed to Anagni. Upon their arrival there broke out a quarrel over the funeral. The Sicilian party wanted Hadrian buried in Anagni and wanted to proceed to an election there and then in order to avoid any interference. The imperial party insisted on a funeral in Rome. The presence of Roman senators proved decisive: they demanded that the body be taken to Rome and the election be held in the city according to canonical custom. When it became clear that this demand could not be resisted, both the Sicilian and the imperial party rushed to Rome to rally support.

[1] 'Of all the throng of cardinals only two or three were found who, following after Christ, piously desired to aid His servant in that cause. These were Octavius and John of St Martin. . . . All the others, led astray by gifts, followed the ways of Balaam, the son of Bosnor.' William of Tyre, *A History of Deeds Done Beyond the Sea*, XVIII, 8.

[2] Psalms, 65, p. 494, 10. *Cp.* P. Classen, *Gerhoch of Reichersberg*, Wiesbaden, 1960, p. 136.

[3] Hauck, IV, p. 236, note 4, for further sources.

[4] W. Ohnsorge, *Eine Ebracher Briefsammlung*, QuF, XX, p. 36, No. VIII. In 1151, when this letter was written, Octavian was not a controversial figure.

[5] *Hist. Pont.*, 38.

[6] P. Classen, *op. cit.*, p. 136.

[7] Peter of Blois, PL, CCVII, pp. 141–3.

The Sicilian party ensconced themselves in the Castle of St Angelo whose men had been faithful to Hadrian. When Octavian was invited to join them there for deliberation, he refused to come because, probably rightly, he feared for his safety.[1]

On 4 September all the cardinals met at the funeral and appear to have agreed there to meet in St Peter's for the election. But when they were assembled in the room behind the altar, it turned out, as was to be expected, that the cardinals were too deeply divided to reach a decision and elect a new pope. The Sicilian party was in a slight majority and they favoured Roland – the obvious choice; for he was both the founder and the leader of their party for years. The wrangling dragged on for three days, and still no decision could be reached. Finally Octavian's party suggested that an outsider be elected – or alternatively that either party be appointed to select a pope from among the members of the other party. Both alternatives amounted to a compromise, for, in either case, neither Roland nor Octavian could hope to be chosen. When an agreement was reached on this matter, the discussion was postponed to the following day.[2]

During the adjournment, when Octavian's friends were eating or sleeping, Roland's party decided to take the initiative. They based their decision on the knowledge that Roland had, after all, had a majority of votes. Cardinal Otto, the prior of the deacons, whose office it was to place the papal mantle upon the new pope, was ready and forced the mantle on Roland. Roland himself had

[1] I follow Giesebrecht, V, pp. 228–9.

[2] Giesebrecht, V, p. 230, accepts the first alternative; Ribbeck, *Der Traktat über die Papstwahl des Jahres 1159*, FDG, 25, 1885, p. 360, the second. *The Treatise on the Schism*, Sudendorf, No. XXII, pp. 62 ff., composed by an author friendly to Roland's cause, reports that when no agreement about a new pope was possible, Octavian's party suggested that an outsider be elected. Ribbeck observes that this plan is not mentioned in any other source, but it happens to correspond exactly to the procedure laid down in the *pactum* made between Hadrian and the cardinals (i.e. the second conspiracy), *op. cit.*, p. 360. Roland's party agreed, and the discussion was postponed to the next day. But when Octavian's friends were asleep or eating, Roland's party proceeded to an immantation of Roland. Ribbeck, *op. cit.*, points out that this report fits in well with a letter from Arnulf of Lisieux to Ymar, cardinal bishop of Tusculum, a friend of Octavian. The letter is in Watterich, II, pp. 466 ff.: Arnulf blames Ymar for having been so greedy for wine and food that he absented himself too soon from the election meeting! Ribbeck adds that Ymar absented himself in good faith, because he believed that the meeting had been adjourned. At any rate, the *Treatise* and Arnulf's letter corroborate one another.

scruples and resisted, and Octavian in person tried to stop the immantation.[1] There was a confusion and tumult, in the course of which the mantle was said to have been torn in shreds.

When it became known that the cardinals were actually struggling with each other, the clergy and many other people who were waiting outside broke into the room. It is not likely that they should have done this spontaneously. And if one is seeking the precise moment at which Otto von Wittelsbach and his soldiers interfered physically, it must have been then.[2] The crowd broke through the barriers at the altar. The riot had been prepared, for Octavian's chaplain suddenly produced a purple mantle and Octavian was declared to the assembled crowd to have been elected Pope Victor IV. The immantation took place immediately and in such haste that the mantle was thrust upon Octavian upside down. Then Victor was placed upon the throne of St Peter, a *Te Deum* was intoned, and the imperial cardinals and the assembled crowd rushed forward to kiss the new pope's feet.

The issue thus forced, Roland abandoned his scruples. He and his cardinals withdrew to the Castle of St Angelo and were forced to admit that the city's populace rejoiced in the election of Victor.

[1] If one accepts Ribbeck's reasoning in the preceding note, there was every reason why Roland, mindful of the adjournment, should have tried to stop the immantation.

[2] The participation of the crowd and clergy in papal elections, though frowned upon by Gregorian purists, was neither uncommon nor strictly illegal. A decree which expressly forbade the participation of the Roman clergy in papal elections, was issued only in 1179 by Alexander III. The 1179 decree was an attempt to legitimize his own election of 1159, in which the clergy appear to have been on Octavian's side. *Cp.* Mühlbacher, *Die streitige Papstwahl des Jahres 1159*, p. 170. – Alexander never claimed that the clergy and populace had been on his side. He always sought to prove his claims by insisting that he had had a majority of the votes of the cardinals. There are several sources which mention that the Roman citizens entered the hall where the election was being held, sword in hand and acclaimed Octavian: two letters by Alexander, Gerhoh of Reichersberg, a letter by a canon of St Peter's and Arnulf of Lisieux. For all of them see F. Tourtual, *Böhmens Anteil an den Kämpfen Kaiser Friedrichs in Italien*, Göttingen, 1865, Vol. II, p. 210, note 320. Unfortunately Tourtual does not mention that all these sources, with the possible exception of Gerhoh, were friendly to Alexander. But, at any rate, the story is completely plausible. Even if one wants to discount Otto von Wittelsbach's part in the crowd movement, the Romans themselves had reason to favour Octavian. They had made overtures both to Conrad III and to Frederick and had been repulsed because in those days Conrad and Frederick had been on friendly terms with Eugene III and Hadrian. It now occurred to them that they were likely to to get further with the emperor if they elected a pope like Octavian who would not continue the anti-communal policies of Eugene and Hadrian.

But given the fact that a majority of the electors had in the first instance voted for him, Roland refused to admit defeat. The city, however, was for Victor, and Roland had to remain in hiding in the castle for several days. Nevertheless, he considered himself the rightfully elected pope. As soon as it became known in the city that there had been a 'double' election, the old factions took sides. The two chief chapters of Rome, the canons of St Peter and the canons of the Lateran, used the opportunity to start their old quarrel as to which chapter held the primacy. Those of St Peter opted for Victor, and those of the Lateran for Alexander. And similarly the noble factions took sides. The Frangipani declared for Alexander, even though at one stage they had opposed the Gregorian reform and had sided with the imperialists. But the Pierleoni, together with the prefect of the city, the Teobaldi and the Stefaneschi, came out for Victor.[1] With the city thus divided, both Alexander and Victor thought it wiser to depart. Alexander was first smuggled out of the castle and, after finding brief refuge in Trastevere, stole away. Victor, too, left. But he, at least, did not have to sneak out.

On 18 September, at Cisterna, near Aricia, Alexander was formally immantated and proclaimed the new pope. On the following Sunday, the canonically appointed consecrator, the bishop of Ostia, Cardinal Ubald, consecrated and crowned him. On the same day Alexander ordered Octavian, upon pain of excommunication, to give up his claims. When Octavian, after a week, had refused to comply, he and his electors were formally declared excommunicated.

Alexander's determined stand proved effective. Most of the local bishops rallied to him and Victor had great difficulty in getting himself consecrated on 4 October at Farfa. Thereupon the two popes took up residence in different places: Alexander in Anagni and Victor in Segni.

[1] P. Brezzi, *Lo scisma inter regnum et sacerdotium al tempo di Federico Barbarossa*, ADR, 63, 1940, pp. 46–7. – Boso, p. 379, maintains that public opinion suddenly changed in favour of Roland. But Hauck, *op. cit.*, p. 243, note 4, rightly doubts this. He says that all that happened was probably that the Frangipani faction stirred up a popular commotion, the confusion of which allowed Roland to flee. But there was, at that time, no sudden change of public opinion.

It was not long before the news of these troublesome events reached Frederick who was then deeply immersed in the siege of Crema. Frederick was probably furious. Furious at the double election and equally furious when he was apprised of Otto von Wittelsbach's part in it. He had sent Otto in good faith to make an alliance with the Romans. He had never dreamt that Hadrian would die and that Otto would give so narrow a meaning to his mission as to make sure that Octavian would be elected pope – or at any rate would make sure of Octavian's election in the teeth of such an opposition. As to Frederick's reaction there can really be no doubt. The promotion of Octavian's cause, regardless of all other considerations, had been Otto's contribution.[1] In this policy, Otto had followed his master Rainald. And soon there was no doubt in the world as to Rainald's active authorship of this policy.[2] But at that time Frederick's relations with both Eberhard of Bamberg and Eberhard of Salzburg were still close and cordial; and there is no reason why one should believe that Frederick was not as open to their opinion as to that of Rainald. And the opinion of the two Eberhards was unequivocally in favour of a free election.

Moreover, within weeks, Frederick faced a situation which made it clear to him that a schism in the church would only complicate his plans in Lombardy and that Victor's partisanship for the empire would be no compensation unless his claims to the papacy could be universally and peacefully and canonically vindicated. Towards the end of the year, the Cistercian Order was making a determined effort to save the city of Milan from Frederick's threatening wrath. St Bernard had had a special affection for Milan, and now the abbots of Cîteaux, Morimund and Clairvaux

[1] It is significant that Victor, in the first instance, appealed to Rainald, not to Frederick. *Cp. Chron. reg. Col.*, ad 1161. He hoped that Rainald would persuade Frederick to support him. *Cp.* Hauck, *op. cit.*, p. 247. With the help of Otto von Wittelsbach, Rainald had presented Frederick with a *fait accompli*. He was to use the same tactics when Victor died in Lucca in 1164. *See* below, p. 236.

[2] There is an overwhelming list of opinions that Rainald was responsible for the schism: John of Salisbury, especially PL, 199, 268 D; Roger of Hoveden, *Chronicle*, MGH, SS, 27, p. 142; *Historia Vizeliacensis*, MGH, SS, 26, p. 148; Alexander III, Bouquet, 15, p. 818; Gerald of Cambrai, *Instructio Principis*, MGH, SS, 27, p. 407; *Historia Welforum*, MGH, SS, 23, p. 153; *Annales Melrosenses*, MGH, SS, 27, p. 435; Robertus de Monte, *Chronicle*, MGH, SS, 6, p. 616; *Chronicon Montis Sereni*, MGH, SS, 27, p. 435.

together with ten other Cistercian abbots approached both Frederick and Milan to negotiate an agreement. Frederick, mindful of the ultimate objectives of the Great Design, was only too ready.[1] But the Milanese, mindful of their agreement with Hadrian, were not in a position to negotiate freely. They were bound to the Roman *curia*, and at that time, for all practical purposes, the *curia*, to them, was Alexander III.

Frederick, therefore, was completely sincere when he decided there and then to submit the disputed election to a universal council.[2] He might have had personal preferences for Octavian. But he could see no advantage in a schism or in a pope foisted upon the church by the empire, no matter how sympathetic such a pope might prove to the Great Design. For a schism would draw all of Christendom into the battle between the Lombards and Frederick and turn this purely local conflict into an international issue. Frederick, at the end of 1159, did not want to be diverted from the Great Design to a conflict in which all kings of Christendom would have to take sides, and in which the bishops of Germany and Italy might be tempted to opt for Frederick's enemies.

By the end of 1159, the double election as such could not be undone. But Frederick decided to take the next best step and summon a council to adjudicate upon it. But with such a decision Frederick was caught in an unfortunate position. If the emperor summoned a council he claimed implicitly the right to arbitrate between two claimants to the papacy. This would immediately be interpreted by his enemies as an attack on the freedom of the church. Moreover, when Frederick summoned both Octavian and Roland to attend the council, the latter had every reason for not

[1] Giesebrecht, V, p. 235. Frederick used this opportunity for consulting these Cistercians about the schism and was assured by them that he was entitled to call a council to decide a disputed papal election. S. Mitterer, *Die Cisterzienser und der Kirchenstreit zwischen Alexander III und Kaiser Friedrich I*, CCh, 34, 1922, p. 4. Perhaps, at this delicate moment, the Cistercians did not wish to jeopardize the chances of peace for Milan by antagonizing Frederick over the question of the papacy.

[2] Frederick's first reaction to the double election is contained in a letter to Eberhard of Salzburg: Frederick begged Eberhard to keep calm and not to commit himself to either side in haste. He let it be known in Germany, Burgundy and Aquitaine that he would recognize as pope only the man who had been elected in the correct manner, and that he wanted to act in concert with France and England. MGH, Const. I, p. 252, No. 181.

wanting to appear. He could have no confidence in Frederick's impartiality and feared that a decision against him would be a foregone conclusion.[1] He was probably wrong in this fear – but given Frederick's interests and the influence of Rainald and Otto von Wittelsbach, it was a natural reaction. And so he decided at once to refuse to recognize the authority of such an imperially convoked council to sit in judgement on his claim. His reasons were dictated by political considerations. But the grounds upon which he based his refusal were a shrewd piece of propaganda: he declared that a pope – and this was an ancient canon law – could not be judged by an emperor, and that, therefore, as an upholder of the freedom of the church, he could not attend the proposed council. If Frederick had had some reasonable way of convincing Alexander, at this moment, of his impartiality, Alexander might have been persuaded to attend. In such a case, he could have been confident of his cause, for he had had a majority of the votes. The council would have accepted him as the rightful pope and all would have been well. Alexander would have continued to side with Milan against Frederick; but after the final subjection of Milan, some kind of understanding between empire and papacy could, no doubt, have been reached. Frederick would have been free to pursue the Great Design and give his undivided attention to the problems of government in Lombardy. But the only way of winning the confidence of Alexander and his supporters would have been to fall in completely with their wishes. And these wishes were that Frederick should interpret his duty to protect the church of Rome and its bishop in one sense and one sense only, that is by declaring himself openly in favour of Alexander.[2] But

[1] But before the decision to summon a council was taken, not even Alexander had believed that Frederick favoured Octavian. His electors wrote to Frederick (*Gesta*, IV, lxiii) and begged him to protect Alexander. This was a conciliatory letter and quite unprecedented. The pope, instead of announcing his election to the emperor, as was customary, implored the emperor's protection. The letter was written by some cardinals in early November 1159 and suggests that at that time they considered the issue an open one and were by no means convinced that Frederick would be partial to Octavian. *Cp.* W. Holtzmann, *Quellen und Forschungen zur Geschichte Friedrich Barbarossas*, NA, 48, 1930, pp. 388–9.

[2] For these wishes see Giesebrecht, V, pp. 238–9. Alexander replied to Frederick's invitation to the council that he recognized Frederick as a very special *advocatus* and defender of the holy church; but expressed surprise that Frederick should have taken

this Frederick could not do, because Rainald was against it, and Rainald, in order to win Frederick to his point of view, probably argued that all might still be well provided Victor's claims could be vindicated by the council and accepted by Christendom. For in this case, Milan would lose the support of the papacy and the Great Design could continue without further hindrance. It was Frederick's mistake to allow himself to be won for what seemed, at first glance, the way of least resistance.

The council was summoned to Pavia for 13 January 1160. It is significant that its opening had to be postponed, because Frederick at that time was still busy with the siege of Crema. It was not until 3 February that Frederick was able to reach Pavia and to open, after the appropriate celebrations of his victory over Crema, the session of the council.

A large number of bishops had responded to the summons and assembled in Pavia. The archbishops of Mainz, Cologne, Hamburg and Magdeburg were present and together with several German and Italian bishops they swelled the number of bishops to a total of about fifty. The archbishop of Trier had fallen ill on his journey; but, and this was a severe blow to Frederick, the archbishop of Salzburg had refused to come.[1] The Burgundian bishops preferred, on the whole, to be represented by delegates. The king of England, Henry II, had sent a message that he would accept the decision of the council; but the king of France had written that

---

it upon himself to summon a council without his (Alexander's) knowledge, as if he were his (Frederick's) vassal. The church must be free and Frederick ought not to usurp power over it. Watterich, II, p. 383. Alexander's cardinals seem to have been willing to attend the council if they were given the presidency. *See* Gerhoh, *De Investigatione Antichristi*, c. 60.

[1] Eberhard of Salzburg started on his journey to Pavia, but turned back at Treviso and sent an excuse to Frederick that he had been taken ill. (*Gesta*, IV, lxxiii.) It looks as if Eberhard had at first decided to attend and then changed his mind. But there is another letter, Tengnagel, No. 38, to Bishop Roman of Gurk, from which it appears that Eberhard had never intended to go to Pavia and that his journey to a place near Treviso had been undertaken for a different reason. W. Schmidt, *Die Stellung der Erzbischöfe und des Erzstiftes von Salzburg zu Kirche und Reich unter Friedrich I*, AOG, 34, 1865, p. 19, points out that therefore Eberhard had never intended to go to Pavia and that he had sided in favour of Alexander immediately. Eberhard's decision therefore did not depend on the views of other bishops but on his belief that Alexander alone had been elected in the correct manner. His immediate decision is further proof that it was widely believed that Octavian was Frederick's, or possibly Rainald's, puppet; and that this was believed long before Pavia.

he would like more detailed information as to the problem and the council's business.[1] Further, there were envoys from the kings of Poland and Hungary and Denmark, as well as a largish number of lay princes. But above all, Victor IV had come, in person. Alexander III, however, did not appear. He was not even represented and none of his cardinals – the majority of the college – had come. Of Alexander's supporters only Cardinal William, by birth a Pavian, a personal friend, was present. Rumour had it that in Rome he had voted, possibly by proxy, for Octavian; but that he had since changed sides. At any rate, he did not attend as Alexander's representative and had come more probably as an observer.

Given this composition of the council, most people's first feeling was that a decision would have to be postponed, for there was nobody who could speak for Alexander. But Frederick was anxious to proceed with the war against Milan; and before doing so he wanted to settle the schism. It was therefore decided to examine briefly the question of the majority of votes – an examination, the result of which showed quite clearly that Alexander's claims were superior to those of Victor. But the partisans of Victor flooded the council with testimonies to prove that no matter what the voting among the cardinals had been, the approval and support of the clergy and the people of Rome for Octavian had been overwhelming[2] and that as a result Octavian had indeed been the first to wear the papal mantle. There is no denying that by this argument the supporters of Victor strengthened their case, for the

[1] There is no reason to doubt that when Frederick wrote to the kings of France and England, he wanted to hold a council in Pavia and recognize as pope the man whom everybody agreed to be the rightful pope, he was completely sincere. The letter of September 1159 is in Watterich, II, pp. 453–4. Nevertheless one might note that the letters of invitation did not all strike the same tone. The one addressed e.g. to the bishop of Brixen contains a high-sounding introduction to the effect that there is a universal empire, that it is *one* and that there must be *one* emperor and *one* pope. But the letter addressed to the kings of England and France wisely omits any reference to the universality of the empire; and merely states that there ought to be no more than *one* pontiff of the church. Both letters are in MGH, Const. I, Nos. 182 and 183. See the astute remarks about the employment of these rhetorical devices by N. Rubinstein, *Political Rhetoric in the Imperial Chancery*, MAe, 14, 1945, p. 29.

[2] The most important document to this effect submitted to the council was a letter from a canon of St Peter in Rome. *See* Giesebrecht, V, p. 246 and his comments on the text, VI, pp. 392–3.

presence of Otto von Wittelsbach had indeed been the immediate cause for this overwhelming popular acclamation of Octavian.

There was, of course, a weighty doubt. Ever since the days of Nicholas II it had been laid down that a pope was to be elected not by a popular vote (which had at best always been an acclamation and, at worst, nothing more than a riot) but by a college of cardinals. If Victor was now proclaimed the rightful pope because he had had a more spontaneous crowd of supporters among the clergy and people of Rome, he would stand out as a pope who opposed the Gregorian reform movement. In order to counter the charge that Victor's record in regard to the reform movement was not clean and wipe out any blemish which might thus attach itself to him, evidence was brought forward that Roland and Hadrian had conspired not only to aid Milan – which was no more than a political move[1] – but also to secure the election of a successor to Hadrian who would continue to pursue an anti-imperial course. Such a conspiracy was an offence against the canon that a papal election ought to be a free election, and with this type of testimony the supporters of Victor were on much firmer ground. If Victor's claim was based solely on the fact that he had enjoyed a popular acclamation in Rome (no matter how engineered), Alexander's majority among the cardinals had been due to an uncanonical conspiracy. And thus Alexander's claim to stand for the freedom of the church was not exactly justified either.

It had to be admitted that Roland had been elected by the *major pars*; but in view of the conspiracy, not by the *sanior pars*.[2]

[1] Even before the Council of Pavia, the Alexandrian cardinals complained that Otto von Wittelsbach made it physically impossible for Alexander to communicate with his supporters. The letter is printed by W. Holtzmann, *Zur Geschichte Friedrich Barbarossas*, NA, 48, pp. 398 ff. It was only natural that Octavian's supporters should make the most of such evidence of a conspiracy as there was. See especially the speech edited by Sudendorf, I, pp. 62–6. But the most startling piece of evidence produced were several letters written by Alexander and his cardinals to the bishops and cities of Lombardy. These letters are mentioned by Provost Henry of Berchtesgaden in a letter to Bishop Eberhard of Salzburg, *Gesta*, IV, lxxxii. There is no certainty how these letters fell into the hands of Octavian's friends. But it seems probable that Otto von Wittelsbach's men managed to capture a messenger from the archbishop of Milan. *See* Tengnagel, p. 393.

[2] Gerhoh of Reichersberg was as anxious for the freedom of the church as John of Salisbury. But he had very serious doubts as to the legitimacy of Alexander's election. He objected to the Anagni conspiracy and considered the fact that money had passed

All in all, the claims of Alexander and Victor were fairly even, though for very different reasons. But since Alexander's case was not represented, the members of the council ended up by deciding for Victor. Victor's case was certainly not hopeless; and given the fact that most members of the council were favourable to Frederick and that they knew that Victor would suit him better than Alexander, they decided for Victor. Frederick himself took great care to keep well in the background during the deliberations and the final verdict was first brought forward by the ecclesiastical members of the council. A majority voted for Victor. The patriarch of Aquileia and several Italian bishops adhered to this decision, but with the proviso that they were doing so because the matter was urgent for the empire and that they would like the question to be re-submitted to the church universal. Eberhard of Bamberg and the bishops of Passau and Ratisbon stipulated the same condition.

Only then did Frederick himself come forward and declare that he recognized the bishops' verdict, and thus Victor was acclaimed. On the following day Victor was accorded papal honours: there was a festive procession and Frederick, waiting at the portals of the cathedral, held the pope's stirrup and led him to the altar where he kissed his feet. The council was closed on 13 February, under the chairmanship of Victor. At this last session, Roland and the most important of his supporters were excommunicated. After the candles had been extinguished, the king of Sicily and the Milanese were formally asked to answer for their opposition to empire and church.

The council concluded, the storm broke loose. Frederick was aware that the decisions of the council were one thing and the adherence of Christendom to these decisions another. But he had

---

hands as proof of Alexander's simony. He further held Alexander to be a simonist because Alexander demanded money from his supporters and had absolved Frederick's subjects from their oaths of fealty. See his *De Investigatione Antichristi*, I, 55, p. 364, and 68, p. 385, and 69, p. 388. He held, therefore, that there was no telling where the right was in this dispute (*ibid.*, I, 53, p. 359). Only a general synod could decide (*ibid.*, I, 56, p. 365). Gerhoh rejected the argument, in this case, that a pope cannot be judged by anybody and that therefore a synod was against canon law. He pointed out that the dispute was precisely as to who was pope (*ibid.*, 56, p. 367; 57, 370), and therefore Gerhoh did not mind that such a synod would have to be summoned by a secular ruler (*ibid.*, 56, p. 366).

probably not anticipated the vigour and persuasiveness of Alexander's propaganda campaign. On Shrove Tuesday, 24 March 1160, Alexander excommunicated both Frederick and the other authors of the schism. He recognized almost immediately that such an excommunication no longer produced the same effect which had been produced a century earlier, when Gregory VII had excommunicated Henry IV.

But Alexander had other resources. He sent legates and letters to every corner of Christendom and appealed to the better conscience of clergy and laity. He took his stand upon the Gregorian reform movement and made out that he had been a victim of secular tyranny, of the emperor's attempt to nominate a pope. He took great pains to discredit the council of Pavia. Frederick, it was alleged, had blackmailed the bishops and had personally invested Octavian with the papacy. This version of the proceedings was designed to rouse all dormant fears about the independence of the papacy. Alexander further took great pains to point out that the claim that 153 bishops had been present at the council was ridiculous. This high figure had been arrived at because for every metropolitan who had attended, all his suffragans were counted; and of those countries whose rulers had written, all bishops were deemed to have been present. Worst of all, Rainald, who had just been elected archbishop of Cologne, was counted even though he had not only not been consecrated, but had not even been ordained a priest. And the archbishop of Ravenna had simply been represented by his father, a Lombard count.[1] Thus Alexander was able to make the most of people's sympathies for the Gregorian ideals[2]

[1] Haller, pp. 154–5.

[2] M. Pacaut, *Alexandre III*, Paris, 1956, pp. 120–1. To all right thinking people there was indeed ample room for reform in the church. According to Gerhoh of Reichersberg, at the *curia* almost everything was being done for money. He considered the Roman clergy particularly unspiritual, venal and corrupt. Eugene III, he said, had been quite exceptional in his personal honesty. *Cp.* his *De Investigatione Antichristi*, MGH, LdL, III, pp. 161, 312, 355, 359, 372, 378, 388, 391. He alleged that the power to bind and loose was exercised for money, preferments and privileges, exemptions of monasteries were given for money. Litigations were decided by bribes, usury flourished and papal officials lived in great luxury and held whole monasteries to ransom. John of Salisbury, *Policraticus*, Webb ed., pp. 67 ff., concurred: the Roman church is not a mother, but a step-mother and the papacy is dominated by venality, vanity and bribery. And William of Tyre, *A History of Deeds Done beyond the Sea*, XVIII, 8, found it remarkable that Cardinal Octavian, of all people, was incorruptible.

and presented himself as the victim of a secular plot to subject the church to purely mundane ends.[1] Frederick was depicted as a persecutor of God[2] and Octavian as the son of the devil.[3] By contrast, Alexander represented himself as a lover of God and a protector of the liberty of the church.[4] In order to underline Frederick's role as the persecutor of the church, Alexander exploited the fact that because of his forced exile from Rome, he was a pauper. Nothing could be more likely in that age to enlist the sympathies of earnest Christians than a pope who actually proclaimed that he was literally destitute[5] and the poor man of Christ, *pauper Christi.*[6] If this argument was designed to raise the support of the common people, he turned to the kings and rulers of Christendom by making the most of the idea that an emperor who oppressed the church was likely to claim universal hegemony.[7] Alexander indeed pointed out that Frederick's final aim was to get the power of *both* swords, the spiritual and the secular, in order to subdue all kings and princes. And for the benefit of the citizens of Lombardy he used yet another facet of the same argument. He reminded them that an emperor was always the head of an oppressive feudal aristocracy, the chief exponent of simony, the enemy of civic liberties,[8] and thus he saw to it that the Lombards connected Frederick with the traditional enemies of their beloved St Ambrose, the Arian heretics.

Every one of these themes was taken up by Alexander's sup-

[1] On 1 April 1160, Alexander wrote to Bishop Arnulf of Lisieux that Frederick had already once invaded the patrimony of St Peter with violence during the pontificate of Hadrian. He omitted to mention that that violence had then been exercised as much on behalf of Hadrian as on behalf of Frederick. But the memory of Frederick's violence in 1155 now helped to underline Frederick's support of a 'schismatic, a simonist and an obvious intruder', i.e. Victor. (*See* PL, CC, p. 88.) In another place Alexander sought to prove that Frederick had already planned to put up Victor as an anti-pope to Hadrian. *Cp.* W. Schmidt, *Die Stellung der Erzbischöfe und des Erzstiftes von Salzburg zu Kirche und Reich unter Friedrich I,* AOG, 34, 1865, p. 25.

[2] Watterich, II, p. 382.

[3] H. Karge, *Die Gesinnung und die Massnahmen Alexanders III,* Greifswald, 1914, p. 20. Victor was depicted as the tool of a secular magistrate. *See* P. Brezzi, *op. cit.*, p. 79.

[4] Watterich, II, p. 384.

[5] *Cp.* F. Heer, *Aufgang Europas,* Wien-Zürich, 1948, pp. 341, 352.

[6] *ibid.*, p. 617.

[7] Bouquet, 15, p. 761; JL, Nos. 10627 and 10628.

[8] Chiapelli, *La formazione storica del commune cittadino in Italia,* ASI, 14, 1928–30, p. 54.

porters. Walter of Chatillon, in one of his poems, called Frederick the precursor of Antichrist.[1] John of Salisbury and Arnulf of Lisieux spread that Frederick was aggressive, proud and overbearing and that his ultimate aim was to subjugate the whole of Christendom to his tyranny.[2] John of Salisbury poured scorn on the council of Pavia and ridiculed it.[3] He explained that Alexander was far from being a papal caesar and was in reality *vicarius crucifixi.*[4] He too made the most of Alexander's personal discomforts as a refugee, and came close to describing him as a type of the 'suffering servant'.

This whole propaganda was very cleverly staged. It was Victor's ill luck that, as the favourite of the emperor, he could not appeal to similar righteous sentiments. By the nature of the case, he could not appear other than an imperial protégé and as something resembling a *proprietary* pope – and there was no worse stigma in that enlightened age of Gregorian reform. He tried to compete as best he could with Alexander, and spoke of himself as a defender of the liberties of the church,[5] and at the synod of Dôle, in 1162, he tried to capture public opinion by decreeing that in future his court would entertain only those cases which could not be decided in the locality in which they had arisen.[6] But such protestations could not ring true when they came from a man who owed the papacy to the emperor – and at a synod summoned for June 1161 to Cremona and held at Frederick's request in Lodi, the worst fears were only confirmed.

The main decisions of the synod concerned the excommunication of a whole row of leading Lombards who had made themselves obnoxious to Frederick: the archbishop of Milan, the bishops of Piacenza and Brescia and Bologna, the consuls and councillors of these cities as well as another unknown bishop.[7]

[1] F. Böhm, *Das Bild Friedrich Barbarossas und seines Kaisertums in den ausländischen Quellen seiner Zeit*, Bresslau, 1936, p. 93.

[2] *ibid.*, p. 92.

[3] Especially 59, Giles ed., p. 63. For Alexander's own words see Karge, *op. cit.*, p. 21. William of Newburgh described the proceeding at Pavia thus: 'Whatever favoured the cause of Alexander, as there was no person to plead for him, was either suppressed in silence or craftily perverted, or turned against him.' (*Hist. Aug.*, ii, 9.)

[4] F. Heer, *op. cit.*, p. 352.

[5] H. Karge, *op. cit.*, p. 23.

[6] This decree was ineffective; Haller, p. 173.

[7] Giesebrecht, V, p. 269.

Nothing was more likely to prove Victor a tool of imperial policy. By contrast, Alexander's friends in France prevailed upon both Louis VII and Henry II of England to hold a synod in Toulouse in the autumn of 1160.[1] At that synod the decisions of Pavia were questioned and neither the Sicilian conspiracy nor Hadrian's agreement with Milan were so much as mentioned. And when it was declared that Octavian had been recognized by Frederick even before Pavia, Alexander's cause shone very brightly.[2] Not all suspicions of the rightfulness of Alexander's claims were dispelled[3] but one can gauge the way the wind was beginning to blow by an exchange of letters between Abbot Eberhard of Eberbach and Abbot Adam of Ebrach. Eberhard wrote to Adam to ask which pope he ought to recognize and added that in view of the decision of the synod of Toulouse, which was, after all, a council of the Gallican church, the decision to accept Victor's invitation to the council to be held in the following year in Cremona was not an easy one.[4] In France, the effect of Toulouse was overwhelming. The Cistercians and Carthusians decided definitely for Alexander, and even the monks of Cluny began to waver: their Abbot Hugh, who had at first stood against Alexander, was forced to leave the monastery and seek refuge with Frederick.[5]

[1] P. Classen, *Gerhoch von Reichersberg*, Wiesbaden, 1960, p. 197, note 29. I follow Classen in believing that the synod took place. Gerhoh, MGH, LdL, III, 365, is the only place in which the synod is mentioned. Haller, pp. 160 and 505, and W. Ohnsorge, *Die Legaten Alexanders III*, 1928, pp. 15–38 as well as *Eine Ebracher Briefsammlung*, QuF, 20, 1929, p. 5 and 32, No. 3, believe also that the synod took place. – F. Barlow, *The English, Norman and French Councils called to deal with the Papal Schism of 1159*, EHR, 51, 1936, denies that such a synod ever took place and F. Güterbock, *Le lettere del notaio Bucardo*, BISI, 61, 1949, p. 5, follows Barlow. *Cp.* also H. Böhmer, *Der Dialogus de pontificatu sanctae Romanae ecclesiae*, NA, 21, 1896, p. 679, and F. Barlow, *The Letters of Arnulf of Lisieux*, Camden, 3rd series, 61, 1939, p. XL and p. 48.

[2] The mere fact that the synod had examined the proceedings of Pavia implied a denial that Pavia had been an ecumenical council. An examination 'revealed' that there had been misrepresentations and a lack of neutrality. It was alleged that Frederick had recognized Victor *before* Pavia. – For the growing feeling in favour of Alexander in France, see the letters by Abbot Fastrad of Clairvaux to Bishop Omnibonus of Verona in Mansi, XXI, 1155. Also Watterich, II, 511.

[3] *Cp.* P. Classen, *op. cit.*, p. 198. For Gerhoh's doubts see p. 220, note 2 above.

[4] W. Ohnsorge, *Eine Ebracher Briefsammlung*, QuF, XX, 1928–9, pp. 4–5.

[5] The enthusiasm with which several lay and spiritual lords had flocked to Frederick in 1157 (*Cp.* Ch. IV, p. 119, note 3) had ensured that in the early 60s the monks of Cluny came out in favour of Victor. *Cp.* I. Schnack, *Richard von Cluny. Seine Chronik und sein Kloster in den Anfängen der Kirchenspaltung von 1159*, Berlin, 1921, and P. Fournier,

For the rest, Victor and Alexander competed by sending legates to every corner of Christendom to argue their cases. But Victor's spokesmen were almost always imperial ambassadors – and this was likely to weaken his case – whereas Alexander used his own legates. With the kings of England and France, Frederick had a certain amount of political influence; but both kings knew perfectly well that the majority of the clergy were favouring Alexander because he was the protagonist of the reform movement, and thus Rainald's journey to France and Garsidonius' journey to England remained fairly ineffectual. In the eastern regions of Europe, the competition was even more bitter. The king of Hungary had at first been very favourable to Victor[1] and so had the archbishop of Zara.[2] But Eberhard, the archbishop of Salzburg, and Venice[3] were firmly attached to Alexander. Frederick therefore decided to act prudently. It so happened that the patriarch of Aquileia had died, and that in August 1161 one Ulrich, a friend of Eberhard of Salzburg, was elected to succeed him. Far from brutally opposing this choice, Frederick pretended to welcome it and commissioned one of his diplomats to accompany Ulrich to his new

---

Le royaume d'Arles, Paris, 1891, p. 35, and G. Duby, *La société aux XIe and XIIe siècles dans la région Mâconnaise*, Paris, 1953, p. 537.

[1] W. Holtzmann, *Beiträge zur Reichs- und Rechtsgeschichte des hohen Mittelalters*, Bonn, 1957, p. 148. But it was soon to show itself that Frederick had been far too sanguine in regard to the king of Hungary. Immediately after Pavia, Alexander too had sent legates to Hungary and though they failed to win over King Geza II through the force of their proof that Alexander was the rightful pope, Geza began to waver when he heard of the decision of Toulouse in the autumn of 1160, *ibid.*, p. 149. And towards the end of the following year Burchard ascertained personally that the reason why Geza had been won over was that Alexander had issued a generous privilege to Hungary according to which the king was allowed to bestow the *pallium* on bishops and the clergy were not allowed to enter into relations with the *curia* without the king's permission, *ibid.*, pp. 151–2. One can see that, when expedient, Alexander was always able to depart from the strict observance of the Gregorian ideals for the sake of which he claimed to be persecuted by the emperor.

[2] P. Kehr, *Rom und Venedig*, QuF, XIX, p. 137.

[3] P. Kehr, *op. cit.*, pp. 136–7; Hadrian had been generous to Venice and the relations between the city and the papacy had been cordial. Venice rallied at once to the support of the man she took as the genuine successor of Hadrian, i.e. Alexander. Under the leadership of Alexander's legate Hildebrand, the Alexandrian refugees from all over Lombardy congregated in Venice. For Hildebrand's indefatigable activities see G. Dunken, *Die politische Wirksamkeit der päpstlichen Legaten in der Zeit des Kampfes zwischen Kaisertum und Papsttum in Oberitalien*, EHS, 209, Berlin, 1931, pp. 70–8 and pp. 83–7; also W. Ohnsorge, *Die Legaten Alexanders III*, 1928, p. 45.

see, to guide and influence him. When Ulrich reached Venice, he told the assembled supporters of Alexander there that Frederick was anxious to hold another general council in order to settle the schism. Alexander's legate in Venice was a bit sceptical; but Eberhard of Salzburg, though an open opponent of Victor, was a man with whom Frederick would not easily sever relations. And Eberhard continued to plead with Alexander's legate in Venice for Ulrich and for trusting Frederick's intention to hold a new general council.[1] Frederick knew that in the east everything was in the balance, and he behaved with great discretion.

He had every reason to be discreet. For after the fall of Crema his next and obvious aim was to reduce Milan to obedience. It took him almost two years to achieve this purpose,[2] and by the time he stood on the ruins of the city, the schism had become an international issue and Alexander's cause had sufficiently progressed for Frederick's whole authority to be called into question. 'Who has made', wrote John of Salisbury, 'the Teutons the masters of the world?'[3] He was, of course, referring to the schism and to Frederick's efforts to impose his own pope upon the church. But, by implication, the world which was rallying to Alexander was also rallying to the Lombards, and the destruction of Milan began to assume vast dimensions. Without the schism, the destruction of Milan would have been no more than a harsh punitive measure. With the schism, it came to be seen as the act of a brutal tyrant. Alexander himself, in countless letters and embassies to every part of Christendom, had seen to it that Frederick's behaviour should be interpreted in such terms.[4]

[1] W. Ohnsorge, *op. cit.*, pp. 44 ff. P. Kehr, *Kaiser Friedrich I und Venedig während des Schismas*, QuF, 17, 1924, p. 232, surmises that Ulrich and Burchard were trying to negotiate with Alexander's cardinals about a possible way of ending the schism. Ulrich had been invested with the *regalia* by Frederick but had managed to avoid personal contact with Victor. Doeberl, p. 195, No. 41, and Sudendorf, II, pp. 135 ff. He was therefore in an excellent position to act as a go-between.

[2] *See* p. 182 above. Ten days after the destruction of Milan, Alexander wrote to Eberhard of Salzburg that Frederick, no doubt, was at the height of his success. But it would be of no use to him to gain the whole world if he lost his soul. Quoted by F. Heer, *op. cit.*, p. 617. Frederick might not have worried too much about losing his soul; but he would have agreed with Alexander that under the conditions the triumph was not much use to him.

[3] W. J. Miller, H. E. Butler, C. N. L. Brook ed., *The Letters of John of Salisbury*, London, 1955, Vol. I, p. 206.

[4] Giesebrecht, V, p. 276.

Rainald von Dassel and his friend Burchard, one of Frederick's leading professional diplomats,[1] too, made the most of this situation. Rainald had always been less interested in the Great Design than Frederick and had always merely seen it as an opportunity to push Frederick into grand anti-papal schemes and into plans for universal hegemony. Burchard wrote, just before the final fall of Milan, at Christmas 1161, that the whole of Christendom, misled by Roland, was preparing a general coalition against Frederick, and that it was high time that counter measures against Byzantium, Hungary, Spain, Barcelona and Denmark were taken. Burchard seems to have had no fears at all lest such ambitions should prove too unrealistic. With the victory over Milan, he hoped, everything would fall into Frederick's lap.[2] A council was to be called in Rome, Roland deposed,[3] the empire would be triumphant and the king of England would make an alliance with Frederick.[4] Burchard also advocated violence against

[1] Burchard, the notary, came from Cologne and was educated in the monastery of Siegburg. He always maintained his connections with Siegburg and he may, originally, have met Rainald there. It is most probable that he was brought into the imperial chancellery by Rainald. *Cp.* P. Scheffer-Boichorst, *Der Kaiserliche Notar und der Strassburger Vitztum Burchard*, ZGO, NF, 4, 1889. Scheffer-Boichorst, however, does not think that the notary Burchard was the writer of the *Cologne Chronicle*, who wrote about 1176. *See* his *Gesammelte Schriften*, Berlin, 1905, Vol. II, pp. 226–37. Burchard was deeply devoted to Rainald and must be presumed to have shared his views – or *vice versa*. *Cp.* F. Güterbock, *Le lettere del notaio Bucardo*, BISI, 61, 1949, p. 63. Güterbock insists that the notary Burchard was not identical with the Burkhard from Strassburg who went on an embassy to Saladin in 1175. (*ibid.*, p. 41.)

[2] 'Victo autem Mediolano, per Dei gratiam vicimus omnia.' Döberl, p. 200. With this doctrine, Rainald's extreme policy against Milan becomes intelligible. One should recall, for example, the satisfaction with which Burchard recorded the fact that the imperial ambassador to the king of Hungary had not been well received and the pleasure with which he reported Frederick's alleged comment: 'grates ago Deo, quod honesta occasione amicum perdo vilissimum. Hoc ait significans regulum istum.' (Sudendorf, II, pp. 134 ff, No. 5; Döberl, IV, p. 195, No. 41.) W. Holtzmann, *Beiträge zur Reichs- und Papstgeschichte des hohen Mittelalters*, Bonn, 1957, pp. 150–1, note 2, shows quite conclusively that the Hungarian king who rejected the imperial ambassador was none other than Geza II. Giesebrecht, V, p. 271, was wrong in believing that Geza had died in May 1161. Geza did not die until after the destruction of Milan.

[3] F. Güterbock, *op. cit.*, p. 57.

[4] The Archipoeta's famous imperial hymn,

Salve mundi domine
cesar noster ave . . .
Princeps terre principum,
cesar Friderice . . .

originated most probably at that time. It was commissioned by Rainald and recited

Eberhard of Salzburg[1] whom he called 'a pious bishop and a crazy old man'.[2]

Nowhere can we see the divergence of opinion between Frederick and Rainald better than in regard to the line to be taken with Eberhard of Salzburg. Frederick hoped to remain on friendly terms with him. Rainald and Burchard wanted to have him eliminated by force. When Milan surrendered in the spring of 1162, Rainald's pressure brought about a situation in which Frederick could not but agree to the total destruction of the city,[3] and Rainald remained undaunted by the fact that with this deplorable event the future of the Great Design was jeopardized. But given the views expressed in Burchard's letter of Christmas 1161, it is likely that Rainald used the fear of a universal coalition against Frederick, supposed to have been inspired by Alexander, as an argument in favour of the total physical elimination of Milan, in order to make sure that Frederick's hands would be free by the spring of 1162 to devote himself to what he and his friend Burchard considered to be wider and more rewarding tasks. One cannot but suspect that the news of a universal coalition building up against Frederick was to a large extent Burchard's own fabrication; for there is not a shred of evidence to support it.[4]

---

before Frederick in the middle of May, 1162, in Pavia. *Cp.* Brinckmann, *Die Dichterpersönlichkeit des Archipoeta*, GRM, 1925, p. 107. H. J. Kirfel, *Weltherrschaftsidee und Bundespolitik*, Bonn, 1959, p. 95, thinks it was recited in Novara in 1163. However this may be, there is no doubt that the poem expressed Rainald's and Burchard's political thought and we may surmise that Frederick listened to it with pleasure during a banquet, while his mind was seeking distraction from his real worries, i.e. what to do next. It is very improbable that Frederick himself should have seriously harboured the thoughts expressed in the poem at the very time when his fertile mind was seeking a practical way of drawing the king of France into a plot to capture Alexander, *see* p. 229 below.

[1] F. Güterbock, *op. cit.*, p. 21. [2] *ibid.*, p. 55. [3] *See* p. 183 above.

[4] Unless one considers Boso's (p. 405, line 15) and Helmold's (I, 91) general remarks that Frederick began to fear for his crown and that all other kings feared him as 'evidence', the idea of active steps being taken against Frederick at this time was too ludicrous. I rather suspect that both Boso and Helmold had heard of the rumours that were being spread by Burchard. It is true that Manuel wrote a letter to the king of France to invite him to join a coalition with Sicily, Byzantium and Alexander against Frederick. The letter is in Dölger, No. 1445. Reuter, *Geschichte Alexanders III und der Kirche seiner Zeit*, 1860–4, Vol. II, p. 175, attributed this letter to the year 1161. He was followed by Kap-Herr, *Die abendländische Politik Kaiser Manuels*, Strassburg, 1881 and by Chalandon, *Les Comnène*, II, 2, p. 560. W. Ohnsorge, *Die Legaten Alexanders*, 1928, Excursus I, shows convincingly that the letter belongs to the year 1163.

When Milan was destroyed, Frederick had indeed to turn his attention to the problem of the schism. Alexander, after a brief and unsuccessful attempt to return to Rome, had been forced to withdraw to Palestrina, for Victor's adherents in Rome were too strong. It was this knowledge of their strength which made Frederick confident that after the fall of Milan a new council in Rome would settle the matter definitely in favour of Victor. But when the fall of Milan became imminent, Alexander realized that he would no longer be safe in Italy. He left by ship and landed on 11 April 1162, in France. There was no point, therefore, in holding a council in Rome to depose him. Alexander was not likely to recognize such a council any more than he had recognized the council of Pavia and Frederick, therefore, had to think of plans to settle the matter by other means. Above all, no plan was feasible which did not include a means of capturing Alexander. As long as Alexander was free, there would be no way of forcing him to abandon his claims.

Frederick therefore decided to change his tactics. He abandoned all hope of a negotiated settlement with Alexander.[1] Instead he wanted to capture Alexander and confirm the decisions of Pavia in favour of Victor. Only in this way would it be possible to counter the growing opposition to the empire. In order to achieve this purpose, he got in touch with Henry of Champagne, count of Troyes, a kinsman and supporter of Victor and a very influential and well connected nobleman in the kingdom of France.[2] The two of them concocted a plan which, if it had succeeded, would have appeared as a masterpiece in the annals of diplomacy – for it was a heads-I-win and tails-you-lose plan.

[1] In July or August 1162, when the letters of invitation to the meeting near St Jean-de-Losne were being issued, Eberhard of Salzburg wrote that Frederick obviously had changes in mind. (Tengnagel, No. 75, p. 433.)

[2] There is doubt as to who took the first step. Helmold (I, 91) and Boso (p. 405) say that the initiative was taken by Frederick. The *Cologne Chronicle* and Hugh of Poitiers say that Henry of Troyes thought of the plan first. In an undated letter of the summer of 1162, Frederick himself attributed the idea to Henry of Troyes. (MGH, Const. I, No. 210.) W. Heinemeyer, *Die Verhandlungen an der Saône im Jahre 1162*, DA, 20, 1964, p. 160, takes this as conclusive proof that Henry of Troyes was the author of the plan. I am not so certain; but the question is of no great importance. Henry of Troyes was a relative of Octavian's, and the idea might indeed have been his in the first instance. Then Frederick took it up and made it his own.

Through the mediation of Henry of Troyes, Frederick negotiated an agreement with Louis, the king of France. Louis had his own reasons for not being happy at having Alexander in France[1] and was therefore prevailed upon to enter into the following agreement: both Frederick and Louis were to attend a general council of the churches of their kingdoms to be held on the Saône, and each king was to produce one of the two popes. The council was to examine the validity of their respective claims. This examination was to be conducted by a board of arbitration, chosen in the presence of the two popes. The decision of the board was to be binding on both kings and their clergy. But if either pope failed to attend in person, the other was to be recognized automatically as the rightful pope.[2]

To all intents and purposes Frederick declared by this treaty that he was completely open-minded about the final decision. But no sooner was the treaty agreed upon than he took a number of steps which reveal its duplicity. First of all, he sent a number of messages, finely graded in their announcement of his impending plan according to the ears of the recipient. He wrote to the German bishops to reassure them, because they had mainly supported Victor and he did not want them to become anxious as to the results of the council. He told them that at the forthcoming council the king of France and the church of France would recognize Victor.[3] To Archbishop Heraclius of Lyon, Frederick wrote in a more judicious manner. He said that he was planning to meet the king of France in order to implore God's grace for the end of the schism and unity of the church; and merely added that he hoped that Victor would thus be confirmed as pope.[4] A letter

[1] Alexander's legates had very hastily issued a dispensation to Henry II to solemnize the marriage between a child daughter of Louis VII and one of his sons, because he was anxious to obtain the castles in Normandy which had been promised as dowry. The legates only thought of winning Henry for Alexander's cause. But when in November 1160 Henry availed himself of the dispensation and seized the castles, Louis was extremely put out and considered that the legates had played a dirty trick on him. They, however, had not meant to deceive. They had merely been too eager, at this difficult moment, to oblige all and sundry.

[2] These terms are fairly well established from several sources by W. Heinemeyer, *op. cit.*, p. 167.

[3] MGH, Const. I, 290, line 29, No. 208.

[4] *ibid.*, p. 292, line 2, No. 210.

to Duke Mathew of Lorraine was even more circumspect: Frederick wrote that he hoped the proposed meeting would restore unity and that Victor might then be able to assume his proper functions as pope.[1] And it seems that among the outspoken supporters of Alexander he caused yet another version to be spread. To them he communicated his intention of holding a meeting with the king of France in a completely neutral manner. He wanted to depose both claimants and have a new pope elected in order to restore unity.[2] Obviously, Frederick told everybody what he knew they would like to hear. His real intentions, however, soon became clear. He was planning to pack the proposed council to make quite sure that Victor would be recognized as the rightful pope.[3]

By not observing the explicitly stipulated open-mindedness in regard to the outcome of the council, Frederick assured himself of victory whatever happened. If Louis produced Alexander, the council would be packed to vote for Victor and Alexander could be apprehended, condemned and locked up. And if Louis failed to produce Alexander – and Frederick must have reckoned with that possibility – Louis was obliged by the terms of the agreement to recognize Victor.

But Frederick had not sufficiently reckoned with the activities of his opponents. Plans which depend too exclusively on minutely timed details become vulnerable. In consonance with Frederick's intention to pack the council, Eberhard of Salzburg was not invited.[4] But someone kept him fully informed. Eberhard wondered whether he ought to attend without being asked;[5] but in any case he wrote to Archbishop Henry of Reims, a firm supporter of Alexander, to warn him[6] and let him have a copy of Frederick's circular letter to the bishops. Henry of Reims immediately passed

[1] MGH, Const. I, p. 291, line 15, No. 209. W. Heinemeyer, *op. cit.*, p. 169, lists these letters and notes the graded expressions; but he fails to draw the obvious conclusion – that Frederick was being dishonest.

[2] There is no real proof that Frederick spread this rumour as well. But since Boso mentions it, it is clear that in Alexandrian circles Frederick's intentions were reported thus. Boso, p. 405.

[3] W. Heinemeyer, *op. cit.*, p. 169. *Cp.* Gretser, 592, No. 73.

[4] W. Heinemeyer, *op. cit.*, p. 169.

[5] Tengnagel, p. 436, No. 75 and p. 435, No. 73.

[6] *ibid.*, p. 432, No. 71.

this news on to King Louis,[1] and expressed both indignation and surprise that Louis should have allowed himself to be drawn into such a plan. At the same time he wrote reassuringly to Eberhard that the French church was firm in her obedience to Alexander.[2]

As a result of such and probably similar interventions, Louis was immediately exposed to the whole pressure of his own clergy,[3] to which Alexander himself, of course, lent his full support. He wrote to both Bishop Hugh of Soissons[4] and to Henry of Reims and asked them to dissuade Louis. He also hoped for a personal interview with the king.[5] In order to counteract this pressure, Rainald wrote to Louis' chancellor, Hugh of Soissons, and pointed out that Frederick's friendship was of unique value to his king and implored him to co-operate with Frederick's plan to restore peace and unity to the church.[6]

The meeting of the two kings was to have taken place at the bridge over the Saône at St Jean-de-Losne towards the end of August 1162. Frederick had assembled, nearby at Dôle, a most impressive array of his followers, both lay and spiritual, and Louis had taken up residence with a large following on the other side of the river, in Dijon. But as was to be expected, Alexander refused to be produced and this refusal put Louis, according to the agreement he had made, into a very embarrassing position. For if he could not produce Alexander, he was bound to recognize Victor, who, of course, was waiting with Frederick. But such a recognition would have placed Louis in an intolerable position *vis à vis* his own clergy. There is no doubt that Louis had been duped by Frederick's initial protestation that the council would act as a genuine and completely open-minded court of arbitration. Now that he had found out that Victor's triumph would be a foregone conclusion, there was nothing for him to do but to go back on his promise.

[1] Bouquet, XVI, 30f., No. 101.

[2] *ibid.*, p. 177, No. 31.

[3] For Cistercian pressure see M. Preiss, *Die politische Tätigkeit und Stellung der Zisterzienser im Schisma 1159–1177*, 1934, as well as the sources quoted by W. Heinemeyer, *op. cit.*, pp. 172, note 66, 173, note 70.

[4] JL, No. 10750.

[5] JL, No. 10752.

[6] Bouquet, XVI, 202, No. 11. Victor's seneschal wrote to Louis VII in a similar vein: Bouquet, XVI, p. 29, No. 94.

And this was precisely what Louis decided to do. He did not come to the meeting.

Frederick's 'heads-I-win and tails-you-lose' plan had been based on the assumption that either Louis would produce Alexander or would not produce Alexander. But Frederick had not reckoned with the possibility that Louis would neither produce Alexander nor attend the meeting.[1]

To be precise, Louis came to the meeting in such a way as to fulfil the minimum requirements of the agreement in a purely formal way. Instead of keeping to an appointed hour he passed the meeting place in a casual way as he was hunting.[2] By that time, Frederick had arrived and gone. Louis waited for several hours.[3] Eventually Rainald appeared and, realizing that all was lost, told Louis that he had broken the agreement[4] – a ridiculous charge in view of the duplicity with which Frederick had assured Louis that the council was to be neutral when he was intending to pack it. Then Rainald all but admitted this duplicity, extravagantly stating that a pope was a kind of imperial proprietary bishop and that any decision as to who was to be pope belonged exclusively to the emperor as the lord of Rome. But Louis remained unperturbed. He pointed out that with his doctrine that the election of a pope was a matter for the emperor alone Frederick's envoy had departed from the original terms of the agreement. He then asked the French nobles who had accompanied him to confirm that he was therefore no longer bound by it. Finally, to demonstrate that he had fulfilled his part of the agreement, he washed his hands in the river[5] and rode away.[6]

[1] Louis's double-cross was richly rewarded by Alexander's arrangement of an alliance between him and Henry II on 18 September. *See* W. Heinemeyer, *op. cit.*, p. 180.

[2] Hugh of Poitiers, MGH, SS, 26, p. 147, line 36.

[3] Helmold, I, 91.

[4] Frederick and Henry of Troyes carried the game to absurd lengths. Henry had pledged his honour and allegiance on the plan. He had promised that he would become Frederick's vassal if Louis did not keep his word. In order to establish before the world that Louis had broken his word, Henry now paid homage to Frederick. W. Heinemeyer, *op. cit.*, pp. 178–9. But Heinemeyer believes that Louis broke his word and that Frederick was genuinely entitled to Henry's homage.

[5] Helmold, I, 91.

[6] Boso (p. 407) and Hugh of Poitiers (*op. cit.*, p. 148) report this incident as if it had taken place after the session of the council. W. Heinemeyer, *op. cit.*, p. 183, accepts

When it became clear that the whole plan had miscarried Frederick and Rainald were furious. In order to cover up their failure, they at once proceeded to hold the council[1] – but by now it was no more than yet another imperial council which could never hope to find universal recognition. Victor again defended the canonicity of his election and declared that his opponent was afraid of doing so. Then Frederick spoke: he sharply attacked the king of France and explained that he had invited him and other *provinciarum reges*[2] out of sheer kindness and had not really ever wanted to reach a decision without them. But they had refused to attend because they wanted to injure the empire by imposing a pope on Rome and by exercising jurisdiction in a city which did not belong to them. Rainald spoke after Frederick and went even further. He roundly declared that the question as to who was to be bishop in Rome was no business of these *reges provinciales* who would be quick to resent any attempt on the emperor's part to interfere with an episcopal election in any of their cities. One could not wish for a more outspoken statement of the claim that Rome was an imperial city and its bishop

---

this order of events and thinks there were two occasions on which Louis appeared. But he gives no reason for his view. I agree with Haller, p. 112, that there was one meeting only and that Boso and Hugh garbled the reports which reached them.

[1] The only source for this council is *Saxo Grammaticus*, MGH, SS, 29, p. 114. The date, 7th or 8th of September. *Cp.* W. Heinemeyer, *op. cit.*, p. 181.

[2] This expression is clearly offensive to the kings of Christendom. W. Heinemeyer, *op. cit.*, p. 182, seeks to excuse it. I entirely agree with H. J. Kirfel, *Weltherrschaftsidee und Bündnispolitik*, BHF, 12, Bonn, 1959, p. 23, that this political pretentiousness and radicalism was an *ad hoc* expression of Frederick's and Rainald's anger, and that it is quite impossible to argue that Frederick really claimed universal power and considered other kings inferior. The expression occurs in Saxo Grammaticus' report of the events in question. The *Cologne Chronicle* ad 1161 says 'aliarum autem provinciarum reguli et populi' decided in favour of Alexander. But this was clearly inspired by Rainald. Similarly, the notary Burchard used the same term in a letter to the abbot of Siegburg. *See* F. Güterbock, *Le lettere del notaio Bucardo*, BISI, 61, 1949, p. 56. There is no shred of evidence that Frederick ever appropriated the expression or that it was ever used on any other occasion.

Alexander and his friends made the most of the term. They tried to persuade the whole world that Frederick and Rainald were really contemptuous of all other kings. *See* e.g. John of Salisbury's letter, Giles ed., I, especially 189, 330. Alexander encouraged other kings in the belief that Frederick called them *reguli* and that Frederick claimed universal power and denied sovereignty to other kings. *Cp.* R. Holtzmann, *Dominium Mundi aud Imperium Merum*, ZKG, 61, 1942. – The legend about Frederick's gift of a horse to the Roman law teacher Martinus because Martinus had told him he was the

therefore Frederick's proprietary pope. To make himself clear beyond doubt, Rainald repeated his speech in French and German.

At that synod, Frederick and Rainald really let fly. Their speeches contained the claim that the emperor was the sole authority to decide a papal election. There also were offensive references to the other kings of Christendom as provincial kinglets. In short, both Frederick and Rainald propounded a doctrine of imperial hegemony which was completely anachronistic by 1162. One can understand these extravagant and unrealistic outbursts only as the direct consequence of the double-cross. One can hardly believe that the doctrine propounded was seriously entertained by either of them; for it was barely two months since Rainald had written most obsequiously to Louis' chancellor.[1] Moreover, the doctrine was incompatible with the Great Design. But by the autumn of 1162 the schism had forced both Rainald and Frederick into such an impasse that they were beginning to become frantic.[2]

---

absolute master of the world, is a thirteenth-century travesty of a real incident concerning Henry VI. The legend found its way into a Milanese redaction of the Morena chronicle in 1220 or 1221. *Cp.* F. Güterbock, *Zur Edition des Geschichtswerks Otto Morenas und seiner Fortsetzer*, NA, 48, 1930, p. 146. – Frederick's unpopularity in Europe was not due to his claims to universal lordship, but to his attempt to foist his own pope upon the church. *See* W. Holtzmann, *Das mitterlalterliche Imperium und die werdenden Nationen*, Köln, 1953, p. 296. – K. Burdach sought to establish a connection between Walter v.d. Vogelweide's expression 'armen Künege' of 1198 and Frederick's alleged political philosophy. *See* his *Zum zweiten Reichsspruch Walthers von der Vogelweide*, SPA, 1902, pp. 897 ff. Whatever Walther's meaning was, there can be no such connection, because the idea of *reguli provinciarum* was not part of Frederick's political philosophy. In this whole question I follow the judicious interpretations of H. J. Kirfel, *Weltherrschaftsidee und Bündnispolitik*, BHF, 12, Bonn, 1959, pp. 47–68. E. H. Kantorowicz, *Kingship and Scientific Jurisprudence*, in: Clagett, Post and Reynolds ed., *12th Century Europe and the Foundations of Modern Society*, Madison, 1961, p. 103, asserts that Frederick put forward universal claims and that he derived them from Roman law. Kantorowicz, unfortunately, does not see Frederick as a politician, let alone a statesman; but as a mere executive agent of a school of jurists. R. Holtzmann, *Der Weltherrschaftsgedanke des mittelalterlichen Kaisertums*, HZ, 159, 1939, p. 257, seeks to establish a distinction between *auctoritas imperandi* and *potestas*. The former is much vaguer and Holtzmann argues that only the former was claimed by medieval emperors and that no German medieval emperor claimed to have power over other kings in virtue of his office.

[1] Note 4, p. 231.

[2] I agree with W. Heinemeyer, *op. cit.*, p. 189, that politically Frederick and Rainald had lost. But I cannot see why Heinemeyer imagines that legally Louis had been at fault. Frederick had obviously tried to deceive Louis and with this intention the whole question of legality becomes absurd. Louis, when he noticed the intended deception, had double-crossed Frederick. That was all. As so often, Helmold spotted the truth: '. . . cunning was outwitted by cunning, for the French, superior in genius, accomplished by counsel . . .' (I, 91).

Their speeches at the council were the expression of their impotence; but they set, for the time being, an official seal upon Rainald's intemperate outbursts in front of the king of France on the bridge of St Jean-de-Losne.[1] By the end of 1162, Frederick stood revealed as an emperor who had unreasonable pretensions to universal power and who was, given the way he had treated Milan and the papacy, a brutal tyrant. If there had been little foundation for the intelligence fed to him at the end of 1161 by Rainald's friend Burchard, it was the sort of intelligence which had provided its own verification. By acting on it in the course of 1162, Frederick had pushed himself into a situation in which he was making the most tyrannous and absurd claims – none of which had anything to do with the Great Design. And thereupon the rest of Christendom began indeed to wonder whether it would not be advisable to take steps to protect themselves.

Soon after the events of St Jean-de-Losne, Frederick and Rainald parted company. Rainald returned to Italy and Frederick went from Burgundy to Germany in order to attend to various matters there. He remained in Germany until the autumn of the following year and when separated from Rainald, he once again allowed a more reasonable attitude to the schism to prevail. In March 1163, for instance, he came together with both Eberhard of Salzburg and Hartmann of Brixen, and there can be no doubt that he listened to their advice to make peace with Alexander.[2] There was nothing much he could do; but he wanted to keep in touch. By contrast, there developed a tension between him and Victor, because the latter resented the manner in which Frederick forgave Bishop Udalrich of Treviso whom Victor had excommunicated.[3]

[1] Whatever the precise date of Rainald's outburst, it is remarkable that the content of it as reported by Boso and Hugh of Poitiers tallies exactly with Saxo's report of the proceedings of the synod. There can therefore be no doubt that these views were authentic and were the views expressed by Rainald.

[2] Giesebrecht, V, pp. 376, 395.

[3] Giesebrecht, V, p. 396. It is worth noting that by this time Frederick began to notice that Victor's influence in Germany was decreasing. Bishop Stephen of Metz died in late 1163 and was succeeded by his nephew Dietrich who refused to be consecrated because he did not wish to commit himself. R. Jordan, *Die Stellung des deutschen Episkopats im Kampf um die Universalmacht unter Friedrich I*, Würzburg, 1939, p. 99. Albert of Verdun had supported Victor, but his clergy had not and in 1161,

Rainald had busied himself during the whole of 1163 with the administrative problems of Lombardy. He had been joined by Victor who took up residence in Cremona, and in April 1164 both Rainald and Victor crossed the Apennines. When Victor reached Lucca, he fell ill and died. Rainald rushed to Lucca, and without hesitation improvised the election of a successor. His choice fell on Guido of Crema, a kinsman of Victor and by that time the only remaining cardinal, except Cardinal John, who had originally voted for Octavian in 1159.[1] All the other cardinals still faithful to Victor had been created by him. If there had been grounds for believing in the canonicity of Octavian's election in 1159, there could be none as to the elevation of Guido, who took the name of Paschal III.[2] The election did not take place in Rome and Paschal had to be consecrated on 26 April by Bishop Henry of Liège – who had no business to consecrate a pope. He happened to be handy because he was then employed as *podestà* of Milan. One could not imagine a more obvious proof of the purely political nature of the proceedings.

It seems that Frederick did not approve. He had remained in

Albert had resigned. His successor Richard refused to be consecrated, *ibid.*, p. 100. Hillin of Trier went over to Alexander in late 1164 or early 1165, *ibid.*, p. 100, a most remarkable defection in view of the fact that at one stage Hillin had been thought of as a possible primate of an independent German church (*see* p. 188 above). Hartmann of Brixen, by the time of his death in 1164, had gone over to Alexander, *ibid.*, p. 107, again a remarkable defection because Hartmann had been on close and friendly terms with Frederick. Conrad of Mainz declared for Alexander in late 1164, *ibid.*, p. 107. Frederick must have been dismayed at discovering how tenuous Victor's hold over the German episcopate was. After 1165, Frederick sought to counteract such lukewarm support for his pope by causing a large number of his relatives to be appointed to sees, i.e., to Metz in 1173, to Brixen in 1165 and again in 1170, to Passau in 1169, and again in 1172, to Speyer in 1167. In most cases such bishops were consecrated by Christian of Mainz, *ibid.*, p. 127. According to Hauck, IV, p. 291, note 3, Hermann II of Bamberg, appointed in 1170 was also related to Frederick. But according to Guttenberg, *Germania Sacra*, II, 1, p. 154, this was not so.

[1] Cardinal Guido of Crema had been personally instrumental in putting the *cappa rossa* on the shoulders of Octavian in 1159. *See* V. G. Mollet, 'Pasqual III', *Enciclopedia Cattolica*, IX; and H. Böhmer, *Realencyclopaedie f. protest. Theologie und Kirche*, pp. 724–5.

[2] According to Boso, p. 397, Paschal was elected by two cardinals. This does, of course, not exclude Rainald's authorship of the election. The *Annales Pisani*, ad 1165, MGH, SS, XIX, p. 250, attribute the election to Rainald. An anonymous letter to Alexander makes Frederick say that the election was due to Rainald. Watterich, II, p. 548. *Cp.* Archipoeta in J. Grimm, *Kleine Schriften*, III, p. 65, No. 7, verse 7. J. Ficker, *Rainald von Dassel*, Köln, 1850, p. 55, accepts this version.

Germany until the autumn of 1163 and then gone to Lombardy.[1] When he heard of Victor's death he dispatched a letter to Rainald instructing him to prevent the election of a successor to Victor.[2] But by the time the letter reached Rainald, if it ever did, it was too late. Rainald had hurried, perhaps because he suspected that Frederick might use the opportunity of ending the schism and of coming to face-saving terms with Alexander. When Frederick was informed of Rainald's impetuous action, he could not disown it and when he met Rainald in May he found he had to throw his whole weight behind Rainald's new pope.[3] It is unlikely that Rainald at that time was able to persuade Frederick of the wisdom of his policy – for in the following year there came an occasion on which Frederick blamed Rainald bitterly for having saddled him with a new pope.[4] But Frederick could not afford to quarrel with Rainald and given the precarious situation in Lombardy he was forced to rely on Rainald's self-assurance, his military command of the situation in Italy such as it was, and his intrepid and indefatigable services.

Thus, by the middle of 1164 the whole question was still unresolved and both Rainald and Frederick decided to return to Germany. The position in Lombardy was completely unsettled, the Lombards groaning under the weight of the imperial commissioners' exactions and corruption. It was clear that Frederick needed further military help from Germany. But this is where the rub lay: according to the Great Design, those parts of Germany which did not form part of Frederick's central kingdom were supposed to be left more or less alone. Now, however, it became clear that Frederick needed further help and could not afford to disregard the fact that Alexander's cause was making slow but steady progress in Germany.

Archbishop Eberhard of Salzburg, the fulcrum of Alexander's

[1] He had come without an army, for he had not been able to persuade the princes to give him military assistance. He had begged even Ebehard of Salzburg, but to no avail. *Cp.* J. Ficker, *Vom Reichsfürstenstand*, II, 1, pp. 316–17.

[2] Giesebrecht, V, p. 397. W. Martens, *Rainald von Dassel*. ADB, 27, p. 732. In *Rad. De Diceto Ymaginibus Historiarum*, MGH, SS, 27, p. 263, the story is told that Frederick was annoyed that Rainald had caused the election of Paschal without permission.

[3] J. Ficker, *op. cit.*, pp. 58–9.

[4] *See* p. 241 below.

party in Germany, died in June 1164. The chapter of Salzburg, in agreement with the archiepiscopal *ministeriales* and the clergy of the diocese, had elected another supporter of Alexander, Bishop Conrad of Passau, to succeed him. But by the time Conrad arrived at the imperial court in Pavia in September, Frederick had been saddled with Rainald's pope and when Conrad refused to recognize Paschal III, Frederick refused to invest him. If Conrad had presented himself six months earlier Frederick would most probably have had no objection to him. But now that he had to rely on further military aid from Germany and was committed to the support of Paschal, he decided to take more radical steps against Alexander's supporters in Germany. After his return there he reaffirmed his decision not to invest Conrad, at a court held in Bamberg in November.

This was the first occasion on which Frederick departed from the spirit of the Great Design in so far as it contained a tacit assurance that he would not play the role of an active ruler in Germany in the lands outside the regions encompassed by the Great Design. But given the way the situation had developed by the end of 1164, he had no alternative.

Rainald, too, returned home. He had written to the citizens of Cologne to prepare them and announced that he was bringing with him the relics of the Three Wise Men which Frederick had donated to him after the destruction of Milan. Rainald took his way through Burgundy where he was active on behalf of his new pope. His success there was very moderate;[1] but Alexander considered such as it was sufficiently dangerous to write to the archbishop of Reims to suggest that Rainald be seized on his way from Burgundy to Cologne.[2] Whatever efforts were made in that

[1] On his visit to Vienne, Rainald had the Archipoeta in tow. The latter provided a splendid description of the festivities which greeted Rainald, but they seem to have stood in inverse proportion to the diplomatic success scored by Rainald:

Fama tuba dante sonum
excitata vox preconum
clamat viris regionum
advenire virum bonum,
patrem pacis et patronum,
cui Vienna parat tronum.

The Archipoeta had very personal reasons for wishing to flatter and please Rainald.

[2] PL, CC, p. 417.

direction, Rainald managed to reach Cologne safely and entered the city, together with the relics, in triumph. It was a tremendous occasion, for with the transfer of these relics to Cologne, that city from now on enjoyed the magic which had belonged to Milan[1] and, more materially, the tourist trade which those relics began to stimulate.[2] Cologne had every reason to be thankful to its archbishop and tended to forget that he was not a pastor of souls.[3] Rainald was at the height of his power and he decided then to render his greatest service yet to Frederick by dealing a crushing blow to Alexander.

The following year during Lent he went on an embassy to the king of England to arrange a marriage for two of Henry II's daughters. One was to be married to Henry the Lion; and the other to one of Frederick's sons. In this way Rainald proposed to draw Henry II into the orbit of imperial politics. He knew of King Henry's quarrel with Thomas à Becket and calculated that Henry would be ready to join in obedience to Pope Paschal III. He thought himself so near success that he even discussed the possibility of a crusade with King Henry. If he had failed two years earlier to manœuvre the king of France into the camp of the imperial pope he now felt certain of the king of England.

In the meantime, Frederick had summoned an imperial court for Pentecost to Würzburg and intended to discuss with all his princes what was to be done. Frederick was genuinely anxious to open the debate on as broad a basis as possible and had even taken up connections with the king of France again, which fact, after the events of 1162, is a remarkable proof of Frederick's sincere desire to find ways and means of an amicable settlement with Alexander.[4] The court was formally opened the Saturday before

[1] P. Munz, *Frederick Barbarossa and the 'Holy Empire'*, JRH, III, 1964, p. 31.

[2] W. Neuss and F. W. Oediger, *Das Bistum Köln von den Anfängen bis zum Ende des 12. Jahrhunderts*, Köln, 1964, p. 230.

[3] Apart from the ostentatious transfer of the relics of the Three Wise Men to Cologne, there are very few instances of Rainald's interest in his see. He assisted in the foundations of two monasteries; ordered a day to be set aside as a holy day for the celebration of the Ascension of Mary; made a donation for the poor on every Maundy Thursday and another one to the cathedral to assist in the celebration of the feast of the Epiphany, *ibid.*, p. 229.

[4] Wichmann of Magdeburg had been in touch with the king of France. *Cp.* G. Rill *Zur Geschichte der Würzburger Eide*, WDGB, 20, 1958, p. 10. It is fairly certain that

Pentecost and for two days the discussions proceeded along those lines.

On the Monday Rainald suddenly arrived back from his mission to Henry II. He burst into the assembly, produced two ambassadors from the king of England and declared that Henry II and his clergy[1] were ready to recognize Paschal. This announcement was like a bombshell, for the promise of such powerful support immediately weakened the party who were arguing in favour of Alexander.[2] If the king of England and his clergy would adhere to Paschal, there could be no reason for making compromises with Alexander. And in order to sway the assembly and clinch the matter while it was still under the spell of his sudden announcement, Rainald proposed that Frederick should take an oath never to recognize Alexander. His successors were to take a similar oath and the bishops and princes were to follow the example. Within six weeks all abbots, prelates and all vassals were to take a similar

---

Rainald too had been instructed to visit the king of France. But such a conciliatory move did not suit Rainald, and he wrote to Louis from Rouen to apologize for not visiting him. Rainald pleaded lack of time because he wanted to return to Germany in time for the Würzburg court. (Bouquet, XVI, p. 122, No. 369.) If Rainald was in Rouen from 16 April to 20 April and did not have to be back in Würzburg till 24 May (Pentecost Monday) there would have been ample time for a visit to the king of France. Rainald was making excuses because he did not seek conciliation and wanted to arrive in Würzburg only with Henry II's assurances of support for Paschal. G. Rill, *op. cit.*, pp. 8–9, speculates that Rainald used the extra time for a furtive visit to London and thus returned to Würzburg with even firmer assurances from the English clergy than is commonly supposed.

[1] G. Rill's speculation about Rainald's visit to London, p. 239, note 4 is without foundation. It is improbable that such a visit should have gone completely unrecorded in England. And Rainald was not a man to travel incognito.

[2] The only elaborate account of the proceedings of the court is pro-Alexandrian. It is a letter written by a friend of Alexander and addressed to him. It is in Watterich, II, 547; Döberl, 205 ff; Robertson, V, 184. The accounts of William of Canterbury and Gervase of Canterbury are based on it. This letter describes the first conciliatory mood of the assembly and then presents the arrival of Rainald as putting an end to it. But Gerhoh too reports that at first the mood of the court was conciliatory, MGH, LdL, III, p. 408. One could also argue that the sudden flight of so many people proves that these men had come because they expected a conciliatory spirit to prevail. Frederick's letter about the proceedings to the abbot of Stablo and to others is in Mansi, XXI, 1221, 1213. But it is explicit only about the final decisions. Alexander, in a letter to Rotrud of Rouen reiterated that Frederick had been led astray by Rainald, Robertson, V, 352. Ficker, *Rainald von Dassel*, Köln, 1850, p. 131, believes that the letter to Alexander was written by no less a person than Conrad, the archbishop of Mainz. He considers the information it contains authentic. Nitzsch, pp. 285–7, follows Ficker. So, in the main, does Giesebrecht, V, pp. 464–5. The present account is based on it.

oath. If they refused, they were to forfeit their property and they were to be exiled. Freemen who refused to swear were to be exiled as well as mutilated.

This proposal was outrageous. For it was not customary for a king to take an oath on anything.[1] But legal niceties apart, Frederick had every reason to be angry with Rainald. Just as the discussions were progressing well, Rainald's announcement so weighted the arguments against reconciliation with Alexander that all hope for reaching a compromise had to be abandoned. No matter what anybody's personal feelings were, Paschal had been recognized by Frederick; and now that it seemed that Paschal might be able to command sizable support in England, the assembled princes and bishops could not really think of any very good argument why Frederick should withdraw his support from Paschal. It was a very awkward situation.

Wichmann was the first to answer. He could not advance a reason why he should not take the oath. But he gave vent to his irritation by declaring that he would not do so unless Rainald had himself consecrated archbishop of Cologne. Rainald had been elected six years ago; but had been unwilling to be consecrated as long as there was a shadow of a doubt as to who was the rightful pope – lest he be consecrated by the wrong one and thus in danger, at the end of the schism, of losing his see. When Rainald refused to promise to be consecrated, it was Frederick's turn to lose his temper. 'You acted like a traitor and deceiver when you saddled me with a new pope,' he said. 'And now you refuse to go into the trap you are preparing for others.'[2] Frederick added that the least Rainald would have to do was to comply with Wich-

[1] G. Rill, *op. cit.*, p. 18. Such oaths, though known in England and Italy, were not customary in Germany. Contemporaries certainly looked upon the imposition of the oath as an act of tyranny. Nobody admitted that Frederick was entitled to demand an oath of this kind. *Cp.* e.g. *Continuatio Aquicinctina*, MGH, SS, VI, p. 411; *Annales Laubienses*, MGH, SS, IV, p. 24; *Vita Gebehardi*, MGH, SS, XI, p. 46. This feeling of revulsion is well in agreement with the account of the proceedings of the court in the letter to Alexander. In the long run, the German bishops' canonical obligations triumphed over oaths of this kind; and, at any rate, the disaster of the following year, p. 252 below, annulled the prestige of the oath.

[2] The speech is reported in the letter to Alexander discussed on p. 240, note 2. Giesebrecht, VI, p. 443, believes it may contain exaggerations, but accepts it in substance. In view of Frederick's disapproval of the 'election' of Paschal in Lucca (*see* p. 238 above) the present report of the speech is perfectly credible.

mann's request and have himself consecrated. Rainald was thus driven into a corner and had to promise. Thus the oath was agreed upon. Frederick took the oath and so did the secular princes. The latter had nothing much to lose in committing themselves to Paschal since their fiefs and lordships did not depend on papal approval.

But the bishops with very few exceptions, were most loth to commit themselves. Frederick permitted them to swear conditionally and a wide variety of conditions was allowed.[1] A great many princes and bishops, when they realized that they would have to take the oath, secretly left the court. In the end, the only people unconditionally committed were Rainald and Frederick himself. It was not a very promising beginning to an attempt to end the schism. Not only had the meeting failed to achieve unanimity; but the imposition of such an oath was like asking high and low to bind their consciences and stigmatizing those who refused. The oaths did not manage to settle the schism in the church; but they did make it clear that the policy of persecuting the supporters of Alexander was inconsistent with the tacit assumption of the Great Design that Frederick would ignore the rest of Germany.[2]

There was nothing for Frederick to do but follow the course set by Rainald. To begin with, the emperor with a vast entourage prepared to celebrate Christmas in Aix-la-Chapelle by an enormous demonstration. Immediately after Christmas, the bones of Charlemagne were lifted from their resting place and deposited in a golden casket which was put in the middle of the cathedral. Frederick donated a large chandelier to the cathedral to be hung over the casket. The idea to have Charlemagne canonized might have originated with Rainald.[3] It was designed to provide divine

[1] Frederick was willing to make concessions in regard to the oath and allowed many bishops to swear conditionally. He was fully aware of the enormity of his and Rainald's policy. Bishop Albert of Freising was even allowed to postpone the oath. (*App. ad Rahewin*). A similar postponement was allowed to the bishop of Verdun. (Hartheim, *Concilia Germaniae*, III, 398). All this shows that Frederick was aware that the Würzburg policy was inconsistent with the tacit assumptions of the Great Design.

[2] For the persecution of the supporters of Alexander, *see* p. 290 below.

[3] Rainald seems to have got the idea from Henry II. *See* R. Folz, *Le souvenir et la légende de Charlemagne dans l'empire germanique mediévale*, Paris, 1950, p. 204.

sanction for the greatest of Frederick's predecessors and by honouring Charlemagne some of the glory was to be reflected upon Frederick. 29 December was the day of the elevation and was listed later as one of the days holy to Charlemagne, together with his birthday and the day of his death.[1] For centuries there had been unofficial cults of Charlemagne[2] and the canonization of 1165 which Paschal III, of course, approved, merely provided an official sanction for these cults. Moreover, the kings of France had been building up the memory of Charlemagne in order to vindicate their claims to lordship over the whole of France and to encourage the loyalty of their various subjects to themselves as the heirs of Charlemagne. The French *Song of Roland* had served the same end. If the primary object of the canonization was now to establish the great predecessor of Frederick as a saint and thus invoke divine sanction for whatever policies Frederick was about to pursue, Rainald and Frederick had also a more narrowly political and immediate object in view: they wanted to prove that Frederick was superior to the king of France. Now that England was – at least temporarily – on the side of Paschal, France stood out in favour of Alexander.[3] It seemed, therefore, particularly necessary to proclaim to the world that France had no claim to Charlemagne. Louis might claim direct descent from Charlemagne and he might have the holy oil and his kingship might be considered especially sacred. But Frederick now had Charlemagne as his personal saint, and with the canonization Aix-la-Chapelle, the place where the kings of Germany were crowned, was elevated at the expense of St Denis.[4]

When the celebrations were concluded they were, naturally, followed up by several literary productions. Frederick issued a special charter for Aix-la-Chapelle and into it he inserted

[1] W. Levison, *Das Verzeichnis der königlichen Tafelgüter von 1164–65 und seine Handschriften*, NA, 41, 1919, p. 563.

[2] R. Folz, *Études sur le culte liturgique de Charlemagne dans les églises de l'empire*, Paris, 1951.

[3] After the court of Würzburg, Alexander was frequently charged with being a friend of France. Stumpf, Nos. 4045, 4046.

[4] The canonization followed very much along the lines of other twelfth century canonizations, e.g., that of Bishop Anno of Cologne, of Henry II, of Edward the Confessor; *Cp.* M. Schwarz, *Heiligsprechungen im 12. Jahrhundert*, AKG, 39, 1957, pp. 57–8.

Charlemagne's *privilege* for the city.[1] Before long somebody composed a *Life of Charlemagne* to justify the canonization.[2] In this book Charlemagne was presented as a real saint, a patron and defender of the church, called to and blessed for this task by God. He was depicted as a model of all Christian and ecclesiastical virtues, a ruler who held both swords and was likened to a martyr and a confessor.

The glory which should have reflected upon the emperor who had caused Charlemagne to be canonized was intended to make up for the precarious political situation. By the beginning of 1166, Frederick had gravely jeopardized the Great Design in Germany by imposing a rule upon conscience. The persecution of the supporters of Alexander in Germany began slowly, moderately and half-heartedly[3] and its effects were no doubt exaggerated by Alexander's propaganda. But the fact remains that the oath had been taken by some and that it had been agreed to impose it upon all and thus a large number of people were forced either to commit perjury or to prevaricate, or live in fear lest Pope Alexander managed to emerge victorious after all and cause all those who had

[1] M. Buchner, *Das fingierte Privileg Karls des Grossen – eine Fälschung Rainalds von Dassel*, ZAGV, 47, 1925. The original of the charter for Aix-la-Chapelle is lost and is known only in a copy issued by Frederick II in 1244. The charter contains the official proclamation of the canonization and confirms as well as quotes a charter which Charlemagne granted to Aix-la-Chapelle as *caput et sedes regni*. The charter attributed to Charlemagne was a forgery which had originated probably in 1158–9 at the imperial court. *See* E. Meuthen, *Karl der Grosse – Barbarossa – Aachen*, in: *Karl d. Grossen Lebenswerk und Nachleben*, W. Braunfels ed., Düsseldorf, 1965, IV. R. Folz, *La Chancellerie de Frédéric Ier*, MA, LXX, 1964, p. 27, compares this charter to similar charters issued to other cities intended by Frederick to be capital cities, i.e. Monza, Arles and Vienne. The forged charter, attributed to Charlemagne, emphasized that the empire was superior to the papacy. This doctrine was very relevant to the events of 1158–9 and was still relevant in 1166.

[2] R. Folz, *Le souvenir et la légende de Charlemagne dans l'empire germanique mediévale*, Paris, 1950, p. 219, is of the opinion that the whole of the *Vita S. Karoli* was written in the eighth decade of the twelfth century in order to justify the canonization of Charlemagne. *Cp.* also P. Lehmann, *Das literarische Bild Karls des Grossen*, in: *Erforschung des Mittelalters*, Vol. I, pp. 179–181. – It is worth reflecting on the different ways in which the memory of Charlemagne was used on both sides of the Rhine. In France, where royal administration was making rapid progress in the second half of the twelfth century, Charlemagne's picture was distorted in order to serve the cause of French 'nationalism'. *Cp.* e.g. O. v. Simson, *The Gothic Cathedral*, London, 1956, Ch. 3. In Germany, where Frederick's policy was reaching an impasse and where he could do nothing more solid than stage a propaganda campaign, Charlemagne's image was used in the manner described, for supporting archaic traditions.

[3] For a fuller account of the persecutions, *see* p. 290. below

taken the oath to lose their offices. Once the decision in favour of the oath had been taken it became painfully obvious that Frederick was no longer able to abide by at least one of the elements in the Great Design. It had been a peripheral, if not a central, part of the Great Design that outside the regions of the three rivers Frederick was to leave well alone. Not that he had ever made an official pronouncement on this matter: but the *privilegium minus* with its territorial concessions of sovereignty to Henry Jasomirgott and the establishment of Henry the Lion in both Bavaria and Saxony had implied that as far as the rest of Germany was concerned Frederick would be content with a mere suzerain lordship. Now, at Würzburg, it had become clear that he was forced by the exigencies of Alexander's continued and stubborn opposition to demand more. Not that the oath itself was a great interference. But the mere fact that he had demanded it and was determined to deprive those who had refused showed that he could no longer afford to remain content with being a mere suzerain. The schism had stiffened resistance in Lombardy. That resistance necessitated a new military effort. And the military effort was not likely to be successful unless Frederick could quell all secret and silent sympathy for Alexander. The force of circumstances was, by the end of 1165, obliging Frederick to abandon the peripheral, but nevertheless very important part of the Great Design. In order to restore confidence in it, it would be necessary to get rid of Alexander and thus encourage everybody to take the oath willingly and make all those who had taken it feel they had nothing to fear because there could never be a chance of recognition for Alexander. By the end of 1165, the Würzburg oath had shaken much of the confidence in Frederick's Great Design, but it had not brought Frederick one step further towards ending the schism. Alexander was still at large. Indeed, just as Frederick and Rainald were celebrating their fairly hollow triumph of the canonization of Charlemagne in Aix-la-Chapelle, Alexander had been able to return to Rome and take up his residence there.

In Rome, the death of Victor seems to have had an immediate and disastrous effect upon the imperial cause. For unlike Victor, his successor Paschal lacked the right connections in the city. With the help of money from Sicily, Alexander's vicar managed to influence the citizens and by October 1164 they had elected a senate consisting almost entirely of supporters of Alexander.[1] And thus for the first time in decades, an amicable agreement between pope and city was concluded and Alexander was invited to return to Rome.

In order to forestall such a triumph for Alexander's cause, Christian of Mainz[2] was ordered to move with an army into central Italy and help Pope Paschal, who was residing at Viterbo, to install himself in Rome. Christian's military power was not overwhelming. He could do little more than devastate the countryside and hope to terrorize Rome into submission. He had promised imperial support for Pisa's claim to Sardinia and in return Pisa had paid him the sum of 13,000 lire which enabled him to get an army together. But the arrival of a Norman army from the kingdom of Sicily[3] prevented Christian from assaulting Rome. He was, however, successful in interfering with the food supply to the city. And by September 1165 Christian had been sufficiently successful to persuade the Romans to come to terms: they agreed to recognize and receive Paschal by the end of September unless Alexander himself had returned by then.[4] The supporters of Alexander understood that time was crucial for they realized that once Paschal was settled in Rome, it would be much more difficult to dislodge him from the papal throne. So far he had been little more than a pretender.[5]

[1] Haller, pp. 192–3.

[2] Strictly speaking, Christian, at this time was not yet archbishop of Mainz. Next to nothing is known of his origins. Since the sixteenth century it is customary to call him Christian von Buch. His mother was the sister of Count Frederick I von Beichlingen. We first hear of him in 1159 when he was sent as an ambassador of Victor IV to Denmark. The attempt to have him made archbishop of Mainz in 1160 was unsuccessful. (*See* p. 180, note 4.) Christian, however, became chancellor in 1162 and was a constant companion of Frederick. He remained in Italy in 1164 and when Archbishop Conrad of Mainz refused to take the Würzburg oath in 1165, Christian succeeded him in September 1165. He was invested by Frederick in the following year and consecrated in March 1167.

[3] P. Brezzi, *Roma e l'impero medievale*, Bologna, 1947, p. 354.

[4] C. Varrentrapp, *Erzbischof Christian von Mainz*, 1867, pp. 22–3. P. Brezzi, *op. cit.*, pp. 354–6, dates the agreement with the Romans for May, 1165.

[5] John of Salisbury, reporting these events to Thomas of Canterbury (Giles ed., I, 201), wrote that Frederick would now make, as a reward, Christian ('non Christianum

Alexander therefore decided to accept the Romans' invitation speedily. He had to travel by ship in order to avoid northern Italy and after a very hazardous journey, which testifies to his physical courage as well as to his political determination, he arrived in Rome in November, just in time to swing the wavering citizens to his side. At this moment Frederick must have once more regretted the execution of Arnold of Brescia. With the help of Victor Frederick had been able to make himself agreeable to the Romans.[1] But this relationship between emperor and Rome had depended on Victor's personal standing in the city and had ceased with his death and the influx of Norman money. If an Arnold of Brescia had now been at hand to stir up the people and appeal to their smouldering resentment of papal administration, ecclesiastical lordship and the wealth of the church, it might have been possible at this moment to persuade the Romans to abide by the letter of their agreement with Christian and receive Paschal, instead of Alexander. For Alexander was late in arriving.

The Romans decided to procrastinate and wait for Alexander, for Christian's devastations in central Italy had been terrible and it was feared that his arrival in Rome would put an end to communal liberty. After all, the imperial record in Lombardy was not exactly designed to inspire confidence in Rome. Alexander, on the other hand, could now be considered the protector of Rome's communal liberty. The only genuine allies of Christian were those cities and lords who were afraid of the Roman commune and its expansionist policies.

Upon his arrival in Rome, Alexander had been very hopeful. 'All this,' he wrote, 'augurs well for the peace and prosperity of the church.'[2] His optimism was to be short lived. For the Romans demanded money[3] and Alexander had none. William I of Sicily died early in 1166. On his deathbed he had caused 40,000 florins to be sent to Alexander, because he was determined to

---

sed antichristum') archbishop of Mainz. John stresses the devastations and the distress of the Romans.

[1] *See* p. 204 above.

[2] PL, CC, p. 400. Similarly to the archbishop of Genoa, Pflugk-Harttung, III, p. 214.

[3] *Cp.* John of Salisbury, letter 183, PL, CXXIX, and *Policraticus*, VIII, 23.

enable Alexander to carry on the fight against Frederick.[1] But William's successor was a boy of eleven who began an era of political turmoil in southern Italy and no further assistance was to be had from that quarter. Alexander's financial straits were pitiable. He wrote to a friend in Reims to complain of the usurious rates of interest he had to pay on money advanced to him in Rome. All the gifts which had been given to the church were thus being devoured. He asked his friend to try to raise another 100 marks of silver.[2]

Frederick and Rainald and Christian of Mainz therefore decided to take the bull by the horns. Frederick had never been able – and probably never seriously considered[3] – to invade France in order to seize Alexander.[4] But now that Alexander was back in Rome and his position there known to be precarious because of lack of

[1] F. Chalandon, *Histoire de la domination Normande en Italie et en Sicile*, Paris, 1907, II, p. 303. *Cp.* John of Salisbury, PL, XCCIX, p. 138, No. 145. *See* also H. Reuter, *Geschichte Alexanders III*, Leipzig, 1860–4, Vol. II, pp. 257–8.

[2] The letter is from 18 January 1166, and is in JL, 11256. *Cp.* F. Schneider, *Zur älteren päpstlichen Finanzgeschichte*, QuF, 9, p. 7. – Ever since 1160 Alexander had been in such despair that he seriously entertained the idea of accepting help from the Greeks. This would only be given on condition of a reunification of the two churches. At a later stage negotiations were to reach a concrete shape: reunification was to be effected in the following way: When Greek troops entered Rome, Manuel would appoint Alexander patriarch of Constantinople, the old patriarch having died in 1169. But the idea of being an imperially appointed patriarch acutely embarrassed Alexander. Boso, pp. 419–20. *Cp.* S. Runciman, *The Eastern Schism*, Oxford, 1955, p. 121. In 1167 the matter was urgent. There is a source which describes how papal legates had already drafted a treaty for a reunion of empire and church, east and west, and how Manuel had already issued a *Chrysobull* to that effect. But at the last moment, Alexander, fearing the charge of simony, refused to consent. *Cp.* A. Dondaine, *Hugues Etherien et Léon Tuscus*, AHDL, 19, 1953, pp. 67–134. *See* Watterich for Manuel's demands and Alexander's refusal, II, 404, 410–11. Lamma, *Comneni e Staufer*, Rome, 1955, II, p. 130, points out that such a move, though politically most opportune for Alexander, was impossible because Alexander had proclaimed that he stood for *libertas ecclesiae*. However, it is worth bearing in mind that Alexander, when he was still *magister* Roland, had argued vehemently in favour of the doctrine that a pope can not only depose an emperor but also transfer the empire and that he had then based his argument on the transfer of 751 A.D. *Cp.* F. Thauer, ed., *Die Summa magistri Rolands*, Innsbruck ,1874, pp. 11 ff.

[3] Though Louis VII, in 1162, seems to have feared an invasion.

[4] As soon as Frederick heard that Alexander was planning to return to Rome, he made frantic efforts to seize him. William of Newburgh reports that Frederick tried to bribe the governor of Montpellier to capture Alexander (*Hist.* ii, 17) and later he employed pirates to seize the papal ship; Robertus de Monte, *Chronicle*, 1165. *See* also John of Salisbury, writing to Thomas of Canterbury, Robertson, V, 218. Thus we see that the imperial expedition to Rome was only the last of a long series of efforts.

money, it was thought that rapid military action might enable Frederick to capture him; and thus settle the matter in the most radical and final way possible.

For this purpose, in October 1166 Frederick assembled an army and led it into Italy. On his arrival in Lombardy he found that the position already precarious in 1163 and 1164 had deteriorated further. The resistance of Verona, the financial inducements offered by Venice[1] and the growing discontent caused by the imperial commissioners, had led most cities close to open rebellion. But Frederick was single-minded in his pursuit of Alexander. He calculated that he could cope with all his troubles once he had dealt with Alexander.

It is worth noting how completely the direction of imperial policy had changed. In 1162 Frederick's chaplain Burchard had advised that all efforts ought to be directed against Milan, for Milan once out of the way, the opposition of Alexander would collapse.[2] Four years later the position had become completely reversed. Now it was Alexander upon whom all attention was concentrated. As a result, Frederick was perhaps less cautious in his passage through Lombardy than he ought to have been. He held a court in Lodi and demanded that the assembly take the Würzburg oath. For the rest, he took dozens of hostages from all those towns whose loyalty he had the slightest reason to suspect. But that was all. By March 1167 he was ready to march on Rome and capture Alexander. For this purpose the army was divided into two parts. One remained under Frederick and moved down the Adriatic coast; the other, under Rainald, approached Rome through Tuscany. And thus Lombardy was left in the rear. How far Frederick was aware of the risk he was taking is not clear. If his hold over Lombardy had been in doubt a year before, it was now hanging by a mere thread. For he had not only refused to entertain complaints, often only too justified, against his commissioners; but the passage of the imperial army itself had aroused ill-feeling and antagonism.

[1] *See* p. 271, note 1.
[2] *See* p. 226 above.

While Frederick was encamped before the hostile Ancona, Rainald had approached the city very rapidly. On 27 May he met a large Roman army, said to have been 30,000 men strong, at Tusculum. Rainald entered the city to seek shelter. But soon Christian of Mainz, who had been following close behind, joined up with him. The two together, with an army counting only a thousand men, inflicted a crushing defeat upon the Romans. With that victory the road to Rome was open.[1]

Rainald and Christian arrived near Rome before the emperor. For a couple of months they stayed outside the city and devastated the countryside. The feeling in the city was desperate. Alexander and his closest supporters and the cardinals had found refuge in a fortress near the Colosseum and the Arch of Titus. But his own position was very unhappy. As long as he could distribute the money he had received from the king of Sicily, the Romans tolerated his presence. But as Rainald's devastations continued, the ill-humour of the Romans increased. They tried to negotiate with Rainald, but found that as the essential condition for a truce was that they were to deliver Alexander, the cardinals and Otto Frangipane, the one great pro-Alexandrian noble, they were powerless, for they could not get hold of Alexander. The latter was besieged in his fortress by the Romans; and the Romans were besieged by Rainald.

On 24 July Frederick finally arrived in person. He immediately began to besiege the city and succeeded in forcing an entry. The Roman army escaped across the Tiber and the next day Frederick attacked the Castle of St Angelo. During the fighting there was a great deal of looting and arson and many valuable pictures and mosaics as well as churches were destroyed. Eventually St Peter's

[1] It is difficult to discover the truth about Tusculum. Boso compares it to the defeat of Cannae. Rainald went to great trouble in order to spread the story of his own military prowess. *Cp.* P. Munz, *Frederick Barbarossa and the Holy Empire*', JRH, III, 1964, p. 35, note 40. Rainald's friend, Philipp of Harveng (Philippus Eleemosynarius or ab Eleemosyna), abbot of Bona Spes, was, like many other people, the lucky recipient of a letter from Rainald about the battle of Tusculum. And we are fortunate in having Philipp's reply to Rainald. It is printed in PL, CCIII, 160 ff. The letter was written after the battle of Tusculum, not as Sinjen, *Les oeuvres de Philippe de Harveng*, p. 149 f. assumes, after the destruction of Milan. The reply shows that Philipp had fallen a total victim to Rainald's propaganda and wrote to Rainald in the most flattering terms as a wise servant of the Christian religion whose victory was due to humility. (sic!)

was captured – it had been used as a fortification and the defenders offered to surrender only when the church itself was in danger of being destroyed.[1]

There Frederick paused. He had not yet captured Alexander – but he was in possession of the Leonine City and of St Peter's and could hardly wait to install at least his own pope there. The following Sunday Paschal was enthroned and two days later, on 1 August, Frederick was crowned once more by Paschal, and his wife Beatrix, though long since known as the empress, received the necessary consecration.[2] Amidst all this splendour, Frederick was mindful of how much he owed to Rainald, and donated two imperial manors together with mint, tolls and court to him.

But the great prize escaped. While the fighting was still in progress Conrad von Wittelsbach, the deposed archbishop of Mainz, appeared in the imperial camp and offered peace terms to Frederick. According to Alexander's biographer, Boso, he is supposed to have suggested that both Paschal and Alexander renounce the papacy. It is very improbable that Frederick would have entertained such a proposal at this moment. It has therefore been suggested with a certain plausibility that these negotiations were being carried on in order to gain time and conceal Alexander's real plan which was to escape.[3] It is not known how Alexander

[1] The Germans got a very bad reputation for carrying the battle into the churches and to the feet of the altars. *Cp.* Helmold, II, c. 10, and Otto of St Blaise, c. 20. But on the other hand the fighting would not have taken place in the churches if the Romans had not used them as fortifications. Gregorovius, *History of Rome in the Middle Ages*, IV, ii, p. 585, wrote of 'the emperor of Christendom and his mail-clad bishops'. The *Cologne Chronicle*, GDV, 69, p. 96, had nothing but praise for Frederick's military glory in the conquest of Rome. But the *Geschichte der Welfen*, GDV, 68 p. 38, paints a grim picture of the massacre and attributed the epidemic to the judgement of God. And the *Chronicle of St Peter at Erfurt*, GDV, 52, p. 38, describes how the Germans broke into churches with axes, burnt them, killed the Romans who had sought refuge in them, covered the altars with blood and had no regard for piety and religion.

[2] The poet Gautier d'Arras in his *Ille et Galeron*, made a charming reference to this event:

> Rome le vit ja coroner,
> Qui nos en puet tesmong douer.
> Rome est de grant antiquité,
> Et ki dame est de la chité,
> Ne puet avoir si grant hautece. . . .
> V. 69 ff.

[3] Giesebrecht, V, p. 548. But Haller, 512, thinks that Boso's story, that the cardinals were really thinking of betraying and abandoning Alexander, is reliable.

got away – some said that he left the tower near the Colosseum disguised as a pilgrim, sailed down the Tiber in a small boat and thus out of Rome. The fact is that when the Romans finally thought of surrendering Alexander, he was nowhere to be found. With Alexander gone and a small Pisan fleet sailing up the Tiber in support of Frederick, there was nothing left for the Romans but to give in. Frederick demanded hostages, an oath of fealty to Paschal and the appointment of a new pro-imperial senate and of pro-imperial officials. The senators did not hesitate, and it was probably at this time that Frederick sought to win the Romans' favour by taking the traditional oaths to the city which secured the continuity of all laws and contracts.[1]

With the flight of Alexander the whole expedition had failed in both its immediate and its ultimate purpose. Nevertheless, Frederick's conquest of Rome, the instalment of Paschal and a crown wearing festival on 1 August had been a considerable triumph for the imperial cause. On the next day, however, there occurred a disaster which eclipsed even Frederick's partial success. An epidemic broke out which virtually wiped out his army, and Frederick was himself taken seriously ill.

The real nature of the epidemic is not known, but it is believed to have been malaria.[2] Such outbreaks were common in the Roman August heat, and Frederick appears to have been less than cautious in risking a campaign in Rome at that time of the year. There was certainly no ignorance of the danger: many years earlier Otto of Freising had written that the heat in Rome in summer was terrible, and that it harmed German soldiers more than the actual fighting.[3] The fact that in 1167 Frederick was willing to take such risks is proof of his desperation.

The disaster was all the more complete because Frederick's most faithful friends and staunchest supporters had been with the

[1] In 1167 Frederick took an oath to the Romans. *Cologne Chronicle* ad 1167; also MGH, Const. I, No. 229, p. 325. Frederick did this in order to make the Romans feel that now that Paschal was installed, they would have nothing to fear from the emperor. The willingness to take the customary oaths at that time contrasts strongly with Frederick's Roncaglia policy towards the cities of Lombardy and with Frederick's refusal to take the oath in 1155.

[2] Kestner, *Alpenpässe und römische Malaria*, HV, 30, pp. 696 ff.

[3] *Gesta*, II, xxxiii.

army. With a very few exceptions, such as Christian of Mainz, they all died. Frederick and the empress and a small retinue left Rome on 6 August without even having entered the city proper. During the following days the others, too weak to move, died: Rainald, Daniel of Prague, the bishop of Verden, Duke Dietbold, Duke Frederick of Swabia, the young Welf. . . .

With a very small contingent Frederick regained Lombardy, only to find that at the news of the Roman disaster open rebellion had broken out. As Frederick was being helped clandestinely across the Apennines in early September, Galdinus, the exiled archbishop of Milan and close friend of Alexander, arrived in Venice, disguised as a pilgrim. Galdinus reached Milan on 5 September; and Frederick, Pavia on 9 September.[1] Frederick pronounced the ban over the rebellious cities and hoped at first for further armed support from Germany. But when he found that the Veronese league had joined with the other cities and formed the Lombard league against him, he decided to return to Germany. It was too dangerous to remain longer. He managed to gain Susa, in the west. The citizens sought to keep him in custody, because they feared reprisals from the Lombards if they allowed such a prize to escape. But eventually Frederick succeeded in leaving the city, disguised as a servant while a friend, pretending to be the emperor, stayed behind.[2] Thus Frederick gained time and was able to cross the Mount Cenis pass to Burgundy. Even in Burgundy he did not feel safe, because the Alexandrian clergy there, following the lead of Guichard, the archbishop of Lyon, had for all practical reasons renounced their allegiance. It was not until he reached Bâle on the Rhine, on 16 March, that he felt

[1] Galdinus had been archdeacon and chancellor of the diocese of Milan. In 1159 he had gone, with his archbishop Hubert, into exile in France. There he made the acquaintance of Alexander with whom he had returned to Italy in 1165, and at the end of 1165 he was made a cardinal. Hubert died in 1166 and Galdinus was chosen to succeed him without Alexander having consulted the church and people of Milan. He was instructed by Alexander to take charge of the re-building and re-grouping of Milan. Since April 1167 he was in constant touch with the Lombard cities and in September 1167 he arrived in Milan. *Cp.* M. Pacaut, *Les légats d'Alexandre*, RHE, 1955, pp. 834–5. For Galdinus's efforts in Milan *see* P. Munz, *Frederick Barbarossa and the 'Holy Empire'*, JRH, III, 1964, p. 31.

[2] Giesebrecht, V, p. 596, and VI, pp. 479–80, for an examination of the sources of the story.

secure. Instead of leading Alexander captive to Germany, Frederick himself returned to it as a refugee.[1]

[1] Frederick had no illusions as to the magnitude of the disaster. He wrote a pitiful letter to Albert of Freising and said: 'credimus . . . fidem tuam condolere et omnia viscera tua conturbari'. MGH, Const. I, p. 325.

CHAPTER VII

Years of Indecision

The experiences of the winter of 1167–8 made Frederick pause for thought. His sense of personal insecurity as he was wandering from city to city through Lombardy and his secret flight from Susa in March 1168, underlined the magnitude and the likely consequences of the Roman disaster. It is impossible to say when the first doubts of the wisdom of pursuing the Great Design and of continuing his opposition to Alexander, which such a pursuit had come to imply, occurred to him. But by January 1168, even before his flight from Italy, Frederick had considered a complete reversal of policies. It so happened that at this time he was visited by Theodoric, a kinsman of his and a very devout lay brother of the Carthusian order. With tears in his eyes Theodoric begged Frederick to end the schism by coming to terms with Alexander.[1] Frederick, surveying his own plight, was moved and wrote to both the abbot of Citeaux and the fugitive bishop of Pavia, inviting

[1] For Theodoric's approach to Frederick *see* John of Salisbury, especially No. 244, PL, 199. Older historians have believed that Theodoric was a natural son of Frederick. Bouquet, XVI, p. 583, pointed out that the person mentioned by John of Salisbury must be the Theodoric whom Frederick in a lost charter of the year 1167 described as 'carissimus et fidelis noster de progenie mea oriundus'. Giesebrecht, VI, 479, thinks that Theodoric belonged to the house of the dukes of Upper Lorraine with whom Frederick was related through his sister Judith. P. Fournier, *Le royaume d'Arles*, Paris, 1891, pp. 55–6, thinks that Theodoric (= Thierry) might have been Frederick's 'natural brother'. However this may be, Frederick was forced to listen to Theodoric because when trying to cross into Burgundy, he had virtually fallen into the hands of Count Humbert III, an enemy of his. Count Humbert only allowed Frederick to proceed when the margrave of Montferrat interceded on Frederick's behalf. Fournier suggests that when virtually a prisoner of Humbert, Frederick allowed Theodoric's approaches in order to pretend that he had peaceful intentions in regard to Alexander. Frederick thus hoped to persuade Humbert to let him proceed. This view of the incident does not seem very plausible. Humbert held up Frederick because Frederick was a friend of Alphonse of Toulouse, his enemy; but not because Humbert objected to Frederick's ecclesiastical policy. One must always resist the temptation to impose a wide meaning on the personal feuds which abounded.

them to visit him with a view to undertaking a peace mission to Alexander. He assured them that he would follow their advice, provided they could find a way of getting round the troublesome Würzburg oath.

We have already had occasion to observe his flexibility and resourcefulness when in early 1156 he had discovered that his first plan was not likely to work successfully. But at this critical juncture in his reign, in the winter of 1167–8, we find him once more beginning to doubt whether the Great Design, his second plan, was likely to work. Or at any rate, he was beginning to count the cost. For this was the real mark of his statesmanship: he always kept an eye on the cost of a plan. And now that the price was getting too high, he began to waver and consider whether he ought not to surrender it. In 1156 it had been easy to give up the first plan; for that plan had, so to speak, merely been inherited from Conrad. It was much more difficult to give up the second plan, the Great Design. For that plan was Frederick's personal creation, and he must have identified himself with it to a very large degree. The real test of his statesmanship was therefore still to come. Would he be able to surrender the Great Design as he had given up the first plan and would he be able to fashion a third one? Under the circumstances it is not hard to understand that it took him some considerable time to make up his mind. For the time being, he simply began to have his doubts and to waver. During the year which followed his desperate flight from Italy, from the beginning in 1168, it is apparent that he was pursuing policies in support of the Great Design, and policies which seem clearly incompatible with it. It is impossible to say how conscious he was of the ambiguous nature of his policies or, for that matter, how much other people noticed this ambiguity. It is tempting to think that the clandestine flight from Susa, was a traumatic experience, and that from that moment onwards he never quite pursued the Great Design with the same determination.

The fact that this long period of indecision in his life occurred is no discredit to Frederick. On the contrary, only a fanatic, an opportunist or a completely irresponsible politician would drop a grand plan at a moment's notice and pursue another with the same dogged determination. Frederick was neither a fanatic nor an opportunist nor was he irresponsible. He began to harbour doubts in the winter of 1167–8, because he understood that he could not spend his life in endless frustration. But while he was trying to decide whether there was yet any hope for the Great Design, he was beginning to toy with alternative policies. Moreover, when he had dropped the first plan and fashioned the Great Design in its stead, this had been done quickly and had been something like a political inspiration. There was something quite original and creative in it – a bold plan to weld together a vast political organization in a certain well defined geographical space. In 1168, twelve years older, he must have suspected that he was not likely to be capable of a similar creative effort. Whatever new plan he was likely to put forward now would be much less original, much less bold and much less based on his ability to mould conditions actively. If the Great Design was to be abandoned as a failure, Frederick was more likely now to turn towards milder and humbler experiments, perhaps towards following existing trends. But in order to do that successfully he would first have to explore very precisely what those trends were and under what conditions he might follow them. Therefore he had to gain time. Such a plan would not be an instantaneous creative effort as the Great Design had been. It would consist of following existing developments and adjusting to them. For these reasons the longish period of indecision that followed is not surprising.

Even without the traumatic experience of the flight from Susa, Frederick had both reason and opportunity, in early 1168, to pause and take stock of the whole situation. Rainald, his closest adviser and collaborator, was dead. With Rainald's death, the main impetus towards the realization of the Great Design through the harrowing of Alexander had disappeared. Now that Frederick was left alone to face the consequences, it must have occurred to him that his pursuit had been a deviation from his main aim and that it ought to be called off. Rainald was no longer at his side to argue that an anti-papal policy was the surest way of laying the foundations for the Great Design. Rainald had been prompted by his obsessive hatred of the papacy. The unfortunate accidents of the double election and a number of subsequent events had given Rainald's advice a certain air of plausibility. But Frederick himself had no personal feelings on this matter and was completely free of the bias which had spurred Rainald. After Rainald's death he thus reflected that the anti-papal twist of the Great Design had been an unfortunate, albeit not wholly accidental diversion. At the same time, he was astute enough to realize that by now the Great Design and the pursuit of Alexander were sufficiently intertwined to make any simple separation of the two causes impossible; and that it would not be feasible to drop the one without dropping the other.

Rainald's own role in this matter is not difficult to understand. He had come from a family and a class whose fortunes and position in society would have debarred him from a major political career. If he had remained content to move within the ambit of his family's status, he would have played a local and very circumscribed role as a member of the lower Saxon aristocracy. Like the Counts Northeim and Sommerschenburg, he would have spent his life feuding and warring, acquiring or losing a castle here and a manor there. But his personal ambition as well as his very considerable political talents made him look for greater prizes. Given his comparatively lowly origin, he realized that he could break out of these confines only by joining the church. And in joining the church, there were two possibilities. He could either aspire to influence and high office by following the paths of men like Arnold von Seelenhofen, the archbishop of Mainz, or of Wibald. But this would mean that he would have had to put aside his worldly pleasures and his flamboyant prowess and assume a somewhat clerical demeanour. Given the time, he would not have had to become exactly a saint or a spiritual reformer; but he would have been compelled to identify himself clearly with the more forward-looking cause of Gregorian reform and the attitudes and ideals for which Pope Eugene III and Hadrian IV had stood. To Rainald, this was out of the question. If he was to change his personality to such an extent as to find the approval of these men, he might as well remain what he was and seek his fortunes in the feuds and opportunities offered to his fellow lower Saxon nobles. There remained, then, only the alternative. He could enter the church, but make himself the protagonist and eventually the prototype of the secular episcopate whose fortunes and successes would depend on the fortunes and favours of the emperor. But these favours were only likely to be forthcoming and remain permanent if the emperor could be persuaded to follow an anti-papal policy and be convinced that he was superior to the pope.[1] Thus it had been that Rainald had recognized that his greatest opportunities would lie in a confrontation with the papacy – from which he was confident the emperor would emerge triumphant.[2] Hence Rainald's close association with Frederick and Frederick's steady reliance on and trust in Rainald. Frederick could not have had any illusions about Rainald's personal interests. But he knew of Rainald's splendid gifts, he appreciated his political talents, his military courage and dexterity, his rhetoric and above all, his devotion. And between 1159 and 1167 Frederick had always judged that whatever anti-papal twists Rainald might be giving to the Great Design, these twists never amounted to a distortion of his own original intentions.

It is nevertheless fair to conclude that as a result of his personal

[1] The expression 'holy empire' was particularly dear to Rainald, and in innumerable places in which it was officially used, one can detect the influence of Rainald's dictation or of his writing. See R. M. Herkenrath, *Rainald von Dassel*, Diss. (typed), Graz, 1962, Excursus V. The expression itself was invented by Rainald and was used very rarely after his death. *See* R. M. Herkenrath, *Rainald von Dassel als Verfasser und Schreiber von Kaiserurkunden*, MIOG, LXXII, 1964, pp. 54, 57, 59, 60. In this connection, E. H. Kantorowicz, *Kingship and Scientific Jurisprudence*, in: M. Clagett *et al.*, ed., *Twelfth Century Europe and the Foundations of Modern Society*, Madison, 1961, pp. 100–101, draws attention to Gulielmus Durandus who, at the end of the thirteenth century, made a positive effort to derive the prince's nonlaical character not from his anointment with the holy oil but from Ulpian's solemn comparison of judges with priests. *Sacer*, Kantorowicz comments, in the language of Roman law meant no more than *imperial*, though in medieval Latin it may have had more Christian-ecclesiastical connotations. 'It was at any rate from Roman law that Barbarossa borrowed the epithet *sacrum* for his *imperium*'. This is worth bearing in mind, provided one substitutes 'Rainald' for 'Barbarossa'. Kantorowicz concludes: '. . . the sacred character of the empire . . . no longer drew its strength from the ideas of the *christus domini*, from the altar or from the church, but it was a secular sacredness *sui generis* apart from the church'. The expression *sacrum imperium*, viewed in this light, was not borrowed from the vocabulary of the church.

[2] In 1158, when Rainald advised against hasty concessions to Hadrian, he wrote to Frederick 'in tali statu Deus vos in praesenti constituit, quod, si vultis, et Romam destruere et de papa et cardinalibus omnem vestram voluntatem habere'. Döberl, p. 123.

ambition, Rainald's hatred of the papacy as represented by men like Eugene III, Hadrian IV and Alexander III, was something of a personal obsession. He hated and resented a papacy which extended its influence towards bishops, especially towards bishops north of the Alps. It was no accident that he first revealed this at Besançon in 1157.[1] In the following year, when he was in northern Italy to prepare the ground for Frederick's proclamation of the Great Design, he had warned his master against a premature reconciliation with Hadrian and against the pope's friends in Germany.[2] And once the final rupture with both Lombardy and papacy had taken place, Rainald knew no bounds. He had been one of the chief promoters of the schism and of Victor.[3] It had been the result of his diplomacy that the destruction of Milan in 1162 had to be permitted.[4] He had been in the forefront at the meeting of St Jean-de-Losne.[5] His precipitate action in Lucca in 1164 had assured a continuation of the schism after Victor's death[6] and his intrigues with the king of England had led to the Würzburg oaths[7] and the Würzburg oaths to the canonization of Charlemagne,[8] an act of useless propaganda, the grandiloquence of which had stood in inverse proportion to its political significance.[9] No doubt he had been as well a major influence in promoting the expedition to Rome in 1167. If Rainald in early 1167 had not hurried on to Rome, Frederick might have stayed longer in Lombardy.[10] But Rainald was anxious for an all-enveloping military triumph. And there was none to be had in Lombardy at that time. So he rushed on to Tusculum; and when the battle took place, Rainald saw to it that its significance was exaggerated beyond all proportions.[11] It is true that he could not have foreseen that Alexander would escape;[12] and even more true, that Rainald could not possibly have anticipated the final and disastrous epidemic.[13] But the whole campaign of 1167 is insolubly linked

[1] *See* p. 187 above.

[2] Sudendorf, II, No. 54; *see* p. 192 above.

[3] *See* p. 213 above. Victor, in the first instance, had addressed himself to Rainald for support. *Cp.*, *Chron. reg. Col.*, ad annum 1161; JL, 14425.

[4] *See* p. 181 above.

[5] *See* p. 232 above. [6] *See* p. 236 above. [7] *See* p. 240 above.

[8] *See* p. 242 above. [9] *See* p. 243 above. [10] *See* p. 249 above.

[11] *See* p. 250 above. [12] *See* p. 252 above. [13] *See* p. 253 above.

with his name and, if it had been successful, would have been the crowning glory of his policies and his views.

There is no indication that Frederick ever felt resentment against Rainald. He expressed disapproval at the hasty election of a successor to Victor[1] and was angry with Rainald's impetuous interference at Würzburg in 1165.[2] But that was all. He understood that it would have been quite impractical to detach Rainald's anti-papal obsession from the Great Design. Any such attempt could only have appeared as hair-splitting. Most people would never have understood the subtle point on which Frederick's sober and calculated judgement differed from that of Rainald and would simply have become confused and puzzled had they been confronted with rumours of disagreement between the emperor and the archbishop of Cologne. And since Frederick had considered it impolitic to make much of his concern and his temporary disapprovals of Rainald during the latter's lifetime, he was too magnanimous to express criticism of Rainald after his death.[3] This magnanimity, however, did not prevent Frederick from taking stock of the situation after his death.

So far as Germany had been concerned, the Great Design had directly involved only Swabia and Alsace. Frederick had not concerned himself directly with the rest of Germany and he had, in fact, encouraged the German princes, lay as well as ecclesiastical, to round off their possessions and turn them into real territorial lordships, much as he had intended to do in the lands of the three rivers. The issue of the *privilegium minus* to Henry Jasomirgott

[1] *See* p. 237 above [2] *See* p. 241 above.

[3] In spite of his services to the magic appeal of Cologne, popular legend was less generous to Rainald. *Chron. Montis Sereni*, MGH, SS, XXIII, p. 153, records that Rainald, when still a boy, was often heard to murmur in his sleep: 'I am'. Once his master asked him what he meant and Rainald replied still sleeping: 'I am the ruin of the world.' – One of the copies of the *Cologne Chronicle* contains the thirteenth century addition for the year 1167. It says that in 1167 it was related that Pope Paschal refused to confirm Philip von Heinsberg as archbishop in succession to Rainald, unless he had the statue of Rainald removed from the church of St Peter in Cologne. The Romans, still smarting under their defeat at the hands of Rainald, were said to have forced Paschal to make this condition, for the statue had been erected in 'honour of the enemy of the Roman church'. Paschal himself had every reason to be grateful to Rainald. The story may well have been an invention. But the details are plausible and Paschal, in Rome after August 1167, was very much in the hands of the Romans who could have no reason for loving Rainald.

was an explicit sanction for developments of this kind.[1] If Frederick did not provide similarly explicit charters for the other princes, it was understood that they were to help themselves. Sooner or later attempts to round off their territories were likely to bring these princes into conflict with one another, for there were lordships which were bound to be coveted by more than one person. Moreover, there were minor princes and bishops who might resist being absorbed; or, if absorbed, might prefer to be absorbed by or pay homage to a major lord whose territorial possessions were not geographically contiguous with theirs – for the theoretical principle of territoriality was neither very clearly enunciated nor yet generally recognized as a natural basis for a political order. There were people old-fashioned enough not to wish to sacrifice their independence to the progressive principle of territorial unity; and others progressive enough to wish to absorb one and the same property into their separate territorial 'states'. Frederick could not have overlooked these ultimate sources of conflict. But he had obviously hoped that they would not eventuate within his lifetime and had certainly not reckoned with rapid progress towards territorial unification in some regions and had therefore not anticipated that the first major clashes would occur as early as the middle sixties.

Above all, he had not reckoned with the possibility that his cousin Henry the Lion would make sufficient progress in Saxony to provoke a major military conflict in the north. But this, unfortunately, was precisely what happened. And once this had happened, the Great Design was shaken at its periphery.

Ever since the end of the reign of the emperor Lothair III (1125–1137), the Welf territorial block of influence had included Saxony and Bavaria as well as the Matildan Lands in Tuscany with which Lothair had been invested jointly with his kinsman Henry the Proud, father of Henry the Lion. The Matildan lands in Italy belonged to an uncle of Henry the Lion, Welf VI, and when Henry the Lion was finally able to take up the duchy of Bavaria in 1156, he showed little interest in these southern lands. In Bavaria, Henry was simply a tribal duke – and there was no telling what

[1] *See* p. 106 above.

this precisely meant. His real power there was confined to one single countship and to a few *Vogteien*.[1] But in Saxony the position was very different. In Saxony he held innumerable countships and a great deal of allodial property. The core of his power was situated in the region between the upper Aller in the east, the Bode in the south and the Fuhse in the west, with Braunschweig firmly in the centre. There he owned so many countships that many historians have quite sensibly concluded that whatever his rights as a duke might have been, they received substance only through his possession of these countships.[2] Moreover, on the other side of the river Elbe there lay the lands of the heathen Slavs whom Henry was converting successfully, if gradually, to Christianity. In these lands he planted bishoprics and there he established his *ministeriales* as rulers of castles, so that to the east of the Elbe he managed to enlarge his territory in a way which left no doubt as to who was the sovereign ruler. And it was natural that he should seek to assimilate his other possessions with this concept of territorial sovereignty[3] and should want to round them off by forcing other bishops, lords and monasteries into subjection and enlarge his own territory by an 'expansionist' policy directed against his neighbours. He confiscated lands where there was no direct male heir and denied the rights of daughters and relatives. He confiscated lands of rebellious nobles, and sought to acquire further countships and *Vogteien*. And after the schism, he deprived bishops who were supporters of Alexander and appointed men of his choice in their place, who would then invest him with their lands.[4] In fact, Henry derived in this way much more immediate

[1] For the paucity of Henry the Lion's possessions in Bavaria *cp.* C. W. Böttiger, *Heinrich der Löwe*, Hannover, 1819, Excursus II; also Heigel and Riezler, *Das Herzogtum Bayern zur Zeit Heinrichs des Löwen und Ottos von Wittelsbach*, p. 248.

[2] This is a matter of considerable importance and is discussed more fully in Chapter VII in connection with Henry's attempts at state-building.

[3] HB, p. 196.

[4] R. Hildebrand, *Der sächsische 'Staat' Heinrichs des Löwen*, EHS, 302, Berlin, 1937. As I have drawn heavily on this work both in Chapter VII and Chapter VIII, I would like to state that the large amount of criticism which has been levelled against it concerns almost exclusively Miss Hildebrand's theory about the nature of Henry's ducal rights, but not the main body of the book which is concerned with Henry's vigorous and aggressive state-building. For a list of critical reviews of Miss Hildebrand's book *see* P. Munz, *Frederick Barbarossa and the 'Holy Empire'*, JRH, III, 1964, p. 35, note 30.

and direct territorial benefit from the schism than Frederick ever did.[1] Henry was indeed so resourceful and determined, that he anticipated Frederick's own territorial conceptions by several years and gave his own territorial twist to concessions which Frederick made to him as early as 1154, under Frederick's first plan.

In 1154, at a court in Goslar, Frederick had issued a charter to Henry, granting him the right to invest bishops in the lands beyond the Elbe. With this charter it was clearly decided that the territorial organization beyond the Elbe was to be left in the secular hands of Henry, and not in the hands of a number of Saxon bishops.[2] In Frederick's intention under the first plan of his reign, the bishoprics which Henry founded east of the Elbe were to be founded by him not in his capacity as duke of Saxony, but as a representative of the emperor and in pursuance of the imperial theory that the empire must extend the faith and the *imperium christianum*. But if Frederick intended Henry to act as the representative of the imperial power, Henry recognized at once that he could turn this charter to serve his own, personal, territorial ambitions[3] for Frederick had no means, and possibly no interest, in

[1] Henry the Lion immediately used the schism in order to obtain Victor's help to get rid of several bishops who had stood in his way in Saxony. In this way, Henry derived much more immediate and direct benefit from the schism than Frederick. *Cp.* W. Ohnsorge, *Päpstliche und gegenpäpstliche Legaten in Deutschland und Skandinavien, 1159–1181*, EHS, 188, Berlin, 1929, p. 10.

[2] K. Jordan, *Bistumsgründungen Heinrichs des Löwen*, Stuttgart, 1939, p. 85.

[3] When Henry gave protection to the German merchants in Gotland, he was also acting, legally, on behalf of the king. The peace given to the merchants was the king's peace. *Cp.* F. Rörig, *Reichssymbolik auf Gotland*, HG, 64, 1940, and for the delegated nature of Henry's right to invest bishops, *cp.* F. Güterbock, *Friedrich Barbarossa und Heinrich der Löwe*, GV, XXIII, 1933, p. 254. – For the practice, however, consider the the following case. When Hartwig of Bremen died in 1168, one of the group of magnates opposed to Henry, Otto von Oldenburg, an old friend and a relative of Hartwig, caused the election, to the Bremen see, of Siegfried, third son of Albrecht the Bear. The latter was connected right and left with the enemies of Henry, not only through his father but also through the house of the Wettiner; and as a canon of the church of Magdeburg he was also associated with Wichmann. Thus Siegfried was 'elected' and tried to install himself while Henry was absent on an embassy in France. But one of Henry's faithful *ministeriales*, Gunzelin, prevented him and chased him away, and Henry's men then caused another man to be elected to the see. Eventually the disputed election was brought before Frederick who rejected both candidates and put forward a neutral man so old and weak that henceforth Henry could pursue his acquisitive instincts without episcopal opposition from Bremen. Thus he was able to assert three months after the accession of this man that the three bishoprics beyond the Elbe were

insisting on fine distinctions. And once the Great Design had taken shape in his mind, he was only too willing to provide further sanctions for the growth of Henry's territorial power.

In 1158 Frederick used his authority to reconcile Henry with Hartwig, the archbishop of Bremen. Hartwig had attempted to restore his metropolitan control over the old bishoprics in the Wendenland. These attempts had been viewed by Henry with suspicion and resentment. For if Hartwig's efforts had met with success, there would have arisen in the north-east of Saxony the same kind of territorial power which Henry had tried his best to prevent from developing in the north-west in the form of the region occupied by the Stade family. Frederick's reconciliation of Hartwig with Henry proved much to Henry's advantage. For Hartwig was forced to concede to Henry the right of investiture in the three Wendish bishoprics. In this way Frederick helped Henry to make sure not only that the Elbe would not become a sort of 'priests' alley' like the Rhine,[1] but also that these bishoprics would recognize Henry as their feudal overlord.[2] It is probably no accident that Henry founded the city of Lübeck[3] in the same year in which he recognized for certain that Frederick was willing to support his territorial aspirations (as distinct from his general position of duke of Saxony and Bavaria) to the fullest extent – and precisely to the

his foundations. *See* J. Harttung, *Das Erzbistum Bremen und Heinrich der Löwe*, HZ, 34, 1865, pp. 339–40. On several occasions he disposed of the property of these sees as if he were the master. The bishops agreed and the archbishop is not so much as mentioned. Henry also insisted that the men of those bishops owed suit of court to *him*. *Cp. ibid.*, p. 340. In almost every respect Henry acted as if the metropolitan did not exist, *ibid.*, p. 342. Thus the archbishop's power and influence were wholly confined to the actual borders of his own diocese and the metropolitan district did not exist. Even in the diocese of Bremen itself Henry interfered brutally, appointed abbots and razed castles to the ground. (*ibid.*, p. 342.)

[1] *Cp.* B. Schmeidler, *Helmold und seine Cronica Slavorum*, ZVLGA, XIV, 1912, p. 234.

[2] K. Jordan, *Heinrich der Löwe und die ostdeutsche Kolonisation*, DALV, 2, 1938, pp. 798–799. G. Glaeske, *Die Erzbischöfe von Hamburg-Bremen als Reichsfürsten*, Hildesheim, 1962, p. 163, remarks that the concession to Henry may have been no more than a recognition of the *status quo*. If one bears in mind that in 1160 Hartwig's right to invest the Wenden bishops was formally confirmed (*see* O. H. May, *Regesten der Erzbischöfe von Bremen*, Hannover-Bremen, 1937, p. 545) the concession to Henry appears as a purely political expedient and is as such all the more telling.

[3] For the parallelism between Henry's and Frederick's foundations of cities see p. 114, note 1. – The foundation of Lübeck proved epoch-making for the commerce in the Baltic. *Cp.* F. Rörig, *Gestaltung des Ostseeraums durch das deutsche Bürgertum*, DALV, 2, 1938.

extent to which Frederick was planning to pursue similar policies in the lands of the three rivers.

Fortified by Frederick's implicit approval of 1154 and the explicit approval of 1158, Henry stepped up his efforts to round off his possessions and to create a territorial sovereignty for himself. Where necessary he was brutally aggressive and if one surveys the policies one will find that he created a vast circle of enemies around, as well as in Saxony, consisting entirely of men who had lost territory and influence through his territorial consolidations and who felt themselves crossed in their own efforts to round off their territories in turn.

In the north he had finally secured the inheritance of the Stade family.[1] The clergy of Bremen had tried to counter Henry's violent attacks by electing Hartwig von Stade as their archbishop. But throughout the long tenure of his office (1148–1169) Hartwig was not able to weaken Henry's predominance.[2] Further to the east where the possessions of the margraves of Brandenburg were, Henry found himself in almost incessant conflict with Margrave Albrecht the Bear. Henry had allodial property in the Altmark – which was a thorn in Albrecht's flesh. Albrecht, as the *Vogt* of the monasteries of Gröningen, Gernrode and Ilsenburg and as the feudal lord or *Vogt* of the bishopric of Halberstadt, had constant occasion for making his power felt in the Harz region, so near the heart of Henry's closest property.[3] Equally in the centre of Henry's power were the territorially fairly compact holdings of the Sommerschenburgs.[4] There was similar friction with the arch-

[1] C. Schambach, *Heinrich der Löwe und die Stader Erbschaft*, NJL, 17, 1940, has sought to prove that Henry took possession of the Stade inheritance only in 1155–6 and not, as commonly supposed, in 1145 as a result of his violent attacks upon Adalbero of Bremen and Hartwig von Stade. H. Woltmann, *Heinrich der Löwe und die Stader Erbschaft*, SA, 34, 1941 and *Heinrich der Löwe und das Erbe der Grafen von Stade*, NJL, 18, 1941; 19, 1942, has convincingly rejected Schambach's revision of the date.

[2] R. Hildebrand, *op. cit.*, pp. 221–2; H. Patze, *Kaiser Friedrich Barbarossa und der Osten*, JGMOD, XI, 1962, p. 21. With the death of Hartwig, Henry's triumph was complete. Not only were the Stade lands not taken from him – a possibility which Rainald had suggested to Hartwig shortly before the latter's death (Helmold, II, 104) – but the whole of the bishopric became completely dependent upon Henry. *See* G. Dehio, *Hartwig von Stade*, Göttingen, 1872, p. 75. Hartwig's successor Baldwin was Henry's willing tool. *Cp.* G. Glaeske, *Die Erzbischöfe von Hamburg-Bremen als Reichsfürsten*, Hildesheim, 1962, p. 181.

[3] R. Hildebrand, *op. cit.*, pp. 244 and 256.

[4] *ibid.*, p. 245.

5 Henry the Lion, duke of Saxony and his second wife, Matilda. c. 1175. (Staatsbibliothek, Berlin.)

6(*a*) Frederick on horseback. (From a coin now in the Staatliche Museum, Berlin.)

6(*b*) Frederick as a Crusader. (Illumination in *Historica Hiersolymitana*. Vatican Library, Rome.)

bishops of Magdeburg, whose allodial property between Magdeburg and Haldensleben was coveted by Henry. Further to the south Henry had managed to possess himself of the inheritance of the Winzenburg family and to make formidable inroads into the Katlenburg and Northeim lands between Weser and Werra so that his territory advanced there right down to Kassel and to the Kyffhäuser.[1] As a result he found himself face to face with the *Landgrafen* of Thuringia who, in turn, were pursuing a territorial policy of their own and resented Henry's expansions southwards. By contrast, Henry seems to have had amicable relations with the archbishop of Mainz, whose own territorial ambitions were negligible at the time. It is possible that Frederick's opposition to the election of Christian von Buch as archbishop of Mainz, after the murder of Archbishop Arnold,[2] had something to do with his determination to countenance Henry's territorial ambitions. For Christian's election had been sponsored, among others, by the *Landgraf* of Thuringia and Frederick probably feared (unjustifiably, as it turned out) that Christian might remain an ally of the Landgraf and join the growing opposition to Henry.

If the archbishop of Mainz had no territorial plans, the same cannot be said of the archbishops of Cologne. The Westphalian part of the archdiocese of Cologne consisted of two tracts, separated from each other by the county of Arnsberg and by Henry's own Westphalian counties.[3] The archbishops of Cologne were eager to create a connection between their Westphalian lands and it was here that a direct clash between their interests and those of Henry was bound to occur.[4] Rainald, however, had not only good reason as archbishop of Cologne to clash with Henry. He also had retained close ties with his brother, Count Dassel, who was trying hard to maintain himself against Henry's encroachments in the Weser-Werra region and with the Northeim family, whose

[1] *ibid.*, pp. 265–70.
[2] *See* p. 180 above.
[3] R. Hildebrand, *op. cit.*, p. 276.
[4] *ibid.*, p. 269. According to a report by Rainald's successor in Cologne, Henry was supposed to have said once that his duchy went as far as Deutz (on the right bank of the Rhine) and even a bit further, i.e. as far as one can throw a spear into the Rhine. *See* H. Hecker, *Die territoriale Politik des Erzbischofs Philipp I. von Köln*, Leipzig, 1883, p. 24 f.

possessions a little to the east of those of the Dassel family were equally threatened.[1]

There was not only the occasion for conflict which might at any time precipitate war on the frontiers of Saxony. There were equally disturbing sources of friction inside Saxony. The Welf family had long since possessed itself of the countships originally in the hands of the bishops of Halberstadt and Hildesheim. But both bishoprics had retained masses of allodial property fortified by castles inside these counties. As a result Henry worked towards an elimination of the lordships which prevented a territorial consolidation of these counties.[2] He was fairly successful in regard to Halberstadt as long as he was able to keep a creature of his, Gero, on the episcopal see;[3] and less so in regard to Hildesheim.[4]

All in all, Henry's progress was steady; and given his persistent if partial successes, it is not surprising to find that by the mid-sixties many minor and major princes were beginning to combine in order to defend themselves against Henry's efforts to give his ducal title a consolidated territorial meaning. As if to underline his intentions and to demonstrate visually his unrelenting power, Henry, in the early sixties, had the statue of the lion erected outside his castle Dankwarderode in Braunschweig.[5]

The first signs of a coalition go back to the year 1163. In that year Count Palatine Adalbert, Albrecht the Bear and the *Landgraf* of Thuringia agreed to attack Henry together. Frederick used his influence to stop other princes from joining the coalition and his efforts seem to have discouraged also the original allies. For in the end, only the count palatine resorted to violence – to pay for his attack with the loss of one of his castles in the Harz.[6] But soon after, the unrest in Saxony became more widespread. Several of Henry's Saxon vassals conspired in order to preserve their ancestral rights from further encroachments and this unrest was

[1] Rainald was related to the Northeim family, *Cp.* Wenke, ZGNKG, 17, 1912. Also Koken, VAHVN, 1840, pp. 147–55. The Northeim family were inveterate enemies of Henry.

[2] R. Hildebrand, *op. cit.*, p. 282. [3] *ibid.*, p. 284. [4] *ibid.*, pp. 286–8.

[5] Giesebrecht, V, p. 512. The castle of Dankwarderode itself was modelled on the imperial palace at Goslar. *See* G. Dehio, *Geschichte der deutschen Kunst*, I, Berlin, 1921, pp. 305 f.

[6] Giesebrecht, V, pp. 457–8; VI, p. 456.

seized by Henry's old enemies to forge a major coalition against him.[1] It consisted, first of all, of no less a person than Rainald, the archbishop of Cologne; then there was Wichmann, the archbishop of Magdeburg. They were joined by Albrecht the Bear and the *Landgraf* Ludwig of Thuringia, as well as by the bishop of Hildesheim and a host of minor princes from Hessen, Thuringia and Saxony.

This coalition was taking shape at the very time when Rainald was forging an alliance with the king of England, an alliance towards the success of which Henry the Lion was contributing a great deal. This coalition was consolidated both before and after the great court of Würzburg in 1165[2] and became effective almost immediately after Frederick's departure for Italy in 1166. Hostilities were begun against Henry on a wide front: the allies moved against Bremen and Haldensleben at the same time. There is no point in following the course of these campaigns in detail. But it is worth adding that in July 1167 the allies held an assembly at Magdeburg and at that assembly they were assured by an embassy from Cologne that Rainald would join their campaigns in person after his return from Italy. The allies now turned against Goslar and were joined, after some hesitation, by Hartwig, the archbishop of Bremen, and by Conrad, the bishop of Lübeck. Eventually the news of Rainald's death temporarily weakened the determination of the vassals and the *ministeriales* of the see of Cologne to continue the fight. During the second half of 1167 when Frederick found himself in extreme personal danger in Italy, he sent two of his most trusted advisers, Christian of Mainz and Berthold von Zähringen, to Germany to seek reinforcements and also charged them to patch up a peace between Henry the Lion and his enemies. In this they were successful.

Such a peace, however, although it led to an end of active hostilities, could not eliminate the sources of conflict. And it became clear then to Frederick that the Great Design, in so far as it implied the formation of territorial states in Germany, had led to severe and, in the long run, insoluble conflict. Studying the situation, he must have had the gravest misgivings. For he

[1] Giesebrecht, V, pp. 512–13.

[2] *See* p. 239 above.

began to understand that his two policies, the policy of pursuing Alexander and the policy of following the Great Design, were incompatible. The first had found Henry the Lion and Rainald firmly united in cementing the alliance with the king of England, whereas Wichmann, to say the least, had been lukewarm. The second had produced a head-on collision between Rainald and Henry and had prompted Wichmann to side with Rainald. When Frederick discovered that the two policies had caused two incompatible sets of alignments, he was forced to conclude that he could not continue with both. And if he needed proof as to whether this was the right conclusion it was provided by the fact that with the exception of Rainald,[1] Bishop Udo of Naumburg and Abbot Hermann of Fulda, none of the enemies of Henry the Lion was prepared to join the expedition to Rome in 1166. The incompatibility was tellingly reflected in the composition of the army which Frederick and Rainald managed to lead to Italy.[2] As late as September 1166 there had been doubt as to whether Frederick would really cross the alps and undertake the planned campaign against Rome.[3] Eventually he decided to go, leaving an explosive situation behind him.[4] He reached Lombardy, only to find that there too the situation had become explosive.

[1] Even Rainald, at this moment, was uncertain. In September 1166, Rainald was sick and, although he had made preparations for the campaign, it was rumoured in his own entourage that he was thinking of making his peace with Alexander. *Cp.* Giesebrecht, V, p. 518–19, and VI, p. 457. The rumour is reported by John of Salisbury in a letter to Thomas à Becket, PL, 199, pp. 203 f., *Ep.*, 191. John says that the sick Rainald, possibly worried by thoughts of death, promised not to go to Italy and to make his peace with Alexander instead, provided it could be made to look as if he had been forced to do so by his own clergy.

[2] According to Helmold, II, 107, Frederick said in Bamberg in 1168 that the conspiracy against Henry in Saxony had given the Lombards occasion for defection. There was clearly no such causal connection, and it is very unlikely that Frederick should have thought so. But there is an oblique truth in Helmold's report. The conspiracy against Henry had proved that the Great Design was not working well in Germany and that its failure was making it very difficult for Frederick to pursue it in Italy. As so often, Helmold got the essence of the matter right.

[3] Giesebrecht, V, 519.

[4] Ironically enough, it was Henry the Lion who remained one of Frederick's firmest supporters in Germany, as well he might, for he had always been one of the chief beneficiaries of the schism and hence could always be relied upon to favour the Great Design which had caused it. In spite of the fact that many of his enemies were also close supporters of Frederick's campaign against Rome, Henry, although he himself did not join the expedition, went to considerable lengths to guard Frederick's rear, as

On his arrival in Lombardy it did not take Frederick long to realize that his ascendancy was anything but assured. Already on his last visit in 1163–4 he had watched how the Veronese were being inveigled into open resistance by the Venetians,[1] and he had had to return to Germany without having been able to break Verona's defiance. Now in 1165 he discovered that the citizens of Brescia were almost hostile; and those of Bergamo, though old enemies of the Brescians, against all expectations, less than friendly. Genoa and Pisa, two potential allies of Frederick, were at each other's throats and no amount of arbitration on Frederick's part

---

the following incident proves. In October 1166, when Frederick assembled his army, he seems to have commissioned Henry von Baumgarten to devastate the property of the monastery of Reichersberg. The monks wrote to Henry as their *Vogt* to ask for help. Henry replied in what can only be described a cynical way. He assured the monks of his love and care and told them he had charged Otto von Wittelsbach to look into the matter. For the correspondence *see* P. Classen, *Gerhoch von Reichersberg*, Wiesbaden, 1960, pp. 400–1. Otto was one of Alexander's most aggressive enemies and a great friend and collaborator of Rainald. To ask him to take care of the monks of Reichersberg in this matter was like appointing the wolf to mind the sheep. *See* MGH, SS, XVII, p. 475.

[1] The Venetians had provided a great deal of money. The legates of Alexander had their headquarters in Venice and they directed their strategy from that city. *Cp.* P. Kehr, *Kaiser Friedrich I und Venedig während des Schismas*, QuF, 17, 1924, pp. 230 ff. With the help of money disbursed by the Venetians, the Verona League was complete by April 1164. *Cp.* H. Kretschmayr, *Geschichte von Venedig*, Gotha, 1905, Vol. I, p. 250. The money which the Venetians disbursed came mostly from Byzantium. *Cp.* G. Ostrogorsky, *Geschichte des byzantinischen Staates*, 1940, p. 275. The main source for Manuel's financial subsidies for the Lombards is Niketas Choniates, VII, 261. Barni, *Storia di Milano*, IV, p. 92, is very suspicious of this source. But P. Classen, 'Mailands Treueid für Manuel Komnenos', *Akten des XI. internationalen Byzantinisten-Kongresses*, München, 1960, pp. 79–85, believes that Niketas Choniates spoke the truth. It seems that Manuel required the consuls to take some kind of oath to him in return for these subsidies and that he made similar offers to other cities in the early 70s. *Cp.* also P. Lamma, *Comneni e Staufer*, Roma, 1955, Vol. II, p. 249. Manuel was a very shrewd political strategist and he must have known that money was a sore point with Frederick and a political instrument with which he could never compete. In the 60s, Manuel fed money to the three cities which had been able to hold out against Frederick. For Venice *see* Dölger, Nos. 1494, 1464, 1479; for Genoa, Dölger, No. 1488; for Pisa, Dölger, No. 1499. – According to the anonymous chronicler of Lodi, Manuel came very close to success in his policy of gaining a foothold in northern Italy at that time. He writes that 'Lombardi, per insolentias imperatoris Frederici tedio et angore fatigati, Manueli Grecorum imperatori submittere eorum regnum deliberaverunt' (MGH, SS, XXVI, p. 446). *Cp.* also P. Lamma, *op. cit.*, II, pp. 42, 116, 154–5. In 1174, Genoa expressly refused to enter into such a relationship with Manuel. *Cp.* C. Imperiale, *Codice diplomatico della Republica di Genova, Fonti per la storia d'Italia*, 79, 1938, Vol. II, 205, No. 95. If Frederick, in the mid-seventies, had not decided to desist from molesting the Lombards, there is no telling how close the relations between the Lombards and the Emperor Manuel might have become.

was able to produce any kind of peace. And at the court he held in Lodi, masses of Lombards carrying the cross, as was the custom, arrived to complain of injustices and extortions.

It cannot have been very difficult for Frederick to see that most of these complaints were only too justified. His original plan – and this had been the central idea of the Great Design – had been to foster in every respect the economic growth of the Lombard cities by providing imperial coinage and imperial peace. In return, he had planned to raise taxes in cash by establishing himself as the source of law and political authority in the cities. He had hoped to achieve this either through the voluntary recognition of his sovereignty by the existing magistrates of the cities or by the election or imposition of magistrates who would exercise their authority as if it were derived from the emperor. By the middle of 1159,[1] this original plan had begun to fail. With the open resistance of Milan and the eventual total destruction of the city in 1162[2] it had become clear that the Great Design could never be implemented through the co-operation of the Lombards themselves. The party in Lombardy which had supported it had failed to remain in the ascendancy. In Milan there had been something close to a real revolution[3] and Piacenza, for instance, had drawn away from Frederick when it had become clear that Frederick would favour Cremona,[4] her old enemy. As a result Frederick and Rainald had been forced to depart from the original intention.

[1] *See* p. 177 above.

[2] *See* p. 183 above. The destruction of Milan, though depriving the Great Design of its very basis, had acted as a powerful warning. Brescia had surrendered completely in the same month; and Piacenza in May.

[3] *See* p. 174 above.

[4] Piacenza, in 1156, had been allied with Milan. In June 1158, Piacenza changed sides. It is likely that this change was due to the fact that the pope had supported the cause of a nunnery on the Po. The nuns had fought a long battle against Piacenza about their right to have a ferry or bridge of their own over the Po. When imperial judges began to support the citizens of Piacenza, Piacenza was persuaded to join the emperor's side. But after Roncaglia, Piacenza changed back to an alliance with Milan, because Frederick showed too much favour to her old enemy Cremona. In revenge, Frederick began to support the nuns. *See* F. Güterbock, *Piacenza's Beziehungen zu Barbarossa*, QuF, 24, 1897, pp. 69 ff. The quarrel with the nuns was more real to Piacenza than international politics or the schism. In 1174, when Frederick's power in Lombardy was very much in abeyance, the old dispute was brought before Alexander's legate Galdinus. Galdinus, anxious to keep Piacenza on the papal side, produced a compromise judgement, fairly favourable to Piacenza, *ibid.*, pp. 96–7.

Instead of allowing the cities to elect their own consuls, who would then be formally invested with their office by the emperor, they had to insist on nominated *podestà*.[1] In some rare cases these *podestà* were native Lombards; but for the most part, and this was to become the fatally irksome factor in the situation, they were country squires imported from Germany. Some were German *ministeriales*, men of un-free status, tied in personal dependence and loyalty to Frederick. They were always solid warriors and tried servants. But they had no education at all and certainly no experience in the administration of foreign and hostile populations. Whatever their sterling qualities at home, they found themselves surrounded by a thousand temptations in Italy. They were not only in a foreign country where they were divorced from the homely sanctions which imposed even upon the most greedy and the most brutal a minimum of restraint; but were also in the midst of riches unheard and undreamt of in the more primitive, rural economy of their native Germany. And when a Markward von Grumbach[2] became controller of Piacenza, there was ground for the worst of fears.

It is reasonable to suppose that Frederick was aware of the danger from the very beginning. For if he had not been, he might conceivably have originally stipulated direct imperial control in the Great Design.[3] The facts that it had not been included and that he had resorted to this system of administration only after the destruction of Milan shows that it was an improvised measure. Once the party which had wanted to co-operate with

[1] FRRGI, II, pp. 182 and 187.

[2] The Grumbach family were closely tied to the Staufen, both to Conrad III and to Frederick. Through them, the Staufen gained influence in the middle Main valley and in Thuringia. A Grumbach had founded the monastery of Ichterhausen; and the charter stipulated that the *Vogtei* was always to belong to the oldest member of the family and was never to be sublet or ceded to an *Untervogt*, so as to ensure that no other lord would ever be able to extend his influence into that region. *Cp.* H. Patze, *Die Entstehung der Landesherrschaft in Thüringen*, Köln-Graz, 1962, pp. 213–14. *Ibid.*, p. 224, Patze stresses the close relationship between Frederick and Markward. But I cannot agree with Patze that Frederick's relation to Markward was one of personal friendship, comparable to Frederick's relation to Count Rudolf von Pfullendorf.

[3] From 1158 onwards, Frederick frequently detached whole regions from the cities and made them *reichsunmittelbar*, and put Germans in charge of their administration. FRRGI, I, par. 127; II, par. 295. This practice was probably part of the original Great Design, but it applied only to the *contado*, not to cities.

him in Lombardy lost control, Frederick had to think of the Great Design as a dictatorial imposition. He was forced to alter his conception of the whole administrative basis of the Great Design in Lombardy.[1] It was then, and then only, that he had to resort to importing these foreign squires. Not all have become as famous as Markward von Grumbach and Arnold von Dorstadt. But we know of a great many others.[2] At first, at least until 1163, Rainald acted as a sort of controller-general of these men. But it appears that he relinquished this post soon[3] and in 1164 he was succeeded in it by Markward von Grumbach who in turn was succeeded in 1166 by Henry von Dietz.[4]

When Markward became *podestà* of Milan in 1164 the Milanese first received him with presents. But he showed himself callous and

[1] There is indeed a complete contrast between the original plan as it is revealed by the Treaty of Milan of September 1158 (*Cp.* p. 163 above) and the system of government by commissioners imposed after the destruction of Milan in 1162. One cannot exaggerate the importance of the fact that the system of 1162 had *not* been part of the original idea. Older historians have usually failed to distinguish between Frederick's original plan and the execution he was forced to improvise in 1162. F. Heer, *Aufgang Europas*. Wien-Zürich, 1949, Chs. VII–VIII, has, unfortunately, given new currency to this older conception. It is equally unfortunate that the criticism which Heer has received from the hands of Th. Mayer, is completely invalidated by Mayer's absurd and bigoted view that, no matter what the facts, 'it is not permissible' to denigrate emperors like Frederick, HZ, 178, 1954, p. 492. According to the original plan, Frederick had wanted to benefit from the economic growth of Lombardy. It was based therefore on the continued existence and prosperity of the cities. This much had even been clear to Rahewin (*Gesta*, IV, viii) who wrote that the money due to Frederick as a result of the new Italian policy amounted to as much as 30,000 talents. As against this, both Nitzsch and Lamprecht believed that it was Frederick's plan to reduce Lombardy to the rural conditions of Germany. Nitzsch saw Frederick as a naïve economist who could not conceive the idea that one simply let one's subjects make money any way they liked and then taxed them. (Nitzsch, pp. 273–5 and 282.) Nitzsch thought that Frederick wanted to extend to Lombardy the administrative system suitable to his estates in rural Swabia. The truth of the matter is that, whatever ruralization took place in Lombardy, it was the last resort of the policy of repression into which Frederick was forced after the schism, when the alignment with Alexander had pushed the cities to extremes of resistance.

[2] For lists of *ministeriales* employed in Italy *cp.* K. Bosl, *Reichsministerialität der Salier und Staufer*, Stuttgart, 1950, p. 618; and P. Darmstädter, *Das Reichsgut in der Lombardei und Piemont, 568–1250*, Strassburg, 1896, pp. 56 ff.

[3] FRRGI, II, par. 297. In 1167 the Bishops Herman of Verden and Daniel of Prague were vicars-general. These bishops were a very different stamp of men from the country squires. They had much closer personal connections with Frederick, were of less servile status, had a more cosmopolitan outlook and were, all in all, less subject to temptation.

[4] It seems that Markward died young; *see* F. Güterbock, *Markward von Grumbach, Vater und Sohn*, MIOG, 48, 1934, p. 39.

severe. He immediately tried to extract as much money as possible. He set up a commission of five Lombards to compile a sort of 'doomsday' book so that he could demand further contributions in kind and eventually he even forced people to carry beams, boards and stones from the ruins of Milan to Pavia for the erection of new houses there.[1] Another source described these *podestà* as *procuratores* who demanded more than seven times as much as was rightfully due to the emperor. They fleeced the rich as well as the poor, the powerful as well as the oppressed. In Milan, they left no more than one third of the produce of the soil. In Crema, even less. They imposed a special tax on hearths and demanded dues from every mill and took one third of the catch of every fisherman and would not allow anyone to catch game or bird.[2] But the tyranny of these German squires concerned not only material goods. According to perfectly credible reports they also raped the wives and daughters of the Lombards.[3]

When confronted with such reports, Frederick was dismayed. Whatever he might have feared of the behaviour of these men, the reality far exceeded his expectations. But there was nothing he could do.[4] Just as he had misgivings about the uneasy situation he had been forced to leave behind in Germany, without being able at this juncture to interfere, so he was now compelled to tolerate or even condone the behaviour of his officials in Lombardy – a behaviour which completely undermined the last chances of success which the Great Design might have had in 1166.

He did make some tentative efforts to cope with the most extreme cases of extortion. In Piacenza for instance the first *podestà*,

[1] F. Güterbock, *op. cit.*, p. 39. According to Morena, a strong supporter of Frederick, Markward was tall and well built, with long black hair, a brave knight and, though full of ambition, generous and open.

[2] Thus the anonymous continuator of the Morena chronicle, MGH, SS, XVIII, p. 643. Similar evidence in *Annales Mediolanenses*, MGH, SS, XVIII, p. 376. *Cp.* also the source material in FRRGI, II, pp. 107 ff. F. Güterbock, *Alla vigilia della Lega Lombarda*, ASI, 95, 1937, has published long lists of depositions made by the citizens of Piacenza about the tyranny and the extortions of imperial *podestà* in 1162–3. These depositions are valuable confirmations of the more emotional accounts by the above chroniclers.

[3] Boso, quoted by F. Heer, *Aufgang Europas*, Wien-Zürich, 1949, p. 626.

[4] This is stated expressly by the anonymous continuator of the Morena chronicle, MGH, SS, XVIII, p. 645. As a supporter of Frederick he could have no reason for describing Frederick's predicament if it had not loomed large.

one Aginulf von Urslingen, had been replaced quite early because he had shown himself too lenient. He had been succeeded by the notorious Arnold von Dorstadt, known in Italy as Arnoldus Barbavaria. Arnold was assisted by a number of officials, German as well as native, who proceeded with brutality and ruthlessness to extort both money and goods, to levy unreasonable fines for minor offences and were not above taking bribes for letting people off. Arnold ruled in Piacenza for a good two years.[1] There was forced labour, blackmail of merchants, confiscation and sequestration.[2] It so happened, however, that in spite of these occurrences, there still was an imperial party in the city. And in the autumn of 1164, Frederick or whoever was then acting on his behalf in Lombardy,[3] recalled Arnold and established a different regime in Piacenza. The leaders of the imperial party were helped into power as consuls, even though in all other cities by this time consuls were strictly barred.[4] Thus we see that wherever possible, more sensible and practical counsels prevailed. But it was not everywhere that a strong imperial party which could be trusted to

[1] Not seven years, as most of the chroniclers say. *Cp.* F. Güterbock, *Alla vigilia della lega Lombarda*, ASI, 95, 1937, pp. 197–8.

[2] We have the names of the complainants who made their depositions under oath. They were small merchants and peasants, and the complaints were about Arnold's officials as often as about him. *See* F. Güterbock, *op. cit.*, pp. 197–8.

[3] In 1166–7, e.g. Bishop Herman of Verden and Bishop Daniel of Prague were imperial vicars in Italy. *See* p. 274, note 3, and Giesebrecht, V, p. 534.

[4] F. Güterbock, *Piacenzas Beziehungen zu Friedrich Barbarossa*, QuF, 24, 1897, p. 87, says that Gisebrecht, V, p. 412, is wrong in thinking that Arnold was forced to flee and was reinstated by force. Giesbrecht's version throws a false light on Frederick's policy. The truth seems to be that by the spring of 1164, when the extortions of the imperial vicars had caused feeling to run very high in Lombardy (F. Güterbock, *Alla vigilia lega Lombarda*, ASI, 95, 1937, p. 208), Frederick took some steps towards conciliation. As a result of this policy, Arnold was recalled and left Piacenza, and his regime was succeeded by milder measures. *Cp.* F. Güterbock, *op. cit.*, p. 210. His successor was assisted by *consules iustitie*, and it is probable that the long depositions about extortions and injustices suffered under Arnold (*cp.* p. 275, note 2) were made in front of him. Arnold left Piacenza in the autumn of 1164, and in the following year one of the new Piacentine consuls was none other than the Ugo Sperone who had been a prominent supporter of Frederick in the late 50s; *see* F. Güterbock, *Piacenzas Stellung zu Friedrich Barbarossa*, QuF, 24, 1897, pp. 72 and 89. Sperone's ascendancy, however, was of short duration. In 1167 he had to flee from Piacenza because of his imperial sympathies, F. Güterbock, *op. cit.*, p. 283. In 1171 he had made his peace with his fellow-citizens and was once more elected consul. His career shows the instability of political opinion in Piacenza. Frederick, whenever he could, was only too ready to avail himself of his supporters. But the latter's hold on power was always precarious.

take charge was at hand.[1] Even so there are clear signs that Frederick was not content with the rule of his commissioners and to those cities which displayed the slightest inclination to remain co-operative he showed immediate generosity and made large concessions in the matter of self-government to the point of even renouncing the *regalia*.[2]

Thus Frederick passed the end of the year 1166 amid complaints and worries not quite knowing what he ought to do. He could not possibly have listened with any great sympathy to the complaints without overhauling the whole of his system of *podestà* and administrators in Lombardy. He had not been able to think of such a reform because he had been anxious to continue to Rome. Nevertheless he tarried. He spent Christmas near Bagnolo; in January he was in Parma; on 1 February, in Reggio. The winter was exceptionally hard and Frederick still kept wondering what he ought to do. For by now the citizens of Cremona had begun negotiations with the Milanese and there were rumours of conspiracy. Cremona, of course, had been the oldest enemy of Milan and had therefore found Frederick's great favour. But now, after half a decade of imperial administration, the Cremonese obviously could bear it no longer. Having been a favoured city, they had obtained encouragement and privileges from Frederick. As recently as the court of Würzburg in 1165, Frederick had remitted a large sum to a Cremonese embassy which had appeared there. But it is not in the least surprising that the Lombard conspiracy should have taken its origin in Cremona. Cremona was, in fact, the least suppressed of the cities, and had been a voluntary

[1] F. Güterbock, *Alla vigilia della lega Lombarda*, ASI, 95, 1937, p. 215, attributes the milder Piacenza policy directly to the availability of an imperial party in Piacenza. Where there was no such party, a conciliatory and mild regime was bound to be interpreted as an admission of defeat.

[2] Frederick often made generous concessions to cities which had remained on his side. He allowed a generous measure of self-government and even would renounce the *regalia*. There exist privileges in this sense for Pisa, MGH, Const. I, No. 205; Genoa, *ibid.*, No. 211; Cremona, *ibid.*, No. 212; Lucca, *ibid.*, No. 214; Pavia, AIS, 112; Mantua and Ferrara, Giesebrecht, V, pp. 403–4; Como, Giesebrecht, V, p. 414. *Cp.* also H. Appelt, *Friedrich Barbarossa und die italienischen Kommunen*, MIOG, LXXII, 1964, p. 319, for this policy in Cremona and Pavia. These examples are further proof that the regime of the imperial commissioners had not been intended as part of the original plan.

party to the Great Design. As a result, the citizens of Cremona had never suffered destruction or casualties and had therefore never been intimidated. In such a city it was very likely that criticism of the imperial administration in Lombardy should be entertained more openly and more vociferously than anywhere else. And when Frederick's army prepared to march south towards Rome, Cremona found the right opportunity. The presence of the imperial army provided a visible threat and a reminder of the terrible days of the years 1159–62. But it had been no more, for Frederick was all bent upon catching Alexander in Rome. And as the army had prepared its departure, the psychological moment had come. The army's presence had combined the maximum provocation with the minimum fear. In the circumstances, Frederick ought to have remained in the north.[1] If he had tarried a bit longer, it is quite possible that the incipient conspiracy might have died down for fear of his presence. But Rainald was already well on his way to Rome. Together with Christian of Mainz he had arrived on 8 March in Pisa. By the end of May he had conquered Civitavecchia and thus the road to Rome lay open. Under these circumstances Frederick had not been able to remain, and early in May, he advanced towards Ancona. He had taken no further precautions to encourage that city to remain loyal. One might almost think that in the spring of 1167 it was Rainald who was hurrying to Rome to force the emperor's hand. For while Frederick was still wondering what to do about the Lombard cities, Rainald was busying himself with the Pisans, whose naval support was necessary for a successful encirclement of Rome.

However this may be, the fact is that at the very time at which Rainald was trying to secure Pisan support for the expedition against Rome, the representatives of Cremona, Mantua, Bergamo and Brescia met and founded an alliance. The terms of the treaty itself are not known; but the formulae of the oaths that were taken in Bergamo in pursuance of that alliance are. The allied cities promised not to harm one another; to stop other people's armies from marching through their territory; to keep the alliance

[1] Giesebrecht, V, p. 533; for a discussion of the exact dates *see* Giesebrecht, VI, p. 462.

for fifty years; to come to each other's assistance if attacked; to give each other diplomatic support at the papal *curia* as well as at the imperial court. These promises, it was expressly stated, were not supposed to interfere with the cities' fealty to the emperor; but, and this was also stated, the emperor was not to be accorded rights other than those exercised by his predecessors during the hundred years preceding the reign of Conrad. According to the Roncaglia decrees such alliances were illegal and therefore the cities had decided to keep the conspiracy secret until a future date.

But secrecy was difficult to keep. When Henry von Dietz, one of the imperial commissioners, heard of the treaty he immediately demanded hostages[1] from the Milanese and a heavy fine lest they join the alliance. Nothing was more likely to encourage them, for the new extortions proved to them, if further proof was needed, how intolerable the present situation was. By the end of March the Milanese approached the allies, Cremona and Bergamo, who, having in the past suffered from Milan's 'imperialism', had to be assured by very special promises that in future Milan would respect their freedom and their territory. And thus Milan was admitted to the league. Thereupon Henry von Dietz, suspecting that these cities were negotiating with the Veronese, had demanded further hostages from Milan. And in imperial Pavia, it seems, a campaign against Milan was being prepared.

The news of such a plan precipitated action. Some time in April the members of the league decided to rebuild the fortifications of Milan by joint effort. And with this decision they went beyond the original challenge to Frederick. Amidst general rejoicing the rebuilding of the city was begun towards the end of April, and the few imperial vicars and commissioners who were present had not the military power to interfere. No effective rebuilding could take place in Milan, however, unless Lodi ceased to be an imperial stronghold. And thus the new Lombard allies sent embassy after embassy to Lodi to persuade them to join

[1] The large degree of unification achieved by the Lombard cities tended to make most of Frederick's methods useless. It had been Frederick's policy to demand hostages from one city and to place them into the keeping of another, rival, city. But when the rivalries between the cities began to lose their importance, this security system was bound to break down. For the hostages system, *see* F. Güterbock, *op. cit.*, pp. 212–13.

the league. Like Cremona, Lodi had been one of the chief recipients of imperial favours; but where Frederick merely used Cremona, he had made Lodi his very special residence and capital and his support there was strong enough for the Lodesans to reject the suggestion. Only a siege of the city by the Lombard allies in the second half of May persuaded the Lodesans to yield. The agreement was most amicable and in order to allay all Lodesan fears, the allies made the most lavish promises guaranteeing Lodi's independence. They even added that if Milan should ever attack her again, the others would come to Lodi's rescue. In return, Lodi swore to observe all the initial conditions of the league. The army which had been assembled to force Lodi into the alliance, then turned its attention against Trezzo which, ever since its first capture by Frederick,[1] had been one of the greatest imperial military strongholds in Lombardy. By August its small garrison was obliged to surrender and by the time this military triumph was assured, both Piacenza and Parma had been persuaded to join the league. Frederick never set much store by the loyalty of Piacenza. But he had counted on Parma, so much so that he kept the Bolognese hostages in that city. In fact, some Parmese knights did resist the league and surrendered only after severe losses. But by September Parma had restored the hostages of Bologna and joined the league.

After the catastrophe in Rome Frederick, with a small retinue, managed to regain Lombardy and on 21 September in Pavia he formally put the members of the alliance to the ban of the empire, although he excepted both Lodi and Cremona. The former had clearly been forced into the alliance against its will. No such excuse, however, could be made for Cremona, the heart and soul of the whole movement. But even at this desperate moment, Frederick did not lose his head: he must have reasoned that he needed some allies and that his only chance of success lay in the possibility of reawakening the old rivalries between the towns. And therefore he decided to forgive Cremona. But without an army from Germany no military success was possible – and such an army was not forthcoming in 1167: most of his closest sup-

[1] *See* p. 160 above.

porters in Germany had died in Rome. As if to test the grand mutual promises the members of the alliance had made to each other, Frederick tentatively moved against Milan, only to find that the promises were solid ones. For all the other cities, like one man, came to the rescue of Milan. Frederick, therefore, desisted from a direct attack and tried the same manœuvre against Piacenza, only to find that there too the mutual promises were effective. To his great consternation he found a complete change had taken place in the political situation of Lombardy. On all earlier occasions he had been able to count on the rivalry of the cities and had always been assured of the support of all those which Milan had antagonized. As a result of this situation he had needed only moderate military support from Germany. But now the cities of Lombardy, for the first time in their history, were completely united in their resistance to Frederick.[1]

Whatever the precise nature of the obligations to the Lombard cities which Alexander III had inherited from Hadrian,[2] the pope was now determined not only to fulfil them but to use his influence and leadership in order to fan the flames of the Lombard movement. Several cardinals were immediately despatched to Lombardy as papal legates, and successfully assumed the direction of affairs. By the end of the sixties they presided at the assemblies of the league.[3] Alexander himself realized that the decisive battle against Frederick was about to begin and that his own fortunes would depend completely on the outcome of the battle. Hence he did not scruple to identify the cause of the Lombards with his own.

[1] The sources do not betray the slightest sign of national consciousness among the Lombards. The cities objected to Frederick because he destroyed their ancient liberties, i.e. the liberties they had been taking since the beginning of the twelfth century. The fact that Frederick was 'German' was incidental. They would have opposed any local lord with the same determination. *Cp.* FRRGI, II, p. 268.

[2] *See* p. 201 above for the conspiracy between Hadrian and the Lombards in 1158.

[3] *Cp.* G. Dunken, *Die politische Wirksamkeit der päpstlichen Legaten in der Zeit des Kampfes zwischen Kaisertum und Papsttum in Oberitalien unter Friedrich I*, EHS, 209, Berlin, 1931, p. 94; Haller, p. 230. During the schism the papal legates assumed a role of unprecedented importance in Lombardy. There they appeared in a region in which practically all bishops were either persecuted or were lacking, in the few isolated cases where a bishop supported Frederick, popular support. This situation created a unique opportunity for them. The fact that hardly any Lombard bishop was on Frederick's side also indicates the absence of class struggle in the cities at that time, and shows how politically homogeneous Lombard society was. *Cp.* p. 150 above.

In 1167 he issued a Bull in which he declared that the purpose of the league was to defend the peace and liberty of the church of God as well as the peace and liberty of the Lombards. But the Bull was not confined to such a general declaration. It also contained a threat of excommunication and interdict in case any Lombard dared to form an association other than the league. Any city which left the league was to cease being a diocesan see, ecclesiastical censures were to be used against people who disobeyed the rectors of the league and people responsible for discord in the league were to be excommunicated.[1]

Alexander, indeed, showed himself a politician of extraordinary dexterity. He was a man of considerable personal courage as was proved by his return to Rome in spite of the most hazardous circumstances[2] and by his flight from Rome in 1167.[3] He was also a dogged and tenacious diplomat, as his dealings with the king of France[4] had shown. And now, as the rebellion in Lombardy was flaring up, with the good politician's quick grasp of the whole situation and its implications, he decided he would be justified in using every resource of his papal spiritual authority to encourage the Lombards and assist their fight.[5]

All his life he had been engaged in the tenacious defence of his position, and it did not now occur to him that there might be anything incongruous in his use of spiritual weapons for purely political purposes. In this he went far beyond anything Gregory VII had ever done. There is some doubt as to whether he actually did renew at that time his excommunication of Frederick, which absolved all Lombards from any oath of allegiance to the emperor they had ever taken.[6] But there is no doubt that he supported the general principles of disobedience by very practical and detailed legal measures. He suggested, for instance, to the

[1] M. Pacaut, *Alexandre III*, Paris, 1956, p. 201

[2] *Cp.* p. 247 above. [3] *Cp.* p. 252 above. [4] *Cp.* p. 231 above.

[5] *See Codice diplomatico Laudense*, II, 60; JW 11747; AIS II, 600.

[6] John of Salisbury, especially No. 218, PL, 199, col. 24 , even maintained that at that time Alexander once more excommunicated Frederick. H. Reuter, *Geschichte Alexanders III und der Kirche seiner Zeit*, 2nd ed., 1860–4, Vol. II, p. 242–3, and H. Prutz, *Friedrich I*, 1870, Vol. II, p. 52, and Watterich, p. 558, have accepted this but disagree as to the date. Giesebrecht, V, p. 566 and VI, p. 473, is convinced that there is no truth in John's report which was merely designed to frighten certain people in England.

archbishop of Milan that only the mildest of penances be imposed upon a certain nobleman who had been guilty of atrocities in fighting for his freedom in pursuance to his devotion to the church, lest others be discouraged from rendering similar services to the church.[1]

Unlike Frederick, Alexander was not a statesman. He had no new conceptions and no grand plans. He was simply determined to defend his position and to cross Frederick's plans. Therefore, his policies had a more circumscribed aim and his ambitions were clearly definable. All he had to do was to use every means at his disposal to defend himself. Since his aims were limited to the defence of his position, he considered them automatically justified by his office, which he took for granted was rightly his. And therefore he never felt called upon to issue a theoretical defence or to justify on general principles the papal stand against the empire. But in terms of purely political achievements, his contribution to the cause of papal power was very considerable; and measured in terms of purely political success rather than political theory, probably more considerable than that of either Gregory IV or Innocent III.[2]

The Lombards' resistance was also immensely stiffened by the arrival in Milan of Archbishop Galdinus, Alexander's special

[1] The penance was to be mild 'ut alii et ipse idem pro austeritate poenitentiae a servitio ecclesiae nullatenus retardentur'. *See* P. Kehr, *Italia Pontificia*, VIa, 63, note 187; also JL, 126288; and *cp.* W. Holtzmann, *Die Register Papst Alexanders III in den Händen der Kanonisten*, QuF, 30, 1940, p. 57. Lest this throws an unfair light upon Alexander, one ought to consider how humanely he was accustomed to use canon law in order to avoid senseless and socially undesirable punishments, also in non-political respects. E.g., when a woman had killed her illegitimate son, the count of Flanders exiled her for seven years. She offered to the pope the penance of a pilgrimage to Jerusalem. Alexander rejected this offer because her presence in Jerusalem could serve no useful purpose. She was to enter a convent or marry. Or: a woman had strangled one of her children and therefore the *dominus terrae* has exiled her. But in view of the fact that she had other children who needed her attention, the pope decreed that she was to be sentenced to another form of penance. *See* Holtzmann, *op. cit.*, pp. 29 and 44.

[2] *Cp.* p. 220 above. Haller, pp. 164–5, reacting against Boso's propaganda that Alexander fought entirely for the Gregorian ideals, sees him as a colourless man without initiative. F. Heer, *Aufgang Europas*, Wien-Zürich, 1949, Ch. VIII, sees him as the representative of the new Italian bourgeoisie. I disagree with all these judgements. He was a resourceful and tenacious politician, with essentially curialist objectives. The Gregorian ideals and the alliance with the Italian bourgeoisie were practical instruments in the validity of which he did not believe any the less because they were instruments.

legate. Galdinus was formerly the chancellor to Otbert, the archbishop of Milan. In 1162 he had gone into exile with his archbishop and both had joined Alexander in France. Otbert died in March 1166 and Galdinus, already a cardinal, was immediately chosen as his successor by Alexander. No sooner had Galdinus heard of the rebuilding of Milan than he set out, with Alexander's blessing, as legate for the whole of Lombardy, to join his city. The journey was hazardous, for Galdinus had to take care not to fall into the hands of imperial soldiers. Disguised as a pilgrim he managed to reach Venice by ship. And from Venice he gained Milan.[1]

On his arrival he set to work at once to deprive schismatic clerics and monks of their positions and influence and restore them to the obedience to Alexander. But most important of all, he began to work for a firm alliance between the original Lombard allies and the other cities and made it clear that any league against the empire could count on firm support from Pope Alexander.

With such encouragement it had been possible on 1 December to conclude a general alliance which was expressly directed against Frederick. The original league was joined by a large number of other cities as well as by the Veronese League as a whole, and by the city of Venice. All in all, there were now sixteen member cities. The basis of the alliance was that they would all resist any demand from Frederick over and beyond the imperial rights exercised between the reigns of Henry IV and Conrad III. That is to say, they were determined to reject all outright innovations made by Frederick as well as his attempts to foist innovations on them in the shape of allegedly old laws. Furthermore, they promised each other help and undertook to abandon all rivalries. The league as such was to be directed by a committee of rectors, who were to be elected by the consuls of the member cities. It was their duty to make provisions for the defence of the member cities and to look after the legal claims of the members against those who were not members and to use all material gains for the benefit of the league. They had the right to impose special contributions upon the various members, the consuls in every city were obliged

[1] *See* p. 253 above.

to carry out the rectors' instructions, and no city was allowed to conclude a truce or a peace without the consent of the rectors.

Under these conditions it is no surprise to find that even those cities who had not joined on 1 December were severely intimidated. From December onwards the league was a much more powerful force in Lombardy than the emperor. Eventually both Opizo Malaspina whose lands were situated on the Apennine slopes and the archbishop of Novara were inveigled to join, and by the end of 1167 not even those sympathetic to Frederick dared to support him openly. As a result Frederick was confined behind the walls of Pavia and found that there was not a single route by which he could safely escape from Italy. John of Salisbury triumphantly wrote: 'He has lost Italy which he did not deserve to keep.' And Godfrey of Viterbo commented laconically: 'The power of the fisc collapsed.'[1]

This then was the general situation which Frederick, at the time of his flight from Susa and after the death of Rainald, was left to contemplate.

After eleven years of strenuous commitment to the Great Design the strongest of doubts were raised in his mind. In the absence of a completely new policy, these doubts began to influence his policies in regard to the old plan. He began to waver and to hesitate. During the years which followed his flight from Italy, he acted ambiguously, now throwing his whole weight behind a definite measure to pursue the Great Design and enforce the Würzburg oath; now steering in the opposite direction, seeking a compromise with Alexander and uneasily watching the growing tension in Germany. The clear political line which he had followed from 1156 to 1167 disappears.

The years of indecision however were not the result of his losing his grip, but of his underlying feeling that if his second plan would not work, he ought to try a third one. In this sense they are a further tribute to his statesmanship. For the indecision was directly caused by his belief that his ultimate aims transcended politics

[1] John of Salisbury: 'Ei fata concesserant Italiam perdere, quam demeruerat divitus retinere.' Especially No. 244, PL, 199, p. 283. Godfrey of Viterbo: 'Fisci pompa ruit', *Gesta Frid.*, v, 834.

anyway and therefore that he ought to desist from pursuing a plan, no matter how grand, when it was obviously proving unworkable. There was too much opposition in Lombardy and for one reason or another the Lombard question had become too inextricably linked with the schism. In Germany, too, the Great Design was revealing an inherent contradiction. If the Lombard part of the Great Design had been capable of speedy realization, these German contradictions need not have mattered. For there was no reason why Frederick should not then have literally confined himself to his new, central European kingdom and left the German princes to fight out their own problems. But as it was, the Lombard question was unresolved; he needed military support from the German princes and therefore could not afford to ignore the growing tension in Germany. No matter where he began to probe, he discovered that all his problems were interconnected.[1]

During the years which followed Frederick pursued a number of inconsistent policies. To begin with, he approached the whole Saxon question in an equivocal way. Outwardly, he took the line that the enemies of Henry had been guilty of a breach of the peace. But instead of proceeding against them, he insisted on no more than a compromise between Henry and his enemies. Even such obvious 'rebels' against Henry as the bishops of Bremen and Lübeck were to be allowed to return to their sees, albeit with the admonition to obey Duke Henry in the future. Henry was probably grateful for the respite; but also puzzled by Frederick's failure to be less than decisive in his support. In 1156 and 1158 this support had been much more outspoken and unequivocal. At any rate, even Frederick's efforts to arrange a compromise were of no avail. By the middle of 1170 Wichmann and Henry were again at each other's throats. Although Frederick continued his efforts, he also began to show a more active interest in territorial acquisitions in the Saxon region[2] and continued to

[1] At this stage, Frederick invites comparison with Napoleon. When, after the Russian disaster, Metternich reminded Napoleon that further resistance in pursuit of his plans would be useless and merely cost thousands of lives, Napoleon lost his temper, kicked his tri-cornered hat which was lying on the floor and stormed: 'What do such lives matter to a man like me!' The comparison is entirely in Frederick's favour.

[2] Th. Mayer, *Kaisertum und Herzogsgewalt im Zeitalter Friedrichs I*, Leipzig, 1944, p. 388.

antagonize Henry further by acquisitions in Bavaria and Swabia which threatened Henry's own properties there. Henry probably did not attribute any deep significance to developments in Bavaria and Swabia. But he must have been concerned at Frederick's interest in the north.

Even before this, in 1169, when Frederick helped to patch up a peace between Henry the Lion and his opponents, he had seen to it that Goslar was taken from Henry and in all probability kept it in his own hands – an open sign of his renewed territorial interests. Henry must have been resentful; and he was certainly puzzled.[1] Even more irritating was Frederick's behaviour in 1172. At the beginning of that year, Henry had undertaken a pilgrimage to the Holy Land. At the time of his departure, he had no living heirs to his lands and titles, only a wife who was pregnant. While Henry was in the Holy Land, Frederick began negotiations with the guardians of several of Henry's Saxon castles and urged them to agree to hand them over in the event of Henry's death in the Holy Land.[2] There was always a chance that Henry might not return from such an arduous pilgrimage and Frederick reasoned that this was a good opportunity of strengthening his own position in Saxony and of weakening that of his cousin. Such policies were,

[1] *Cp.* K. Jordan, *Goslar und das Reich im 12. Jahrhundert*, NJL, 35, 1963, p. 72.

[2] Our knowledge of this incident is derived solely from a notice in the *Cosmidromius* by Gobelinus Persona, written in the fifteenth century. It is most probable that Gobelinus Persona, owes this information to a twelfth century source, since lost. The most likely such source is the continuation of the Paderborn Annals, written down during the years 1182–92. For the date of composition, *see* Scheffer-Boichorst, *Annales Patherbrunnenses*, 1870, pp. 90–1, especially note 3. Scheffer-Boichorst, *op. cit.*, p. 172, note 3, did not believe that Gobelinus Persona drew upon the Paderborn Annals for this piece of information. But both K. Hampe, (*Heinrichs des Löwen Sturtz in poliitsch-historischer Beurteilung*, HZ, 109, 1912, p. 57) and J. Haller (*Der Sturtz Heinrichs des Löwen*, AU, 3, 1911), believe that he did. Nevertheless, Hampe, reacting against the somewhat exaggerated importance attached by Haller to the incident in question, felt obliged to deny that there was any truth in the report. I follow Haller in believing that the report was true, but do not share his view that the incident was the cause of the discord between Frederick and Henry. Moreover, H. Niese, *Der Sturtz Heinrichs des Löwen*, HZ, 112, 1914, p. 555, pointed out very plausibly that at that time Frederick was showing considerable interest in various northern estates. In late 1171 he asked the Askanier to hand over the Plötzkau inheritance. He was very concerned lest the Askanier, in the event of Henry dying without heir, should lay a claim to Saxony. His attempt to secure these castles was probably also meant to forestall any Askanier ambition in that direction. There is no real reason for doubting the genuineness of the information; and Hampe's suspicions are entirely prompted by Haller's far-fetched interpretation of the castle incident as the cause of the quarrel between Henry and Frederick.

of course, in flagrant contradiction to the tacit agreements between the two men. As it was, Frederick's attempts bore no fruit. Henry returned alive and healthy from his pilgrimage, and his wife gave birth to an heir. Henry, on his return, if not earlier, also learnt of other examples of Frederick's renewed activities in the north. In 1173 one of his worst enemies was installed as bishop of Brandenburg and in the same year Frederick demanded the inheritance of Count Bernard von Anhalt, a son of Albrecht the Bear.[1] Such a demand, of course, not only irritated Henry, but also offended Albrecht the Bear, who had his own reasons for welcoming the fact that Frederick was beginning to go back on his understanding with Henry but did not wish Frederick's territorial ambitions to be unfavourable to his family. Frederick's aims were getting very tangled. And as if in order to make the prevailing confusion complete, he solemnly announced in the same year that he was preparing yet another expedition to Italy in order to vindicate his rights and fight for the Great Design.

It was, however, not only in questions of territory that Frederick's policies were beginning to be ambiguous. His attitude to the schism and the policy decided upon at Würzburg in 1165 began to show a similar lack of direction.

The whole schism had, of course, right from the beginning posed a great problem for him. According to the conception of the Great Design he ought to have left the German bishops more or less in peace, especially in those areas situated outside the lands of the three rivers. And indeed, during the early years of the schism, he had treated any opposition from bishops as an unpleasant disturbance; but he never bothered to take any active measures against them. Thus, for instance, he had not objected to the election of Udalrich of Aquileia in 1161, although it was well known that Udalrich was friendly to Alexander. In Germany, the question was also complicated by the fact that the bishops were divided into three, not two groups. There were first the supporters of Alexander; second, the supporters of Victor; and third, a group who were genuinely undecided.[2] Since the purely

[1] *Chron. reg. Col., ad annum* 1173.
[2] *Cp.* P. Classen, *Gerhoch von Reichersberg*, Wiesbaden, 1960, p. 203.

political aspects of the schism were felt less acutely than in Italy, there was in fact a considerable body of honest opinion on both sides. Gerhoh of Reichersberg thought that both Alexander and Victor had been guilty of simony and that therefore it was not clear who ought to be pope.[1] Elizabeth of Schönau had proclaimed that God had revealed to her that Victor was pleasing to Him.[2] Her brother Ekbert had had no great sympathy for Alexander and believed that the whole schism was a deserved punishment for the sins of the church.[3] Hildegard of Bingen had cautiously refrained from committing herself and had advised people to obey their superiors.[4] A man like Bishop Eberhard of Bamberg was in favour of Alexander in principle but thought he had done wrong in absolving men from their oath of fealty.[5] The Premonstratensians had sided with Victor,[6] and the Cistercians with Alexander.[7] Given these various views, and given the fact that most of them were quite honestly held, it would have been very difficult for Frederick to institute determined measures of persecution without appearing a tyrant. In Italy, of course, for obvious reasons of political expediency, Frederick and Rainald showed no such consideration. And there are indeed reports of cruel and brutal acts to stop the schism and of oppression of the followers of Alexander.[8]

[1] Gerhoh of Reichersberg doubted the validity of *both* elections and believed that there was no telling who was the rightful pope. *De Investigatione Antichristi*, I, 53, p. 359. At least on one issue he was on Frederick's side. He held that only a general synod could decide the dispute (*op. cit.*, I, 56, p. 365) and rejected the argument that a pope cannot be judged. For the dispute was precisely as to who was pope. (*op. cit.*, I, 56, p. 367.) And therefore Gerhoh supported the view that in this case such a synod was to be summoned by a lay ruler. (*op. cit.*, I, 56, p. 366.)

[2] Roth, *Die Visionen der heiligen Elisabeth*, p. 140.

[3] *ibid.*, p. 315.

[4] PL, 197, p. 316, letter 95.

[5] Rahewin, *Gesta*, IV, lxxxi.

[6] Hauck, p. 258, note 3.

[7] The decision in favour of Alexander III was taken at a chapter general in 1161.

[8] It is very difficult to form a coherent picture of how persistent and systematic persecution in Italy was. There is plenty of evidence of isolated instances over the years. Already before the synod of Pavia's decision was known, Otto von Wittelsbach had used pressure and violence. His men caught a messenger from the archbishop of Milan to Alexander, seized the letters he was carrying and had him blinded. (These might have been the letters through which Frederick obtained vital information about the alliance between Milan and the papacy, *cp.* p. 218, note 1). Another clerk was also arrested, but we know nothing of what was done to him. For these cases see the letter by Eberhard of Salzburg to Bishop Roman of Gurk, in Gretser, p. 576, note 38; and M. Hausiz, *Germania Sacra*, Augsburg, 1729, II, p. 258. – Then we have the report

In Germany, the Würzburg oath of 1165 altered all this; or, to be more exact, ought to have altered all this. The Würzburg regulations for failure to take the oath were quite unequivocal.[1] Not so Frederick's efforts to implement them. In some instances there was active persecution of the supporters of Alexander. Abbot Erlebold of Stablo, for example, was officially charged with the execution of the Würzburg decisions in the diocese of Cambrai.[2] But there is no evidence of any systematic enforcement in other regions. The only group who were made to feel Frederick's wrath systematically were the Cistercians. But even here it is difficult to gauge exactly the extent of brutality. According to one Cistercian abbot, cruel persecution set in soon after 1161, when the Cistercians had opted in their chapter general for Alexander,[3] and Helmold reports that those monks who failed

---

about Abbot Sampson who travelled to Alexander in the early 60s. He was very conscious of the danger, because at the time when he passed through Italy, all clerks bearing letters to and from Alexander were being arrested. Some were imprisoned, others hanged, some had their noses and lips cut off. Sampson got through because he said he was a mere Scot (sic!) on a pilgrimage. But on the return journey he was searched. He succeeded in disguising a letter from Alexander he was carrying, but the searchers took his money. The report is in Jocelyn of Brakelond, (*Chronica*, Engl. tr., London, 1844, p. 14). – A more systematic enforcement of the provisions against the supporters of Alexander cannot, however, have been possible before the arrival of Frederick's army in 1166. Then there was interference even in Pisa where, so far, Archbishop Villanus, a staunch Alexandrian, had been tolerated. Villanus had personally assisted Alexander in the flight to France in 1162 and had remained a voluntary exile from Pisa while Rainald and Paschal had resided there. In March 1167, however, Rainald forced the Pisans to depose Villanus and to elect a more suitable successor who recognized Paschal. At the same time, Christian of Mainz was active in Genoa. At that time, also, Christian, Guido of Ravenna and Eberhard of Ratisbon and several others were consecrated in Imola (*cp.* Vincent of Prague, MGH, SS, XVII, p. 683). In the same February, Erlebold of Stablo and Bishop Alexander of Lüttich were active in Faenza to secure the oath for the recognition of Paschal and exiled those who refused the oath. It appears that the citizens of Faenza were antagonistic to the oath because at the same time Frederick's officials were making extortions in the region for the support of the army on its way to Rome, and large sums of money were being levied from Imola, Forli and Forlimpopoli. *Cp.* F. Güterbock, *Zum Schisma unter Alexander III*, Kehr Festschrift, München 1926, pp. 382–4. – For the early 70s we know of the activities of Conrad von Lützelhard, Frederick's commissioner in Ancona, who imprisoned several English and French clerks who had travelled to Rome when the news of the impending peace had reached them. *See* Giesebrecht, V, p. 651 and Bouquet, XVI, pp. 696 ff. – Gervasius of Canterbury painted a very lurid picture of Frederick's cruelties: MGH, SS, XXVII, p. 304.

[1] *See* p. 240 above. [2] MGH, Const. I, Nos. 223 ff.

[3] W. Ohnsorge, *Eine Ebracher Briefsammlung des 12. Jahrhunderts*, QuF, XX, pp. 8–9. M. Dietrich, *Die Zisterzienser und ihre Stellung zum mittelalterlichen Reichsgedanken*,

to declare for Victor were to be expelled from Germany.[1] But there must be considerable doubt as to the actual number expelled, and the severity of these persecutions seems to have varied a great deal.[2] Even Boso admits that it had been Rainald, rather than Frederick, who had wanted to pursue a relentlessly vindictive policy against Alexander's supporters in Germany before 1165.[3]

Mindful of the fact that the Würzburg decision contravened the tacit understanding that he was not to exercise direct power in Germany, Frederick proceeded with restraint. The archbishop of Mainz, who had openly defied the Würzburg decision and gone to join Alexander, was, of course, deprived of his see. For the rest, Frederick saw that no more than politic pressure was used to

---

Salzburg, 1934, pp. 33–4, is more cautious and gives a list of odd Cistercians who stood up for Alexander. According to Dietrich, the Cistercians as a body were too shrewd to jeopardize their possessions by open partisanship.

[1] I, 91. 'How many fathers, how many bands of monks, therefore left their monasteries and fled to France is hard to say.'

[2] M. Preiss, *Die politische Tätigkeit und Stellung der Zisterzienser im Schisma 1159–1177*, 1934, is of the opinion that there was not very much systematic persecution of Cistercians. *Cp.* HB, p. 177, note 3. If Frederick displayed special ferocity against the Cistercians, there was some special reason for it. As part of his policy to restore imperial influence over the bishops and abbots – an essential element in his first plan; and a tangential consideration in the Great Design – Frederick was particularly alive to his chances among such new orders as the Cistercians. He took full advantage of the fact that the Cistercian abbeys were exempt and were directly under papal control. And since the emperor was the *Vogt* of the Roman church, it followed that the emperor could claim the *Vogtei* of those abbeys which were under papal supervision. He exploited this notion especially during the first decade of his reign and in doing so he went well beyond any rights which Conrad III had asserted over the Cistercians. In this he was most successful in the regions where the influence of his family was greatest, i.e. in Swabia and eastern Franconia. Elsewhere other 'territorial' princes were not too anxious to allow the emperor the exclusive *Vogtei* over Cistercian abbeys. *Cp.* H. Hirsch, *Die Klosterimmunität seit dem Investiturstreit*, Weimar, 1913, pp. 110–18. Hirsch was criticized by H. Zeiss, *Zur Frage der Kaiserlichen Zisterzienservogtei*, HJ, 46, 1926, because at least one of the charters on which Hirsch bases his theories is not genuine. Hirsch, *Studien über Vogteiurkunden*, 3, Folge, IV, p. 31, admits that Zeiss's doubt about this charter is justified but maintains that there remain enough other charters to justify his view. If Hirsch is right, we can understand how hard a blow it was to Frederick when the Cistercians in 1161 opted as a body for Alexander. None of the other orders had ever been looked upon by him as a special support for the monarchy. Hence the special ferocity of Frederick's reprisals, such as they were. But, on the whole, there is no clear evidence of systematic ferocity. M. Dietrich, *op. cit.*, pp. 35–6, gives examples of imperial charters and diplomas for Cistercian houses in 1164 and even after 1165.

[3] Boso, p. 402. According to the *Chron. Montis Sereni*, MGH, SS, XXIII, p. 151, all those who tried to travel to Alexander were to lose their goods and their lives. There is no evidence at all that this Draconian measure was ever enforced.

ensure the succession of bishops who opposed Alexander whenever sees fell vacant. Thus, for instance, it was not until 1171 that the Alexandrian Dietrich III was succeeded in Metz by an imperialist who supported the imperial pope. This policy was moderately successful. Eventually the sees of Augsburg, Münster, Worms, Lüttich and Bremen were all occupied by enemies of Alexander. And in those sees, it would appear, the lower clergy were threatened with exile if they persisted in their recognition of Alexander.[1] But it was only in 1169 that Frederick finally insisted that the bishops, Albert of Freising and Hartwig of Ratisbon, who had hesitated to be consecrated after their election by a schismatic bishop, should be consecrated by Christian of Mainz. And similarly, in Passau, it was only in 1169 that Albo, a supporter of Alexander, was deposed. Albo had had a bad reputation and could not even enlist the support of other Alexandrian bishops.[2] He was succeeded in the see of Passau, at Frederick's request, by Henry von Berg. Henry was a son of Count Dietbold von Berg and of Gisela, a sister of Count Berthold von Andechs. Frederick was related to both the Berg and the Andechs families; and when Henry resigned his see the following year, Frederick had it conferred on Henry's brother Dietbold. He was determined to keep it in the family, even though Dietbold proved a supporter of Alexander and even though his election (for the sake of which he was first ordained) had the full approval of Alexander.[3] Dynastic and territorial considerations were not allowed to be over-ridden by the schism.

The thorniest question, however, was posed by the metropolitan see of Salzburg. Archbishop Eberhard who had been not only a keen supporter of Alexander but who had been since February 1163 Alexander's special legate for combating the schism in Germany,[4] died on 22 June 1164. The chapter of Salzburg immediately chose Bishop Conrad of Passau a brother of Henry Jasomirgott of Austria and an uncle of Frederick, to succeed him. Conrad was a staunch Alexandrian, but the chapter hoped that so close a relative of the emperor would prove acceptable

[1] *Caesar. Heisterbach Dial.*, II, 18, p. 87.
[2] Giesebrecht, V, pp. 637–8.
[3] *Chronicon Magni Reichersperg.*, MGH, SS, XVII, p. 497.
[4] JL, 10824.

in spite of his ecclesiastical convictions. Conrad, moreover, had quarrelled incessantly with his brother Henry as long as he was in Passau. It was hoped that his promotion to Salzburg would satisfy him sufficiently to make a full reconciliation with his brother possible. On a lesser scale, Henry Jasomirgott's ambitions were creating problems similar to those created by Henry the Lion's ambitions in the north.

But the archiepiscopal see of Salzburg was important enough for Frederick to make at least a formal remonstrance. When Conrad refused to recognize Pope Paschal, Frederick refused to invest him. But this made little difference to Conrad. Alexander sent the *pallium* and in spite of minor disturbances undertaken against various archiepiscopal properties by Frederick's friends who sought thus to enrich themselves,[1] Conrad remained archbishop until his death in 1168.

This time the chapter again elected a supporter of Alexander. Their choice fell on Adalbert, son of the king of Bohemia, who was a close friend of Frederick. Adalbert was also a nephew of Henry Jasomirgott. The choice shows that in this case, too, there was considerable determination to keep the see in the family, even though Adalbert at the time of his election was no more than a deacon. But he was a real enthusiast and supported Alexander from genuine conviction. At first, Frederick made a determined show of resistance. He undertook a military action in order to force Adalbert to surrender at least the *regalia*. Adalbert was no warrior and agreed, but refused to surrender the archiepiscopal title and not even Frederick pressed the matter sufficiently for

[1] There is some doubt as to the precise legal steps taken by Frederick and Paschal against Conrad; but for practical purposes, Frederick issued a more or less open invitation to a horde of enemies of the Salzburg see to go and enrich themselves. The letter is in Sudendorf, I, pp. 79 f., No. 34, These people began to devastate the properties of the see. The Reichersberg Annals describe these raids but also add that the archbishop's *ministeriales* resisted 'these acts of violence by evil men with courage and manliness'. (MGH, SS, XVII, p. 473). The Reichersberg Annals say that these attacks were 'alleged' to have been undertaken by the order of the emperor. For the list of the persons responsible for the attacks *see* P. Classen, *Gerhoch von Reichersberg*, Wiesbaden, 1960, p. 284 and for the damage they seem to have done, *see* R. Jordan, *Die Stellung des deutschen Episkopats in Kampf um die Universalmacht unter Friedrich I*, Würzburg, 1939, pp. 129–30. In spite of these attacks it seems that before Conrad's death relations became more amicable, *Ann. Reichersp.*, MGH, SS, XVII, ad 1168.

Adalbert to be formally deposed.[1] Adalbert merely became a fugitive and during the following years Frederick was so aware of the adherence of the clergy of Salzburg to Adalbert, and of Adalbert's family connections, that he entertained endless proposals to be reconciled with him. Adalbert's manœuvres exasperated Frederick in the extreme. As a result of Frederick's restraint and refusal to force a decision, the matter remained open and was still undecided at the time of Frederick's departure for Italy in 1174. Whatever personal reasons Frederick had for wishing to avoid or at least to postpone an irrevocable and intransigent decision about the see of Salzburg, the whole problem brought home to him how inextricably the tacit parts of the Great Design were wound up with the schism. Adalbert could not be proceeded against without causing serious offence to the king of Bohemia and to Henry Jasomirgott, whose independence the Great Design was supposed to respect. Bishop Eberhard of Bamberg, who had withdrawn from the royal entourage at the time of Rainald's complete ascendancy,[2] had been called back by Frederick in the late 60s.[3] He certainly advised moderation and compromise not only in regard to Alexander but also in regard to the supporters of Alexander in Germany.[4] And similarly, Wichmann of Magdeburg, who was to render Frederick invaluable diplomatic services in the 70s,[5] used his influence to protect Adalbert.[6]

Contradictorily, as Frederick in 1169 stepped up his persecution, such as it was, of the supporters of Alexander in the German church, in that same year he made a major overture to Alexander. If observers had been puzzled by the lack of firmness and by the moderation which Frederick had displayed in spite of the Würzburg decisions and was continuing to display in regard to Salzburg

[1] *See* p. 238 above.

[2] Otto von Wittelsbach tried to win Adalbert over by reminding him that if he refused to abandon Alexander he would never recover the *regalia* and his worldly possessions, even if he managed to remain archbishop. But Otto's well meant advice fell on deaf ears. Cp. *Chron. Magni Reichersp.*, MGH, SS, XVII, p. 490.

[3] *See* p. 295 below,

[4] Giesebrecht, V, p. 631.

[5] *See* p. 295 below.

[6] H. Patze, *Kaiser Friedrich Barbarossa und der Osten*, JGMOD, XI, 1962, p. 63. *See also* R. Jordan, *Die Stellung des deutschen Episkopats im Kampf um die Universalmacht unter Friedrich I*, Würzburg, 1939, p. 135. For Wichmann's letter on behalf of Adalbert *see* Sudendorf, I, p. 74, No. 30.

during the early 70s, they must have been completely bewildered by the discovery that in that very year Frederick tried to reach an understanding with Alexander.

In the autumn of 1168, Frederick sent Henry the Lion, Christian of Mainz and Philip, the new archbishop of Cologne, to France to assist in the peace negotiations between the king of France and the king of England. The negotiations were successful and led in January 1169 to the Peace of Montmirail. In the course of these negotiations, the schism was discussed[1] and these discussions led eventually to the idea that the abbots of Cîteaux and Clairvaux should use their influence to bring about an understanding between Frederick and Alexander.[2] Thus it was agreed, at a court held in Bamberg in March 1169, that the two abbots, together with Eberhard of Bamberg, should journey to Italy and treat with Alexander. A startling move, to say the least. Equally significant at this moment was the re-emergence of Eberhard. But Frederick, who never bore people any grudges, realized that this man who had gradually receded into the background at the time when Frederick and Rainald had thrown their whole weight behind Victor, was the most likely person to gain the confidence of Alexander and bring these negotiations to a happy conclusion.

The two abbots and the bishop set out for Italy. But when they approached Lombardy, Eberhard was compelled to stay behind. The Lombards, highly suspicious of the peace mission, would not allow an imperial counsellor to cross their lands. The two abbots, however, were allowed to proceed. They came from France and as Cistercians were well known as supporters of Alexander.

We have no certain knowledge as to the proposals the two abbots were to make to Alexander. It was rumoured that Frederick wanted Alexander to promote the coronation of his son Henry and that he promised in return that Henry – though not Frederick – would recognize Alexander as the rightful pope. It is very likely that some such proposal was made; for at that time Frederick was anxious to secure the succession of his son. And it can be inferred

[1] *Annales Cameracences*, MGH, SS, XVI, p. 545.

[2] Haller, pp. 226 and 517. John of Salisbury, Giles ed., Vol. II, p. 204. Robertson, VI, 513.

fairly clearly from subsequent proposals that Frederick felt, as far as he personally was concerned, that he could not very well go back on the Würzburg oath; but that as far as others were concerned, he was willing to let them recognize Alexander.

The abbots were received by Alexander and the negotiations dragged on until the middle of the year. There must have been some hope of success, for at the beginning of the following year, Eberhard of Bamberg set out once more. This time he was successful in reaching the pope. But Alexander took good care lest he gave the appearance of negotiating a settlement with Frederick without the Lombards. He understood very clearly that the cause of Lombardy and his own were closely linked and that Frederick ought never to be allowed to drive a wedge between the papacy and the Lombards. Therefore he asked the rectors of the Lombard league to participate in the negotations.

There are two reports of these negotiations.[1] Unfortunately, they do not tally in details. But on the whole it emerges that Eberhard had been authorized to offer two things: first, that the emperor would cease all hostilities against the person of Alexander; and second, that the emperor would recognize all ecclesiastics who had been consecrated by Alexander or his legates or his bishops. Alexander expressed surprise at the ambiguity of these proposals, for if Frederick was willing to recognize Alexander's ordinations as valid, why did he not agree to recognize the author of these ordinations as the rightful pope? Or was the formulation of these proposals meant to be sufficiently equivocal to allow Frederick to recognize Alexander *de facto* without having to say so in so many words, lest he be taken to have broken his Würzburg oath? One could gain the impression that this ambiguity was no insuperable obstacle – for if it had been, Alexander would not have continued the negotiations after the two abbots had made a similarly ambiguous offer. What really made progress in these negotiations impossible was the fact that there was nothing in the proposals that

[1] The negotiations are reported by Boso, pp. 421–2; but Boso assumes that Frederick's overture was a mere manœuvre to gain time and mislead the pope. Whatever Boso's reasons, this belief was not shared by Alexander. *Cp.* his letter of July 19, 1169, from Benevento, PL, 200, pp. 594 ff and JL, 11633. Alexander was confident that Frederick was sincere.

could have led to a peace with the Lombards. Alexander had not only given them every opportunity to express their point of view, but had also made it clear that he considered his case inseparable from that of the Lombards. It was most probably over this aspect of the matter that the negotiations broke down.

In early June 1170, when he was holding a court at Fulda, Frederick learnt of the failure of the peace mission. He thereupon solemnly repeated his intransigent declaration that he would never recognize Alexander. If such a declaration had been forced from him because of the breakdown of the negotiations, his cautious moderation in the Salzburg affair belied his very words.

If Frederick kept two contradictory policies running, this did not mean he was losing his diplomatic skill. In September 1168 his pope, Paschal III, had died in Rome. His position there had been sufficiently strong for a successor to be elected at once. Frederick's party in Rome chose John of Albano who took the name of Calixtus III and whom Frederick recognized after some hesitation.[1] But in the following year, Calixtus III must have got wind of the impending peace negotiations with Alexander and wrote an anxious letter to Frederick,[2] urging him to remove the causes of discord from the church.[3] In order to reassure Calixtus at the very time at which the negotiations with Alexander were being taken up, Frederick wrote back to say that he was planning to end the schism in 1170 through military intervention in Italy.[4] And by March the following year, though the negotiations were still in full swing,[5] Frederick must have convinced Calixtus that he would stand by him, for in early 1170, Calixtus felt sufficiently

[1] The idea of peace had been sparked off by the death of Paschal in the autumn of 1168. Only Boso, p. 420, for obvious reasons, reports that Frederick recognized Calixtus immediately. Calixtus's election was so much the result of the work of a Roman faction, that Frederick thought this was too good an opportunity to miss. Hence his hesitation. *Cp.* W. Holtzmann, *Quellen und Forschungen zur Geschichte Friedrich Barbarossas*, NA, 48, 1930, pp. 404–5. Frederick appears to have told the abbots that if no understanding with Alexander was reached by Pentecost, he would have to recognize Calixtus.

[2] We know of these legates from the *Chron. Magni Reichersp.*, MGH, SS, XVII, p. 489.

[3] The letter is in A. Brackmann, *Dictamina zur Geschichte Friedrich Barbarossas*, SPA, 1927, p. 390.

[4] A. Brackmann, *loc. cit.*

[5] P. Kehr, *Italia Pontificia*, VI, 1, p. 248.

secure as the rightful pope to issue a whole series of charters for German monasteries.[1] Frederick had skilfully kept all doors open and had succeeded in remaining on friendly terms with Alexander's third rival, a man whom he did not even know personally, and in whose personal fortunes he could have had no interest at all.[2]

If Frederick had been able to string along Calixtus, who was completely dependent on him, it proved less easy not to exasperate the German princes. When, after all these tergiversations and conflicting lines of policy it came to the point of the actual preparation of the expedition to Italy which had been announced at a court at Worms in March 1172 and agreed upon in principle by the princes,[3] Frederick discovered to his great consternation that the princes were anything but eager to follow him.

The reluctance of the princes to join Frederick's military expeditions to Italy was nothing new. Strictly speaking, only the bishops, having been invested with their *regalia* by the king, were obliged to render military service.[4] The lay princes had no comparable feudal obligation.[5] But whatever their reluctance on earlier occasions[6] the whole conception of the Great Design had rested on the assumption that eventually Frederick would be able

[1] A. Brackmann, *Germania Pontificia*, II, 1, pp. 182, 185, 203.

[2] Calixtus was so completely at the mercy of the Roman faction who had elected him, that he was not even allowed to surrender the papacy when the schism was well and truly over. *See* p. 202, note 4.

[3] Giesebrecht, V, pp. 707–8, 503–4.

[4] Only the ecclesiastical princes were under an obligation to give military aid to the king for campaigns other than the expedition to Rome to be crowned. A bishop's obligation was more like that of a *ministerialis* than that of a vassal, for he had been entrusted with imperial property. He was supposed to administer it and to provide for the imperial needs from the proceeds. *Cp.* Ficker, *Vom Reichsfürstenstand*, II, 1, 349. In many cases, bishops and abbots had to pawn church property and manors in order to render military aid to Frederick. His campaign constituted a heavy financial burden on the ecclesiastical princes, *ibid.*, 362. In 1167, 1174 and 1176 Frederick's army consisted almost entirely of ecclesiastical princes and their men, *ibid.*, 367.

[5] The lay princes were obliged to render military aid only for a campaign to Rome for the coronation and on such an occasion they could make a money contribution instead only with the king's permission, Ficker, *Vom Reichsfürstenstand*, II, 1, 360. If the emperor had obtained the princes' consent for a campaign, he was entitled to expect their aid. Otherwise, he could only hope to buy their aid, *ibid.*, 316–17, 373–5.

[6] There was not a single occasion on which Frederick had demanded help on which at least some princes had not shown reluctance. For examples see Giesebrecht, V, pp. 134, 136, 157, 165, 290, 381, 404, 584. It must have been not the least of the attractions of the Great Design in 1156 that it had held out, in the not very distant future, a reasonable hope that these demands would be discontinued.

7 Frederick on the Third Crusade and his death in the river Saleph. (Illumination in Petrus de Ebulo, *Liber ad honorem augusti*. Bürgerbibliothek, Bern.)

8 The Imperial Palace at Gelnhausen as it is today.

to stand independently in Lombardy and not continue to make demands for further military aid. By 1172, moreover, even those princes who had for years willingly lent a hand in Italy, must have felt sufficiently uncertain of Frederick's intentions for the future to wonder whether there was any point in giving further military aid. Frederick had shown himself so moderate in the execution of the Würzburg decisions; had come so close to an agreement with Alexander; had shown such renewed interests in territorial questions in the German north, that many princes must have seriously wondered precisely how determined Frederick was to persevere in Lombardy. Therefore, when Frederick set out in the autumn of 1174 he had great difficulty in collecting a large army. Some bishops had to mortgage themselves heavily in order to furnish the required soldiers. Others found excuses and did not come at all. Most lay princes refused altogether and a Bohemian contingent on its way to Italy was decimated by the citizens of Ulm in retaliation for robberies committed by its members. To make up for such deficiencies, Frederick had to rely to a greater extent than ever before upon mercenaries who were not only expensive but also lent an air of ferocity to the whole expedition, an air which was unusual even for the brutal military customs of the twelfth century.[1] All in all, despite Frederick's efforts, the army which he led across the Alps was considerably smaller than the armies of 1158 and 1166.[2]

The plan of the campaign was to attack Lombardy in the western and eastern extremes simultaneously. Frederick was to launch the attack in the west and Christian of Mainz at the other, eastern end. As both men had an army ready, it was calculated that it

[1] Given the social and economic conditions of the age, there were no large numbers of people whom one could hire as soldiers. The mercenaries employed by Frederick were the so-called 'Brabanzonen', bands of men who had been roaming around, unattached and unsettled, a scourge of the countryside, a social phenomenon parallel to the growth of religious sectaries during the second half of the twelfth century. Frederick had first employed them in 1166. Eventually Frederick made an agreement with the king of France not to use them; or, if he did, not to have them march through the kingdom of France. At the Lateran Council of 1179, Alexander III issued a decree forbidding their use. But this decree did not stop the archbishop of Cologne from employing them soon afterwards for the first time in Germany during his campaigns against Henry the Lion. *See* G. Grundmann, *Rotten und Brabanzonen*, DA, 1942.

[2] Giesebrecht, V, p. 727.

would be difficult for the Lombards to defend themselves effectively at points geographically so distant. The towns under immediate attack might not be able to defend themselves alone and the cities in the middle would be hard put to decide towards which end they were to rush their troops, while the remaining cities in the east and west would not be keen to rush soldiers to the opposite end of Lombardy.

Frederick began his campaign in the west by the destruction of Susa, a city which was not even a member of the league but which he wanted to punish for the humiliation it had inflicted on him at the end of 1167. From Susa he directed his steps to Asti – and at his approach the citizens of Asti renounced their allegiance to the league. Thence to Alexandria, a new city on the Po, founded in 1168. Alexandria[1] had grown into a sizable fortress and its citi-

[1] The sources about the foundation of Alexandria are in H. Prutz, *Friedrich I*, 1870, Vol. II, pp. 352–3. According to Boso, and he is the only source for this, the city had been founded on 1 May 1168, 'ad honorem Dei et beati Petri et totius Lombardiae' as a symbol of defiance. Hence Frederick attacked it at once with uncontrolled imperial wrath. But there are several oddities in this story. We know that the formation of the league was a slow process, and it is very unlikely that the league, long before Frederick's appearance in Italy, should have been capable of such concerted action. Hence Boso's story, that everybody rushed to help the common cause by contributing to the foundation of the city, is a little implausible. Moreover, we know that the bishopric of Alexandria was founded only on 30 January 1176 – that is well after the first and second assault on the city (JL, 8423) and eight years after its foundation. If the city had been originally intended as a symbol of resistance, it is more than likely that the Lombards would have prevailed upon Alexander to make it a bishopric from the very start. Finally, Frederick was not the sort of man who would be relentlessly stubborn about Alexandria. And relentlessly stubborn he was. When he was willing to concede everything and make peace with Alexander, the last difficult bone of contention was the survival of Alexandria. If his hatred of the city had been no more than hatred of a symbol, he would certainly have given in on this issue too.

F. Gräf, *Die Gründung Alexandrias*, Berlin, 1887, sought to explain these anomalies in the story. He argued that the city had come into existence simply as a new city, on land which seems to have belonged to the margrave of Montferrat, a close friend of Frederick. It began to prosper at his and at Pavia's expense. When Frederick arrived in Lombardy, Alexandria was prepared to submit to him completely. This is clearly reported by Godfrey of Viterbo, an eye-witness, *De Gestis Friderici*, v. 874. Alexandria thought that a submission to the emperor might secure them a charter or at least a promise of protection against the margrave. Frederick, at first sight, seems to have been favourable to the idea and several sources agree that the attack on the city was begun only after the margrave and Pavia had brought pressure to bear on Frederick. (*Cp.* Romuald of Salerno, MGH, SS, XIX, p. 440; *Chron. reg. Col.*, GDV 69, p. 108. Godfrey of Viterbo, *loc. cit.*) Thereupon Frederick changed his mind and began to lay siege to Alexandria. Against all expectations, the city proved impregnable. And when it turned out that the city was able to resist Frederick, the Lombards began to realize its value to their cause. And it was then, and then only, that the city became the

zens were anxious to submit to Frederick in order to obtain a charter or a privilege which would assure their continued growth. But Frederick was planning to follow his old course of action – and the smallness of his army in 1175 may have made it imperative for him to do so. He wanted to gain the support of at least some Lombards by making his authority available to them to pursue their own ends.[1] And since Alexandria had grown at the expense of the margrave of Montferrat and of the city of Pavia, he gave in to the margrave and the Pavians and instead of coming to terms he undertook to reduce Alexandria to submission. As it turned out, this was a great mistake, for he severely limited his freedom of action in at least one direction. But the fact that he did enter into such an agreement at this stage shows that his indecision was by no means over. He was still bent on pursuing the Great Design and on fighting the Lombards in spite of the fact that in the preceding years he had pursued so many incompatible policies. He was, however, soon to see how much his agreement with the margrave of Montferrat and with Pavia was to stand in the way of his sudden decision to abandon the Great Design and to make peace with the Lombards. For it was his commitment to destroy Alexandria which was to prevent the easy consummation of his decision to change his course.

---

symbol of the Lombards' resistance. If Gräf's explanation is accepted, it looks as if we have here another example of a minor error of judgement on the part of Frederick. Following his earlier strategy, he thought of fighting his campaign in Lombardy in 1175–6 by enlisting the help of Pavia and the margrave of Montferrat. This help had to be paid for by the destruction of Alexandria and in this way Frederick himself first created the cause which the league then espoused as the symbol of their resistance. This story also has the advantage of explaining why Frederick, always subject to the pressure of and dependent on the margrave and on Pavia, had to prove so stubborn about Alexandria. Unfortunately I have not been able to consult the works on Alexandria by G. Jachino, *Le origini di Alessandria nella storia e nelle tradizioni populari*, Torino, 1926, and C. Patrucco, *Perchè e come fu fondata Alessandria*, 1927.

[1] This strategy had led in 1155 to the siege of Tortona undertaken on behalf of Pavia (*cp.* p. 74 above) and in 1159 to the siege of Crema, undertaken on behalf of Cremona. (*Cp.* p. 172 above.) In both these cases, as now in the case of Alexandria, this strategy was fraught with troublesome consequences for Frederick. And yet, it was a strategy which always recommended itself because of the difficulty of getting sufficient military help from Germany. In the last analysis, therefore, it was the reluctance of the German princes to support the Great Design to the hilt, which involved Frederick time and again in difficulties – which, in turn, made the German princes even more reluctant.

Having given way to the pressure of Pavia and the margrave, Frederick laid siege to Alexandria. By the end of October the town was almost enclosed. The siege, however, was as far as Frederick got. The citizens defended themselves all through the winter with stubborn determination. Already by Christmas many members of Frederick's army felt discouraged and there were several serious defections. In the Lenten period there still was no end in sight. Frederick therefore decided upon a desperate and completely unchivalrous measure. During the days when the Truce of God was supposed to be in force, he had tunnels dug under the walls and on the night between Good Friday and Saturday a large number of warriors crawled through them. About two hundred managed to enter the city but while Frederick was waiting for the gates to be flung open to his men from the inside, the citizens rallied and succeeded in demolishing the tunnels, suffocating a large number of Frederick's soldiers. The remainder who had entered the city could not open the gates but fled under heavy losses across the city walls back to their camp. This defeat seems to have decided Frederick to abandon the siege. On the following day, Easter Sunday, he burnt down his camp and all siege apparatus and departed with his army in the direction of Pavia.

The departure was prompted not only by the resistance of Alexandria but also by the fact that the Lombard league had finally succeeded in raising a largish army. The rectors had not got together until February 1175 to decide to meet Frederick in the field with an army. Even then the army had been slow to move and had directed its first attacks upon the fields and territory of imperial Pavia. The devastations reached their height during the Easter days, just at the time when Frederick was trying his last desperate ruse against Alexandria.

Immediately after Easter the Lombard army encamped near Casteggio, opposite Frederick's army which was then in the vicinity of Voghera. Between Casteggio and Voghera there lay plains ideal for battle. Half way between the two armies was the township of Montebello. The Lombards proceeded at once to organize themselves for battle. On 14 April they pushed their *carocci* across the Coppa and the various contingents took up their positions around them. But they waited in vain for the emperor. After a long wait, the soldiers withdrew to their camp, leaving the *carocci* behind under an armed guard. They spent the rest of the day in readiness, but nothing happened. On the following morning, 15 April, Frederick's army finally began to move from its encampment near Voghera. It approached the Lombard positions until within about a quarter of a mile from the *carocci*, halted and then withdrew. By three o'clock that afternoon the Lombards too retired once more. It seems that neither side was anxious to risk their fortunes in an open battle. It is possible that the Lombards were reluctant because Cremona had remained aloof from the enterprise and because they did not feel strong enough. But the manœuvres make it clear that Frederick was even more reluctant.

On the following day both sides faced the implication of their reluctance to fight it out. Negotiations were opened and before the day was over, the Peace of Montebello had been agreed upon and signed.

Frederick had toyed for years with the possibility of scrapping the Great Design. Now that he realized he would have to stake its success upon the fortunes of a battle, the outcome of which was by no means certain, he showed extraordinary strength of mind and clear vision. He refused to drift into a battle in order to make it possible to pursue a policy the advisability of which had been questionable for years. And so he made up his mind to cut his losses and come to terms with the Lombards.

Only a man of superior intelligence and self-assurance could afford to make such a decision. If he had identified himself personally with the success of the Great Design he would now have felt its surrender involved a loss of self-respect. As it was, the Great Design had been an attempt to find a political solution which would make it possible to fulfil the wider and ultimate purposes of empire: the crusade and all it implied in terms of eschatology. He was personally detached from it and could therefore surrender it, when he saw that the cost was getting too high, without loss of face.

It was agreed in the Peace of Montebello[1] that a commission of six men, three from each side, was to draw up the details and the work was to be completed by the middle of May. Pending the details, the emperor was to re-admit the Lombards to his favour and the Lombards were to lay down their arms and beg the emperor formally to forgive their rebellion. It was further agreed that if any questions remained unsettled by the middle of May, the consuls of Cremona were to act as arbitrators and that their decisions were to be binding on both parties.

When the commission of six met, the Lombards made it clear that they expected a complete repeal of the Roncaglia decrees. They demanded that in future Frederick should exercise only those rights exercised by his two immediate predecessors and cease digging up older and obsolete rights. All possessions and privileges which Frederick had taken from the members of the

[1] The negotiations at and after Montebello are reported by Romuald of Salerno, MGH, SS, XIX, p. 440; Boso, p. 429; *Chron. reg. Col.*, GDV, 69, p. 110; *Ann. Magdeburg.*, MGH, SS, XVI, p. 261; *Roberti de Monte Chronica*, MGH, SS, VI, p. 524; *Magistri Tolosani Chronicon Faventinum*, Muratori, ii, 28/1, Bologna, 1938, p. 60; Godfrey of Viterbo, *De Gestis Friderici*, MGH, SS, XXII, p. 328. *Cp.* also MGH, Const. I, No. 242, p. 339. – The reconstruction of the events has been notoriously difficult and controversial. J. Ficker, *Zur Geschichte des Lombardenbundes*, SWA, 60, 1868, was rendered obsolete by Tononi's discovery of a draft for a final peace, *Nuovi documenti intorno alle pratiche di pace tra Frederico Barbarossa e i Lombardi*, ASL, 4, 1877. But his interpretation of this document was challenged by O. Tschirch, *Beiträge zur Geschichte Mailands*, Halle, 1884, Excursus II, as well as by Giesebrecht, VI, p. 522. The most consistent and plausible reconstruction is that by F. Güterbock, *Der Friede von Montebello*, Berlin, 1895. More recently, the discussion has been re-opened by W. Heinemeyer, *Der Friede von Montebello*, DA, XI, 1954. Heinemeyer agrees with Güterbock that the Cremona arbitration was offered *after* the negotiations between Frederick, Alexander and the Lombards had broken down (p. 134), but unlike Güterbock he does not seem to infer from this that the arbitration took place at a time when the basis for the arbitration had been abandoned by both sides. Heinemeyer also agrees that both parties must have believed from the very outset that the negotiations would lead to a positive result (p. 118), i.e. that Frederick was prepared to make peace no matter what the Lombards might demand. But I have decided to follow Güterbock's version rather than Heinemeyer's because Güterbock is less legalistic and has a better appreciation of the political constellation. Heinemeyer, however, has the great merit of having shown beyond reasonable doubt that the break-down of the negotiations between Frederick, Alexander and the Lombards was in the last analysis due to a failure to agree upon the destiny of Alexandria, and that the failure was in the nature of a diplomatic technicality, i.e. the original peace concerned the Lombard league and Frederick kept maintaining that Alexandria could not benefit from this peace because it was not really a member of the league. *See* Heinemeyer, *op. cit.*, pp. 117, 119 and 130. I have tried to incorporate this important point into the sequence of events as adopted by Güterbock. – *Cp.* also P. Munz, *Frederick Barbarossa and Henry the Lion in 1176*, HS, 12, 1965, pp. 15–17.

league were to be restored and the league itself was to remain in existence.

The Lombards would not have put forward such claims at the outset if Frederick had not given them to understand that he was prepared to negotiate on such a basis.[1] If there had been any doubt as to the broad principles of the peace, Frederick would not have dismissed his army. As it was, most of the army departed after the Peace of Montebello. The mercenaries were paid off and even most of the bishops went home. Frederick himself went to Pavia in order to wait for the commission of six to complete their work.

There was one factor, however, which both Frederick and the rectors of the league had left out of account. Alexander's direct and personal influence in the cities of Lombardy had grown to enormous proportions.[2] When it became known that the rectors were willing to make peace with Frederick, the bishops in several cities were able to stir up trouble; for they did not want Pope Alexander, who had faithfully stood by the Lombards, to remain isolated. There were popular commotions and even riots[3] and as a result of these disturbances the rectors were obliged to tell Frederick that they could not proceed with the negotiations unless he also came to an understanding with Alexander.

Formally, this demand was a breach of the original peace terms. It is a measure of Frederick's complete determination that, far from resenting such a breach, he immediately despatched messengers to Alexander in order to satisfy the new demands. Alexander appointed three cardinals to treat with Frederick's men – and thus the negotiations continued beyond the middle of May, by which date the arbitration of the consuls of Cremona was to have been invoked. It turned out that an understanding with

[1] During the negotiations of the final Peace of Venice in 1177 (*cp*. p. 329 below), the Lombard representative from Milan, Girardo Pisto, said as much. He pointed out that the Lombards could have made peace with Frederick on their own terms had they been prepared to abandon Alexander. Girardo Pisto added that it was only fair that Alexander should not now force them to agree to less than they could have had had they agreed to leave him in the lurch. Romuald of Salerno, MGH, SS, XIX, p. 447.

[2] *Cp*. p. 281, note 3.

[3] F. Güterbock, *Der Friede von Montebello*, Berlin, 1895, p. 22.

Alexander could not be reached in a hurry[1] and when the negotiations had not produced a positive result by the autumn of that year, the consuls of Cremona issued their arbitration. But by that time, both parties had abandoned the formal conditions of the Peace of Montebello – the Lombards by insisting that Frederick should make his peace with the pope; and Frederick, by starting to negotiate with the pope. The arbitration of the Cremona consuls issued in September[2] was therefore no longer, formally, an arbitration upon the original points but an attempt to offer a new set of peace terms. And since it so happened that these terms were rather more favourable[3] to Frederick than the rectors had anticipated, they rejected them. On the other hand, Frederick himself had reason to be dissatisfied with the arbitration, for it declared that the league was to be allowed to continue in its obedience to Alexander. This provision, in view of the fact that his own negotiations with Alexander had, by that time, proved inconclusive, was unacceptable to Frederick.

The result was a complete diplomatic deadlock. The rectors had insisted that Alexander be brought in. But Alexander, in order to make quite sure that his and the Lombards' causes remained inextricably linked, had insisted upon the inclusion of the city and fortress of Alexandria – a matter which the original understanding between the rectors and Frederick expressly excluded[4] – in the final peace. And Frederick, having made concession after concession, over and above the terms of the original agreement, felt that the question of the existence of Alexandria was a point beyond which he could not go; especially since from a purely formal point of view, the rectors had originally agreed that it was not to be included automatically among the cities to be restored to the emperor's favour.

Perhaps Frederick was imprudent; perhaps he felt he might as well try to remain stubborn on this one point, as he was willing

[1] F. Güterbock points out how very near a final agreement the negotiators must have been, *op. cit.*, p. 26.

[2] F. Güterbock, *op. cit.*, pp. 30 and 39.

[3] The occasions on which the emperor could demand *fodrum* were increased and the *regalia* which had been left to Frederick were to be retained by him.

[4] MGH, Const. I, p. 341. *Cp.* W. Heinemeyer, *op. cit.*, p. 117.

to concede all others and therefore would have nothing to lose. Whatever the correct explanation, the deadlock could not be solved and in the autumn of 1175 hostilities were resumed. By November Frederick tried to launch another attack on Alexandria and in January 1176 the rectors of the league took a new solemn oath in Piacenza to reaffirm their decision to defend all the member cities. And in order to forestall any opportunity for a further misunderstanding of their intentions the city of Alexandria was now explicitly mentioned as a member city.[1] In the same month, Pope Alexander created a new bishopric for Alexandria and appointed the Roman Subdeacon Adriun as the first bishop.[2] No gesture could be more calculated to broadcast his firm intention to stand by the city.

If it had been difficult for Frederick to raise a large army in 1174, the prospect of finding military support during the winter of 1175–6 seemed completely bleak. For it was now clear that any further fighting in Italy would serve no greater purpose than solving a diplomatic deadlock. Philip, the archbishop of Cologne, proved reliable; and so did Archbishop Wichmann of Magdeburg. Both raised large contingents and crossed the Alps. But for the rest, the German princes and bishops would not come.

Among the many refusals, that of Henry the Lion was singled out by later chroniclers and historians as especially noteworthy.[3] Henry had had personal and first-hand opportunities for discovering how undecided Frederick had been. He had been a member of the embassy which had gone to France to assist in the negotiations between King Louis VII and King Henry II, and there he had heard much about the forthcoming approach that was to be made to Alexander.[4] During the second half of 1170, after the negotiations with Alexander had come to an end, Frederick had sent Christian of Mainz to Constantinople – partly to see whether the Emperor Manuel could be detached from Alexander, partly

[1] C. Vignati, *Storia diplomatica della lega Lombarda*, Milan, 1867, pp. 276–9.

[2] Giesebrecht, VI, p. 525.

[3] It is essential to keep in mind that, without exception, only later chroniclers and historians have attributed special importance to Henry's refusal. At the time, the refusal went unnoticed and was not considered worthy of comment. *Cp.* P. Munz, *Frederick Barbarossa and Henry the Lion*, HS, 12, 1965, pp. 4–10.

[4] *See* p. 295 above.

to try whether the old anti-Greek policy could not be discontinued.[1] In June 1171, a Greek embassy had come to Cologne and returned to Constantinople, accompanied by an official German negotiator.[2] Frederick's attempt to reverse his relations with the Greek emperor looked hopeful. And when Henry the Lion went on his pilgrimage to Jerusalem in 1172, he seems to have participated in the negotiations in Constantinople in a semi-official capacity.[3] Henry arrived in Constantinople at the very moment when a marriage alliance between Byzantium and Sicily was to be concluded. There is almost certain evidence that the Emperor Manuel postponed a final decision in this matter to await the arrival of Henry – for such an alliance would have committed Manuel to a continuation of his old anti-German policy which had begun at the inception of the Great Design in 1156.[4]

When Henry arrived in Constantinople, he at once saw the precarious situation and, not being tied by instructions as was Frederick's official ambassador, sought to persuade Manuel to desist from the intended Sicilian alliance by offering him territorial concessions in southern Italy. Henry's offer was a bit highhanded. But he recognized a dangerous situation and, aware of Frederick's indecision, had seen nothing wrong in saving Manuel's friendship for Frederick by a promise.[5] This, of course, came close to reproducing the alignments which had existed on the basis of the Treaty of Thessalonica and which had been such an essential part of Frederick's first plan in the years 1152–5.[6] Henry simply reasoned that since Frederick was undecided about the future, there was no point in losing Manuel's friendship by continuing to thwart him in Italy. His calculations were not groundless: on his return to Germany, Frederick received him in Augsburg in December 1172 in a most friendly way and was pleased to hear of Manuel's friendship.[7] Henry, however, had underestimated the

[1] Böhmer-Will, *Regesta Archiepiscoporum Maguntinentium*, II, p. 28, No. 72.

[2] W. Ohnsorge, *Die Byzanzpolitik Friedrich Barbarossas und der Landesverrat Heinrichs des Löwen*, DA, 6, 1943, 129. [3] *ibid.*, p. 131. [4] *See* p. 127 above.

[5] W. Ohnsorge, *op. cit.*, pp. 135–6. [6] *See* p. 63 above.

[7] Arnold of Lübeck, MGH, SS, XXI, p. 124, reports that the relations between Henry and Manuel had been friendly and cordial, and Kinnamos wrote that Henry had succeeded in reconciling the two emperors.

degree of Frederick's vacillation and indecision. In March the following year, Christian of Mainz moved against Ancona[1] where a Greek agent had established himself[2] and Henry was to live to see the day when his efforts in Constantinople on behalf of Frederick were to be held against him.[3]

Personally, a continuation of the Great Design would have suited Henry only too well.[4] As long as Frederick encountered difficulties with it, it would have kept him busy in the lands of the three rivers; and if successful, it would have established Frederick in central Europe and ensured Frederick's continued support for Henry's parallel plans in the north.[5] But when Henry heard of the Peace of Montebello and acquainted himself with the lengths to which Frederick was willing to go in order to surrender the Great Design to appease both Alexander and the Lombards, he firmly and abruptly decided that any further support for Frederick would be a waste of time. He had proof of Frederick's renewed

[1] Böhmer-Will, *op. cit.*, II, p. 35, No. 113. A *vaticinium* which belongs to the year 1173, very clearly expressed these anti-Greek feelings, MGH, LdL, III, p. 561, x, especially pp. 564 and 570.

[2] Dölger, No. 1515.

[3] At the time nobody thought that Henry had been guilty of treason. But when he was in disgrace, his Byzantine diplomacy came to be construed against him. *Cp.* C. Erdmann, *Der Prozess Heinrichs des Löwen*, in: Th. Mayer ed., *Kaisertum und Herzogsgewalt im Zeitalter Friedrichs I*, Leipzig, 1944, p. 362. – There is also clear evidence that Frederick wavered in regard to Sicily as much as he wavered in regard to the Greeks. In 1170 Frederick's relations with Sicily were so bad that Eberhard of Bamberg on his peace mission could not enter Sicilian territory and Alexander therefore had to leave Anagni and go to Veroli. But in 1174, Frederick tried to negotiate a marriage alliance with Sicily, Giesebrecht, V, 743.

[4] Henry's relations with Wichmann are a good indication of the uncertainty of the whole political situation and of all these political alignments. During the years of the coalition against Henry, Wichmann was one of his chief enemies. During Henry's pilgrimage, his relations were extremely friendly. *Cp.* W. Biereye, *Die Kämpfe gegen Heinrich den Löwen*, Schäfer Festschrift, 1915, p. 157; W. Hoppe, *Erzbischof Wichmann von Magdeburg*, GSLM, 43–4, 1908–9, pp. 232 ff; J. Hartung, *Die Territorialpolitik der Magdeburger Erzbischöfe*, GSLM, 21, 1886; M. Philippson, *Heinrich der Löwe*, Berlin, 1918, p. 384. The relations must have deteriorated again almost immediately after Henry's return. By 1176, as the Treaty of Anagni was to show (*cp.* p. 313, note 3), Wichmann was again a leading opponent of Henry.

[5] With his usual political perspicacity, Nitzsch, p. 297, said that after 1167 it looked as if Germany was disintegrating into ducal Welf and royal Staufen regions of influence and power. I agree with this view – except that Nitzsch's formulation is too dependent on a national point of view. Nitzsch takes it for granted that 'Germany' is a nature-given unit and hence he spoke of 'disintegration'. It is more realistic to treat Germany merely as a geographical expression and to see that after 1167 it seemed as if Henry was to build a northern 'kingdom' and Frederick a central European one.

territorial interests in the north and when in early 1177 Frederick appealed to him for help, he decided to put the matter to one final, decisive test. He agreed to meet Frederick in Chiavenna[1] and demanded as a condition of his help that Frederick surrender to him the city of Goslar.[2] By this he wanted to test Frederick's intentions for the future.

Frederick naturally refused. Thereupon Henry refused military help against the Lombards, for now he had tangible proof of Frederick's decision to abandon the Great Design and to embark upon a new course in Germany. He was unaware of the nature of the new course and of the fatal results it was to have for him. But he refused because he thought it unreasonable to squander further money and men on a policy which he knew was to be discontinued anyway.

Neither Frederick nor anybody else attributed any great significance to this refusal.[3] For Frederick thought a final settlement with the Lombards and with Alexander was imminent.

Towards the end of May the various contingents, such as they were, began to assemble near Como, from where Frederick was planning to attack Milan. But the Milanese succeeded in assembling a major force which advanced against the imperial host. In the early hours of 29 May the Milanese army stood in the vicinity of Legnano. Their major force was grouped around the

[1] The meeting was considered at the time of so little importance that it was soon forgotten where exactly it had taken place. Some later chroniclers have Chiavenna, others Partenkirchen, and one says near the lake of Como. *Cp.* P. Munz, *Frederick Barbarossa and Henry the Lion in 1167*, HS, 12, 1965, p. 7, note 28.

[2] *See* P. Munz, *op. cit.*, note 49. By 1170 Goslar was in Frederick's hands. *Cp.* K. Jordan, *Goslar und das Reich im 12. Jahrhundert*, NJL, 35, 1963, p. 72. This makes it quite clear that Henry's demand for Goslar in 1176 was made to test how seriously and how far Frederick was willing to pursue his territorial interests in the north. Henry's demand for Goslar as reward for aid was perfectly in order. He was not obliged to give aid and could reasonably expect Frederick to pay for it. Ficker, *Vom Reichsfürstenstand*, II, 1, 371.

[3] P. Munz, *op. cit.*, *passim.* Only later, when chroniclers and historians were at a loss for a direct cause of the fall of Henry the Lion, the refusal was seized as a possible explanation and its importance exaggerated beyond all proportions. In the thirteenth century, at the time of the civil war between the Staufen and the Welfen, the refusal was even considered to have been the first sign of the rivalry of the two families for the crown. And in the nineteenth century, during the great debate between the *Kleindeutschen* and the *Grossdeutschen* the refusal was interpreted as evidence that Henry stood for a *kleindeutsches* ideal and Frederick for a *grossdeutsches* ideal. But all these considerations belong to the history of the history of Frederick and Henry; not to their history.

caroccio; but a contingent of knights had been sent forward in order to explore the situation. Frederick made contact with these knights, and in the fighting which ensued his men gained the upper hand. Thus he was able to lead his army right to the *caroccio* where the main forces of the Lombard league were standing firm. The heaviest fighting began at once; and for hours there was no decision. Eventually the tide of the battle turned in favour of the Lombards – not because they were gaining the upper hand, but because of one of those strange and unaccountable incidents which often upset the precarious psychological balance on a battlefield and cause one of the parties to lose its nerve.

Frederick was in the thick of the fighting from the beginning, clearly recognizable by his splendid armour. Suddenly he received a blow from a lance and was thrown off his horse. At that moment his men thought they were being overcome and began to retreat. Before long the retreat was a disorderly flight and by the time the sun went down it appeared that the Germans had been beaten. Frederick himself was lost sight of. The German encampment fell to the Lombards who looted it completely without further resistance and proudly captured several precious pieces belonging to the emperor's personal effects. Frederick had to remain in hiding for several days and his wife, who had remained behind in Pavia, thought him dead. Eventually he appeared back in Pavia, and discovered that the losses were far smaller than he had anticipated. The disaster resulted from panic rather than from a real military defeat.[1]

In fact, from a purely military point of view, the battle of Legnano had been anything but decisive and Frederick's military situation in Lombardy, in the middle of 1176, was by no means desperate.[2] But he was more determined than ever to bring this whole affair to an end and considered the resumption of hostilities which had found their climax in the battle of Legnano as nothing

[1] Most historians nowadays concede that the battle of Legnano was neither a major military defeat nor a decisive battle. But most of them fail to draw the necessary conclusion. If it was not a decisive defeat for Frederick, he must have had other, independent reasons for immediately taking up peace negotiations. *See* P. Munz, *op. cit.*, pp. 17–19.

[2] *Cp.* F. Güterbock, *Ueber Kaiserurkunden des Jahres 1176*, NA, XXVII, 1902; *Ancora Legnano*, Milan, 1901, p. 19; *Der Friede von Montebello*, Berlin, 1895, p. 86.

but an interlude. He therefore entertained sympathetically a new attempt at arbitration by the consuls of Cremona, even though it now included, explicitly, a demand for the recognition of Alexandria.[1] Frederick faced the necessity of concluding peace with the Lombards and with Alexander simultaneously, and took immediate steps to resume negotiations. Archbishop Wichmann and a great many other bishops urged him to persevere on this course and to settle the matter once and for all. Wichmann was indeed one of the chief promoters of this policy which was to lead, within a short time, to the agreement concluded in Anagni in November 1176.[2]

Wichmann and Conrad of Worms, together with Christian of Mainz and Wortwin, the emperor's protonotary, were sent to Alexander who received them most graciously at Anagni on 21 October. The first official meeting took place the following day in the cathedral. The imperial embassy declared that Frederick had given them full powers to make peace and it was hoped to bring the negotiations which had begun a year earlier to a final conclusion. Alexander replied that nothing would please him more than peace, provided that such a peace eould also be extended to the pope's faithful allies, the Greeks, the king of Sicily and the Lombard cities.[3] The discussions began at once in the

[1] W. Heinemeyer, *op. cit.*, p. 138.

[2] Wichmann was one of the main promoters of an immediate resumption of the peace negotiations. P. Kehr, *Der Vertrag von Anagni*, NA, XIII, 1888, pp. 89–90. *See* also Haller, p. 518. Wichmann was also the chief negotiator of the Anagni agreement, and as a result it contained clauses which were a crushing blow to Henry's territorial ambitions in Saxony. See p. 313, note 3.

[3] Alexander was quite explicit and quite adamant on this extension: 'Qui (nuntii) cum vehementer apud nos institissent ut ad pacem inter ecclesiam et imperatorem complendam intenderemus nec possent obtinere quod sine Lombardis aut sine rege Sicilie vel Constantinopolitano imperatore pacem ad plenum et solidum statueremus.' Pez, 6a, 397, No. 14. There is no evidence that the *nuntii* of Frederick were not prepared to extend the peace to Sicily, the Greeks and the Lombards. Boso, who also mentions these negotiations, makes no mention that the *nuntii* would have preferred a separate peace and were forced by Alexander to give in. I cannot see the strength of Kehr's argument that the above letter proves that Frederick wanted to make a separate peace with Alexander and thus detach him, at this late stage, from his allies. Kehr, *Der Vertrag von Anagni*, NA, XIII, 1888, p. 94, argues that if Boso does not mention the proposal to conclude a separate peace, this proves that the proposal was made so secretly that Boso did not hear of it. The ease with which Frederick's ambassadors fell in with Alexander's wishes is proof again that Frederick was prepared to go to any length.

sacristy of the cathedral. The imperial embassy seems to have preferred private consultations with the pope, because they pointed out that in an open assembly such as had met in the cathedral there were too many people on both sides who were less than anxious to make peace.

And thus the preliminary Peace of Anagni was agreed upon.[1] It consisted first of all of mutual promises to recognize each other's dignities and rights. In this way Frederick undertook to break the Würzburg oaths and put an end to the schism. Secondly, it envisaged a complete understanding which was to be decided upon if necessary by the majority vote of a special arbitration commission. Thirdly, Frederick promised to restore to Alexander all lands and benefices and *regalia*, including the Matildan lands, which he had withheld or seized from him.[2] And finally it was agreed that a number of arrangements were to be made in regard to certain ecclesiastical dignitaries who had either wrongly benefited or wrongly suffered, as the case may be, from the schism. Calixtus III was to be made an abbot of a monastery. The archbishops of Cologne and Mainz were to be recognized by Alexander. Conrad von Wittelsbach, Alexander's faithful ally, was to be compensated by the first vacant see in Germany. Gero of Halberstadt, however, was to be deposed unconditionally,[3] and so forth.

[1] MGH, Const. I, Nos. 249 and 250.

[2] P. Kehr, *op cit.*, p. 97.

[3] The treaty was very much to the detriment of Henry the Lion. (*Cp.* R. Hildebrand, *op. cit.*, p. 255.) Bishop Siegfried of Brandenburg, an old enemy of Henry the Lion, was in Italy after Legnano, and article 15 of the Treaty of Anagni says that his earlier election to the see of Bremen was to be investigated; and if valid, he was to be confirmed as archbishop of Bremen and that everything the see had lost was to be restored to it. Bishop Gero of Halberstadt, an opponent of Alexander, was to be deposed. He was very much a creature of Henry's. He was to be replaced by Ulric. Frederick had no great liking for Ulric. (F. Lucas, *Zwei kritische Untersuchungen zur Geschichte Friedrichs I*, Berlin, 1904, p. 20, note 41.) It is all the more remarkable therefore that he allowed a decision in favour of Ulric. One cannot even believe that Wichmann and Philip of Cologne tried to foist Ulric on Frederick and hoped that Frederick would simply agree to everything they had done in Anagni. For we know that Frederick went over the agreement of Anagni very carefully and, e.g. in regard to Bishop Conrad, he made an alteration. (Lucas, *op. cit.*, p. 19.) Frederick must therefore have known how Wichmann and Philip used their opportunity at Anagni to inflict damage on Henry. Indeed, the deposition of Gero was to be the signal for a renewal of hostilities between Henry and his enemies, hostilities which issued in the major feuds which finally led to Henry's fall. (*Cp.* E. Otto, *Friedrich Barbarossa*, Potsdam, 1943, p. 102.) For Ulric at once dismissed all the clergy appointed by Gero under Henry's patronage and demanded the return of all fiefs of the church which Gero had obsequiously granted to Henry. The

Taken as a whole, the terms of the Peace of Anagni were mainly negative. They incorporated Frederick's intention of abandoning the Great Design and of recognizing Alexander as the rightful pope. But the treaty was not the result of a military defeat. It was the result of Frederick's determination to change his whole course and to end the years of indecision which, ever since the Roman disaster of 1167, had prevented him from working out a constructive political solution. With this negative treaty, Frederick was free to think of a new, his third, political enterprise.

---

next move was even more hostile. On a hill near Halberstadt, the Hoppelberg, Ulric built a fortress as a basis for operations against Henry. It was twice destroyed by Henry and twice rebuilt by Ulric. *See* A. L. Poole, *Henry the Lion*, Oxford, 1912, p. 68. Henry certainly was to live to regret that he had not been in Italy at the time of Legnano. Had he been, he might easily have been able to use his influence too at Anagni. As it was, all negotiations were in the hands of his enemies.

CHAPTER VIII

On the Crest of the Wave . . .

As far as Frederick was concerned, both the agreement of Montebello with the Lombards and the agreement of Anagni with Alexander had been negative. But Frederick was not the man to surrender one major political plan without embarking immediately upon a new experiment. It is impossible to say when precisely he formulated his third plan; but it is clear from his diplomacy in 1177 that he had already decided on yet another political experiment. The agreement of Anagni had been reached in the autumn of 1176. By the time the imperial and Lombard delegates met Pope Alexander in Venice in May 1177 in order to reach a complete settlement, the new plan of action must have been fairly clear in Frederick's mind, for the Venice negotiations show not only that he was determined upon a policy of hard bargaining, but also that he had definite objectives in view. As a result, the final Peace of Venice, which was concluded in July 1177, does not reiterate the negative character of the Montebello and the Anagni agreements, but represents the starting point for the third plan.[1]

[1] Until almost a hundred years ago, historians used to see the Peace of Venice as a simple capitulation. *Cp.* e.g. H. Fechner, *Leben des Erzbischofs Wichmann von Magdeburg*, FDG, 5, 1865. With Kehr's discovery of the draft of the Treaty of Anagni, there came a strong reaction. *Cp.* his *Der Vertrag von Anagni*, NA, 13, 1888. Kehr was able to show that the Venice Peace was much more advantageous to Frederick than the Treaty of Anagni. Eventually historians have ended up by convincing themselves that Frederick gained positive advantages in Venice because he was able to exercise pressure on Alexander. *Cp.* e.g. E. Otto, *Friedrich Barbarossa*, Potsdam, 1943, pp. 96–7. G. Barraclough, *Origins of Modern Germany*, Oxford, 1946, claims that in spite of apparent reverses, Frederick did not lose much in Italy. It is true that Frederick's position in Italy remained strong, but on a completely different basis. Barraclough's argument is like saying that there is not much difference between Britain's position in India before independence and Britain's position after independence. If one subjects the Peace of Venice to a close scrutiny, one will find that it was more favourable to

Frederick's intellectual resourcefulness and political ingenuity were just as remarkable as his physical strength. Now, at the approximate age of fifty, he was ready for the third time in his life to forge a completely new conception of politics and government.

This third plan was based upon the insight that a statesman's greatest chances of success lay in availing himself of existing trends and in twisting them slightly to his own ends. Instead of pursuing an outmoded policy inherited from his predecessor, as he had done in plan one; and instead of trying to mould a new form of central European political organization as he had done in the Great Design, Frederick now decided to ride on the crest of the wave of feudalism – and to turn feudalism, such as it was, into a constitutional principle.

The original social organization of the Germanic tribes had been based, like that of all primitive societies, upon kinship. In the course of time, owing to the migrations,[1] to the corroding influence of Christianity[2] and to the increase in population, the bonds of kinship had weakened, or at least become sufficiently diffuse no longer to serve as the sole effective bond among people whose properties and next of kin were scattered over a geographically very wide area.[3] In order to make up for the decreasing strength of mere kinship bonds, people had begun almost at once to enter into personal relationships with one another – relationships which later historians chose to call feudal. An

---

Frederick than the Treaty of Anagni, not because of any particular provision it contained, but because of its indeterminate character which gave Frederick an opportunity for the future. Frederick's diplomatic victory did therefore not lie in any particular achievement at Venice but in the fact that he was able to persuade Alexander to agree to a mere truce with Sicily and the Lombards and to leave the question of the Matildan lands in abeyance. This was indeed a considerable diplomatic triumph for Frederick – but not of the kind Kehr and other historians since have believed.

[1] *Cp.* P. Munz, *The End of the Ancient World*, HS, XI, 1963, p. 8.

[2] During the twelfth century, the church fought a particularly tenacious battle against Teutonic marriage customs. It campaigned against marriage of people related in the seventh degree. The church was not very successful, and in the early thirteenth century at the fourth Lateran Council, Pope Innocent III had to make concessions to the manner in which Teutons were accustomed to keep their society together and permit marriages beyond the degree of third cousins.

[3] *Cp.* H. Fichtenau, *The Carolingian Empire*, Engl. tr., Oxford, 1957, p. 110.

economically or socially weak man would commend himself to a stronger man. The relationship would be mutually advantageous and provide firm social bonds, sanctioned and reinforced by religious ritual, over small areas. From time to time wise statesmen had tried to use the Christian church and the mystique of kingship to provide either alternative or additional bonds and grounds for obedience, grounds which would command the support of people over larger areas. But given the primitive methods of communication and, outside the church, the absence of even rudimentary education, such large-scale plans had met with very little response, and all the while feudalism spread in proportion to the growing insecurity which resulted from the weakening of the tribal structure based on kinship bonds. By the second half of the twelfth century there were rulers, especially in England and France, who had managed to create a system of feudalism and combine it with the mystique of kingship – for a king could easily be placed at the head of a feudal pyramid, so that allegiance to a king could be given a feudal meaning.

Owing to conquest, the Normans had made enormous progress in that direction both in England and in their Sicilian kingdom in southern Italy. To be a feudal king was never as easy as being an ordinary king, for feudal kings could really only command the allegiance of their immediate vassals, their tenants-in-chief. Their kingship was only a very superior form of feudal lordship, for their vassals were never really quite subjects, but men tied to them through a mutual contract. But in the circumstances, feudal kingship was better than a vague overlordship, based upon a mystique of empire and church, a mystique by which most people remained personally comparatively unaffected. And if feudal kingship could be made hereditary, as in France and England, and based upon the fiction, as in England and in the kingdom of Jerusalem, that by right of conquest all the land was the king's, there might even be a chance of surrounding it with an administrative personnel, the activities of which might eventually tip the precarious balance between tenant-in-chief and king in the latter's favour. During the second half of the twelfth century there was no telling which way this balance might be tipped. The kings of

France had not progressed far in that direction; and England, where Henry II had made great progress, was to suffer a severe setback during the reign of King John.

If it is granted that feudal bonds tended to spring up with particular speed whenever bonds of kinship had become loosened, that is in an age of great social mobility with no economic outlets other than those provided by agriculture,[1] it can be clearly inferred that the Germany of the twelfth century witnessed an extraordinary development of feudalism. From the middle of the ninth century onwards, there had been a group of families, estimated to have been no more than three hundred in number, who had been in possession of all governmental rights in Germany. All countships and dukedoms were the exclusive rights of its members.[2] Their power was autogenous and they owed allegiance to the king only in a formal and somewhat nebulous manner.[3] This group of families consisted of a small number of interrelated clans and such cohesion as there was, was due to the blood-relationships which existed between these clans.[4] But owing to the enormous increase of population during the twelfth century,[5] these bonds of kinship were tending to dissolve. Instead of constant intermarriage between these clans, we begin to find from the second half of the century onwards that many daughters of these dynasts married their father's *ministeriales*, men of servile status who had risen socially and economically and who thus were enabled to share in the inheritance of the older families.[6] This suggests that the estate of the older dynasts was in a state of dissolution. As it enlarged, it became diffuse. Some of its members went down in the social scale, and others up. And as its cohesive force thus disappeared, we may presume feudal bonds to have multiplied in proportion. Feudal relationships seem to have become more universal throughout society, for without them there would have been a drift towards total social fluidity, and thus towards chaos and anarchy.

The view that the old and primitive social structure was dis-

[1] *See* note 3, p. 23.
[2] O. v. Dungern, *Adelsherrschaft im Mittelalter*, Aachen, 1927, p. 4.
[3] Th. Mayer, *Kaisertum und Herzogsgewalt im Zeitalter Friedrichs I*, Leipzig, 1944, p. 412.
[4] O. v. Dungern, *op. cit.*, p. 12.
[5] *See* p. 23 above.
[6] O. v. Dungern, *op. cit.*, p. 56.

appearing[1] gains further support from the fact that new classes began to emerge. The *ministeriales* were really in a state of progressive emancipation. Those *ministeriales* who could afford it became knights.[2] Hence the growth of thousands of knightly manors.[3] These knightly *ministeriales* became capable of making feudal contracts and could enter into real feudal obligations[4] and eventually provided the personnel of a new kind of aristocracy. As they became capable of holding offices, the old distinction between 'free' and 'unfree' broke down. The class of knights, therefore, did not result from a reorganization of an old class of men under the aegis of a new cultural and religious ideal, but really amounted to the formation of a new class of people who had originally belonged to the lower orders. This new class cut across the traditional boundaries. The *ministeriales*, in their process of emancipation, provided the comparative freedom of movement and of personal independence which the ideal of chivalry and knighthood required and which it transformed eventually into a whole ethos. Hence the fusion of knights and *ministeriales*.[5] The class of knights, of course, tended to develop almost immediately their own code of social behaviour and cut themselves off, as an estate of warriors, from those who could not render military service because of their poverty – and thus the peasants ceased to take part in fighting.[6] Through this social mobility and emancipation, knights became so numerous that not all of them ended up with land. They wanted to form a caste whose right to bear arms was protected by special privilege.[7]

The *ministeriales* turned knights were the protagonists of a new

[1] M. Bloch, *Feudal Society*, Engl. tr., London, 1961, p. 426, surprisingly, is far too sweeping when he calls German society archaic.

[2] O. v. Dungern, *op. cit.*, p. 373.

[3] I.e. *Rittergüter*. O. v. Dungern, *op. cit.*, p. 374.

[4] *ibid.*, p. 380.

[5] *ibid.*, p. 364.

[6] P. Schmitthenner, *Das freie Söldnertum im abendländischen Imperium des Mittelalters*, 1934, pp. 9–10; *cp.* also Fehr, *Das Waffenrecht der Bauern im Mittelalter*, ZSSRG, 35. During the second half of the twelfth century the peasants ceased to take part in fighting and were practically excluded from the estate of warriors. This development found its legal conclusion in the law of Frederick, *Constitutio contra Incendiarios*, MGH, Const. I, No. 318, p. 451, c. 20, which actually forbade peasants to wear arms. Frederick's law also sought to make the knights into a closed caste by preventing their ranks being swelled by intrusion from below.

[7] Schmitthenner, *op. cit.*, pp. 9–10.

culture, of courtly literature and of the ideal of chivalry.[1] This culture began to flourish in Germany only during the last decade of Frederick's reign[2] and the fact that it did flourish is additional proof of the social transformation which resulted in a universalization of feudal relationships.

The growth of feudalism and the dissemination of the ideals of chivalry are clearly reflected in this literary revolution. The literature which belonged to the older social order had depicted a life which was coarse, naïve and unsentimental, and had treated of love in the same realistic manner in which it had treated of the *gesta* of the warriors.[3] In the German *Rolandslied* we have an outstanding example of this pre-courtly and pre-chivalrous mentality. Its author attributes gentle and courtly qualities of behaviour and thought only to the infidels – and considers such refinements unbecoming to a Christian. The infidels fight for honour; but the Christians for their salvation and for the kingdom of God.[4] The *Kaiserchronik*, another remarkable example of this

[1] P. Kluckhohn, *Ministerialität und Ritterdichtung*, ZDA, 52, 1910, p. 136. – During the twelfth century the population increase had also led to an increase of wayfaring people, wandering preachers, heretics as well as potential heretics, religious enthusiasts, mercenary soldiers, vagabonds, 'Brabanzonen', etc. They were all people who had come adrift from their families and clans and were now looking around for new niches, new ties and new bonds. And those who could not enter into feudal relationships, kept on drifting. If lucky, they found their way into towns. If their impulses were more on the criminal side, they joined groups like the 'Brabanzonen'.

[2] H. Naumann, *Kurzer Versuch über welfische und staufische Dichtung*, ELJ, 8, 1929, p. 84, argued that the 'Hohenstaufentum' had taken the modern *Minneroman* under its wings. If the *Graf Rudolf* and the first German poem about Flor and Blancheflor originated in the Rhineland during Frederick's reign, this does not prove that Frederick had taken them under his wing. One might as well argue that Shaw's plays ought to be credited to Queen Victoria. The whole concept of 'Hohenstaufentum' is as ridiculous as it is confusing. This is not to deny, of course, that Naumann has spotted correctly that the Rhineland, a sphere of Staufen influence, was much less archaic than lower Saxony, the sphere of Henry the Lion's ascendancy. J. Bumke, *Studien zum Ritterbegriff*, Heidelberg, 1964, p. 13, note 26, rightly criticizes the widespread custom of inferring from the presence, towards the end of the twelfth century, of an ideal of chivalry the existence of a class of chivalrous knights. On pp. 89 and 92 he takes pains to show that the concept of knighthood itself was very slow in coming during the second half of the twelfth century. It can therefore not have had any influence on Frederick during his formative years. In Germany, it was not only late in coming; but also 'mirrored a human ideal, whereas in France it mirrored an aristocratic reality'. A. Borst, *Das Rittertum im Hochmittelalter*, Sae, 10, 1959, p. 228.

[3] *Cp.* the penetrating comments by F. Heer, *Die Tragödie des heiligen Reiches*, Wien-Zürich, 1952, p. 107.

[4] F. Ranke, *Gott, Welt und Humanität in der deutschen Dichtung des Mittelalters*, Basel, 1952, pp. 49–51.

period,[1] is full of simple judgements. Rulers are good or bad according to their attitude to Christianity and the church, and its author was not interested in chivalry and in deeds for the sake of deeds. There is no interest in *minne*, the special courtly brand of love, and in one verse it is even described as a devilish power which ought to be broken by baptism and priestly exorcism.[2] The heroes are unhewn and untutored, displaying tremendous brutality and exhibiting uncontrolled appetites, temper and emotions. If there is a distinction between good and bad, it is based on Christian virtue, but not on a knightly ideal or on courtly education. There are no more than the faintest traces of a courtly form of life with its worship of women, its devotion to romantic passion for an unobtainable woman and its cultivation of refined manners and formal behaviour.[3] In these works, men are governed by the simple ideals of faithfulness to their lord and to God. In his *Chronicle of the Two Cities*, Bishop Otto of Freising provided the following austere list of the signs of progress in the twelfth century: the crusades; the conquest of Jerusalem; the new conception of knighthood according to St Bernard; the spiritual devotion of the new knightly orders; the papal victory embodied in the Concordat of Worms; and the growth of the new monastic orders. Courtly manners and courtly love, the great achievements of the new literature, were not to be found. Otto's list was informed by his serious eschatological preoccupations and ignored the joys of life which the new culture was to embody. The older, clerical Latin poetry which had dominated literature had placed its accent on the brevity of life, the real meaning of which was revealed only by death.

[1] While there is no doubt that the *Kaiserchronik* belongs to the age of pre-courtly literature, E. E. Stengel believes that it was written not earlier than 1161–4; *Die Entstehung der Kaiserchronik und der Aufgang der staufischen Zeit*, DA, 14, 1958. He has weighty reasons, but his opinion is in opposition to that of most historians. It cannot be denied that the *Kaiserchronik* shows traces of *minne*, praising it as a civilizing force and considering at times, women to be the nobler of the two sexes. *Cp.* 4575 ff. There is also praise of temperance in the expression of emotions as especially becoming to Christians. *Cp.* e.g. 2823 ff., 2957 ff. It also debates whether a man ought to value the favour of women more than a fight with a powerful opponent. *See* G. Ehrismann, *Geschichte der deutschen Literatur*, München, 1922, II, i, p. 283.

[2] 13067 f.

[3] G. Ehrismann, *loc. cit.*

The new literature produced a complete reversal of values. It awakened men's sense for the beauties of both body and soul and for the gracefulness of nature as cultivated and formed by man.[1] In the new courtly epic, the infidel knight is as chivalrous as the Christian knight. He is no longer prompted by pride and vanity and his devotion to courtly ideals of life is no longer branded as a devilish inspiration. On the contrary, with the rejection of the old ecclesiastical condemnation of *eros* the new literature adopted a worldly tone. It welcomed love as a central experience; it went to great lengths in order to fan romantic passions through a psychological understanding of the fact that the more unrequited romantic passion is, the more it increases. And, above all, it drew up and agreed upon rules to fit this all-powerful experience into conventional and conveniently measured systems of courtly behaviour. This insistence upon formal and measured standards of comportment was reflected in turn in the evolution of measured and controlled emotions in other spheres of life. And thus the old habit of displaying passions and violent outbursts of emotion came to be displaced by the propagation of the love of restraint and manners.[2] Instead of poets taking cold comfort, as Otto of

[1] The classes who treasured these ideals, took pains to stress their social distance from villains and *Tölpel* who were not only socially inferior but were considered to have been left behind by progress. The villain betrays himself not only by lack of form but also, and mainly, by lack of moral refinement. – During the second half of the twelfth century the traditional theme of Christian writing, *memento mori*, is noticeably replaced by a *memento vivere*. It does not require much psychology to understand that Frederick, in his old age, was not likely to take a great share in this new orientation. – The courtly festival, at which the products of the new literature came to be produced, made literature into a social occasion. It helped to divorce it from the folk-tale and turned it into something for the upper classes, into something self-conscious, into an art.

[2] In 1170–80 Wernher von Elmendorf rendered the *Moralium Dogma Philosophorum* into German. It was a complete system of knightly virtue, and Ehrismann has argued that this work became a veritable textbook, teaching a graduated system of ethical values, i.e. in descending order: religion (wisdom); honour (probity and moral acts), property (material goods) – or, in Christian terms: devotion to God, relative worldly morality, relative earthly pleasures. Thus there emerged something like a philosophical system which helped people to reconcile the obvious conflict between the old value (God, transcendence, *memento mori*) and the new value (*memento vivere*, *minne*, joy). E. R. Curtius criticized Ehrismann for believing in the immediate influence of this systematic way of thought. At best, the obvious conflict between the old and the new was not resolved until well into the thirteenth century. It is indeed a little difficult to believe in the immediate triumph of Ehrismann's 'gradualism'. Curtius believes that the early knightly ethic was quite unsystematic. The early knight was torn between diametrically opposed values, even though from a higher point of view he might have

Freising had done, from the progress of the new monastic orders and the contemplative ideal, they were placing their emphasis upon man's life on earth and thanked God for His Grace which put *minne* for their mistress into their hearts.

Frederick was no more responsible for this literary revolution than he had been for the social transformation upon which it had rested. On the contrary: if the social transformation had indigenous causes, the literary revolution was almost entirely the result of foreign influences.[1] But Frederick had been watching; and he cannot have been unaware of the existence of either, even though the precise nature of their causal relationship may have eluded his grasp. Since he was now entering his sixth decade, it is all the more remarkable that he should have been so aware of what was going on around him as to decide to utilize it for his own ends. There can be little doubt that he personally had no great love for, or sympathy with these developments. If he was able to adjust himself to the social changes, the intellectual and literary revolution must have left him unmoved. Nevertheless he affected an interest, once again demonstrating his adaptability and capacity for change.

His third plan was indeed based on the simple reflection that if feudalism was gaining ground, it ought to be encouraged and eventually turned into a constitutional principle, giving a new foundation for the monarchy. Frederick decided no more and no

---

sensed at times that these values were related to one another. At any rate, the transformation in literature which took place towards the end of Frederick's reign was not likely to allay conflict, but to increase it. Ehrismann's attempt to see it as something leading to an integrated system of ethics is unrealistic and helps to cloud the issue. Frederick's reign did not end in a formation of a harmonious world picture. The transformation it witnessed was a source of new conflict; not a resolution of old conflicts.

[1] With Henry von Veldeke's *Eneasroman* the direct influence of French literature became noticeable. Ehrismann, *op. cit.*, II, ii, pp. 89 f. The Minnesänger Frederick von Hausen was a friend of Christian of Mainz in the early 70s. *See* H. J. Rieckenberg, *Leben und Stand des Minnesängers Friedrich von Hausen*, AKG, 1961, 2, p. 165. But between 1175 and 1186 he is not to be found anywhere, *ibid.*, p. 166. In the late 80s he is back in the imperial circles and at the famous court of Jesus Christ in 1189 he took the cross as a member of Frederick's household, *ibid.*, pp. 167–8. Rieckenberg thinks that Frederick von Hausen spent the years from 1175 to 1186 in Burgundy and acquainted himself there with 'modern' literature which influenced his own writing considerably and decisively, *ibid.*, p. 171. Hence his return to Germany and his role in the formation of the culture of the feudal era.

less than to become a feudal king, stretching the network of feudal allegiances over as wide a field as possible, taking in Germany, Burgundy, Lombardy and a substantial part of central Italy. He wanted to become a monarch to whom a very large number of feudal vassals owed homage, and whose tenants-in-chief were not only the German princes, lay as well as ecclesiastical, but also the towns of Italy and such Italian princes as were left. This was a simple and rough conception of politics for the future. Details were to be worked out as he went along. In fact, many questions seem to have been left completely open. First, what exactly was to be the relation between such a feudal king and the papacy? Second, how could the cities of Lombardy be fitted into a feudal pyramid? Third, how would the German princes respond, especially those who, like Henry the Lion, had built up a quasi-monarchy of their own and whose territorial ambitions had progressed much further than those of Frederick under the Great Design? Fourthly, would it be possible to make such a feudal monarchy hereditary, lest the king, elected by the tenants-in-chief, was a mere puppet in the hands of the feudal magnates? How centralized could such a monarchy become? Finally would it be possible for a large royal domain to be administered by royal officials? Or would it be necessary to grant every piece of land, even the king's land, to an official who would treat it as a feudal tenure and make it hereditary, more or less, in his own family? There can be no doubt that Frederick was sufficiently well acquainted with the centralizing developments of feudalism in France, England and Sicily, to toy with the possibility of such developments for his own domains. But at the time when he was forging his new plans, after the battle of Legnano or perhaps a little earlier, he could not have had any precise idea as to what detailed arrangements he would be able to make – everything had to be worked out piecemeal. His own bargaining power was not great; and he was certainly not in a position to dictate terms.

It was indeed an integral part of this new plan that he should not work out too many details in advance. The plan was built upon the notion that he should swim with the tide; and that meant that he should allow feudalism to continue to develop in all directions, not to prune and train it, but to make use of its own momentum. If he had erred in the Great Design by wishing to coerce too many people, he now decided to follow developments rather than to determine them. And this meant that, to begin with, he had to refrain from making too many detailed plans.

Nevertheless it would be a mistake to imagine that from now on Frederick was a mere bystander, or even that he was not really responsible for forging the outlines of the new plan himself. To begin with, there was an almost complete change of personnel. The agreement of Anagni had been negotiated by Wichmann, Bishop Conrad of Worms, the protonotary Wortwin and Christian of Mainz.[1] But when it came to the final negotiations, which began in Venice in the May of the following year (1177), neither Bishop Conrad nor Wortwin nor Wichmann were among the negotiators. Wichmann had had a personal interest in ending the schism and if necessary in presiding over the surrender of the Great Design. But there is no indication that he continued to assist Frederick in forging more constructive plans for the future. The official imperial delegate in Venice was Christian of Mainz – a valuable warrior[2] but not a man whom we can credit with any great diplomatic astuteness or political inventiveness. And he was eventually joined or perhaps superseded by Frederick's chancellor Godfrey, by Bishop Pontius of Clermont and by Abbot Hugh of Bonnesvaux. The fact that Christian of Mainz continued as negotiator

[1] Giesebrecht, VI, p. 532.

[2] In 1175 and the years immediately after, Christian of Mainz had had considerable military successes in Romagna and had probably complete military control of that region. Neither the Lombards nor Alexander could do much about this. Hence the bargaining strength of Frederick in regard to the Matildan lands. Christian controlled Imola, Rimini, Cesena, Forli and Faenza, and in early 1175 he destroyed S. Cassiano, a Bolognese fortress, in order to please Imola. In that year and the following year Christian even managed to terrorize the region around Bologna, Ravenna and Ferrara. In spite of Christian's successes, however, the bishops of these cities remained firm supporters of Alexander. *Cp.* F. Güterbock, *Zum Schisma unter Alexander III*, in: Kehr zum Geburtstag, München, 1926, pp. 395–6. But Frederick's *de facto* control of this region, W. Lenel, *Der Konstanzer Friede von 1183 und die italienische Politik Friedrichs I*, HZ, 1923, 128, p. 230, was the great vital factor in the Venice negotiations. In Faenza, even the bishop had always been against Alexander so much so that in the spring of 1175 Pope Calixtus was able to take up his residence in that city. Other bishops of this region and some citizens were less consistent in their support of Frederick. *See* F. Güterbock, *op. cit.*, p. 385. In 1177 Ravenna, Rimini, Faenza and Imola appeared as allies of Frederick at the negotiations of Venice, *ibid.*, p. 396.

shows that no palace revolution had taken place in Frederick's council; but the fact that new men had appeared in Venice suggests its own story. The new constructive plan had been put forward by Frederick himself, and he did not wish to continue to use men like Wichmann who had been the instruments of the old one. There can be little doubt that Frederick took a personally active part in the formulation of the new policy.

It seems certain from the course of the negotiations in Venice and from the hard bargaining which took place, that by the spring of 1177 Frederick had a more positive plan in mind than he had had at Montebello and Anagni. Whatever shape in detail the feudal monarchy was to take, Frederick realized that its success would depend very largely upon the actual size of his own holdings, i.e. of something like a royal domain. And he considered therefore that the one point he ought to gain from the impending negotiations for a final peace was the Matildan lands in Italy. They lay to the south of Lombardy. Unlike Lombardy, they contained no flourishing cities of any note and Frederick could expect to administer these lands as a feudal domain.[1]

The Countess Matilda had converted her allodial properties into a papal fief and confirmed the donation in 1102 by charter, while retaining the right of disposal. She had exercised this right in favour of the Emperor Henry V; and after Henry V, Emperor Lothair had paid homage to the pope for these lands and finally succeeded in having his kinsman Henry the Proud, father of Henry the Lion, enfeoffed by Pope Innocent II. King Conrad III had claimed them, but in vain; and from Henry the Proud they had come to Welf VI who did not much care for them. True to his first plan, Frederick confirmed Welf VI in the possession

[1] Considerable confusion reigned about the geographical extension of these lands. Their extents were not clearly known, and it proved impossible to distinguish clearly between allods and fiefs. This fact alone added much to the intractable nature of the problem. J. Haller, *Heinrich VI und die römische Kirche*, MIOG, 1914, XXXV, p. 403, note 1, is confident that the geographical and legal situation was well known in the 80s, for in a monograph written by A. Overman, *Gräfin Mathilde von Tuszien*, 1895, the geographical lay-out and the distinction between allods and fiefs was clearly outlined. Haller's argument is not very convincing. For Overman, writing towards the end of the nineteenth century, was obviously much more learned than Frederick and the pope's negotiators in the 80s.

of these lands in 1152.[1] At the outbreak of the schism in 1159, Welf's son had taken Alexander's side[2] but eventually Frederick managed to win him over, and thus he had joined the campaign of 1167 against Rome, where he, like so many other nobles, died.[3] Thus the road was conveniently open for Frederick to stretch the Great Design to encompass the Matildan lands too, for Welf VI had no other heir, and spent the rest of his days on his Swabian estates, consoling himself with wine, women and hunting. In fact, all through the sixties Frederick had had designs on these possessions[4] and after 1167 he simply increased his activities and sought to acquire them from Welf VI outright. At first, when Welf's son died, Henry the Lion advanced a small sum of money to persuade Welf VI to keep the lands in the family.[5] But Welf was a spendthrift, and when he wanted more money Henry the Lion refused – rightly calculating that he had no interest in acquiring so much property in central Italy.[6] Thereupon Welf VI revoked the arrangement with Henry and made a new one with Frederick who did have reason for acquiring a good title to these lands.[7]

[1] Hadrian's demand for the Matildan lands in 1159 had been preceded by Frederick's efforts to levy dues in the Matildan lands, i.e. to turn his lordship into a reality. But, as Rahewin says, *Gesta*, IV, xiii, Frederick had handed everything he had managed to raise to Welf.

[2] A. Overman, *op. cit.*, p. 65. [3] *ibid.*, p. 66.

[4] Rainald, during his sojourn in central Italy, 1162–4, had done much to strengthen imperial rights in the Matildan lands. *Cp.* A. Overman, *op. cit.*, p. 66. *See* also W. Lenel, *op. cit.*, p. 221. After 1162, Frederick made systematic efforts to undermine Welf's position. *See* J. Ficker, FRRGI, I, par. 137, and II, par. 311.

[5] Th. Mayer, *Kaisertum und Herzogsgewalt im Zeitalter Friedrichs I*, Leipzig, 1944, p. 387.

[6] It is customary to explain Henry's refusal by his proverbial meanness with money. But given Henry's political aspirations, he had other very good reasons for refusing to acquire these lands. At this stage he could not even have wished to burden himself with such responsibilities in Italy for the sole purpose of causing damage to Frederick.

[7] It is significant that the final deal with Welf was made very late, i.e. either shortly before or shortly after the Peace of Venice. J. Ficker, FRRGI, II, par. 310, thinks that Welf surrendered the fief to Frederick in 1169, or a little later. But Adler, *Herzog Welf VI und sein Sohn*, Hannover, 1881, pp. 80, 92, 130, dates the surrender later, in 1175, and says that the final bargain with Frederick was made only in 1179. C. Varrentrapp, *Zur Geschichte der deutschen Kaiserzeit*, HZ, 47, 1882, p. 411, accepts this late date, and so does Hampe, HB, pp. 183, 200. – It is worth mentioning that some historians, anxious to discover a cause for the Chiavenna refusal (p. 310, note 3), have considered whether Henry might not have refused because he had been offended by the way in which Frederick had taken or was trying to take, over Welf's lands.

Frederick decided therefore, when it came to the final negotiations in Venice, to hold out for the Matildan lands. At Anagni he had agreed to restore these lands to the papacy; but now with his new plan in mind he was determined to drive a bargain sufficiently hard for these lands to remain in his hands. His prospects were good – for if he could not hope any longer to maintain himself in Lombardy with military force, his military position in the Matildan lands was strong. Christian of Mainz's army held complete sway there, and there was no one in Italy who could have forced Frederick to surrender his claim by armed intervention.[1] It is more than likely that Frederick appointed Christian his chief negotiator in Venice because Christian had first-hand knowledge of the extent of Frederick's actual power in that area. Christian was a warrior and not a diplomat; and as soon as he had stated, or over-stated, Frederick's initial demands, his task was taken over by others.

Initially Alexander had wanted the peace negotiations to be held in Bologna. But Frederick objected, for Christian had such a bad reputation in that city that he could not have used him as the leader of his delegation. And thus Venice was agreed upon. The Venetians had been strong supporters of the Lombards and of Alexander,[2] but for some time now they had suffered so much from Byzantine opposition that they were forced to draw closer to Frederick and for this reason Venice, in 1177, seemed almost neutral ground.[3]

The congress of Venice was opened in May 1177, and the course of the negotiations[4] shows clearly that Frederick managed to persuade everybody to ignore the most difficult issues. He was willing to come to terms with the Lombards and to make peace with Alexander. But he began by not taking either of these condi-

[1] *See* p. 325, note 2.

[2] *See* p. 225 above. Many of the Lombard bishops had found refuge in Venice, and in 1179 Alexander described it as a *civitas refugii*, JL, 13497.

[3] *Cp.* A. Baer, *Die Beziehungen Venedigs zum Kaiserreich in der staufischen Zeit*, Innsbruck, 1888, pp. 40 ff. In 1172–3 the Venetians had hated the Greek emperor so much that they had even assisted Christian von Mainz's siege of Ancona. *Cp.* C. Cipolla, *Verona nella guerra contro Frederico Barbarossa*, NAV, 10, 2, 1895, p. 422.

[4] The two main sources of the negotiations are Romuald of Salerno and Boso, both eye-witnesses.

tions for granted and thus succeeded in clouding the issue of the Matildan lands sufficiently for this question to be left virtually undecided – a positive gain over the respective clause in the agreement of Anagni.

Christian of Mainz began by formulating the conditions upon which Frederick would make peace with the Lombard league. None of these conditions – Christian put forward three alternatives – were acceptable to the Lombards, because all of them amounted to more than the Montebello agreement had envisaged. The Lombards, naturally enough, were indignant and rejected these conditions and argued that they could not be expected now to grant Frederick more than he had originally demanded merely because they had insisted on Alexander being brought into the negotiations.[1] In other words, they now sheltered behind Alexander and made it clear to Christian that if he persisted with these conditions they could reasonably hope that Alexander would break off all negotiations. Alexander took the hint. He told Christian that there was no point in discussing the legal subtleties upon which Frederick might come to terms with the Lombards, and that Frederick instead ought to make a simple truce with the league and postpone all final settlements to a later date.

This seemed the moment for which Frederick had waited. He now sent new delegates to Venice with a secret proposal. They were to communicate this not to Alexander, but to two cardinals to be nominated by Alexander; and Frederick offered to agree to a truce with the Lombards provided Alexander would agree to the secret proposal if recommended by the cardinals.

The secret proposal concerned the Matildan lands. Frederick suggested that the lands remained his for another fifteen years and at the end of that period the question should be reopened. However, he did not wish the Lombards to know he was willing to make a truce with them provided Alexander made a concession in regard to the Matildan lands. For if his willingness to divert his attention from Lombardy to the Matildan lands became public knowledge, his bargaining position (in case

[1] *See* p. 306 above.

Alexander or the cardinals rejected the proposal) would have been very much weakened.

The cardinals listened to the proposal, advised Alexander to accept it and eventually Alexander insisted, reasonably enough, that he should know what it was before he gave his consent. When this became known, Frederick's chancellor Godfrey, one of the new delegates, feigned anger and departed. But the other two delegates, Bishop Pontius of Clermont and Abbot Hugh of Bonnesvaux, remained behind. They had obviously been told not to break off negotiations if the ruse of secrecy should fail. For the most part, all sides were clear as to the general terms of the peace. Frederick was willing to grant the Lombards everything they wanted, and Alexander had to recognize that the Matildan lands were in Frederick's (or, more precisely, in Christian's) hands and that he could not force Frederick to give them up. And since Frederick was willing to concede everything to the Lombards anyway, Alexander had no bargaining power either.

It remained therefore to arrange a vague understanding to the effect that Frederick was first to conclude a truce with the Lombards and that the Matildan lands were to be left with Frederick pending a future decision. The only real problem was how to bring Alexander and Frederick together to celebrate their peace.

Over this technical question the congress nearly came to grief. When Christian realized Frederick was carrying on private negotiations behind his back with Alexander,[1] he suggested that Frederick move closer to Venice so that he could be kept *au courant* of everything that went on and eventually Alexander agreed that Frederick should take up residence in Chioggia.

This practical move seems to have been misinterpreted by some of Frederick's partisans in Venice. They thought Frederick was preparing to come to Venice to confront Alexander, peace or

[1] Giesebrecht, V, p. 830. Christian was getting a bit impatient. He failed to understand the diplomatic astuteness with which Frederick wanted to make capital out of the fact that he was in *de facto* possession of the Matildan lands. Christian seems only to have seen Frederick's prevarications and appears to have feared that Frederick might go back on the Anagni agreement. Hence, at the last minute, as Giesebrecht plausibly reports, V, p. 834, Christian reminded Frederick that he for one felt obliged to abide by the Anagni agreement.

no peace. Alexander sent an embassy to Chioggia to suggest that Frederick took an oath there and then, to confirm the peace with him, a truce with the Lombards for six years, and one with Sicily for fifteen years. While Frederick was still thinking about this proposal, his partisans in Venice raised a commotion and tried to force the doge to invite Frederick to the city without his having taken the oath.[1] Naturally, the Sicilian and Lombard delegates were alarmed and in great haste prepared their departure lest they should fall into Frederick's hands before he had taken the oath. It required the doge's and Alexander's great *sangfroid* to deal with the crisis and prevent a premature dissolution of the congress just when it was on the point of reaching a satisfactory conclusion. And thus it was possible for a final settlement to be agreed upon. On 21 July 1177 a draft document was signed in Chioggia; it was made public in Venice the following day and sworn to in front of Alexander by Frederick's ambassadors.

Early on Sunday, 24 July Pope Alexander said Mass in St Mark's Cathedral and then sent several cardinals to meet Frederick who had travelled in the doge's galley to the Lido. Frederick declared formally that henceforth he would recognize Alexander as the only rightful pope and the cardinals absolved him and received him into the bosom of the church. And when the princes who were with him had followed his example, the doge arrived in a galley in order to accompany Frederick to Venice.

In front of the central gate of St Mark's Cathedral a throne had been erected upon which Alexander awaited Frederick who arrived towards ten o'clock. When he had disembarked, he was led in a festive procession to the steps of the throne where he took off his purple coat, prostrated himself and kissed Alexander's

[1] There is no doubt that such a commotion took place in Venice. It is, however, not clear who its authors were and what they hoped to gain. The only source is Romuald of Salerno, MGH, SS, p. 449. Giesebrecht thinks, (V, p. 834), that Romuald exaggerated the importance of the incident, and is sceptical about Romuald's belief that the commotion encouraged Frederick to postpone agreement to the final terms. Fechner, *Beiträge zum Friede von Venedig*, Berlin, Diss. 1886, thinks that Romuald exaggerated the importance of the incident in order to show that Alexander was saved from Frederick's treachery only by the presence of the Sicilian fleet. A. Baer, *op. cit.*, took the populist riot very seriously and believed that Frederick had promised to help the democratic party into power in Venice if they made it possible for him to enter Venice before the conclusion of the treaty with Alexander.

feet. Alexander, tears in his eyes, raised him up and gave him the kiss of peace. The crowd intoned a *Te Deum* and the bells were rung. Thus Frederick led Alexander from the throne and into the cathedral, where Alexander, in front of the main altar, gave his blessing to him.

On the following day, the feast of St James, Frederick once more led Alexander into the cathedral to say Mass. After the *credo* Frederick again prostrated himself before the pope. And when Mass was completed, Frederick held Alexander's stirrup and even offered to lead his horse. But Alexander would not allow him to do this and blessed him instead.

On 1 August finally, there took place the festive and formal oath upon the peace. On that day Frederick with many princes went to the patriarch's palace in which the pope was residing and there, in the presence of the Lombard ambassadors and the representatives of the king of Sicily, the ceremony took place. Frederick sat on the pope's right and listened to Alexander's address. After the address, Frederick rose, took off his coat and replied in German that henceforth he would be an obedient son of the church and would grant both the Lombards and the king of Sicily his peace as agreed. Thereupon Count Henry von Dietz, in the name of the emperor, took the oath upon the Gospels, several relics of saints and a splinter of the Holy Cross. The oath was then repeated by the German princes who accompanied Frederick and who then signed and sealed the charter. The Sicilian ambassadors and the Lombard delegates in turn took an oath to observe the truce.

Thus the years of indecision came formally to an end and the Great Design was rendered to oblivion. But the indeterminate character of the peace agreement, and especially the fact that no more was said in article eleven about the Matildan lands in central Italy than that eventually arbitrators were to be appointed to settle the matter[1] was a great triumph for Frederick's new policy and his third plan. He was now free to retain the Matildan lands and had thus gained a flying start for the feudal monarchy: a large

[1] MGH, Const. I, No. 260, p. 363, article 11, says nothing at all about the Matildan lands as such. It merely states that arbitrators are to be appointed to settle outstanding questions between empire and papacy. Nothing could be more indefinite than this article.

addition to those of his possessions which were to fulfil the function of a royal domain.[1]

In the summer of the following year Frederick left Italy to return to Germany. He did not choose a direct route but travelled through Burgundy in order to proclaim there the end of the schism and to secure once more the bonds of loyalty which had been loosened during the last decade. As was to be expected, many nobles in Burgundy had used the schism as a pretext for enriching themselves at the expense of those bishops who were faithful to Alexander; and, in turn, both clergy and those nobles who were jealous of those who enriched themselves, had increasingly turned towards the king of France and implored his protection.[2] Frederick now used this opportunity to establish himself ceremonially in Burgundy as feudal suzerain. He went to Arles and there, reviving a custom which had been in abeyance for several centuries,[3] the archbishop crowned him king of Burgundy.[4] From

[1] It is instructive to glance at the principles underlying Frederick's administration of these regions after the peace of Venice. Frederick respected the few cities. If they were not supposed to enter into leagues with each other, they were allowed self-government which was, however, to be restricted to the city itself and was not to extend far into the *contado*. They also had to keep away from the property of the church and nobles. Any military establishment was kept away from the cities, but the countryside was dominated by a large number of smaller fortified places which dominated the roads, supported by a system of tolls and road-dues. The whole was a model of a feudal domain. *Cp.* W. Lenel, *Der Konstanzer Frieden von 1183 and die italienische Politik Friedrichs I*, HZ, 1923, 128, pp. 238–40. Unfortunately Fedor Schneider's work on this period has never been published.

[2] P. Fournier, *Le royaume d'Arles et de Vienne*, Paris, 1891, pp. 48 ff. After the initial successes of Frederick's policy under the Great Design in Burgundy (*cp.* p. 118 above) the Great Design had had the effect that Frederick had begun to compete with the king of France for the loyalty of many Burgundian nobles. This competition became specially marked from 1161 onwards. *Cp.* R. Folz, *L'empereur Frédéric Ier et le royaume de Bourgogne*, SHDB, 18, 1956, p. 113. From 1166 onwards those nobles who had suffered most from the pressure of the lords whom Frederick had supported had begun to side more and more with Alexander and to invoke the protection of the king of France. Both in 1166 and again in 1171 the king of France had been very tentative in his support. *Cp.* G. Duby, *La société aux XIe et XIIe siècles dans la région Mâconnaise*, Paris, 1953, pp. 540. But by 1180, Philip Augustus had become more bold, *ibid.*, pp. 540–5. By that time the Great Design had been abandoned and there was now much more scope for an outright competition between Frederick and Philip for the feudal allegiance of the Burgundian nobility.

[3] Fournier, *op. cit.*, p. 62.

[4] F. Güterbock, *Zur Geschichte Burgunds im Zeitalter Barbarossas*, ZSG, 17, 1937, pp. 176 ff. Frederick was crowned in Arles on July 30, and Beatrix a little later, in Vienne, so that both the archbishop of Arles and the archbishop of Vienne, who was the archchancellor of the kingdom of Burgundy, could share in the honour.

there he travelled leisurely northwards and spent most of the autumn in the Rhône valley.

It seems that this journey was to inaugurate for Burgundy the era of the new plan. Frederick made the greatest possible use of the Burgundian bishops in order to foster their loyalty to him as their feudal suzerain. He showered them with privileges and charters in order to protect them against the encroachments of the Burgundian nobility.[1] If he alienated thus a large section of the lay magnates, he nevertheless maintained the closest ties with those who were directly related to his wife Beatrix. In fact, Frederick himself, after the autumn of 1178, never returned to Burgundy, but left the direct exercise of suzerainty to Beatrix who went to reside in Burgundy several times, issued charters and privileges there,[2] and died there, in Jouhe near Dôle, in 1184. After her death Frederick had himself crowned king of Burgundy once more in 1186 at Milan,[3] but three years later, when he was preparing his departure for the Holy Land, he caused the whole of Beatrix's heritage to be transferred to their son Otto, who became the count palatine of Burgundy,[4] thus fulfilling a promise,

[1] P. Fournier, *op. cit.*, pp. 68 ff. H. Hirsch, *Urkundenfälschung aus dem Regnum Arelatense*, Wien, 1937, believed that many of these charters were forged in such a way as to give the impression that they were much older and that they dated from the very beginning of his reign. See his conclusions on p. 152. U. Brumm, *Zur Frage der Echtheit der ersten Stauferdiplome für südburgundische Empfänger*, MIOG, 57, 1949, who has re-examined the charters, believes that Hirsch's scepticism was not justified and that they are indeed as old as they proclaim. If Hirsch is right, the present Burgundian policy was new and was merely, for obvious reasons, made to look old. If Ursula Brumm is right, the policy was not new. Present scholarly opinion inclines to agree with U. Brumm and shares the doubts about Hirsch raised earlier by J. de Fontréaulx, *Les Diplômes de Frédéric Ier rélatifs au royaume d'Arles*, AdM, 1939. I cannot quite agree with R. Folz, *L'empereur Frédéric Ier et le royaume de Bourgogne*, SHDB, 18, 1956, p. 116, note 2, that one can ignore the whole question and confine oneself to tracing the stages of the restoration of imperial power in Burgundy. Clearly the date of the charters is relevant to one's conclusions as to these stages.

[2] Giesebrecht, V, p. 897.

[3] P. Fournier, *op. cit.*, p. 75; H. Hirsch, *op. cit.*, p. 153. See p. 368 below.

[4] Jean-Yves Mariotte, *Le Comté de Bourgogne sous les Hohenstaufen*, Paris, 1963, p. 49. The count palatine in Burgundy was a new institution. A count palatine was an imperial tenant-in-chief, he was *reichsunmittelbar* and resembled in almost every respect the new type of duke who emerged after 1180. For the new type of duke see note 1, p. 354 below. – Otto had a bad press because the Marbach Annals mention that he used to murder people, and Wackernagel, *Geschichte des Elsass*, p. 99, has accepted this judgement at its face value. But Th. Mayer, *Die historisch-politischen Kräften im Oberrheingebiet*, ZGO, N.F. LII, 1938, pp. 17–18, points out that if one examines the names of his

which had been more or less explicitly made in various documents, to treat Burgundy as a family heritage.[1] This decision was, for Burgundy, the clearest expression of the new policy of the third plan.

Frederick returned to Germany towards the end of October 1178, and his first concern there was to explore how his new conception of feudal suzerainty could be translated into practice. In general theory, the most obvious approach was to consider the princes, lay as well as ecclesiastical, as tenants-in-chief.[2] But in practice, there were far too many who might claim to be princes. This older class of princes – 'old' to distinguish them from the new imperial princes who were to emerge first as a result of Frederick's pursuit of his third, feudal plan – consisted of men who were princes because they belonged to certain families who had prestige, property and power. They became counts as a result of their position,[3] but these countships were autogenous and had not been formally conferred on them. Their franchises and immunities were theirs in their own right.[4] These princes had formed an aristocracy of birth and they had held their society together because they were a corporate organization of a comparatively small number of interrelated clans. This corporate body had been in a state of progressive dissolution ever since the beginning of the twelfth century; and, as we have seen on several occasions,[5] the whole setting in which Frederick deployed his political experiments had been determined by this dissolution and the need for finding alternative forms of social and political organization.

---

victims, one sees that he did not murder for pleasure or profit, but for political reasons: his victims were all members of the Alsatian and Lotharingian nobility who were reluctant to be subjected to the new territorial state which Otto was trying to establish. Even the Marbach Annals mention that after his death Otto was deeply mourned by his subjects because of the peace he had secured for them. – According to Fournier, *Le Royaume d'Arles*, Paris, 1891, p. 77, note 1, Otto did not really assume power in Burgundy until 1189.

[1] The date on which these promises had first been made is uncertain. Mariotte, *op. cit.*, p. 49, note 19, mentions the first such promise in 1173.

[2] The custom of investing bishops with *regalia* and of bishop's homage was well established in Burgundy, and it may well be that the custom spread to other parts of the empire from Burgundy. *Cp.* H. Hirsch, *op. cit.*, pp. 155–6.

[3] Keutgen, *Der deutsche Staat im Mittelalter*, Jena, 1918.

[4] Th. Mayer, *Kaisertum und Herzogsgewalt im Zeitalter Friedrichs I*, Leipzig, 1944, p. 412; O. v. Dungern, *Adelsherrschaft im Mittelalter*, Aachen, 1927, p. 4.

[5] *See* p. 318 above.

The dissolution of the older princely estate had resulted in the evolution of an upper crust of families who now wanted very much to protect themselves against the possibility of the lower princes claiming equal privileges and status. Having risen socially and economically, they were anxious to give political expression to their achievements and wanted to exclude all the other princes from joining their ranks.[1] There existed, therefore, as a natural result of the process of dissolution of the older corporate estate of princes, a widespread desire among the upper strata of the German nobility to find ways and means of turning themselves into an exclusive order. They had tried to achieve this by elaborating a strict feudal order in which ordinary counts were the vassals of dukes, and by securing territorial overlordship in given areas as a result of which they exercised some kind of territorial sovereignty over all people who happened to be living in that area. The development towards a number of territorial sovereignties, which had resulted from these aspirations of the upper section of the older princes, had been countenanced by Frederick because it had suited the Great Design. From the point of view of constitutional theory, this whole development had implied a certain withdrawal of the monarchy from a position of direct overlordship over the ancient tribes and a corresponding limitation of royal suzerainty to those princes who had managed to establish some kind of territorial sovereignty in their own areas of power as well as to those lands which belonged directly to the monarchy and which could be said to form some kind of royal domain.[2] With this process the ordinary counts and dynasts were tending to cease being real princes. They became the feudal vassals of the class of men who alone remained genuine imperial princes and could be considered tenants-in-chief.[3]

[1] H. Mitteis, *Der Staat des hohen Mittelalters*, Weimar, 1948, p. 302.

[2] H. Brunner, *Land und Herrschaft*, 3rd ed., 1943, p. 220.

[3] There was an intimate connection between the new ducal territorial state and feudal law. The new imperial prince became the head of a territory and this development was made possible through feudal law, for he became the king's feudal tenant and was invested with his duchy. At the same time he became the lord of the dynasts in the new duchy who now owed allegiance to the king only through him. Hence feudalism and the territorial duchy developed hand in hand. *Cp.* Kallen, *Das Kölner Erzstift und der 'ducatus Westfalie et Angarie'*, JKGV, 31–2, 1957. – The princes who

It suited Frederick's third plan to continue to countenance this development. For Frederick discovered that the social transformation which was taking place was building itself naturally and spontaneously into a feudal pyramid. It remained for him to swim with the tide and to establish himself at the apex of that pyramid.

The one great obstacle to the transformation of the upper layer of new princes into a class of feudal tenants-in-chief was the 'state' which Henry the Lion had built up in Saxony. His power and influence and pre-eminence had reached such a peak that he stood out from the other princes who could not, although they very much would have liked to, consider themselves his peers.

Territorial state-building, as we have seen, had been very much part and parcel of the Great Design. The lands of the three rivers were to be turned into something like a territorial state by Frederick himself. And the whole conception of the Great Design had therefore strongly countenanced this development. Frederick's own efforts in this direction had suffered a complete check. Those of Henry Jasomirgott and a number of other princes had only been very moderately successful. Those of Pope Hadrian had been completely undone by the turmoils created by the schism. The tendency to regard as irrelevant all considerations other than

---

became the new imperial princes were mostly dukes, albeit not dukes in the ancient tribal sense, but in a purely technical sense, i.e. in the sense that they had more power and greater rights than counts. Thus the bishop of Würzburg, by the charter of 1168, had become a duke in this technical sense. But these new imperial princes were not created by the king. Many bishops, having no tribal following at all, were the first of these *de facto* new dukes. Eventually the dukes realized that their position was not so very different from that of these bishops. Finally, some other princes took their position to be similar to that of these bishops. The status of these new princes was defined in terms of feudal law. The spiritual princes received 'sceptre fiefs', and the lay princes 'flag fiefs', immediately from the king. It is this feudal immediacy which constitutes the tenancy-in-chief and defines the new imperial princes. *See* H. Mitteis, *Der Staat des hohen Mittelalters*, Weimar, 1948, p. 300. For the gradualness of this transformation see E. E. Stengel, ZSSRGer, 66, p. 312, and also Schönherr, *Die Lehre vom Reichsfürstenstand des Mittelalters*, 1914, p. 131, and G. Tellenbach, *Vom karolingischen Reichsadel zum deutschen Reichsfürstenstand*, in Th. Mayer ed., *Adel und Bauern*, Leipzig, 1943, p. 67. When the transformation was complete, the archbishop of Cologne, for instance, came to be known also as duke of Westphalia (M. Jansen, *Die Herzogsgewalt der Erzbischöfe von Köln in Westfalen*, München, 1895), and the archbishop of Magdeburg as the head of *ducatus transalbinus* (J. Ficker, *Vom Reichsfürstenstand*, II, 3, p. 482, and E. Rosenstock, *Herzogsgewalt und Friedenschutz*, p. 201).

those of territorial power and administration had been very much part of what has been described as *naturalism.*[1] It was a tendency which manifested itself with enormous power in the areas of Norman influence, in England and in Sicily, and, to a slightly lesser extent, in the dominions such as they were of the king of France. This influence spilt over into Germany and was one of the formative factors in the conception of the Great Design. Frederick had battled for two decades to give it concrete shape. But now that he had decided to change his plan, he found that in northern Germany it had begun to strike root. The extent of its success there may no longer have suited his third plan, but he had only himself to thank for having countenanced and propagated it for so long.

Alone among the princes of Germany, Henry the Lion's attempts at state-building had made spectacular progress by the late 1170s. As a result he had made a very large number of enemies who had on several earlier occasions made common cause against him.[2] But he had always managed to resist and when as a direct result of the end of the schism, as embodied in the Anagni agreement and the Peace of Venice, new warfare broke

[1] *See* Chapter II p. 27 above. A. Brackmann, *Der mittelalterliche Ursprung der Nationalstaaten*, SPA, 1936, p. 137, argued that with Frederick, Henry the Lion, as well as in the Zähringer region financial and political considerations became paramount. The church tended to lose its paramount importance and *Lady World* came more and more to the fore. Brackmann attributed the growth of this naturalism to Norman influences. – This naturalism was finding an ally in spiritualism: Arnold of Brescia e.g. had attacked the clergy and flattered the laity by insisting that only laymen were allowed to own property. *See Gesta*, II, xxviii. Naturalism, however, was in sharp contrast to sacerdotalism. Consider for instance the conflict at the time of the crusade against the Wenden in 1147 when St Bernard insisted on conversion or extermination. Pope Eugene III forbade the conclusion of treaties or the levying of tribute unless the Wenden were first converted. But the Saxon lords had established a *modus vivendi* with the Wenden princes and were reluctant to have these relations subject to purely sacerdotal criteria. They were much more interested in receiving tribute than in conversion and were certainly not keen on devastating the lands of the Wenden merely because the latter refused to be converted. *Cp.* K. Jordan, *Die Bistumsgründungen Heinrichs des Löwen*, Stuttgart, 1939, p. 80. According to Helmold, c. 84, Niclot, the prince of the Obodrites replied in 1156 to Henry the Lion's invitation to accept Christianity as follows: 'Let the God in heaven be your God; for us it is enough to worship you.' In other words, Niclot wanted his relations with Henry to be based on political and military circumstances and suggested that religion be left out. In many ways this secular attitude suited Henry, for Helmold, c. 68, reports that Henry's expeditions against the Slavs were undertaken for money, not for Christianity.

[2] *See* p. 268 above.

out in Saxony,[1] he was, as ever, fully confident that he would be able to ride the storm.[2]

The tribal character of dukedom in Saxony had ceased to exist centuries ago when Henry, duke of the Saxons, had become king. The office of duke, given to the Billunger family and held by them for a considerable time, had not been a tribal office in the old sense of that term. Only in the days of King Lothair (1125–37), some effort had been made to reunite the older tribal ducal office with the newer 'ducal' functions, such as they were.[3] Lothair had indeed been something like a tribal duke by the simple magnitude of his possessions in Saxony.[4] But from the time he became king he had often been absent from Saxony and the other Saxon dynasts considered themselves under his power in his capacity as king rather than in his capacity as duke. Thus his (tribal) ducal power had suffered in consequence, even though his actual influence had not.[5] He had, therefore, been able to take what were perhaps the first steps towards the achievement of some kind of territorial lordship: he had used *ministeriales* for the administration of many of his lordships (*Hoheitsrechte*).[6] It might almost be true to say that his dukedom in Saxony stood as the forerunner of a new age.[7]

When Henry the Lion became duke of Saxony, he availed himself of whatever there was left of his rights and his pre-eminence as a traditional tribal duke,[8] and it is a measure of his political

[1] *See* p. 313, note 1.

[2] As early as 1152, when Archbishop Hartwig had urged Vicelin to obtain investiture from Frederick rather than from Henry the Lion, Vicelin had refused to do so because he was certain that Henry's ire would be terrible: 'for in this country only the authority of the duke is heeded'. Helmold, I, 73. – In c. 69, Helmold reports that one of Henry's men said: 'if you do not obey your labours will be frustrated, for neither the Caesar nor the archbishop can help your cause if my lord (i.e. Henry) opposes it; for God gave him all his land'.

[3] There is no telling what a tribal duke's rights exactly were.

[4] Lothair's dukedom was founded upon countships, *Vogteien* and allodial property, as well as on his powerful personality. Thus his ducal power almost assumed once more the character of a tribal dukedom. *See* G. Tellenbach, *Vom Karolingischen Reichsadel zum deutschen Reichsfürstenstand*, in Th. Mayer ed., *Adel und Bauern*, 1943, p. 60.

[5] K. Jordan, *Herzogtum und Stamm in Sachsen während des hohen Mittelalters*, NJL, 30, 1959, *passim*. *Cp*. Th. Mayer, *Kaisertum und Herzogsgewalt im Zeitalter Friedrichs I*, Leipzig, 1944, p. 405.

[6] H. W. Vogt, *Das Herzogtum Lothars von Supplingburg*, Hildesheim, 1959, p. 135.

[7] 'Zwischen den Zeiten', H. W. Vogt, *op. cit.*, p. 198.

[8] F. Hildebrand, *Der Sächsiche 'Staat' Heinrichs des Löwen*, EHS, 302, Berlin, 1937, has argued that the Saxon duchy had been a territorial, as opposed to a tribal unit, ever

astuteness that he used those powers and rights wherever he could and that he supplemented them, wherever he could not, by more modern methods, i.e. by violence, by legal subterfuge and by deploying his wealth and his following in order to increase his holdings and his power.[1] Henry's aim was to turn his 'duchy' into

---

since the tenth century, and that Henry simply continued this line. But this view is an over-simplification and has not found much support. Hampe, HB, p. 197, note 2, thinks that Hildebrand went too far in denying that Henry's power had any basis whatever in tribal custom. G. Läwen, *Die herzogliche Stellung Heinrichs des Löwen in Sachsen*, 1937, agrees with Hildebrand that little was left in the middle of the twelfth century of any tribal basis for ducal power and that Henry did not rely on any tribal ducal rights for his state-building. But Läwen, like most other historians, disagrees with Hildebrand's theory that the Saxon territorial, as distinct from a tribal association, goes back to the tenth century, i.e. to the reign of Otto I. But even though one is forced to admit that Henry's power had no tribal basis, it is nevertheless true that a duke always had a flying start over any count, because of tribal custom, such as it was. For a duke had a military authority which placed him both legally and politically above a mere count. Hence a dukedom was a bit more than the sum total of the countships a duke might hold. *Cp.* also K. Jordan in DA, 1, 1937, p. 573. He objects to Hildebrand's equation of duke and count and insists that Henry did exercise rights in Saxony which can only be explained on the assumption that he was a (tribal) duke. No mere count, no matter how many countships he held, could have held a *curia* at which other magnates attended. For these 'ducal' *curiae* see J. Ficker, *Vom Reichsfürstenstand*, II, iii, pp. 291 f. – Hildebrand can therefore not be completely right in saying that Henry's power in Saxony consisted in the mere fact that he controlled so many countships. A dukedom, even at the time of Henry, was a bit more than the sum total of the countships a duke might hold. But even so it is true that this extra power which Henry enjoyed in virtue of his being duke was nebulous. The expression *ducatus* was used by him only twice. *Cp.* K. Jordan, *op. cit.*, p. 24. And only once or twice did he hold a ducal *curia*, *ibid.*, p. 25. The real basis for his (ducal) power was the sum total of his rights and possessions, which he tried to increase by violence and conquest, if necessary. His contemporaries were very conscious of this. *See* Helmold, II, 102: 'The duke's power now increased beyond that of all who were before him and he became a prince of the princes of the earth. He trod upon the necks of rebels and broke up their strongholds, he extirpated the men who had revolted and made peace in the land; he built very strong fortresses . . .'. It is, however, only fair to add that Hildebrand has examined all the known cases in which Henry exercised 'justice' in a *curia*, and found that he always acted in his capacity of *Vogt* or count – never in his capacity of duke of the tribe.

[1] R. Hildebrand, *op. cit.*, argues that the tribal duchy was never revived. From the tenth century to the issue of the Gelnhausen charter in 1180 the ducal office was defined territorially and consisted in the sum total of countships in the hands of the Billung family, of Lothair and Henry. L. Hüttebräuker, ZSSRGer, 57, p. 582, doubts whether Hildebrand is right in thinking she has disproved the older view of Weiland, *Das Sächsische Herzogtum unter Lothair und Heinrich dem Löwen*, 1866. She says that Henry did not rule over a defined territory, but merely exercised a large number of different and disjointed rights. Hildebrand thinks that a count ruled over a certain territory by holding the money, market and customs *regalia* and by exercising judicial functions. But in reality, no count was such a territorial lord (*Landesherr*). The various judicial and regalian functions were usually not in one hand in any one region. To be a count did

a territorial state.[1] His ultimate object was to make good his right to invest bishops and to hold fiefs from them which he, in turn, placed in the hands of his own men, mainly *ministeriales*; to acquire as much allodial property as possible; and to hold as many countships as he could and have them administered by his own men. In this way he sought to give the Saxon duchy a territorial definition and to replace the old association of clans by a kind of territorial sovereignty over the inhabitants, high and low, of a given territory.[2] In this he went very far beyond any attempt to

---

not necessarily imply that one was a territorial lord. Hence Henry could not hope to establish a territorial lordship (*Flächenstaat*) by simply holding a large number of countships in his hands. Where he had no allodial property, he, on the contrary, often tried to advance his fortune and power in virtue of his tribal ducal authority. Hüttebräuker, *ibid.*, p. 584, denies therefore that Henry could ever have aimed at a territorial state. She believes that Henry merely aimed at an increase in power. On the whole, the controversy between Hildebrand and Hüttebräuker seems merely a problem of degree. Once Henry's power had reached a certain point, the territorial state had emerged, whether he had consciously planned it or not. The fact that Henry had farther to go than Hildebrand, with her notion of territorially unified countships which he merely had to gather in his own hand, supposes, does not prove that he was not, in fact, slowly creating a closed territorial unit. Historians have made it very difficult for themselves by seeking to understand what Henry did in purely legal terms, i.e. by wondering whether he used tribal powers or the sum total of the powers he enjoyed by holding many countships. The crux of the matter is that Henry was no lawyer and simply wanted to increase his powers.

[1] A. Brackmann, *Die Wandlung der Staatsanschauungen im Zeitalter Friedrichs I*, HZ, 145, 1932, p. 8, and *Der mittelalterliche Ursprung der Nationalstaaten*, SPA, 1936, p. 137, points to the Norman example which had a strong influence on Henry's thinking.

[2] It is Hildebrand's great merit, *op. cit.*, to have established this – no matter whether one agrees with her other theory about the absence of ducal tribal authority. In fact, if her own theory that there was nothing left of the tribal character of Henry's duchy is correct, Henry would appear much less original than he probably was. R. Hildebrand is unfortunately inclined to a rigid dogmatism, and fashions an image of Henry as a little dictator. Thus e.g., she denies all active participation to the citizens of Lübeck. She sees it all as a cut and dried case of *étatisme* and thinks of Henry as a sort of military Prussian monarch who knows best what is good. But there is worse. Quite gratuitously she throws in on p. 7 and p. 429 an acknowledgement to the *völkische Bewusstsein* which has made her rehabilitate Henry. She ends up by stating not only that Henry aimed at a territorial state – which is a reasonable conclusion – but also that Henry helped the growth of a 'tribal-territorial' state – which is not only untrue but also a complete contradiction of her own theory. It is a great pity that in so intelligent a book Dr Goebbels was allowed to display his cloven hoof. Hildebrand also owes very much more to Philippson that she cares to admit on p. 8, note 2. Philippson, *Heinrich der Löwe*, 2nd ed., 1918, has a very good chapter, Bk. III, Ch. I, on Henry as an aggressive state-builder. But Philippson was a Jew; and hence Hildebrand's dismissal of him. Unlike Hildebrand, Philippson was a very shrewd judge of politics. He says on p. 192 that the means employed by Henry were both morally and politically questionable, for he failed to establish a firm party of trusted friends in that he always sought to increase his power at the expense of friends as well as of enemies. Henry's lack of

re-establish the old kind of tribal duchy and it is difficult to see him, as so many earlier historians have done, as a romantic reactionary who wanted to turn the clock back and who, eventually, fell victim to the other Saxon dynasts' resistance.[1] But if Henry went a longer way towards success in his state-building than the other princes, and if his aims in that direction were more clearly formulated, it must not be forgotten that he lived in the second half of the twelfth century and that the technical devices at his disposal were as primitive as those of anybody else; certainly more primitive than those of, say, Henry II of England. Wherever he established his administrators there was always the tendency for them to become his vassals and, as vassals, to form a hereditary feudal nobility who might pay homage to their lord; but who were not his subjects or officials in any modern sense of the term.[2] Henry's

---

prudence and his moral failure were completely beyond Hildebrand's grasp. She can see his failure only in theoretical terms, i.e. that his state did not fit into the traditional framework of the empire.

[1] Weiland, *op. cit.*, and Heigel and Riezler, *Das bayrische Stammesherzogtum Heinrichs des Löwen und Ottos von Wittelsbach*, 1867, see in Henry's fall the necessary consequence of his attempt to restore his position as a tribal duke. They believe that he fell a victim to the dynasts' resistance. It is certainly true that the Saxon dynasts considered themselves his equals and resented him from the beginning of his 'reign' in 1142. *Cp.* K. Jordan, *op. cit.*. They too were dynasts aspiring to improve their position. They might have been prepared to owe feudal allegiance of some kind or other to Henry. But his efforts to depress their status and to charge *ministeriales* with the administration of the countships which he assembled in his hands, was bound to provoke resistance. One does, therefore, not have to believe, as Weiland and Riezler did, in Henry's archaism in order to understand that the Saxon dynasts were provoked by him beyond endurance. It is worth quoting Helmold, II, 103: 'But because glory begets envy, and because nothing in the affairs of men is permanent, all the princes of Saxony were jealous of the great glory of the man.'

[2] In theory, the 'state' of Henry was administered by vice-counts and was divided into vice-counties. But each vice-count was a feudal vassal of Henry and these men formed thus a hereditary caste over which Henry had no firm and secure control. True, he had a firm circle of friends among them. There was Count Conrad von Rode, Eilbert and Bernhard von Wölpe, Bernard von Lippe, Gunzelin von Schwerin, and others. But his enemies among the Saxon dynasts also formed a firm circle: there was the count of Arnsberg, Christian von Oldenburg and the counts of Ravensberg. Henry tried to exile the latter and deprive them of their lands. But he never quite succeeded and they formed a lively opposition to him in Saxony. His most effective method was to insist on severe and punctilious observance of all feudal dues. There was a more extreme method: he tried to use *ministeriales* as counts. When the Leinegau came into his possession as part of the Winzenburg inheritance (*see* p. 267 above), he placed it under Berthold von Wolbernehausen and in the Stade lands he used *ministeriales* as *Vögte*. His most assured success was in the colonial lands beyond the Elbe, which he had conquered from the Slavs. These districts were ruled by his own men like prefects, who were military and judicial rulers. His castles, throughout Saxony, were

state-building effort, therefore, contained its own limitations.[1] If Frederick had fully understood this, he might have ignored Henry. As it was, he became unduly alarmed by his successes and judged that Henry's territorial power had advanced too far beyond the stage at which he could be treated as a mere tenant-in-chief.

Frederick's lack of confidence in the efficacy of Henry's limitations is perhaps understandable, if the determined astuteness of Henry the Lion's commercial policy is taken into account. Henry's financial wealth was common knowledge in the second half of the twelfth century[2] and so was the unusual splendour of his court. If Frederick's Lombard plans under the Great Design had been successful, he would undoubtedly have become the richer of the two. For the money that was to be had in Lombardy by far surpassed the profits that could ever be made by the most successful commercial ventures in the economically backward and undeveloped lands of the German north. But as it was, in the late

---

administered by *ministeriales*, and at times he imported them from Bavaria. It is significant that he never used Saxon *ministeriales* in Bavaria. *Cp.* O. Haendle, *Die Dienstmannen Heinrichs des Löwen*, 1930. In all this, Henry endeavoured to follow Norman examples, but unlike the Norman rulers of England and Sicily, he could never claim, not even in theory, to own the land by conquest. The process of feudalization was therefore tilted against him, and not, as in the case of the Normans, in his favour.

[1] Henry entrusted many castles in the lands of the Obodrites to *ministeriales*. They were supposed to be vicars and *praefecti*, not feudal vassals. This policy was a first attempt to create a state administration (as opposed to feudal tenures) in colonial lands. *See* R. Hildebrand, *op. cit.*, pp. 385 f. It is significant that these policies were frustrated and checked by the rebellion which began against Henry towards the end of 1166. In order to secure himself against surprises in his rear, Henry had to make friends again with the prince of the Obodrites and restore much of his inheritance to him. He took it as a fief from Henry. *See* Helmold, c. 103. And thus the plan to establish a state-like organization in the colonial lands with the help of Saxon *ministeriales* had to be abandoned. Even Schwerin, which Henry had not restored to Pribislav, had to be given to one of these *ministeriales* as a fief. *See* K. Jordan, *Die Bistumsgründungen Heinrichs des Löwen*, Stuttgart, 1939, pp. 99–100. On p. 135 Jordan attributes Henry's reversion to feudal tenures in the colonial lands to the Slav rising of 1164; on p. 99, he attributes it to the rising of the Saxon nobles. – *Cp.* R. Hildebrand, *op. cit.*, p. 389: in spite of all efforts, Saxony remained a feudal state in which the independence of the lesser dynasts grew. Even the *ministeriales* proved unreliable, *ibid.*, p. 391, and not even the clergy could be de-feudalized, *ibid.*, p. 423. We have here a very clear illustration of the truth of J. R. Strayer's general observation, *Feudal Institutions*, in: M. Clagett, ed., *12th Century Europe and the Foundations of Modern Society*, Madison, 1961, pp. 84–5, that the lack of specialized administrative personnel helps to explain why the effective sphere of government had been no larger than the castellany. If a ruler delegated authority, he would probably succeed only in creating a new lordship. If he did not delegate it, he might lose all control over outlying districts.

[2] R. Hildebrand, *op. cit.*, p. 302, note 1.

70s Frederick's failure stood in marked contrast to the success of Henry's commercial policies in the German north.

Henry was very alive to the possibilities of commercial development, such as it was, and did everything in his power to encourage the slowly developing merchant classes of northern Germany. The most striking aspect of his economic acumen is that he sought to co-ordinate his political enterprises with his economic plans.[1] He understood, for instance, that it was vital for him to control places which were situated at important commercial cross-roads,[2] so that he could make full use of any rights he had to levy tolls. He furthered the growth of commercial centres like Stade and Bremen,[3] and at the same time did his best to prevent the growth of rival centres. In the case of Hamburg, he tried to prevent development by simple pressure.[4] In order to counter the commercial aspirations of the citizens of Magdeburg, he founded the city of Haldensleben,[5] and in order to assist the development of Lübeck, he eventually destroyed his own city of Bardowiek.[6] There are also instances where he deliberately founded a city of his own in order to divert commerce from a city over which he could not gain influence. He furthered the development of Göttingen in order to eliminate the growth of the nearby village of Grone[7] and sought to isolate Hildesheim by the development of Hanover[8] and of Hagenstadt within the precincts of Braunschweig.[9] Last, and not least, he founded what came to be the most flourishing and forward looking centre for the development of commerce in the north, the city of Lübeck.[10]

[1] J. Bärmann, *Die Städtegründungen Heinrichs des Löwen*, Köhn-Graz, 1961, p. 296, places the emphasis differently: Henry's city policy served the larger aim of his territorial policy.

[2] R. Hildebrand, *op. cit.*, pp. 308–10, 327.

[3] R. Hildebrand, *op. cit.*, p. 318; J. Bärmann, *op. cit.*, p. 189. For the way in which Bremen obtained a charter from Henry the Lion see also H. Meyer, *Freiheitsroland und Gottesfrieden*, HG, 1931, 32. After Henry's fall, the citizens wanted Frederick to confirm their liberties and since they could not very well ask him to confirm a charter granted by Henry, they persuaded him that their freedom went back to Charlemagne.

[4] J. Bärmann, *op. cit.*, 1961, p. 19; R. Hildebrand, *op. cit.*, p. 318.

[5] R. Hildebrand, *op. cit.*, pp. 331 ff.

[6] *ibid.*, p. 324. [7] *ibid.*, p. 328. [8] *ibid.*, p. 340.

[9] *ibid.*, pp. 340–9.

[10] *ibid.*, pp. 350–8. *Cp.* p. 114, note 1. Henry authorized an association of entrepreneurs to found Lübeck. *Cp.* F. Rörig, *Heinrich der Löwe und die Gründung Lübecks*,

Henry's commercial and economic policies were an integral part of his territorial aims. This is not only proved by the choice of sites such as Stade and Bremen in the north-west, Lübeck, in the north-east, his acquisitions in the region between Weser and Elbe and between Thuringia and Braunschweig, but also by the way he endeavoured to administer the cities he had founded or brought under his sway. In most cases, he tried to have the city administered by a city 'judge', appointed by himself,[1] with little participation in administration by the citizens. He did not favour self-government for fear that it would come into conflict with his own attempt to establish some form of territorial sovereignty.[2] In this respect again, there is a striking similarity between Frederick's aspirations in Lombardy and Henry's policies. Frederick's failure and Henry's success can be accounted for by the fact that Henry was operating in a much more virgin territory. The merchants and commercial classes of northern Germany were much more backward and inexperienced than those of Lombardy. Their efforts

---

DA, I, 1937, p. 446. The foundation of Lübeck shows an alliance between Henry's political authority and his commercial initiative. *Cp.* F. Rörig, HG, 58, 1933, p. 32. Henry was shrewd enough to mobilize the commercial entrepreneurs of his age to do something that was of interest to them as well as to him. As a result, the citizens of Lübeck, unlike so many feudal lords and *ministeriales,* made at least a strong attempt to remain faithful to him in the early 80s.

[1] J. Bärmann, *op. cit.*, p. 246.

[2] *ibid.*, p. 300. Henry's attitude to old cities and his foundation of new cities were part of his territorial policy. This is proved especially by the choice of sites. He selected sites which commanded commercial routes. Those parts of his lands where no commanding posts over routes of commerce were necessary, like Westphalia, received no help or encouragement for cities. The idea was to advance the fortunes of cities where he could derive markets, tolls and customs, i.e. *regalia,* which in turn were to serve the purposes of his territorial sovereignty. *Cp.* Bärmann, *op. cit.*, p. 296. The duke was always the overlord of the city. The administration of each city was headed by a city judge appointed by Henry, *ibid.*, p. 246, and there was a comparative absence of the citizens' participation in city government. Henry certainly did not favour self-government, *ibid.*, p. 300. But the protection he afforded and his promises to pay compensation for losses suffered on the way to and from markets through robbers proved powerful incentives to merchants. If he did not favour self-government, his policy proved nevertheless attractive to many merchants who were only too eager to cooperate. Hildebrand, *op. cit., passim,* is insensitive to this cooperation. One can see, for instance, that in the new colonial lands, though Henry provided the initiative and kept a great deal of authority, city life flourished because of the efforts of the leaders of commercial guilds. Henry was always shrewd enough to avail himself of the merchants' own self-interest. Lübeck owed its existence to the efforts of merchants; but they would not have gone to Lübeck if Henry's helping hand had not been extended there and if they had had no hopes to improve their status and income there. *Cp.* F. Rörig, *Heinrich der Löwe und die Gründung Lübecks,* DA, 1, 1937, pp. 418–19, 423–4.

were in their earliest stages of development, and they had, therefore, much reason to be grateful to Henry and to require his guidance and protection. Whereas in Lombardy the development had progressed far beyond the preliminary stages, and Frederick's attempt to interfere perhaps inevitably caused strong resentment. As it was, Frederick was not only forced to compare his own failure with Henry's success, but also to couple such a comparison with his own knowledge of the wealth and power he had almost won in Lombardy. The comparison caused him to believe that a man like Henry would never join the ranks of the new imperial princes as a tenant-in-chief.

There was probably another factor which entered into Frederick's considerations at this time. Quite apart from the resistance of the citizens themselves, one of the greatest obstacles to Frederick's establishing his rule in Lombardy had been his lack of trained and educated personnel. Frederick must have known that Henry was not likely to find better trained and educated men to carry out his work of administration in his 'state'. But he did realize that the men Henry was using were for the most part loyal. They worked near their own homes, surrounded by their own kin, and were in close and constant touch with their master Henry. Thus they were never likely to play as disastrous a role as Frederick's commissioners had played in Lombardy. For this reason, Frederick held, Henry the Lion constituted a tangible threat to the feudalization of the monarchy.[1] He therefore decided

[1] This is, of course, very much a modern view of the situation, based on a sociological and political analysis which was beyond the grasp of people in the twelfth century. Historians have advanced a number of views as to the reasons for the fall of Henry. J. Haller believed that Henry thought himself too much of a territorial ruler and no longer as a prince of the empire. Hence his destruction was necessary. C. Erdmann, *Der Prozess Heinrichs des Löwen*, in Th. Mayer, ed., *Kaisertum und Herzogsgewalt*, Leipzig, 1944, attributed the main initiative to Frederick. But H. Mitteis, *Zur staufischen Verfassungsgeschichte*, ZSSRGger, 65, 1947, rejects this. He argues that Frederick could not possibly have been interested in the feudalization which was the result of the destruction of Henry. Mitteis simply assumes that feudalization cannot have been in Frederick's mind. But if one supposes that feudalism was his third and last plan, Erdmann's view and his narrative of the process of destruction becomes eminently plausible. R. Hildebrand, *op. cit.*, p. 300, attributes the fall of Henry to the fact that a well organized state could not exist within the securely coherent empire. This view overestimates, first, the successes of Henry and secondly, the coherence of the empire as a going concern. As a result, Hildebrand sees the clash between Henry and Frederick as a clash between two principles, the territorial and the imperial principle. This is a

to discontinue the old policy of supporting Henry's aspirations – a policy which had been an important part of his first plan as well as of the Great Design.

For his new plan, Frederick had no Otto of Freising to write another history to explain that the new policy was not really new, and that Frederick and Henry had been enemies all along. As it was, the decision was clearly understood by Frederick's contemporaries as a new departure, but they did not understand the real reason for it. The chroniclers of the 1180s, none of whom was a real historian, let alone a historian of the stature of Otto of Freising, were therefore reduced to speculation, and with few exceptions decided that Henry's refusal to help Frederick in Italy (in 1176) was the cause of Frederick's hostility. Authors of the succeeding generation, who included major chroniclers like Arnold of Lübeck and Burchard of Ursberg, wrote in the shadow of the civil war which had broken out in 1198 and therefore formed the theory that the conflict between Frederick and Henry had been a preliminary skirmish in the great battle for the crown, which was being fought between Frederick's son Philip of Swabia and Henry's son Otto of Brunswick.[1]

On his return to Germany in the autumn of 1178, Frederick found that once again, as a direct result of the Peace of Venice, a bitter

very plausible view. By promoting feudalism and by allowing its growth, Frederick wanted to give the empire a new coherence. But it is putting the cart before the horse to maintain that there was such a coherence and that Henry's policies offended against it.

[1] *See* P. Munz, *Frederick Barbarossa and Henry the Lion in 1176*, HS, XII, 1965. Modern historians have been very slow in ridding themselves of these amateurish explanations provided by twelfth and thirteenth century chroniclers. Bünau, writing in the early eighteenth century, and H. Mitteis, writing in the twentieth century, both see the conflict between Frederick and Henry as a dynastic conflict. Mitteis, therefore, believes that what requires explanation is not why the conflict broke out in 1179, but why it did not break out sooner. In the nineteenth century, Sybel and Ficker believed that the clash occurred because Henry rebelled against Frederick's Italian policy. To Sybel he rebelled in the interests of Germany; to Ficker, in the interests of his personal ambitions. Ranke and Giesebrecht, on the other hand, tended to see the conflict in terms of Germany's position in the world. To Ranke, Frederick's friendship with Henry had made German predominance possible. Giesebrecht agreed with this view, but added that in the end the continuation of this friendship would have defeated German predominance because Henry had become too powerful within Germany. As a curiosity I would like to add that Luther believed that Henry had been bribed by the pope to rebel against the emperor. (*See* U. Jentzsch, *Heinrich der Löwe im Urteil der deutschen Geschichtsschreibung*, Jena, 1932, p. 28.)

feud had broken out between Henry the Lion and his enemies. One of the provisions of the Peace, already contained in the Anagni agreement, had been that Bishop Gero of Halberstadt was to be deprived as a schismatic and Bishop Udalric, who had been ejected from the see because of his obedience to Alexander, be reinstated.[1] Gero had been one of Henry's creatures, and during his administration Henry had been invested with a large number of valuable Halberstadt fiefs. Udalric's return put an immediate end to this state of affairs and was a severe blow to Henry. When Henry refused to restore the fiefs, Udalric imposed spiritual penalties and Henry proceeded to attack one of the episcopal castles. Udalric was able to enlist the support of Archbishop Philip of Cologne, Rainald's successor, and by the beginning of 1178 a new and formidable coalition had joined against Henry. On 11 November at Speier, where many princes had gathered to welcome Frederick upon his return from Burgundy and Italy, Henry and his old enemies[2] preferred charges against each other. If Frederick had persevered in his old policy, he would have seized this opportunity of bringing about a reconciliation. Instead he avoided negotiation and ordered Henry to appear in January before an imperial court in Worms to answer the charges.

At this juncture there was no telling how the affair would develop. And Frederick, least of all, could have had no inkling of the length to which he would have to go in order to chasten Henry. But from that moment onwards, Henry was on the defensive and sought to forestall any legal action. Frederick, at first, did not foresee the need for military action, and did not envisage that Henry might have to be destroyed altogether. But as Henry evaded action after action, Frederick mounted his attack, hoping that Henry's final destruction would smooth the path towards a feudal monarchy and that the remaining princes, and especially the immediate beneficiaries of Henry's fall, would emerge automatically as the new tenants-in-chief.

Henry did not appear at Frederick's court in Worms in January 1179 and it seems that sentence was passed on him then for con-

[1] *See* p. 313, note 3.
[2] *See* pp. 268–9.

tumacy.[1] It was not to be effective immediately and Henry was given another chance to answer at a court to be held in Magdeburg in June.[2] If he failed to appear at Magdeburg too, the sentence of outlawry was to become effective.[3]

The proceedings against Henry were taken under ancient tribal law. Henry was being judged by a bench of his own tribesmen, that is by Swabians; for Henry, like Frederick, was a Swabian. The original sentence in Worms had been pronounced by a number of Swabian nobles. They had then been summoned[4] to Magdeburg because in Magdeburg, although it was far from Swabia, a large number of Henry's opponents from eastern Saxony could gather and testify against him. To make a condemnation possible, it was necessary to bring Swabian tribesmen and Saxon accusers together. But when the court met in Magdeburg on 24 June, there was a great surprise in store for everybody. Not only did Henry not appear; but his judges-to-be also failed to appear. As a result, no sentence of outlawry could be formally proclaimed.[5]

Henry himself had taken steps to prevent an effective court of Swabians from meeting in Magdeburg. Just as Frederick had followed Henry's activities in Saxony, Henry had watched Frederick's in Swabia. He had thus become aware that Frederick had made many enemies among the lower dynasts of Swabia at whose expense his policy of turning the country into a territorial

[1] I follow C. Erdmann, *Der Prozess Heinrichs des Löwen*, in: Th. Mayer ed., *Kaisertum und Herzogsgewalt im Zeitalter Friedrichs I*, Leipzig, 1944. Erdmann's account, although it has not gone completely unchallenged (*Cp.* e.g. H. Mitteis, *Zur staufischen Verfassungsgeschichte*, ZSSRGger, 65, 1947) is the most consistent of all accounts and manages to explain all problems raised by the text of the Gelnhausen charter. It therefore supersedes all previous accounts by F. Güterbock, *Der Prozess Heinrichs des Löwen*, 1909; *Die Gelnhäuser Urkunde und der Prozess Heinrichs des Löwen*, 1909; *Nochmals die Gelnhäüser Urkunde*, NA, 49, 1932; as well as K. H. Ganahl, *Neues zum Text der Gelnhäuser Urkunde*, MIOG, 53, 1939.

[2] C. Erdmann, *op. cit.*, p. 313. On this occasion two technical, legal devices were introduced from Italian judicial custom. This introduction was due to Frederick's personal initiative and proves that he took a very active part in the proceedings, even at this early stage.

[3] *ibid.*, p. 305. I am using the term 'outlawry' confidently. Strictly speaking there was a difference between *Acht* (*proscriptio*) and *friedlos* (*exlex*). But the legal usage in the second half of the twelfth century did not always make such subtle distinctions. *See* Erdmann, *op. cit.*, 353.

[4] *ibid.*, p. 310.

[5] *ibid.*, p. 315.

'state' had been pursued. On at least one occasion as early as 1175 Henry had lent support to one of Frederick's enemies,[1] and now that he was in dire straits, he entered into a conspiracy with a large number of Swabian nobles in order to prevent the assembly in Magdeburg.[2] Henry now very shrewdly tried to use against Frederick the same tactics which Frederick was employing against him.[3]

As a result of the Swabian conspiracy, the Magdeburg court proved ineffectual. All Frederick could do was to set the date for yet another court to be held in Kayna, because Margrave Dietrich von Landsberg, an old enemy of Henry's who had duly appeared at Magdeburg, had challenged Henry to a duel on a charge of high treason.[4] Henry, confident in the success of his counter-blow, resumed his acts of violence in Westphalia and proceeded as if nothing had happened. But here he was underestimating Frederick's determination and resourcefulness. Henry felt that as long as he could prevent another meeting of a court of his Swabian peers Frederick would remain legally powerless against him; and as far as military action was concerned, he reckoned that as long as he was not an outlaw and had only to fight those nobles whom he had actually hurt or offended, he could well stand his ground. Henry, clearly, seems to have made an old mistake: he assumed that political customs and methods do not change.[5]

But customs were changing – and it seems to have occurred to Frederick that if the old method of a trial by tribal peers could not prevail against Henry, he might start an entirely new kind of legal action, that is, a trial in feudal law, a trial in which Henry would be judged not by his tribesmen, but by Frederick's other tenants, or rather by those princes whom Frederick might persuade to consider themselves his tenants-in-chief; for up to now there did not exist a

[1] Th. Mayer, *op. cit.*, p. 397.

[2] C. Erdmann, *op. cit.*, p. 317.

[3] *ibid.*, p. 319. There is a weak point in Erdmann's theory: why did Frederick not attempt to summon those Swabian nobles who were faithful to him? This would have been the most obvious solution.

[4] *ibid.*, p. 323. Dietrich had a personal grudge against Henry, *ibid.*, p. 335.

[5] In the end, Henry was very aware that Frederick had employed extra-legal methods and that, according to traditional custom, he ought not to have been outlawed. *See* Arnold of Lübeck, *Chronica Slavorum*, II, 10.

clear legal definition of such a rank.[1] This, of course, was a rather revolutionary concept. A feudal, as opposed to a tribal, court would not be able to outlaw Henry and deprive him of all his property. It could only strip him of his ducal title and of his fiefs, which he could be deemed to hold in some kind of feudal tenure, but could not claim jurisdiction over Henry's allodial property which was considerable. But this did not matter to Frederick. For his plan was merely to put an end to Henry's extraordinary power in Saxony, which had made Henry unsuitable as a feudal tenant-in-chief. He had no personal animosity against him, and no real grounds for wishing to make him a pauper. The switch to feudal proceedings suited Frederick very well. It would fulfil the real purpose of destroying Henry's 'state', and at the same time establish a court of tenants-in-chief, a rudimentary *curia regis*. In this way the destruction of Henry's extraordinary power would automatically result in the definition of a class of new princes, i.e. men who were entitled to judge a prince like Henry and who would, in that sense, be the immediate beneficiaries of Henry's fall. So as it turned out, Henry's manœuvres to prevent a tribal judgement had actually played into Frederick's hands.

In the meantime, however, Frederick decided to allow matters to run their own course. Margrave Dietrich had charged Henry with treason and challenged him to a duel. The margrave did not state the precise nature of the treason,[2] but it is clear that with this charge a new kind of trial was started, for there had been no such charge in Worms. The treason to which Dietrich referred

[1] C. Erdmann, *op. cit.*, p. 321; *cp.* also pp. 341–2.

[2] The exact nature of the treason supposed to have been committed by Henry has caused much speculation by contemporary chroniclers, as well as by later historians. Their first guess was that Henry was guilty of treason because he had refused to help Frederick in Italy in 1176. But it is now certain that Henry was not legally obliged to help (J. Ficker, *Vom Reichsfürstenstand*, 1911, II, i, p. 370), and that therefore his refusal could not be construed as treason and that Frederick himself did not attribute any importance to the refusal; *see* P. Munz, *Frederick Barbarossa and Henry the Lion in 1176*, HS, XII, 1965, p. 12. There are all sorts of other guesses. Frederick may have felt that Henry's relations with Henry of England or with the emperor of the Greeks were treasonable. It is Erdmann's great merit to have shown that the most important treason with which Henry was charged was the Swabian conspiracy which he had caused, *op. cit.*, pp. 337 ff. – W. Biereye, *Die Wendeneinfälle der Jahre 1178–1180*, HZ, 115, 1915, pp. 322–3, surmises that Dietrich came forward to challenge Henry because the latter had inveigled the heathen Slavs to devastate many north-eastern regions of Germany in order to weaken his enemies. Dietrich had a very personal grudge.

must, therefore, have been an act which had taken place since the first trial at Worms. It seems more than likely that the act which was considered treasonable, a *reatus maiestatis*, was the Swabian conspiracy.[1] In this matter Frederick had an advantage over Henry because he was king and emperor. Henry might resent Frederick's support of his Saxon enemies, but by no stretch of the imagination could he claim that such support was illegal or 'treasonable'; whereas Frederick, as king and emperor, could well demand that Henry's support of Frederick's enemies in Swabia be considered a crime against his own majesty.

The court met in the middle of August in Kayna, a small place in the east Salian region. Kayna was chosen as a venue for the duel, because it was situated in an area in which Dietrich had many relatives.[2] But although there was now a new charge and a new type of trial, the success of the court depended again upon the presence of Henry's Swabian peers. Henry did not appear to fight the duel. This refusal to answer the charge amounted to an establishment of his guilt;[3] but since no more Swabian peers appeared in Kayna than had in Magdeburg, the court could not proceed to a formal proclamation of outlawry. There were several north-Swabian nobles there, but north-Swabian nobles were not really Swabian nobles[4] and thus Henry had once again been able to frustrate Frederick's plan. The only action that was achieved in Kayna was that the assembled princes decided to take concerted military action against Henry.[5] It was then that Frederick, thwarted for the second time, decided to change his tactics and initiate proceedings against Henry in a feudal court, which would consist of men other than Henry's Swabian peers, and if it pronounced sentence against Henry, the military action of the princes would assume the proportions of a royal campaign to execute the judgement of a court of law. Frederick, therefore, summoned a new court, this time an imperial court, to meet at Würzburg in the middle of January the following year (1180).

The new feudal court in Würzburg was attended by a large number of princes from Swabia, Franconia and Saxony. This time

[1] C. Erdmann, *op. cit.*, pp. 333–9.
[2] *ibid.*, p. 323.
[3] *ibid.*, p. 326.
[4] *ibid.*, p. 324.
[5] *ibid.*, p. 323.

Frederick himself appeared as plaintiff and opened the proceedings by charging Henry with all kinds of misdemeanours[1] and ending up with the most important one, the charge of treason which had first been proffered at Magdeburg by Dietrich. Not all the charges were strictly speaking breaches of feudal law. Feudal law, at that time, was still imperfectly formed and it cannot therefore come as a surprise that although the court was summoned under feudal law, it also dealt with charges which ought perhaps to have been heard in a different kind of court. But Frederick and his advisers could not stand on legal niceties.[2] And therefore, at Würzburg, the imperial court proceeded to pronounce judgement in the lapidary sentence of the charter which was issued a little later at Gelnhausen when the judgement was executed: Henry was guilty of contumacy and was deprived, by the unanimous judgement of the princes, of the duchies of Bavaria as well as of Westphalia and Angaria (i.e. Saxony).[3]

The new trial under feudal law had finally produced the desired result. Henry was given one more chance to defend himself, but when he failed to do so within the short period allowed, a charter was issued at Gelnhausen on 13 April 1180. By that charter the Saxon duchy was divided into two parts – the eastern part was given to Bernard von Anhalt and the western part to Archbishop Philip of Cologne. In June of the same year, at another court held in Ratisbon in Bavaria, the sentence of deposition was repeated and Henry again allowed a period in which to defend himself. At the end of that period, Frederick's old and trusted warrior, Otto von Wittelsbach, was formally installed as the new duke of Bavaria proper.[4] Styria was made into a separate principality and the counts of Andechs too came henceforth to be known as imperial princes and termed dukes. The princes who benefited

[1] Erdmann surmises that the refusal at Chiavenna was one of the charges. In view of the fact that Frederick had not considered the refusal important, it seems very improbable, though not impossible, that Frederick should now have dug up this matter. *See* P. Munz, *op. cit., passim.*

[2] Erdmann himself says that feudal law was still unformed, p. 341. It is a weakness of Erdmann's summing up that it is too legalistic. The men concerned were not trained jurists and did not know nearly as much feudal law as H. Mitteis, Erdmann's authority, or as Erdmann himself.

[3] The so-called Gelnhausen charter is in MGH, Const. I, No. 279, pp. 384–6.

[4] C. Erdmann, *op. cit.*, p. 348.

directly from the fall of Henry were thus raised in status. The role they had played in the last, feudal, trial defined their status in the feudal hierarchy. And as a direct result of the splitting up of Henry's two duchies, the number of these new tenants-in-chief was greatly increased.

In order to accomplish his purpose, Frederick had had to pursue it for almost two years. Henry's intransigence and his counter-attacks necessitated a much tougher political battle than the one which Frederick had originally intended in early 1178. But when Frederick discovered the Swabian conspiracy and began to understand the lengths to which Henry was willing to go in order to thwart his policies, he rose to the occasion. Without his new overall plan, Frederick would probably have been helpless in face of Henry's shrewd handling of his case. But with the new feudal concept, he was able to find the energy and understanding to give the proceedings an entirely new twist. And as a result he not only managed to have Henry legally sentenced, but also managed to have it done in such a way that the foundations for the new feudal monarchy had been laid. His third plan had enabled him to seize the opportunity offered by Henry's resistance in order to guide the widespread hostility to Henry into channels which led to a new constitutional order. Feudal law became the pillar of the constitution, because henceforth all those who had received a fief from the emperor were to be the new imperial princes, i.e. the emperor's tenants-in-chief. The paradigm of the new tenant was the prince who received a fief as a result of Henry's fall, but there were several other princes whose status, in 1180, was assimilated to the paradigm. By implication the dynasts who had had autogenous authority and who had formed an official class of princes, were depressed in status: they became mediatized, that is, they became the vassals of the new imperial princes.[1] With this develop-

[1] O. v. Dungern, *Constitutional Reorganization and Reform under the Hohenstaufen*, in G. Barraclough ed., *Medieval Germany*, Oxford, 1938, p. 229; Th. Mayer, *Kaisertum und Herzogsgewalt*, Leipzig, 1944, p. 412; Th. Mayer, *Die Ausbildung der Grundlagen des modernen deutschen Staates im Mittelalter*, HZ, 159, 1939, pp. 482–4. 'As long as the king was the lord of the tribes which formed the realm, nobody could be a territorial lord in the ordinary sense of the term. The territorial lordships originated precisely at the moment at which the king withdrew to a position from which he exercised feudal suzerainty . . .' H. Brunner, *Land und Herrschaft*, 3rd ed., 1943, p. 266.

ment, Frederick had actively assisted in the abolition of the old order, in which the German monarchy had, in theory, been an association of tribes; and, in practice, an association of a limited number of princely families whose standing and power were rooted in the remnants of tribal law.

This constitutional transformation was the most far-reaching and constructive change the German monarchy had ever undergone. Frederick had realized that there was no point in continuing to patch and to tinker. He had, perhaps only dimly, understood the drift towards feudalism, and had decided that the most practical basis for the German monarchy would be to establish itself at the apex of the pyramid which was thus emerging. The proceedings against Henry had begun as an attempt to diminish his power sufficiently to fit him into the pyramid, and had ended, thanks to Frederick's astuteness, in a fairly clear formulation of the new order. Frederick, true to his third plan, had gone with the tide; but also, true to his statesmanship, had guided the tide into a constructive and purposeful direction.

As an immediate result of the new order there emerged also a new military constitution, the so-called *Heerschildordnung*. This *clipeus militaris* had originally been the right to demand military service from one's vassals and had come, by implication, to mean the right to have vassals of a certain kind, for a man's right to demand military service depended on the kind of vassals he had. Now, with the clear definition of the feudal hierarchy, the degrees of the *clipeus militaris* also emerged in clear definition and, in turn, helped to define the hierarchical order. First, there was the king, entitled to the military service of his tenants-in-chief. These tenants-in-chief formed the second and third degree of the *Heerschild* respectively, according to whether they were ecclesiastical or lay princes. And they were entitled to demand military service from their vassals who, therefore, formed the fourth degree.[1]

The new order, of course, contained new problems. Any feudal monarchy was a precarious balance between the rights of the king and the rights of the tenants-in-chief. It lay in the nature of this

[1] H. Mitteis, *Der Staat des hohen Mittelalters*, Weimar, 1948, pp. 301–2; *Lehnrecht und Staatsgewalt*, Weimar, 1958, pp. 437 ff.

balance that king and tenants-in-chief would seek to upset it in their own favour. The king would be tempted to make kingship hereditary in his family, to seek ways and means of gaining control and influence over his so-called sub-vassals and to reserve the right to dispose of the fiefs of the tenants-in-chief in the case of the death of a tenant or, at least, in the case of a vacancy through the demise of a family. The tenants-in-chief, on the other hand, would try to usurp more power over their own vassals, to treat their fiefs like their property and to reduce the homage they owed the king to a formality. A king like Frederick, who had neither a permanent capital nor established offices of government and administration, nor a trained personnel, could not hope to upset the balance in his favour to any great extent. When Henry was disposed of and his fiefs were forfeit, Frederick, in theory, might have kept them in his own hands and turned them into a royal domain, to be administered directly by royal officials. If he had taken such a step, his power would have increased considerably. As it was, he had no men to whom he could have entrusted the administration of such a large domain and no offices from which it could be supervised.[1] Therefore he had no choice but to part with these lands by investing princes with them.[2] The fact that there had been a definition

[1] Th. Mayer agrees that Frederick had no administrative machinery at his disposal. So does H. Heimpel, *Kaiser Friedrich Barbarossa und die Wende der staufischen Zeit*, Strassburg, 1942. W. Kienast believes that Frederick had all the necessary machinery, see his review of Heimpel, HZ, 167, 1943, p. 404. K. Bosl, *Die Reichsministerialitat der Salier und Staufer*, Stuttgart, 1950, p. 167, also thinks that Frederick could not have kept the lands of Henry, even if he had wanted to.

[2] Theoretically the grant was of 'royal grace', but at the same time *ex sententia principum. Cp.* H. Mitteis, ZSSRGger, 59, p. 405. H. Mitteis is therefore of the opinion that there was a law which compelled Frederick to hand out these lands and reinvest other princes with them, i.e. that there was *Leihezwang*. Mitteis seems to be of the opinion that if Frederick had wanted to, he could have taken over Saxony as easily as Philip Augustus took over Normandy. Whether Frederick was legally entitled to do this or not, he had no administrative machinery to do so. Mitteis points out that since there were no tribal duchies left in 1180, the old legal principle that a king could not be a tribal duke (because this would have impaired the super-tribal character of kingship) was no longer valid. Therefore, when Frederick handed out the lands of Henry, he must have been guided by a new legal principle, i.e. by *Leihezwang*. It does not seem to have occurred to Mitteis that Frederick might have been guided by considerations other than legal ones, i.e. by political necessity. *See* also H. Mitteis, *Politische Prozesse des früheren Mittelalters*, SHA, 1926–7, 3, pp. 116 ff. Mitteis was much criticized. *See* e.g. W. Kienast, HZ, 167, 1943, p. 404 and 158, 1938, p. 14. W. Goez, *Der Leihezwang*, Tübingen, 1962, explains that *Leihezwang* was not an established custom and that Frederick granted away the lands of Henry for political reasons. Eventually Mitteis

of the new type of imperial prince, coupled to the absence of anything approaching even remotely a formal capital and a formal household with appointed officials, encouraged these new princes to treat their fiefs as real territories. Frederick's feudalism became, therefore, unwittingly the constitutional foundation of the new territorial unit which developed within the German monarchy.[1] But all these problems were in their infancy in the early 1180s. Frederick, for the time being, could afford to shelve them and hope that one of his successors would deal with them.[2] As far as he was concerned, he had every reason to be satisfied, for with the fall of Henry the Lion a general pacification of Germany and a political equilibrium became possible.

---

himself admitted, DA, 8, 1950, p. 327, that *Leihezwang* resulted as a natural development of German feudal custom which tended to favour vassals. – From the point of view of the present argument, the controversy as to whether there was or was not *Leihezwang* in 1180 is largely academic. Frederick, in the absence of a suitable administrative machinery, had to grant away the lands of Henry, whether there existed a law to this effect or not. Goez points out rightly that when the Gelnhausen Charter was issued, Henry was still in possession of his duchy. Frederick's problem, therefore, was to find ways of making sure that he would be deprived and the sentence enforced (pp. 230–1). Hence Frederick gave the fiefs away, i.e., he promised them to other princes provided they would go and get them and it is natural that the princes, when they promised to undertake a campaign against Henry, wanted their profits guaranteed in advance. Hence they insisted that Frederick hand out the fiefs. He complied not because he felt legally obliged to do so but because he considered it politically expedient. Frederick handed the fiefs out not because of a legal principle, which may or may not have existed at that time. H. Mitteis, ZSSRGger, 59, p. 404, admits that the Gelnhausen Charter does not mention the legal obligation but believes that the omission was due to the chancellor's desire to give the impression that Frederick, in handing out the fiefs, was acting from free will. On p. 405, Mitteis goes so far as to claim that if there was no legal obligation for Frederick to hand out the fiefs, Frederick made a 'mistake' in handing them out; and since Frederick was unlikely to have made a mistake, he presumes that he *was* under a legal obligation. He cannot entertain the possibility that at times Frederick was guided by politics and expediency rather than by legal precepts.

[1] H. Mitteis, *Zur staufischen Verfassungsgeschichte*, ZSSRGger, 65, 1947, p. 337.

[2] There is one well known case which shows that the problems raised by Frederick's third plan were by no means in the distant future. Philip von Heinsberg, who had succeeded Rainald as archbishop of Cologne, began to avail himself of his enlarged power and of his pre-eminence as the bishop of Germany's largest and most flourishing city. In the middle 80s he defied Frederick and entered into alliances with Pope Urban III and the king of France, alliances which were designed to challenge Frederick. Philip did not make his final submission until March 1188, just prior to Frederick's departure for the Holy Land. The ease with which one of the foremost of the new imperial princes managed to defy Frederick ought to have been a warning. *Cp.* W. Neuss and F. W. Oediger, *Das Bistum Köln von den Anfängen bis zum Ende des 12. Jahrhunderts*, Köln, 1964, pp. 230–40.

The pronunciation of a sentence against Henry in Würzburg and the formal proclamation of that sentence at Gelnhausen in April 1180 had not only given a legal sanction to his old enemies but also encouraged other princes to join forces with them. And thus it was decreed that on 25 July an imperial campaign was to be launched. Frederick led an army into Saxony and by the end of the year the whole of southern Saxony had been wrested from Henry. In the summer of 1181 Frederick advanced into the northern parts and into the colonial lands beyond the Elbe, where Henry's power had remained strongest. But here too, Henry could not withstand the concerted efforts of an imperial army, and when Frederick laid siege to Lübeck the citizens, despairing of Henry's power to help them, had to submit. Through a sentence pronounced in Erfurt in November, where he appeared and threw himself at Frederick's feet, Henry was exiled for three years and permitted to retain only certain of his hereditary estates situated around Braunschweig and Lüneburg. At the end of the three years he was not to return to Germany without the emperor's express permission. The whole edifice of Henry's magnificent power and achievements, his 'state', had collapsed like a house of cards. The comparative speed with which the imperial campaign against him was brought to a conclusion shows, of course, how strong the feeling against Henry had become and underlines once more the extent to which Frederick, in his third plan, was swimming with the tide.[1]

[1] *Cp.* A. K. Hömberg, *Westfalen und das sächsische Herzogtum*, Münster, 1963, p. 51, for the ease with which Frederick achieved his military victory over Henry in 1182. The princes who had joined the first campaign were all immediate beneficiaries of the fall of Henry. *Cp.* W. Goez, *Der Leihezwang*, Tübingen, 1962, p. 232. A precise list is to be found in G. Gattermann, *Die deutschen Fürsten auf der Reichsheerfahrt*, typewritten diss., Frankfurt, 1956, Vol. 1, p. 106. It is significant that with very few exceptions, the southern princes did not join. In some cases it had not been left to chance that Henry's enemies were ready to gang up against him in 1180. Consider, for instance, the case of the bishopric of Bremen. After the death of Bishop Baldwin in June 1178, the electors in Bremen had rushed to choose one Berthold. They wanted to act before Henry had a chance to interfere and had wanted to prevent the succession of too open an enemy of Henry, lest there would be fighting. But Henry's enemies would not accept Berthold. They claimed that the election was irregular because there had been, ever since 1168, an *electus* in the person of Siegfried von Brandenburg, a member of the Askanier family. It was true that at the time of the election, Berthold had only been an acolyte. Now he managed to obtain a papal dispensation and was made a sub-deacon. In his capacity of sub-deacon he was elected once more and the more intransigent of Henry's enemies

Nothing can illustrate the progress of formal feudalism and the growing suffusion of German life with courtly culture better than the great festival which took place in Mainz at Pentecost 1184, for the knighting of Frederick's two sons, Henry and Frederick. To do justice to this splendid occasion, a festival city was erected outside the city on the other bank of the Rhine. Frederick had a wooden palace built, complete with church and houses for the accommodation of his guests. There were so many that innumerable tents sprang up around the buildings, as well as special storehouses to contain the food and wine which was being brought from the surrounding countryside. Invitations had been issued to the spiritual and lay princes of the whole empire and the leading citizens of the towns of Lombardy. The guests came in great numbers from every corner of Germany, Italy and Burgundy, and they all brought with them a large following dressed in beautiful garments, their servants in liveries and their horses bedecked with decorative colours. Last, but not least, the festival had attracted not only the ordinary jugglers and entertainers and singers, but such poets as Guiot of Provins, Doetes of Troyes and Henry von Veldeke, who made their first public appearance on German soil and thus introduced their new literary style to this exalted audience.

On Sunday, 20 May, Frederick and Beatrix and their son

---

were prevented by a show of violence from interfering. Finally, Frederick gave Berthold the *regalia*. But at the Lateran Council in 1179 the whole matter was brought before Alexander III who declared Berthold's election invalid on technical grounds. By this time, Frederick was anxious to prepare the ground for his attack on Henry: the first election was set aside because as an acolyte, Berthold might have been married, and the second election was declared invalid because Berthold had obtained the *regalia* before his consecration. *Cp.* J. Harttung, *Der Erzstift Bremen und Heinrich der Löwe*, HZ, 34, 1875, pp. 348–51. Thus the road was cleared for the installation of Siegfried in Bremen, an important step for the advancement of the Askanier at the expense of Henry. Frederick by this time was swimming with the tide by using papal influence and canonical arguments of the strictest persuasion in order to support the ambitions of the princes who were opposed to Henry. For other examples of the painstaking care Frederick took to detach some of Henry's closest followers from him see Giesebrecht, V, pp. 906, 912, 926–7, 930. Frederick had no easy task. But the tide was with him. How much, is proved by the fact that when he finally succeeded in marshalling a real phalanx against Henry, he had even succeeded in cutting across Henry's family ties: practically all the princes who had passed judgement on Henry must have been related to him or allied to him by marriage. *Cp.* Lerche, *Die Eheverbindungen des Welfischen Hauses*, p. 80.

Henry wore their crowns in a festive procession and, in the evening of that same day, at a banquet, dukes and margraves, all members of the new class of princes, acted as cup-bearers, marshals and chamberlains. On the next day, after early morning mass, Frederick's two sons received their swords and took the oath of knighthood. For the main political object of the celebrations was to prepare the ground for their succession. Henry from now on became a real co-regent and Frederick was made, officially, duke of Swabia. There were rich presents to reward wandering knights and singers.[1] Then there was another banquet and finally a great tournament in which Frederick himself took part; and on the following day, more banquets and tournaments. The gaiety of that Tuesday, however, was marred by a sudden storm which destroyed the wooden church and several other buildings, killing fifteen people. It seems that under the impact of this disaster the original plan for further tournaments in the following weeks was abandoned, for on the Wednesday after Pentecost the princes began to depart.[2]

[1] One should note the contrast between Frederick's feudal monarchy and the feuda monarchy in England. The king of England expected defined aids, on such an occasion, from his barons. But there seem to have been no such aids for Frederick. The presents were given, according to Gislebert, MGH, SS, XXI, p. 539, *militibus, captivis et cruce signatis*.

[2] The splendour of the festival was described by several poets:

Dem Kaiser Friedrich
Geschah soviel Ehr'
Dass man immer mehr
Wunders davon sagen mag
Bis an den jüngsten Tag
Ohne Lügen, ja fürwahr
Es wird noch über hundert Jahr
Von ihm gesaget und geschrieben.

Henry von Veldeke, *Eneid*, 13222–52.

. . . cum de toto simul orbe vocatos
Quanta nec ante fuit nec creditur esse futura
Mogontina suos aspexit curia patres.

Ligurinus, 353–5.

Mar lor membre du Roi Artu,
D'Alixandre et de Juliu,
Et des autres Princes vaillanz
Qiu jà tindrent les Corz si granz.
Quel cort tint ore Asuérus!
Ele dura cent jorz et plus;

In order to understand the pursuit of Frederick's third, feudal monarchy plan in Italy from 1183 onwards, where conditions were so different from those in Germany, we must now consider his Italian policies. For the new German order could not possibly be simply extended to Italy with its cities and the papacy. In Italy, the concept of feudal suzerainty had to be adapted to local conditions. As always, Frederick proved himself inventive and adroit in the adaptation of his general plan.

The year before the festival of Mainz the six years' truce with Lombardy had come to an end and been replaced by a negotiated peace, concluded and sworn to in Constance. The final settlement of Constance had been preceded by careful negotiations[1] and in the end it was agreed by both sides that the Lombards would recognize in theory Frederick's full imperial suzerainty. In return, Frederick abandoned his claim to the *regalia* and agreed to the continued existence of the league. These two provisions between them were to annul in practice what the Lombards had conceded in theory. Their recognition of Frederick's imperial suzerainty implied in theory that the consuls would have to be invested, if not elected, by him; that in matters of justice there was to be an appeal to an imperial court; that the *fodrum* was to be paid when demanded, and that the consuls were to take periodic oaths of fealty. But Frederick's surrender of the *regalia* and his official recognition of the league[2] with all its oaths and provisions for self-government, amounted to nothing less than a declaration that he would not insist on any of these implications in practice. In order to adapt his conception of feudal monarchy to the conditions of Lombardy, Frederick was merely

---

Et de l'Emperéor Ferri
Vos puis bien dire que je vi
Qu'il tint une Cort à Maience;
Ice vos di-je sanz doutance,
C'onques sa pareille ne fu.

Guiot de Provins, *Bible*, 272–81.

[1] We know of these protracted negotiations from a document, the so-called *Petitio Imperatoris a Rectoribus Castigata*, MGH, Const. I, No. 288, pp. 396–9.

[2] The Peace of Constance was written into the constitution of the league and became part of its fundamental law. *See* H. Kauffmann, *Die italienische Politik Kaiser Friedrichs I nach dem Frieden von Constanz*, Greifswald, 1933, p. 16.

anxious to be recognized as suzerain in principle.[1] The ultimate formula agreed to at Constance can, therefore, be summed up as follows: the recognition of Frederick's imperial lordship, without the implementation of any rights which follow from such a lordship, equals a feudal relationship; or, better, equals a relationship which was the Italian equivalent of the German feudalism of the third plan. The recognition without the execution equals a feudal relationship, because it substitutes, at least in practice, the principle of mutual obligation for imperial lordship. In this way Frederick had managed to turn the indefinite arrangements with the Lombards at the Peace of Venice, into a positive programme. The loyalty of the Lombard cities was won by Frederick's well considered renunciation of any interference with their special interests.

The Peace of Constance was eminently satisfactory to both sides. Early in 1186 Frederick participated personally in an official meeting of the rectors of the league[2] and later that year he concluded a special treaty with Milan, one of the chief provisions of which was that Milan, and, by implication, the other members of the league were to assist Frederick in vindicating his claims to the Matildan lands.[3]

If Frederick had been able to turn the provisional truce with the Lombards into a substantial agreement based on a quasi-feudal relationship and use it to vindicate his claims to the Matildan

[1] W. Lenel, *Der Konstanzer Friede von 1183 und die italienische Politik Friedrichs I*, HZ, 128, 1923, p. 200. J. Ficker, *Zur Geschichte des Lombardenbundes*, SWA, 60, 1868, p. 334, had been anxious to show that Frederick had been able to modify the final text in his favour. But Ficker's desire to rehabilitate Frederick and to show that his Italian policy was ultimately successful, or more successful than his nineteenth century detractors had been willing to grant, deflected, in the end, attention from Frederick's real achievement, which consisted in the adaptation of his relations with the Italian cities to the feudal pattern which was working itself out in Germany. – In FRRGI, II, p. 193, par. 299, Ficker himself admits that, for instance, the provision that there was to be a yearly investiture was never carried out, and that in practice the relationship between emperor and the cities was thus ordered in terms of feudal conceptions. – *Cp.* H. Mitteis, *Der Staat des hohen Mittelalters*, Weimar, 1948, p. 321: the essence of the Peace of Constance was that the cities were placed like major vassals. Unfortunately, Mitteis considers this a dangerous relapse into apparently out-dated feudal thinking. Far from being a relapse, it was the application to Lombardy of the constructive thinking of the third plan.

[2] H. Kauffmann, *op. cit.*, p. 47.

[3] H. Kauffmann, *op. cit.*, p. 53, calls this treaty rightly an appendix to the Peace of Constance.

lands, it was not equally easy to persuade the pope to accept Frederick's claims to these lands or to various other central Italian territories. The Treaty of Venice had been as indeterminate on this question as the truce with the Lombards had been provisional. But Frederick had shrewdly reckoned with two factors. First, there was no doubt that he was the *de facto* owner of the Matildan lands;[1] and secondly, Pope Alexander was completely dependent on Frederick's military support, which alone had enabled him, after the congress of Venice, to return to Rome. In fact, when Frederick left Venice, Alexander had been led back to Rome by Christian of Mainz who from then on had become his special military protector.[2] It was under Christian's protection that Alexander was able, in 1179, to hold the Lateran Council,[3] and for several years to follow he remained dependent on Christian. When owing to local intrigues Christian was captured and held captive for a long time,[4] Alexander had to leave Rome once again and died, in exile, in August 1181. His successor Lucius III, also relied on Christian who, fortunately for the papacy, had eventually regained his liberty. And after Christian's death in August 1183, Pope Lucius begged Frederick to send another imperial legate to protect him.[5]

[1] *See* p. 328 above.

[2] J. Ficker, FRRGI, II, par. 337. *See* also S. Löwenfeld, *Die unmittelbaren Folgen des Friedens von Venedig*, FDG, 25, 1885.

[3] W. Lenel, *op. cit.*, pp. 209, 245.

[4] J. Ficker, FRRGI, II, p. 216, par. 306. Christian, it seems, had made himself widely unpopular in central Italy. In 1172, when Christian had been supposed to act as arbitrator in Tuscany between warring parties, the Annals of Pisa report that *multa mala Tuscis intulit*, MGH, SS, XIX, p. 265 and Davidson in his *History of Florence* thinks that Christian's behaviour was, to say the least, ambiguous, for he was intent on procuring enough money for his own very luxurious standard of living. He was unpopular enough for Frederick to find it impossible to hold the peace conference in 1177 in the region in which Christian held sway (*see* p. 325 note 2, above) and we know of his worldly appearance from the chronicler Albert of Stade who describes him on horseback, a hyacinth coloured tunic over his armour and a gilded helmet on his head. His donkeys alone were reputed to have cost more than the emperor's whole outfit, MGH, SS, XVI, p. 347. When reading the *Annales Stadenses* for the years 1172–5, it is not difficult to understand that he had enough personal enemies in this region to have finally brought about his captivity. But C. Varrentrapp, *Erzbischof Christian I von Mainz* 1867, pp. 94–5, is of the opinion that the real instigator of the conspiracy to which Christian fell victim was the Greek emperor. It was he who had assisted the personal enemies of Christian, of whom there were legion, with money in order to sabotage the consolidation of Frederick's power in central Italy after the Peace of Venice.

[5] J. Ficker, FRRGI, II, p. 143, par. 279; P. Scheffer-Boichorst, *Kaiser Friedrichs I letzter Streit mit der Kurie*, Berlin, 1866, p. 46, notes 2 and 3.

Given the fact that the papacy was so dependent on his military protection, Frederick calculated that he would sooner or later be able to come to a satisfactory agreement with the pope about the Matildan lands. If he was such a faithful *Vogt* of the church of Rome and its pastor, he had every reason to believe that the pope could be persuaded to let him have these lands. And indeed, no sooner had Frederick brought the campaign against Henry the Lion to a happy conclusion than, in the spring of 1182, he sent a message to the pope in which he suggested how the question could be settled. He proposed that he should be left in possession of the lands, and that he would pay compensation to the pope to the tune of a tenth of all revenues and of a ninth, to the cardinals.[1] This, in view of the circumstances, was an eminently reasonable proposal – for the pope was dependent on Frederick for his position in Rome, whereas he had no means of forcing Frederick to abandon the Matildan lands. This suggestion was contained in a message carried to Lucius by Archbishop Conrad of Salzburg, the same Conrad von Wittelsbach who, as a supporter of Alexander, had been ejected from the see of Mainz and who after the Peace of Venice, had been given the see of Salzburg. Conrad was, therefore, a man whom the *curia* had every reason to trust and the fact that on this occasion he was chosen as ambassador proves that Frederick believed quite sincerely that his suggestion ought to be acceptable to the pope. Conrad met Lucius in Velletri in May and returned to Germany in June. The negotiations dragged on.[2] In June 1183 the pope sent two cardinals

[1] Our knowledge of these proposals and of the course of the negotiations about the Matildan lands until the time of the congress of Verona is derived from a letter by Frederick to the pope written in the summer of 1183, MGH, Const. I, p. 420, No. 296. Scheffer-Boichorst, *op. cit.*, pp. 23 ff., and Lenel, *op. cit.*, pp. 210 ff., differ considerably in the information they cull from this document. In my view, these differences are fairly irrelevant to the course of events as presented by me. The one thing that is clear from the document is that negotiations took place and did not reach a satisfactory conclusion.

[2] Scheffer-Boichorst, *op. cit.*, p. 28, says that Lucius rejected Frederick's proposals. There seems to be no evidence for this opinion. Scheffer-Boichorst simply inferred that Lucius rejected Frederick's proposals because it suited his theory of a growing estrangement between Lucius and Frederick. But as this theory is, at least partly, based upon the inference that Lucius became hostile to Frederick, Scheffer-Boichorst is obviously here arguing in a circle. Giesebrecht, VI, p. 6, is a little more cautious than Scheffer-Boichorst, but follows him. J. Haller, *Heinrich VI und die römische Kirche*,

to negotiate with Frederick at the court of Constance, at which the peace with the Lombards was being concluded. On this occasion, Frederick appears to have made even further concessions. He was now prepared to cede to the papacy certain parts, and suggested that an arbitration committee be set up to decide what should be left to the church and what should be left to the empire.[1] When it emerged that the question of the details was a thorny one it was finally agreed that a congress should be held in the following year in the vicinity of Lake Garda.[2]

Unfortunately for Frederick, the position of strength from which he negotiated began to crumble in that same summer of 1183. Christian of Mainz died in August, and with his death imperial power in central Italy suffered a sudden, albeit temporary eclipse.[3] The restoration of the patrimony of St Peter which had been one of the results of the Peace of Venice, was undone. Lucius had to flee to Verona, where it had been agreed the congress should be held. He arrived as a refugee, begging for help.[4]

With Lucius in dire straits, Frederick could no longer be quite so confident of persuading the pope to agree to his suggestions. Frederick still held the Matildan lands; but Lucius must have

---

MIOG, 34, 1914, p. 394, note 1, points out that Scheffer-Boichorst's statement that Lucius rejected the proposals is pure conjecture.

[1] The exact nature of the various proposals, whether they were supposed to be supplementary to one another or alternatives, is unfortunately not clear, *See* W. Lenel, *op. cit.*, p. 210 and Scheffer-Boichorst, *op. cit.*, p. 29.

[2] Scheffer-Boichorst, *op. cit.*, p. 30.

[3] It is Lenel's great merit to have understood clearly that Christian's death jeopardized imperial policy by causing an eclipse of imperial power and protection for the pope in Rome. *See op. cit.*, p. 232. Scheffer-Boichorst was completely oblivious to this. His view that Christian's career ended in a triumph of imperial power was first expressed in *op. cit.*, p. 4, repeated more elaborately in his review of Varrentrapp's *Erzbischof Christian I von Mainz*, in GGA, 1867, pp. 2011 ff., and in his *Gesammelte Schriften*, EHS, 43, 1905, 277 ff., and has been accepted without much criticism by HB, p. 213 (Hampe adds though that with Christian's death, imperial power suffered a minor decline) and by J. Haller, *op. cit.*, p. 389. Lenel shows that Scheffer-Boichorst's view was based on a fairly arbitrary interpretation of notices in two German sources, the *Translatio S. Annonis* and the *Annales Reinhardsbrunnenses*. He adds that if these sources are considered in conjunction with Italian sources, one must come to the conclusion that imperial power in central Italy was re-established only after 1185. As my own interpretation of the congress of Verona depends on this temporary eclipse of imperial power in central Italy, Lenel's analysis of the state of affairs at Christian's death is of the greatest importance.

[4] Scheffer-Boichorst, *op. cit.*, pp. 45–6.

been very conscious of the fact that at this particular juncture it looked as if he owed very little to Frederick. It is hardly surprising therefore to find that at the congress of Verona in 1184 the negotiations about the Matildan lands were once more inconclusive.[1] They were inconclusive not because a new quarrel between empire and papacy was brewing up[2] but because Frederick was at this moment no longer in a position to parade as the protector of the papacy. Given Frederick's impotence, it is understandable that even so friendly a man as Lucius should have hesitated before signing away papal rights in perpetuity, when it was so doubtful whether he would get anything substantial in return.

At this critical moment, when the whole future of the relations between emperor and pope were once more in doubt because of the military eclipse Frederick had suffered in central Italy, Lucius rose to the occasion. As bishop of Ostia and as cardinal he had had a long attachment to both Hadrian and Alexander. He was widely respected and a man of undoubted probity.[3] He had been one of the negotiators of the Treaty of Benevento in 1156 and, although he had been faithful to Alexander throughout the schism, he had, ever since the early 1170s, been in favour of a peaceful understanding with Frederick.[4] He now considered that he ought to help Frederick to regain his hold in central Italy lest he,

[1] Scheffer-Boichorst, *op. cit.*, p. 61, believed that the congress of Verona ended in open disagreement about the Matildan lands. He was led to this conclusion by his belief that Lucius had become hostile to Frederick. But the truth of the matter is that there was no disagreement, at least not about the Matildan lands, merely a failure to agree. The matter was not settled in Verona, and negotiations were continued. *See* Haller, *op. cit.*, p. 399; Kauffmann, *op. cit.*, p. 34; Lenel, *op. cit.*, p. 248. As far as the Matildan lands were concerned, the Congress was neither a success nor a failure, but simply inconclusive.

[2] Scheffer-Boichorst, *op. cit.*, p. 62, argued that Lucius became hostile to Frederick because at the congress of Verona he had learnt that Frederick had made a marriage alliance between his son Henry and Constance, the aunt of the king of Sicily. He considered this an attempt at encirclement of the papacy and resented that this had been done behind his back. Haller, *op. cit.*, pp. 414 ff., has shown that these negotiations had not only not been carried on behind his back, but had been started by Lucius himself. Haller's theory is startling, but although other historians have been a little reluctant in accepting it, they have all been forced to admit that it is irrefutable. *Cp.* the review of Haller by A. Hofmeister, HZ, 115, 1916, p. 204, and Lenel, *op. cit.*, p. 248.

[3] Haller, III, p. 252.

[4] K. Wenck, *Die römischen Päpste zwischen Alexander III und Innocent III*, in: Kehr Festschrift, 1926, p. 421, maintains very implausibly that since Lucius was the author

Lucius, should remain a permanent exile from Rome. Lucius had fully understood Frederick's change of plan. He knew that Frederick was becoming a feudal monarch in Germany as well as in Lombardy and that he was willing to protect the papacy against the unruly citizens of Rome. He knew that this new plan included permanent peace with the kingdom of Sicily, and he believed that the best hope for the papacy was to co-operate. When he discovered that through the death of Christian the new plan was in danger of being upset, he decided to take an active step towards consolidating it. He suggested to the king of Sicily, William II, that his aunt Constance be married to Frederick's son Henry.[1] Through Lucius's intervention negotiations were opened, perhaps already in 1183, and were near conclusion when Lucius was on his way to Verona in 1184.[2] And in August 1184, at Augsburg, the betrothal of Henry was officially announced.

This was a triumph for Lucius's statesmanship. The marriage alliance between Henry and Constance gave a new reality to the Peace of Venice and cemented the bonds between emperor, pope and king of Sicily, upon which that peace had been based. If the

---

(sic!) of the Treaty of Benevento, he could not have changed his mind since 1156 and therefore was hostile to Frederick. Oddly enough, on p. 424 Wenck says that it was natural that Lucius, whose policy in 1156 had led to warfare between empire and papacy, should wish, towards the end of his life, to establish permanent peace between empire and papacy. This would indicate that Wenck believes after all that Lucius changed his mind in the course of his long life.

[1] I follow Haller in believing that the marriage was first negotiated by Lucius. The only strong reservation to Haller's story must be in respect to his argument that when the marriage was first negotiated, there could be no possible thought that it might lead to Henry's and Constance's succession to the kingdom of Sicily. For Haller, p. 430, believes, that at that time nobody could imagine that King William would die without heirs of his own. Hence, Haller thinks, the marriage was a mere political alliance and was not concluded in the hope that Henry or his son would inherit the kingdom of Sicily. Haller's belief that William was *not* impotent is based on a curious argument. On p. 421 Haller says that contemporaries did not consider William to be physically weak, and that one chronicler even called him a hard tyrant. *Pace* Haller, it is well known that sexual impotence has nothing to do with physical weakness; and that there are many cases of men trying to overcompensate sexual impotence by aggressive and brutal behaviour. However this may be, given the uncertainty of health and life in the middle ages, every reasonable person must at that time have known that the marriage alliance could very easily lead to succession. This does not prove that the alliance was forged in order to allow Henry and Constance to succeed; but it does show that Haller must be wrong in insisting that the possibility of succession was not in Frederick's and Lucius's mind.

[2] Haller, *Heinrich VI und die römische Kirche*, MIOG, 35, 1914, p. 414.

military ascendancy of Frederick in central Italy had suffered a temporary eclipse and had allowed the Roman citizens to eject Lucius from his see, with the help of the new alliance between emperor and Sicily the pope would soon be restored to Rome. By comparison, it was a matter of small consequence that Lucius and Frederick failed, at Verona, to agree upon the detailed arrangements for the future of the Matildan lands. As long as the main outlines of the Peace of Venice remained secure – and Lucius's intervention had assured this – everything else could be left pending.

Lucius, unfortunately, did not live to witness the complete triumph of his policy.[1] But in spite of his death and in spite of Frederick's purely personal quarrel with his successor, Urban III, the consummation of this policy was celebrated in January with a festive wedding in Milan. A large number of magnates were invited. They came from Lombardy, from Burgundy and from Sicily. In the park which lay between the Porta Romana and the Porta Tosa a large wooden assembly hall had been erected. The church of St Ambrose, the oldest and principal church of the city which had luckily survived the destruction of 1162, was splendidly decorated. The grille which usually protected the golden altar had been opened, and there, on 27 January, the marriage was solemnized. The wedding was followed by a festival crown wearing, at which the archbishop of Vienne placed the crown on Frederick's head, the patriarch of Aquileia placed the crown on Henry's head, and Archbishop Conrad of Mainz[2] placed the crown on the head of the new queen. Thus the clergy of Italy, Burgundy and Germany were united in this act.[3] The festivities ended with

[1] Lucius unfortunately died in Verona soon after the congress of Verona in November 1185. He was succeeded by Urban III (1185–1187) a Milanese who harboured a personal grudge against Frederick, probaby on account of the sufferings inflicted on his native city and family by Frederick in the 60s. Wherever he could, he tried to cross Frederick's policies but died without having been able to cause a serious permanent conflict.

[2] Conrad von Wittelsbach, formerly archbishop of Salzburg. At the death of Christian, Conrad had returned to his original see of Mainz. Giesebrecht, VI, p. 122, presumes that it was he who crowned Constance.

[3] There was one shadow upon the festivities. Archbishop Humbert of Milan, later Pope Urban III, ought to have crowned Henry king of Italy. But in view of his personal hatred of Frederick and the empire (note 1, above) he refused to act.

a sumptuous banquet in the wooden hall. Whatever difficulties there remained, Frederick's triumph was complete.[1]

[1] During the 80s, when Frederick was at the height of his success there appeared two new historians. The so-called Ligurinus produced a work in verse which took all its information from the *Gesta*. He wrote in order to stimulate patriotic enthusiasm for Frederick and true to his statement in the prologue that he wanted to sing the emperor's praises rather than stick to the truth, he began his fifth book with the announcement that Frederick's return from the coronation was a triumph. W. Stach, *Politische Dichtung im Zeitalter Friedrichs I.*, NJDW, XIII, 1937, takes this work as proof of the emergence of an aggressive national party who were impatient of the sober and legalistic spirit in which the *Gesta* had been written. There is no doubt that the author wielded a more fiery pen than either Otto of Freising or Rahewin and one might perhaps agree with K. Langosch, *Politische Dichtung um Friedrich Barbarossa*, 1943, p. 55, that the work betrays a more purely German point of view than the *Gesta*. Its author certainly shows more open hostility to the papacy than the *Gesta*. But the details of Stach's argument that the Ligurinus portrayed Frederick as a lusty power politician in order to obliterate the more sober picture given in the *Gesta* appear, on examination, to be very far-fetched. The other great works about Frederick written in the 80s are the *Gesta Frederici* and the *Speculum Regum*, both by Godfrey of Viterbo. They show a more Italian orientation and present Frederick very much as the happy and triumphant emperor of the 80s. In the latter work, Godfrey hopes to promote the cause of unity and the future reign of Frederick's son Henry by the argument that Romans and Germans are all descended from Troy and are, therefore, appropriately joined in the Roman Empire.

CHAPTER IX

. . . Towards Jerusalem

'Quid dormis? vigila.'[1]

During the second half of the twelfth century, ever since the failure of the second crusade, the position of the kingdom of Jerusalem had deteriorated gradually and steadily. The failure of the second crusade (1147) had been widely lamented and kings and popes were vaguely aware of the necessity of a new crusade – or at least of the necessity of a concerted effort to support the precarious military position of the kingdom of Jerusalem. The matter was frequently talked about, but as long as there was no actual crisis, matters had been allowed to drift. Merchants and pilgrims who had first hand knowledge of the Holy Land had been impressed by the general wealth and luxury prevailing in the east which by far surpassed anything that could be seen at home. They were not the men to be able to form a precise estimate of the threatening nature of Saladin's power and of his ability to unite a massive Moslem force under the common banner of a holy war. His victory over the Christian army at Hattin on 5 July 1187, which led to the rapid surrender of Accon and Ascalon and the conquest of Jerusalem on October 3, proved a shock to Latin Christendom. The news of the disaster at Hattin

[1] 'Why are you asleep? Awake!' Opening line of the so-called *Carmen Sangalliense*, written in 1187 under the immediate impact of the news of the battle of Hattin. *Cp.* Hagemeyer, *Archives de l'orient latin*, I, Paris, 1881, pp. 580 ff. The same chord is struck in the appeal for a crusade in the *Carmina Burana*, 49:

> Tonat evangelica clara vox in mundo:'
> qui dormis in pulvere, surge de profundo!
> luce sua Dominis te illuminabit
> et a malis omnibus animam salvabit.

The appeal here is based on the old argument of St Bernard: to take the cross is to do penance. During the preparation of the third crusade, the accent had to be shifted to less devotional levels.

was said to have been the last blow which killed the ailing Pope Urban III, and his successor, Gregory VIII, who received the news of the fall of Jerusalem in Ferrara in the middle of November, hastened to make the most of this shock in order to stir the kings of Christendom into action.[1] He despatched William, the archbishop of Tyre, to the kings of France and England and Cardinal Henry of Albano to Germany, in order to persuade Philip Augustus, Henry II and Frederick to take the cross and reconquer Jerusalem. Although there was also, at that time, a certain amount of popular enthusiasm for a crusade,[2] the rulers took care not to encourage it, for past experience had taught the futility of vast popular expeditions, badly armed and insufficiently provisioned. If the kingdom of Jerusalem was to be restored, a well ordered military campaign was required, and such a campaign would have to be led by kings and planned as a military enterprise. Another outburst of popular religious zeal would never achieve the necessary goal.

Constantly aware of the plight of the kingdom of Jerusalem, the idea of a crusade had never been far from Frederick's mind. In 1165, when Rainald enlisted the help of Henry II of England against Pope Alexander,[3] Frederick and Henry II had promised each other, in the event of a successful termination of their respective quarrels with the pope and the archbishop of Canterbury, to launch a crusade. And again, in 1184, at the time of the congress of Verona,[4] Frederick and Pope Lucius III had discussed the

[1] 'Given human weakness', Pope Gregory VIII who had succeeded Urban III, wrote to Frederick, 'there is nothing to be expected in the cause of the Holy Land, unless the powerful princes can be enflamed with holy spirit . . .', JL, 10008.

[2] There were, for instance, the usual popular excesses against Jews, so that Frederick decreed that violence against Jews would be punished by the loss of a hand and the bishops threatened excommunication and declared that people who had been guilty of attacks on Jews could not gain remission of sins by a crusade. *See* Giesebrecht, VI, 185. The Jews were warmly appreciative, *ibid.*, p. 678. The crusading songs of the *Carmina Burana* reflect a more edifying aspect of popular devotion and enthusiasm: they were informed by the desire for repentance. Another curious feature of the popular interest in the fate of Jerusalem is the diffusion of pictures for propaganda purposes. Conrad of Montferrat, the governor of Tyre, sent a painting to Europe which depicted an Arab horse defecating in the temple of Jerusalem. *Cp.* Bohadin, *Vita Saladini*, tr. Schultens, p. 135. Another picture of this type is mentioned by Ibn Alatsyr. It shows Christ being cruelly beaten by Arabs. *Cp.* Reinaud, *Extraits des historiens Arabes*, 497.

[3] *See* p. 239 above.

[4] *See* p. 365 above.

desirability of a crusade. If these earlier projects had been somewhat vague, they were taken up more concretely at the beginning of 1188 when Frederick became acquainted with the extent of the disaster in the Holy Land.

It was, however, not only the realization that the infidels had re-conquered Jerusalem which caused the revival of these earlier projects in Frederick's mind. In the middle 80s, for the first time since his accession in 1152, he was able to survey his dominions with satisfaction. After the failure of his earlier policies, his third plan seemed successful. There had been resistance and obstacles, but none which Frederick had not been able to overcome. And by the middle of the ninth decade of the century, he could feel for the first time the taste of genuine security and success.

All through his life, Frederick had realized that the ultimate and most formidable task of the emperor of Christendom was to protect the church and defend the holy places in Palestine against the infidels. His belief in this ultimately trans-political end of empire had provided him with the detachment necessary to scrap one political plan after another and to view each of his political enterprises as a mere experiment, a means to an end. When, towards the end of 1187, he realized the extreme urgency of a new crusade, he must have considered himself fortunate that the latest experiment had succeeded sufficiently for him seriously to entertain the thought of a departure to the Holy Land. Given his age and his knowledge of the physical hardships that awaited him at the best of times, he cannot have had any great illusions as to the likelihood of returning to Europe alive. But his departure was not an afterthought indulged in when he happened to have nothing better to do. It was the crowning act of his reign, an act which he had planned all along, and for the sake of which he had undertaken experiment after experiment. And now that, finally, one of these experiments had proved comparatively successful, he was free to turn his mind to the real task that lay ahead.

The essential purpose of the imperial dignity, as distinct from royal dignity, had always been the protection of the church.[1] At

[1] *Cp.* G. Tellenbach, *Römischer und christlicher Reichsgedanke in der Liturgie des frühen Mittelalters,* SHA, 1934–5.

the beginning of his reign, Frederick had written to Pope Eugene III that he wanted to be zealous in securing to the church all the functions of her dignity,[1] and towards the end of his reign he justified his assumption of the imperial title by telling the ambassadors of the Greek Emperor Isaac that the transfer had been necessary because Greek emperors had been slack in carrying out their duty of protecting the church.[2]

Many modern historians have looked upon the empire as if it were a territorial state and a political institution and written its history as if the main task of an emperor had been to guard its frontiers, to protect its inhabitants and safeguard its power. They have been so preoccupied with the political thinking which pertains to the modern nation state and its power politics that they have distorted the 'political' thinking of the middle ages. A medieval emperor's main task was the protection of the church and of the *populus christianus*. Any other purpose he had was his in virtue of other titles and functions. This did not mean that an emperor could not have such other purposes *qua* emperor. But it meant that these other purposes were not primarily imperial ones. If an emperor or a pressure group, as they did from time to time, came forward with purely secular conceptions of imperial power, they stood out as anomalies.[3] Frederick both at the beginning of his reign and at its end was very conscious of this meaning of 'empire'. But this consciousness is by itself not enough to explain what he considered the ultimate purpose of his reign. In order to understand the purpose for the sake of which he had undertaken his political experiments, we must dig deeper and seek to understand his and his contemporaries' knowledge of history and of its meaning.

[1] MGH. Const. I, No. 137, p. 190.

[2] '. . . propter tardum et infructuosum Constantinopolitani imperatoris auxilium contra tyrannos ecclesie.' MGH, SRG, V, p. 50.

[3] One must think, e.g., of the so-called Aix-la-Chapelle group in the reign of Charlemagne, with their pronouncedly secular and utilitarian conception of empire. *Cp.* P. Munz, *The Imperial Coronation of Charlemagne*, Dunedin and Leicester, 1960, pp. 10–15, or of Widukind's idea that Otto the Great was emperor because the army made him one. Whenever such secular conceptions of empire were put forward, there was a corresponding neglect of the foremost traditional function of the emperor, i.e. a neglect of the idea that his primary duty was to protect the church. This duty was not denied, but tended to be overshadowed by more practical concerns.

In the very early middle ages, when the Teutonic tribes first invaded the Roman Empire and became converted to Christianity, they had managed to persuade themselves in the flush of their victory and their enthusiasm that they were appointed by God to accomplish all sorts of tasks which the Romans had failed to accomplish. The papacy was powerless in its attempt to hold fast to the older view that the Roman empire was continuing in spite of its temporary military eclipse in the west.[1] To historical thinkers like Alcuin,[2] Regino of Prüm and Widukind of Corvey,[3] the Teutonic kingdoms represented a new beginning with a grand future. But as the power of these original tribal kingdoms began to wane, and as the disintegration of kinship ties began to corrode the original social structure of these kingdoms, historical thinking returned to its earlier transcendental grooves and with them, to the earlier, universal Roman orientation. Minds which were spiritually sensitive turned to the monastic seclusion and withdrawal of Cluny, or to the inward forms of religious devotion taught by St Bernard of Clairvaux. But those who were spiritually less subtle and less sensitive, plunged into historical speculation for eschatological purposes and took their cue from the writings of Adso, the abbot of Montier-en-Der who, towards the end of the tenth century had composed a long treatise *De Ortu et Tempore Antichristi*. Adso did not share the optimistic outlook of Alcuin, Regino and Widukind. He based his speculations upon the idea that the Roman empire had never completely disappeared, even though at the present time it was being administered by Frankish kings. And in order to determine the future of that empire and to find out how long it would last and by what means it would come to an end, he availed himself of a vast body of earlier, late-Roman apocalyptic prophecy.[4] Drawing upon this material, he explained

[1] H. Grundmann, *Die Grundzüge der mittelalterlichen Geschichtsanschauungen*, AKG, 24, 1934, pp. 326–36.

[2] H. Löwe, *Von Theoderich dem Grossen zu Karl dem Grossen*, Darmstadt, 1956, p. 50. *Cp.* J. Adamek, *Vom römischen Endreich der mittelalterlichen Bibelerklärung*, Würzburg, 1938, p. 66; and the remarks by R. Wenskus, *Brun von Querfurt*, 1956, pp. 95–6.

[3] H. Beumann, *Widukind von Korvei*, Weimar, 1950, pp. 218–19.

[4] Most of it went back to the age of Constantine or the fourth century A.D. At that time there originated the story about the Tiburtine Sybil, a daughter of King Priam, who had been brought to Rome. On her arrival 100 senators had the same dream: they dreamt of nine suns each of which looked different. They told their dream to the

that the last and greatest of all kings would eventually journey to Jerusalem and deposit his crown and sceptre on the Mount of Olives.[1] Soon after this voluntary surrender, Adso explained, the reign of the Antichrist would begin and that reign would be brought to an end by the Second Coming and the end of all history. In Adso's mind, the Roman empire had a great eschatological significance, for as long as it lasted, the reign of the

---

Sybil who interpreted as follows: the nine suns are nine ages. In the fourth age, Christ will be born. In the ninth age (the words of the Sybil are extremely obscure) the history of the German-Italian rulers will take place. Finally, the interpretation seems to say, the world will come to an end after the ninth age. *Cp.* E. Sackur, *Sibyllinische Texte und Forschungen*, Halle, 1898, p. 129. The ninth age is characterized as completely dark, with only one ray of light. The actual names of the kings of the ninth age were added during the middle ages. Adso used one of these medieval versions. The king who rules at the end age, will be a king of the Greeks or the Romans. He will be tall and pleasing in appearance and he will reign for 112 years. During his reign there will be abundance of fruit and great wealth. He will devastate the lands of the heathen and plant the cross on their temples. All those who refuse to be converted will be killed. After 112 years even the Jews will be converted. During his reign the Antichrist will appear and 22 nations will rise. He will fight them and destroy them. Thereupon he will come to Jerusalem and divest himself of his royal vestments and of the diadem, and will surrender his rulership over Christendom to God and Jesus, E. Sackur, *op. cit.*, pp. 163–4. The emperors of the ninth age are mentioned only by their initials. Each of them will perform one of the roles pertaining to the last age of history. One of them is the emperor of peace who will defeat all enemies of Christianity, and he is the one during whose reign the Antichrist will appear and who will go to Jerusalem. *Cp.* also Adamek, *op. cit.*, pp. 64–5. – All these prophecies were inspired by the archetypal belief that one day strife will cease, harmony reign and time stop. Each writer used a slightly different technical nomenclature. They all copied from each other, but not necessarily slavishly. The archetypal belief had a continuous vogue, not because of a text which happened to be current, but because people wanted to believe and therefore clung to certain texts like the prophecy of the Tiburtine Sibyl, copied it and reinterpreted it. It is a vain and rather absurd belief sported by countless philologists, that an exact investigation of who owed what to whom will throw much light on the matter. If the text had not been known, people would have invented one. It was not because Gerhoh and Adso and others happened to know of the Tiburtine Sibyl that they believed that the end of time was near. They believed it anyway and Gerhoh explored Adso because he was preoccupied with the belief. Much ammunition was provided throughout the ages by Virgil's Fourth Eclogue, and one historian, F. Kampers, *Die Geburtsurkunde der mittelalterlichen Kaiseridee*, HJ, 36, 1915, has called that Eclogue the birth-charter of the medieval legend of the last emperor; as if there would have been no legend if medieval authors had not had their Virgil! The ultimate explanation of the persistence and pervasiveness of the legend is to be found in psychology, not in philology. Virgil, for example, only provided some concrete details which were used time and again.

[1] This story is a variation of an old archetype. Heracles surrendered his mantle in Delphi, Otto III gave his coronation coat to the monastery of Alessio, Henry II gave his golden imperial coat to Cluny. *Cp.* F. Kampers, *Vom Werdegang der abendländischen Kaisermystik*, 1924, p. 122.

Antichrist could not begin, and therefore the end of all time could not take place.

It is difficult to determine whether Adso considered his arguments as grounds for rejoicing in the continuing existence of the empire, or whether he preferred to see them as grounds for hoping that the empire would come to a speedy end. But there can be no doubt as to the enormous literary success of his treatise. It inaugurated a new era in historical thought, which stood in marked contrast to the more worldly orientation of the non-eschatological writings of men like Alcuin, Strabo, Regino and Widukind, who had all looked upon their various kings and emperors as the guarantors of peace and prosperity for the *populus christianus* rather than as possible path-finders for, or claimants to the role of the final emperor. And in the period immediately preceding the first crusade, more and more people began to identify the final emperor's journey to Jerusalem with a crusade for the reconquest of the Holy Sepulchre.[1]

By the time Frederick was a young man Antichrist speculation was the universal topic of conversation.[2] In 1105 the Synod of Florence had felt it necessary to state that the Antichrist was not yet actually present. But Pope Lucius II expected him soon, and Gerhoh of Reichersberg wrote to Pope Innocent II that if he was not yet there, he was certainly on his way. St Bernard considered the opponents of his friend Innocent II at least the partisans of Antichrist.[3] Hugh of St Victor (b. 1096) believed that all history moves from east to west and that now, with history mostly taking

[1] C. Erdmann, *Endkaiserglaube und Kreuzzuggedanke*, ZKG, LI, 1932, p. 413. In the eleventh century, before the first crusade, there were only faint traces of such an equation of a crusade with the impending end of the world. The equation was directly due to the first crusade. *Cp.* C. Erdmann, *Die Entstehung des Kreuzzuggedankes*, Stuttgart, 1955, pp. 278–9.

[2] Discussion and speculation was, naturally, extremely confused and vague. P. Classen, *Gerhoch von Reichersberg*, Wiesbaden, 1960, p. 217, for instance, distinguished three possible meanings. (1) The Antichrist is the head of the *corpus diaboli* or *corpus malorum*. He can be either a metaphysical force or a person, but not yet manifest in history, unlike Christ, Who is manifest. (2) Every member of the *corpus diaboli* can be an Antichrist. There can be many Antichrists. (3) The Antichrist can be the false Messiah of the last age, prophesied in the Bible. He will appear bodily.

[3] On a famous occasion, when St Bernard met Norbert of Magdeburg, he was taken aback to hear that Norbert expected the Antichrist within his own life-time. PL, 182, 162.

place in the west, the end must be near. The musings of Hildegard of Bingen (1098–1179) were full of similar eschatological motifs. Wherever Frederick turned for information during his formative years, he must have heard about the Antichrist and the impending end of time.

At least once in his life, possibly already in the course of the festivities which surrounded his coronation in 1152,[1] there was performed before Frederick the *Ludus de Antichristo*. In this play the completion of the four ages of world history was presented visually. The emperor, after many vicissitudes, received the submission of the kings of France, Greece, Babylon and Jerusalem. His work thus fulfilled, he laid down crown, sceptre and empire on the altar of the temple in Jerusalem: his task as defender of the church was accomplished:

> Suscipe quod offero nam corde benigne
> tibi regi regum imperium resigne,
> per quem reges regnant, qui solus imperator
> dici potes et es cunctorum gubernator.[2]

In the second part, the reign of the Antichrist begins. The Antichrist appears, accompanied by Hypocrisy and Heresy, the one designing to win over the laity and the other to destroy the clergy. Again, after countless dramatic vicissitudes, the Antichrist manages to subject the whole world to his poisonous rule. But just as he is celebrating his universal triumph, he is struck down by Jesus Christ.

If this was high drama, there was also in existence a formidable body of learned literature in which the doctrine of the ages of the world was expounded and the position of the present age as the one immediately preceding the Antichrist's or at least the reign of the last emperor was being determined. Abbot Rupert of Deutz (d. 1135), for example, believed in a sevenfold division of history. The sixth epoch was the epoch of piety, which lasted from the Teutonic migrations to the Investiture Contest, that is to the

[1] K. Hauck. *Zur Genealogie und Gestalt des staufischen Ludus de Antichristo*, GRM, 33, 1951, pp. 22–3. Hauck's view is now widely accepted. *Cp.* K. Langosch, *Geistliche Spiele*, Darmstadt, 1957, p. 268.

[2] F. Wilhelm, ed., p. 11.

end of the eleventh century. The present epoch was therefore the seventh, the epoch of the fear of God, which would usher in the Last Judgement.[1] Honorius Augustodunensis, a contemporary of Rupert, divided world history into ten ages. For the sake of symmetry, there were five before and five after Christ. The five ages after Christ are characterized by the Apostles, the martyrs, the church fathers, the monks and the Antichrist, and Honorius believed that the twelfth century was part of the fourth age, the age of monasticism, with the age of the Antichrist just about to come. Perhaps the most impressive and systematic of these writers was Bishop Anselm of Havelberg, a professional diplomat close to Frederick's inner circle. He was finally elevated to the see of Ravenna, where he died in 1158. According to Anselm's speculation, there were eight stages of world history, four of which had passed by the twelfth century. There were four to come. First, the age of the expectation of the end, in which the church was expecting the completion of its earthly development. Second, the age of the preparation of the end of the world, that is, the age of the Antichrist. These two ages were part of the ordinary course of history in the twelfth century. The following final two ages were transcendental. The third age to come was the *magnum silentium* and the fourth age, the *annus jubilans*, the age of eternal beatitude and the eternal present.[2]

The method employed by all these writers was strictly symbolical. They paid no attention whatever to actual historical

[1] In another place, Rupert treats us to a slightly different version: In reality the Roman empire had been brought down by the birth of Christ. But the vanquished dragon spat out water and thus caused the Arian heresy. The empire was therefore only quasi-dead, and through the efforts of Constantine at the Council of Nicea its mortal wound had been healed. Hence only five empires have really fallen so far. The sixth is still in existence and the seventh, the empire of Antichrist, is to come. *See* A. Dempf, *Sacrum Imperium*, Darmstadt, 1954, p. 238.

[2] After J. Spörl, *Grundformen hochmittelalterlicher Geschichtsanschauung*, München, 1935, pp. 26–7. Anselm is not easy to follow. *Cp.* also W. Berges, *Anselm von Havelberg in der Geistesgeschichte des 12. Jahrhunderts*, JGMOD, 5, 1956, and K. Fina, *Anselm von Havelberg*, AP, 1957, XXXIII. Fina's expositions do not contribute much towards clarification. A. Dempf, *op. cit.*, points out that Anselm contributed something over and above the conventional twelfth century speculations on the subject by demonstrating that in the course of history there is an ever increasing clarity and understanding of the sacraments as a means of salvation. Hence there is a progress towards the knowledge of truth. One might think that with this theory Anselm contributed something towards an understanding of the actual mechanism of change in history.

events, but simply thought in terms of symbols, e.g. various beasts, horses of different colours, the sacraments or the Persons of the Trinity, and assigned to each presidency over one of the ages in question. The only strictly historical relevance of this symbolic interpretation of world history was the conclusion which invariably consisted in the belief that the twelfth century was the age of the last emperor or, at any rate, the age immediately preceding the age of the Antichrist.

But lest the impression is gained that all this thinking took place in the nebulous regions of symbolic speculation and had no genuine relevance to history, one should glance at the writings of Gerhoh of Reichersberg, a contemporary of Frederick. Unlike the writers mentioned, Gerhoh was not a systematizer. He too employed the symbolic method to the full[1] but with such skill that in his hands it became a pointed criticism of his own age. He saw history exclusively as the battlefield of transcendental forces. Man as such had no effectiveness at all: every human action was merely a manifestation of a transcendental force. David, for instance, was a manifestation of the fourth gift of the Holy Spirit opposing a diabolical force. But Gerhoh was so interested in contemporary events, that he made himself pay much closer attention to the concrete details of contemporary history than any of the other writers. It is true, for instance, that he saw Gregory the Great as the representative of a new epoch of history rather than as a personality whose actions and whose character brought about this period.[2] Gerhoh believed that certain transcendental forces manifested themselves by putting Gregory into the world. Gregory is thus not a man who acted in history, but a sign that a certain transformation was taking place. However, if one allows that Gerhoh, at least by modern standards of viewing history, may have put the cart before the horse, this close attention to detail enabled him to wield the symbolic method as a powerful hammer of contemporary criticism. He held, for instance, that simony was not a sin committed by certain historical characters but a *sign* which pointed to the fact that the great secession from faith,

[1] Gerhoh acknowledged his debt to Rupert. *Cp.* E. Meuthen, *Kirche und Heilsgeschehen bei Gerhoh von Reichersberg*, Leiden–Köln, 1959, p. 117.

[2] MGH, LdL, III, 509, 27.

prophesied in II, Thessalonians, 2, 3, was now taking place.[1] Gerhoh taught, therefore, that if one understood the phenomenon of simony correctly as a symbol, one could learn from II Thessalonians, 2, 3, what was happening to the world at the present moment at which simony was so rampant, and at what stage of universal development one happened to be. In his *De Corrupte Statu Ecclesiae*[2] he equated Zion with speculation and speculation with the *ecclesia peregrinans*, that is, with looking towards the goal.[3] The goal is Jerusalem, i.e. the vision of peace. Each man singly as well as the church as a whole, strives away from Babylon, the essence of which is confusion, that is the confusion of world and church, expressed by the existence of a secular clergy and by the use of church property by laymen. The citizens of Babylon are the servants of *avaritia*, *concupiscentia* and *libido*. On earth, Zion and Babylon are mixed together, and church and world cannot be separated. Only God, at the Last Judgement, can distinguish the citizens of Zion from those of Babylon.' But in the meantime the church must attempt to make a beginning with the distinction in so far as this is already possible; and Gerhoh, almost anticipating Dante in presumptuousness, was going to do it on behalf of the church. He hoped to clear away a certain amount of this confusion by insisting that all clergy ought to become regular clergy – although he was willing to concede that there were some citizens of Zion among the secular clergy and some citizens of Babylon among the regular clergy. He further sought to eliminate part of the confusion by insisting that the church may own property and that the Donation of Constantine ought to be regarded as genuine.[4] He held, however, that the clergy must employ laymen for the administration of this property. Bishops ought to owe their position only to clerical authority and only clerical courts may judge disputed elections. He would allow the king to invest bishops with

[1] MGH, LdL, III, 274, 25.

[2] The title is not the original title, but was added by a later editor. *See* Van den Eynde, *L'ouevre littéraire de Géroch de Reichersberg*, SPAA, II, 1957, p. 92.

[3] After P. Classen, *Gerhoch von Reichersberg*, Wiesbaden, 1960, pp. 142 ff.

[4] Gerhoh here put his finger on a very vital point of the debates of the twelfth century. He realized how much support naturalism was receiving from spiritualism. And since he disapproved of naturalism, he disapproved of pure spiritualism. For the meaning of these terms, *see* p. 27 above.

the *regalia* – but considered such investment a pure formality because it referred to property which belonged to the church anyway, i.e. he denied that there were any proper *reglia* as far as bishops were concerned. And laymen who administered church property had to swear fealty to the church. Finally, he insisted that all decisions as to which wars were just and good for the defence of *patria* or church were to be left in the hands of the pope. Popes could depose and excommunicate kings and princes, but must never conduct wars themselves or exercise capital justice. Bishops were allowed armed retainers only for their personal protection. The lay powers were the *ordinata potestas*, and their duty was to execute the decisions of the church.[1]

Given these views, Gerhoh made himself an outspoken critic of contemporary events. He believed that in 1155 Pope Hadrian had called upon the iron sword of Frederick to defend the church and that Frederick's victory (*sic*) over the Romans[2] had resulted in the defeat of Babylon.[3] If this was an unrealistically sanguine interpretation it was dictated by his firm conviction that the ideal state of affairs was the harmony which had existed between Emperor Constantine and Pope Sylvester: with these two there had been no confusion of duties.[4] With these presuppositions,

[1] Gerhoh's views as formulated in the 40s and 50s were contained in his *De Ordine Donorum Spiritus Sancti* (1142–3); his work on Psalm 64 (1150) and his *De Novitate Huius Temporis*. (1156). These views were very Gregorian. The state, he held, had no independent rights. The pope has the imperial power and can depose and appoint princes. All the same, Gerhoh envisaged the possibility that any one pope might be an enemy of the church and he did not believe that a pope should actually rule an emperor. In 1156 the *De Novitate Huius Temporis* was presented to Hadrian and it was made clear that Gerhoh and his friends did not expect Hadrian to quarrel with Frederick but expected him to reform the church. The German Gregorians did not receive the news of the Besançon quarrel with joy.

[2] *See* p. 87 above.

[3] *Cp.* Classen, *op. cit.*, p. 156.

[4] MGH, LdL, III p. 152. Gerhoh was anxious that the temporal power should pay all respect to the spiritual power. For this reason he was in favour of the emperor's marshall service to the pope. (*See* p. 81 above). *Cp.* MGH. LdL, III, 283 and 336. However, he thought that holding the stirrup went too far. This is in agreement with his whole attitude. He wants the emperor to show respect, i.e. to act as marshall; but he thinks that the pope ought to be humble, i.e. not demand that the emperor hold the stirrup. Gerhoh therefore also took exception to the notorious Lateran paintings (*see* p. 142, note 1 above), because they depicted the emperor as the vassal of the pope and did not show the pope in a position of humility. *See* MGH, LdL, III, p. 393, lines 10–36. In line 35 Gerhoh even says that if people take the marshall's service for more than a sign of respect and consider it proof of the emperor's feudal dependence on the pope, the pope ought not to demand it because the pope must be humble. To demand

which Gerhoh had all worked out in the 40s and 50s, he wrote in the early 60s his major work *De Investigatione Antichristi – The Search for the Antichrist.* There is no need to relate the detailed arguments of the work. Its title and purpose speak for themselves. Gerhoh believed that the Antichrist was already in full action, and managed to detect the results of his activities in all the many evils which he castigated, i.e. the simony committed by Pope Alexander when he became a party to the conspiracy of Anagni, the schism of the church and the refusal, for instance, of the Greeks to recognize either of the two rival popes. In his enthusiasm, Gerhoh perhaps went too far. For at least some of his signs of the Antichrist had disappeared with the conclusion of the Peace of Venice in 1177, and in the 80s there certainly reigned the peace[1] which was necessary for a crusade and which might be likened to the peace described in the *Ludus de Antichristo*, the peace which made possible the emperor's surrender of his crown and sceptre on the altar of Christ in Jerusalem. This surrender, it will be recalled, was to precede, not follow, the advent of the Antichrist.[2]

It is the enormous merit of Bishop Otto of Freising to have written history in a much more realistic manner than any of these writers. Otto certainly belonged to the same school of thought and had acquired the basic presuppositions of his view of world history from the symbolic method. He took it for granted that the key to the course of history is to be found in the symbols provided by the Bible. But unlike the other writers, Otto paid much more attention to historical detail, and in his early and major work, *The Chronicle of the Two Cities*, he had written something which was much more akin to real history than to a symbolic interpretation of history. It is true that he considered the Gregorian ideal and the emergence

t is a sign of pride and the pope, as a spiritual lord, cannot possibly be the feudal lord of the emperor.

[1] Gerhoh's tracts were very much tracts for the time. His pessimism as to the end of history reached its climax in 1167 in his *De Qyarta Vigilia Noctis*. He believed that the fourth vigil had begun. Avarice reigns supreme, for the pope is compelled to buy the fealty of the Romans with money. He held, therefore, that the new Antichrist, as distinct from the Antichrist of the earlier ages, i.e. Nero, Julian the Apostate and Henry IV, will be avaricious. It is clear that Gerhoh here attributed universal historical significance to Alexander's temporary difficulties with the Romans.

[2] Gerhoh considered the *Ludus* a frivolous play. But A. Dempf, *op. cit.*, p. 258, remarks rightly that in substance it did not differ from his own views.

of the contemplative orders and of the crusaders as the manifestations of a new age, because his symbolic way of thinking had taught him that a new age had to dawn in preparation for the final age. But once he had gained this insight into the significance of these phenomena, he proceeded to treat them as genuine historical events rather than as ciphers or signs.[1] As a result, Otto's work had to be taken far more seriously as a realistic assessment of the nature of the twelfth century and a prediction of the immediate future. If the other writers are of interest to us because they reveal the general mental climate in which Frederick must have moved, Otto's work is of even greater interest, because it gives much more detailed precision to the course of events while still interpreting the twelfth century up to the beginning of Frederick's reign in the same spirit, i.e. as a preparation for the crusade to Jerusalem. Frederick, as we know[2] was deeply impressed by Otto. So deeply, in fact, that when he and Rainald were looking around for someone to write a political tract for the inauguration of the Great Design, he decided to enlist Otto's services. Otto's abilities stood him in good stead. In the *Gesta Friderici* which he composed in the late 1150s at Frederick's request, he shed the last remnants of the symbolic method and gave an account of contemporary history in as realistic a vein as any modern historian might desire. The new age, the Great Design, was not presented as the manifestation of a sign by which one could recognize this or that epoch of world history. The advent of the new age had not been deduced *a priori* from a consideration of the beast of the apocalypse or the Persons of the Holy Trinity,

[1] Otto's reputation has been inflated beyond all reason by the many historians who have seen in him mainly a trumpeter for the imperial pretensions which Frederick is alleged or imagined to have had. Equally unjustly, his work has never received its full due by some other historians who are wont to compare the *Chronicle* with much earlier attempts at world history. Otto is bound to suffer by comparison with St Augustine. To do him justice, one must appreciate Otto in his own context, that is, compare him with the symbolist thinkers of the twelfth century. One will then see the enormous importance of the step he took in the direction of rational historical contemplation without ever severing his connection with the basic eschatological preoccupations of the symbolists. To quote him: 'I must now, I think, make answer to those who will perhaps attempt to belittle this labour of mine as without value by claiming that I do not properly combine the deep and mystic proofs of the Scriptures with the historical accounts of so many successive misfortunes . . .'. (*Chronicle*, Prologue to Book VIII).

[2] *See* p. 130 above.

but was described as the result of a human plan, i.e. of Frederick's determination to create a central European kingdom.

In the middle 1180s the Great Design belonged very much to the past; and so did, presumably, Frederick's interest in Otto's *Gesta Friderici*. If anything, this work must now have been a considerable embarrassment to him, and it is more realistic to assume that at this stage in Frederick's life he was once again more mindful of Otto's *magnum opus*, the *Chronicle of the Two Cities*. In this work, the historical account of the first seven books had been concluded by a long, eighth book on the coming of the Antichrist, in which Otto too had taken his cue from the passage of II Thessalonians 2, 3, about the falling away from the church and had proceeded to speculate as to how and when the reign of the Antichrist might be expected. On thinking this matter over, Frederick was perhaps also mindful of the description of the state of the world (in the first, introductory book of the *Gesta*)[1] which had preceded the second crusade: 'Suddenly by the right hand of the Most High so great a change was brought about that, all these tumults of wars being lulled to rest, in a short time you might have seen the whole earth at peace and countless numbers from Gaul and from Germany accepting crosses and undertaking military service against the enemies of the cross.' When Frederick dwelt on this description, and it seems reasonable to suppose that he did, it must have reminded him forcefully of another, more dramatic scene in which this moment of peace was presented in the *Ludus de Antichristo* – and, for that matter, it must have underlined the auspicious moment he had reached in his own career in the middle 80s when he was fully enjoying the fruits of his third political experiment, the feudalization of the empire.[2] For it would be a

[1] I, xxix.

[2] Peace as a precondition for a crusade was very much a leading political concept of the twelfth century. A disturber of the peace is a disturber of the peace necessary for the crusade, i.e. an enemy of Christianity. *Cp.* for instance John of Salisbury, a rationalist if ever there was one, *Historia Pontificalis*, M. Chibnall, ed., pp. 11–12. We are too often tempted to assess twelfth century political thought in terms of more modern, utilitarian political notions, like justice or the commonweal. The preoccupation with this kind of peace found also a powerful reflection in Otto of Freising's *Gesta*, especially II, ii; xxviii, last paragraph; xxxii; lvi. In all these places, Otto assesses such early triumphs as Frederick did achieve in the first part of his reign (1152–6) in terms of 'peace'.

mistake to see Frederick as a mere visionary, captivated by the Antichrist speculations of his century. If there had been nothing more to influence him than the vision of Hildegard of Bingen who saw the devilish head of the Antichrist being carried in the lap of the figure of the naked and bleeding church, the flesh of her legs torn by persecutions, Frederick might not have been deeply moved. He might have paid greater attention to the systematic speculations of Rupert of Deutz or Honorius Augustodunensis. But a mind like Frederick's, which had been absorbed for a lifetime in practical politics, required something more concretely detailed and more precisely relevant – and that detail and relevance had been provided by both Gerhoh and Otto of Freising. The writings of these two men had succeeded in giving just enough actual relevance to symbolic speculation to appear plausible to the cool, calculating political mind of Frederick. They had given so much contemporary substance to the abstract scheme of Abbot Adso, and had explained at the hand of so much contemporary history that the reign of the Antichrist was near, that Frederick could be satisfied that a new crusade was not so much a religious adventure – something which would have been utterly alien to his whole nature – as a realistic task for the sake of which he had become emperor and for the sake of which he had undertaken all his political experiments.

And so it was that when in early December 1187 Bishop Henry of Strassburg addressed the court which Frederick was holding in his city, Frederick listened with tears in his eyes. Several earlier efforts made by the pope's special legate Henry of Albano had met with very little response. When the first appeals for a crusade had been made, the preachers had taken up an old and well worn theme. They had argued that since Jesus had taken up the Cross for us, we must now take it up for Him.[1] They had pleaded for repentance and for the necessity of taking up the Cross in order to reach heaven,[2] and Henry of Albano had bemoaned the fact that the Cross was now in the hands of the infidels.[3] At Strassburg, in December 1187, Bishop Henry struck a different note. He used

[1] F. W. Wentzlaff-Eggebert, *Kreuzzugsdichtung des Mittelalters*, Berlin, 1960, p. 139.
[2] *ibid.*, p. 141. [3] *ibid.*, p. 142.

a typically feudal argument. He appealed to the assembled knights with a voice charged with emotion to take the Cross and avenge the insults incurred by Jesus, because, so he argued, he was certain that none of them would allow their own feudal lords to be insulted without vengeance. Would they allow, he continued, their heavenly Lord to ask for help and not go to his rescue? This tone met with instant response. After listening in silence, a knight came forward and begged to be allowed to take the Cross. His example was followed by others. Frederick himself, though moved to tears, still hesitated. He wanted first to reassure himself that if he took the Cross his absence from Germany would not immediately jeopardize the political equilibrium which he had achieved.

Having reassured himself, a new court, a *curia Jesu Christi*, was summoned to Mainz for Pentecost, 1188. Frederick refused to preside, because it was felt that at this court Christ Himself was the head of the assembly. Henry of Albano read a letter from the pope describing the plight of Christendom in the Holy Land. But the most impressive speech was delivered by Bishop Godfrey of Würzburg. God, he explained, wanted to give the knights a personal opportunity of redeeming themselves by military service. It is significant that it was this appeal to knighthood and to the feudal concept of service which carried the day. Frederick himself took the Cross from Godfrey; and so did his son, Duke Frederick of Swabia, Ludwig of Thuringia, several bishops and princes, and a large number of counts and knights – it was estimated that 13,000 men in all took the Cross on that day. At mass, the *laetere Jerusalem* was sung with deep meaning.[1] The departure for the Holy Land was fixed for St George's day of the following year.

Frederick made ample and serious preparations for the crusade. If one compares him with Philip Augustus and with Richard the Lionheart who also, at that time, undertook a crusade, the comparison is entirely in Frederick's favour. Philip Augustus did not

[1] S. O. Riezler, *Der Kreuzzug Kaiser Friedrichs I*, FDG, X, 1870, p. 17, estimates that in Mainz 13,000 men took the cross, 4,000 of whom were knights. The tremendous effect of the *curia Jesu Christi* of Mainz is attested by numerous chroniclers: *Chronicon Magni Presbiteri*, MGH, SS, XVII, p. 509; *Gestorum Treverorum Continuatio*, MGH, SS, XXIV, p. 388; *Continuatio Sanblasiana*, MGH, SS, XX, p. 319; *Historia de Expeditione Friderici* (by the so-called Ansbert), MGH, SRG, V, pp. 14–15. *See* also the essay by F. W. Wentzlaff-Eggbert, *Der Hoftag Jesu Christi 1188 in Mainz*, Wiesbaden, 1962.

really want to go at all. He was forced by political and religious pressures to take the Cross, and returned to France as soon as he had satisfied appearances. Richard, on the other hand, was an adventurer.[1] His preparations were elaborate, but the political circumstances of his kingdom did not really allow a prolonged absence, and throughout his crusade his behaviour was prompted time and time again by personal and idiosyncratic considerations. Frederick alone went about the crusade in a careful and business-like spirit.[2] To begin with, he saw to it that the crusading army would be a fairly disciplined body of knights. Only men who had a certain, specified amount of property were allowed to take part, and after the departure of the army, on several occasions Frederick caused stringent measures for the maintenance of discipline and chastity to be issued.[3] Equally important were his careful

[1] 'There were grave flaws in Richard's character.' S. Runciman, *A History of the Crusades*, Cambridge, 1954, III, p. 34.

[2] He left nothing to chance. When the abbot of the imperial monastery of Murbach hesitated in his support of the crusade, Frederick demanded as compensation that the abbot cede him one of the monastery's manors which was able to supply 250 men. A. Waas, *Geschichte der Kreuzzüge*, Freiburg, 1956, Vol. I, p. 188, considers this not to have been an isolated instance.

[3] A. Waas, *ibid.*, and Riezler, *Der Kreuzzug Friedrichs I*, FDG, X, 1870, p. 17. When passing through Vienna, Frederick ordered 500-odd thieves and n'eer-do-wells, who had attached themselves to the army, to be sent back, Riezler, *op. cit.*, p. 27. In Pressburg, he appointed a special judge for every contingent, *ibid.*, p. 27. In Belgrade he held a court of justice, by the sentence of which several nobles were executed and some men had their hands cut off, *ibid.*, p. 28. In Philippopolis he again took draconic steps for the maintenance of order and several thieves were executed, *ibid.*, p. 46. This policy was not only expedient, but also increased the reputation of the crusading army with the infidels and made them realize that their enemies' discipline was something to be reckoned with. An Armenian informed Saladin to this effect: 'Although the German army contains all manner of people, there is harsh discipline and tremendous severity. A man guilty of a crime is sacrificed like a sheep, without ado. A noble, charged with the maltreatment of one of his men, is hauled before the priests who unanimously sentence him to death. In spite of intercessions, the emperor has him executed. They abstain from sensuous pleasures with the greatest care. A man guilty of indulgence is ostracized and punished mercilessly. All this through their mourning for the Holy Sepulchre. It is a fact that many of them have vowed to wear for a long time no shirt but only their iron armour. . . . Their perseverance in spite of every kind of deprivation is singular and unbelievable.' Quoted by Bohadin, *Vita Saladini*, tr. Schultens, p. 122. William of Huntingdon, *Hist. Angl.*, Rolls series, 74, London 1879, pp. 280–1, had attributed the failure of the second crusade to the sinfulness of the crusaders. Their 'incontinence, which they practised in open fornications and even in adulteries . . . and finally in robbery and all sorts of evils, came up before the sight of God . . . Who withdrew his favour from the armies which consequently were defeated.' Similarly St Bernard: 'It seems as if the Lord, provoked by our sins, had forgotten his compassion and had decided to judge the world according to his justice before the appointed

diplomatic preparations. After many deliberations it was decided to travel by land. Frederick knew this would involve a laborious journey; but, on the whole, he felt the hazards of such a journey to be less than the dangers of the sea. But a journey across land required careful negotiations with the potentates whose countries the army would have to pass through. And there, as it was later to appear, Frederick was very much out of his depth. Nothing in his own long political experience had ever taught him the importance of a system of balance of power. He had had conflicts with the kings of England and of France, but the nature of the power of these rulers had been such that a major armed conflict was beyond all possibility, and there had therefore never been any need for Frederick to think in terms of a system in which his power and that of other rulers would be balanced.

In his relations with the kings of Bohemia, Sicily, Poland and Denmark, the question of a balance of power had not arisen either. These rulers were either enemies, or they made a feudal submission; or, as in the case of the king of Sicily, Frederick eventually concluded a treaty of peace and even friendship. But in the east the situation was very different. The Byzantine empire had shrunk to a comparatively small region, of which Constantinople was the geographical centre. Most of Asia Minor was occupied by the Seljuk Turks, and Egypt, Syria and the Holy Land were ruled by Saladin who had arisen as a major power. There also existed in southern Asia Minor an Armenian principality, and only Antioch and Tyre had remained as the last vestiges of Latin Christian

---

time. . . .' *De Consideratione*, PL, 182, p. 743, II, i. Otto of Freising, *Chronicle*, I, 65, also had been of the opinion that the second crusade had failed because of the crusaders' sinfulness. It is very likely that Frederick was very mindful of these explanations of the failure of the second crusade and one must therefore see in his constant preoccupation with the high moral standard of his army a conscious attempt to make up for the disasters of the second crusade:

> Dem Kriuze zimt wol reiner muot
> und kiusche site:
> . . . .
> ez wil niht daz mau sî
> der werke drunder frî:
> waz touc ez uf der wât,
> ders an dem herzen niene hâte?
>
> Hartmann von Aue, MF, 209, 25–36.

power. In order to obviate the necessity for permanent armed conflict, the rulers of these 'countries' had tried to establish something like a balance of power, and it appears that they had taken special measures to preserve this balance when they had learnt of Frederick's intentions. The Byzantine Emperor Isaac had entered into an understanding with Saladin,[1] and the rulers of the Turks, who were placed between Isaac and Saladin in Asia Minor, were playing a double game. They were offering help to Frederick on one side, and had a marriage alliance with Saladin on the other.[2] A further complication was added by the fact that the rulers of the Serbians and Bulgarians stood in a somewhat equivocal position to their own 'subjects', on whom they had only a very tenuous hold and whose attitude to the crusading army they could not control. It was, therefore, never to be clear whether the hostilities with which Frederick was to meet in those parts were the result of the rebelliousness of their subjects or of the faithlessness of these rulers. These same rulers stood in an equally equivocal position to Emperor Isaac. They were trying to maintain their independence of him so that it was not clear whether any hostility shown to Frederick in those regions was a sign of their friendship for Isaac or a sign of their rebellion against him. For Isaac, when he learnt that Frederick had put out feelers to the rulers of the Serbians,[3] had himself decided to play a double game.[4] While he had reached an understanding with Saladin, he

[1] Riezler, *op. cit.*, p. 36. Saladin and Isaac made concessions to one another. Those of Isaac, who was obviously the more immediately threatened party, were very far-reaching.

[2] Riezler, *op. cit.*, p. 62.

[3] G. Ostrogorsky, *History of the Byzantine State*, J. Hussey tr., Oxford, 1956, p. 361. Whatever the justification of Isaac's initial fears, the negotiations between Frederick and the Serbian Grand Zupan in the winter of 1189–90 provided solid ground for Isaac's suspicion that Frederick might actively help the Serbians. *Cp.* Riezler, *op. cit.*, p. 48.

[4] The German chroniclers of the time and later German historians have been quick to look at the whole situation from a purely German perspective. They are all convinced that Isaac was a treacherous villain. *Cp.* e.g. Riezler, *op. cit.*, p. 47. But from a Byzantine point of view there was nothing treacherous in Isaac's policy. He found himself in a most unenviable situation and clearly had no reason for trusting the Germans who had made treaties not only with him but also with his enemies, the Serbian Grand Zupan and the ruler of the Seljuk Turks. Isaac was far too shrewd a diplomat to be able to fathom the truth, i.e. that Frederick was completely simple-minded and honest and genuinely wanted nothing but to assure a safe passage to his army. If one consults Nicetas Choniates, one will gain a better perspective: 'As if the barbarians,

had also made overtures to Frederick. His own military power was weak and he was naturally apprehensive, as well he might be, of the presence of a large German army in his empire. In order to cover himself against all eventualities, he decided to prevaricate and reinsure himself in both directions. Given the precarious balance of power in the east, this was nothing but good diplomacy.

All this was completely beyond Frederick's comprehension. To begin with, he thought in simple terms of Christian *versus* infidel, and the idea that Isaac might be in league with Saladin was, to his mind, monstrous treason. Frederick, however, had no real excuse for such simplicity of mind; for he himself had found that the ruler of the Seljuk Turks had been willing to negotiate with him, a Christian. All in all, Frederick simply plotted his course geographically. He knew he would have to cross the dominions of the king of Hungary, the lands 'ruled' by some Serbian potentates, the empire of Byzantium and the regions controlled by the ruler of the Seljuk Turks, and finally attack Saladin. He therefore decided on a simple course. There was no doubt as to the friendliness of the king of Hungary.[1] He was pleased to receive a friendly embassy from the rulers of Serbia.[2] He opened negotiations with Isaac for the support of his army and for a peaceful passage through the Greek empire,[3] reached a friendly understanding with the chief ruler of the Seljuk Turks,[4] and sent a formal

lusty for battle, who surrounded us were not enough of a plague, there also approached from afar another ferocious misfortune, Frederick, the king of Alamans . . .' (525) Nicetas Choniates seems, however, to have understood Frederick's simplicity of mind and the honesty of his purpose, for he attributes the growth of Isaac's suspicions to wrong information (526 and 528), and then goes on to say that as a result of this misleading information, Isaac himself became somewhat confused and began to issue contradictory orders. (526).

[1] Riezler, *op. cit.*, pp. 27–8.

[2] *ibid.*, p. 30. Riezler is careful to point out that in spite of all friendliness, Frederick refused to accept a feudal oath of fealty from the Grand Zupan of Serbia and would not hear of a conspiracy against the Greeks.

[3] The first agreement with Isaac was made in Nuremberg, Christmas 1187, when Frederick received a Greek embassy. His son Frederick and the duke of Austria took an oath on Frederick's behalf to assure the Greeks of their peaceful intentions. Thereupon the Greeks faithfully promised a free passage to Frederick's army. Finally Frederick sent an embassy of his own to Constantinople. *See* Riezler, *op. cit.*, p. 22.

[4] The arrival of the embassy from Konya was a great sensation in Nuremberg at Christmas 1188. According to the *Annales Col. maximi*, the embassy consisted of 1,000 men and 500 horses. Riezler, *op. cit.*, p. 22.

declaration of war to Saladin.[1] This diplomatic scheme, to his mind, was straightforward: a friendly agreement with the rulers whose lands he had to cross, and a declaration of war on the ruler whose lands were situated at the end of the line.

These preparations made, the crusading army assembled in early May in Ratisbon and departed on 11 May.[2] Frederick himself travelled by ship on the Danube, but the major part of the army moved on foot and on horseback towards the kingdom of Hungary. The march through Hungary was completed without difficulties. Frederick seems merely to have been somewhat disappointed at the poor rate of exchange which the Hungarians insisted on for his Colognese *denarii*: they considered their own *denarii*, the value of which barely equalled those of Verona, to be the equivalent of those of Ratisbon.[3] But the warm reception meted out by the king of Hungary and the clement climate made up for the financial disappointment. The crusading army was in the best of moods when it crossed from Hungary into what they considered to be Byzantine territory but which was in reality a land controlled by men who were trying to overthrow the rule of the Greeks. Against expectations, there was no embassy from the Greek emperor to welcome the crusaders, and before long the crusaders realized that the local population was anything but friendly. Their progress was made difficult by robbers and

[1] This famous exchange of letters may be spurious. Most historians doubt whether Frederick's letter was genuine. They think that it may have originated in England in order to rouse enthusiasm for the crusade. *Cp.* H. E. Mayer, *Der Brief Kaiser Friedrichs I. an Saladin vom Jahre 1188*, DA, 14, 1958. But A. Waas, *op. cit.*, p. 190, note 114, is of the opinion that both letters are genuine. There is nothing inherently improbable in Frederick having written or dictated the letter. It is, however, rather grandiloquent. It contains a reminder to Saladin that much of Asia and Africa used to be part of the Roman empire and that Frederick had therefore a right to these provinces. Some modern historians have taken this passage as proof that in Frederick's political thinking he, Frederick, was the master of the world. If Frederick wrote such things, he was too sober to mean them literally. He might have tried them on Saladin to give himself a more imposing air than he had and to intimidate a ruler whom he considered an oriental despot.

[2] The sources for the expedition are the *Historia de Expeditione Friderici Imperatoris* by the so-called Ansbert; the *Historia Peregrinorum*, the *Epistola de Morte Friderici Imperatoris*. They have all been edited by A. Chroust, *Quellen zur Geschichte des Kreuzzuges Kaiser Friedrichs I*, MGH, SRG, V, Berlin, 1928. In a long introduction Chroust also analyses the relationship of these accounts to one another.

[3] Riezler, *op. cit.*, p. 28.

marauders, by the bad roads and the climate, which in conjunction with the bad supply of food caused the outbreak of an epidemic. Frederick considered all these difficulties as a breach of faith on the part of Isaac; but to a very large extent they were not caused by Isaac, because the inhabitants of Serbia and Bulgaria were no longer under his control. And although he did eventually send a friendly embassy to meet the army near Nissa to assure Frederick that the governor of Brandiz, for instance, had disobeyed orders when he had been hostile to the crusaders, Frederick was now very much on his guard against Isaac and suspected that he would not remain faithful to his original agreement.

Towards the end of August, the army finally reached Philippopolis and found ample food in that fertile region. They helped themselves freely and thus confirmed the fears of Isaac. Wily politician that he was, he now began to suspect Frederick of being equally wily. This, of course, was a misunderstanding for Frederick had no other thought than to pass through Byzantine territory as peacefully and rapidly as possible. But Isaac was accustomed to the tortuous tergiversations of Byzantine politics. He could not understand Frederick's simplicity of purpose and before long there was every possibility of Isaac's error of judgement producing its own verification. Isaac indeed convinced himself, or was persuaded to believe, that the real object of Frederick's expedition was not so much to destroy Saladin and reconquer Jerusalem, as to take possession of the Byzantine empire.[1] Thus it came about that by the end of August the first serious clashes occurred between Frederick's army and Greek contingents and by the end of October the situation had deteriorated so much that Frederick found himself at open war with Isaac. The Greek army was powerless against the crusaders and by November the whole of Thracia was controlled by the latter who then decided to winter there. As the situation had developed it is not surprising that there was a considerable body of opinion in Frederick's army who urged Frederick to avail himself of the opportunity of destroying the power of Byzantium. It took all of Frederick's strength of mind to

[1] *Cp.* p. 389, note 4 above, on Niketas Choniates's version, and Riezler, *op. cit.*, pp. 34, 39.

resist such pressure.[1] He himself did not abandon hope of an understanding with Isaac until November[2] and if he then began to toy with the idea of a conquest of Constantinople it was only to assuage his own army and to gain time.[3] But Frederick himself remained steadfast in his purpose, even though he did write home that he now was in a position where he might easily have possessed himself of the city of Constantinople. But, he added, justice and his principles as a pilgrim made it impossible for him to give way to such a temptation.[4]

As a result of Frederick's steadfast determination, the crisis passed. In February 1190 a definitive agreement was reached with Isaac. According to its provisions, the German army was to cross into Asia Minor near Gallipoli with the help of ships provided by the Byzantines. The Greek army was to remain at a distance of at least four days' march, and all Byzantine ships which were not used for the crossing were to remain during the specified days at anchor in their ports. The inhabitants of the region where the crossing was to take place were to supply food for payment – the rate of exchange was officially fixed – and the Germans were not to pay prices higher than those charged normally to the Greek army. Only if Greek officials failed to provide sufficient food for sale were the Germans to be allowed to forage, though they were not to deprive people of their land.[5]

Now everything went smoothly,[6] and during Easter week,

[1] K. Zimmert, *Der deutsch-byzantinische Konflikt vom Juli 1189 bis Februar 1190*, BZ, 12, 1903, p. 63. The article is much better and much more perceptive than the title suggests. When a German emperor quarrels with the Greek emperor while he is trying to lead a crusading army through the latter's dominions, this is not a case of a conflict between Germany and Byzantium.

[2] *ibid.*, p. 69. [3] *ibid.*, p. 77.

[4] AIS, I, 152, No. 162.

[5] Isaac had a bit of a bad conscience at having extricated himself thus from his predicament, for he had now failed in his promises to Saladin. He therefore wrote him a letter in order to belittle the importance of Frederick's passage across the Hellespont and to assure Saladin that sufferings and deprivations had so weakened the army that it was not likely to reach Saladin's dominions. The letter is in Bohadin, *op. cit.*, p. 131.

[6] There were only some picturesque hitches. The hostages whom Isaac had promised to provide went into hiding and had to be replaced by some men of lower status. Riezler, *op. cit.*, p. 50, making Frederick's point of view his own, comments that their fears were groundless. Niketas Choniates, 538, however, reports that in the end Isaac forgave them when he realized that they had disobeyed his orders because they had

18–24 March, the German army crossed the Hellespont without incident. On 28 March Frederick himself, accompanied by five galleys, and to the sound of trumpets, set foot on Asia Minor.

The army, considerably weakened by the hardships suffered in the Balkans and in Greece,[1] immediately proceeded on its march. The route took them through Sardes, Philadelphia and Laodicea. When the army left the coastal regions and entered central Anatolia, new difficulties had to be faced. Frederick now discovered that his understanding with the old Sultan of the Seljuk Turks who ruled this region was of no avail.[2] The Sultan's sons were allies of Saladin, and as a result nothing was done to provide food and provisions for the crusaders. When they proceeded to help themselves, the Turks retaliated and a number of battles had to be fought. Although the crusaders managed to stand up to such resistance, they were forced from their chosen route into barren

had good reasons to be afraid of the Germans. – During Easter Sunday there arose such a storm, that the crusaders had to make a virtue of necessity. They were forced to rest and celebrate Easter. The same storm brought them a windfall. Several Venetian ships had arrived at the Hellespont laden with victuals. Their Italian masters had refused to sell their cargo to the crusaders and had preferred to sail to Constantinople because their goods were likely to fetch higher prices there. But the storm forced them back and enabled the crusaders to buy their goods.

[1] Riezler, *op. cit.*, p. 52, insists that the crusaders had suffered few real losses, but even he admits that Frederick was short of money and that the loss in horses had been beyond expectation and was serious. Also, the king of Hungary had ordered the Hungarian contingent to return to Hungary. He had obviously become very concerned at the growing hostility between Frederick and Isaac during the winter, and wanted at all costs to avoid getting involved in a conflict with the Byzantine emperor, his father-in-law.

[2] Owing to the great distance involved, Frederick's diplomatic exchanges with the Sultan had been hazardous. The Sultan had sent an embassy to Frederick to Nüremberg in 1188. Frederick, thereupon, had sent an ambassador to the Sultan. But the ambassador had tarried in Konya and had started on the return journey only in December 1189. When passing through Constantinople, he was arrested by Isaac and could deliver the Sultan's letter to Frederick only after the final peace treaty between Isaac and Frederick in February 1190. But by that time there seems to have been something like a palace revolution among the Turks, and power had passed into the hands of the sons of the aging Sultan. The son who became master of Konya reassured Frederick of his friendship and during the following months took pains to explain that any attacks on Frederick's army by Turks had not been authorized by him. But eventually the truth came out. Saladin, in order to win his support, had given him a daughter in marriage with an enormous dowry, and after Frederick's victory at Konya this dowry fell into Frederick's hands. – Runciman, *op. cit.*, III, pp. 14–15, does not seem to be aware of these complicated factors and simply states that the old Sultan proved treacherous.

mountain regions where they suffered from hunger and thirst. Frederick then decided to take the bull by the horns and attack the major stronghold of the Seljuk Turks, the city of Konya. The army was, by that time, in a desperate state. Men and horses had died like flies. Hunger and heat had caused enormous suffering, and when there had been food there had been no fuel to cook it. Eventually tents, saddles and clothing, even arms, had to be sacrificed as fuel, and by the time Frederick was encamped before Konya no more than 600 knights on horseback were left to him.[1] It was almost a miracle that the battle which took place on 17 May turned into a complete victory for the crusaders. The victory enabled the army to rest for four days in the parks of the city and to acquire new horses and other supplies. On 26 May the march was continued across the steep and barren slopes of the Taurus mountains to reach, on 30 May, the frontier of the Christian state of the Armenians. The ruler of the Armenians, a prince by the name of Leon II, was most friendly to Frederick, and it is reported that Frederick intended to crown him king of the Armenians.[2] The lord of one of the outlying Armenian castles entertained Frederick, and the crusaders were welcomed by an Armenian embassy at a bridge across the river Saleph. Leon II himself intended to receive Frederick festively in Seleucia, and in the meantime sent food and other supplies. Since the river Saleph takes its course to Seleucia through a succession of gorges, Frederick decided to lead his army on a more direct route across the mountains to the coast. On 10 June the army was crossing the last of the mountains, and towards evening they saw the city of Seleucia in the distance and rejoiced at the prospect of a rest among the friendly Armenians. Frederick himself had ridden ahead with a small retinue and reached the valley by midday, and as he was resting by the river Saleph he wanted to refresh himself in the

[1] Riezler, *op. cit.*, p. 60, Waas, *op. cit.*, p. 195, estimates that during the march through Anatolia, the army was reduced by one half.

[2] Riezler, *op. cit.*, p. 67. It seems, however, that even the Armenians were uneasy and had kept in touch with Saladin as well as with Frederick. Again, this was hardly a case of treachery. Living so closely to the might of Saladin, they could not be expected, except by Frederick's simple, straight and undiplomatic mind, to stake their whole future on the success of the crusader's army. *Cp.* Waas, *op. cit.*, p. 195, and Runciman, *op. cit.*, p. 15.

water. Whether it was the sudden shock of the cold water or the strong current which was too much for Frederick's strength, he drowned. His men tried to reach him, but when they dragged him to the bank, Frederick was dead.[1]

[1] Thus the *Historia de Expeditione Friderici*, MGH, SRG, V, pp. 91–2. The river Saleph is the ancient Calycadnus and the modern Gök-su. There are several different accounts of the accident. For a discussion of these accounts see Riezler, *op. cit.*, pp. 126 ff., and Waas, *op. cit.*, p. 196, note 130. Apart from the ordinary inaccuracies, some of these differences can be accounted for by the obvious doubts which the emperor's death was bound to stir up. Was it conceivable that so honourable a man could die without the last sacrament? And if so, was his soul likely to be saved? And why did God allow him to die so near his goal, which if he had reached it, would have assured him of salvation? Many years later, the chronicler Albert of Stade, MGH, SS, XVI, p. 351, provided a version of Frederick's death, which was designed to allay even the gravest of these doubts. According to his account, Frederick was submerged in the floods of the river exclaiming: 'Benedictus crucifixus Dei filius, quod aqua me suscipit, quae me regeneravit, et me martirem faciat, quae me fecit christianum!' Riezler, *op. cit.*, p. 132, describes this as 'ridiculous gossip'. I would prefer to comment: *se non è vero, è ben trovato!* Much later, blinded by his hatred of the Ghibellines, the chronicler Giovanni Villani considered Frederick's death in Asia Minor to have been a well deserved punishment for his hostility to the Roman church. RIS, XIII, p. 132.

Epilogue

With the death of Frederick there disappeared from the political scene of the late twelfth century one of its most indefatigably enterprising and imaginative minds. Some of his followers took the emperor's body to Antioch and buried it in the cathedral. Some were so disheartened that they committed suicide and some renounced the Christian faith and went over to the heathen. One contingent, under Duke Frederick of Swabia, laid siege to Acre – but soon the arrival of English and French knights who had made their way to the Holy Land by sea, took the initiative from the Germans and Duke Frederick himself died of a disease.

On his departure to the east Frederick had left his son Henry in Germany as regent – and Henry therefore succeeded his father as a matter of course when the news of Frederick's death arrived in Germany. But Henry lacked his father's physical and mental stature. He never quite recovered from a serious illness in 1191 and died in 1197. During his short reign he tried to make the most of the arrangements he had inherited from his father. But determination was not enough. It so happened that the king of Sicily died towards the end of 1189 and that Henry's wife, Constance, was his only heir. Her succession, however, was not peaceful and Henry had to fight lengthy battles in order to overcome a national party who tried to resist what they considered to be Henry's intrusion. In Germany, Henry had to face the return of Henry the Lion in October 1189 and the consequent renewal of all the hostilities occasioned by his presence in northern Germany. One can only guess how Frederick, faced with these new problems, would have reacted. Henry had no resources other than his tenacity of pursuing the old policies and his determination to fight for the arrangements he had inherited. Unable to fashion new plans for the new problems, he pursued old plans with stubbornness and was often guilty of cruelty and breaches of faith. Eventually he sought to round off his father's third plan for the complete feudalization of the German monarchy by suggesting to the princes that the monarchy, like fiefs, should become hereditary. With this proposal he meant to put the finishing touch to Frederick's third plan, the feudal monarchy in Germany. For as long as the princes retained the right of freely electing their king, one could never hope for a genuinely stable feudal monarchy. In return, Henry promised the princes that they could treat their fiefs as fully hereditary, not only in the direct line, but also in collateral lines.

The princes, however, were on the whole reluctant to enter into such an arrangement. By consenting to make the monarchy hereditary, they had much to lose; and by formally obtaining the right to leave their own fiefs to their brothers and nephews as well as to their own sons, they gained very little, for this was precisely what they had always been doing. It then became clear that the feudalization of the monarchy, far from being a source of strength, was becoming a fatal weakness. The princes treated their fiefs more and more like hereditary territories of which they were the effective rulers and they remained free to elect as king a man whom they could rely upon never to be able to build up effective organs of centralized government. The following century saw a long series of statutes by which the king divested himself of one residual right after another in favour of the territorial princes, both lay and ecclesiastical.

In England, ever since the Norman Conquest, the feudal monarchy had been based upon definable rights. Every fief was subject to certain contributions and even at the height of the barons' reaction against the monarchy in the thirteenth century, this initial tendency could never be completely wiped out. But in Germany there had been no conquest. Frederick, in surveying the scene, had simply recognized that feudal relationships were proliferating and he had done no more than allow this indigenous development to run its course. And when his son Henry tried to give it the decisive twist which would have favoured the monarchy, he saw that he was powerless.

It is doubtful whether he actually lived long enough to see it clearly. When his formal proposal was shelved at a court in

Würzburg in April 1196, he left under the impression that the princes would ultimately consent. But when he died in Palermo in September of the following year at the age of thirty-two, there was no question of a hereditary succession. His own son was only one year old; and his brother Philip soon had to face a formidable claim to the crown by Otto, the son of Henry the Lion. And thus began a long civil war. By the time Henry's son Frederick was old enough to play his part, all opportunities had been lost. Frederick II, the grandson of Frederick Barbarossa, more or less washed his hands of Germany and spent all his energies in an attempt to extend his Sicilian kingdom to central and northern Italy.

The early death of Henry coincided almost exactly with the accession to the papacy of one of the most determined and powerful men ever to sit on the papal throne, Innocent III. Innocent availed himself fully of all the forces which the growth of spiritualism and sacerdotalism had placed at the disposal of the papacy; and the civil war in Germany gave him every opportunity he could possibly wish for. By the turn of the century, therefore, Frederick's carefully laid plans had almost come to nought.

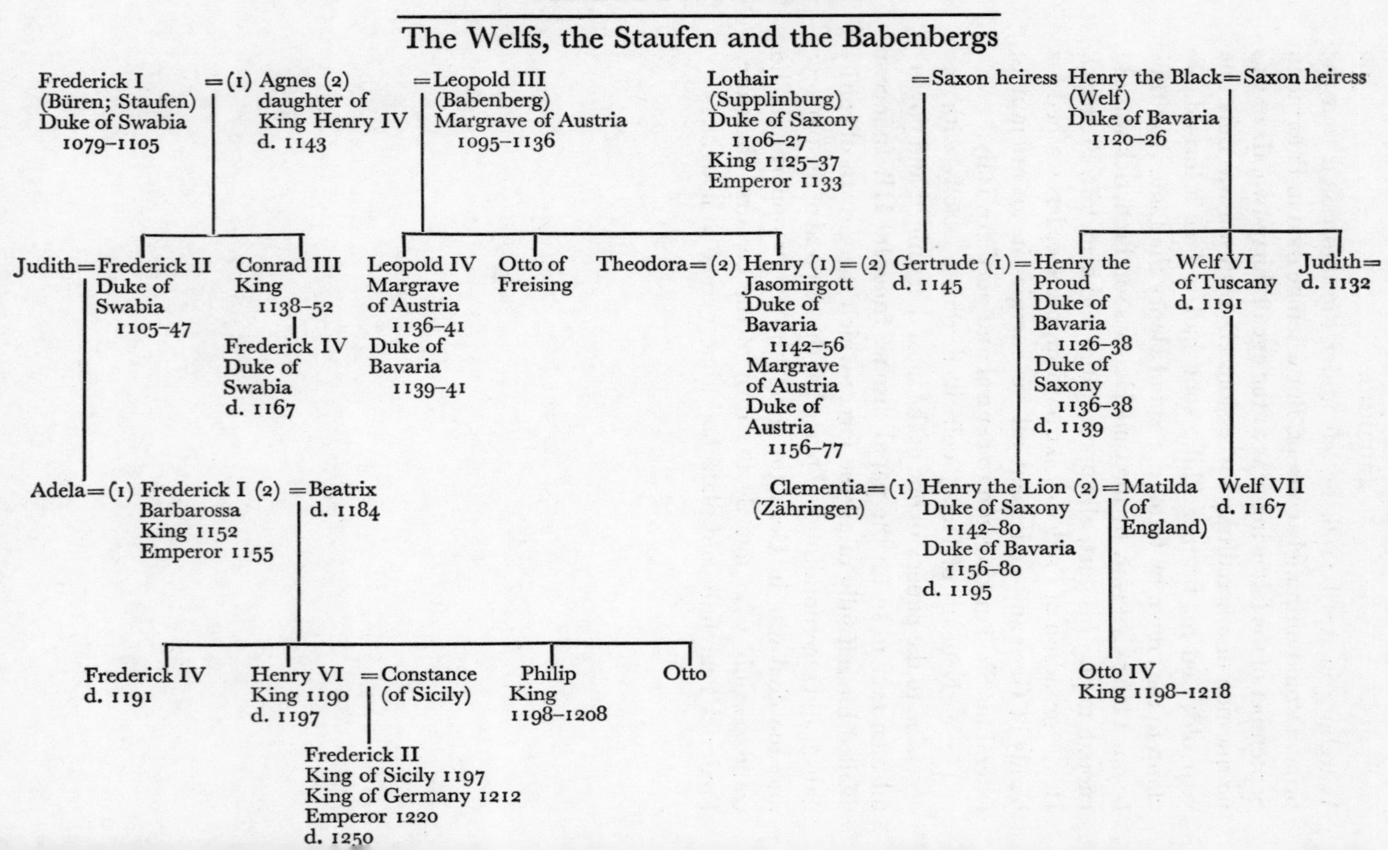
GENEALOGICAL TABLE
The Welfs, the Staufen and the Babenbergs
Frederick I (Büren; Staufen) Duke of Swabia 1079–1105
=(1) Agnes (2) daughter of King Henry IV d. 1143
=Leopold III (Babenberg) Margrave of Austria 1095–1136
Lothair (Supplinburg) Duke of Saxony 1106–27 King 1125–37 Emperor 1133
=Saxon heiress
Henry the Black=Saxon heiress
(Welf) Duke of Bavaria 1120–26
Judith=Frederick II Duke of Swabia 1105–47
Conrad III King 1138–52
Frederick IV Duke of Swabia d. 1167
Leopold IV Margrave of Austria 1136–41 Duke of Bavaria 1139–41
Otto of Freising
Theodora=(2) Henry (1)=(2) Gertrude (1)=Henry the Proud
Henry Jasomirgott Duke of Bavaria 1142–56 Margrave of Austria Duke of Austria 1156–77
Gertrude d. 1145
Henry the Proud Duke of Bavaria 1126–38 Duke of Saxony 1136–38 d. 1139
Welf VI of Tuscany d. 1191
Judith= d. 1132
Adela=(1) Frederick I (2) =Beatrix
Frederick I Barbarossa King 1152 Emperor 1155
Beatrix d. 1184
Clementia=(1) Henry the Lion (2)=Matilda
Clementia (Zähringen)
Henry the Lion Duke of Saxony 1142–80 Duke of Bavaria 1156–80 d. 1195
Matilda (of England)
Welf VII d. 1167
Frederick IV d. 1191
Henry VI =Constance
Henry VI King 1190 d. 1197
Constance (of Sicily)
Philip King 1198–1208
Otto
Otto IV King 1198–1218
Frederick II King of Sicily 1197 King of Germany 1212 Emperor 1220 d. 1250

Select Bibliography

The majority of the sources for the reign of Frederick Barbarossa have been printed in the *Monumenta Germaniae Historica*. For the charters it is still necessary to use the old editions by Stumpf, *Die Reichskanzler*, Vols. II and III, Innsbruck, 1865. For the history of the church and the relations with Byzantium additional sources are in the following: Jaffé, Watterich, Boso, Tengnagel, Pez, Döberl, Böhmer, Dölger, Migne, Sudendorf, Mansi, JL, Bouquet, RIS, Robertson. (See *List of Abbreviations* for titles.) The monumental digest of the chronicles of the period by W. v. Giesebrecht, *Geschichte der deutschen Kaiserzeit*, Vols. V and VI, Leipzig 1888 and 1895, is indispensable. Apart from Giesebrecht, there are comparatively few modern works devoted to Frederick I's reign as a whole:

H. PRUTZ, *Friedrich I*, 1870.

K. HAMPE, *Friedrich Barbarossa*, in: *Herrschergestalten des deutschen Mittelalters*, 6th ed., Heidelberg, 1955.

E. OTTO, *Friedrich Barbarossa*, Potsdam, 1943.

F. HEER, *Aufgang Europas*, Wien-Zürich, 1949.

F. HEER, *Die Tragödie des heiligen Reiches*, Wien-Zürich, 1952.

K. JORDAN, *Friedrich Barbarossa*, Göttingen, 1959.

H. HEIMPEL, *Friedrich I. Barbarossa*, in: *Neue deutsche Biographie*, Vol. 5, 1961.

M. PACAUT, *Frédéric Barberonsse*, Paris, 1968.

In addition there are lengthy chapters devoted to the reign of Frederick in Vol. VI of the *Cambridge Medieval History*; in K. Hampe, *Deutsche Kaisergeschichte*, 11th ed., Heidelberg, 1963; in B. Gebhardt, *Handbuch der deutschen Geschichte*, 8th ed., Vol. I, Stuttgart, 1954; and in G. Barraclough, *The Origins of Modern Germany*, Oxford, 1946. R. Folz, L'idée de l'Empire mediévale, Paris, 1953.

The following bibliography is a select one and does not include general works and handbooks and histories of the period or general books on the history of ideas, law and economics of the twelfth century. Similarly, the many local histories of cities and special regions have been omitted. It does not include works which appeared before 1900, unless they have proved of permanent value. With a few exceptions, the vast controversial literature which has grown up around the debate on the authenticity of the *Privilegium Minus* and the meaning of the Gelnhausen Charter has been omitted.

E. M. ALMEDINGEN, *The English Pope Adrian IV*, 1925.

H. APPELT, *Friedrich Barbarossa und die italienischen Kommunen*, MIOG, LXXII, 1964.

H. APPELT, *Kaiserurkunden und Fürstensentenz unter Friedrich Barbarossa*, MIOG, LXXI, 1963.

H. APPELT, *Friedrich Barbarossa und das römische Recht*, RHM, 5, 1961–2.

E. ASSMANN, *Bleibt der Ligurinus anonym?*, DA, 12, 1956.

J. BACHMANN, *Die päpstlichen Legaten in Deutschland und Skandinavien* (1125–1159), EHS, 115, Berlin.

F. BARLOW, *The English, Norman and French Councils Called to Deal with the Papal Schism of 1159*, EHR, 51, 1936.

J. BÄRMANN, *Die Städtegründungen Heinrichs des Löwen*, Köln, Graz, 1961.

G. BARRACLOUGH, 'Frederick Barbarossa and the twelfth century' in *History in a Changing World*, Oxford, 1955.

G.V. BELOW, *Die italienische Kaiserpolitik des Deutschen Mittelalters, mit besonderem Hinblick auf die Politik Friedrich Barbarossas*, HZ, Suppl. X, 1927.

E. BERNHEIM, *Der Charakter Ottos von Freising und seiner Werke*, MIOG, VI, 1885.

W. BIEREYE, *Die Kämpfe gegen Heinrich den Löwen in den Jahren 1177–1181*, Festschrift für D. Schäfer, 1915.

W. BIEREYE, *Die Wendeneinfälle der Jahre 1178, 1179, 1180 und die Herausforderung Heinrichs des Löwen durch Markgraf Dietrich von Landsberg*, HZ, 115, 1915.

K. BOSL, *Reichsministerialität der Salier und Staufer*, Stuttgart, 1950.

A. BRACKMANN, *Die Wandlung der Staatsanschauungen im Zeitalter Kaiser Friederichs I*, HZ, 145, 1932.

A. BRACKMANN, *Die Ursachen der geistigen und politischen Wandlung Europas im 11. und 12. Jahrhundert*, HZ, 149, 1936.

A. BRACKMANN, *Der mittelalterliche Ursprung der Nationalstaaten*, SPA, 1936.

A. BRACKMANN, *Dictamina zur Geschichte Friedrich Barbarossas*, SPA, 1927.

P. BREZZI, *Lo scisma inter regnum et sacerdotium al tempo di Federico Barbarossa*, ADR, 63, 1940.

P. BREZZI, *Ottone di Frisinga*, BISI, 54, 1939.

P. BREZZI, *Caratteri, momenti e protagonisti dell'azione politica di Frederico Barbarossa*, RSI, 5, 1940.

BRINCKMANN, *Die Dichterpersönlichkeit des Archipoeta*, GRM, 1925.

U. BRUMM, *Zur Frage der Echtheit der ersten Stauferdiplome für südburgundische Empfänger*, MIOG, 57, 1949.

M. BUCHNER, *Das fingierte Privileg Karls des Groszen—eine Faelschung Rainalds von Dassel—und die Entstehung der Aachener Vita Karoli Magni*, ZAGV, 47, 1925.

M. BUCHNER, *Pseudo-Turpin, Rainald von Dassel und der Archipoet in ihren Beziehungen zur Kanonisation Karls des Groszen*, ZFLS, 51, 1928.

J. BUMKE, *Studien zum Ritterbegriff im 12. und 13. Jahrhundert*, Heidelberg, 1964.

A. BUSSON, *Conrad von Staufen, Pfalzgraf bei Rhein*, ANHVN, Köln, 1868.

H. BÜTTNER, *Die Alpenpasspolitik Friedrich Barbarossas bis zum Jahre 1164/5*, in: *Grundfragen der alemannischen Geschichte*, ed. Th. Mayer, Konstanz, 1955.

H. BÜTTNER, *Staufer und Zähringer im politisch Kräftespiel zwischen Bodensee und Genfersee*, Zürich, 1961.

H. BÜTTNER, *Churrätien im 12. Jahrhundert*, SZG, 13, 1963.

H. BÜTTNER, *Kloster Disentis, das Bleniotal und Friedrich Barbarossa*, ZSKG, 47, 1953.

H. BÜTTNER, *Die Erschliessung des Simplon als Fernstrasse*, SZG, 3, 1953.

H. BÜTTNER, *Erzbischof Heinrich von Mainz und die Staufer 1142–1153*, ZKG, 69, 1958.

A. CARTELLIERI, *Das deutsch-französische Bündnis von 1187*, HV, 27, 1932.

M. CHAPUIS, *Recherches sur les institutions politiques du Pays du Vaud du XIme au XIIIme siècle*, Lausanne, 1940.

P. CLASSEN, *Gerhoch von Reichersberg*, Wiesbaden, 1960.

P. CLASSEN, *Das Konstantinopeler Konzil von 1166 und die Lateiner*, BZ, 1955.

P. CLASSEN, '*Mailands Treueid für Manuel Komnenos*,' *Akten des XI internationalen Byzantisten-Kongresses*, München, 1960.

G. CONSTABLE, *The Second Crusade as Seen by Contemporaries*, Tr, 9, 1953.

E. R. CURTIUS, *Der Archipoeta und der Stil mittelalterlicher Dichtung*, RF, 54, 1940.

P. DARMSTÄDTER, *Das Reichsgut in der Lombardei und Piemont, 568–1250*, Strassburg, 1896.

J. DEER, *Die Siegel Kaiser Friedrichs I Barbarossa und Heinrichs VI in der Kunst und Politik ihrer Zeit*, Festchrift H. R. Hahnloser, Basel und Stuttgart, 1961.

G. DEHIO, *Hartvich von Stade, Erzbischof von Hamburg-Bremen*, Göttingen, 1872.

G. DEIBEL, *Die italienischen Einkünfe Friedrichs I*, NHJ, 1932.

G. DEIBEL, *Die finanzielle Bedeutung Reichsitaliens fur die staufischen Herrscher des 12. Jahrhunderts*, ZSSRGger, LIV, 1934.

A. P. D'ENTRÈVES, *Ottone di Frisinga e la storiografia del medio evo*, RIFD, 20, 1940.

M. DIETRICH, *Die Zisterzienser und ihre Stellung zum mittelalterlichen Reichsgedanken*, Salzburg, 1934.

O. V. DUNGERN, *Die Staatsreform der Hohenstaufen* (Festschrift für E. Zitelmann), München–Leipzig, 1913.

G. DUNKEN, *Die politische Wirksamkeit der päpstlichen Legaten in der Zeit des Kampfes zwischen Kaisertum und Papsttum in Oberitalien unter Friedrich I*, EHS, 209, Berlin, 1931.

E. EICHMANN, *Die römischen Eide der deutschen Könige*, ZSSRGkan, IV, 1916.

E. EICHMANN, *Officium Stratoris et Strepae*, HZ, 142, 1930.

E. EICHMANN, *Die 'formula professionis' Friedrichs I*, HJ, 52, 1932.

I. ENGEL, *Das Schisma Barbarossas in Bistum und Hochstift Freising, 1159–77*, München, 1930.

V. EPIFANIO, *Sul preteso assedio di Benevento e sul concordato tra la chiesa e lo stato normanno del 1156*, ASPN, XXVIII, 1945.

C. ERDMANN, *Der Prozess Heinrichs des Löwen*, in: Th. Mayer, ed., *Kaisertum und Herzogsgewalt im Zeitalter Friedrichs I*, Leipzig, 1944.

C. ERDMANN, *Die Entstehung des Kreuzzuggedankens*, Stuttgart, 1935.

C. ERDMANN, *Endkaiserglaube und Kurezzugsgedanke im 11. Jahrhundert*, ZKG, 51, 1932.

A. ERLER, *Die ronkalischen Gesetze des Jahres 1158 und die oberitalienische Städte-Freiheit*, ZSSRGger, 61, 1941.

GINA FASOLI, *Governanti e governati nei communi cittadini italiani fra l'XI ed il XII secolo*, SBaG, 20, 1962–3.

H. FECHNER, *Wichmann*, FDG, 5, 1865.

H. FEIN, *Die staufischen Staedtegründungen im Elsass*, 1939.

H. FICHTENAU, *Von der Mark zum Herzogtum. Grundlagen und Sinn des Privilegium minus für Österreich*, München, 1958.

H. FICHTENAU, *Bamberg, Würzburg und die Stauferkanzlei*, MIOG, 53, 1939.

J. FICKER, *Rainald von Dassel*, Köln, 1850.

H. FILLITZ, *Der Cappenberger Barbarossakopf*, MJbK, 3. folge, 14, 1963.

P. W. FINSTERWALDER, *Die Gesetze von Ronkalia*, ZSSRGger, 51, 1931.

W. FÖHL, *Studien zu Rainald von Dassel*, JKGV, 17, 1935; and 20, 1938.
W. FÖHL, *Bischof Eberhard II von Bamberg*, MIOG, 50, 1936.
R. FOLZ, *La chancellerie de Frédéric Ier et la canonisation de Charlemagne*, MA, Vol. LXX, 1964.
R. FOLZ, *Le souvenir et la légende de Charlemagne dans l'empire germanique mediévale*, Paris, 1950.
R. FOLZ, *L'empereur Frédéric Ier et le royaume de Bourgogne*, SHDB, 18, 1956.
A. FRUGONI, *Arnaldo da Brescia nelle fonti del secolo XII*, Roma, 1954.
F. GEISTHARD, *Der Kämmerer Boso*, EHS, 293, Berlin, 1936.
G. GLAESKE, *Die Erzdischöfe von Hamburg-Bremen als Reichsfürsten*, Hildesheim 1962.
H. GLEBER, *Papst Eugen III*, Jena, 1936.
W. GOEZ, *Der Leihezwang*, Tübingen, 1962.
F. GRÄF, *Die Gründung Alessandria's*, Berlin, 1887.
G. W. GREENAWAY, *Arnold of Brescia*, Cambridge, 1931.
H. GRUNDMANN, *Der Cappenberger Barbarossakopf*, Köln, 1959.
H. GRUNDMANN, *Rotten und Brabanzonen*, DA, 5, 1942.
H. GUNIA, *Der Leihezwang*, Düsseldorf, 1938.
I. F. GÜTERBOCK, *Zur Geschichte Burgunds im Zeitalter Barbarossas*, ZSG, 17, 1937.
F. GÜTERBOCK, *Barbarossa auf Burg Rivoli*, NA, 45, 1924.
F. GÜTERBOCK, *Die Rektoren des Lombardenbundes in einer Urkunde für Chiaravalle*, QuF, 18, 1926.
F. GÜTERBOCK, *Die Lukmanierstrasse und die Passpolitik der Staufer. Friedrichs I Marsch nach Legnano*, QuF, 11, 1908.
F. GÜTERBOCK, *Zum Schisma unter Alexander III. Die Überlieferung des Tolosanus und die Stellungsnahme der Romagna und Emilia*, in: F. Kehr zum Geburtstag, München, 1926.
F. GÜTERBOCK, *Der Prozess Heinrichs des Löwen*, 1909.
F. GÜTERBOCK, *Die Gelnhäuser Urkunde und der Prozess Heinrichs des Löwen*, 1920.
F. GÜTERBOCK, *Zur Edition des Geschichtswerks Otto Morenas und seiner Fortsetzer*, NA, 48 and 49.
F. GÜTERBOCK, *Le Lettere del notaio Bucardo intorno alla politica del Barbarossa nello scisma ed alla distruzione de Milano*, BISI, 61, 1949.
F. GÜTERBOCK, *Markward von Grumbach, Vater und Sohn*, MIOG, 48, 1934.
F. GÜTERBOCK, *Alla vigilia della lega Lombarda*, ASI, 95, 1937.
F. GÜTERBOCK, *Piacenzas Beziehungen zu Barbarossa*, QuF., 24, 1897.
F. GÜTERBOCK, *Ueber Otto von St Blasien, Burchard von Ursberg und eine unbekannte Welfenquelle mit Ausblick auf die Chiavennafrage*, in: R. Holtzmann Festschrift, Berlin, EHS, 238, 1933.
F. GÜTERBOCK, *Barbarossa und Heinrich der Löwe*, VuG, XXIII, 1933.
F. GÜTERBOCK, *Tortonas Abfall vom Lombardenbund*, NA, 45, 1924.
F. GÜTERBOCK, *Der Friede von Montebello*, Berlin, 1895.
F. GÜTERBOCK, *Ancora Legnano!*, Milano, 1901.
F. GÜTERBOCK, *Otto und Acerbo Morena*, ASI, Vol. 13, 1930.
F. GÜTERBOCK, *Legnano*, HV, 14, 1911.
O. HAENDLE, *Die Dienstmannen Heinrichs des Löwen*, 1930.
K. HADANK, *Zur Kontroverse über Legnano*, HV, 11, 1908.
J. HALLER, *Zur Zusammenkunft von Chiavenna 1176*, MIOG, 33, 1912.

J. HALLER, *Der Sturtz Heinrichs des Löwen*, AU, 3, Berlin, 1911.

J. HALLER, *König Heinrich VI und die römische Kirche*, MIOG, 35, 1914.

K. HAMPE, *Welfen und Waiblinger*, 11, 1935.

K. HAMPE, *Heinrichs des Löwen Sturtz in politisch-historischer Beurteilung*, HZ, 109, 1912.

K. HAMPE, *Zur Geschichte Arnolds von Brescia*, HZ, 130, 1924.

J. HARTUNG, *Die Territorialpolitik der Magderburger Erzbischöfe Wichmann, Ludolf und Albrecht, 1152–1232*, GSLM, 21, 1886.

J. HARTTUNG, *Der Erzstift Bremen und Heinrich der Löwe*, HZ, 34, 1875.

J. HASHAGEN, *Otto von Freising als Geschichtsphilosoph und Kirchenpolitiker*, Leipzig, 1900.

F. HAUSMANN, *Reichskanzlei und Hofkapelle*, MGH, 14, 1956.

K. J. HEILIG, *Ostrom und das deutsche Reich um die Mitte des 12. Jahrhunderts* in: Th. Mayer, ed. *Kaisertum und Herzogsgewalt im Zeitalter Friedrichs I*, Leipzig, 1944.

H. HEIMPEL, *Kaiser Friedrich Barbarossa und die Wende der staufischen Zeit*, Strassburg, 1942.

O. V. HEINEMANN, *Albrecht der Bär*, Darmstadt, 1864.

W. HEINEMEYER, *Der Friede von Montebello*, DA, 11, 1954.

W. HEINEMEYER, *Die Verhandlungen an der Saône im Jahre 1162*, DA, 20, 1964.

R. M. HERKENRATH, *Rainald von Dassel als Verfasser und Schreiber von Kaiserurkunden*, MIOG, LXXII, 1964.

R. M. HERKENRATH, *Rainald von Dassel*, Diss. (typed) Graz, 1962.

H. HEUERMANN, *Die Hausmachtpolitik der Staufer von Herzog Friedrich I bis Köning Konrad III*, Berlin, 1939.

R. HILDEBRAND, *Der sächsische 'Staat' Heinrichs der Löwen*, EHS, Berlin, 1937.

N. HILLING, *Paria litterarum*, in: H. Finke Festgabe, Münster, 1925.

H. HIRSCH, *Urkundenfälschung aus dem Regnum Arelatense. Die Burgundische Politik Friedrichs I*, Wien, 1937.

N. HÖING, *Der angebliche Briefwechsel Papst Hadrians IV und Kaiser Friedrich I. Ein Werk aus dem Kreis des Bischofs Eberhard II von Bamberg*, AfD, 3, 1957.

N. HÖING, *Die 'Trierer Stilübungen'*, AFD, 1, 1955; and 2, 1956.

A. K. HOMBERG, *Westfalen und das sächsische Herzogtum*, Münster, 1963.

A. HOFMEISTER, *Puer, Iuvenis, Senex*, in: Kehr Festchrift, *Papsttum und Kaisertum*, München, 1926.

A. HOFMEISTER, *Zur Epistola de morte Friderici imperatoris*, NA, 41, 1919.

A. HOFMEISTER, *Studien über Otto von Freising*, NA, 37, 1911.

R. HOLTZMANN, *Dominium mundi und imperium merum*, ZKG, 61, 1943.

R. HOLTZMANN, *Die Wahl Friedrichs I zum deutschen König*, HVj, 1898.

R. HOLTZMANN, *Das Carmen de Federico I imperatore aus Bergamo und die Anfänge einer staufischen Hofhistoriographie*, NA, 44, 1922.

R. HOLTZMANN, *Der Weltherrschaftsgedanke des mittelalterlichen Kaisertums*, HZ, 159, 1939.

R. HOLTZMANN, *Der Kaiser als Marschall des Papstes*, SSWG, Neue Folge, 8, 1928.

W. HOLTZMANN, *Die Register Alexanders III*, QuF, 30, 1940.

W. HOLTZMANN, *Quellen und Forschungen zur Geschichte Friedrich Barbarossas*, NA, 48, 1930.

W. HOLTZMANN, *Beiträge zur Reichs-und Papstgeschichte im hohen Mittelalter*, BHF, 8, 1957.

W. HOPPE, *Erzbischof Wichmann von Magdeburg*, GSLM, 43, 44; 1908, 1909.
G. JACHINO, *Le origine di Alessandria nella storia e nelle tradizioni popolare*, Turin, 1926.
W. JANSSEN, *Die päpstlichen Legaten in Frankreich vom Schisma Analekts II bis zum Tode Coelestins III 1130–1198*, Graz, Köln, 1961.
J. JASTROW, *Die Welfenprozesse und die ersten Regierungsjahre Friedrich Barbarossas 1138–1156*, DZG, 10, 1893.
V. JENTZSCH, *Heinrich der Löwe im Urteil der deutschen Geschichtsschreibung*, Jena, 1932.
E. JORANSON, *The Palestine Pilgrimage of Henry the Lion*, in: Medieval historical essays in honour of J. W. Thompson, 1938.
K. JORDAN, *Goslar und das Reich im 12. Jahrhundert*, NJL, 35, 1963.
K. JORDAN, *Herzogtum und Stamm in Sachsen während des hohen Mittelalters*, NJL, 30, 1959.
K. JORDAN, *Heinrich der Löwe und die ostdeutsche Kolonisation*, DALV, 2, 1938.
K. JORDAN, *Bistumsgründungen Heinrichs des Löwen*, Stuttgart, 1939.
R. JORDAN, *Die Stellung des deutschen Episkopats im Kampf um die Universalmacht unter Friedrich I*, Würzburg, 1939.
W. KAEGI, *Chronica Mundi. Grundformen der Geschichtsschreibung seit dem Mittelalter*, Einsiedeln, 1954.
G. KALLEN, *Das Kölner Erzstift und der 'ducatus Westfalie et Angarie' 1180*, JKGV, 31–2, 1957.
W. KAMLAH, *Der Ludus de Antichristo*, HV, 28, 1933–4.
H. KARGE, *Die Gesinnung und die Massnahmen Alexanders III*, Greifswald, 1914.
H. KAUFFMANN, *Die italienische Politik Friedrichs I nach dem Frieden von Constanz*, 1933.
K. A. KEHR, *Zur Friedensurkunde Friedrichs I von Venedig*, NA, 27, 1902.
P. KEHR, *Kaiser Friedrich I und Venedig während des Schismas*, QuF, 17, 1924.
P. KEHR, *Zur Geschichte Victors IV*, NA, 46, 1926.
P. KEHR, *Der Vertrag von Anagni im Jahre 1176*, NA, 13, 1888.
P. KEHR, *Die Belehnung der süditalienischen Normannenfürsten durch die Päpste, 1059–1192*, APA, 1934.
F. KESZYCKA, *Kaiserin Beatrix*, Freiburg, 1923.
A. KESTNER, *Alpenpässe und römische Malaria*, HV, 30, 1934.
G. KIRCHNER, *Staatsplanung und Reichsministerialität*, DA, 10, 1954.
H. J. KIRFEL, *Weltherrschaftsidee und Bündnispolitik*, BHF, 12, 1959.
H. W. KLEWITZ, *Die Abstammung der Kaiserin Beatrix*, DA, 7, 1944.
H. W. KLEWITZ, *Die Festkrönungen*, ZSSRGkan, 28, 1939.
H. W. KLEWITZ, *Geschichte der Ministerialität im Elasss bis zum Ende des Interregnums*, Frankfurt, 1929.
H. M. KLINKENBERG, *Der Sinn der Chronik Ottos von Freising*, in: G. Kallen Festschrift, *Aus Mittelalter und Neuzeit*, Bonn, 1957.
P. KLOPSCH, *Zum 'Kaiserhymnus' des Archipoeta*, Eu, 54, 1960.
P. KLUCKHOHN, *Ministerialität und Ritterdichtung*, ZDA, 52, 1910.
J. KOCH, *Die Grundlagen der Geschichtsphilosophie Ottos von Freising*, in: W. Lammers ed., *Geschichtsdenken und Geschichtsbild in Mittelalter*, Darmstadt, 1961.
H. KOEPPLER, *Frederick Barbarossa and the Schools of Bologna*, EHR, 54, 1939.
H. KRABBO, *Albrecht der Bär*, FbpG, 19, 1906.

G. LADNER, *I mosaici e gli affreschi ecclesiastico-politici nell'antico palazzo lateranense*, RAC, II, 1935.

G. LÄWEN, *Die herzogliche Stellung Heinrichs des Löwen in Sachsen*, 1937.

P. LAMMA, *Comneni e Staufer*, Roma, 1955.

K. LANGOSCH, *Politisch Dichtung um Friedrich Barbarossa*, 1943.

K. LANGOSCH, *Der politische Literaturkreis um Friedrich Barbarossa*, GA, 11, 1944.

K. LANGOSCH, *Studien zum Archipoeta*, DA, 5, 1942.

G. LE BRAS, *Le droit romain au service de la domination pontificale*, NRHD, 1949.

W. LENEL, *Der Konstanzer Friede von 1183 und die italienische Politik Friedrichs I*, HZ, 128, 1923.

W. LEVISON, *Otto von Freising und das Privileg Friedrichs für das Herzogtum Österreich*, NA, XXXIV, 1909.

M. MACCARONE, *Papato e impero dalla elezione di Federico I alla morte di Adriano*, Rome, 1959.

J. D. MACKIE, *Pope Adrian IV*, Oxford, 1907.

H. K. MANN, *Nicolas Breakspear, Hadrian IV*, 1914.

J.-Y. MARIOTTE, *Le Comté de Bourgogne sous les Hohenstaufen*, Paris, 1963.

H. E. MAYER, *Der Brief Kaiser Friedrichs I an Saladin vom Jahre 1188*, DA, 14, 1958.

TH. MAYER, *Friedrich I und Heinrich der Löwe*, in: Th. Mayer, ed., *Kaisertum und Herzogsgewalt im Zeitalter Friedrichs I*, Leipzig, 1944.

TH. MAYER, *Die historisch-politischen Kraefte im Oberrheingebiet im Mittelalter*, ZGO, LII, 1938.

TH. MAYER, *Die Ausbildung der Grundlagen des modernen deutschen Staates im hohen Mittelalter*, HZ, 59, 1939.

TH. MAYER, *Die Entstehung des 'modernen' Staates in Mittelalter und die freien Bauern*, ZSSRGger, 57, 1937.

TH. MAYER, *Der Staat der Herzoge von Zähringen*, 1935.

W. METZ, *Staufische Güterverzeichnisse*, Berlin, 1964.

E. MEUTHEN, *Kirche und Heilsgeschehen bei Gerhoh von Reichersberg*, Leiden-Köln, 1959.

H. MITTEIS, *Zur staufischen Verfassungsgeschichte*, ZSSRGger, 65, 1947.

W. MOHR, *Zum Geschichtsbild Ottos von Freising*, in: *Perennitas*, P. Th. Michels zum Geburtstag, Münster, 1963.

P. MUNZ, *Frederick Barbarossa and Henry the Lion in 1176*, HS, XII, 1965.

P. MUNZ, *Frederick Barbarossa and the 'Holy Empire'*, JRH, Vol. 3, 1964.

H. NAUMANN, *Kurzer Versuch über welfische und staufische Dichtung*, ELJ, 8, 1929.

H. NIESE, *Der Sturtz Heinrichs des Löwen*, HZ, 112, 1914.

W. OHNSORGE, *Beitrag zur Geschichte Kaiser Manuels I*, in: Festschrift für Brackmann, 1931.

W. OHNSORGE, *'Kaiser' Konrads III zur Geschichte des staufischen Staatsgedankens*, MIOG, Vol. 46, 1932.

W. OHNSORGE, *Die Byzanzpolitik Friedrich Barbarossas und der Landesverrat Heinrichs des Löwen*, DA, 6, 1943.

W. OHNSORGE, *Zu den aussenpolitischen Anfängen Friedrich Barbarossas*, QuF, 32, 1942.

W. OHNSORGE, *Päpstliche und gegenpäpstliche Legaten in Deutschland und Skandinavien, 1159–1181*, EHS, 188, Berlin, 1929.

W. OHNSORGE, *Eine Ebracher Briefsammlung des 12. Jahrhunderts*, QuF, 20, 1929.

W. OHNSORGE, *Die Legaten Alexanders III in ersten Jahrzehnt seines Pontifikats*, 1928.

I. OTT, *Der Regalienbegriff im 12. Jahrhundert*, ZSSRGkan, 35, 1948.

E. OTTMAR, *Das Carmen de Friderico I imperatore aus Bergamo und seine Beziehungen zu Otto-Rahewins Gesta Friderici, Gunther-Ligurinus und Burchard von Ursbergs Chronik*, NA, 46.

E. OTTO, *Otto von Freising und Friedrich Barbarossa*, HV, 31, 1937.

E. OTTO, *Friedrich Barbarossa in seinen Briefen*, DA, 1942.

A. OVERMANN, *Gräfin Mathilde von Tuszien, ihre Besitzungen, Geschichte ihres Gutes von 1115–1230 und ihrer Regesten*, 1895.

M. PACAUT, *Louis VII et Alexandre III*, RHEF, 39, 1953.

M. PACAUT, *Les Légats d'Alexandre (1159–1181)*, RHE, 1955.

M. PACAUT, *Alexandre III*, Paris, 1956.

H. PATZE, *Kaiser Friedrich Barbarossa und der Osten*, JGMOD, 11, 1962.

CH.–E. PERRIN, 'La Seigneurie rurale en France et en Allemagne du début du IXe à la fin du XIIe siècle', *Les Cours de la Sorbonne*, Centre de Documentation, 1951.

CH.–E. PERRIN, *La Société rurale allemande du Xe au XIIe siècle d'après un ouvrage récent*, RHDFE, 4e ser., 24, 1945.

H. C. PEYER, *Friedrich Barbarossa, Monza und Aachen*, DA, 8, 1950–1.

M. PHILIPPSON, *Heinrich der Löwe*, 2nd ed., Berlin, 1918.

A. L. POOLE, *Henry the Lion*, Oxford, 1912.

R. C. POOLE, *The early Lives of R. Pullen and N. Breakspear*, in: Essays presented to T. F. Tout, Manchester, 1925.

M. PREISS, *Die politsche Tätigkeit und Stellung der Zisterzienser im Schisma 1159–1177*, 1934.

F. RANKE, *Gott, Welt und Humanität in der deutschen Dichtung des Mittelalters*, Basel, 1952.

P. RASSOW, *Honor Imperii*, 1940.

E. REHFELDT, *Die politische Stellung Wibalds von Stablo und Korvei im Zusammenhang mit seinen Grundanschauungen*, Greifswald, 1913.

H. REUTER, *Geschichte Alexanders III und der Kirche seiner Zeit*, 1st ed., 1845; 3 Vols., 1860–4.

R. RIBBECK, *Friedrich I und die römische Kurie in den Jahren 1157–1159*, Leipzig, 1881.

R. RIBBECK, *Der Traktat über die Papstwahl des Jahres 1159*, FDG, 25, 1885.

H. J. RIECKENBERG, *Leben und Stand des Minnesängers Friedrich von Hausen*, AKG, 2, 1961.

S. RIEZLER, *Der Kreuzzug Kaiser Friedrichs I*, FDG, X.

G. RILL, *Zur Geschichte der Würzburger Eide von 1165*, WDGB, 20, 1958.

F. RÖRIG, *Heinrich der Löwe und die Gründung Lübecks*, DA, 1, 1937.

N. RUBINSTEIN, *Political Rhetoric in the Imperial Chancery during the 12th and 13th Centuries*, MAe, 14, 1945.

S. RUNCIMAN, *The Eastern Schism*, Oxford, 1955.

E. RUNDNAGEL, *Die Ehescheidung Friedrich Barbarossas*, Festschrift R. Holtzmann, 1933.

R. SCHAMBACH, *Das Verhältnis Rainald von Dassels zum Empfang der höchsten Weihen*, ZHVN, 80, 1915.

C. SCHAMBACH, *Rainald von Dassel*, ZHVN, 1913.

P. SCHEFFER-BOICHORST, *Friedrichs I letzter Streit mit der Kurie*, 1866.

W. SCHLESINGER, *Egerland, Vogtland, Pleissenland*, in: W. Schlesinger, *Mitteldeutsche Beiträge zur Verfassungsgeschichte*, 1961.

W. SCHLESINGER, *Die Anfänge der Stadt Chemnitz und anderer mitteldeutscher Städte*, 1952.

F. J. SCHMALE, *Die gesta Friderici I imperatoris Ottos von Freising und Rahewins*, DA, 19, 1963.

B. SCHMEIDLER, *Helmold und seine Cronica Slavorum*, ZVLGA, XIV, 1912.

K. SCHMID, *Graf Rudolf von Pfullendorf und Kaiser Friedrich I*, Freiburg, 1954.

K. SCHÖNHERR, *Die Lehre vom Reichsfürstenstand des Mittelalter*, 1914.

E. SCHRADER, *Vom Werden und Wesen des Würzburgischen Herzogstums Franken*, ZSSRGger, 80, 1963.

E. SCHRADER, *Zur Gesichtsbestimmung des Privilegium minus*, ZSSRGger, 69, 1952.

W. J. SCHRÖDER, *Der Ritter zwischen Welt und Gott*, Weimar, 1952.

H. SCHRÖRS, *Untersuchungen zu dem Streit Kaiser Friedrichs I mit dem Papst Hadrian IV, 1157–58*, Freiburg I.B., 1916.

E. SCHULZ, *Entstehungsgeschichte der Werke des Gottfried von Viterbo*, DA, 46, 1957.

H. SIMONSFELD, *Friedrich Rotbart und Eskil von Lund*, HV, 15, 1912.

G. B. SIRACUSA, *Il regno di Guglielmo I in Sicilia*, Palermo, 1929.

J. SPÖRL, *Grundformen hochmittelalterlicher Geschichtsanschauung*, München, 1935.

J. SPÖRL, *Rainald von Dassel auf dem Konzil von Reims*, HJ, 60, 1940.

E. E. STENGEL, *Die Entstehung der Kaiserchronik und der Aufgang der Staufischen Zeit*, DA, 14, 1958.

H. THIEME, *Staufische Stadtrechte im Elsass*, ZSSRGger, 58, 1938.

H. THIEME, *Die Funktion der Regalien*, ZSSRGger, 62, 1942.

F. TOURTUAL, *Böhmens Anteil an den Kämpfen Kaiser Friedrichs in Italien*, Göttingen, 1865.

F. TOURTUAL, *Bischof Hermann von Verden*, 1866.

W. ULLMANN, *The Medieval Interpretation of Frederick I's Habita*, in: Studi in memoria di Paola Koschaker, Milano, 1951.

W. ULLMANN, *The Pontificate of Adrian IV*, CHJ, 11, 1955.

W. ULLMANN, 'Cardinal Roland and Besancon', *Misc. Hist. Pont.*, Rome, 1954.

C. VARRENTRAPP, *Zur Geschichte der deutschen Kaiserzeit*, HZ, 47, 1882.

C. VARRENTRAPP, *Erzbishof Christian I von Mainz*, 1867.

O. VEHSE, *Benevent als Territorium des Kirchenstaates bis zum Beginn der avignonesischen Epoche*, QuF, 22, 1930–1.

O. VEHSE, *Die päpstliche Herrschaft in der Sabina bis zur Mitte des 12. Jahrhunderts*, QuF, xxi, 1929–30.

C. VIGNATI, *Storia diplomatica della lega lombarda*, Milan, 1867.

P. WAGNER, *Eberhard II, Bischof von Bamberg*, Halle, 1876.

D. WALEY, *The Papal State in the 13th Century*, London, 1961.

K. WELLER, *Die Staufischen Städtegründungen in Schwaben*, WVH, 36, 1930.

K. WELLER, *Geschichte des schwäbischen Stammes bis zum Untergang der Staufer*, 1944.

F. W. WENTZLAFF-EGGEBERT, *Der Hoftag Jesu Christi 1188 in Mainz*, Institut fur europäische Geschichte, Mainz, Vorträge Nr. 32, Wiesbaden, 1962.

H. WIERUSZOWSKI, *Roger II of Sicily, Rex-Tyrannus, in 12th century Political Thought*, Sp, XXXVIII, 1963.

A. WILMART, *Nouvelles de Rome au temps d'Alexandre III (1170)*, RB, XLV, 1933.

F. WINTER, *Erzbischof Wichmann von Magdeburg*, FDG, 13, 1873.

H. WOLTMANN, *Heinrich der Löwe und das Erbe der Grafen von Stade*, NJL, 18, 1941.

H. ZATSCHEK, *Beiträge zur Geschichte des Konstanzer Vertrags*, 1153, SWA, 210, 3, 1930.

H. ZATSCHEK, *Wibald von Stablo Studien zu Geschichte der Reichskanzlei und Reichspolitik unter den älteren Staufern*, MIOG, Suppl. X, 1928.

K. ZEILLINGER, *Zwei Diplome Barbarossas für seine römischen Parteigänger*, DA, 20, 1964.

H. ZEISS, *Zur Frage der kaiserlichen Zisterzienservogtei*, HJ, 46, 1926.

P. ZERBI, *Papato, Impero e 'Respublica Christiana' dal 1187 al 1198*, Milano, 1955.

P. ZERBI, *Un inedito dell'Archivio Vaticano e il convegno di Verona*, Ae, 28, 1954.

K. ZEUMER, *Par litterarum*, NA, 35, 1909; 38, 1912.

K. ZIMMERT, *Der deutsch-byzantinische Konflikt vom Juli 1189 bis Februar 1190*, BZ, 12, 1903.

Appendix

The following works are indispensable for an understanding of the Kyffhäuser legend:

J. ADAMEK, *Vom römischen Endreich der mittelalterlichen Bibelerklärung*, Würzburg, 1938.

L. BECHSTEIN, *Die Sagen des Kyffhäusers*, 1835.

M. W. BLOOMFIELD and M. E. REEVES, *The Penetration of Joachism into Northern Europe*, Sp. 29, 1954.

M. BROSCH, *Die Friedrichssage der Italiener*, HZ, 35, 1876.

H. EBERHARDT, *Die Kyffhäuserburgen in Geschichte und Sage*, BDL, 96, 1960.

W. ERBEN, *Untersperg-Studien. Ein Beitrag zur Geschichte der deutschen Kaisersage*, MGSL, 54, 1914.

F. GRAUERT, *Zur deutschen Kaisersage*, HJ, 13.

K. HAMPE, *Eine frühe Verknüpfung der Weissagung vom Endkaiser mit Friedrich II und Konrad IV*, SHA, 1917.

O. HOLDER-EGGER, *Italienische Prophetien des 13. Jahrhunderts*, NA, 15, 1890.

P. HOSP, *Ketzertum und deutsche Kaisersage beim Minoriten Johann von Winterthur*, FS, 3, 1915.

F. KAMPERS, *Die deutsche Kaiseridee in Prophetie und Sage*, München, 1896.

E. KANTOROWICZ, *Zu den Rechtsgrundlagen der deutschen Kaisersage*, DA, 13, 1957.

L. MICHELSEN, *Die Kiffhäuser Kaisersage*, ZThGA, I, 1854.

G. NEUMANN, *Kyffhäuser Studien*, ZThGA, 42, 1940.

D. VÖLTER, *Die Sekte von Schwäbisch-Hall und der Ursprung der deutschen Kaisersage*, ZKG, IV, 1880.

G. VOIGT, *Die deutsche Kaisersage*, HZ, 25, 1871.

Index